TO THE STUDENT: A Study Guide for this textbook is available through your college bookstore under the title *Study Guide/Managing Effective Organizations.* This Study Guide can help you with course material by acting as a tutorial, review, and study aid. If the Study Guide is not in stock, ask the bookstore manager to order a copy for you.

Managing Effective Organizations
An Introduction

Managing
Effective Organizations
An Introduction

Richard M. Steers
University of Oregon

Gerardo R. Ungson
University of Oregon

Richard T. Mowday
University of Oregon

Kent Publishing Company
A Division of Wadsworth, Inc.
Boston, Massachusetts

Dedicated
with sincere appreciation
to our families

Editor: David V. Anthony
Production Editor: Eve B. Mendelsohn
Interior Designer: Glenna Collett
Cover Designer: Trisha Hanlon
Production Coordinator: Linda Siegrist
Cover Photo: © David F. Hughes/The Picture Cube

Kent Publishing Company
A Division of Wadsworth, Inc.

Printed in the United States of America
1 2 3 4 5 6 7 8 9 —
93 92 91 90 89 88 87 86 85

Library of Congress Cataloging in Publication Data

Steers, Richard M.
   Managing effective organizations.

   Bibliography: p. 681
   Includes indexes.
   1. Management.   I. Ungson, Gerardo R.
II. Mowday, Richard T.   III. Title.
HD31.S6876   1985   658.4   84–23390
ISBN 0–534–03277–X

Text Credits

p. 115: F. E. Jerstad, "An Administrator's Manual of Planning," in R. J. Alio and M. W. Pennington, eds., *Corporate Planning: Techniques and Applications,* 1979: AMACOM, a division of American Management Associations, p. 257.

pp. 123–124: Reprinted by permission from *Organizational Behavior Contingency Views,* by Don Hellriegel and John W. Slocum, Jr. Copyright © 1976 by West Publishing Company. All rights reserved.

Chapters 9 and 10: Portions of the material in these chapters were adapted from *Introduction to Organizational Behavior,* Second Edition, by Richard M. Steers. Copyright © 1984 by Scott, Foresman and Company. Reprinted by permission.

pp. 528–529: W. F. Glueck, *Management* (Hinsdale, Ill.: Dryden Press, 1980), p. 427. Reprinted by permission of Holt, Rinehart and Winston.

pp. 633–634: From Grover Starling, *The Changing Environment of Business,* Second Edition (Boston: Kent Publishing Company, 1984), pp. 507–508. © 1984 by Wadsworth, Inc. Reprinted by permission of Kent Publishing Company, a division of Wadsworth, Inc.

Illustration Credits

p. 2 Courtesy of Bethlehem Steel; p. 26 Courtesy of Remington; p. 50 Courtesy of Industrial Motivation, Inc.; p. 92 Photo by Jeff Roberts; p. 130 Photo by Bill Pappas; p. 166 Illustration by Ernest H. Shepard from *Winnie-the-Pooh* by A. A. Milne, copyright 1926 by E. P. Dutton, Inc.; renewed 1954 by A. A. Milne. Reprinted by permission of the publisher; p. 202 Drawing by H. Martin; © 1981 The New Yorker Magazine, Inc.; p. 234 Courtesy of Logisticon; p. 268 Courtesy of Ford Motor Company; p. 304 Courtesy of Charlton Photos; p. 338 Photo by Elizabeth Zeschin; pp. 374 and 486 © Peter Menzel; p. 412 Drawing by Leo Cullum; © 1983 The New Yorker Magazine, Inc.; p. 446 Courtesy of Monsanto; p. 518 Courtesy of Black & Decker (U.S.) Inc.; p. 550 Reprinted from *U.S.News & World Report* issue of Feb. 11, 1980. Copyright, 1980, U.S.News & World Report, Inc.; p. 578 Photo by Loren McIntyre; p. 620 Jim Anderson/Stock Boston; p. 646 Courtesy of General Electric Co.

Preface

The emergence of management as a profession and science during the 1920s provides a pivotal event in explaining the historical development of the United States industrial structure. Effective management was a response to the inefficiencies, bottlenecks, poor controls, and administrative malaise that plagued the early enterprises. Many of these problems were solved using managerial techniques and tasks advanced by pioneering management scientists such as Frederick Taylor, Henry Fayol, Henry Gantt, and Frank and Lillian Gilbreth. The resulting era of productivity was associated with systematic planning, high volume standardization, effective coordination within and between organizational hierarchies, and rigid control of both the worker and the production process.

In the following sixty years, the practice of management has developed further into a discipline. Homilies about good management practices are now systematized into tools, tasks, skills, and techniques. The study of management is typically organized around the key functions of planning, organizing, directing, and controlling; and consequently, most current textbooks on management have adopted this perspective.

Our text was inspired by spirited discussion among academics and practioners on various shortcomings of management education and on new challenges faced by American managers. The inability to effectively integrate into the world economy and to retain our international competitiveness raised questions about management education and renewed debates on the role of government. Furthermore, books that presented critical comparisons between American and Japanese styles of management were fast becoming best-sellers. Our attention centered on the question: What managerial competencies are needed for the executive to become and remain effective in these modern times?

Modern managers need to develop strategies to offset the shock of changes from emerging markets, international competition, and government policy. New design templates are needed to improve an organization's internal adaptive capabilities. Behavioral and social skills need to be developed to meet the requirements of managing complex organizations and changing corporate cultures. This book combines state-of-the-art theories and research with contemporary management concerns. It focuses on the issue of effective organizations and how to manage an organization so that it becomes effective.

In this book, we offer an integrated concept of management that builds on three managerial competencies: technical, behavioral, and strategic. In contrast to many textbooks that examined management from the inside out, this book is intended to provide a broader managerial perspective that is responsive to current problems and opportunities. Our purpose, however, is not to replace the traditional focus on planning, organizing, directing, and controlling, but to elaborate on it. The book offers several essential features in order to achieve these goals:

First, it presents a triadic model of management/organizational effectiveness: (a) *Technical competencies* (Chapters 4–8) include planning for a changing environment, designing organizations, managerial decision making, developing control systems, and operations and production control. (b) *Behavioral competencies* (Chapters 9–14) include encouraging motivation and performance, effective leadership, management of work groups, effective communication, handling conflict and power, and human resource management. (c) *Strategic competencies* (Chapters 15–19) include strategic analysis, managing organizational change, dealing with government and society relations, and understanding international considerations.

Second, this book allows the instructor flexibility in structuring the course to his or her perspective. He or she can emphasize the traditional management functions of planning (Chapters 1, 2, 3, and 4), organizing (Chapters 5, 11, and 13), directing (Chapter 6, 9, 10, 12, and 14), and controlling (Chapters 7, 8, and 11). Each chapter presents a comprehensive treatment of the subject matter, including contemporary trends that have impacted the managerial function. Alternatively, the instructor can opt to present the traditional view as illustrated above and supplement it with recent managerial issues. In such a case, strategic analysis (Chapter 15) can complement chapters on planning; organizational change (Chapter 16) provides an excellent tie-in with the chapters on organizing; and social issues (Chapter 19) offers additional background material for chapters on directing and controlling. Finally, the instructor can make full use of the triadic model of this book, emphasizing how technical, behavioral, and strategic competencies define the modern managerial role.

Third, a strong pedagogy supports the content of the book. Each chapter contains a short introductory vignette, a chapter outline, key terms, chapter objectives, boxed features providing real-life examples of specific points, a chapter summary, chapter discussion questions, and a case study with questions. In addition, many chapters have exercises that allow the student to apply the material discussed in the text. A complete glossary of important terms used in the text can be found at the end of the book.

Fourth, this book has several chapters that are not found in many management textbooks. A whole chapter is devoted to operations and production management (Chapter 8) — a topic that is becoming more important on account of declining productivity in the United States. Chapter 15 ("Strategic Adaptation to the Environment") covers the changing structure of the United States economy and offers practical guidelines for dealing with these changes. Chapter 17

("Understanding the Role of Government") discusses the changing role of government and how managers can operate effectively in regulated and deregulated environments. Finally, Chapter 18 ("International Considerations in Management") offers an overview of the complexities and requirements of operating in a global economy.

In writing this book, we benefited from the counsel, advice, and criticisms provided by the following reviewers: Allen Bluedorn, University of Missouri; David Gray, University of Texas at Arlington; Marvin Karlins, University of South Florida; James C. McElroy, Iowa State University; Kenneth R. Thompson, University of Arkansas; Phil Van Auken, Baylor University; and Malcolm Walker, San Jose State University.

We also wish to thank Kenneth D. Ramsing, University of Oregon, for writing Chapter 8 ("Operations and Production Control") and George Z. Vozikis, University of Miami, for writing Chapter 18 ("International Considerations in Management"). We acknowledge the assistance of Ann Hall for her work as developmental editor, and of Charlie Cole, University of Oregon, for developing supplementary material. Eve Mendelsohn of Kent Publishing Company took the arduous task of coordinating the three of us — even at times when we were on sabbatical, on leave, or on vacation — to ensure that the book was as complete as possible. Margaret Kearney provided invaluable help in obtaining permissions and drafting some of the chapter vignettes. Dave Anthony and Jack McHugh, Editors at Kent Publishing Company, provided encouragement at different phases of this project.

We think that no book in management can be written without acknowledging the intellectual works of the early management theorists. We are grateful to them and to our professors who taught us about their works. Finally, we express our appreciation to our colleagues, friends, and families for their support: to Dorothy Wynkoop, our Departmental Secretary, for her inspiration on how work should be done; to Sheila and Kathleen for their support and good cheer; to Judith Herzfeld for her patience, care, and encouragement; and to Mary, Graham, and Garrett for their understanding.

Richard M. Steers
Gerardo R. Ungson
Richard T. Mowday

About the Authors

Richard M. Steers   *Gerardo R. Ungson*   *Richard T. Mowday*

Richard M. Steers is Associate Dean and Professor of Management at the University of Oregon. His primary research interests are in employee and job performance, organizational adaption and effectiveness, employee turnover and absenteeism, and organizational commitment. He is author of ten books and over sixty articles and has served on four editorial boards including those of the *Academy of Management Review* and the *Administrative Science Quarterly*. In 1984 he was elected Vice-President and Program Chair of the Academy of Management. Professor Steers is Kent's Consulting Editor in management.

Gerardo R. Ungson is Assistant Professor of Management at the University of Oregon. His research interests in macro-organizational theory include organizational adaption and effectiveness, strategic decision making, and information processing and decision making. He has published in *Contemporary Psychology,* the *Administrative Science Quarterly,* the *Academy of Management Review,* and the *Journal of Management.* Professor Ungson is also on the Editorial Review Board of the *Academy of Management Review* and is co-editor of *Decision Making: An Interdisciplinary Inquiry* (Kent, 1982).

Richard T. Mowday is Associate Professor of Management at the University of Oregon. His research focuses on organizational commitment, turnover and absenteeism, the early employment period, and the psychological processes of employee reactions to work organizations. He has co-authored several books and serves on the editorial review boards of the *Academy of Management Journal,* the *Journal of Management,* and the *Journal of Vocational Behavior.* He is an international consulting editor for the *Journal of Occupational Psychology* and Chairperson-Elect of the Organizational Behavior Division of the Academy of Management.

Contents

Managing Effective Organizations
An Introduction

The Nature of Management and Organizations

CHAPTER 1

A Challenge for Management

During the past five years, the country's big steel producers have lost billions of dollars and laid off hundreds of thousands of steelworkers. In 1953, 682,000 steelworkers held high-paying jobs. Presently, the industry only employs 396,000, and analysts are predicting a further decline to 185,000 by the year 2000.

The problems are enormous: insufficient capital, high labor costs, raw materials problems, shrinking markets, and foreign competition. The major producers are also facing increasing competition from minimills. These are small domestic steel producers that use a production process called continuous casting. Long ribbons of molten steel are produced and then cut into slabs. Eighty-six percent of Japan's steel and 61 percent of Europe's is continuously cast, compared to 26 percent of the steel produced in the United States. The major advantage of continuous casting is that it greatly increases product yield.

In order to survive large domestic steel producers must reduce their steelmaking capacity by closing facilities that cannot be modernized, and they must invest in continuous casters to compete with the minimills. Many steel executives want government assistance and tougher trade laws to control foreign imports.

Even if the industry does survive, one thing is certain: Most laid-off steelworkers will not get their jobs back, and the next few years are going to be tough ones for the survivors.

Sources: "Big Steel's Big Chill," by Harry Anderson with Richard Manning, *Newsweek,* October 10, 1983, p. 71; "Time Runs Out for Steel," *Business Week,* June 13, 1983, pp. 84–94.

Chapter Outline

- Declining United States Industrial Performance
- Challenges for the Modern Executive
- Plan of the Book

Key Terms

- recession
- stagflation
- key competencies
- technical competencies
- behavioral competencies
- strategic competencies
- inflation
- rising entitlements

Chapter Objectives

After studying Chapter 1 you should be able to

1. Discuss how industry in the United States is losing ground in the world marketplace.
2. Identify the social and policy reasons for American productivity problems.
3. Understand why recent economic periods have been so turbulent.
4. Explain limitations in the present practices of management that are contributing to productivity problems in the United States.
5. Identify three key competencies needed by today's managers and trace their historical development.
6. Describe four stages companies seem to go through in developing their management processes.

Introduction

We have heard a great deal in recent years concerning a general decline in productivity in North America and western Europe. We hear that our companies and industries are losing their competitive edge. We hear that managers have lost the ability to make their organizations truly effective. Some people have suggested that truly effective organizations in many instances simply are not possible.

Although few would deny that many organizations face a crisis in productivity and organizational effectiveness, most managers are not yet willing to give up the fight. There are, in fact, many ways to improve the situation.

This book has as its central theme the study of what can be done to resolve this crisis. But before we begin to consider remedies, it is important to understand the nature and extent of the problem. We foster such understanding in our first chapter by considering two related issues: the causes of our declining productivity and some limitations on corporate management. We then begin to explore what it takes to be an effective manager.

Declining United States Industrial Performance

During the past two decades, industry in the United States has lost considerable ground to competition in world markets. In the 1970s the United States lost 23 percent of its share of the world market, compared with a 16 percent decline in the 1960s. The losses in the 1970s were particularly significant because they occurred in the wake of a 40 percent depreciation in the value of the dollar, which decreased the cost of American goods in foreign markets and made foreign imports more costly. It is estimated that this decline in the American competitive position during the 1970s alone resulted in $125 billion in lost production, plus the loss of about two million jobs in industry ("The Reindustrialization of America," 1980).

The scope of this problem is shown dramatically in Figures 1.1 and 1.2, which chart the declining share of American products in domestic and foreign markets. Few industries have escaped this decline. The American aircraft industry, long a leader and innovator, had 66 percent of the world market ten years ago but has only 58 percent today. We expect its market share to decrease further as European and Japanese aircraft corporations continue to develop and become more aggressive.

The share of the world market in plastics held by the United States declined from 28 percent in 1962 to 13 percent in 1980. Also affected were the drug industry (from 28 percent in 1962 to 15 percent in 1980), agricultural machinery (from 40 percent in 1962 to 24 percent in 1980), and textile machinery (from 15 percent in 1962 to 7 percent in 1980) ("The Reindustrialization of America," 1980). In many respects we have lost our competitive edge in the marketplace.

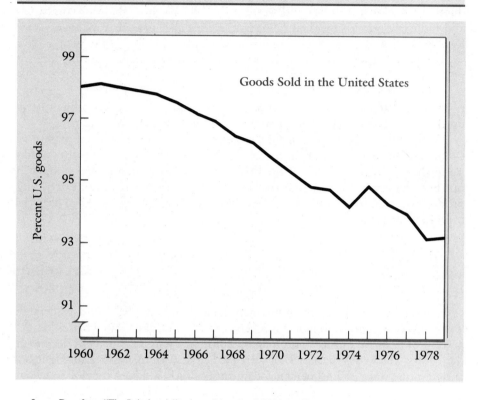

Figure 1.1
United States Share in Domestic Market, 1960 to 1979

Source: Data from "The Reindustrialization of America," 1980, p. 58.

Although our productivity has not declined, it is increasing at a slower pace than that of our competitors. From 1948 to 1968 output per hour worked increased at an annual rate of 3.2 percent. From 1969 to 1973, however, output increased at a rate of only 1.9 percent per year. The annual rate of increase from 1974 to 1984 has been a minuscule 0.7 percent. In absolute terms the United States remains the most productive nation in the world. But the rest of the industrialized world is rapidly catching up and may soon surpass the United States. This productivity growth by other nations is dramatically demonstrated in Figure 1.3.

Social and Policy Explanations
for the Decline

There are several reasons for our productivity problems. These relate largely to societal trends and government and business policies. The problem has been

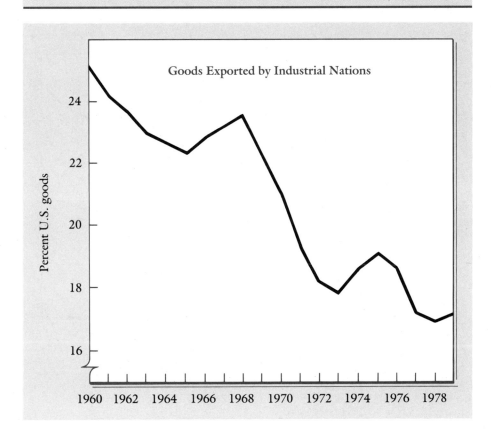

Figure 1.2
United States Share in Foreign Markets, 1960 to 1979

Goods Exported by Industrial Nations

Source: Data from "The Reindustrialization of America," 1980, p. 59.

a long time in coming, and the solutions will not be arrived at quickly. Among the more important factors hampering productivity growth over the past decade are the following:

A Diminished Investment in Innovation. Until very recently, many United States corporations refused to make major commitments to long-term research and development. This problem — and the recent upsurge in research and development — are shown in Figure 1.4. Unfortunately, in many cases we have begun our investments much later than have several of our foreign competitors.

Many fear that today's corporate leaders are becoming increasingly conservative and timid about innovation. They rise through the ranks by doing what

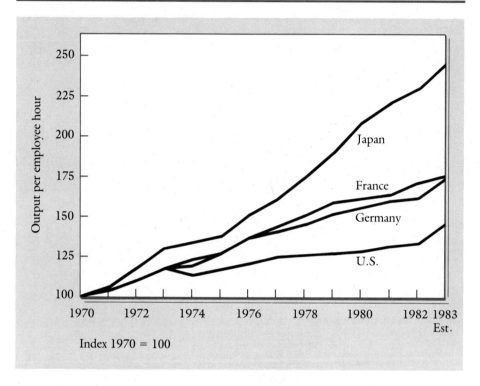

Figure 1.3
Growth in Productivity: The United States and Its Competitors, 1970–1983

Index 1970 = 100

Source: Data from Bureau of Labor Statistics.

everyone else does, and when they reach senior levels of management, they often spend more time enjoying or protecting the fruits of their labor than helping the organization grow and develop. Modern industry was founded by people who took moderate and sensible risks, yet many feel such individuals are becoming a rare commodity.

An Erosion of Personal Savings. Personal savings provide much of the capital for investment in industry. Unfortunately, Americans have never been big savers, compared with individuals in countries such as Japan and West Germany. In fact, personal savings in the United States have remained at between 4 to 7 percent of income during the past decade, whereas Japanese families saved about 20 percent of their income and the Germans saved about 15 percent (Fig.

Figure 1.4
Research and Development Spending in the United States, 1970 to 1983

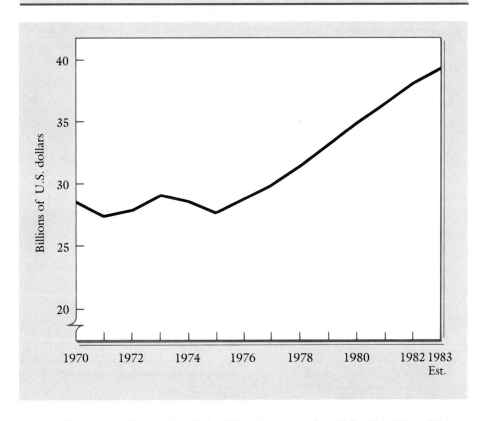

Source: Data from Data Resources Inc., National Science Foundation, John W. Kendrick of George Washington University.

1.5). As a result, relatively more money is available in these other countries for investment in plants and equipment.

The latest figures on plant and equipment investment are ominous for United States firms. In the hotly contested area of semiconductors and integrated circuits, for example, the gap in capital spending between the United States and Japan has been narrowing since 1976. At that time the United States was investing $4.43 to every $1 invested by the Japanese. By 1981 the ratio had shrunk to $1.84 for the United States to $1 for Japan. Experts have predicted that Japan's aggressive capital spending will give it an added 5 percent of the United States and European markets in 1985 ("Chip Wars," 1983).

Figure 1.5
Changes in Personal Savings and Plant Investment, 1970 to 1979

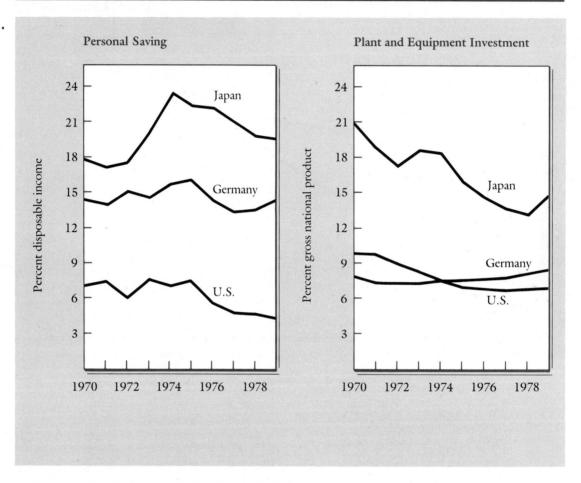

Source: Data from "The Reindustrialization of America," 1980, p. 61.

Lack of a Consistent Government Policy. Contemporary organizations face a maze of government bodies and regulations that constrain competitive efforts. Although many government actions may have good intentions, the result has often been chaos for corporations. An example of this conflict and contradiction in government policy can be seen in Figure 1.6. These few examples concern only the federal government and do not include state and local regulations.

In many cases American corporations have focused primarily on domestic markets and have been either disinterested or ineffective in world markets. The

---

Figure 1.6
Contradictions in United States Government Policies

HOW WASHINGTON'S CONTRADICTORY POLICIES HOBBLE U.S. INDUSTRY

On the One Hand . . .	*On the Other . . .*
The Environmental Protection Agency is pushing hard for stringent air pollution controls.	The Energy Department is pushing companies to switch from imported oil to dirtier coal.
The National Highway Traffic Safety Administration mandates weight-adding safety equipment for cars.	The Transportation Department is insisting on lighter vehicles to conserve gasoline.
The Justice Department offers guidance to companies on complying with the Foreign Corrupt Practices Act.	The Securities and Exchange Commission will not promise immunity from prosecution for practices Justice might permit.
The Occupational Safety and Health Administration chooses the lowest level of exposure to hazardous substances technically feasible, short of bankrupting an industry.	The Environmental Protection Agency uses more flexible standards for comparing risk levels with costs.
The Energy Department tries to keep down rail rates for hauling coal, to encourage plant conversions.	The Transportation Department tries to keep coal rail rates high, to bolster the ailing rail industry.
The Environmental Protection Agency restricts the use of pesticides.	The Agriculture Department promotes pesticides for agricultural and forestry uses.

Source: "The Reindustrialization of America," reprinted from the June 30, 1980 issue of *Business Week* by special permission, © 1980 by McGraw-Hill, Inc.

---

lack of expertise in international marketing is compounded by what many business people feel is a restrictive United States government policy on international sales. One estimate is that $5 billion to $10 billion in exports is lost annually because of government regulations. The United States has lost ground as a world leader in marketing.

A Prolonged Period of Inflation and High Interest. Economic conditions also have hampered industry. Many economists argue that continued inflation, high interest rates, and relatively heavy taxation create conditions that make long-term economic growth and stability increasingly difficult.

There are several reasons for the turbulence of recent economic periods. In their book *Five Economic Challenges,* Heilbroner and Thurow (1981) point out that inflationary periods until the 1950s were regularly associated with wars and were always relatively brief. In times of war, governments usually spend more money than they can take in through taxation. Spending rises rapidly, leading to

Feature 1.1
Cooperating Companies Take on the Japanese

To meet the growing challenge of competition from the Japanese in computers and semiconductors, two major cooperatives have been formed in the United States. The Semiconductor Research Corporation (SRC), located in North Carolina's Research Triangle, funds research by other organizations, mainly universities. The Microelectronics and Computer Cooperative (MCC), located in Austin, Texas, is funding its own research and development. Both cooperatives are trying to provide the kind of support that Japanese industry is receiving from the Japanese government.

MCC was conceived in 1982 by William C. Norris, Chairman of Control Data Corporation. Norris, and the task force of electronics executives that he assembled, chartered the new cooperative, wrote its bylaws, and hired retired Admiral Bobby R. Inman, a former director of the National Security Agency and deputy director of the CIA, as president and chief executive officer. Within a few months thirteen members had joined MCC, and research in four major areas was planned: computer-aided design and manufacturing (CAD/CAM), computer architecture, software technology, and packaging.

The idea behind MCC is that members pay an entry fee ($200,000) and then provide researchers and funding for a minimum of three years. In return for their investment of talent and financial support, members receive a three-year lead in being licensed on any MCC patents that result from the research. As more companies join and support a project, the costs for that project go down.

MCC hopes to have 255 researchers by 1985 and an operating budget of $75 million. Inman believes that MCC's future success lies in the commitment of its member companies to provide top-notch researchers.

Semiconductor Research Corporation is already enjoying a measure of success. Formed a few months before MCC, by mid-1983 it had committed $8.25 million to support research at thirty universities. Some of SRC's directors are urging the cooperative to begin its own research and development project. Specifically, they would like to see SRC develop a 4-megabit computer chip, which could store more than 4 million bits of digital data, before 1990, the current projected date for producing such a chip. To be first in this endeavor would do much to put the United States out in front again — ahead of the Japanese — in the worldwide production of computer chips.

Sources: "High-Tech Companies Team Up in the R&D Race," *Business Week,* August 15, 1983, pp. 94–95; "MCC Moves Out of the Idea State," by John Walsh, *Science,* June 17, 1983, pp. 1256–1257.

inflation. Inflationary periods were short, however, and from 1866 to 1900 and 1925 to 1933, prices actually fell.

The record since the 1950s is strikingly different. The wars in Korea and Vietnam brought about price increases, but inflationary rises were not followed by long periods when prices declined. In fact, inflation has been chronic since that time and often has been accompanied by a significant level of unemployment (Figs. 1.7 and 1.8).

Traditional theories of economics proposed that inflation and unemployment do not normally occur together. Inflation was thought to persist when a

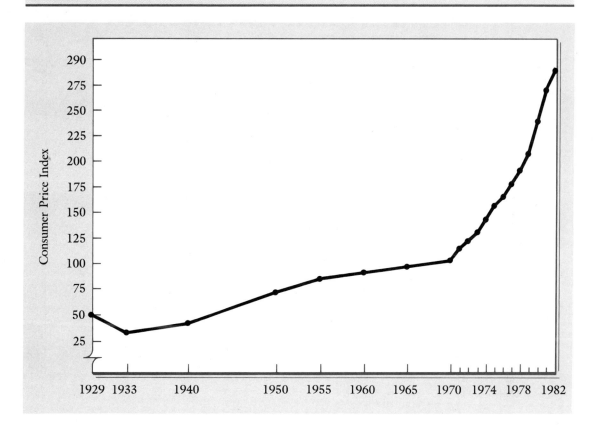

Figure 1.7
Consumer Price Index, All Major Expenditure Classes,
1929 to 1982 (1967 = 100)

Source: Data from *Economic Report to the President,* 1983, p. 221.

system was close to full capacity and employment was high. Thus, inflation could be reduced by stepping back from full capacity and lowering employment. A slowing down in the growth of the economy is called a **recession,** and this period is often characterized by high unemployment. It was commonly believed that employment could be increased by loosening monetary and fiscal policies to accelerate economic growth. In this context, inflation and high unemployment were conditions that occurred in different times. It is little wonder that the presence of both inflation and high unemployment, referred to as **stagflation,** bewilders economists and others who have attempted to predict our economic course. Our inability to predict the future correctly has caused havoc in many industries and has contributed to our declining competitive position.

Figure 1.8
Unemployment Rate, 1948 to 1982

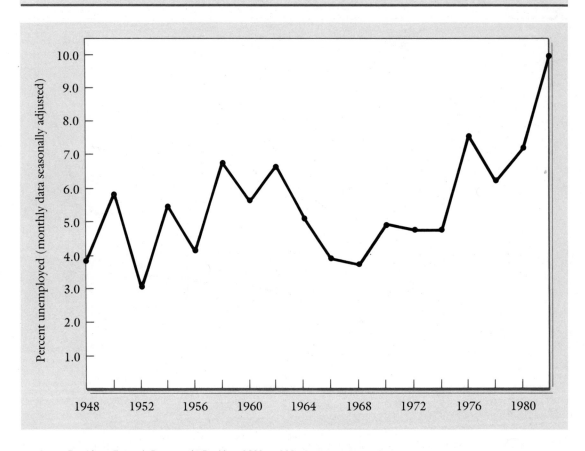

Source: Data from *Economic Report to the President,* 1983, p. 199.

Outdated Production Facilities. As noted in *Business Week* ("The Reindustrialization of America," 1980, p. 74), "The closing of . . . major steel complexes, as well as similar plant closings in the automobile, tire, and other manufacturing industries, is the final dramatic concession from today's chief executives that management has not been doing its job in keeping its plants up-to-date in order to meet foreign competition. Such a concession represents decades of maximizing profits for the short-term, while ignoring the long-term consequences."

Simply put, the United States is not modernizing its plants fast enough to keep up with technological change. American plants fail to compete with the modern plants of Japan and western Europe.

A Highly Adversarial Collective Bargaining Relationship. Organizations often find themselves in an "us"-versus-"them" relationship with their own employees. Instead of cooperating with each other, labor and management often see themselves as adversaries, with a basic lack of trust standing between them. There is a long tradition of such a relationship in this country. It is no surprise that the Japanese, who have a tradition of cooperation rather than conflict, can harness their human resources to benefit employees as well as investors.

Social Expectations that Are Difficult to Meet. Some people believe society has entered a phase of rising entitlements, with an increasing feeling among individuals that they have legitimate claims against society and that society owes them something. Earlier social attitudes, which touted the need to work hard or rewarded performance, have been replaced among some people by the feeling that they are entitled to certain benefits merely because of their membership in society. Philosophy aside, such attitudes can hardly ease the economic problems of our society. Feelings of entitlement among individuals in a society make it harder to improve the long-term quality of life for everyone; the work falls on fewer and fewer shoulders.

Managerial Explanations for Productivity Problems

There have been many suggestions for overcoming our productivity problems based on the points just presented. They include increasing the level of investment, reducing the burden of government regulations, and increasing the level of personal savings.

In their book *Minding America's Business,* Ira Magaziner and Robert Reich (1983) have criticized these proposals, contending that they place too much emphasis on financial matters — government expenses, capital, and research and development. These authors believe that too little attention has been paid to how these expenditures can bring about a more competitive position, a question that relates to the fundamentals of effective management. Government policies, whether fiscal or monetary, can only set the stage. In the final analysis it is how managers respond to and capitalize on these policies that spells the difference between economic revitalization and a prolonged economic slump.

Shortcomings in our present competitive position are also linked with management failures or limitations. From our vantage point there are five key interrelated limitations in the present practices of management that must now be addressed and corrected.

Failure to Develop Basic Managerial Competencies. An important theme constantly echoed by managers and theorists is the need to go back to the fundamentals of managing. Success comes from good planning, tight cost control, good communication, and sound decision making. Vanport Manufacturing's success in marketing forest products in Japan, for example, did not occur overnight. The company devoted enormous attention to the special aesthetic and structural requirements of Japanese home builders and carefully designed or retrofitted sawmill machinery to manufacture to Japanese specifications. In contrast, the demise of the World Football League can be attributed to poor planning, incorrect assumptions about its competitors, inadequate financial controls, and wholly unsupported optimism.

The *Business Failures Record* (1977) listed the known causes of business failures as follows: incompetence (44.6 percent), unbalanced experience (22.6 percent), lack of managerial experience (26.9 percent), and neglect, fraud, and disaster (1.8 percent). Note that the first three causes are linked to poor management. In recessionary periods or tight economic times, there is even less room for error. The more successful companies will be those that have committed the fewest mistakes.

Emphasis on Short-Term Strategies and Immediate Results. Despite widely publicized claims to the contrary, many United States corporations place considerable stress on the here-and-now. They want immediate profits and

---

Feature 1.2
Bankruptcy Court Perspective: Managers Are to Blame

It usually begins with the same symptoms — profits drop off, a manufacturer can't raise the capital to replace or improve its plant, store openings are delayed, lenders are reluctant to roll over credit. It is the road to bankruptcy court.

Business failures in 1981 and 1982 reached a post-depression high, according to Dun & Bradstreet Corporation. In 1982 alone, 89 of over 10,000 businesses failed.

Take E. A. Adams Inc. of Pawtucket, Rhode Island, for example. It was flush with $19 million in sales in 1980. Then the long-time owners sold the business to some of their own executives. The new owners embarked on a series of new acquisitions, and before long the revenues weren't big enough to pay the interest rate on borrowings. Creditors moved to stop further borrowing. Bankruptcy court records show the company had assets of $6.3 million and secured debts of $10.3 million at one point. The company eventually was liquidated, a victim of managers who tried to acquire too much at a time of high interest rates and slipping jewelry sales.

Executives of failing companies usually try to shift the blame to the economy, unions, foreign competition, and so on, but people who watch bankruptcy proceedings say the managers themselves are to blame for most failures.

"Management is the key," said Frederic T. Hersey, a Boston certified public accountant whose firm counsels distressed companies. "There is no question about that. You can see it in the same industry where some companies make it even in a bad economy but others don't."

Sydney Parlow, a consultant who acts as a court-appointed trustee in bankruptcy cases, puts it more bluntly. "That's why these companies get in trouble," he said, "because some idiot thinks he can do everything."

Source: "Saving a Company through Chapter 11," by Dan Hall, *New England Business*, May 2, 1983, pp. 10–14.

search for ways to achieve them — often at the expense of long-term stability and growth. For instance, the automobile industry has long been criticized for failing to respond adequately to the need for a long-range overhaul of both its designs and its manufacturing processes. Instead it has all too often relied on strong advertising in the hope of convincing the public to buy what Detroit already offers. This strategy hasn't worked.

A further example of this shortsightedness can be seen in the tool industry. Cyclical downturns have long prevented machine tool companies from gambling in prosperous times with the construction of new plants and manufacturing capacity. As a result, when a major sales opportunity emerged in 1978 when Detroit began building smaller cars, the machine tool companies weren't ready. With lead times stretching to two years, German and Japanese manufacturers entered the market and now hold an estimated 25 percent of it.

Inadequacies in Managing Human Resources. Commenting on the comparisons that are currently made between the United States and Japan, Ario Morita, chairman of the Sony Corporation, said, "There is no magic to the Japanese success in the world market . . . what American managers need to do is a much better job in managing their most important resource — people." The difference between the United States and Japan in developing human potential cannot be overemphasized. The Japanese place great importance on the task of recruiting and hiring employees. Major Japanese firms consider the employment contract as relatively permanent, extending until retirement. No such explicit guarantees are given to employees in the United States. The organization does not promise job security.

In difficult times American firms commonly lay off workers. For example, at the end of 1981 it was estimated that more than 250,000 employees had been laid off in the automobile industry; in the steel industry, 150,000. Only in the most adverse circumstances do these firms consider reducing compensation for their top executives. The pattern is normally reversed in Japan. When Japan's Toyo Kogyo Company, the manufacturer of the Mazda rotary engine cars, was at the brink of bankruptcy, its first action was to cut executive bonuses. Then it resorted to offering early retirement for more senior employees. It was only after these steps were taken did the company terminate employees (Tsurumi, 1983).

Absentee and turnover statistics present additional evidence of the magnitude of the problem. In many industries daily absence rates approach 15 to 20 percent and cost an estimated $26.4 billion annually (Mirvis and Lawler, 1977). Mowday, Porter, and Steers (1982) also report that monthly turnover rates in 1979 were highest (4.4 percent) in small firms of up to 500 employees; lower in manufacturing sectors (1.6 percent), and somewhat higher in the western region of the United States (2.4 percent). Worker layoffs, job turnovers, and absenteeism contribute to our productivity problems. More careful attention to managing and developing employees would greatly alleviate the problem.

Lack of an Integrated Strategic Analysis. Managing the internal activities of an organization is only part of the modern executive's job. He or she must also monitor important changes in the external environment, assess competitive actions, and develop offensive and defensive competitive strategies.

McKinsey and Company, a well-known management consulting firm, has suggested four phases that companies go through in developing their management process: financial planning, an emphasis on budgets and schedules; forecast-based planning, which highlights prediction; externally orientated planning, featuring competitive analysis; and strategic planning, with an emphasis on creating the future. They estimate that most corporations are still in the second phase, forecast-based planning, and struggling to make major changes in their systems to move them solidly into the third phase, externally oriented planning. The future success of corporate managers depends on how effectively they can develop and manage integrated strategic systems.

Lack of an International Orientation.   The growth of the international sector has had a significant impact on the economy of the United States. On the domestic front the number of goods imported and exported grew from approximately 12 percent of the gross national product in 1970 to an estimated 24 percent in 1980. This trend might signal opportunities for American firms, but the disappointing fact is that the United States had become less competitive in the world markets through the years. In 1963 the United States produced about 40 percent of world output, in 1970 about 37 percent, and in 1975 to 1976 only 35 percent. In contrast, Japan, which produced only 5.48 percent of world output in 1963, registered an impressive 9.14 percent in 1977. Even more impressive is the production of the so-called gang of four: Hong Kong, Korea, Taiwan, and Singapore. Their share of world output rose from 0.4 percent in 1967 to 1.4 percent in 1976.

Given the vastness of the domestic market, it was natural for firms in the United States to give priority to the home front. Countries with a more limited domestic market, notably Japan, were forced to emphasize opportunities overseas. Japanese are noted for carefully scanning the worldwide market. They have done so by sending study teams to the targeted countries, formulating detailed feasibility studies, and even hiring experts to help diagnose the specific needs of future customers. For example, when Toyota entered the smaller car market in the United States, it faced a formidable competitor — Volkswagen. Toyota then commissioned an American marketing researcher to interview Volkswagen owners to determine what they liked and disliked about their cars. Then Toyota designed a car to include all the benefits of the Volkswagen and none of the weaknesses. The Japanese followed this pattern to penetrate markets for such products as calculators, motorcycles, watches, and television. It is no wonder that the noted marketing professor Philip Kotler called the Japanese "the world's champion marketers" (Kotler and Fahey, 1982).

The insularity of firms in the United States might have worked in the early 1950s and the 1960s, when they faced little competition. Since then Japan and West Germany have become strong competitors. Also, the newly industrializing countries of Taiwan and Korea, as well as Hong Kong and Singapore, have be-

**Feature 1.3
Can It Come Home Again?**

American industry is beginning to pay attention to a system it pioneered and then forgot.

Called the "flexible manufacturing system," it's a new kind of automated manufacturing process that can be programmed to change its procedures for different production requirements. Conventional "fixed automation" systems follow a set sequence to make a product.

Japan and Europe latched onto the new flexible system, but companies in the United States either ignored it or turned to a less risky, more primitive form of automation in which tools are grouped by the product they make instead of their function.

"Many United States companies are ready to buy a brand new 1959 Cadillac in 1983," said Jim Baker, head of General Electric's automation group.

General Electric is one American company stung by foreign competition that is beginning to use the flexible manufacturing system at its Erie, Pennsylvania, locomotive plant. The company does most of its locomotive business overseas. Its foreign rivals have access to cheap labor and a variety of government support. Without automation the company predicted it would have to move its operation overseas or get out of the business.

The Japanese, with their chronic labor shortage and their emphasis on long-term rather than immediate gains, have plunged into the development and application of the flexible systems. American companies have held back because of a labor surplus and because management seems to like short-term gains and less risk. The historic American dominance of world markets has also done nothing to push companies into making radical, expensive changes.

But now the competition is beginning to hurt. American companies, says Baker, have to stop whining about their problems and about the advantages foreign companies have, and start automating.

Source: "Flexible Manufacturing: Where the U.S. Lags Behind" and "Flexible Systems Invade the Factory," by Paul Kinnucan, *High Technology,* July 1983, pp. 32–42.

come contenders not only in labor-intensive industries but in high technology, which appears to be the battleground of the future. With growing opportunities in the international market and the maturing of our primary industries — automobiles, steel, nonferrous metals, textiles, coal, other metals, and machinery, — the modern executive can no longer afford the luxury of staying within the domestic market. An effective global strategy has become a requirement if the modern executive is to survive.

Challenges for the Modern Executive

The nature of these problems and their magnitude suggest that managerial initiative and innovation are keys to future organizational success. Managers must play a central role in facilitating organizational effectiveness. Thus, we need to develop new managers who have both the insight to see and understand the nature of such problems and the courage and initiative to develop comprehensive strategies for change. These managers not only will be making their organizations more effective, but also will be improving the quality of their employees' working life and the nation's economic development. The challenge to management is indeed an important one.

The modern executive's principal task is to respond to new external developments and the demands of society. To meet this challenge, the executive must develop three key **competencies:** technical, behavioral, and strategic (see Fig. 1.9). A short historical look at their evolution will provide perspective.

Technical Competencies

The growth of the management profession should be viewed against the backdrop of economic events in the last decades of the nineteenth century. This period was a time of great mergers, trusts, cartels, and holding companies. Railroads structured the economy. The coming of the automobile helped establish the consumer goods industry.

The growing size and complexity of operations created acute problems for management. The larger numbers of employees necessitated greater integration and coordination. The growing sophistication of machinery led to new questions concerning aspects of work not related to machines. Not surprisingly, the engineers, notably the American Society of Mechanical Engineers, and the railroad managers defined the new requirements of management. One particular engineer, Frederick Taylor, led the way in examining the efficiency of non-machine relations. Other writers, such as Fayol (1949), Urwick (1947), and Barnard (1938), devoted their attention to defining the roles of top managers. From these efforts came the elements of planning, organizing, directing, and controlling that to this day provide the foundation of management. We refer to these as **technical competencies.**

Technical competencies focus on the requirements of the task and are a prerequisite for a good manager. Graduating students must be trained in the fundamentals of their particular field. A finance major is expected to know how to develop discounted cash flow analysis; a marketing major needs to know how to conduct a consumer research project; a management major should know the details of planning and control. Technical skills constitute the first of three competencies required of a modern executive.

Behavioral Competencies

At all times, but particularly since the 1950s, managers have had to direct behavior effectively within their organizations. The pioneering work of the Hawthorne researchers challenged the assumption that people in organizations are motivated solely by economic incentives, an assumption that provided the

Figure 1.9
Requirements for Effective Management

TECHNICAL COMPETENCIES *(Part II)*	BEHAVIORAL COMPETENCIES *(Part III)*	STRATEGIC COMPETENCIES *(Part IV)*
Planning	Motivational skills	Managing strategic adaptation
Organizing	Effective leadership	Managing organizational change
Directing	Managing work groups	Responding to government regulations
Controlling	Effective communication	Understanding international considera-
	Managing conflict and power	tions
	Human resource management	Understanding social issues

basis for the planning, organizing, controlling, and directing functions. The researchers found instead that performance depended as much on the organized social group. These findings stimulated research in the behavioral sciences to investigate more complex motivations. Contemporary areas of importance include leadership, motivation, group performance, power and politics, communications, and human resource management. We refer to these as **behavioral competencies.** It should be noted, as shown in Figure 1.9, that behavioral competencies build upon technical competencies.

Behavioral competencies focus on the requirements of social relationships. A good manager is not only a good technician, but also an individual equally adept at dealing with people. Every so often we hear the story of a highly trained, promising student with a master's degree in business administration who was fired shortly after entering a firm because of his or her inability to relate to the older and senior employees. As one executive recruiter said, "Newly minded MBAs are excellent technicians but are terribly naive in the area of social and political relationships." The modern executive needs to master these behavioral skills.

Strategic Competencies

New challenges confront the manager in the 1980s, challenges arising principally from significant changes in the outside world. We are faced with more turbulent economic periods, a more restless work force, more domestic and international competition, increased government involvement in the private sector, and declining industrial performance. The modern executive must master the skills to diagnose the environment, analyze competitors' actions, compete in international markets, and manage organizational change. We refer to these as **strategic competencies.**

These competencies emphasize the requirements of interorganizational linkages, and, in so doing, they build upon both technical and behavioral competencies. Perhaps the most important criterion differentiating a good and a very good manager is the ability to think in strategic terms. General Electric, a company that has been consistently ranked by *Fortune* as one of the best-managed firms in the United States, is also considered to be one of the best strategic firms in the business.

Plan of the Book

One of the primary concerns of this book is the ways in which managers can become more effective. We will proceed by building on our discussion of managerial competencies and discussing how these competencies can improve effectiveness. The book has five parts, covering (1) the nature of management and organizational effectiveness, (2) technical competencies, (3) behavioral competencies, (4) strategic competencies, and (5) the future of management (Fig. 1.9).

The Nature of Management and Organizations. We start our examination in Chapter 2 with a study of the nature of management and the ways in which managers can help their organizations become more effective. Because managerial goals are linked to organizational goals, it is important to understand completely the context in which managers operate. The nature of organizations and effectiveness are discussed in Chapter 3.

Technical Competencies of Management. In Part II we focus on technical competencies that are required for effective management. The section builds on the traditional functions of planning, organizing, directing, and controlling that were formulated by theorists such as Fayol, Urwick, Roethlisberger, and Barnard. Recent research findings and modern management practices are also included. We examine planning in a complex environment in Chapter 4, designing effective organizations in Chapter 5, managerial decision making in Chapter 6, control systems in organizations in Chapter 7, and operations management and production control in Chapter 8.

Behavioral Competencies of Management. In Part III we turn to motivational and behavioral processes in organizations, and the nature of groups and group effectiveness. We review relevant theories of motivation and performance in Chapter 9. In Chapter 10 we examine the nature of leadership and how it relates to managerial effectiveness. Chapter 11 is concerned with the nature of groups and ways to manage effective work groups. In Chapter 12 we review processes of communication and their importance to the management function. Chapter 13 covers conflict, power, and political processes in organizations. Finally, in Chapter 14 we examine human resources management and how such management promotes managerial effectiveness.

Strategic Competencies of Management. In Part IV we discuss special topics of strategic management related to the problems faced by managers. In Chapter 15 we present a framework of strategic analysis in growing, maturing, and declining industries. Chapter 16 focuses on the management of change and organizational development. Chapter 17 presents a system for assessing the effects of government regulation and deregulation, as well as recent developments in industrial policy. Chapter 18 covers the international dimensions of strategic management. Chapter 19 is devoted to a discussion of social and ethical issues that confront the modern executive.

The Future of Management. The function of management has evolved to meet the requirements of new external and internal events. It is important, therefore, for the modern executive to be responsive to future events that may have impact on the management function. In Chapter 20 we look briefly at these developments.

Summary

American industry has lost considerable ground competing in the world marketplace in the last twenty years, because of a diminished investment in innovation, an erosion of personal savings, lack of a consistent government policy, prolonged inflation and high interest rates, outdated production facilities, adversarial collective bargaining, and social expectations that are difficult to meet.

Managers are responsible as well. They have failed in the fundamentals of good management: good planning, tight cost control, good communication, and sound decision making. They have often emphasized only short-term strategies, have inadequately managed human resources, have failed to develop an integrated strategic analysis, and have lacked an international orientation.

Strong action must be taken. To respond to new external developments and the demands of society, executives must develop technical, behavioral, and strategic competencies. Skills in these areas are required to help overcome some crucial problems related to our declining productivity and the difficulties facing managers.

Questions for Discussion

1. Present some of the reasons for the decline in the relative competitiveness of United States industries during the past decade.
2. In 1983 some American scholars argued that the short-term orientation of corporate executives reduced their investment in production facilities, research and development, and employee training. Such reductions served to undermine the competitiveness of United States firms. Others have defended the actions of these executives by arguing that United States firms are evaluated on a quarterly basis, and that the corporate executives were actually acting in the best interests of their stockholders. Present your critical comments on both points of view.
3. In what ways do our present managerial practices contribute to our declining competitiveness?

4. Define as clearly as you can the following terms and concepts:
   a. technical competencies
   b. behavioral competencies
   c. strategic competencies
5. In what ways do technical, behavioral, and strategic competencies affect managerial effectiveness?

Exercise 1.1
Forecasting the Future

This exercise is designed to show you how attempts at forecasting and monitoring can operate on an industry-wide basis. This exercise can range from an overnight assignment to a term project, and you can do it either individually or in groups.

First you or your group must select an industry — for example, automobile, telecommunications, high technology and electronics, or food retailing, and then choose three of the following categories:

1. communications
2. health and biomedicine
3. science
4. social developments
5. business and economics
6. politics and government
7. technology

Next, select one or more of the following publications to monitor over a specified period of time:

Advertising Age	*Electronic News*	*New Scientists*
American Journal of Sociology	*Esquire*	*Newsweek*
	Forbes	
American Review of Political Science	*Fortune*	*Popular Science*
	Futures	*Psychology Today*
American Scholar	*The Futurist*	
		Science
Behavior Today	*Harper's*	*Scientific American*
Business Economics	*Harvard Business Review*	*Social Policy*
Business Horizons	*The Humanist*	
Business Week		*Time*
	Industry Week	*Technological Forecasting and Social Change*
Conference Board Record	*Inforsystems*	
		Technology Review
Daedalus	*Journal of Consumer Affairs*	
Datamation		*Wall Street Journal*
	MBA	*Wharton Magazine*
Economist	*Money*	

During this period of time, review each issue for articles that relate to the chosen category of research. If an article is relevant, abstract it and submit it to your instructor for review. The article should involve an idea or event that is indicative of either a trend or shift in the macroenvironment. In addition, the implications of the article should have some relation to the long-range concerns of both United States society and the selected industry. As the final step in the exercise, prepare a summary of the most significant abstracts and present them in class.

CHAPTER 2

The Nature of Management

A well-groomed, fiftyish-looking man in a bathrobe appears on the screen. "My wife bought me a Remington shaver," he says with a smile, "and I liked it so much I bought the company."

The man in that television ad is Victor Kiam, and the story he's telling isn't some advertising executive's pipe dream. Kiam, who began his career selling Pepsodent and Lifebuoy soap in New Orleans, did buy Sperry Rand's Remington shaver division for $25 million in 1979. Remington had once been at the head of the shaver market. But it had been losing ground and had accumulated $30 million in losses over five years.

Kiam cut overhead and costs. In his first week at the Bridgeport, Connecticut, head-quarters he fired seventy executives and saved the company $2 million. He lowered prices and began spending more on advertising, and he turned the company around.

The company's 1981 sales jumped to about $80 million, 40 percent more than the year before. Pretax profits were about $6 million. The company's market share bounced from 19.5 percent two years before to 40 percent. The company's work force increased from 550 to 900. "We don't need a lot of chiefs," he said. "We need people who can produce."

Source: Adapted with permission from "Smooth Performance — Remington's Shaver Turnaround," *Fortune,* January 11, 1982, p. 11.

Chapter Outline

- What Is Management?
- Variations in Managerial Work
- Managerial Skills and Abilities
- How Managers Spend Their Time
- The Managerial Role Constellation
- Managerial Demands, Constraints, Choices

Key Terms

- management
- executive management
- middle management
- first-line management
- line manager
- staff manager
- technical, human, and conceptual skills
- managerial role constellation
- interpersonal roles
- informational roles
- decisional roles
- demands
- constraints
- choices

Chapter Objectives

After studying Chapter 2 you should be able to

1. Define the term *management* and discuss its four primary functions.
2. Understand the differences among executive, middle, and first-line management and how they work together.
3. Explain the difference between line and staff managers.
4. Discuss the technical, human, and conceptual skills successful managers need at different levels.
5. Define the term *managerial role constellation* and discuss the different roles managers must play.
6. Talk about managerial jobs in terms of their demands, constraints, and choices.

Introduction

In Chapter 1 we examined several of the major problems facing contemporary organizations. A central theme was the fact that in many cases *managers can make a difference* in the effectiveness and productivity of an organization. This is not to say that managers can overcome all problems. Several severe problems, such as the state of the economy, are clearly beyond their reach. But even with these constraints the quality and degree of ingenuity of management is vitally important.

Because management is so important in helping organizations become more effective, we focus on that subject in this chapter. We begin by defining the concept of management and discussing several of its more common functions. You will encounter different types of managerial work. We will introduce you to the managerial role constellation, based largely on the work of Henry Mintzberg. Finally, a model of management following the work of Rosemary Stewart will be discussed.

What Is Management?

Definition of Management

Perhaps the best place to begin our examination of managerial work is with a definition. Exactly what is management? Around the turn of the century, the early management theorist Mary Parker Follett said that management is the "art of getting things done through people." In other words, the manager coordinates the work of others to accomplish aims that might not be achievable by an individual. We will define **management** as the process of planning, organizing, directing, and controlling the activities of employees in combination with other organizational resources to accomplish stated organizational goals.

Underlying this definition are the assumptions that achieving organizational goals is helped greatly by coordinating various work activities, and that a central figure or figures are needed to ensure that the parts of a group or organization work together. This does not mean that all good management is either highly centralized or highly decentralized, authoritarian or participative. The concept of management exists in virtually all organizations seeking to attain goals, whether in the public or the private sector and whether in a socialist or a capitalist economy. The nature of management varies, but all organizations have a managerial structure.

Functions of Management

Given this definition of management, exactly how do managers go about managing? What do they do to help attain organizational goals? We can identify four primary functions of management that characterize the activities of most managers. Although the amount of time spent on each of these functions can vary considerably, these categories serve as a general introduction to the variety of work performed by managers. The four functions are:

1. *Planning.* To make the best possible use of an organization's scarce resources, managers must engage in a variety of planning activities. There usually are two levels of planning: *strategic,* which focuses on long-term plans for dealing with the environment, and *internal,* which deals with activities within the organization, such as production scheduling.

2. *Organizing.* Managers must bring together individuals and tasks to make effective use of people and resources. Organizing involves designing and monitoring appropriate organizational structures to know when change and development are needed.

3. *Directing.* A manager must be able to make employees want to participate actively in achieving an organization's goals. He or she should understand group processes and the relationship between individual and group behavior, as well as how employees respond to authority and leadership.

4. *Controlling.* Control systems can be found throughout organizations. They include production, information and financial controls, and budgets. Control systems provide standards for monitoring and evaluating the use of resources.

We can see that being a manager — accepting these responsibilities — is no easy matter. Managers are responsible not only for their own actions, but also for those of their subordinates and their organization, and they must somehow coordinate all these factors with the interests of society. It is not surprising that many choose not to accept the responsibility of becoming a manager when given the chance.

Variations in Managerial Work

People tend to talk about managers as though they all performed roughly the same functions. Such is not the case. Managers are different in several ways. We can categorize them by *level* in the organizational hierarchy and by *type*.

Management by Level

For convenience of analysis, there are usually considered to be three distinct levels of management: **executive, middle,** and **first-line,** or supervisory, **management** (Fig. 2.1).

Executive Management. Executive managers are those relatively few senior administrators who are responsible for establishing long-term objectives as

Figure 2.1
Levels of Management

well as general operating policies to ensure that the objectives are met. Executive managers can usually be identified by their titles, such as chief executive officer (CEO), president, and vice-president.

Middle Management. Middle managers are largely responsible for interpreting the general, long-range objectives set down by executive management and translating them into concrete, specific goals for various divisions and departments. Middle managers often supervise the activities of other, lower-level managers.

First-line Management. First-line managers, or supervisors, are largely responsible for carrying out the day-to-day activities within the various departments to ensure that short-term goals are met. Such positions are often the place where new college graduates receive their first assignments.

Management by Type

In addition to different levels of management, there are two general types of managers: line and staff.

Line Managers. Line managers are directly responsible for a main product line or service of the organization. They are directly involved in the production of goods or services. Production and marketing managers are two examples.

Staff Managers. These managers generally serve a supporting role in the organization. Examples of **staff managers** include personnel, purchasing, and research and development managers, accountants, and public relations officers. Although they are not directly involved in production, production would not continue for long without their services. Ideally, line and staff managers serve a complimentary role. Each helps the other as they pursue corporate objectives together.

The difference between line and staff management can be seen in the highly simplified organizational chart shown in Figure 2.2. Line management extends from the president down through the vice-president of manufacturing, general manager, plant managers *A, B,* and *C,* and, finally, product supervisors *A, B,* and *C*. In contrast, personnel and finance vice-presidents are shown as examples of staff management.

Figure 2.2
Line and Staff Management

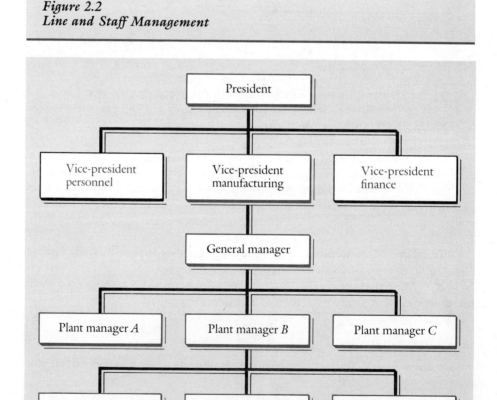

Feature 2.1
High Tech Stress

Paul Smith has paid for his success with a new kind of high tech malady that experts are calling "TechnoStress."

Smith at age 37 was the director of data processing for a large West Coast manufacturer. He successfully supervised a $12 million computer conversion, the largest ever attempted by his company. His boss and his peers praised him. "Paul's a genius," they said.

But the costs were great for Smith. He spent almost every waking hour on the project. There were communication problems with executive management who didn't understand the scope of the job. Technical specialists often didn't respond to his leadership, and some quit. Demands of the computer users were unrealistic. The whole conversion nearly fell apart several times. And there were complaints from people who had to put in extra time.

The family paid, too. Smith often worked through the weekend and was preoccupied the little time he was home, his wife said. His children and his wife understood little about what he was doing. And added to all this were the health problems — chronic fatigue, hypertension, a nervous stomach, too much drinking.

His attitude? If he didn't do it, there would be lots of people waiting to take his place.

Unfortunately Smith is not an exception. He is a victim of a unique brand of mental assault called TechnoStress. Experts estimate that his problem exists in perhaps half the data processing centers in the United States, not because of personal deficiencies but because of the kind of work that is done. The combination of high stress and high technology is taking its toll.

Source: Adapted with permission from "Paul's 'Success' Story," *Data Management,* September 1983, p. 11.

Managerial Skills and Abilities

Using the three-part description of management levels discussed, we can move one step further and ask questions about the skills managers need. Robert Katz (1974) has suggested that successful managers must exhibit three distinct types of skills:

1. **Technical skills.** Managers must have the ability to use the tools, procedures, and techniques of their special areas. An accountant should have expertise in accounting; a production manager must have mastered operations management techniques. These skills are the mechanics of the job.

2. **Human skills.** Human skills involve the ability to work with people. They also require understanding of human motivation and group processes. These skills are necessary for the manager to become involved with and lead his or her work group.

3. **Conceptual skills.** These skills represent the manager's ability to organize information to better understand or improve his or her performance on the

Feature 2.2
Consolidated Foods Turns to Growth from Within

When John H. Bryan took over as chief executive officer of Consolidated Foods in 1975, the price of the company's common stock had fallen by half since 1968, when Consolidated's chairman and largest share-holder Nathan Cummings had retired. Few believed that Bryan would be able to get along with Cummings, who was still on the board and who had already gone through two successors prior to Bryan. But the critics were wrong. Not only has Bryan gotten along with Cummings, but he has also brought the stock back up to previous levels and increased sales from $2.5 billion in 1975 to over $6 billion in 1982.

How did he do it? The first thing Bryan did was to take a tour of the 125 companies that made up Consolidated Foods. He then decided that Consolidated should concentrate solely on consumer goods and services, and thus sold 49 of the companies that did not fall into this category. At the same time he introduced tough cost controls over the companies he kept — among them Sara Lee (frozen baked goods), Shasta (soft drinks),

Hillshire Farms (specialty meats), Hanes & L'eggs (hosiery), and Bali (bras).

Under Bryan's leadership, Consolidated has turned its attention to internal growth. The company is working at increasing unit volume and improving marketing and advertising strategies — efforts that are ongoing today. Management is encouraging its divisions to be more aggressive about risk taking and exploring new ideas, with a promise of back-up funding for smart investments. However, Consolidated is demanding accountability before its divisions spend big money.

The success of these measures is evident in the company's recent 18 percent return on equity — 5 percent higher than the industry average. And Consolidated Foods is now one of the most diversified and profitable companies in the nation.

Sources: "A Sprawling Company's Organization Man," by Grover Heiman, *Nation's Business,* April 1983, pp. 48–50; "A Leaner Consolidated Foods Rediscovers Marketing," *Business Week,* August 29, 1983, pp. 58–59.

job. They include the manager's ability to see the organization as a whole and to understand how the various parts fit together to work as a well-integrated unit. These skills are necessary to coordinate the departments and divisions successfully so the organization can pull together.

Managers at different levels require or use these three managerial skills in different proportions. As shown in Figure 2.3, executive managers concentrate primarily on the use of human and conceptual skills. Technical skills are less important, although still necessary. In middle management conceptual skills become less important and technical skills required for day-to-day operations become somewhat more significant. Finally, for first-line managers, technical skills are highly important, whereas conceptual skills diminish considerably. Note that the human skills of understanding and dealing with people are always important.

Although this analysis is very general and exceptions can easily be identified, the general model emphasizes that different skills may be necessary as a manager

Figure 2.3
Differences in Skills Required for Successful Management
According to Level in the Hierarchy

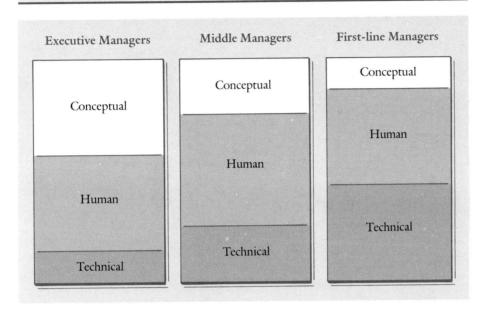

moves up through the hierarchy. This fact becomes apparent in management education: junior management courses tend to be technical in nature, whereas executive programs focus more on the development of conceptual skills. Both emphasize human relations skills.

How Managers Spend Their Time

We can now go one step further and consider the question of how managers spend their time. Figure 2.4 shows that managers at different levels in the organization's hierarchy generally emphasize different tasks. A study by Mintzberg (1973) found that executives concentrate most of their efforts on planning, change, and organization, a finding consistent with the points concerning executive managerial skills we have discussed (Katz, 1974). Planning and organizing are largely conceptual activities. The findings also show that executives focus

Figure 2.4
Variations in Managerial Time Allocation According to Managerial Level

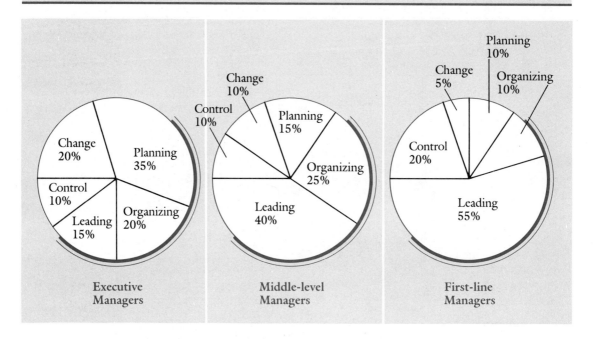

Source: Data from Mintzberg (1973). Illustration adapted from Szilagyi (1981, p. 27). Reprinted by permission.

primarily on strategy formulation, on developing long-range plans to help the organization survive and prosper.

In contrast, middle managers concentrate on leading or organizing and spend somewhat less time on planning and change. This finding by Mintzberg, also consistent with Katz's model, shows that middle managers divide their time about equally between conceptual and human skills. These managers focus their energies on strategy implementation, a task requiring both organizational and leadership skills.

Mintzberg also found that first-line managers focus largely on leadership activities and to a lesser extent on control activities. This finding is consistent with Katz's assertion that first-line managers concentrate on technical and human skills. They spend far less time in activities requiring conceptual skills, such as planning, and in developing change strategies.

A separate study of managerial time allocation (Horne and Lupton, 1965) investigated how managerial time distribution varied by function rather than by level. The study looked at managers in production management, marketing, finance, and personnel. Four managerial activities were used, including planning, organizing, controlling, and a miscellaneous "other" category. The results,

---

Feature 2.3
Inefficiency at the Top

A study of eleven major American banks has found that more than 30 percent of middle management could be eliminated with no harmful impact on the quality of service the banks provide.

The study was done by SMC Hendrick Inc., a management consultant firm in Framingham, Massachusetts, specializing in computerized analysis of the way businesses are organized. More than 48,000 bank managers and workers were surveyed.

Managers, the survey found, spend nearly half their time on work that could be done by technicians, clerks, and other non-management personnel. The productivity problem costs banks millions of dollars in overhead annually.

Bank managers spend only 55 percent of their time actually managing, according to Hendrick's Charles K. Rourke. The remaining 45 percent is spent on secondary, technical aspects that could be done by skilled workers. Many banks allow managers to be only 50 percent effective in ther jobs, Rourke said. He called such inefficiency one factor in increasing overhead and decreasing productivity in the banking industry.

The survey added that each bank manager oversees an average of only four employees, but that in better-organized banks the number grows to seven employees.

Source: "A Consultant's View: Managers Manage Too Few, Too Much," *New England Business,* May 17, 1982, pp. 30–32.

---

shown in Figure 2.5, demonstrate again that different managers spend their time on different areas. Production managers, who are line managers (as we have discussed), spend the greatest percentage of their time on controlling activities, whereas personnel managers, who are staff managers, spend the largest proportion of their time on planning. The diversity of management emerges once again.

Figure 2.5
Variations in Managerial Time Allocation According to Function

FUNCTION	MANAGERIAL ACTIVITIES			
	Planning (%)	*Organizing (%)*	*Controlling (%)*	*Other (%)*
Production	17	19	46	18
Marketing	14	17	53	16
Finance	15	12	60	13
Personnel	33	26	20	21

Source: Horne and Lupton, 1965, p. 23. Reprinted by permission.

The Managerial Role Constellation

To this point, we have been considering various aspects of a manager's job. We examined levels of management, different managerial skills, and the ways managers spend their time. We now come to a crucial aspect of management: the constellation of behaviors or roles required of a successful manager. We will refer to the **managerial role constellation** as the set of roles that managers must perform if they are to be successful in their jobs.

In discussing this topic we will present a role model developed by Henry Mintzberg after an intensive study of five chief executive officers of major corporations. Although there may be implications for lower-level managers, this section speaks primarily to managers at the executive level. Mintzberg begins by arguing that the ten different roles required of a manager cannot be isolated. They represent a unified whole. He says:

> These ten roles form a *gestalt* — an integrated whole. In essence, the manager is an input-output system in which authority and status give rise to interpersonal relationships that lead to inputs (information), and these in turn lead to outputs (information and decisions). One cannot arbitrarily remove one role and expect the rest to remain intact [1973, p. 58].

According to the model, managerial roles are a result of the manager's authority and status (Fig. 2.6). We will define a **role** as an organized set of behaviors related to an identifiable office or position (Sarbin and Allen, 1968).

A manager's personality may affect *how* a role is performed, but not *whether* it is performed. The managerial role constellation consists of three distinct but related categories of roles: interpersonal, informational, and decisional. Each role category has several specific behaviors associated with it.

Interpersonal Roles

The first general role requirement lies in the area of interpersonal relations. In varying degrees all managers must represent the organization to others. They must deal with others both inside and outside the organization to achieve certain goals. **Interpersonal roles** are characterized by three activities (see Fig. 2.6).

The *figurehead* role consists largely of such ceremonial work as greeting and receiving visitors and symbolically representing the organization. Managers also serve a *leader* role through motivational and leadership activities and human resources management. Finally, managers serve as a *liaison* to the community, establishing an image, gathering resources, and so forth. Interpersonal roles generally represent the manager's efforts to deal with others on behalf of the organization.

Informational Roles

The second general area of managerial responsibility lies in the **informational roles** managers perform. Many managers, particularly at the senior level,

Figure 2.6
The Managerial Role Constellation

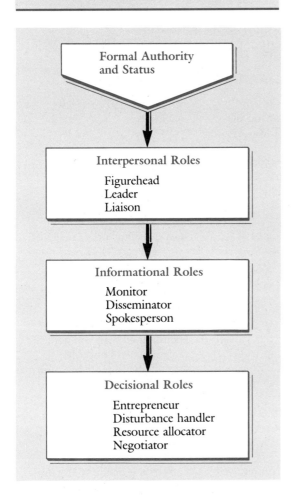

Source: Figure 8 from *The Nature of Managerial Work* by Henry Mintzberg. Copyright © 1973 by Henry Mintzberg. Reprinted by permission of Harper & Row, Publishers, Inc.

receive a great deal of important information from inside and outside the organization because of their position in the hierarchy.

Decisional Roles

The third major area of management concern focuses on **decisional roles** of managers. There are four such areas of responsibility. First, managers serve an

Figure 2.7
Ten Roles in the Managerial Role Constellation

ROLE	DESCRIPTION	IDENTIFIABLE ACTIVITIES FROM STUDY OF CHIEF EXECUTIVES
Interpersonal		
Figurehead	Symbolic head; obliged to perform a number of routine duties of a legal or social nature	Ceremony, status requests, solicitations
Leader	Responsible for the motivation and activation of subordinates; responsible for staffing, training, and associated duties	Virtually all managerial activities involving subordinates
Liaison	Maintains self-developed network of outside contacts and informers who provide favors and information	Acknowledgments of mail; external board work; other activities involving outsiders
Informational		
Monitor	Seeks and receives wide variety of special information (much of it current) to develop thorough understanding of organization and environment; emerges as nerve center of internal and external information of the organization	Handling all mail and contacts categorized as concerned primarily with receiving information (e.g., periodical news, observational tours)
Disseminator	Transmits information received from outsiders or from other subordinates to members of the organization; some information factual, some involving interpretation and integration of diverse value positions of organizational influencers	Forwarding mail into organization for informational purposes; verbal contacts involving information flow to subordinates (e.g., review sessions, instant communication flows)
Spokesperson	Transmits information to outsiders on organization's plans, policies, actions, results, etc.; serves as expert on organization's industry	Board meetings; handling mail and contacts involving transmission of information to outsiders

Figure 2.7 (continued)

ROLE	DESCRIPTION	IDENTIFIABLE ACTIVITIES FROM STUDY OF CHIEF EXECUTIVES
Decisional		
Entrepreneur	Searches organization and its environment for opportunities and initiates "improvement projects" to bring about change; supervises design of certain projects as well	Strategy and review sessions involving initiation or design of improvement projects
Disturbance handler	Responsible for corrective action when organization faces important, unexpected disturbances	Strategy and review sessions involving disturbances and crises
Resource allocator	Responsible for the allocation of organizational resources of all kinds — in effect the making or approval of all significant organizational decisions	Scheduling; requests for authorization; any activity involving budgeting and the programming of subordinates' work
Negotiator	Responsible for representing the organization at major negotiations	Negotiation

Source: Table 2 from *The Nature of Managerial Work* by Henry Mintzberg. Copyright © 1973 by Henry Mintzberg. Reprinted by permission of Harper & Row, Publishers, Inc.

entrepreneurial role in developing strategic models for future organizational actions. They also act as *disturbance handlers,* representing the decision maker of last resort for problems. Managers also serve as *resource allocators* by distributing available resources where they are most needed to meet the organization's needs. Finally, managers often are *negotiators* for resources outside the organization, and settle internal conflicts. As noted by Sayles (1964, p. 131), "Sophisticated managers place great stress on negotiations as a way of life. They negotiate with groups who are setting standards for their work, who are performing support activities for them, and to whom they wish to 'sell' their services."

It is clear that managerial work is highly demanding yet highly challenging. These ten managerial roles, summarized in Figure 2.7, clearly show the complexity of the manager's job. In reviewing these various roles, Mintzberg (1973) takes issue with those who claim that managers are essentially generalists in organizations filled with specialists. He argues:

> This is only partly true. Managers are generalists when considered in terms of the set of specialist functions performed by their organizations. But when compared with other kinds of work, managerial work is also specialized. Managers must perform ten roles that involve their own kinds of specialized behavior [p. 94].

Managerial Demands, Constraints, Choices

We have seen that managers serve a variety of roles within the organization and that the manager's job is not easy. Occasions for conflict and stress are numerous. It also has been suggested that the successful use of management is a key ingredient in organizational effectiveness. How can we put all these facets together to understand the essence of management?

One answer to this question lies in the management model presented by Rosemary Stewart (1982). Stewart has done several in-depth studies of managers in various types of public and private organizations. She used a variety of research methods, including in-depth interviews, questionnaires, observations, diaries, and group discussions. As a result of these studies, Stewart argues that management can best be understood by analyzing the manager's job along three dimensions: demands, constraints, and choices (Fig. 2.8).

Demands

Demands focus on what a manager has to do. Stewart (1982, p. 2) notes, "There are many things that a manager ought to do because they are in the job description, or because his or her boss thinks them important, but 'demands' is a narrower term; 'demands' are only what *must* be done."

Demands can be categorized into two types. First, managers face certain demands in that they must meet *minimum criteria* of performance. A field sales representative, for example, may have a basic minimum quota that must be met in order to keep his or her job. Managers also face demands concerning the necessity for certain *kinds of work*. They must, for example, attend meetings, follow certain procedures, and interact with co-workers or customers.

These demands can vary across jobs. The managers in the four jobs outlined in Figure 2.9 each face a series of demands from various sources, but the intensity of these demands varies considerably among the four.

Constraints

The second way to compare managers' jobs focuses on the number of **constraints** associated with the job. Constraints are factors internal and external to

Figure 2.8
Different Kinds of Demands, Constraints, and Choices
in Managerial Jobs

DEMANDS

Overall, meeting minimum criteria of performance
Doing certain kinds of work. Such work is determined by:
  The extent to which personal involvement is required in the unit's work
  Who must be contacted and the difficulty of the work relationship
  Contacts' power to enforce their expectations
  Bureaucratic procedures that cannot be ignored or delegated
  Meetings that must be attended

CONSTRAINTS

Resource limitations
Legal and trade union constraints
Technological limitations
Physical location
Organizational constraints, especially extent to which the work
of the manager's unit is defined
Attitudes of other people to:
  Changes in systems, procedures, organization, pay, and conditions
  Changes in the goods or services produced
  Work outside the unit

CHOICES

In *how* the work is done
In *what* work is done
  Choices within a defined area:
    To emphasize certain aspects of the job
    To select some tasks and to ignore or delegate others
  Choices in boundary management
  Choices to change the area of work:
    To change the unit's domain
    To develop a personal domain:
      To become an expert
      To share work, especially with colleagues
      To take part in organizational and public activities

Source: Rosemary Stewart, *Choices for the Manager,* © 1982, p. 3. Reprinted by permission of Prentice-Hall, Inc., Englewood Cliffs, N.J.

the organization that limit what the jobholder can do. At least six types of constraints can be identified, as shown in Figure 2.8. Together these constraints largely define the boundaries for managerial actions.

Figure 2.9
Profiles of Behavioral Demands of Four Jobs

	JOB TITLE			
BEHAVIORAL DEMANDS MADE	*Police Inspector*	*Hospital Administrator*	*Bank Manager*	*Store (chain) Manager*
By subordinates	⊠	⊠	□	⊠
By peers and other seniors	⊠	■	□	□
By dependence of boss(es)	□	■	□	□
By external contacts	■	⊠	■	□
By short-term contacts	■	⊠	■	□
By conflicting demands	■	■	□	□
On private life	■	□	⊠	□
By exposure	■	⊠	■	⊠

■ = high demands; ⊠ = medium demands; □ = low demands.

Source: Adapted by permission of the publisher from "To Understand the Manager's Job: Consider Demands, Constraints, and Choices" by Rosemary Stewart, *Organizational Dynamics,* Spring 1976, p. 23. © 1976 by AMACOM, a division of American Management Associations, New York. All rights reserved.

Choices

The third factor in Stewart's model is **choices,** those activities that job-holders can do but do not necessarily have to do. Choices represent opportunities for one manager to do work differently from a co-worker. This area of the manager's job is perhaps the most intriguing because it provides the most options. As Lord Armstrong (1977) notes:

> The people who are doing the job, whether it is at the coal face or in the branch of a bank, are not actually doing what the book says that they should do. They may be achieving approximately the same result, frequently doing it better than the book says, but sometimes skipping it and doing it in a slip-shod way. But nevertheless they have adapted it to themselves, how they like to work, how they like to behave, how it looks to them, and sometimes what they think the organization wants [cited in Stewart, 1982, p. 1].

The level of demands, constraints, and choices varies considerably among jobs, as is seen in Figure 2.10. In this illustration the job on the left has few choices but many demands and constraints. A first-level supervisor on an assembly line has such a position. The nature of the technology, combined with a union contract, gives the supervisor little freedom, but the production demands of the job are still strong: production goals must be met.

In contrast, the job on the right suffers from fewer demands and constraints and has far more choices available. The presidency of a medium-sized company

Figure 2.10
Differences in Demands, Constraints, and Choices for Two Jobs

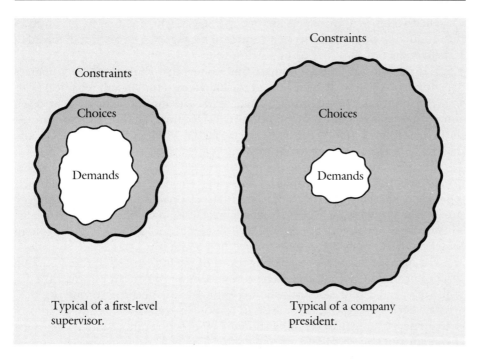

Typical of a first-level
supervisor.

Typical of a company
president.

Source: Rosemary Stewart, *Choices for the Manager,* © 1982, p. 7. Reprinted by permission of Prentice-Hall Inc., Englewood Cliffs, N.J.

is an example. A variety of constraints exist for such a manager, yet their nature and extent are less confining than those of our assembly line supervisor. The president also has a far greater variety of choices than does the supervisor.

A framework like this can be used to compare managerial jobs across organizations and hierarchies. Such a technique will provide a better understanding of the nature of managerial work than than would a single definition.

Summary

In this chapter we have seen that management is crucial in helping an organization become more effective. Managers plan, organize, direct, and control the activities of others in combination with other organizational resources to meet the organization's goals. Some central figure is required for the parts of an organization to work together. The challenge is great.

Managers can be differentiated by their level in the hierarchy and by type. Managers are divided by level into executive management, generally top administrators who formulate long-term goals and operating policies; middle management, which interprets the long-range goals and translates them into concrete goals for specific divisions; and first-line managers, who carry out the daily operations of the company and ensure that the short-term goals are met.

The two types of managers are line managers, who are directly involved in the production of goods or services, and staff managers, who are not involved in actual production but play a supporting role.

Managers use technical, human, and conceptual skills in varying degrees depending on the level they occupy in the hierarchy. Human and technical skills are very important for first-line managers. At the middle management level, conceptual skills become more important and technical skills less important. At the executive level conceptual skills are crucial. Different skills may be necessary, therefore, as a manager ascends through the hierarchy.

Managers must also perform different roles. The managerial role constellation is the set of roles that managers must fill if they are to be successful at their jobs. There are three categories of roles: interpersonal, informational, and decisional. The interpersonal role involves representing the organization to others. The manager must serve a ceremonial or figurehead role, must play the role of leader, and also must act as a liaison to the community.

The manager must meet the obligations of the informational role by acting as a monitor of information for decision-making purposes, an information disseminator, and a spokesperson who explains the organization to outsiders.

The decisional role has four areas of responsibility. Managers must act in an entrepreneurial role in developing strategic models for future action. They must also be disturbance handlers, resource allocators, and negotiators.

Rosemary Stewart has given us a framework to compare managerial jobs across organizations and hierarchies. She analyzes jobs along three dimensions: demands, constraints, and choices.

Questions for Discussion

1. What are the underlying assumptions of the definition of management?
2. How do managers go about managing?
3. In what ways can managers make a difference in the effectiveness and productivity of an organization?
4. What is the relationship between the responsibilities of an executive manager and a middle manager? A middle manager and a first-line manager?
5. How does line management differ from staff management? What goals do they share?
6. Are the three types of skills necessary for successful managers equally important at each level of management? Explain.
7. How do executive managers and middle managers differ in the ways they spend their time?
8. Are managers specialists or generalists?
9. Discuss the relationship among choices, demands, and constraints for managers.

Exercise 2.1
Interviewing Managers

Your assignment is to interview at least three managers who are employed full time. You should use the interview schedule below in your interviews, but you are not restricted to it. The purpose of these interviews is to give you a chance to learn about some critical managerial skills from the standpoint of those who have to use them.

Treat the interviews as confidential. We are not interested in the name of the individual, only in the opinions, perceptions, and behaviors that he or she has. You should guarantee the manager that no one else will be able to identify him or her from these responses.

Keep notes on your interviews. These notes should be in as much detail as possible so that you can reconstruct the interviews in class. For the last question in the interview schedule, actually put numbers to the side of the items.

Questions for Manager Interviews

1. Describe a typical day at work.
2. What are the most time-consuming activities that occupy your work day?
3. What are the most critical problems that you face as a manager?
4. What are the most critical skills needed to be a successful manager?
5. What are the major reasons why managers fail?
6. If you could design a college course to help students become successful managers, what would the course include?
7. Using the scale at the left for your responses, rate the extent to which you use the following skills or behaviors during the course of your work day.

	Managing personal stress
	Managing time
	Setting goals
Scale	Making individual decisions
	Defining or recognizing problems
5 – Constantly	Verbal communication skills
4 – Frequently	Delegating
3 – Sometimes	Motivating others
2 – Seldom	Managing conflict
1 – Very Rarely	Interviewing
	Gaining and using power
	Orchestrating change
	Appraising others' performance
	Facilitating group decision making
	Listening
	Disciplining others
	Self-awareness
	Empathizing
	Team building
	Solving problems
	Conducting meetings

Source: Interpersonal Skill Development for Managers, by David Whetten and Kim Cameron, Lexington, MA: Ginn, 1981, p. 29. Reprinted by permission.

Case Study
New Supervisors

CHICAGO — The way Peter Schmidt tells it, his first 18 months as a boss have been pretty traumatic. "Sometimes I feel like I'm being drawn and quartered" on the job, he says.

As chief accountant at a medium-sized gear company here, Mr. Schmidt supervises a handful of bookkeepers who previously worked without supervision. One underling has frequently chastised him "for not picking up the in-house system quickly enough," he says. Another tries to boss him around. "She's old enough to be my mother — and she acts like it," he maintains.

So, like many a troubled manager these days, Mr. Schmidt has turned to consultants for help. . . . He and 170 other new supervisors are jammed into a ballroom at the O'Hare Motor Inn, waiting for . . . enlightenment.

Promptly at 9 A.M., seminar leader Jay Terry strides to the podium. He's a fast-talking former teacher and corporate personnel man who promises six hours of practical advice.

"You probably know all the technical information you need to do your job," he begins. On the other hand, most new supervisors need to learn a lot about dealing with people on the job.

One of the best ways to motivate employees, Mr. Terry says, is to tell them exactly what you are trying to accomplish as boss. But few supervisors communicate this "big picture" effectively, he adds. To prove it, he gives a quick test. "How many of you know the five most important things that measure the success of your immediate boss?" Mr. Terry asks. Only a few hands go up. "That's the first thing you should ask your boss when you go back to work tomorrow."

But it probably isn't a good idea for a new boss to ask employees about *their* individual goals right away. Probing too early, he says, can make a subordinate suspicious. Until boss and subordinate have begun to trust each other, the employee is apt to wonder, "are we setting goals to catch me or to help me grow and develop?"

One way to help a subordinate grow is to learn the proper way to praise him, Mr. Terry says. The wrong way is to give the employee a quick slap on the back and say, "good job" or "attaboy." Better to say, "I'm happy about the way you processed those invoices so quickly. You really saved us a lot of bucks. Thanks." Taking the latter approach, the boss has told the subordinate how he feels ("I'm happy") and told him exactly what he's happy about, so the employee knows how to repeat the praise-worthy behavior.

Mr. Terry also suggests that there's a right way and a wrong way to interrupt a subordinate while he's working. The wrong way is to stroll over to his desk and say, "Are you busy right now?" "That's a hard question to field," Mr. Terry says. If the employee says, "No, I'm not busy," he sounds like he's goofing off. If he says, "Yes, I'm busy," he sounds a little rude. Better to ask, "Is this a good time to interrupt?"

Mr. Terry isn't just a corporate Amy Vanderbilt, however. He's all for being the tough guy on certain occasions. Consider how he recommends dealing with chronically tardy subordinates:

Tell the employee, "We have a problem and it has to be resolved. I'm upset that you keep coming in late because it really screws up the invoice processing," or the telephone load, or whatever. The key thing is to let the employee know how you feel and to let him know that his tardiness messes up the office and makes life difficult for the people around him.

The latecomer is likely to offer some kind of excuse. The boss, Mr. Terry says, should brush aside all excuses until the employee admits he's creating a problem. Only then is the employee likely to vow to get better. About 5 percent of the time, however, the latecomer simply won't admit he's causing a problem. In that case, the boss should say that the latecomer is passing up any chance of being promoted and might be fired.

What's more, the boss must be willing to back up his threat, or he loses credibility and authority. That's a particular problem for new supervisors, who frequently find their authority put to the test right away.

Al Sporny, manager of a tire store in downtown Chicago, is one seminar participant who remembers facing such a test his first day as a manager. On the same day that Mr. Sporny was promoted from mechanic to service manager, the tire store decided to extend hours until 9 P.M. on certain evenings. But despite Mr. Sporny's orders, none of the mechanics would agree to take a night shift.

"So I fired the ringleader," the 33-year-old Mr. Sporny recalls, and he told the other mechanics, "If I have to fire all of you, I will." Mr. Sporny said the blowup prevented him from sleeping for two nights. The ringleader "had a family; he had a girl six months old," Mr. Sporny recalls. "But it was his career or my career." Fortunately, he adds, the remaining mechanics agreed to work nights, and the ringleader humbly asked for his job back. He agreed to work nights and was reinstated.

Power plays should be a last resort, of course. By frequently barking commands at subordinates, Mr. Terry says, a boss separates himself from the people who work for him. "Power erodes relationships," he says, and dries up sources of information that the boss needs to do his job.

Most of the time, Mr. Terry says, the best way to run the show is by suggestion. The boss sells his idea, and the source of his power is competence rather than his position as boss.

Case Questions

1. As a manager, what are useful antecedents of good performance by an employee/subordinate?
2. As a manager, what are useful consequences of good (or bad) performance by an employee/subordinate?
3. Why do employees "test" their new supervisor? How can a supervisor succeed in passing this test?

Source: Editorial by Bernard Wysocki, *The Wall Street Journal,* July 7, 1979. Reprinted by permission of *The Wall Street Journal,* © Dow Jones & Company, Inc. 1979. All Rights Reserved.

CHAPTER 3

Organizations and Organizational Effectiveness

Cedartown Paperboard Company, a paper converter in Cedartown, Georgia, saved about $80,000 because of some BAD ideas.

The BAD idea is actually a very successful program designed to involve employees in holding down their company's operational costs. The program encourages employees to pass on to management suggestions that will save at least a dollar a day on their particular job.

BAD, which stands for "Buck-a-Day," is copyrighted and marketed by Industrial Motivation Inc. in New York.

Cedartown Paperboard, a $20 million company, is one of the program's success stories. Drivers of the company's thirteen tractor-trailer trucks suggested that they take advantage of cash customer discounts for diesel fuel instead of using the company's credit cards, saving the company about $10,000 annually. Another $10,000 was saved when an employee noticed three men were assigned to a machine similar to one operated by only two men. The extra man was reassigned.

Kinney Vacuum Company of Canton, Massachusetts, expected to save more than $57,000 from the 264 ideas its 153 employees handed in. Suggestions ranged from replacing an inaccurate shipping scale to not hiring a foreman to replace one who left.

"The BAD program saved money and improved interaction between management and the work force," said Kinney's vice president of manufacturing, Albert Smegal.

Besides the satisfaction that they were contributing something of value to help meet the company's cost-cutting goal, what did the employees who made the suggestions receive? For their first idea they were given a mug that said, "I had a BAD idea"; for the second, a rubber dollar signifying how far a dollar can be stretched.

Source: Adapted with permission from "BAD Ideas Pay Off," *INC.* Magazine, September 1983, p. 122.

Chapter Outline

- What Is an Organization?
- The Nature of Organizational Goals
- Goal Formulation Processes
- Goal Succession and Displacement
- Organizational Effectiveness:
  A Unifying Framework
- A View of Organizational Effectiveness

Key Terms

- goal relevancy
- official goals
- operative goals
- operational goals
- external environment
- side payments
- goal succession
- goal displacement
- suboptimization
- Iron Law of Oligarchy
- organizational effectiveness
- efficiency
- goal optimization

Chapter Objectives

After studying Chapter 3 you should be able to

1. See the link between organizational goals and a company's personality.
2. Discuss the functions of goals for an organization.
3. Identify what organizational goals can do for an individual.
4. Consider the effect of goal dysfunctions on organizations.
5. Discuss the importance of relative power distributions and prior commitment to organizational goals.
6. Understand the differences between goal succession and goal displacement.
7. Distinguish between potential and actual efficiency.

Introduction

This book is about managing organizations, so it is important that you understand not only the nature of management, which we explored in Chapter 2, but also something about organizations themselves. In this chapter we will examine the nature of organizations. We will be setting the stage for discussions in coming chapters of ways to improve both organizational design and employee job performance. As a result, you will learn about improving productivity and making organizations more effective.

The present chapter discusses several related topics. We begin by defining the concept of organization itself. Next we consider organizational goals, including functions and dysfunctions of goals and types of goals. Then we examine how organizational objectives are determined. We look at the related topics of goal succession and goal displacement. Finally, the complex topic of organizational effectiveness is examined.

What Is an Organization?

Definition of an Organization

There are many definitions of the term **organization.** In an early definition Chester Barnard (1938, p. 73) labeled it "a system of consciously coordinated activities of two or more persons." Following this point of view, we can add that organizations have stated purposes or goals, communication networks and other coordinating systems, and people who are willing to cooperate with one another on the jobs necessary to meet the organizational goals. Etzioni (1964, p. 4) described organizations as "planned units, deliberately structured for the purpose of attaining specific goals." Goals and objectives are in the forefront again in this definition. We also see here the concepts of coordination and planning among individuals in the pursuit of those goals.

Characteristics of an Organization

We can identify five characteristics of organizations (Porter, Lawler, and Hackman, 1975):

1. *Social composition.* Organizations consist of people who develop social relations and patterns of interaction.

2. *Goal orientation.* Organizations exist for stated, and sometimes unstated, purposes.

3. *Differentiated functions.* For efficiency, organizations typically divide the work so members can specialize in one or two areas.

4. *Rational coordination.* Work activities are coordinated in some rational manner.

5. *Continuity.* Most organizations are born with the intention of staying alive, although that doesn't always happen.

Organizations are best seen as many people working together for a common aim. This does not mean that every member has identical aims or that there are no disagreements. There may even be interest groups or factions within the organization. Simply put, organizations exist and survive because members have decided to join together to accomplish what no one could do alone.

Because goals and objectives are so important in our definition of organizations, we will consider them in detail in this chapter. Then in Chapter 4 we will turn to how organizations are designed or structured to go after these goals. The crucial role of management in ensuring organizational survival and effectiveness will be a constant theme.

The Nature of Organizational Goals

All organizations have goals that they pursue, overtly or even covertly. Organizational goals and the way they are formulated are important in understanding organizational behavior.

The Goal Concept

Organizations marshal physical, financial, and human resources to meet their objectives. It has been suggested that the goals of an organization can provide unique insight into its character and behavior (Perrow, 1970). They are a useful frame of reference for understanding and evaluating what an organization does.

On the surface, an **organizational goal** may be defined as a desired state of affairs that organizations attempt to realize (Etzioni, 1964). In other words, goals answer the question of where the organization is going. A company whose basic objective is to make a profit tends to direct its resources and energies into areas that will bring in corporate income. A nonprofit hospital, in contrast, might organize its resources with an eye to improving community health or patient care. Goals may represent policy statements that show how an organization intends to arrange and use its scarce resources.

But this simple approach leaves several questions unanswered. When we speak of an organization's goals, whose goals are we talking about? Do we mean the goals set by executive management, or what all members of the organization want? There is also the problem of multiple and often conflicting goals. Few organizations pursue only one goal. A business may want a profitable return on investment while it improves social welfare in the community. How an organization determines the relative importance of its goals, given limited resources, is the main issue.

Feature 3.1
The Journalists Judge Organizational Goals

Business management, union bosses, government officials, and workers all have their own ideas about the goals companies should have. Now you can add journalists too.

A poll taken by the Opinion Research Corporation asked journalists on the staffs of newspapers, magazines, wire services, and radio and television stations to indicate what they felt were the most important responsibilities of corporations. Most of the journalists polled specialize in business and financial news. Here are their answers, including the percentage who say each activity is a major corporate responsibility:

- Provide a safe work environment — 95 percent
- Keep the environment clean and free from pollution — 92 percent
- Maintain high ethical standards — 86 percent
- Pay stockholders reasonable returns on investments — 82 percent
- Look at long-range development instead of short-term profits — 77 percent
- Retain adequate earnings to expand capacity and create more jobs — 75 percent
- Improve productivity of existing plants and factories — 75 percent
- Satisfy customer needs at reasonable prices — 74 percent

- Make corporate decisions with social responsibility in mind — 74 percent
- Provide customers with product-related information — 71 percent
- Hold down costs — 67 percent
- Effectively compete with foreign companies — 60 percent
- Hire and train minorities — 57 percent
- Replace out-of-date plants and equipment — 53 percent
- Hire and train the disadvantaged — 53 percent
- Provide rewarding and satisfying jobs — 51 percent
- Find and develop additional sources of energy — 51 percent
- Contribute money to support education, cultural affairs, health, and charities — 50 percent
- Develop new products to improve the nation's living standard — 44 percent

Remember, these responses come from journalists. Consider how different the list would be if you asked corporation executives, union leaders, or consumer advocates.

Source: Adapted with permission from "How the Media Would Set Your Priorities," *Nation's Business*, October 1982, p. 82. Copyright: U.S. Chamber of Commerce.

The simple definition of goals we began with may be useful on an abstract level, but it lacks the precision we need to understand more fully the relationship between goals and effectiveness. For that we must examine the way organizations use their goals. We will briefly look at several positive and negative consequences of goals.

Functions of Organizational Goals

Formally stated, objectives can affect organizational behavior in many ways, from the behavior of the entire organization down to that of the individual employee. Although goals can sometimes have very positive results, they also can have negative consequences for organizational performance and effectiveness.

Functions for Organizations.   Let us first consider the positive effects of goals on an organizational level (Steers, 1977). As outlined in Figure 3.1, goals can serve at least five functions for the organization as a whole:

1. They often focus attention or give direction to managers attempting to acquire and make use of organizational resources. Legitimate goals provide guidelines for members of an organization.

2. Goals are often a reason for organizing. The activities, practices, and processes necessary for reaching goals can restrict the behavior of members and groups. Organizational goals can dictate such basic social processes as communication patterns, authority and power structures, the division of labor, and status.

3. Goals can serve as a standard by which to judge how effectively and efficiently an organization achieves its purposes. For example, a company whose primary goal is making a profit can determine fairly easily at year's end how successful it has been in achieving its goal.

4. An organization often uses goals to justify itself and its activities to such diverse groups as investors, members, customers, and the public. Goals are of central importance in motivating and adapting in a dynamic and uncertain environment.

5. Goals can assist the organization in acquiring needed human resources. People who identify with the humanitarian goals of the Red Cross, for example, may join that organization at very low salaries because they identify with the organization's objectives.

Functions for Individuals.   Goals can also be useful for individual members of the organization.

1. Goals can provide job direction, so an employee can more clearly focus his or her attention and efforts on specific corporate objectives.

2. Goals often provide a rationale for working and sometimes can impart a sense of meaning to an otherwise pointless job. They can answer the question "Why am I doing this?"

3. Goals may serve as a vehicle for personal goal attainment. A commission-based salesperson can satisfy both his or her own monetary goals and the company's profit goal by increasing sales.

4. Goals may assist individuals by providing a sense of psychological security, a feeling that the organization is going somewhere and will remain in operation for some time. The perception of organizational longevity or continu-

Figure 3.1
Functions and Dysfunctions of Organizational Goals

	FOR ORGANIZATION	FOR INDIVIDUAL
Functions	Focus attention	Focus attention
	Rationale for organizing	Rationale for working
	Standard of assessment	Vehicle for personal goal attainment
	Source of legitimation	Personal security
	Recruitment through identification	Identification and status
Dysfunctions	Means to end can become real goals	Rewards may not be tied to goal attainment
	Measurement stresses quantitative goals at expense of qualitative ones	Difficulty in determining relevant performance evaluation criteria
	Goal specificity problem (ambiguous goals fail to provide direction; highly specific goals may constrain action and creativity)	Inability of individuals to identify with abstract, global goals
		Organizational goals may be incongruent with personal goals

Source: Reprinted from Steers, 1977, p. 21.

ity, whether or not justified, can provide comfort and security to an employee in an ever-changing, unstable environment.

5. Goals can provide a source of identification and status for employees. How often, when you ask someone what he or she does for a living, is the reply, "I work for XYZ Company"? The sense of self-identity is closely related to the organization and its goals.

It is doubtful that any one goal of an organization could simultaneously serve all these organization-wide and individual functions. Instead, different goals usually have different functions for different people at various points. For example, an employee may ignore the profit motives, joining and remaining with a company primarily because he or she feels the organization is doing more than its competitors to help society. But the executive management of the same company may feel it has a greater responsibility to its own welfare. Although a company may claim to have both profit and social welfare goals, each may be more important to different elements of the organization, for quite different reasons.

Dysfunctions of Goals

An issue often overlooked in organization theory concerns dysfunctions that can result from the existence of stipulated goals. A major problem for many managers is their assumption that specifying and elaborating organizational goals will have entirely positive effects. This assumption ignores certain negative aspects of goals (see Fig. 3.1).

Dysfunctions for Organizations. There are a number of dysfunctions of goals on an organization-wide basis.

1. The means set forth for attaining an organization's goals may become goals themselves. This occurrence is usually called a **means-ends inversion.** For example, a city that has a goal of improving traffic safety may institute a quota ticketing system among its police officers, requiring them to issue a certain number of traffic tickets per month. Although the quota was originally intended as a means to an end — public safety — the quota itself could become the goal in the eyes of organizational members, the police. The focus and effort would then shift from the original objectives.

2. Etzioni (1964) points out that *measurement tends to stress the measurable.* Qualitative goals, such as improving employee morale, may be ignored by managers; highly quantitative and measureable goals, such as increasing profits and sales, may become accentuated.

3. The degree of goal specificity may not be appropriate. Goals that are too ambiguous may fail to provide needed direction; highly specific goals can limit creativity and innovation. Intended or desired objectives must be sufficiently specific without being overly constraining.

Dysfunctions for Individuals. Although many of these organization-wide dysfunctions also would apply on an individual level, problems unique to individual employee behavior also emerge. Some of these problems do not necessarily follow from the mere existence of goals, but their behavioral implications are closely related to such goals.

1. When rewards such as pay and promotions are not specifically designed to reward goal-directed behavior, people may not try to reach those goals. Instead, employees will tend to do things that have the greatest payoffs in terms of their personal needs and goals.

2. Even when goal-directed performance is rewarded, it is often difficult to identify the performance criteria that are directly related to attaining organizational goals. Consider the example of a personnel manager in a large company. If profit is the company's main goal, what criteria should be used to evaluate a personnel manager based on that organizational goal?

3. Employees may fail to identify with broad, abstract goals. How can a factory worker contribute to a company goal of organizational growth?

Feature 3.2
The Labor-Management Revolution in Detroit

If United States auto manufacturers have learned anything from having lost their number one status in the worldwide auto industry to the Japanese, it is a lesson in how important the labor-management relationship is in the production process. Japanese managers are involved in every phase of production and encourage workers to submit new ideas for improving productivity. Soichiro Honda, a former mechanic who founded the famous Honda company, says, "An industry prospers only when everybody involved in it thinks about how it can be improved" ("Detroit Faces the Rising Sun," p. 158).

American auto manufacturers are getting the message. They have admitted that the time has come to heal the rift between labor and management. Labor has made some major concessions in wages and benefits. Management has set up employee involvement groups and implemented many of the ideas that have come out of them.

Getting middle managers to cooperate still seems to be a problem, however. W. Edwards Deming, whose process-control techniques have been popular in Japan, warns that this group has been responsible for keeping top management and workers apart. Ford's chairman Philip Caldwell agrees. "We have a lot of plant managers who were really production supervisors because that's what we told them to do," he said. "Now we're trying to make them whole people" ("Detroit's Merry-go-round," p. 76).

Deming is not overly optimistic about the timetable for changing management policies in Detroit. He estimates the process will take thirty years. John Latini, the plant manager in Ford's Wayne, Michigan, assembly plant, takes the opposite view. "It's the most exciting time ever in the auto industry," he says. He believes that the cooperation that is now developing between labor and management is the factor that will close the gap between the United States and Japan. "I tell the Japanese, 'You've awakened a sleeping dog. And now he's going to bite you!'" ("Detroit Faces the Rising Sun," pp. 171–172).

Sources: "Detroit Faces the Rising Sun: A New Day Dawns for the Motor City," by D. Reed, *Reader's Digest*, September 1983, pp. 89–94, 153–172; "Detroit's Merry-go-round," *Business Week*, September 12, 1983, pp. 72–81.

4. Goals of the organization may be in conflict with the personal goals of employees. This conflict can be seen time and again in arguments between management and unions about whether stockholders or employees should receive an increased proportion of corporate income.

We have briefly reviewed several functions and dysfunctions of organizational goals on organization-wide and individual levels. These factors certainly would not apply in all cases; we are presenting them simply to demonstrate the pervasive influence of goals and objectives on the way groups and individuals behave in organizational settings. Throughout this discussion **goal relevancy** has been a key factor. Although certain goals may be important to particular segments of the organization, such as executive management, they may simply not be important enough to, for example, shop floor workers to justify an expenditure of time or effort on the part of these employees. In cases like this, employee support for and participation in goal-directed activities must be obtained in other ways.

Types of Goals

To this point we've discussed the concept of organizational goals in general terms. Now we can examine several types of goals and consider how each type affects behavior in organizations.

Organizational goals are most commonly divided into official, operative, and operational types (March and Simon, 1958; Perrow, 1961). **Official goals** are formal statements of purpose made by executive management concerning the nature of an organization's mission. They are typically vague and aspirational: maximize profit, contribute to community welfare, and so on. They usually have an infinite time horizon and are set forth more for securing support and legitimacy from the outside world than to make it any easier to accomplish specific tasks.

In contrast, **operative goals** represent the real intentions of an organization. They reflect what an organization is actually trying to do, regardless of what it claims to be doing. Operative goals may or may not be widely publicized. In some cases management uses appealing and widely publicized official goals to conceal less attractive operative goals.

Operational goals are those goals with built-in standards that can be used to determine whether the goals are being met. An operative goal is said to be operational if management can fairly precisely specify how to measure its attainment. Operative goals such as "maximize profit" or "manufacture electronic equipment" would not be considered sufficiently operational. "Manufacture and sell one million television sets this year" would, because it has clearly measurable assessment standards concerning volume and time.

The remainder of this section will focus on operative and operational goals and the relationship between them, because it is against these types of goals that organizational effectiveness must ultimately be judged.

Relative Importance of Goals

A separate but related aspect of goals concerns the relative importance of the various goals to management. It was pointed out earlier that organizations pursue multiple goals at the same time. We can gain greater insight into an organization's nature and character if we can tell which goals are more important. Consider the findings of a survey carried out by England (1967) in which business managers were asked to rate the importance of a series of potential corporate goals. As outlined in Figure 3.2, organizational efficiency and high productivity were much more important for these managers than employee or social welfare.

Figure 3.2
Organizational Goal Preferences of United States Managers

TYPE OF GOAL	% RATING GOAL AS HIGHLY IMPORTANT	% INDICATING GOAL IS SIGNIFICANT FOR CORPORATE SUCCESS
Organizational efficiency	81	71
High productivity	80	70
Profit maximization	72	70
Organizational growth	60	72
Industrial leadership	58	64
Organizational stability	58	54
Employee welfare	65	20
Social welfare	16	8

Source: Data from England, 1967, p. 108.

These findings show that we can better understand an organization's intentions by dividing its goals into *first-order* and *second-order goals* (Steers, 1977). Given scarce resources, most managers would initially pursue first-order goals. Then, if resources allowed, second-order goals would receive attention. It is important when considering operative and operational goals to ask which goals are of the first order. Answers to questions like this provide still further clues about an organization's intentions and actions.

Goal Formulation Processes

The fairly simple approach to the concept of organizational goals that we began with earlier in this section becomes more complex when we consider the factors that can influence the selection and modification of goals over time. Goal formulation is interwoven with organizational design and effectiveness. We view effectiveness in terms of how well organizational goals are attained. What goes into determining these goals, their nature, quality, and rationality can have a major influence on whether they will be achievable and effective in the long run.

There are at least two ways to view the process of formulating goals. One approach involves focusing on factors outside the organization that can influence the selection and modification of organizational objectives. Two models of goal formulation will be examined to provide a clearer understanding of the basic processes involved. The first model, by Thompson and McEwen (1958), deals with external forces affecting goal formulation. The second, by Cyert and March (1963), deals principally with internal forces. Following this discussion, we will summarize and tie together the major variables, both external and internal, that can affect the goals of an organization.

Thompson and McEwen Model

Organizational Power in Environmental Relations. In this fairly abstract approach, Thompson and McEwen have suggested that the process of formulating goals can be understood best by looking at the relationship between an *organization* and its **external environment.** Environment here means those factors outside the organization that have the potential to influence organizational actions and success, such as market and economic conditions, competitors, and government agencies and regulations. According to this model, the managers of an organization formulate goals to establish and maintain a favorable balance of power with the external environment. The more power the organization has, the more autonomy it has in making decisions concerning future actions.

In stressing the close relationship between setting goals and the world outside the organization, Thompson and McEwen suggest a continuum of organizational power in environmental relations. This continuum ranges from total organizational control over the environment to complete environmental control over the organization, as shown in Figure 3.3. It suggests that all organizations can be placed somewhere along this continuum, depending on how much power they have in dealing with their environment. For example, a multinational oil company, which has large quantities of resources and produces products vital to a modern society, would typically possess a considerable amount of power in dealing with its environment, such as government agencies and environmental protection groups. Such a firm would be placed toward the left end of the continuum in Figure 3.3. In contrast, a grass-roots consumer group, which relies on the often uncoordinated efforts of many small but interested parties of concerned citizens, would typically have little power in dealing with its environment. The many unsuccessful attempts by consumer groups to secure desired legislation demonstrate this point. Such groups wuld be placed toward the right end of the continuum. Other organizations, such as small businesses, public utilities, and political parties, would be found toward the center of the power continuum.

Power and Bargaining Strategy. The amount of power an organization has largely determines what *bargaining strategy* it should adopt to deal most successfully with its environment. Most organizations must bargain with their environment to fulfill their goals. For instance, organizations need to secure resources and markets. Thompson and McEwen believe that choosing the proper method of bargaining is vital to the success of the effort. They identify four bargaining strategies, depending on the amount of power an organization has. When an organization has a great deal of power in relation to its environment,

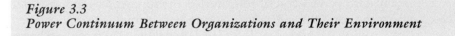

Figure 3.3
Power Continuum Between Organizations and Their Environment

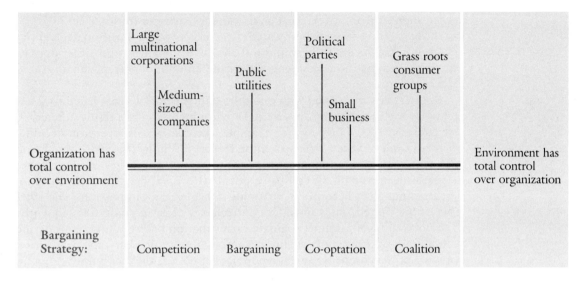

Source: Reprinted from Steers, 1977, p.27, based on Thompson and McEwen, 1958.

as in the case of a large multinational corporation, the model suggests that the best strategy is one of *competition* with the environment. In other words, the organization is generally free to determine its own goals and pursue them with little concern for outside factors. But as the forces in the external environment become more powerful, management must shift its strategy toward increasing cooperation with the environment. Without such cooperation the organization would be unable to secure the resources it needs to attain its goals. Depending on the relative distribution of power, this cooperation can take one of three forms:

1. *Bargaining,* by which the organization tries to set up some exchange.
2. *Co-optation,* in which new and possibly hostile elements are absorbed into the leadership of an organization to avert threats to its stability or existence.
3. *Coalition,* in which two or more organizations join for a common purpose.

This model becomes less useful for our purposes when we examine its implications for formulating goals. Thompson and McEwen point out that the way management formulates its objectives is largely determined by the *relative* bargaining position of an organization. Goal formulation is seen as a strategic problem. The more power an organization has, the less its management must rely on the inputs and controls of outside sources.

Rationality also plays a crucial role, in that environmental support is purchased only at the cost of organizational autonomy, by moving from competition toward coalition. In other words, organizational independence and power become the currency, the medium of exchange an organization uses to buy needed support from its external environment. An organization's ability to select the bargaining strategy best suited to its relative power position depends on how well it can successfully sound out the environment for possible support. The more accurate the assessment, the greater amount of currency that is saved for future bargaining.

Business history is filled with examples of organizations that failed to assess accurately their relation to the external environment and as a result suffered severe consequences. Consider, for example, the case of a labor union deciding whether or not to vote a strike. If union leaders misjudge the environment and push a strike that union membership fails to support, or if they initiate a strike that has little impact on the company, possibly because of large existing inventories, attaining goals becomes increasingly difficult, if not impossible. The 1981 strike of the United States air traffic controllers is a case in point. Consequently, most union leaders carefully evaluate each situation before acting, considering such things as the strength of support among union members, the production potential of the company, and the popular support of the community. Any organization that fails to assess accurately the nature and strength of its environment, and to act accordingly, invites open conflict, to the detriment of organizational goal attainment.

Cyert and March Model

The Thompson and McEwen model does not consider the role played by individuals in determining or modifying an organization's objectives. This important role has been acknowledged by Cyert and March. Focusing principally on the internal determinants of goals, they begin their analysis by suggesting that any organization is really a coalition of groups and individuals with diverse needs, desires, talents, and orientations. In their approach, goal formulation is seen as a function of three interrelated processes.

The first is a continual bargaining process within organizations, similar to the Thompson and McEwen notion, in which potential coalition members use **side payments** to induce others to join with them on certain goals. Such side payments can take the forms of money, status, power or authority, and position. Any conflicts between coalition members are usually settled through this side-payment system: for a price, an employee or group adopts the goals. In exchange for wages, employees produce; in exchange for dividends, stockholders invest. The more power any member of a coalition has, the more payments he or she has available to help the group accept his or her objectives.

Second, organizational goals are affected by the prior commitments, policies, and agreements with others that have been made by an organization. These internal controls constrain major changes in an organization's goals by limiting the resources an organization has. For example, a company that commits itself to paying generous shareholder dividends may be reducing the financial resources it has to enlarge plant production capacity or to invest in research and development of future products.

Finally, goals are sometimes modified when members of an organization agree to alter them in response to changes in the environment. Perhaps the clearest examples of this are the attempts of political parties to modify their platforms based on what their leadership believes are the important issues of the day.

Inherent in all three of these processes is the notion of **organizational slack,** the excess of an organization's total resources beyond the necessary side payments. According to Cyert and March, slack consists of those payments to coalition members over and above what is necessary to maintain an organization. Slack is somewhat like a bank account that can be drawn upon when needed. A company experiencing economic difficulty may institute a moratorium on hiring to reduce its total employment, thereby reducing the slack in the system. In more favorable times the same company may hire more people that it really needs, consciously or unconsciously, to build up its reserves (slack) once again. Slack can take many forms, such as the payment of wages higher than those required by market conditions, the doling out of executive bonuses, or the installation of carpeting in the employees' dining room. In most cases such investments are made with the intent of retrieving increased commitment and contribution at some future time.

Points of Agreement in the Two Models

Comparing these two models of goal formulation shows a high degree of overlap, despite the different approaches initially taken to the subject. Although the two begin their analysis in different places, their conclusions and implications are largely in agreement. For example, both models explain the constant difficulty most organizations have in specifying their operational goals in detail. With a turbulent environment and recurring conflicts among coalition members over their organizational aspirations, it is easy to see why such goals would be in a constant state of flux. Although it may be easy to secure agreement on relatively abstract and nonoperational official goals, clarifying those objectives into more specific and more constraining operational goals can become a sizable task. Such a conclusion has implications for any model of organizational effectiveness. If agreement and commitment cannot be achieved on operational goals, how then is it possible to measure whether the organization's goals are being met?

Both approaches to goal formulation concern the role of management in such unstable environments. A basic role of management is to facilitate and maintain enough agreement among coalition members and sufficient external support and resources to make a coordinated, smooth effort in one direction. This task of maintaining stability is not simple, considering the diversity of internal and external forces and people involved. Management's skill in appropriately coordinating and utilizing its resources to accomplish tasks is a major ingredient in an organization's effectiveness and efficiency.

The two models also bear a resemblance to each other in the key factors they cite as having the strongest influence on organizational goals. The two models taken together lead to the conclusion that two of the most potent forces in the goal formulation process are relative *power distributions,* both within an organization and between an organization and its environment, and the nature of an organization's *prior commitments.* When we discuss external environmental support, side payments, organizational slack, and coalitions of organization members, we are in effect raising questions about how power is distributed throughout an organization and its environment. An organization that has little slack, for example, is generally less powerful in bargaining with its environment than is one that has a great deal of slack. When power is concentrated in the hands of a small coalition, its members can issue whatever side payments they choose to gain the support necessary for their plans and goals. But when power is diffused and controlled by many coalitions, formulating or modifying goals is more a result of compromise. Individual or group contributions to the goal formulation process are largely determined by the relative strength of the individual or group power base.

Prior commitments by the organization also play a major role in determining and modifying goals. These can include a wide range of past decisions or obligations made on behalf of an organization concerning plant capacity, commitment to minority hiring policies, and investments in research and development. Commitments like these directly affect future decisions on allocation or distribution of available resources. These commitments can be made as a result of learned behavior, as in the case of an organization that previously made a disastrous investment and vowed to steer clear of that area in the future. In this sense commitments serve as constraints on organizational decision making that can affect future goals almost without regard to relative power positions.

We have reviewed two prominent models of organizational goal formulation and have seen how both ultimately rest on the concepts of power and commitments. The success or failure of an organization is largely determined by its capacity to understand the nature of these two factors and by its ability to act consistently with this understanding. Managers in effective organizations must fully understand the nature of their past experiences and modify their present and future behavior if they are to maximize their organization's performance and ensure survival.

Goal Succession and Displacement

Changes occur almost inevitably in the ends that organizations seek. When such changes are conscious attempts by management to shift the course of an organization, the process is termed **goal succession.** When a shift is not intended by management, we usually refer to it as **goal displacement.**

Feature 3.3
New Goals for Marine Midland

Marine Midland Bank is trying to move from Buffalo into the big time.

Although it is the nation's fourteenth largest bank, Marine Midland had been plagued through the years with a poor image. And recently the bank had financial troubles to worry about as well.

In the early and mid-1970s managers of Marine's New York City bank, which was then quasiautonomous, made some bad loans and started a merchant banking operation in London that lost money. The 1974 and 1975 recession brought in bad loans totalling $233 million, and Marine was put on the Federal Reserve Board's list of seriously troubled banks.

Then along came salvation in the form of the Hong Kong and Shanghai Banking Corporation. The Hong Kong bank handed over $236 million and eventually wound up with 51 percent of the stock in the bank's holding company. But the new people wanted change.

A Marine planning group first established the bank's new financial goals. After studying the records of eight of its peers, they decided to shoot for a 60 percent average return on assets, an average return on equity of 15 percent, and equity amounting to 4 percent of assets.

They pulled the new goals together with the slogan, "60–15–4 — You'll make the difference." The phrase was engraved on desk clocks and ball point pens, which were presented to the bank's officers. Bank Chairman Edward W. Duffy promised that if the goals were achieved on schedule, the pens could be exchanged for their weight in gold.

The bank reorganized along functional lines and streamlined its management to fit, and it set about creating a new image by writing a style statement covering its philosophy on innovation, decision making, communications, performance appraisal, and rewards.

Marine's cultural change went on for two and a half years before management informed the bulk of the bank's 10,000 employees. They felt the new image had to be understood by the executives before it could be passed down. "There is no such thing as a grass-roots revolution," one officer said. "The people lower down will begin to believe and behave a certain way only because they realize that the leadership believes that way and behaves that way."

They explained the changes to employees at four meetings throughout New York State, but it was clear that the road to enlightenment would be rocky. Chief Planner W. James Tozer, Jr., discovered that some people only three or four levels below him weren't even sure what their sector was called. There were also grumblings about "these fast-trackers" and complaints about the new "analytical, fact-based decision making."

But the problems and a slowing economy weren't enough to stop the spirit of the Marine executives. "We'll stick to our targets," one said.

Source: "In Search of Style at the 'New Marine,'" *Fortune,* July 26, 1982, pp. 40–45.

Goal Succession

A clear example of goal succession is provided in a case study of the National Foundation for Infantile Paralysis (Sills, 1957). The foundation's initial primary goal was to secure funding for research to eliminate one specific childhood disease, infantile paralysis. Through its March of Dimes campaign, this foundation contributed to the virtual eradication of the disease. It attained its primary organizational goal. But the result was a major crisis in the organization, because its efforts had eliminated its major purpose for existence! After considerable thought, the foundation revised its goals, shortened its name, and set a new course: funding research into a whole series of childhood diseases. This is an explicit example of intentional goal succession. More subtle examples of succession or partial succession can be found in the decisions by several major businesses, such as Xerox Corporation and International Business Machines Corporation, to broaden or shift their original organizational objectives to focus on several specific contemporary social problems, and to devote a share of corporate resources to their solution.

Goal Displacement

The concept of goal displacement is much less tangible. Goal displacement occurs when there is a diversion — unintended by management — of organizational energies or resources away from the original goals of the organization. The simplest form of goal displacement is a means-ends inversion, which, as mentioned earlier, occurs when rules or subgoals aimed at facilitating goal attainment themselves become the de facto goals in an organization. There are many reasons for goal displacement. Several of the more important ones can be summarized briefly (Steers, 1977).

The Need to Operationalize Abstract Goals. Although it is initially possible to set forth goals in broad, abstract terms, people in an organization have to act in concrete ways. Abstract goals must be operationalized, or translated into language specific enough to allow employees to act and to measure results. The concrete decisions, plans, and actions that emerge from the original goals are often inconsistent in some way or at least do not contribute to the original, abstract aims of the organization. For instance, the ostensible purpose of a research and development laboratory may be basic or applied research benefiting its parent company and, it is hoped, society. This goal, however, may become operationalized in terms of the number of patents secured in a year or the number of publications produced by the staff.

Delegation Process. Operationalizing goals is initially horizontal, that is, it occurs at only one level of the organization. A problem often arises when the final operational goals are delegated down through the organization to individual employees to be acted upon. Sills (1957) refers to the delegation process as the ultimate source of displacement. As employees or groups of employees are given various responsibilities, their interpretation of the organization's goals, plans, and policies largely determines the true operative and operational goals of any enterprise.

Uncertainty Associated with New or Intangible Goals. Uncertainty about the nature and implications of new or intangible goals can often result in increased employee anxiety and insecurity. People tend to fear changes in their everyday activities. As a result, in making decisions concerning goals, employees often prefer to follow past practices, because they generally are safe and more comfortable. They are not necessarily goal oriented, however.

Necessity for Coordinated and Controlled Activities. Efforts by an organization to coordinate the employees' activities to achieve goals often lead to the establishment of policies, rules, and sanctions to guide and reinforce desired behavior. When employees think the control systems are excessively strict, unreasonable, or unnecessary, they may respond in a variety of nonproductive ways, including staging work slowdowns, striking, using sabotage, or "working to rule," complying so rigidly with the letter of the law that goal progress is slowed by excessive red tape and documentation.

Measurements and Evaluations. Organizations strive to be rational in trying to achieve their goals. As a result of attempts to measure or evaluate the rationality, however, employees can be directed primarily toward satisfying quantitative, measurable goals at the expense of nonquantitative goals, as we discussed earlier (Etzioni, 1964). The more qualitative the goal, the easier it is to displace.

Prior Commitments and Decisions. As Selznick (1949) has pointed out, the pursuit of organizational objectives involves decisions aimed at attaining them. These decisions and actions often emerge later as commitments that can become either goals in themselves or constraints on the existing goals. Commitments like this can divert attention and resources from the intended goals.

Absence of Goal Consensus. Departments within an organization, such as production and marketing, may place greater value on and work harder to achieve goals that affect them directly, at the expense of other goals that may benefit the organization as a whole. Such **suboptimization** can lead to interdepartmental rivalry, conflict, and competition for scarce resources instead of cooperation on mutual, organization-wide objectives.

Personal Goals and Aspirations. Employees, including executives, can intentionally or unintentionally subvert the original goals of an organization to satisfy their own personal goals. Individuals or groups may take actions designed to maintain or enhance their own power or attempt to modify organizational goals to win support and legitimization from the environment or from other groups or members. Michels (1949) refers to this behavior among leaders as the **Iron Law of Oligarchy,** observing that revolutionary leaders tend to become more conservative in their objectives once they gain power in order to protect and maintain their new positions. Displacement may occur when the goals of the organization conflict with personal goals and individuals choose to pursue the latter instead of the former.

Organizational Effectiveness: A Unifying Framework

Organizational effectiveness is the *ultimate criterion* against which management is judged. Without such effectiveness, the welfare of both the organization and its employees can be severely threatened. Understanding organizational effectiveness is crucial. In the sections that follow, we shall examine several of its aspects. First we will consider problems in assessing organizational effectiveness; then we will define effectiveness and discuss the relationship between effectiveness and efficiency. Finally, a model of effectiveness, including its implications for management, will be presented.

Problems of Assessment

Many people would agree that the pursuit of effectiveness is a primary responsibility of management, but there is a lack of consensus on what the concept means. The economist or financial analyst typically equates organizational effectiveness with high profits or return on investment. For a line manager effectiveness is often measured by the amount and quality of goods or services produced. The research and development scientist may speak in terms of the number of patents, new inventions, or new products developed by an organization. And to many labor union leaders, effectiveness means job security, high wages, job satisfaction, and quality of working life. Although there is general agreement that effectiveness is something all organizations should seek, the criteria for assessment remain unclear.

Because managers conceptualize organizational effectiveness differently, there is also disagreement over the most appropriate strategy for attaining effectiveness. A principal reason for this disagreement probably stems from the narrow views that many people have of effectiveness. Many people have only one evaluation criterion, such as profit or productivity. But no organization would survive long if it pursued profits to the exclusion of its employees' needs and goals, or those of society. Organizations typically pursue multiple and often conflicting goals. These goals also tend to differ according to the nature of the organization and its external environment.

Another reason for the lack of agreement about the nature of effectiveness is the ambiguity of the concept. Organizational analysts often incorrectly assume that it is relatively easy to identify the various assessment criteria, but the criteria are somewhat intangible. They depend largely on who is doing the evaluating and the specific frame of reference. The problems are pointed up in attempts to identify relevant aspects of effectiveness that can serve as useful evaluating criteria. A review of seventeen different approaches to assessing organizational effectiveness found a general lack of agreement (Steers, 1977), as shown in Figure 3.4. Only one criterion, an organization's ability to adapt to a changing environment, was mentioned in more than half the studies. It was followed rather distantly by productivity, job satisfaction, profitability, and acquisition of scarce and valued resources. There is clearly little agreement as to what criteria should be used to assess current levels of effectiveness.

A possible resolution to this problem that minimizes many of the assessment obstacles is to view effectiveness in terms of a *process* rather than an end state. Most earlier approaches place a heavy emphasis on identifying the end states of a course of action. Although this may be useful, end states tell us little about the ingredients that facilitate effectiveness, nor do they help the beleaguered manager better understand how effectiveness results. We need to reexamine our notions about organizational effectiveness and the kinds of analytical models managers use to make their own organizations more effective and efficient.

What Is Organizational Effectiveness?

The concept of organizational effectiveness has been used in a wide variety of contexts by such analysts as Goodman and Pennings (1977), Cameron and Whetten (1982), and Steers (1977). Some equate the term with profit or pro-

---

Figure 3.4
Frequency of Occurrence of Evaluation Criteria in Seventeen Models of Organizational Effectiveness

EVALUATION CRITERION	NO. OF TIMES MENTIONED (N = 17)	% OF TOTAL
Adaptability/flexibility	10	59
Productivity	6	35
Job satisfaction	5	29
Profitability	3	18
Acquisition of scarce and valued resources	3	18
Absence of organizational strain	2	12
Control over external environment	2	12
Employee development	2	12
Efficiency	2	12
Employee retention	2	12
Growth	2	12
Integration of individual goals with organizational goals	2	12
Open communication	2	12
Survival	2	12
All other criteria	1	6

Source: Data from Steers, 1975, p. 549.

ductivity, whereas others view it in terms of job satisfaction or the quality of working life. A few investigators suggest that variables such as these are actually intervening variables that make effectiveness more likely.

If we recognize that organizations are unique and often pursue widely divergent goals, we realize that such definitions are too situation specific and value laden to be of much help. It is more useful initially to define **organizational effectiveness** as an organization's ability to acquire and efficiently use available resources to achieve its goals. This definition requires some elaboration.

To begin with, we are focusing on *operative,* rather than official, goals. It is more appropriate to evaluate the relative level of effectiveness in terms of an organization's real objectives than against a list of goals meant principally for public consumption. For example, we often see public advertisements by corporations claiming that "progress is our most important product" or "the things we do improve the way we live." Such statements, or official goals, often give the impression that the company's primary objective is progress, whereas in fact other goals, such as profit, growth, and an acceptable rate of return on investment, probably represent more accurate statements of intent — that is, they are the real operative goals.

Effectiveness is best judged against whatever objectives the organization truly intends to pursue. This approach has the added advantage of minimizing the influence of the outside analyst's value judgments in the assessment. For example, although many would argue that job satisfaction is a desirable end, it remains for the organization, not an outside analyst, to set such an objective. Inherent in this definition is the assumption that organizational effectiveness is best judged in terms of an organization's ability to compete in a turbulent environment and successfully acquire and utilize scarce resources. This assumption in turn implies that managers must deal effectively with their external environments to secure needed resources. This approach also recognizes that efficiency is a necessary ingredient in determining organizational effectiveness but is not the only criterion.

Efficiency and Effectiveness

Organizational effectiveness is the extent to which operative goals have been achieved. **Efficiency** represents the cost/benefit ratio incurred in pursuing those goals (Barnard, 1938). In other words, efficiency is a measure of how many inputs — raw materials, money, and people — are necessary to attain a specific output or a particular goal, such as achieving a certain level of production. If two companies making the same product finish the fiscal year with equal production levels but one attained the level using fewer resources, that company can be characterized as more efficient: it achieved the same level of output with fewer inputs. An example of such a comparison appears in Figure 3.5, which shows the number of employees required to make automobiles in American, European, and Japanese companies. It should be remembered, however, that the

Figure 3.5
Employee Efficiency Ratios for Various Automobile Companies, 1980

COMPANY	NO. OF CARS PRODUCED	NO. OF EMPLOYEES	EFFICIENCY RATIO
British Leyland	500,000	130,000	4:1
General Motors	4,000,000	517,000	8:1
Volkswagen	1,600,000	150,000	11:1
Renault	1,700,000	100,000	17:1
Toyota	2,000,000	45,000	44:1

Source: Data from Morrison, 1981a, p. 284.

Japanese make extensive use of robots to replace humans on more mundane jobs. Although such comparisons admittedly are crude, they do point to the importance of efficiency in discussing goal attainment and organizational effectiveness.

Numerous factors go into determining the efficiency of an organization. These factors can include relative labor costs, productivity per man-hour, costs of raw materials, and technological advances. In the past decade, for example, many businesses have moved their factories in order to be in states with lower labor costs or to be closer to their sources of raw materials to reduce transportation costs. These relocations are attempts to improve organizational efficiency, if not organizational effectiveness.

Nature of the Relationship. Although the concept of efficiency is clearly related to effectiveness, the precise nature of that relationship is unclear. Some argue that efficiency is a necessary yet insufficient ingredient in determining organizational effectiveness. This viewpoint is probably an oversimplification, however. The actual relationship between effectiveness and efficiency may depend on other variables, such as the availability and cost of necessary resources. For instance, after World War II a German general complained that the Allies, and in particular the United States, had not "beaten," but rather "smothered," Germany. The general was saying that although the Allies had been very effective in attaining their goal, they did not necessarily pursue that objective efficiently.

A more recent example can be seen in the case of the United States space program. In the early 1960s the United States set a national goal of achieving a safe lunar landing and return by the end of the decade. In 1969, after eight years of research and an investment of more than $26 billion, the mission was accomplished. The program was said to be highly effective. But how do we judge whether the program was efficient? Does the expenditure of $26 billion represent a favorable or an unfavorable cost/benefit ratio? Because of the magnitude of the problem and the absence of comparative data, it is almost impossible to answer this question with any certainty. Several prominent spokespersons at the time, referring to the high profits made by some of the aerospace corporations involved in the project, argued that the project could have been accomplished at a much lower, more efficient cost. Whether such assertions are correct can probably never be determined.

Thus, in at least some cases, efficiency is not a prerequisite for effectiveness. If an organization such as the United States government has unlimited or at least sizable resources, or if the country finds itself under threat in wartime, efficiency may be far less crucial than effectiveness. When resources are more limited, however, as is the case in most business organizations, efficiency may emerge as a central determinant of organizational effectiveness. Under these more constrained circumstances, efficiency allows an organization to stretch limited resources, permitting increased productivity, growth, and expansion with the same inputs. In fact, efficiency may mean survival for organizations in highly competitive markets.

Two Types of Efficiency. To go one step further, it is helpful to distinguish between two types of **efficiency:** potential and actual (Katz and Kahn, 1978). **Potential efficiency** represents the top level of efficiency at which organizations theoretically can function, given their unique characteristics, processes, products, and goals. **Actual efficiency** represents the cost/benefit ratio that an organization actually achieves. Consider the effects of some of the regulations of the Interstate Commerce Commission. For decades the commission, a bureau of the United States government, set regulations that many people felt reduced competition and led to inefficiency. Certain trucking firms were required to transport their cargoes from point A to point B not by the most direct route, but through out-of-the-way point C instead. Costs were increased for the trucking firms, their customers, and ultimately the consumer. In such cases the actual efficiency level of the trucking firm was clearly below the potential efficiency level.

Managers themselves can have a major influence on how close actual efficiency is to the potential level. An organization may have sufficient resources in terms of money, materials, and technological expertise, but poor decision making or other inept actions by management can easily lead to lowered efficiency. This key role of management is particularly evident in highly competitive situations involving rival industries in which all firms have sufficient resources. In these situations the gap between actual and potential efficiency is the area in which managerial expertise and innovation can make the greatest difference.

Efficiency is thus closely linked to organizational effectiveness. Whether it is a determinant of effectiveness depends on several additional factors, such as the availability of resources. Efficiency has been defined here as the extent to which resources are utilized rationally in the pursuit of organizational goals. Factors such as employee turnover and absenteeism, the wasting of human resources, are more an indication of organizational inefficiency than of ineffectiveness. Although they may contribute indirectly to effectiveness, they are not useful criteria for its assessment.

A View of Organizational Effectiveness

On a very general level, it may be enough to define effectiveness in terms of attaining operative goals. But to understand more fully the process of creating effective operations, we must take a more dynamic approach. The approach we use here is a process model of effectiveness. Its aim is to provide managers with a framework for analyzing the major processes involved in effectiveness. This approach contrasts sharply with earlier models that merely listed the supposedly necessary criteria for assessing success. Our model consists of three related components: the notion of goal optimization, a systems perspective, and an emphasis on human behavior in organizational settings (Steers, 1977).

The Goal Optimization Approach

Most of the current approaches used to assess effectiveness ultimately rest on the concept of goal attainment. An advantage of using operative goals to assess effectiveness is that success can be measured in terms of an organization's own intentions. Because different organizations pursue widely different goals, it is logical to recognize this uniqueness in any evaluation.

There are several variations on this approach to evaluating effectiveness. The most fruitful views effectiveness in terms of **goal optimization.** Instead of assessing success in terms of whether maximum goals have been reached, it recognizes a series of constraints, such as money, technology, and personnel, that inhibits reaching such goals. In this situation, managers set and pursue optimized goals, desirable goals within the constraints of available resources. A business may, for instance, feel that a 10 percent return on investment is a realistic goal in view of resource availability and the existing market environment, even though it would like a higher return. We suggest that it is against feasible goals, not against ultimate or ideal goals, that effectiveness is best evaluated. It is important not to confuse goal optimization with suboptimization, in which, for example, an organization may intentionally set a 5 percent return-on-investment objective even though 10 percent may be feasible given current conditions and resources.

The use of a goal optimization approach to assess effectiveness has several advantages over conventional approaches. First, it implies that reaching maximum goals is probably not possible and may be detrimental to an organization's well-being and survival. In most situations there is little chance for a company to maximize productivity and job satisfaction at the same time, for example. Instead, compromises are made that provide for an optimal level of attainment of both goals. The use of a goal optimization approach allows multiple and often conflicting goals within the same organization to be recognized.

Second, the use of a goal optimization model recognizes that managers place different weight on the various goals. For instance, a company may employ five times the resources in pursuing its profit goal that it devotes to its affirmative action employment goal or its job satisfaction goal.

Third, this approach recognizes a series of constraints that can impede progress toward attaining goals. Many of these constraints, including, for example, limited finances, personnel, and technology, may be impossible to reduce or eliminate, at least in the short run. Consider the true case of a slide rule manufacturer that lost 75 percent of its business within two years of the introduction of small, cheap, electronic calculators. Manufacturing slide rules requires a radically different technology than that used in the manufacture of electronic calculators. As a result, this firm, which had a competitive advantage using one technology, lost its edge when market demand shifted. If the company had anticipated changes accurately and far enough in advance, it might have been able to develop new applications for existing technology, assuming the technology could not be changed. The firm might have devoted its energies to developing new precision measurement instruments not based on electronics. It is impor-

---

Feature 3.4
The Liquor Industry Shifts Its Goals

Liquor sales in the United States — the world's largest market — have slumped significantly, falling back to 1977 sales levels. From 1979 to 1982, Scotch sales alone fell more than 25 percent.

Interestingly, the recession is not the only reason for the downturn. Another major factor is a heightened health awareness among Americans, which has turned many hard-liquor drinkers to wine, beer, and soda. "We're becoming a nation of more moderate people," said William M. Wilbur, president of Joseph E. Seagram USA, a subsidiary of Seagram Company, the world's largest producer of wines and spirits. "We're more careful about what and how much we eat and drink, and that has major implications for our industry" ("Distillers Must Cope," p. 110).

The liquor industry is moving in several directions to combat slumping sales. Some distillers of scotch are selling their bulk whisky to cut-rate bottlers who mix it with inferior whiskies and sell it at reduced prices. A lot of this bulk whisky has gone to Japan. Other distillers are developing new products and targeting new market segments. Seagram's, for example, has joined forces with Coca-Cola Bottling Company to produce a line of non-

alcoholic mixers. And Heublein Spirits is targeting sixteen new products, some featuring lower proofs, at blacks, Hispanics, and working women. Other companies are jumping into the rum, brandy, cordial, cognac, and imported vodka markets.

Heublein's chairman and chief executive Hicks B. Waldron isn't optimistic. "At best," he says, "the industry's growth will be flat for the next five years" ("Distillers Must Cope," p. 110). Drexel Burnham Lambert analyst Arthur Kirsch is of a like opinion: "The entire whisky part of the spirit business is going to continue to fall from favor" ("Scotch on the Rocks," p. 75). Perhaps the most perceptive comment of all comes from Heublein's president Robert R. Weiss: "You can't sit in front of the TV and watch ads against drunk driving and see states getting more stringent on minimum-drinking-age laws without realizing that the public's consciousness is being raised against alcohol abuse" (Distillers Must Cope," p. 112).

Sources: "Distillers Must Cope with a Sobering Future," *Business Week,* May 2, 1983, pp. 110–112; "Scotch on the Rocks," by Susan Dentzer with Ronald Henkoff and Frank Gibney, *Newsweek,* May 16, 1983, p. 75.

tant to recognize such constraints and the ways in which an organization responds to them in assessing the success or failure of an organization.

Fourth, the goal optimization approach has the advantage of making evaluation criteria more flexible. As the goals of an organization or the constraints associated with them change, a new optimal solution emerges that provides new evaluation criteria. The methods of assessment remain current and reflect the changing needs and goals of the organization over time.

A Systems Perspective

A second important property of a process model of effectiveness is the use of an open-systems perspective for analysis. This emphasizes the interrelationships of parts of an organization and its environment as they together influence effectiveness. Using such a perspective we can identify four major categories of influences on effectiveness (Fig. 3.6):

1. Organizational characteristics such as structure and technology.
2. Environmental characteristics such as economic and market conditions.

Figure 3.6
Major Influences on Organizational Effectiveness

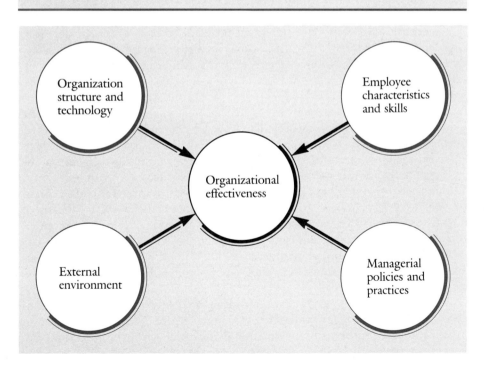

3. Employee characteristics such as level of job performance and job attachment.
4. Managerial policies and practices.

These four sets of variables must be considered in relation to one another to achieve effectiveness. The interrelationship among these primary variables is a central concern throughout this book. Managers have the responsibility of understanding the nature of their external environment and setting realistic goals to accommodate that environment. The more effective organizations will be those that successfully adapt structure, technology, work effort, and policies to aid in efficiently attaining goals.

A Behavioral Emphasis

The third aspect of the process model emphasizes individual behavior as it affects organizational success or failure. This position is in opposition to the stand taken by many that effectiveness is best examined exclusively on a "macro," or organization-wide, level. We believe analyses should include consideration of how the behavior of individual employees influences organizational goal attainment. If an organization's employees largely agree with the objectives of their employer, they are likely to exert a relatively high level of energy toward achieving those goals. If, however, organizational goals conflict with the employees' personal goals, there is little reason to believe that employees will exert their maximum effort. There are many reasons why employees may attempt to thwart managerial efforts.

To see the importance of individual behavior in organizational decision, consider the controversy over automobile seatbelts. To improve traffic safety the United States government passed a law requiring car manufacturers to install seatbelts in all new cars. The law failed to have the desired consequences: many people simply did not use them. Then additional laws were passed requiring manufacturers to install warning lights and buzzers to remind drivers to use the seatbelts. When these measures also proved ineffective, laws were passed requiring manufacturers to install devices that made it necessary to connect seatbelts before the ignition could be activated. These devices could be circumvented with a degree of ingenuity and have since been dropped. Thus, although the initial goal was laudatory, the processes or means used to achieve the goal were largely ineffective because they ignored behavioral patterns of most drivers. Now there is talk of passive restraint systems. Perhaps a more effective strategy, less costly and time consuming, would be simply to pass a law nullifying accident insurance claims for drivers injured while not wearing seatbelts. This would make auto safety and responsibility a matter of individual behavior and choice.

In any case, when we examine organizational effectiveness it is important to recognize the people who ultimately determine the quality and quantity of an organization's response to environmental demands. The role of individual employees is a theme throughout this book.

Implications for Management

Two general conclusions emerge from this analysis that have important implications for management. First, organizational effectiveness is best understood as a *continuous process* rather than an end state. Marshaling resources for goal-directed effort is an unceasing task for most managers. Because of the changing nature of the goals of most organizations, managers have a continuing responsibility to recognize environmental changes, to restructure available resources, to modify technologies, and to teach employees to utilize resources for continually changing objectives.

Our analysis also has emphasized the central role of *contingencies* in any discussion of organizational effectiveness. Managers must recognize the unique qualities of their own organization — its goals, structures, technologies, people, and environment — and respond in a manner consistent with this uniqueness. The arbitrary use of rules or principles in a diverse organization does not foster success. Instead, the organization and its management must teach employees to recognize and understand the nature of a particular situation and respond appropriately. When viewed this way, organizational effectiveness becomes largely a function of how well managers and employees can pool their talents and efforts and overcome the obstacles that inhibit goal attainment. A goal optimization approach to understanding effectiveness allows managers to ask intelligent questions concerning the appropriateness of resource allocation decisions. Is there a better way to allocate the limited resources? Important questions for managers to consider include:

1. *How well are we applying our limited resources toward attaining our goals?* Many organizations make resource allocation decisions independent of goal decisions, resulting in *unfunded goals* and *funded nongoals*. This behavior is most clearly seen in the frequent practice of various legislatures of passing authorization and appropriation bills separately, thus making it possible for a bill (goal) to become law without the resources to implement it.

2. *Is there a clear relationship between the amount of resources we spend on the various goals and the relative importance of each goal?* If, for example, an organization truly believes it places equal weight on making a profit and on improving the quality of working life, are such beliefs reflected in the allocation of resources? We are not suggesting that equivalent amounts of resources must be spent on each goal but, rather, that sufficient resources should be spent to attain both objectives.

3. *What kind of return on investment are we getting on our resources per goal?* If organizations pursue multiple goals, it would seem logical to examine the efficiency of effort invested in each goal. It may be that an organization is highly efficient in achieving its less important goals and relatively inefficient in achieving its more important goals. When there are such inefficiencies, decisions must be made concerning the desirability of continuing to pursue a particular goal. When a goal, such as hiring the hard-core unemployed, is

considered worthwhile, companies may pursue the goal despite a low return on investment.

4. *Is the entire organization working together for goal attainment?* Is the entire organization pulling together and coordinating its activities for the benefit of the entire organization? Or are different departments and special interest groups looking after their own interests?

5. *Is the fit between the organization and its environment changing?* Organizations should continually raise questions concerning their niche in the external environment. We saw in the example of the slide rule manufacturer how a company can lose a major share of its market by failing to adjust to changes in market demand. In these circumstances, without the necessary technology to compete with manufacturers of electronic calculators, the firm might have found it desirable to establish its place in the market by specializing in drafting equipment or other instruments not based on electronics. A relatively successful example of such organization environment fit can be seen in the American Motors Corporation, which for many years has specialized in small cars and Jeeps, while General Motors, Ford, and Chrysler have stressed medium-sized and large cars. As the other auto makers shift their focus toward smaller cars, American Motors, with its fewer resources, may find it necessary to adjust its efforts toward newer markets. Flexibility in the face of environmental change remains an important area of concern for effective organizations.

Summary

The nature of organizations is examined in this chapter. Organizations exist for stated and sometimes unstated purposes and consist of people who develop social relations and patterns of interaction. They divide work so members can specialize, they coordinate work rationally, and they are created with the intention of surviving.

Organizational goals consist of official goals, formal statements about the group's mission; operative goals, which represent an organization's real intentions; and operational goals, which are stated in observable or measurable terms. We can also better understand an organization's intentions by dividing its goals into first- and second-order goals. Goals have functions and dysfunctions for both the organization itself and individual employees.

The Thompson and McEwen model of goal formulation states that the process is best understood by looking at the relationship between an organization and its external environment, consisting of such factors as market and economic conditions, competition, and government agencies and regulations. Managers formulate goals to create and maintain a favorable balance of power with the environment.

The Cyert and March model acknowledges the important role played by individuals in determining or modifying an organization's objectives. Cyert and March suggest that an organization is a coalition of groups and individuals and that goals are affected by continual bargaining, prior commitments, and changes in the environment. Both this and the Thompson and McEwen models ultimately rest on power and commitments.

Changes in goals are inevitable. In goal succession, changes are made consciously by management to shift the organization's course. In goal displacement, the changes are unintended by management.

Organizational effectiveness is the ultimate criterion against which management is judged, but there are many concepts of effectiveness. Looking at effectiveness as a process rather than an end state minimizes many assessment obstacles. Effectiveness also must be examined in terms of an organization's operative, not official, goals.

Organizational efficiency is the cost/benefit ratio of pursuing organizational goals. There is potential efficiency and actual efficiency.

The most fruitful way of evaluating effectiveness is with a process model. Such an approach uses the goal optimization method, which recognizes constraints that inhibit reaching maximum goals instead of assessing success in tems of whether desired goals have been met.

A second property of the process model is an open-systems perspective, which emphasizes the interrelationships of parts of an organization and the environment as they together influence effectiveness. The process model also emphasizes individual behavior as it affects organizational success or failure.

Questions for Discussion

1. What characteristics do organizations share?
2. What function do goals serve for the organizations as a whole and for the individuals in an organization?
3. What is meant by the term *means-end inversion*? Give an organizational example of means-end inversion.
4. In what ways can goals be dysfunctional?
5. What factors are necessary for goals to be realized by individuals?
6. How can a manager increase the relevancy of goals for employees?
7. What are the differences between official and operative goals? Are official goals operational? Can operative goals be operational? Give examples of each type of goal.
8. Describe the types of companies that hold a great deal of power over their environments. What types of companies hold little power over their environments? Why?
9. In what ways can an organization that has little power bargain with its environment?
10. What is meant by the term *side payments*? How are side payments used in an organization?

11. In what ways are the Thompson and McEwen model and the Cyert and March model of goal formulation similar?

12. Explain how goal displacement can occur.

13. Differentiate the terms *organizational effectiveness* and *organizational efficiency.* Use examples to help explain the difference. How are the two concepts related?

14. Why is the goal optimization approach beneficial in determining organizational effectiveness?

15. Explain the relationship between realizing goals and allocating resources.

Exercise 3.1
Setting Individual Objectives

Introduction

You are beginning an exercise especially designed to give you and others a chance to experience the crucial steps in setting individual objectives within a Management by Objectives (MBO) system. The setting for the exercise is Alsim, Inc., a large manufacturing and wholesaling firm.

In this exercise a number of decisions are necessary. *First,* you will be asked to make an individual decision. *Second,* you will have the opportunity to exchange ideas with your associates in a group discussion. *Third,* the group will then agree upon a solution. The group discussions will be most helpful for learning about MBO if all issues and viewpoints are thoroughly examined and full agreement on a solution is reached. Avoid, if possible, using majority rule to make group decisions.

The basic purpose of this exercise is to stimulate discussion between you and your associates. The more involved you become in the situation depicted by the exercise, the more meaningful will be your contribution to group discussion. The answers given are offered as guides to your thinking. These answers cannot always be "right," because groups typically define the situations depicted differently. Whether the exercise is successful really depends on how much you learn about MBO.

Background

Alsim, Inc. is a large and diversified manufacturing and wholesaling firm. Current sales are in excess of $600 million as a result of a forty-year history of successful and growing operation. However, current economic conditions have made funds for expansion and modernization very limited.

Alsim is organized into four major divisions, each headed by a vice-president. These divisions are Consumer Products, Industrial Products, Sales, and International. For the purpose of this exercise, you will imagine that you are a newly appointed plant manager in the Industrial Products Division. This division consists of ten plants located in the Midwest and the Southeast.

Your plant (the Middletown Plant) is one of the oldest in the Industrial Products Division. With the exception of a few equipment replacements, the plant was constructed in the mid-1950s. Most other divisional plants and those of your com-

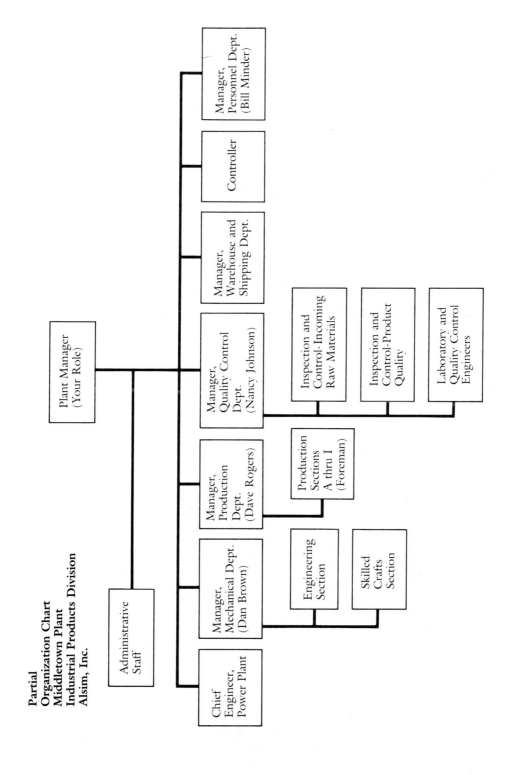

**Partial
Organization Chart
Middletown Plant
Industrial Products Division
Alsim, Inc.**

petitors were built in the past seven years. For the previous year, before you assumed this new position, performance of the Middletown Plant has been below forecast. Neither production goals nor cost goals had been fully met.

The plant employs approximately 500 people of which about 70 were classified as managerial and professional. You directly supervise a three-man administrative staff and seven department heads. The labor force has been recruited largely from nearby rural areas, and there have been numerous hourly employees that have assumed first-line supervisory positions. Although the local union has not been militant, the labor wage rates have consistently risen with the national trend. Thus, it is becoming increasingly difficult to keep production costs at a competitive level. However, the plant's ability to handle special orders and meet increasingly stringent product specifications has kept its profitability at an acceptable, if unimpressive, level.

You have been Plant Manager since the first of the year, and you've been spending considerable time over the past four months with your staff in developing improved operating procedures throughout the plant. To date there has been some progress in reducing the excessive machine downtime and lowering inventory costs. The Industrial Products Division has been directed by corporate management to implement a Management by Objective System in each of its plants. You welcome the introduction of MBO as a means of insuring continued improvements in your plant operations. MBO has been used very successfully for several years in other Alsim divisions, and corporate management is committed to implementing MBO throughout the company by the end of the coming year.

The Implementation program has been underway at your plant for six weeks, and, with the help of MBO consultants retained by corporate headquarters, you feel you are making good progress in implementing MBO with those managers who report directly to you.

For purposes of this exercise, you are acting as the Plant Manager of the Middletown Plant.

Defining Key Result Areas

Dave Rogers is the Manager of the Production Department for your plant and reports directly to you, as plant manager. In preparation for setting his objectives, Rogers has provided you with a list of his major job responsibilities. You have previously reviewed the list and concur with Dave's analysis. The major job responsibilities for Dave Rogers are presented in the accompanying list.

Soon you will be meeting with Dave Rogers to jointly determine his objectives. It is important that you be very well prepared to discuss with Rogers the Key Result Areas in which you expect him to set objectives.

As an individual, and *without* discussion with your associates, decide which *four* of the major job responsibilities for Dave Rogers should be his Key Result Areas. Indicate your choice by placing a check mark (✓) in the Individual Choice column opposite the four major job responsibilities that are Key Result Areas for Dave Rogers.

After each member of the group has made his or her individual choice, discuss Rogers's job responsibilities as a group. The group should then select the four major job responsibilities that the group believes are Dave's Key Result Areas. Indicate the group choices by check marks (✓) in the Group Choice column opposite the appropriate job responsibility.

MAJOR JOB RESPONSIBILITIES FOR DAVE ROGERS, PRODUCTION DEPARTMENT MANAGER	KEY RESULT AREAS	
	INDIVIDUAL CHOICE	GROUP CHOICE
1. Schedule the work force	_____	_____
2. Maintain quality control	_____	_____
3. Prepare cost estimates for special runs	_____	_____
4. Decide first-level union grievances	_____	_____
5. Supervise nine shift foremen	_____	_____
6. Approve shipments	_____	_____
7. Order necessary raw materials	_____	_____
8. Supervise production clerks	_____	_____
9. Direct prevention maintenance program	_____	_____
10. Direct safety program	_____	_____
11. Train the workforce	_____	_____
12. Supervise housekeeping	_____	_____

Questions

1. When should a manager pay more attention to *general* goals rather than *specific* goals?

2. How do we translate *activities* into *goals*?

3. One student pointed out the problem associated with having demanding goals as follows: "The deadline rather than the achievement of a necessary task becomes the goal. The deadline can be used as an excuse for turning in incomplete work, simply by saying: 'I didn't have the time to do a complete job.' How do you deal with this problem?" Discuss the student's point of view.

Source: "Setting Individual Objectives," by E. Allen Slusher and Henry P. Sims, Jr. Reprinted by permission.

Case Study
Ocean Electronics, Inc.

In June of 1967, Ralph Roberts graduated from Florida Atlantic University with a master's degree in ocean engineering. Ralph was not the typical June graduate; at age 36 he had spent twelve years in the United States Navy. During those twelve years Ralph had learned a great deal about naval electronics. The more he studied electronics, the more ideas he had about ways to improve existing equipment. With little opportunity to have his ideas studied, Ralph made an important decision; he left the Navy and, with the aid of his G.I. benefits, entered the University of California at Santa Barbara to major in ocean engineering. His academic record was spotty. His science, engineering, and math courses all showed outstanding performance, yet his studies in the social sciences and humanities were never more than average, and often below average.

Upon graduation from the University of California at Santa Barbara, Roberts looked to continue his education and came to the newly founded Florida Atlantic University in Boca Raton, Florida. The location had been responsible for the formation of an excellent department of ocean engineering. Ralph's record in his major allowed him to be accepted, and his record at Florida Atlantic University was much above average. His faculty viewed Ralph as an outstandng student. His knowledge of practical ocean engineering, gained through his years in the Navy, lent much to his research projects. It was during his research for his master's thesis that Ralph made some interesting findings. The results of these findings were the basis of a series of ocean electronics sounding instruments whose rate of accuracy was three times better than existing equipment. Encouraged by his professors, upon graduation Ralph sought financial assistance to establish a production facility to gain the rewards of his research. He believed that much of the profits could be diverted into the development of an ocean research company to allow Ralph to continue his work.

Jim Stanton was contacted in May of 1967 by the chairman of the ocean engineering department about forming a corporation to support the work of Ralph Roberts. Stanton talked to Roberts, asking him what he wanted in terms of selling the new electronics process. Roberts commented that, "I want freedom to do research and a company which will encourage my research by plowing back profits into the firm." Stanton and two Miami associates formed Ocean Electronics, Inc., giving Ralph Roberts 20 percent ownership for his patents and put up a total of $1,400,000.

Stanton stated that, "We thought we saw a good investment, and we put up the needed money. It will be fnancially rewarding to all involved."

Jim Stanton: *(to interviewer)* My associates, David Rubin and Tim O'Leary, and I wanted to invest in a company which could take advantage of the rising market for specialized electronics. Ralph has some patents which we felt provided the nucleus for forming a mutually profitable business venture. We gave Ralph 20 percent ownership in the company, which, in 1969, netted him $15,000 in dividends, plus his salary of $10,000 a year. Our prediction for 1970 indicated that his share of distributed earnings will be in the neighborhood of $26,000. That's not a bad neighborhood, is it?

Interviewer: No, I guess not. What was your role in the early formation of the company and its management?

Jim: When Ike Lawson, the chairman of the ocean engineering department at Florida Atlantic University, called me and told me of Ralph, I made an appointment to visit the campus and meet with both Ike and Ralph. At the meeting I was impressed with the capabilities Ralph had shown in his work and told him that I would see if capital could be raised. I subsequently met with David Rubin and Tim O'Leary, and they agreed to join in the venture.

Now, as far as management, I am chairman of the board and in the early stages was active in its management.

Interviewer: What do you mean, *active?*

Jim: Well, Ralph was busy making operational the new inventions, so I hired both Ron Able, the manager of sales, and Herb Schultz, the production manager.

Interviewer: Was Ralph ever involved with these decisions?

Jim: Yes, he concurred on all decisions. He was president of the company but, as I said, involved at that time with our technical problems.

The Other Executives

The other executives of Ocean Electronics are listed in Exhibit 1.

Manager of Production, Herb Schultz, Age 47

Herb had been hired in December of 1967 by Jim Stanton. Herb had been the assistant manager of production of a medium-sized electronics firm located in the southwest United States.

Interviewer: Why did you come with a new firm? Ocean was just being established and its future was not secured.

Herb: Well, I like this business. Production is a real

Exhibit 1
Ocean Electronics, Inc., Organizational Chart

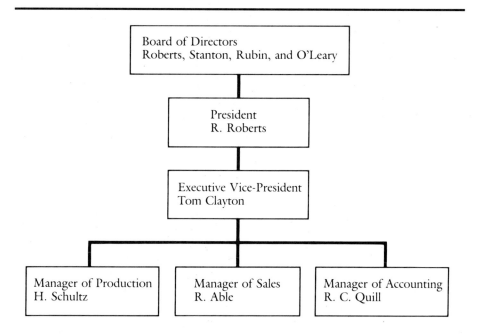

challenge. Before, I was the assistant manager; I want to be the top man.

Interviewer: Are you happy you made the change?

Herb: You bet. I came here and started from scratch. I have ordered all our production equipment, installed it, designed the work layout, hired and trained the men; in general, I feel it's my area.

Interviewer: What is the work force in your production area?

Herb: At present we have two other engineers and fifteen technicians. We have grown from just myself and no one has ever been laid off. In fact, only two men have left the shop, and both had offers we just couldn't match. They left with our best wishes for success.

I think we have a very compatible work group. We have never failed to meet a production schedule. Each technician respects his fellow workers and this respect breeds cooperation.

Interviewer: Does Ralph ever interfere with your operation?

Herb: In the past six months Ralph has been causing us a few headaches. He [Ralph] never really cared how we assembled the instruments. He did worry about quality — he always has — and so have I. My men are proud of our quality. Because of the nature of electronic instruments of this type, we inspect each before shipment. Lately he has been making all sorts of ridiculous requests. Two months ago he wanted us to stop assembly of one line so that he could alter the model to include some new improvement he had just developed. Well, it took all Ron Able and I could do to convince him that it would be better to include the changes on next year's line. The cost to redesign our assembly processes in mid-production seemed to have no impact on his opinion.

Interviewer: Can you still work with Ralph?

Herb: If Ralph would only go back to the way it

was; he does the research, and I assemble the instruments.

Manager of Sales, Ron Able, Age 37

Ron also came to the company when it was being formed. Ron had been in the ocean instruments industry with a major producer and was hired because of his proven selling ability. He had many major Washington contacts, which had given him the reputation of being the top man in the field when it came to government contracts.

Interviewer: What brought you to Ocean Electronics, Inc.?

Ron: Money. I thought that Ocean Electronics was going to be a winner. The new technology that Ralph was developing was going to set the pace in the future. It is easy to sell the best, and Ralph Roberts had the patents for the next generation of ocean instruments.

Interviewer: How successful has Ocean Electronics, Inc. been?

Ron: Very successful, I believe; and what's more, this is only the beginning. From what I see around the industry, we have the finest electronic ocean instruments in the world. The established firms are really sitting up and taking notice of our products. In fact, I will predict that the 1970 sales will be at $1,400,000, and that 1971 will approach $3,000,000.

Interviewer: How would you describe the customer relations of Ocean Electronics, Inc.?

Ron: To be truthful, spotty.

Interviewer: Can you explain further?

Ron: Many of the sales we make are to government agencies, primarily the Department of Defense.

They have very exacting standards, and if you wish to compete for a contract, you had better have a product which matches their specs. To this point we are great; the technical specialists of the Department of Defense evaluate our product and make a recommendation that it be purchased over its competitors; then, since we are still small and new, we are investigated as to ability to comply with the contract. In other words, will we be able to do what we said we could? These personnel are not technical types in general. On occasion, Ralph has given these men a tough time. Not by design, but Ralph is just not too aware of how to handle these visitors.

Interviewer: What specifically did he do?

Ron: On a number of occasions while we were entertaining visitors, Ralph would begin on his favorite conversation: his research and his electronic instruments. When most of the visitors showed no technical knowledge of the workings of the product or the nature of his research, Ralph would put them down and just leave, seldom even a good-bye.

Interviewer: Has this happened with civilian clients as well?

Ron: Yes, it has. Most people don't mind eccentrics, but they prefer polite ones.

By June of 1970, Ocean Electronics, Inc. was two and a half years old and was a financial success (Exhibit 2).

Company facilities had been expanding, and in 1970 the physical plant comprised two buildings located in an industrial park in Pompano Beach, Florida. One building, the larger, was now used ex-

Exhibit 2
Ocean Electronics, Inc., Income Statement

	1/1/68 thru 12/31/68		1/1/69 thru 12/31/69		1/1/70 thru 6/30/70	
Sales (net)		$245,000.00		$671,000.00		$584,000.00
Less expenses						
Administrative	$ 29,000.00		$ 44,000.00		$ 38,000.00	
Operating	160,000.00		361,000.00		261,000.00	
Research	25,000.00	214,000.00	75,000.00	480,000.00	81,000.00	380,000.00
Net profit		$ 31,000.00		$191,000.00		$204,000.00
Dividends		-0-		75,000.00		

clusively for production. It had originally served as the entire facility until the recent completion of the office building and research laboratory. The research laboratory had been designed by Ralph and included the finest in modern electronic equipment. The company also owned two boats, which were used as test beds for new equipment and for the personal use of the executives.

Tom Clayton, the executive vice-president, had been hired in 1969 by the board of directors to oversee the general operations of the company. Ralph had not really been opposed to Tom's being hired, because he felt that this would take a lot of troublesome problems off his back.

Ralph: *(to interviewer)* I just didn't realize that business had so many time-consuming problems. In research, you work at one problem until it's solved. This day-to-day business stuff was really getting to me. Last year Jim Stanton brought up to the Board of Directors the idea of hiring an executive vice-president. Jim said he knew of someone with excellent qualifications who would administer the day-to-day business problems and coordinate with the functional area (sales and production).

Interviewer: What was your reaction to his suggestion?

Ralph: Well, in 1967 when we started, everything was great. I worked on perfecting my inventions and packaging them in a size that fits the needs of boat and ship owners. Each product, though identical in theory, differed in its application, depending on the size of the ship. For instance, an ocean-going freighter is not as limited as to size and weight as a 30-foot pleasure boat. The 30-foot boat, on the other hand, won't need the range and accuracy of the ocean-going freighter. Then there are military uses that completely differ again. Anyway, while I was getting all those technical problems solved, Jim Stanton brought together Ron Able and Herb Schultz. He knows about business, and if he said they were qualified it was all right with me; besides, I was really busy.

Interviewer: What happened after you perfected the product?

Ralph: When I was satisfied with the product, we began production and started our sales campaign. About this time Jim Stanton let me take over the reins. By mid-1968 we were showing a profit and the outlook was very promising. Ron and Herb were in almost every day about one thing or another. Delivery schedules, production runs, pricing policies, discounts; it was all new to me. What worried me most was our lack of research. I didn't have the time to get any research done. From the middle of 1968 until we hired Tom Clayton was a miserable time for me. I felt a little lost sometimes. I guess Ron and Herb saw this, and they tried to help. When Tom came, it got me back where I wanted to be.

On a warm July afternoon, Ralph was speaking to Tom Clayton about the proposed cut in the research budget.

Ralph: I don't understand the stockholders; we must do research to prosper. It was my research that got this whole thing started.

Tom: Ralph, look at their side. They put up over a million dollars to get this company going and they want to get a return on their investment.

Ralph: [Interrupts] Return, hell, they want to milk it dry.

Tom: Now that's not so. You own 20 percent of the company yourself. And, besides, the proposed budget for research for 1970 was $110,000 and all of it is yours. That was more than a 45 percent increase over last year.

Ralph: But I'm on to something, and we need to buy the equipment now. You don't turn research ideas on and off like water from a faucet.

Tom: We understand that, but there are other things to consider.

Ralph: [Interrupting] You and your bastard costs. I'm going back to the lab. (Ralph leaves.)

Case Questions

1. Are different parties (people, groups) using different definitions of "organizational effectiveness" for Ocean Electronics, Inc.?
2. How would you help Tom Clayton resolve this difficulty?

Source: This case was prepared by Professor Thomas W. Zimmerer, Department of Management, Clemson University. Published in P. E. Connor, *Organizations: Theory and Design* (Chicago: SRA, 1980), pp. 457–462. Reprinted by permission of the author.

Technical Competencies of Management

CHAPTER 4

Planning in a Complex Environment

Nabisco, Keebler, and Sunshine — for years the cookie shelves in supermarkets have displayed these well-known brand names. Lately, however, these traditional favorites are being squeezed out by new offerings of both domestic and foreign cookie manufacturers. Proctor & Gamble, for example, best known for its household products and disposable diapers, is test marketing a chocolate chip supermarket cookie that it describes as being "crispy on the outside, chewy on the inside, and tastes more homemade than the bestselling brands" ("Cookie Monster," p. 55). Pepsico is another United States company that has made inroads into the cookie market.

The established brands are fighting back, with announcements of their own new chewy, gooey creations and some new marketing strategies. Nabisco is pushing its new line of "Al-most Home" cookies. The company is also test marketing an older brand to which it has added twice as many chocolate bits. Sunshine is experimenting with reducing the size of some of its cookies so they can be priced below $1 per package.

Because supermarket shelf space is so limited, the cookie war is heating up. Retailers are being wooed by old and new brands alike. In the words of Jane Armstrong, consumer marketing vice-president at Chicago's Jewel Food Stores, "We'll be watching the movement and start weeding out" ("The Monster That Looms," p. 92).

Source: "Cookie Monster: P & G Bites Nabisco," *Time,* January 31, 1983, pp. 55–56; "The Monster That Looms Over Cookie Makers," *Business Week,* August 8, 1983, pp. 89–92.

Chapter Outline

- What Is Planning?
- An Overview of the Organizational Planning Process
- Contingency Planning and Other Methods
- Environmental Scanning

Key Terms

- planning
- strategic gap
- strategic/corporate-level plans
- business/divisional-level plans
- unit/functional-level plans
- mission statement
- strategies
- product/market expansion matrix
- market development
- product development
- concentric diversification
- conglomerate diversification
- product portfolio strategy
- stars
- cash cows
- dogs
- problem children
- cost leadership strategy
- differentiation strategy
- focus strategy
- competitor analysis
- experience curve
- contingency planning
- dialectical processes
- environmental scanning

Chapter Objectives

After studying Chapter 4 you should be able to

1. Understand the characteristics of planning.
2. See why some businesses don't plan and the benefits for those that do.
3. Differentiate several types of organizational planning.
4. Explain the need for contingency planning.
5. Relate the procedures for developing a formal environmental scanning program.
6. Explain a variety of scanning techniques.

Introduction

Dwight Eisenhower once said, "Plans are nothing; planning is everything." He recognized that an organization need not only to plan, but to plan effectively. Kentucky Fried Chicken was successful in Japan because of its arduous efforts to scan the Japanese market, to examine changing eating habits, and to move into cooperative ventures with the Japanese government. In contrast, the Bay of Pigs fiasco was a poorly conceived plan based on several false assumptions. Among the worst errors was the assumption that the attacking forces could safely retreat to the Escambray Mountains. It turned out that this protective enclave was 80 miles away across a tangle of swamps and jungle that made human passage virtually impossible (Janis, 1972).

One of the most significant characteristics of the world today is the speed and the texture of change. Managers are increasingly faced with new problems that defy traditional methods of attack and resolution. Jerome Jacobson, senior vice-president of Bendix Corporation, observed, "Annual financial plans for a number of companies are going to hell this year. . . . [I]n a rapidly changing economic environment, some plans are out of date in three to six months . . ." (Branch, 1975, p. 46). Peter Drucker (1980, p. 4) says it this way: "In the twenty-five years after World War II, planning became fashionable. But planning, as commonly practiced, assumes a high degree of continuity. Planning starts out, as a rule, with the trends of yesterdays and projects them into the future — using a different mix perhaps, but with very much the same elements and the same configuration. This is no longer going to work."

Planning is not an easy task. In fact, the growing complexity of problems that makes planning a necessity also makes planning difficult. The effective manager will be one who is able to design superior planning systems. General Electric, Texas Instruments, Intel, General Motors, and Dana Electronics, consistently cited by *Fortune* magazine as being the best-managed corporations in the United States, have systematic and well-managed planning programs. Conversely, the lack of planning can lead to failure. The experiences of Texas Instruments and W. T. Grant are briefly discussed in Feature 4.1.

Managers will be faced with fundamental questions in the future: How can we best build flexibility and adaptiveness into our planning system? What types of plans can work in a complex, ever-changing environment?

The first part of this chapter introduces you to the fundamentals of the planning process. We discuss the meaning of planning and the benefits of a well-conceived planning program. Second, we present a general model of the planning process: the key dimensions, types of plans, and design considerations. Through the years a number of planning models have been introduced by General Electric, the Boston Consulting Group, and other management consultants. Our discussion provides a taste of each of these planning models. We also present more recent methods, such as contingency planning, future analysis, and computerized simulations, that are designed to improve planning in highly uncertain and turbulent times. The final section of the chapter is devoted to en-

Feature 4.1
The Consequences of Good and Bad Planning

W. T. Grant is a good example of a firm that lacked direction on the type of store it should be.

There was a lot of dissension over whether the company should embark on the K Mart route or go after the Montgomery Ward and the J. C. Penney positions. As a result, daily operations were erratic. From 1963 to 1973 Grant's opened 612 stores and expanded 91 others. But it failed to expand its management organization.

As one official said, "Our training program couldn't keep up with the explosion of stores, and it didn't take long for mediocrity to begin to show." The company eventually went bankrupt.

Texas Instruments, makers of semiconductors, calculators, and other products, is one of the most feared competitors in the consumer electronics business. It is so successful, in fact, that the company has been favorably compared to the Japanese.

Bruce Henderson, president and founder of the Boston Consulting Group, attributes Texas Instruments's success to its commitment to a long-term point of view, its emphasis on a strong sense of belonging, company loyalty, work, and its efforts to remain the low-cost leader in the industry. In doing so it has built a strong, profitable business in consumer electronics, a feat that a number of American companies tried but failed to do.

Sources: "How Grant Lost $175 Million Last Year," *Business Week,* February 24, 1975, pp. 74–76; "Texas Instruments Shows U.S. Business How to Survive in the 1980s," *Business Week,* September 18, 1978, pp. 66–84.

vironmental scanning, an important area that should be emphasized in corporate planning.

What Is Planning?

In its simplest conception, **planning** is the process by which managers define goals and take necessary steps to ensure that these goals are achieved. The notion of goals implies a desired future state. Planning arises from the recognition that some intervention is needed to bring about a change from the current or existing state to some desired or alternate future state. The difference between the present level and the future state is commonly referred to as a **strategic gap** (Figure 4.1). It takes time and preparation to bridge this gap. In situations in which no such preparation is needed, planning is not necessary. Let's look at some of the characteristics of planning.

1. *Planning is a process.* Effective plans have no natural end points and are continuously monitored to capitalize on opportunities or to anticipate emerging threats. As a process, planning involves the systematic analysis of the changing environment. It includes a statement of future actions and goals, and mechanisms designed to implement actions to accomplish goals.

Figure 4.1
A Simple Planning Model

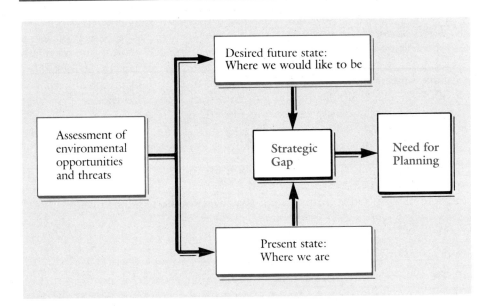

2. *Planning is anticipatory, or future oriented.* Plans are made in anticipation of future trends and events. If we want certain events to take place in the future, it is important to obtain necessary resources and to inform, if not involve, all concerned parties. Because this preparation is likely to take time, plans have to be made far in advance.

3. *Planning involves an interdependent set of decisions.* Complex problems often result in a set of interdependent decisions — for example, marketing normally is in charge of forecasting sales, production is responsible for ensuring that quality products are made on time, finance ensures that financial resources are available, and administration must make sure that there are qualified people to do the work. Such interdependence may lead to problems. Marketing might commit the company to sales orders that production is not able to produce in time. Finance might not have the necessary resources. Administration might still be training people to be part of the team. It is imperative, therefore, that planning occur across these interdependent units to meet organizational goals and minimize conflict.

4. *Planning involves many persons and departments.* As implied in the last point, for plans to succeed, the planning team should work effectively. Poor planning programs are often caused by poor communication between people, a high level of distrust among the organizational personnel, and disruptive

conflict between the parties involved. Good teamwork is necessary for plans to operate. Thus, plans should have the support of top management, whose responsibility it is to create a supportive structure conducive to planning.

5. *Planning involves actions that lead to future states that would not occur if no plans were made.* For many years people have mistaken plans to be projections representing extrapolations from past data. But such projections reflect actions or assumptions that may not be applicable or relevant in the long term. Commenting on erroneous forecasts made by economists, a chief executive officer of a large timber and pulp organization noted that the forecasts were premised on the continuation of economic policies of a previous administration that were no longer in effect. Good planning involves actions or interventions that lead to a desirable future.

From these points we can summarize planning as an anticipatory, or future-oriented, process involving multiple parties in interdependent decisions and actions that lead to future states that would otherwise not occur.

Why Don't Firms Plan?

Despite the numerous advantages of planning, there are many firms that do not plan or that have abandoned planning. Understanding some of their reasons may help you to appreciate the difficulty in introducing planning in organizations. Louis Gerstner, a leading management consultant, presents some reasons why firms fail to engage in planning (1980, pp. 8–9):

1. *"It is risky."* Developing a plan can spell the difference between success and failure for an executive. In targeting the compact-car market, George Romney, president of American Motors Corporation in 1954, knew that failure in this market would be costly for the company.

2. *"It is difficult and too complicated."* Planning involves complex decisions and interdependencies between people. It entails patience and commitment from those involved. Designing a plan is also not a simple process. Many of the key variables are complex, if not ambiguous. Some plans require a tremendous amount of available information. Taken together, these factors deter some executives from adopting planning systems.

3. *"It requires leadership."* Most strategic decisions are controversial, and key executives frequently must make unpopular decisions. President Reagan's experiences with his economic program, based on the controversial theory of supply-side economics, provide an example of the difficulties underlying the implementation of any plan. Without both the support and the leadership of top management, plans are likely to fail.

4. *"It is costly."* Indeed the planning process is costly. In addition to time and effort, the use of support systems — that is, computer-assisted programs —

may add to the cost. These expenses are one reason why many smaller firms have not adopted planning systems.

Although many of these objections are valid, the fact remains that firms may have little choice but to plan in today's ever-competitive environment. Planning, a luxury in the 1960s and 1970s, may be a necessity in the 1980s. The task, therefore, is to study the planning system carefully and to learn the basics of designing a planning system.

Does Planning Pay Off?

What are the benefits of planning? Will firms that plan perform better than those that don't? In eleven studies of the question, the answer generally seems to be that planning does pay off.

In a study of eighteen matched pairs of medium-to-large companies in the petroleum, food, drug, steel, chemical, and machinery industries, Thune and House (1970) found that those firms involved in formal strategic planning significantly outperformed those that did not plan, using measures of success such as return of equity, earnings, per-share growth, and return on investment. In a follow-up study, Herold (1972) reported that firms in the Thune and House sample that had formal planning continued to outperform nonplanners for four years after the initial study.

Wood and LaForge (1979) observed seventy large commercial banks to see whether the use of strategic planning systems improved financial performance. They reported that firms that had strategic planning systems outperformed firms that did not.

Ansoff, Avner, Brandenberg, Portner, and Radosevich (1970) investigated the relationship between performance and methods of growth in a large sample of American manufacturing firms for the period 1947 to 1966. On virtually all relevant financial criteria, the planners in the sample outperformed the non-planners.

Lindsay and Rue (1980), surveying 199 corporations in fifteen industrial classifications, found that firms tend to adopt more complete, formal, long-range planning processes as the business environment becomes more complex and unstable.

Firms that plan receive other benefits in addition to financial success. Philip Kotler (1980, p. 243) argues that planning

1. Encourages systematic thinking ahead by management,
2. Leads to better coordination of company efforts,
3. Leads to the development of performance standards for control,
4. Causes a company to sharpen its guiding objectives and policies,
5. Results in better preparedness for sudden developments,
6. Brings about a more vivid sense of interacting responsibilities in the participating executives.

An Overview of the Organizational Planning Process

There are several types of plans in an organization: strategic/corporate level, business/divisional level, and operational or unit/functional level. The types of plans introduced by an organization depend on the complexity of business operations. Small businesses may appropriately adopt unit/functional plans, which basically represent the action program of each functional unit, such as marketing, finance, research and development, and manufacturing. Large firms with diverse products may use divisional plans in addition to functional plans. Still larger firms may adopt corporate-level plans, which encompass the entire

Figure 4.2
Relationship Between Organizational Structure and
Strategic/Corporate, Business/Divisional, and
Unit/Functional Planning

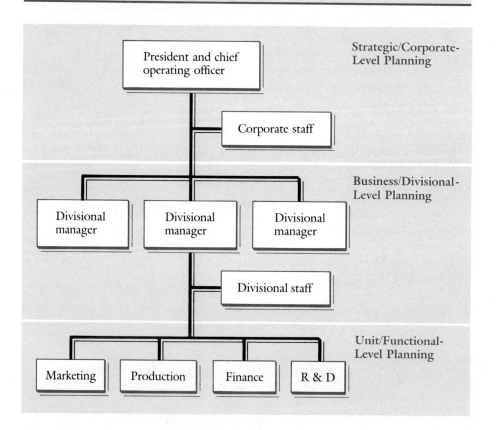

organization. Key components of each type of planning are a *formal statement of goals and objectives* and the development of *formal strategies.* Corporate, divisional, and functional plans are traditionally differentiated by their *focus, strategic orientation, time horizon,* and the *level of organization* at which the plans are formulated (Fig. 4.2). Turning to Figure 4.3, we see how these plans are interrelated and supportive of one another. **Strategic/corporate-level plans** guide the development of **business/divisional-level plans; unit functional-level plans** are then formulated to support divisional- as well as corporate-level plans. Typically, feedback provided by managers of lower levels (i.e., divisional or functional levels) is used to revise corporate-level plans.

Strategic/Corporate-Level Plans

Strategic plans are normally developed at the same corporate level, with input from staff groups and managers in lower echelons of the organization. The primary task is to define the overall business plan for the corporation. Plans are also closely aligned with the concept of company mission. The fundamental questions asked in preparing a corporate strategic plan are: What is our real business? Who are our customers? How are we going to compete in order to maintain or improve our strategic position? What rate of return on assets are we trying to achieve? What are our social responsibilities? A company's business is usually defined in its **mission statement.** Examples of mission statements are:

- *Dayton-Hudson Corporation:* Dayton-Hudson is a diversified retailing company whose business is to serve the American customer through the retailing of fashion-oriented quality merchandise. Serving the consumer over time requires skilled and motivated employees, healthy communities in which to operate, and maximum long-range profit. We are committed to meaningful and comprehensive employee development; to serving the business, social, and cultural needs of our communities; and to achieving levels of profitability equivalent to those of the leading firms in the industry.
- *Hewlett-Packard Company:** Our company . . . has developed over the years a very specific and carefully defined management philosophy. . . . It is important for us to recognize that . . . our own management is not consistent in every aspect with what other people do, nor consistent with every aspect [of what] the best scholars in management might say. . . . We do not believe that the thinking of other people should be necessarily accepted without the most careful consideration and without some actual testing in practice. . . . We have developed over the years a rather unique and, I think, effective way of working with our people. . . .

Because mission statements are long range, they are often made in very general terms. Objectives are more specific and concrete. Some examples include

* From an address by Dave Packer to a training class, quoted in "Human Resources at Hewlett-Packard," Intercollegiate Clearing House, Harvard Business School, Case 0-482-125.

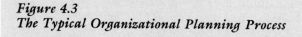

Figure 4.3
The Typical Organizational Planning Process

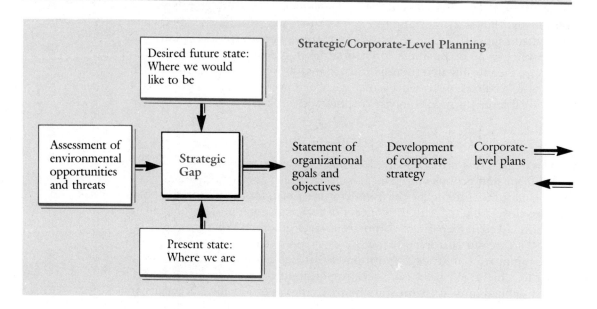

"Our objective is to make $8 million in profits by three years from today" and "Our target market share is 15 percent this year and 17.5 percent next year." The more specific, concrete, and measurable objectives are, the greater their chances of affecting people's actions. Examples of good and bad organizational objectives are presented in Figure 4.4.

Strategic Orientation. In the broadest sense, **strategies** are a pattern of decisions made by firms to achieve their corporate missions and objectives. Corporate-level strategies involve decisions concerning which market in which to compete, or the selection of product/markets based on internal resources.

Management and marketing theorists have proposed a number of methods to help a business select and define its product/market. Three such methods — the product/market and expansion matrix; the strategic business planning grid, or "stoplight strategy"; and the product portfolio analysis — are discussed in this section.

Product/Market Expansion Matrix. Kotler (1980) has popularized the use of the **product/market expansion matrix,** which essentially represents management's choices of growth opportunities in its present and future products and markets (Fig. 4.5).

Figure 4.3 (continued)

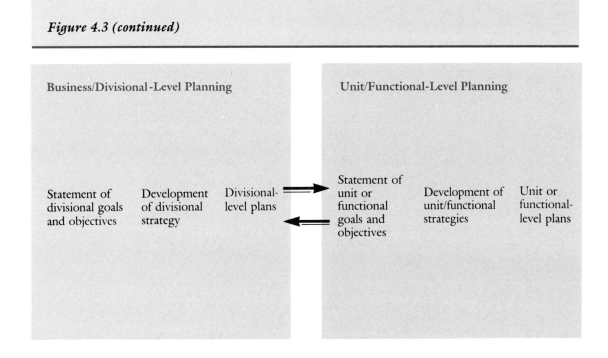

If the company decides to remain with its current market and product, the appropriate growth strategy is that of **market penetration.** In this strategy, the company seeks increased sales for its current products through more aggressive advertising, product design, and sales campaigns. Head Ski used such a strategy in the early 1960s to promote the sales of metal skis in a time when fiberglass skis were becoming more popular.

Market development occurs when a company seeks increased sales by taking its current products into new markets. One popular way, represented by the strategies of Pepsico in Russia and Coca-Cola in China, is through international expansion. Facing maturing markets in the United States, cosmetics firms such as Avon and Mary Kay are considering third-world countries in Asia and Africa for future markets.

In **product development,** a company seeks increased sales by developing new and improved products for its current markets. In addition to skis, Head Ski started to sell ski accessories and clothing as part of its product line.

Diversification is the process by which a company seeks increased sales by developing new and improved products in new markets. Sometimes diversification means adding products and services technologically related to existing products. Some examples include Exxon Corporation's move into goethermal, nuclear, and synthetic sources of energy. Other diversification efforts have no relationship to the company's technology, products, or markets. Mobil Corpo-

---

Figure 4.4
Examples of Good and Bad Organizational Objectives

OBJECTIVE	REMARKS
Good (Clearly Defined) Objectives	
1. "We plan to make Product X the number-one-selling brand in its field in terms of units sold by 1985."	Leaves little doubt as to the intended sales objective and market standing.
2. "We strive to be a leader, not a follower, in introducing new products and in implementing new technologies by spending no less than 5 percent of sales revenue for research and development."	Indicates an attempt to remain on or near technological frontiers, and says how this attempt is to be financed.
3. "Our profit objective is to increase earnings per share by a minimum of 8 percent annually and to earn at least a 20 percent after-tax return on net worth."	Clear, concrete, and readily measured.
4. "We seek to produce the most durable, maintenance-free product that money can buy."	An obvious focus on being the leader in quality.
5. "It is our objective to help assure that the wood products needs of this country are met by planting two seedlings for every three we cut and by following exemplary forest management practices."	A specific commitment.

---

ration's diversification strategy involved moving into the real estate market and purchasing Montgomery Ward. In contrast to Exxon, Mobil did not place its full resources into energy-related business. Exxon's type of diversification has been labeled **concentric diversification,** and Mobil's **conglomerate diversification.**

General Electric's Stoplight Strategy. Strategic planning involving forty-three district businesses is no easy task. Imagine yourself as a manager who, at the end of the annual review period, is examining detailed forecasts from forty-three different businesses, each with projected measures of sales, profits, return on investment, and growth rates. The task is to identify those businesses that you intend to continue to support, divest, or develop.

The General Electric Company thinks it has found a partial solution to this task in its strategic planning grid, or **stoplight strategy** (Fig. 4.6). The

Figure 4.4 (continued)

OBJECTIVE	REMARKS

Bad (Poorly Phrased) Objectives

1. "Our objective is to maximize sales revenue and unit volume." — Not subject to measurement. What dollar figure constitutes maximum sales? Also may be inconsistent; the price and output that generate the greatest dollar revenue are almost certainly not the same as the combination that will yield the largest possible unit volume.

2. "No new idea is too extreme, and we will go to great lengths to develop it." — Too broad. No firm has the money or capability to investigate any and every idea that it comes across; even to try is to march in all directions at once.

3. "We seek to be the most profitable company in our industry." — Vague. By what measures of profit: total dollars? earnings per share? return on sales? return on equity investment? All of these?

4. "In producing our products we strive to minimize costs and maximize efficiency." — What are the standards by which costs will be said to be minimum and efficiency maximum? How will management know when the objective has been achieved?

5. "We intend to meet our responsibilities to stockholders, customers, employers, and the public." — In what respects? As determined by whom? More a platitude than an action commitment.

Source: From Arthur Thompson, Jr. and A. J. Strickland, III, *Strategy and Policy: Concepts and Cases,* p. 13. Copyright © 1981 by Business Publications, Plano, Texas. All rights reserved.

two dimensions of the grid serve to represent industry attractiveness and the company's competitive position. *Industry attractiveness* includes such measures as volatility of market share, technology needs, employee loyalty, competitive stance, and social need. Three categories, low, medium, and high, are obtained by rating each business on these measures. The second dimension, the *company's competitive position,* represents the strengths and weaknesses of the company based on an evaluation of internal resources and performance, including sales, profits, and return on investment, over time. Businesses are classified in terms of these dimensions as warranting growth (green light), borderline or cautious investment (yellow light), or no growth (red light).

Figure 4.5
Product/Market Expansion Matrix

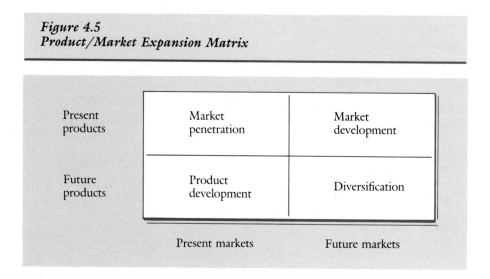

	Present markets	Future markets
Present products	Market penetration	Market development
Future products	Product development	Diversification

Figure 4.6
General Electric's Stoplight Strategy

Industry Attractiveness

Company's Competitive Position	High	Medium	Low
High	Green: "Invest and grow." STARS	Green: "Invest and grow." STARS	Yellow: "Move into this area cautiously." PROFIT PRODUCERS
Medium	Green: "Invest and grow." STARS *A*	Yellow: "Move into this area cautiously." PROFIT PRODUCERS	Red: "No growth" LOSERS
Low	Yellow: "Move into this area cautiously." PROFIT PRODUCERS	Red: "No growth" LOSERS	Red: "No growth" LOSERS *B*

Source: "Piercing the Future Fog," 1975.

If a business is seen as attractive and if General Electric's strengths are seen as high, as in area A, a green light is given, suggesting an "invest and grow" strategy. Such a business is labelled a "star." If both industry attractiveness and

Feature 4.2
Stevens Takes a New Tact

A leading American textile company, J. P. Stevens, has teamed up with one of America's most successful fashion designers, Ralph Lauren, in what many believe is one of the boldest and riskiest ventures the retail world has ever seen. Through the years Lauren has built a product line that started with men's clothing and now includes women's and children's apparel, furs, cosmetics, luggage, footwear, and eyeglass frames, to name a few. Stevens, of course, is a household name in sheets and towels. Lauren and Stevens together are introducing a new collection of household furnishings that will include 2,500 items ranging from bed linens and bath towels to rugs, wall coverings, flatware, table linens, and glassware — all to be offered at designer prices and in four themes: Log Cabin, Thoroughbred, New England, and Jamaica. David M. Tracy, vice chairman of Stevens, describes the venture as "the next plateau of life-style marketing" ("The Business of Being Ralph Lauren," p. 112).

Lauren views the collaboration as a way to add to his already extensive empire. Stevens executives view the Lauren line as a way of shifting the focus away from the company's past labor-relations problems and toward a future in which Stevens is the leading supplier of decorative home furnishings. Part of the plan involves displaying the new Lauren line in wood-paneled boutiques that Stevens is requiring its selected retailers to provide. Retailers are enthusiastic despite the exorbitant expense of up to $250,000 required to build the structures. "This is an outstanding step forward in home furnishings," said Bloomingdale's chairman, Marvin S. Traub ("J. P. Stevens Takes the Designer Route," p. 118).

J. P. Stevens needed to take a step forward. The company's 2.9 percent return on equity was the lowest among the ten largest public textile companies, despite the fact that it is the second-largest producer in the industry. A costly modernization program, a major reorganization, and price competition in the company's shirt, towel, and sheet markets all combined to reduce net income. The company is hoping that the Lauren line will boost sales and add a little glitter to its reputation. As Tracy said, "We're sending off some shock waves" ("J. P. Stevens Takes the Designer Route," p. 118).

Sources: "The Business of Being Ralph Lauren," *New York Times Magazine,* September 18, 1983, pp. 112–114, 124–132; "J. P. Stevens Takes the Designer Route," *Business Week,* September 19, 1983, p. 118.

General Electric's strengths are low, as in area B, a red light is given, indicating that the business is a "loser." While it may continue to generate earnings, it no longer warrants additional investment. If industry attractiveness is high but General Electric's strengths are low, a yellow light signals the business is a "question mark." That is, it could soon move to a green or red light status, depending on whether General Electric decides to invest in the area. Finally, a business classified as low in industry attractiveness but high in competitive position is labeled a "profit producer." That is, it generates earnings that can be used to invest in more promising businesses.

In practice the grid is used as a preliminary means of analysis rather than an automatic and irreversible plan. After critiques of the grid at various levels of the organization, the final grid is approved by a corporate policy committee consisting of the chairman, three vice-chairmen, five senior vice-presidents, and the vice-president of finance. It is claimed that this exercise is particularly beneficial in helping to avoid costly errors ("Piercing the Future Fog," 1975).

Product Portfolio Strategy. The Boston Consulting Group has extended the notion of experience curves to cover the management of the array of products, or the portfolio, at a company's disposal. The essence of the **product portfolio strategy** is that some products should assist the growth of other products to ensure a balanced growth pattern and an acceptable level of risk for the company. In specific terms, to support growth some products should generate cash and others should use it. The specific classification of products depends on the market growth of the products as well as their market dominance.

Market growth refers to the percentage of increase in sales for some defined period. In the Boston Consulting Group analysis, this is measured in terms of the annual growth rate in constant dollars. *Market dominance* is commonly represented in terms of market share, although the measure is not a very good indicator. For example, if a firm has a 50 percent share and its next largest competitor has 45 percent, its so-called dominance is not the same as it would be if it faced five other competitors having equal shares of 10 percent each. Measures used by the Boston Consulting Group are therefore expressed in relative terms, such as the company share compared with its largest competitor's share. Another measure would be to compare the company share with the share of its three largest competitors.

By juxtaposing market growth and market dominance, one can arrive at a four-cell portfolio in which to classify all products (Fig. 4.7). The four cells imply patterns of strategies that apply to the products within each category:

- **Stars.** These are fast-growing products that are also market leaders. Unfortunately, a great deal of cash is needed to sustain or improve the rate of growth. Appropriate strategies consist of reinvesting earnings into product improvements, advertising, or distribution channels. In General Foods, for example, "stars" are the instant breakfast drink Tang, powdered soft drinks such as Kool-Aid, and the semimoist dog food Gaines Burgers (Cox, 1967, pp. 375–384).

- **Cash cows.** Products that are growing slowly yet have high market shares usually yield substantial cash flows. Therefore, the amount of cash generated is normally far in excess of the amount required for reinvestment, and such excess cash can be used to support other products in the company. "Cash cow" examples are General Foods's ground coffees Maxwell House and Yuban, decaffeinated coffees Brim and Sanka, and instant coffees Yuban, Maxim, and Maxwell House (Cox, 1967, p. 381).

- **Dogs.** Products that are growing very slowly and have low market shares are classified as "dogs." Note that with slow-growing markets there is hardly any incentive to reinvest to gain more market share. Ready-to-eat cereals are considered "dogs" in General Foods, given the firm's relative low market share of 16.6 percent (Cox, 1967, p. 381).

Figure 4.7
Market-Share/Market-Growth Matrix

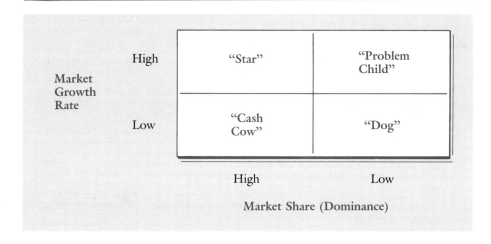

• **Problem children.** Products that are growing fast yet have low margins because they have low market shares are classified as "problem children." Without sufficient investment the products may become "dogs" as growth slows. With heavy investment and as market share improves, however, these products may become "stars." In General Foods the dry dog foods are considered "problem children" (Cox, 1967, p. 381).

Business/Divisional-Level Plans

At the divisional level the key task is to determine how a particular business can best compete in a particular market. Questions include: How can the division improve its competitive position? How can the division develop business activities that are synergistic or complementary to those of other divisions?

It is important to recognize the interrelatedness of corporate-level and division-level plans. Based on corporate-level goals and objectives, a division develops plans that support the overall corporate plan. The Pontiac and Chevrolet divisions of General Motors have different plans, but both should support the corporate goals of General Motors.

Porter (1980) suggests that there are three generic strategies to outperforming other firms in an industry:

1. Overall **cost leadership.** This strategy, based on the experience cost curve concept, places the company in a low-cost position, enabling it to earn above-average returns despite the presence of strong competitive forces. Cost leadership is attained through aggressive construction of efficient scale facilities, rigorous cost control, and cost minimization in functional areas. Texas

---

Feature 4.3
Motorola's "Cash Cow"

The beleaguered semiconductor industry, hit by a severe recession and price-cutting, had a star performer in the early 1980s. While most manufacturers were struggling with the economy, Motorola, Inc. was selling discretes — that is, individual resistors, capacitors, and transistors — which competitors had forsaken for second-generation integrated circuits. These more complex devices consist of many circuits etched onto a single silicon chip. "Discretes haven't gone through the pricing horrors of the high-technology products," points out one of Motorola's competitors. "It's a real cash cow for Motorola" ("Motorola's New Strategy," p. 132).

Although the company's semiconductor group isn't trouble-free — Motorola's profit decline of 6 percent in 1981 was blamed on semiconductor problems — its increased market share has been such that the company made significant progress in catching up to the industry leader, Texas Instruments.

In 1983, Motorola finally tied Texas Instruments for world sales of chips.

Realizing that discretes are not part of the future, Motorola has joined their competitors in the production of integrated circuits, which now accounts for 65 percent of its semiconductor business. Motorola has also diversified, recently venturing into the field of computers, information processing, and cellular mobile telephones.

But each of these steps is taken with caution and forethought. As Motorola's vice chairman, William Weisz put it, ". . . the company that survives is the one that isn't afraid to take a critical and introspective look on a regular basis. . . . and we don't try to shoot off our mouths too much" ("Underpromise, Overperform," p. 90).

Sources: "Underpromise, Overperform," by J. Bettner, *Forbes,* January 30, 1984, pp. 88–90; "Motorola's New Strategy: Adding Computers to Its Base Electronics," *Business Week,* March 29, 1982, pp. 131–132.

Instruments, Black and Decker, Honda Motorcycle, DuPont, and General Electric are among the many firms that have used this strategy.

2. **Differentiation.** This strategy involves offering unique and distinct products and services to broad markets. By providing distinctive, often non-price value (e.g., performance, support, and reliability), the company intends to protect or insulate certain market segments through customer loyalty. Hewlett-Packard, Mercedes Benz, and Apple Computers have successfully utilized this strategy.

3. **Focus.** This strategy involves concentrating resources and attention on a particular market segment. By servicing one or a few as opposed to several segments of the market, a firm can potentially earn above-average returns in its industry. One example would be Design and Manufacturing, which solely produced quality dishwashers for Sears, Roebuck and Company.

There has recently been a growing focus on **competitor analysis** as part of the corporate and divisional plan. Divisional managers may soon find that the key to success lies in their ability to keep ahead of competitors, to monitor their strategic movements, and to respond quickly to their actions. Two analytical frameworks can be used for such situations, the **experience curve** analysis and competitive action analysis.

Proponents of the *experience curve analysis theory* have demonstrated that the total unit cost of producing and distributing a product declines by a consistent percentage with a twofold increase in accumulated output over time. Estimates of this consistent decline, expressed in constant dollars, are about 20 to 30 percent. Unit costs may decline because of many factors: economies of scale, specialization, productivity improvements, replacement of less efficient production methods, or new technological developments.

Used as a tool for analyzing competitors, the experience curve theory has a number of strategic implications. We present a representative picture of a hypothetical industry in Figure 4.8. Because of accumulated experience the major-volume firm, *A,* has the greatest potential for the lowest unit costs and the largest profits. In the event of price wars, the dominant firm has a clear strategic superiority over the other firms in the industry. This strategy is evident in the

Figure 4.8
Experience Curve, Showing Relative Profit Levels of Competitors

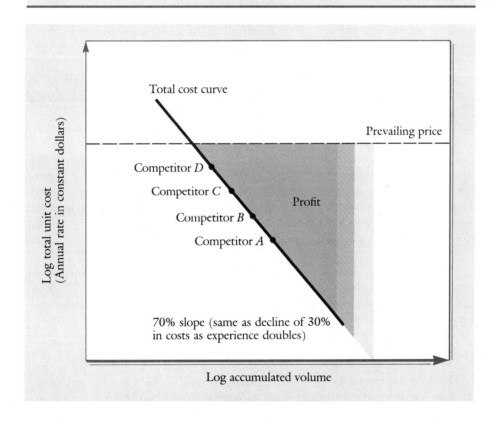

world motorcycle industry, in which the dominant firms, Japanese manufacturers, were able to penetrate the low-cost end of the market and undercut both their American and their British competitors. A second strategic implication is that the slope of the experience curve may be as important as the relative position of firms on the curve. The slope can indicate the length of time it will take for lesser-volume firms to reach, if not overtake, the major-volume firm. Using this analysis, General Electric realized that it would take considerable time to overtake its chief rivals and consequently pulled out of the mainframe computer business.

The second analytical framework is competitive action analysis, popularized by Porter (1980). In his model, Porter emphasizes four major components that purportedly have an impact on a competitor's response profile: goals, assumptions, strategy, and capabilities. Knowing competitors' *goals* will allow predictions about how satisfied the competitor is with its progress toward achieving those goals. The less satisfied the competitor, the more likely it is to pursue those goals with a more vigorous strategy. For example, knowing General Motors's major goal, which is to remain the market leader, may help predict future pricing strategies and explain present overtures toward Nissan Motors of Japan.

It is also important to know what *assumptions* the competitor makes about itself as well as about the industry. These assumptions can point up biases or blind spots. Anheuser-Busch's assumption about its dominance in the beer market and the superiority of its product provided the bias that Miller was able to exploit by aggressively marketing new products.

Knowing a competitor's strategy can also validate suppositions about its goals and assumptions. As we said earlier, *strategy* can be considered the pattern of actions in such areas as pricing, advertising, and financing employed by a competitor. Appraising what the competitor intends to do is much more difficult and may require closer surveillance.

Porter's fourth component is the *capabilities* of particular competitors. This component can be studied through use of the experience curve. In the competitive semiconductor market, for example, the cost superiority of Japanese producers will enable them to pursue price reduction strategies aggressively in the future. American companies, although not in the same cost position, have been able to develop new products faster than their Japanese counterparts and may be expected to follow this strategic course.

Knowing these four components, one can make better predictions about how a competitor would respond to specific actions (Fig. 4.9). Although a relatively new technique, competitor response analysis may provide important insights into appropriate competitive strategies in a given industry.

Unit/Functional-Level Plans

Unit/functional-level plans are principally concerned with the best use of strategic variables that are under the control of each functional or unit manager.

Figure 4.9
Competitor Analysis

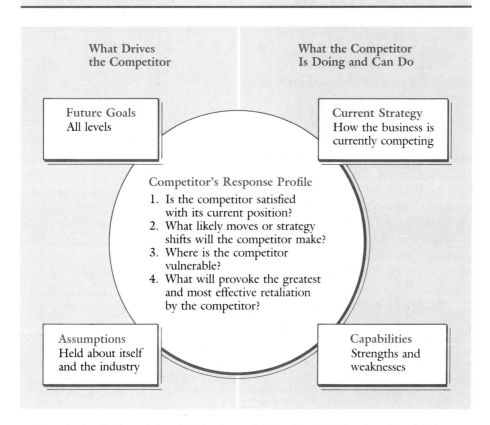

What Drives the Competitor	What the Competitor Is Doing and Can Do
Future Goals All levels	**Current Strategy** How the business is currently competing

Competitor's Response Profile

1. Is the competitor satisfied with its current position?
2. What likely moves or strategy shifts will the competitor make?
3. Where is the competitor vulnerable?
4. What will provoke the greatest and most effective retaliation by the competitor?

Assumptions Held about itself and the industry	Capabilities Strengths and weaknesses

Source: Reprinted with permission of The Free Press, a division of Macmillan, Inc., from *Competitive Strategy* by Michael E. Porter. Copyright © 1980 by The Free Press.

For example, a marketing manager would be involved in decisions about pricing, advertising levels, new product development, recruitment and training of salespeople, and distribution channels. Manufacturing managers might be involved in product scheduling, inventory control, quality considerations, and machinery set-up time.

Strategy at the unit/functional level is concerned with getting the best mix of the strategic variables under the control of the functional manager — for example, the mix of marketing variables, price, promotions, and advertising that will lead to the desired level of sales. The choice of acceptable expenditure levels for production or research and development must also be considered. Manufacturing strategy involves the proper scheduling of production to meet sales deadlines and to minimize total production costs. Personnel or human relations strategies involve developing appropriate selection, recruitment, and training programs. It is important to emphasize that functional strategies should be consistent with the divisional and corporate strategies of the organization. A summary of planning systems and their respective characteristics is presented in Figure 4.10.

Contingency Planning and Other Methods

Contingency Planning

Because the future can never be predicted with certainty, **contingency planning** is often a crucial part of the planning process. Contingency plans add another element of flexibility that helps a firm anticipate changes and quickly alter strategies and objectives if necessary. For example, executives in the wood products industry differ in their predictions of the length of the recession and the recovery period in which increased demand for housing may boost wood product sales. By adopting contingency plans that are based on different forecasts of recessionary and recovery periods, wood products firms may totally avoid unexpected crisis decisions that typically lead to poor performance.

Figure 4.10
Characteristics of Planning Systems

TYPE OF PLAN	FOCUS	STRATEGIC ORIENTATION	LEVEL OF ORGANIZATION	TIME FRAME
Corporate strategic plan	Definition of corporate mission, philosophy, and objectives	Services offered; customer benefits; key markets; social responsibilities; distinctive competence	Corporate/corporate staff	Long range
Divisional plan	Definition of competitive strategies for markets faced by division	Competitive analysis; strengths and weaknesses; allocation of tasks and resources	Divisional managers	Medium range
Unit functional plan	Definition of strategic variables that are under the control of unit or functional managers	Marketing mix strategies; manufacturing strategies; R & D strategies; personnel strategies	Unit or functional managers	Short range

Contingency plans can be optimistic or pessimistic scenarios of future events, depending on whether predicted events are favorable or unfavorable to the strategic plan. Simulations can be developed to examine how sensitive present plans would be to such events as changes in raw materials costs, the entry of new competitors into the industry that may increase industry capacity and lead to price wars, new government regulations that may result in significant compliance costs, natural disasters, and labor problems resulting in increased labor cost.

People involved in contingency planning develop better strategic vision and skills. First, they are better able to understand the underlying competitive forces in the external environment that affect their organizations. Second, they develop their skills in recognizing how contingent actions affect the success of their firms.

Integrating a contingency plan into the overall planning process at the very least requires that possible threats and opportunities resulting from substantial change be identified, in the way that the external environment was analyzed in Chapter 2. Finn Jerstad (1979, p. 257) suggests the following lead question:

> Describe briefly what other strategies you must implement and what other key steps you are ready to take if a substantial change occurs in your markets or industries which creates an immediate threat or opportunity for your organization.
> A. Changing the Objectives
> If the changes in the future are substantial, they may cause you to change the . . . objectives in the plan period. . . . How will [these changes] affect your objectives if and when they do occur? Describe briefly alternative strategies and key changes you must implement in order to attain the revised objectives.
> B. Maintaining Objectives
> . . . If under changing conditions in the market place, the economy, life styles, etc., you still think that the stated . . . objectives can be reached, state these changes you must make (1) in major strategies and (2) by steps.

For a while, contingency plans were considered theoretical exercises. Now it is claimed that contingency plans are becoming standard operating procedures. Here are the contingency plans of several companies ("Piercing the Future Fog," 1975):

- *Mead Corporation.* The company has three short-term contingency plans — *A, B,* and *C* — standing for aggressive, basic, and conservative. Mead's *B* plan was scrapped early. The *C* plan was considered too optimistic, and a new *B* plan was quickly formulated.
- *Frontier Airlines.* The company developed a "reasonable size shrink" plan based on anticipated leveling off of passenger demand. The first planned shrinkage has already gone into effect and the second "shrink" has become operational.
- *General Electric.* The company concentrates on eight to ten key influencing factors in the external environment — rate of inflation, consumer spending

on nondurables, interest rates, and so on — and evaluates their cumulative effects on the company's strategic plan.

- *Hewlett-Packard Company.* The company makes use of different scenarios based on four models: economic, intermediate range, econometric, and aggregate sales. It is reported that the decision to use in-house financing on long-term debt involved about one hundred different scenarios built from its own H-P2000 computer.

Other Planning Aids

As planning has become more complex, not surprisingly, more novel planning aids have been developed to help the decision maker. Contingency planning and multiple scenarios are only two of many planning aids. Two other methods, dialectical processes and computerized planning systems, have been growing in popularity.

Dialectical Processes. Mason, Mitroff, and Barabba (1982) have proposed the use of **dialectical processes** for highly complex problems. In their approach the assumptions underlying specific problems are first identified. Then two groups are assigned to develop scenarios based on those assumptions and on directly opposite assumptions. The groups examine what each might have missed under each set of assumptions. Out of this dialectical process comes a new set of assumptions, which is used as a basis for a new strategy. The benefit of this process is that it systematically identifies biases and results in a more comprehensive analysis.

Computer Simulation. As computer technology continues to improve, the use of simulation models in planning systems has become less expensive and more accessible. **Computer simulation** models are important because they allow the examination of multiple decisions and their possible outcomes. In addition, the models analyze the sensitivity of decisional variables. For example, one can incorporate the assumptions of competitors (see p. 112 of this chapter) and examine their possible responses to selected decisions. As in any model, the simulations are only as good as the assumptions on which they are based, yet simulations do provide valuable help for managers faced with complex and unconventional problems. Simulations can be used to test the validity of commonly held assumptions and beliefs.

Environmental Scanning

Scanning is generally defined as acquiring information. In the context of organizational planning, **environmental scanning** involves monitoring changes and developments in the environment that have potential impact on the organization. The task of scanning the environment is normally given to executive management, although managers from all organizational levels may be involved in this activity. On the occasion of his retirement, the founder of Honda Motor Company, Soichiro Honda, was able to say, "The deputy president and I have not signed any papers nor attended any executive meetings for the past ten

---

Feature 4.4
Texas Instruments: Beating on the Roof

Texas Instruments, plagued by shriveling profits and managerial mistakes, is trying to regain its ability to hit the right targets, at the right time, for the right market, by reorganizing from top to bottom.

The company habitually reorganizes when business drops off. "When you've got ten tons of canaries — or executives — in a five-ton truck, you beat on the roof now and then to make sure at least half of them are up and flying," said one former employee.

One of the underlying problems management is trying to fix is a system originally intended to encourage entrepreneurship and innovation by linking design, production, and marketing and making them the responsibility of one person. Product-customer centers, units of varying size, were created whenever there was a clear product-customer match. The managers were responsible for profits and losses, but they didn't have authority to tell departments what to do. As the company grew the centers became insignificant supplicants.

The planning system known as OST, for objectives, strategies, tactics, will also go under the knife. Under the system, top executive management and the board of directors are responsible for setting eight or so business objectives, such as becoming a leader in semiconductors. Other executives and engineers map out the routes to achieve those goals. The lowest operating manager may be assigned one of 200 to 300 tactical action programs that spring from those strategies.

Managers handled both their daily operating tasks and the tactical action plans. But as the product-customer centers fell behind, people had less time for their tactical action plans and less incentive because the plans often had nothing to do with their operating responsibilities. The company grew sluggish. Products fell behind schedule.

Texas Instruments President J. Fred Bucy feels the planning system had "drifted out of alignment" with the operating system. Management is now trying to ensure that managers' planning jobs fall in their operating sphere.

But management itself is thought to be another problem area.

"Proposed products were defined and redefined there (at headquarters) ad infinitum," said one former employee. "Eventually you were just given a product that was a square peg and told to fit it into the round hole of a market."

There have been changes — improvements in marketing and more responsiveness to distributors and consumers. The company is working on improving sales in minicomputers and has begun moving from a components into a systems orientation along with the rest of the industry. And more problems will fade when the market picks up.

Source: "Texas Instruments Regroups," by Bro Uttal, *Fortune*, August 9, 1982, pp. 40–45.

years. We have done what presidents should do; we have spent our time correctly judging future trends. That is our job."

Unfortunately, this situation may not hold true for many firms in the United States. In spite of the obvious importance of scanning to corporate planning, the process by which managers scan the environment remains poorly understood. Aguilar (1967) reported that few managers are able to spend adequate time scanning the environment. Whatever scanning is done is fragmented and often unsystematic. Most firms in the United States still largely rely on ad hoc, informal methods of scanning. Only very recently have firms such as General Electric, the Coca-Cola Company, and Xerox implemented formal scanning methods.

This final section of the chapter builds on some of these experiences and presents procedures for developing a formal environmental scanning program. This program is oriented around four key questions: What sources should be used in scanning? What criteria should be used in deciding whether a trend will be transient or long lasting? How can better objectivity be developed in scanning? What scanning methods should a firm employ?

Concentrated or Comprehensive Scanning

The first question deals with what should go into a scanning program. A comprehensive program will inevitably be very expensive and time-consuming, as Aguilar's (1967) study shows (Fig. 4.11). But a concentrated scanning program might not be sufficiently effective in identifying the range of developments crucially affecting the organization. The problem becomes worse when developments occur outside the industry beyond the scope of the firm's scanning programs. Note the following examples:

• Advances in computer technology and information processing did not occur until after mathematicians developed binary arithmetic.
• Present competition in the dry cleaning industry comes from synthetic fibers and chemical additives that have cut the need for dry cleaning. But the most severe challenge may come from technological developments in the field of ultrasonics that may make the chemical dry cleaning process obsolete.
• Competition in the airlines industry is not limited to struggles among carriers; it also encompasses changes in telecommunication technology that may severely reduce the need for travel.
• The solid-state revolution in digital display watches was spearheaded not by established watch companies such as Timex, Bulova, Benrus, and Gruen, but by semiconductor companies including Texas Instruments, National Semiconductor, Litronix, Hughes Aircraft, and Fairchild Camera and Instrument. The breakthrough in digitals was also a result of advances in space technology.

The cost/benefit ratio has to be weighed in setting the scope and designing an environmental planning program.

Figure 4.11
Scanning the Environment

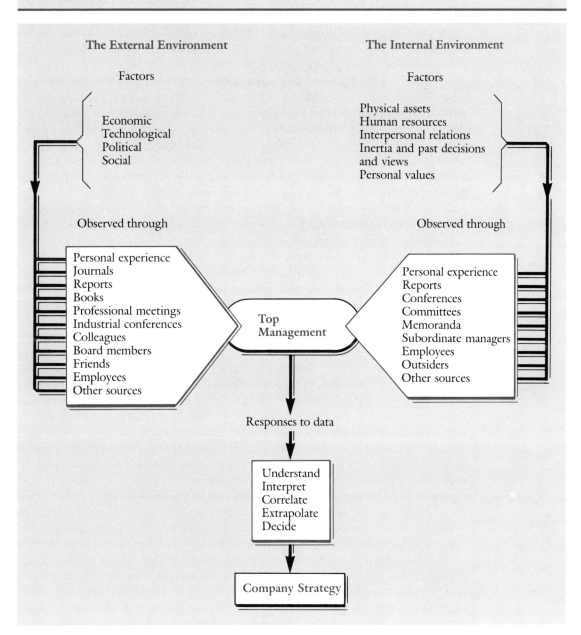

Source: Aguilar, 1967, p. 11. Reprinted by permission of The Trustees of Columbia University in the City of New York.

Transient and Long-Lasting Trends. One of the key tasks in developing a scanning program is to develop criteria that can distinguish between transient and lasting trends. Contingency plans also should be developed in the event that a trend thought to be transient becomes more lasting.

Some trends, such as urbanization, energy conservation, and environmental protection, appear to be lasting. Others — pet rocks, rubber baby panties, and ladies's millinery equipment — have shorter life spans and are more transient. Investment is a lasting trend and can be quite profitable, as it was, for example, when McDonald's turned the fast-food market into big money, the Japanese exploited the small car market, and the semiconductor companies moved into the digital watch market. But a similar investment in a short-lived trend can prove financially disastrous. The *Saturday Evening Post's* investment in papermills and other production facilities, spurred by the postwar paper shortages, proved to be a disadvantage when it needed the capital to exploit market opportunities, such as the acquisition of the Columbia Broadcasting System (CBS).

Automobile industry executives have readily recognized the growing preference for foreign-made cars, the sudden and seemingly lasting fuel shortages, and the growing need for more transportation, but the prospects of an efficient electric car remain clouded by concerns about its marketability and its road performance. Whether automobile executives will invest in electric cars is an unanswered question, yet the electric car may well result in the prosperity of some automobile companies and the doom of others.

Developing Objectivity in Scanning. Numerous authors have addressed the problem of organizational inability to perceive or discern changes in the environment. Leavitt (1964) discussed how organizational success breeds myopic tendencies, which in turn foster reactive, wait-and-see strategies rather than proactive strategies designed to change things. The movie industry confined its business to movies, for example, instead of exploiting new opportunities in the entertainment business. Similarly, the railroads narrowly viewed their business as rail transportation and did not capitalize on other methods of transportation. Such singularity in business definition may be one reason why the movie and railroad industries failed to adapt to their environments.

Learning in organizations occurs through *programming.* When certain activities appear successful, organizations turn them into standard programs. The programs are built into formal roles, making activities consistent among different people at different times (Hedberg, Nystrom, and Starbuck, 1976). Merely saying that organizational scanners develop a broader view of their business oversimplifies the complex process of organizational learning. Some companies, especially Japanese companies, have begun to use think tanks to combat the myopia resulting from years of programming (Feature 4.5). Such efforts may be incorporated in scanning programs to ensure more objectivity.

Selection of Scanning Methods. In the past, environmental scanning methods have been largely associated with demand analysis and market re-

Feature 4.5
Environmental Scanning in Japan

Japanese firms collect and process information more thoroughly than their foreign counterparts.

In fact, the Japanese trading companies such as Mitsubishi, Mitsui Bussan Sumitomo, Marubeni, C. Itoh, and Nissho Iwai are considered unparelleled in their international information network. There are several reasons. First, most of Japan's foreign trade is conducted through these companies, each of which is represented in virtually every country. Second, information gathering is given high priority.

In gathering detailed economic information, private companies even are superior to the Japanese government, particularly in areas where they have substantial economic interest. When a Japanese airliner was highjacked in 1973 in Abu Dhabi, the foreign ministry relied on Mitsubishi Trading Company telexes to keep informed.

In another case, the American government was shocked to learn in 1973 that Soviet officials in the United States had arranged with an American company for a large sale of wheat to the Soviet Union.

But a Japanese trading company was not surprised. Officials in the Moscow office had wired the Tokyo office that several high trade officials who would make such arrangements were not in Moscow. Upon request from the Tokyo office, company officials in New York found out that the Soviets were going through a New York airport en route to Colorado. Regional trading company officials were able to confirm that a meeting with American executives was in the works.

As a result, Japanese officials were able to make adjustments to the grain market before the purchase became public and caused a price increase in grain.

To obtain more specialized information, Japanese government agencies have supplemented their own research institutes by supporting a small number of private institutes. Each research center is assigned to a ministry, which controls annual appropriations and supervises the collection of information. Government agencies also help sponsor other agencies through assignments of small cores of experts.

Source: Adapted by permission of the author and publishers from *Japan as Number One*, by Ezra F. Vogel, Cambridge, Mass.: Harvard University Press, Copyright © 1979 by the President and Fellows of Harvard College.

search. Now organizational theorists and corporate managers are devoting more attention to scanning. Jain (1981) has proposed a variety of scanning techniques:

1. *Extrapolation methods.* These techniques require information from the past to explore the future. The future is assumed to be some function of the past. There are a variety of extrapolation techniques, including trend analysis, forecasting, and regression analysis.

2. *Historical analogy.* When past data cannot be effectively used to analyze an environmental trend, the trend is studied by establishing historical parallels with other trends. This method assumes that sufficient information is avail-

able from the other trend. Turning points in the progression become guide-posts for predicting the behavior of the trend being studied.

3. *Intuitive reasoning.* This technique calls for a rational intuition by the scanner. Intuitive thinking requires free thinking unconstrained by past experience and personal biases.

4. *Scenario building.* This procedure involves constricting a time-ordered sequence of events that have a logical cause-and-effect relationship to one another. The resulting forecast is based on the interrelationships among the events.

5. *Cross-impact matrices.* When two different trends in the environment point to two conflicting futures, the trends are studied to see their potential impact on each other.

6. *Morphological analysis.* This technique is used to identify all possible ways to achieve an objective. It can be used to anticipate innovations and to develop ideal patterns for achieving desired objectives.

7. *Network methods.* Two types of network methods are popular: contingency trees and relevance trees. A contingency tree is a graphic display of logical relationships among environmental trends that focuses on branch points, at which several alternate outcomes are possible. A relevance tree is a logical network similar to a contingency tree, but assigning degrees of importance to various environmental trends with reference to an outcome.

8. *Missing link approach.* This approach combines morphological analysis and the network method. Many developments and innovations that appear promising may be hindered because something is missing. Under such circumstances this technique may be used to study new trends to see if they reveal the missing links.

9. *Model building.* This approach is similar to network methods but relies more on developing mathematical representations of the environmental phenomena in question. Simulations are good examples of model-building techniques.

10. *Delphi technique.* The Delphi technique is the systematic solicitation of expert opinion in varying stages, using feedback to develop new forecasts.

The choice of a scanning method depends on the specific needs of the organization. Without a conscious effort to develop one of these methods, however, scanning may evolve in an ad hoc and unstructured fashion, as described by Aguilar (1967). Some firms, notably General Electric, have attempted to institutionalize the scanning process to achieve long-lasting results. General Electric's successful approach, as described by Hellriegel and Slocum (1976), is presented next.

General Electric's Assessment Strategy

The General Electric Company has tried to give greater attention to the external environment by creating a Public Issues Committee as part of its board of directors. This committee has a chairman who is a board member from outside the company. A majority of members are also from outside the company. A senior executive vice-president from the corporate executive staff serves as the formal link between company management and the committee. Within General Electric a business environment studies unit has been created to serve the committee and management. The unit's primary role is to identify and evaluate issues requiring broader consideration by top management and the board of directors.

Dilemmas. The top management of General Electric is faced with the traditional demands of economics: the need for the firm to be concerned with efficiency, productivity, profits, and the new and emerging expectations and pressures of society. Because the company assumes that these expectations and pressures exceed its resources and capabilities, at least in the short run, its managers are faced with fundamental questions: What demands should they respond to? What constituencies and pressure groups should they listen to? Implicit in their approach is their desire to allocate scarce resources in a way that will yield the greatest benefit to the firm. Resources spent on passing fads, even if there are strong currents of pressure behind them, might have been better spent on other purposes, such as higher salaries, bigger profits, or more comfortable offices.

Assessment Approach. Because General Electric assumed it was impossible to respond to every pressure equally, the management felt it needed a way to analyze pressures and establish priorities. They grouped environmental pressures into eight broad categories: marketing and finance, production, employee relations and working conditions, governance, communications, community and government relations, defense production, and international operations. They identified the charges or complaints and the demands and threats within each category. Ninety-seven different demands and threats were identified, and then analyzed in terms of priority.

Each demand was assessed along two dimensions. One dimension was called the *degree of convergence with trends.* Thirteen societal trends expected to be of major importance during the next ten years (through 1982) were identified: increasing affluence; a rising level of education; proliferating technology; the emergence of a postindustrial society or a services economy; the growing interdependence of institutions, including business-government partnerships; an increasing emphasis on individualism; growing pluralism, an increase in groups and organizations, and a diversity of lifestyles; the "equity revolution"; a growing emphasis on quality of life, including ecology, culture, and education (Maslow's levels four and five); a redefinition of work and leisure patterns; a continued increase in foreign competition; the growing and changing role of government; and continued urbanization.

Each demand was evaluated for its degree of convergence or collision with each of the thirteen trends, along a rating scale of 1 to 10. A rating of 10 meant high convergence between a demand and a trend; a rating of 1 meant no convergence, or collision with a trend.

The second dimension was the *degree of pressure or power behind each demand.* Each demand was evaluated for its relative importance or interest to each of fourteen constituencies or pressure groups in the environment: customers and consumer groups; shareholders; unions; blue-collar workers; managers and professional staff; federal, state, and local government; small businesses; minority groups; women's groups; college youth; environmental groups; populists; academic critics; and moralists, including church groups.

Each demand was given a 4, 3, 2, or 1 score according to whether it was estimated to fall in the first, second, third, or lowest quartile of a group's demands or interests. In combining the point values for the fourteen constituencies or pressure groups, the company also recognized that not all groups are equally powerful or equally active in working to enforce their demands.

Findings. General Electric's detailed findings concerning high- and low-priority issues have not been publicly disclosed. Some of the general issues or demands most germane to organizational behavior that received a high-priority analysis, however, include job enlargement; flexible work scheduling; equality of opportunity; participation and individualization; external constraints on employee relations, particularly in equal employment opportunity, health and safety, and federalization of fringe benefits; coalition bargaining by unions; broader public representation on the board of directors; disclosure of information; and accountability and personal liability of managers and directors in matters relating to organizational governance (Hellreigel and Slocum, 1976, pp. 66–68).

Summary

Planning has evolved to be a crucial function for the manager. As external environments become more complex and turbulent, managers are increasingly faced with new problems that defy traditional methods of attack and resolution. Therefore, managers should not only master the fundamentals of planning, but also acquaint themselves with newer methods designed to make the planning system more flexible and adaptive.

Planning is the process by which managers define goals and take necessary steps to ensure that these goals are achieved. Planning arises out of the recognition that some intervention is needed to bring about a change from the current or existing states to an alternate and desired future state. Planning is a process that is anticipatory, or future oriented, involving multiple parties in interdependent sets of decisions, and actions leading to future states that would not occur without planning.

Plans in organization can be described as corporate, divisional, and unit/functional. The plans can be differentiated according to the level of the organization at which the planning system is developed, the focus of the plans, and the strategic orientation. Corporate plans define the company's major goals and objectives (mission). Strategic orientation is directed at the selection of product/markets. Divisional plans are directed at enabling the division to outperform other firms or divisions in the industry, given a particular market's strategic orientation. Porter's three generic strategies — cost leadership, differentiation, and focus — provide some indication of how to compete. Unit/functional plans are concerned with the optimal use of strategic variables under the control of the functional manager. Strategic orientation is directed at developing the proper mix of such strategic variables to arrive at target performance levels.

Contingency planning involves developing alternate plans in anticipation of environmental events that change the firm's strategic plans. A number of contingency plans employ multiple scenarios based on optimistic and pessimistic developments. Other planning aids are future studies, dialectical processes, and computerized simulations.

The process of acquiring information about the firm's external environment, known as environmental scanning, is becoming more important to the planning function. Four questions, relating to the sources of information, the criteria for differentiating trends, the need for greater objectivity, and the types of scanning methods, are suggested for purposes of developing a formal environmental scanning program.

Questions for Discussion

1. Why has planning evolved as a crucial function for the manager?
2. What is planning? Describe some of the key components of planning.
3. Differentiate corporate, divisional, and unit functional plans in terms of level, strategic orientation, and focus.
4. What is contingency planning? Describe a number of contingency plans.
5. What is environmental scanning? Discuss the importance of scanning to the planning function.
6. Describe how one might develop a formal environmental scanning program.
7. What is the General Electric assessment program? Describe some of the key findings of this program.
8. The Japanese are apparently highly successful in their scanning activities. Discuss the reasons for this success.

Exercise 4.1
Planning and Assessment

This is a group-oriented exercise designed to make you more aware of how organizations might evaluate pressures emanating from their business/societal environments. The exercise is based on an actual program used by General Electric (for details, see General Electric's Assessment Strategy, pp. 123–124).

Step 1. Participants are divided into groups of three to five.

Step 2. Each group performs the following tasks:

    a. List (agree on) twelve major societal trends that you believe will be instrumental in shaping values and work patterns for the next ten years. (Suggested discussion time: 10 minutes.)

    b. List (agree on) twenty major complaints students have about the educational system at present. (Suggested discussion time: 10 minutes.)

Step 3. Each group evaluates each societal trend for its degree of convergence or collision with the major complaints about the educational system. A rating of 10 indicates high convergence, and a rating of 1 indicates no convergence.

Step 4. Each group evaluates the degree of pressure behind each complaint — that is, the relative importance of each complaint to the following pressure groups (constituents):

    State legislature
    Faculty
    Graduate students
    Undergraduate students
    Alumni and donors
    Parents
    Business community

Each complaint should be rated a 4, 3, 2, or 1, 4 indicating high pressure and 1 indicating low pressure. For each complaint, combine the point values for all seven pressure groups. (Suggested discussion time : 10 minutes.)

Step 5. Using the two key dimensions, the degree of convergence and relative importance of each complaint, develop a matrix and specify the four quadrants: low convergence–low importance; low convergence–high importance; high convergence–low importance; and high convergence–high importance. Position each of the complaints in one of these quadrants.

Questions

1. How effective is this method in formulating priorities for pressures from the business environment?
2. How might you structure your planning system to accommodate complaints positioned with the high convergence–high importance area? The low importance–low convergence area?

Case Study
Planning at the Philippine Consulting Corporation

Prior to 1964, management consulting in the Philippines was highly fragmented, with a few returning MBAs from abroad and a few professors engaging in consulting on a part-time basis. The first organized effort at consulting came about with the incorporation of the Philippine Consulting Corporation (PCC), a private, nonstock, nonprofit organization with a basic objective of providing a full range of services to the business community for better management of corporate resources.

This organization was initially assisted by the Fry Consultants of Chicago, who designed the first product/service line for the company. This arrangement gave added impetus to the organization in its sales effort, because the business community was quite receptive to foreign consultants.

At the time, manufacturing companies in Manila were experiencing problems in their production planning and control, and enormous inventory costs. The marketing effort of the PCC was steered toward designing production and inventory systems for these companies; such provided 80 percent of their total revenues during the first year.

The next three years saw the establishment of three major consulting outfits, one of which was to displace the PCC as the top company in the country. ABC, an accounting firm, opened a Management Services Division in 1965. Because this was an accounting firm, several quarters decried the resulting "unethical" situation. Nonetheless, the firm continued and was able to market its services successfully to its clients.

In 1969 two companies were formed: the Decision-Analyses Corporation, to provide computerized services to the community, and Personnel Consultants, Inc., to provide personnel management services to the market.

It was in the beginning of 1970 that Mr. Celestino Rivera took over as chief executive of the PCC. As an assistant to the chief executive over the years, he had pushed to extend PCC services to cover such service areas as management science, feasibility studies, and organizational development, to no avail. By the time he assumed office, he had realized many of the mistakes the company had made and resolved to correct them.

His prime concern was the market for PCC. A marketing research report presented the following highlights:

SITUATION ANALYSIS
JANUARY 1970

MARKET SHARE (SALES)

1. ABC Corporation	40%
2. Philippine Consulting Corporation	30%
3. Decision-Analyses	9%
4. Personnel Consultants	8%
5. MAC Consultants	7%
6. Others	6%
	100%

PRODUCT LINE ANALYSIS

1. Feasibility Studies	22%
2. Marketing programs, research, etc.	18%
3. Personnel studies	15%
4. Organization studies	10%
5. Production studies	8%
6. Economic research	3%
7. Industrial research	1%
8. Various services	17%

Mr. Rivera was not highly optimistic about market prospects. The firm had failed to secure government contracts (all contracts awarded to some competitor for "political" reasons). Moreover, his review of PCC's clientele indicated that many sales were affected through "repeat" projections — i.e., the same client would ask for a marketing program, a feasibility study, and so forth. In a few years the firm would have totally saturated its client base.

He was likewise concerned about the lackluster performance of the Management Development Department. The department was the market leader in the offerings of public seminars in 1965; by 1970, revenues had dropped to 17% (various services), owing to the proliferation of similar offerings by competing firms, universities, and other organizations.

Of particular concern to Mr. Rivera and the PCC staff was the gradual growth of in-house consulting. Staff members had brought up the fact that many of their own clients had organized internal consulting departments. PCC consultants expressed concern that in the future these clients would no longer need consulting services. It was apparent that PCC's competitors would not be consulting firms but their own clients who were organizing in-house consulting departments.

Case Questions

1. Describe the environment of PCC. What sectors of this environment are particularly threatening? Why?

2. Discuss how the growth of in-house consulting might affect the corporate strategy of PCC.
3. What are PCC's strategic options?
4. Define a corporate mission for PCC, and describe the nature of business-level strategies that might support this mission.
5. What recommendations would you make to Mr. Celestino Rivera of ways in which PCC might restructure its planning function to accommodate important changes in its environment?

This case was prepared by Gerardo R. Ungson, University of Oregon, Eugene, Oregon, 1984. All names of firms and persons have been disguised, and market data are approximated.

CHAPTER 5

Designing Effective Organizations

arry V. Quadracci often refuses to tell his employees what to do.

He has the right — he's president of the successful printing company Quad/Graphics Inc. in Pewaukee, Wisconsin. It's just not his philosophy.

Once, for example, the company's shipping department needed more haul-back revenues to expand its trucking fleet. Quadracci handed each of the drivers the keys to one of the company's Peterbilt trucks and told the drivers they were now owner-operators in a new company division called DuPlainville Transport Inc. He also told them it was their duty to make their return trips profitable.

The drivers asked the company president what they should haul back. "How should I know?" Quadracci shrugged. "I don't know anything about driving an eighteen-wheeler. I'm not going to find your loads."

"Believe me, it was a big challenge for everybody," said fleet manager Larry Lynch. "We got stung a few times, but we got rolling."

Source: Adapted with permission from "Management by Walking Away," by Ellen Wojahn, *INC.* Magazine, October 1983, pp. 68–76.

Chapter Outline

- The Nature of Organizational Structure
- The Concept of Organizational Design
- Historical Approaches to Organizational Design
- Overall Implications for the Design of Organizations

Key Terms

- span of control
- functional structure
- product-management structure
- divisional structure
- geographic structure
- matrix/mixed structure
- inertia
- scientific management theory
- administrative management theory
- human relations movement
- contingency theory
- unit/small-batch technology
- mass/large-batch technology
- process technology
- neocontingency design theory
- strategic choice
- adaptive cycle

Chapter Objectives

After studying Chapter 5 you should be able to

1. Describe organizations in terms of their formal characteristics, types of grouping, and organizational inertia.
2. Discuss the characteristics of bureaucratic structures.
3. Explain the principles of scientific management.
4. Explain the main ideas of the administrative management theory.
5. Contrast the ideas of the human relations school with other management theories.
6. Explain some general implications for designing effective structures.

Introduction

Students of business will quickly see that organizational structures are widely diverse: there is Procter & Gamble, which pioneered management on the basis of individual products in 1927; General Motors, split into divisions by Alfred P. Sloan, Jr.; the Peace Corps and multinational businesses, with their geographic structures based on location; small businesses, with their simpler, more functional organizations; and a maze of hybrids.

What accounts for this variety of organizational structures? Is one type better than another? What guidelines can we use to design structures? These are some of the many questions that face managers who have the fundamental task of designing organizational structures.

A poorly designed structure creates problems. Responsibilities may be duplicated, leading to high administrative costs. Lack of coordination between units can cause conflict and wasteful slack. The structure may be too formal and restrictive, resulting in low employee morale and commitment. People and tasks may be mismatched, which can necessitate costly training programs.

Managers must know how to organize effectively. What a tragedy it would be to see a well-conceived strategy fail because the structure for putting it into action was poorly designed.

In this chapter you will be introduced to organizing. First, we will describe different organizational structures. Second, the problem of organizational design will be discussed. Third, we will show how different schools of management have approached the problem of organizational design. At the end of the chapter, we will discuss some implications for the design of organizations.

The Nature of Organizational Structure

For a long time, *organizing* has meant designing organizational structures. There are a number of ways to describe organizational structures, as well as a number of ways to conceptualize the historical development of organizational design theory. Let us start with the concept of organizational structure, and then move on to discuss how structures have been used by managers and academicians.

The Concept of Structure

Structure generally refers to stable and relatively fixed relationships that exist among jobs in an organization. Structure represents the skeleton of the organizational system. In discussing the stable relationships among jobs, we refer to how tasks are allocated within the organization over time, including the way tasks are differentiated by horizontal and vertical levels. Structure also encompasses the ways in which different jobs are coordinated and controlled. Thus, we may also say that structure consists of stable or enduring relationships reflecting task differentiation and coordination.

Perspectives of Organizational Structure

Structure has been described in three related ways (Fig. 5.1), emphasizing *formal characteristics,* including the division of labor, span of control, formalization, and authority; *types of groupings* (functional, product, divisional, geographic, or matrix); and *inertia* (mechanistic or organic). Let us examine each in detail.

Formal Characteristics. For many years sociologists have attempted to describe the formal and enduring characteristics of organizations. Borrowing largely from the work of Max Weber (1947), four characteristics have been identified:

1. *Division of labor (specialization).* Tasks are organized in groups that allow and encourage specialization based on some criteria. The logic here is that if people are grouped by their specialties and skills, the organization will be more effective than if people try to do a little of everything.

2. *Span of control.* This characteristic refers to the number of subordinates who directly report to a superior. Traditional theory specifies that the **span of control** should be kept small to be manageable.

3. *Formalization.* The scope and diversity of rules vary in each organization. The clearer, the more detailed, and the more specific the rules are, the more formal the organization.

4. *Number of authority levels.* Organizations range from **flat structures,** in which a large number of subordinates report to one superior, to **tall structures,** in which fewer subordinates report to several superiors. Small spans of control in effect create relatively tall structures; larger spans, flatter structures.

Figure 5.1
Perspectives on Organizational Structure

ORGANIZATIONAL STRUCTURE HAS BEEN DESCRIBED IN TERMS OF . . .

Formal Characteristics	*Types of Groupings*	*Inertia*
Division of labor	Functional structures	Mechanistic (bureaucracy)
Span of control	Product-management structures	
Formalization	Divisional structures	Organic (human relations)
Number of authority levels	Geographic structures	
	Matrix/mixed structures	

Many theorists, such as Blau (1970), have emphasized the study of these formal and observable characteristics of organizations. Others have pointed out that informal characteristics such as rituals, myths, and rites may be as important in understanding how an organization functions (Argyris, 1974). Still others have indicated that top managers do not always agree on formal characteristics, such as the number of authority levels, making the interpretation of that type of data more difficult (Perrow, 1965). Even so, many researchers have used formal characteristics to define and determine organizational structures.

Types of Grouping. A second way of describing organizational structures is according to their departmentalization. The following five types are common:

1. *Functional structures.* In small companies the way to organize is to foster specialization by creating functional groupings. The different functional groups are coordinated by clear programs that delineate areas of responsibility and integration. Small businesses such as restaurants, machine shops, and subcontractors are some examples of **functional structures** (Fig. 5.2).

2. *Product-management structures.* Popularized by Procter & Gamble in 1927, **product-management structures** differentiate organizations by product

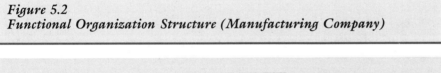

Figure 5.2
Functional Organization Structure (Manufacturing Company)

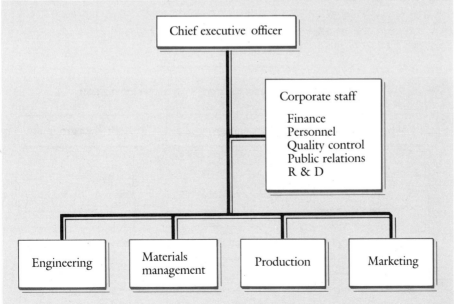

(Fig. 5.3). The product manager has full responsibility for the design, manufacturing, and marketing of his or her product. This structuring allows the organization to manage each product on its own life cycle, not merely as similar or equivalent products are managed. Manufacturers such as General Foods, The Kellogg Company, and Colgate-Palmolive have adopted this type of structure.

3. *Divisional structures.* As particular product lines become associated with specific markets, it becomes necessary to group the product line into divisions. The Pontiac and Chevrolet divisions of General Motors are examples of divisional organizational structures (Fig. 5.4). Each division performs all the functions required to carry out its operations. **Divisional structures** are particularly efficient in dealing with their markets, because they are autonomous and independent from the rest of the organization. Some inefficiency may occur, however, because each division maintains its own inventories. Duplication of resources also may result.

4. *Geographic structures.* A structure based on geographical location is particularly appropriate for firms that serve markets in different areas. The rationale is to be as close as possible to the action. In the United States it has been popular to split the market into eastern, southern, western, and northern re-

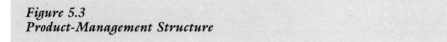

Figure 5.3
Product-Management Structure

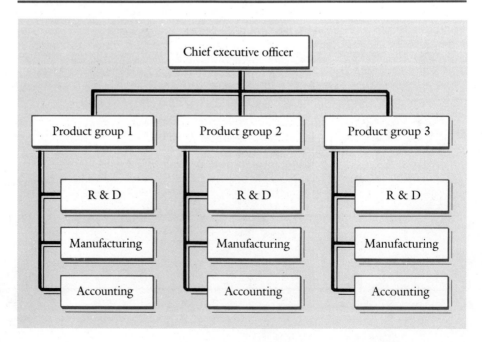

Figure 5.4
Divisional Organizational Structure

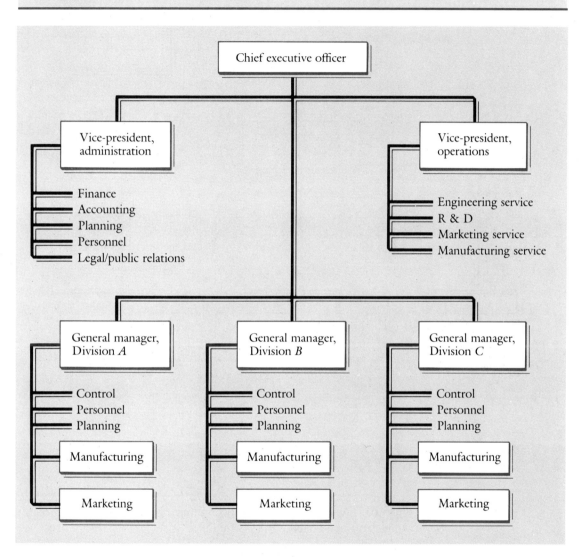

gions. Because each region has a different growth rate, the **geographic structure** allows each regional unit to monitor changes in its own area (Fig. 5.5). As with the divisional organization, inefficiencies may exist, and control may become a serious problem.

5. *Matrix/mixed structures.* **Matrix/mixed structures** combine the elements of functional and product-management structures in an ad hoc or temporary manner to maintain flexibility in the face of complex environmental condi-

Figure 5.5
Geographic Structure

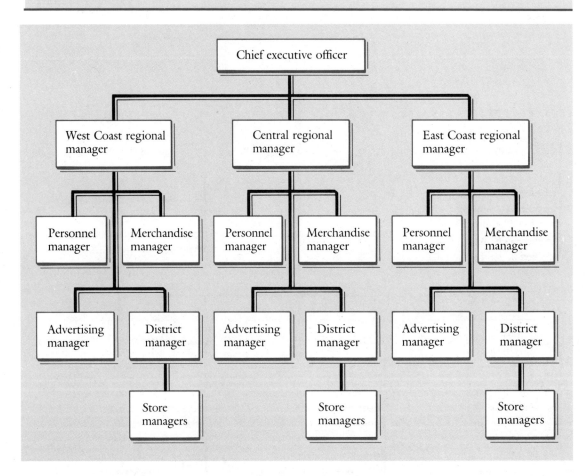

tions (Fig. 5.6). These structures have been referred to as *project-management organizations* and have been adopted by firms in the aerospace, consulting, banking, and pharmaceutical industries (see Davis and Lawrence, 1977). Matrix organizations are particularly appropriate in complex environments that mandate the sharing of resources within the firm. Matrix structures, however, also can lead to problems, ambiguous roles, power struggles, and excessive overhead if not effectively managed.

Organizational Inertia. Still another way of describing organizational structure is by its **inertia** or its responsiveness to conditions in the external environment. In studying twenty Scottish and British rayon milling and electronics

Figure 5.6
Matrix Organization Structure

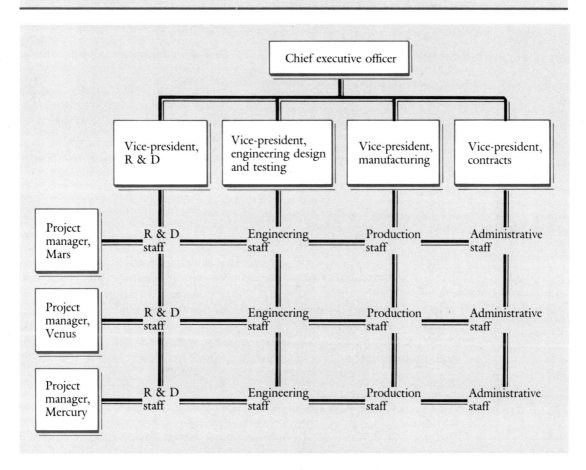

firms, Tom Burns and G. M. Stalker (1961) discovered two different management systems, which they termed mechanistic and organic (Fig. 5.7). *Mechanistic structures* seem to be more appropriate for firms with relatively stable environmental conditions, whereas *organic management systems* seem more suited to changing environmental characteristics.

Apart from structural differences in the two systems, Burns and Stalker found that traditional Scottish firms with mechanistic management structures had a difficult time adopting more organic structures, because of the relative inflexibility of mechanistic systems in adapting to new requirements.

Thus, organizational structure can be described in terms of formal characteristics, type of groupings, and organizational inertia. As you read more about

Figure 5.7
Mechanistic and Organic Management Structures

MECHANISTIC STRUCTURES	ORGANIC STRUCTURES
Rigid classification of roles into specialized, functional tasks	Flexible and adaptable classification of roles
Precise definition of duties, responsibilities, and powers	Duties, responsibilities, and powers are loosely defined
Well-defined system of communications hierarchy	Loosely defined system of communications hierarchy
Knowledge and control of tasks are centralized at the top of the organization	Knowledge and control of tasks are located anywhere in the organization
Vertical communication	Lateral communication

Source: Burns and Stalker, 1971, pp. 119–122.

organizational design, you will discover that these perspectives are interrelated. What is important is the fundamental meaning of organizational structure: stable relationships among jobs that reflect task differentiation and coordination in organizations. Knowing this definition well will help as you encounter the jargon used by organizational theorists. Next we will consider the significance of organizational structure for managers by discussing the organizational design problem.

The Concept of Organizational Design

Organizational design basically involves choices about how to allocate tasks and responsibilities most efficiently in line with both organizational goals and strategies, and individual needs and aspirations. In the preceding chapter we noted that fundamental questions involve what markets to compete in and how to do so effectively. In this chapter we will examine how organizational structures are designed to support or accommodate these strategies. Such division must reconcile the needs of top management, whose prime responsibility is to formulate corporate strategy, and the needs of the organizational members, who implement the strategy. We refer to these needs as *organizational* and *individual imperatives.*

The needs and values of top management and its employees are not always consistent and may be difficult to reconcile (Argyris, 1962). The following cases exemplify the problem:

• In a large university, the faculty senate recently proposed a change from a ten-week term system to a fifteen- to sixteen-week semester system of instruction.

It was believed that such a change would help students who felt that the ten-week term system did not give them enough time to learn all the required class materials. When the senate presented the change to the rest of the faculty, however, there was tremendous opposition. The faculty said that the new schedule cut into their research and vacation times and would only create more problems.

• In 1975 the automobile industry reported record-high profits and sales, but the industry also had many strikes and high absenteeism.

• A new graduate with a master's degree in business administration was assigned to promote more competitiveness among divisions of a large manufacturer of consumer durables. The company had been losing sales for a number of years to its competitors, who had aggressive marketing problems. Within a year the graduate had instituted a new system of profit control centers that was responsible for the company's reassuming its original market position. But key managers, who were accustomed to less rigid controls, opposed the new move and quickly resigned.

In the first example, the semester system sponsored by the faculty senate (organizational imperative), which was designed to accommodate the requirements of better education (strategy), was not in accord with the values and needs of the rest of the faculty (individual imperatives). Similarly, the strategy and organizational procedures adopted by automobile firms, although they contributed to some success in sales and profits, did not favor the development of highly motivated employees. Finally, the graduate successfully implemented top management's strategy — more competitiveness — at the cost of alienating some key managers.

The organizational designer must bridge the gap between individual and organizational imperatives by developing consistency, coherence, and congruence between them. Because perfect congruence may be unachievable, the designer's task is to integrate organizational and individual requirements in the best possible manner (Fig. 5.8). Various schools of thought have attended to this problem in different ways.

Historical Approaches to Organizational Design

The organizational design problem is not new. Management philosophers, sociologists, behavioral scientists, and managers have been considering how to bridge the gap between the organization and its employees for some time. Different answers have been provided, some emphasizing management prerogatives, some employee welfare. This lack of agreement has prompted recent authors to classify schools of research as embodying universalistic or contingency approaches. **Universalistic approaches** attempt to define the one best way to organize. **Contingency approaches,** in contrast, attempt to outline conditions or circumstances, often referred to as *contingencies,* that favor either organizational prerogatives or employee welfare.

Figure 5.8
The Organizational Design Problem

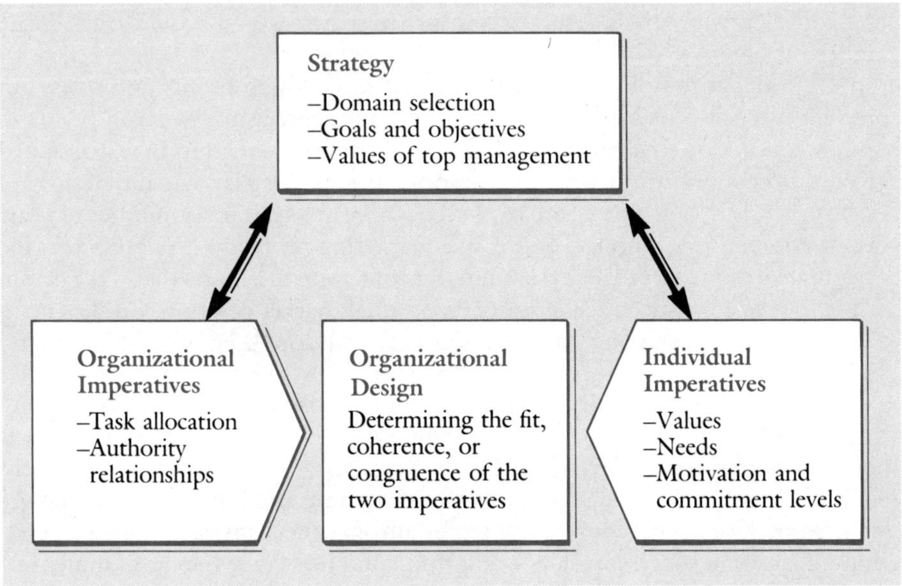

Strategy

–Domain selection
–Goals and objectives
–Values of top management

Organizational
Imperatives

–Task allocation
–Authority
 relationships

Organizational
Design
Determining the fit,
coherence, or
congruence of the
two imperatives

Individual
Imperatives

–Values
–Needs
–Motivation and
 commitment levels

For perspective, the different schools of thought concerning organizational design and their respective time periods are presented in Figure 5.9.

Bureaucratic Organizational Theory

Bureaucratic organizational theory can be traced to the work of Max Weber (1864–1920). A prodigious writer, Weber had a sweeping interest in the historical development of civilizations and the sociology of economic life. His interest in the theory of authority structures, or why people do what they are told, became the basis for his theory of organizations. Central to this interest was a distinction between power, the ability to force compliance in others, and authority, which causes people to obey commands and directives voluntarily.

Antecedents of the Theory. Weber (1947) classified organizations as exhibiting three types of authority structures: charismatic, traditional, and rational-legal. People generally follow *charismatic* leaders because they are able to relate to or empathize with a distinctive personality trait. Adolf Hitler, Franklin D. Roosevelt, Henry Ford, and Anwar Sadat are among the many historical figures who used their charismatic qualities to lead. In *traditional* organizations, such as monarchies and feudal systems, the authority structure is based on precedent and usage. The third form, *rational-legal,* provides the means to achieve

Figure 5.9
Historical Approaches to Organizational Design

Prevailing Work and Theory	1890	1910	1930–1950	1965	1965–1970	1975–Present
	Weber's work on bureaucracy	Taylor's work on scientific management	Hawthorne experiment: Birth of human relations movement	Harvard's school of contingency design	Examination of contingency variables: Environment, technology, size, power, control	Strategic choices

Perspectives on the Organizational Design problem	I. Universalistic theories with emphasis on managerial perogatives.	II. Universalistic theories with an emphasis on employee perogative.	III. Contingency theory with an emphasis on contingency design variables.	IV. Neocontingency theory with an emphasis on strategic choices or managerial discretion.

**Feature 5.1
Management by Walking Away**

Every May the entire management of Quad/Graphics Inc. walks out for an entire day, leaving the workers in charge of millions of dollars of equipment and projects for *Newsweek, Harper's,* and *Playboy.*

Every year it pays off. The problems are minor and the workers' morale is high.

The company's "Spring Fling," as they call it, is the embodiment of an unusual management style that has been dubbed "management by walking away." Quad/Graphics President Harry V. Quadracci has developed a company that can just about run itself, with workers whom he can trust. And he did it by emphasizing responsibility of a very nontraditional kind.

"We don't believe that responsibility should be that defined," he said. "We think it should be assumed and shared. Nothing should be 'somebody else's responsibility.' Anybody who sees that something needs to be done ought to assume the responsibility for doing it. Our people," he adds, "shouldn't need me or anybody else to tell them what to do."

Quadracci's philosophy is undoubtedly one reason for the company's great success. Just eleven years old, Quad/Graphics expected a sales volume of $75 million in 1983 and is considered the wonderchild of its industry. Quadracci believes the company is one of the ten largest magazine-printing companies in the country. Its growth is clearly outdistancing that of most of its competitors.

"Harry is formidable, and his organization is *very* formidable — not only in terms of printing technology, but in how he treats his people," said one magazine executive.

Quadracci has instituted a three-day, thirty-six-hour work week, which has resulted in a 20 percent increase in productivity. The company also has an employee stock ownership plan, profit sharing, an employee education and training program, and a $3 million employee sports center.

Quadracci says the "assumed responsibility" system is working well — sometimes almost too well. He recalled one incident in which managers in the company bindery caught some lunch-hour marijuana smokers, which resulted in the firing of five employees.

Quadracci disapproved of the department's tactics but said nothing. Then when one of the five asked for his job back, he made the rare move of saying that it would be "all right" with him if the offender were rehired. But the bindery workers said no.

"They told me," Quadracci said, "the kid had broken the cardinal rule — he had violated their trust. He failed to assume responsibility for his own actions, so how could they trust him to assume responsibility for the success of the company?"

Source: Adapted with permission from "Management by Walking Away," by Ellen Wojahn, *INC.* Magazine, October 1983, pp. 68–76.

---

goals in a rational and legal way. Authority is exercised through governing rules and procedures. The rational-legal authority structure forms the basis of the bureaucratic organization.

Characteristics of Bureaucratic Structures. Bureaucratic structures attempt to order their activities in a manner that ensures consistency of outputs and behavior. The bureaucratic structure has the following components:

1. *Hierarchy.* Jobs are highly specialized and arranged in a hierarchy. Each job embraces every job below it.

2. *Rules and regulations.* All tasks are performed according to consistent sets of rules. Formalizing the means of achieving desired performance minimizes or eliminates individual differences.

3. *Authority levels.* Each job has a specific jurisdiction, with a superior or supervisor in charge. Jobs are performed according to their scope, jurisdiction, and authority.

4. *Impersonality.* There is a clear separation between business and personal activities. To ensure that personalities do not interfere with the job, the superior must maintain social distance from subordinates and clients.

5. *Technical qualifications and career orientation.* Employment and promotions are based on technical qualification and achievement. Therefore, seniority is the main variable in promotion. As bureaucracies develop, the number of professionals and specialists within the organization grows.

Implications for Organizational Design. The bureaucratic structure attempts to reconcile the needs of the organization and its employees. It serves organizational imperatives by providing predictability and consistency in products and behavior. The inherent logic of bureaucracy led Weber to conclude that it was superior to other forms of organization, particularly in its precision, stability, and reliability. Contrary to some interpretations of bureaucratic theory, the structure was thought to promote the well-being of both the organization and its employees. The bureaucratic structure was seen as protecting employees from nepotism, arbitrary firing, and favoritism, practices that were prevalent at the time. In effect, the bureaucratic structure supported employees as much as it did executive management.

Postscript. In later studies of bureaucratic structures, Merton (1940) reported a number of unintended consequences arising from the need for consistent and reliable outputs. In **trained incapacity,** actions successfully applied to previous problems result in incorrect responses when applied to new problems. Rules may become ends in themselves instead of means to an end, a situation known as a **means-end inversion.** For example, in complying with numerous government regulations, sometimes there is more emphasis on completing the required reports than on what is being regulated. **Occupational psychosis** occurs when people develop special preferences as a result of routine daily activities. One example is people's refusing to take action on a task they consider outside their job description. Final criticism of bureaucracies is that managers tend to be impersonal toward their employees and clients.

But before you conclude that bureaucracies are synonymous with inflexibility, red tape, and rigid behavior, consider what the other side has to say. Charles Perrow (1979) argued that the unintended consequences just discussed are not natural to bureaucracies but, rather, are a result of poor management. Good managers in bureaucracies are able to avoid or minimize these consequences.

The reality of life is that about 70 to 80 percent of the firms in the United States can be described as bureaucratic. It makes sense to know and understand the mechanisms and processes of such structures even if you do not fully agree with their philosophies.

Scientific Management Theory

Scientific management theory was developed by Frederick Taylor (1856–1917), who went from laborer to foreman to chief engineer at the Midvale Steel Works before becoming an engineer at the Bethlehem Steel Works. At the time there was considerable interest in the emerging power of large organizations. The era included the first wave of mergers, cartels, holding companies, and trusts. These events raised some new problems for management. The more traditional ways of managing, geared to smaller companies, seemed no longer applicable.

Taylor believed that the key to success was to develop a science that would concentrate on doing the job right. Physics was popular at the time. He felt that the way to reconcile differences between management and the individual was to create a *social physics* of work. Taylor anchored his theory on three specific problems that he believed to be the leading causes of inefficiency: (1) workers' ill-founded belief that increased output would lead to unemployment, (2) deficient management systems that made it necessary for workers to restrict output, and (3) inefficient rule-of-thumb approaches to work (Pugh, Hickson, and Hinings, 1973).

Principles of Scientific Management. Taylor (1911) laid the groundwork for scientific management with the following principles:

1. *Scientific approach to work.* Central to Taylor's theory is *maximum specialization,* or the removal of all extraneous elements of the job. For example, shoveling, which is relatively simple, has fairly complex components. Taylor's scientific approach involves determining an optimal work load by breaking down the job into finite components: pick up shovel, place right hand on barrel, place left hand grip two inches above the barrel, stoop at a direction diagonal to the ground, and so on. Wasteful or duplicate motions are eliminated.

2. *Incentives for rewards.* Taylor believed that fixed rate systems are not conducive to high productivity. In addition to a fixed rate, he advocated an incentive system in which the worker would receive more pay for more output.

3. *Scientific selection and progressive training.* Taylor believed that it was management's responsibility to bring in the best person for the job and provide him or her with opportunities for advancement. Any person could become a

first-class worker with scientific management training but that innate talent would make the process easier.

4. *Separation of planning from performance.* Taylor's theory held that work should be strictly divided between management and workers. Management was assumed to be good at planning, setting standards, developing and administering incentive programs, and supervising workers. Workers were better off concentrating on the physical aspects of the job without having to worry about its mental aspects, which were management's responsibility. Both managememt and workers had to abide by the principles of scientific management to be successful.

Implications for Organizational Design. It may seem that scientific management favors management prerogatives over those of the worker, but the theory was developed to meet the needs of both parties. For management, scientific management was supposed to bring about higher productivity, improved worker morale, and more efficient management. For the workers, it would mean higher wages arising from greater productivity, and higher morale as a result of improved work practices. Many workers at the time were recent immigrants with somewhat different work attitudes and values than workers of today, and they might have found financial rewards particularly appealing. In terms of our organizational design framework (see Fig. 5.2), science founded on efficient work practices was assumed to reconcile effectively the differing expectations of workers and management.

Postscript. Taylor's efforts to make jobs more efficient were initially praised, and his theory was widely discussed by both management and workers. Then Taylor, a fairly ambitious man, attempted to apply his principles to a government arsenal. Labor problems erupted, and a special committee of the House of Representatives was formed in 1911 to investigate scientific management.

Over time, Taylor's methods were refined by Frank and Lillian Gilbreth, Bedaux, Gantt, and others. The theory has evolved and now falls under the domain of industrial engineering. Like bureaucratic management theory, scientific management has acquired the bad reputation of being antiworker, or of reducing workers to robots. This reputation unfortunately obscures the fundamental intent of scientific management, which is improving the lot of management and workers by increasing the size of the surplus, rather than dividing it.

Administrative Mangagement Theory

Principles of Administrative Management. Scientific management was directed at the worker and his or her task on the shop floor. But one of the central questions was the role of top management. Henri Fayol (1841–1925), a mining engineer, examined this question, as did later theorists such as Urwick,

---

Feature 5.2
Greyhound Strike Is Bitterest in Company History

Nowhere is conflict between top management and employees more evident than in collective bargaining negotiations.

In November 1983, 12,700 members of the Amalgamated Transit Union went on strike against Greyhound Lines Inc. to protest what they considered to be the "union-busting" company demand that they accept a sizable pay cut. John Teets, chairman of the board of the Phoenix, Arizona–based Greyhound Corporation, said the proposed 9.5 percent wage cuts were necessary to make the company competitive with other bus lines.

The strike was the bitterest walkout in Greyhound's history. Strikers vandalized equipment, picketers were arrested, and one picketer was run over and killed by a bus. Eventually the strike was settled when the union accepted terms that would cut Greyhound's labor costs by about 13 percent in a three-year period. Transit union leaders found some solace in the fact that they had successfully fended of two "final" offers that would have cut the average Greyhound worker's wage-and-benefit package of about $15.15 an hour by up to 28 percent.

Speaking for the company, Teets said, "This contract gives us the parity we were seeking and still makes the employees the best paid in the industry." With labor costs amounting to about 62 percent of total costs, the new contract would cut the bus line's operating expenses by about 8 percent over the following three years.

Even so, the company will have to deal with the grumblings and heightened mistrust of the transit union in the future. Despite the impressive array of propaganda from company headquarters, union leaders are skeptical about the company's financial position.

If the company was in such drastic shape, they argued, Teets should have taken a cut in his $457,000-a-year salary. Union leaders also are angry that Greyhound never offered trade-offs in return, such as better job security or a profit-sharing plan.

"What Teets did was solidify the union to an extent I would never have believed," said Darrel Horn, president of the Amalgamated Transit Union Local 1055 in Portland, Oregon. In that sense, added James Hodges, president of the union's Local 1313 in Kansas City, Missouri, "I feel we won our strike."

Sources: "Jobless Hope Greyhound Strike Means Jobs for Them," *The Oakdale Tribune,* November 4, 1983, p. 1; "If Anyone Won the Strike, Greyhound Did," *Business Week,* December 19, 1983, pp. 39–40.

Barnard, and Brown. **Administrative management theory,** which Fayol's approach is commonly called, is concerned with general principles that guide the management of the entire organization. Fayol (1949) outlined fourteen principles of management:

1. *Division of work.* Much like scientific management, this theory holds that specializing ensures efficiency and productivity.

2. *Authority.* Managers have the right to give commands and orders, and the responsibility to see that the orders are carried out.

3. *Discipline.* Management must be able to provide good leadership, and workers must obey management's orders.

4. *Unity of command.* Workers should be supervised by only one boss.

5. *Unity of direction.* Workers involved in the same activities should have one guiding plan with the same objectives.

6. *Subordination of individual interest to the general interest.* All individual goals should be secondary to the goals of the firm.

7. *Remuneration.* As much as possible, pay should be used to motivate people to work.

8. *Centralization/decentralization.* Decisions may be centralized in upper echelons of organizations or delegated to lower echelons, depending on circumstances.

9. *Scaler chain.* For effective management, organizations must have a hierarchy with vertical and horizontal communication.

10. *Order.* Organizations must have material order in physical arrangements and social order in reporting relationships.

11. *Equity.* All employees should be treated justly and with kindness. Indiscriminate or arbitrary actions by management impair relationships with employees.

12. *Stability of tenure.* The more time they have in the company, the more effective employees and managers become. A successful firm, then, is characterized by an abundance of stable and tenured personnel.

13. *Initiatives.* Management should encourage workers to take the initiative. Such behavior does not undermine the manager's job.

14. *Esprit de corps.* Management should promote harmony among personnel. Coordinating efforts, encouraging the use of a person's abilities, and rewarding merit, all within the guidelines of authority and discipline, are important managerial tasks.

Implications for Organizational Design. Fayol's principles are directed at managers. His underlying assumption is that good or enlightened management is able to motivate workers to perform according to management guidelines and expectations. If workers fail to produce, the fault lies with managers. The fourteen principles are designed to make managers more aware of their responsibilities and better at executing them.

Postscript. Fayol's work has influenced managers' administrative efforts and given us a broader perspective of the functions of management. There has been considerable controversy over the meaning of the term *principle* (see Mouzelis, 1967) and over whether the fourteen points apply to all situations, yet we still see many of Fayol's principles reflected in the action of today's managers. For example, the principle of unity of command has endured until recently as an

Feature 5.3
Geico Muddles Along

When John J. Byrne became chairman of Geico Corporation in 1976, he pulled the auto insurer out of bankruptcy and set about creating a new corporate culture based on consensus management and inflexible operating rules.

He soon realized one of those rules stood in the way of company growth. He could have changed it quickly. Instead, he waited four years until his lieutenants were ready to go along.

Byrne describes his management style as "muddling through."

His philosophy is a curious mixture of management by objective, consensus management, and old-fashioned opportunism. He simply believes that management should not make policy decisions on its own but, rather, create an environment in which subordinates can be trusted to set their own goals by consensus.

He's willing to accept group decisions but remains at the center of the decision-making process. Long before decisions must be made, he drifts from office to office, gathering opinions and making known his own until he is certain about the outcome of the vote.

A key ingredient in this philosophy is the company's annual "challenge sessions," which bring together the company's top managers and heads of the company's twenty-eight planning centers, including line and staff managers. At each session the executives distribute copies of their proposed budget and goals for the coming year; then each takes a turn at the head of the table, listening while his or her colleagues criticize the budget.

By the end of the grueling three-week session, each executive has accepted personal responsibility for a detailed corporate operating plan including specific goals he or she is expected to attain.

People who don't meet their goals don't get any bonuses and overly cautious goals rarely survive the inquisition, so goals are generally realistic.

Performance is what counts with Byrne. So long as an employee gets results, "I don't care if he shines his shoes with a brick," he said.

Source: "Muddling to Victory at Geico," by Stratford P. Sherman, *Fortune,* September 5, 1983, pp. 66–80.

important design consideration. Fayol's work stands apart as one of the first formal treatises on the functions of a manager.

Human Relations Theory

Elton Mayo (1880–1949) is considered the founder of the **human relations movement.** As a professor at Harvard University, Mayo was interested in the effects of rest pauses on fatigue, accidents, and labor turnover. After a successful experiment at a Philadelphia spinning mill in which introducing rest pauses apparently lowered turnover, Mayo (1971) conducted a series of investigations, called the Hawthorne experiments, designed to study the effects of illumination on the worker. Contrary to initial expectations, there was no significant difference in output between the group that had varied lighting and the group whose lighting was kept constant throughout. One finding was that production increased regardless of whether group scheme plans, rest pauses, or shorter work hours were introduced. It became clear to Mayo and his colleagues that the continually increasing production was a result of changes in experimental conditions per se. A subsequent explanation was that the workers in the experiment felt a tremendous increase in work satisfaction because they were able to communicate openly with one another and because they felt they were being treated as a special group by management and researchers.

Theoretical Implications. After several years Mayo concluded that work satisfaction depends on the informal social pattern of work groups. In effect, how much is produced depends on norms concerning cooperativeness and acceptable levels of productivity. Under such conditions the effects of the physical environment are unimportant. This finding was verified in the third stage of the experiment, called the Bank Wiring Observation Room experiment, in which workers purposely restricted their output to comply with social norms on the unacceptability of rate-busting.

Implications for Organizational Design. In contrast to Taylor's theories, bureaucratic management theory, and administrative management theory, which all highlighted the importance of top management, the human relations school concentrated on the workers. Problems in management-worker relationships were considered to be primarily a result of workers' values and social norms and not of the complexities of the situation. Management's interest in cost reduction and efficiency, and the workers' interest in sentient relationships, would only aggravate a potentially conflicting situation.

Another area of contrast between the human relations movement and earlier theories is the emphasis on informal, as opposed to formal, elements of structures. Scientific management, bureaucratic management, and administrative management theories were based on the idea of the worker as reactive, easily manipulated, and motivated primarily by monetary rewards. The worker of the human relations movement was proactive, resourceful, and motivated by favorable social relationships.

Postscript. Human relations theory has been influential in programs for developing and training employees. A number of leadership models have adopted the fundamental beliefs of human relations theory, which generally assumes that good leadership is the key to increased employee productivity.

Still, research findings have not demonstrated conclusively that group or leadership training is related to higher productivity. Campbell and Dunnette (1968) conducted a thorough review of the effectiveness of group training. They concluded that training helped individuals but did not result in more enduring benefits for the organization. Similar conclusions come from leadership research. After years of study it is difficult to conclude whether leaders have significant impact on their organizations. It is well to recognize that these conclusions are based on scientific experiments, which may not have great bearing on how people actually act. Nevertheless, the human relations movement remains appealing, and consultants and academicians are still in demand to conduct a vast array of training programs for organizations.

Contingency Theory

In the 1960s a fresh perspective was developed in organizational theory that considered organizations to be open systems continuously interacting with the environment (Katz and Kahn, 1978; Thompson, 1967). Burns and Stalker (1971) examined the effect of the changing electronics market on traditional Scottish firms. Woodward (1965) led a research team in a survey of manufacturing firms in the South-East Essex area in England. It was the work of Harvard University professors Paul Lawrence and Jay Lorsch (1967), however, that made the term **contingency theory** popular. They rejected existing principles of organizational design — bureaucratic, administrative, scientific, and human relations management theories — as either too universalistic or too prescriptive. Instead, they advocated searching for the situational patterns or relationships that determine organizational structure. They then defined the contingency theory framework:

> During the past few years, there has been evident a new trend in the study of organizational phenomena. Underlying this new approach is the idea that the internal functioning of organizations must be consistent with the demands of the organizational task, technology, or external environment, and the needs of its members if the organization is to be effective. Rather than searching for the panacea of the one best way to organize under all conditions, investigators have more and more tended to examine the functioning of organizations in relation to the needs of their particular members and the external pressures facing them. Basically, this approach seems to be leading to the development of a 'contingency' theory of organization with the appropriate internal states and processes of the organization contingent upon external requirements and member needs. [Lawrence and Lorsch, 1967, p. 1]

Technology as a Contingency Variable. Joan Woodward (1916–1971), a professor of industrial sociology at the University of London, pioneered the South-End Essex research study of manufacturing firms.

The original objective was to test classic management theory, which held that certain types of management structures are superior to others. Contrary to bureaucratic management theory, Woodward (1965) found that the number of authority levels, span of control, clarity of rules and regulations, formality of communications, and pattern of functional specialization showed no systematic relationship to such measures of effectiveness as market share and its rate of change, profitability, changes in stock prices, company reputation, and employee turnover. But when she classified the firms by modal technology and reanalyzed her data, she was able to find a link between organizational structure and effectiveness. By **modal technology** we mean the technology of the primary flow of products in each manufacturing unit. Three types of modal technology were described:

1. **Unit** or **small-batch technology.** This technology refers to production that directly meets customer requirements, including prototypes and building large equipment in stages. Examples are custom-made suits and special equipment.

2. **Mass** or **large-batch technology.** This technology includes mass production, large batches, and assembly line production. Firms that make automobiles or television sets use this technology.

3. **Process technology.** This technology refers to the continuous processing of products. Examples are intermittent production of chemicals, production of liquids and gases, and oil refining.

Firms adopt modal technologies based on their objectives, what they want to do, and the markets they want to service. For example, firms specializing in custom-made suits should not use mass production, and businesses that produce liquids or crystalline substances would find mass production technology infeasible.

Woodward's findings revealed that more successful firms had characteristics that were about average for their category of modal technology. A rough assessment also indicates that unit and process technologies more clearly exemplify human relations theory, whereas mass-production technology has structural dimensions characteristic of bureaucratic management theory. Therefore, successful mass-production firms have taller pyramids with narrow bases and are highly formalized. Successful firms in unit or process technologies tend to have flatter, wider-based pyramids and to emphasize informal coordination (Fig. 5.10).

These findings have been explained in terms of the controls each of the modal technologies requires. In unit or small-batch production, it is difficult to predict the results of the work, which depend on the idiosyncrasies of the workers. Control becomes the responsibility of the production personnel. The emphasis is at the work level, where most client-firm relationships are established, so typically there are few managers and fewer staff specialists. Coordination is informal, which explains why there is so much verbal and so little written communication.

Similar control mechanisms are required in process technologies. Because performance can be predetermined by setting machines to specified standards, control is much more predictable than in unit or small-batch technologies. Operations tend to be more sophisticated, so there are many staff specialists, with a low ratio of direct to indirect labor. Coordination comes through taller hierarchies and is managed through committees rather than by means of on-line instruction. There is a great deal of verbal communication and a need for inter-

Figure 5.10
Characteristic Organizational Structures
for Different Modal Technologies

MODAL TECHNOLOGY	CHARACTERISTIC ORGANIZATIONAL STRUCTURES
Unit: Small-Batch or Unit Technology	
1. Production of units to customers' requirements 2. Production of prototypes 3. Fabrication of large equipment in stages 4. Production of small batches to customers' orders	Low number of management levels High ratio of direct to indirect labor Low amount of written communication High amount of verbal communication
Mass: Large-Batch or Mass Technology	
1. Production of large batches on assembly lines 2. Mass production	Average number of management levels Average ratio of direct to indirect labor High amount of written communication Low amount of verbal communication
Process: Batch- or Continuous-Process Technology	
1. Process production of chemicals in batches 2. Continuous-flow production of liquids, gases, and solids	High number of management levels Low ratio of direct to indirect labor Low amount of written communication; high amount of verbal communication

departmental meetings and coordination. There is little need for formalized, written instructions.

Mass production technologies represent the middle of the road between unit and process technologies. Control is achieved at the work level by line supervisors. The number of staff specialists is not unduly large or small, and coordination is achieved through written rather than oral instructions.

Thus, technology is considered a contingency variable that is the major determinant of organizational structure. Unlike classic management theory, which favored either the bureaucratic or the human relations type of structure, the Woodward researchers argued that structure and organizational success depend to a large degree on the technology employed by the particular firm.

Environment as a Contingency Variable. The Harvard group, led by Paul Lawrence and Jay Lorsch, attempted to determine what influence an organization's environment has on its structure. Their sample included plastics, food processing, and container-manufacturing firms. Key variables included:

1. *Management's perception of the environment.* This variable included the clarity of information received, the rate of environmental change, the time it took

---

Feature 5.4
Beatrice Foods's New Game Plan

The chairman of Beatrice Foods Company, James L. Dutt, is giving himself two years to transform the company into a giant.

He faces a formidable challenge. He must toss out a long-time strategy of decentralization and growth by acquisition, which served the company well until recently. From selling butter and eggs ninety years ago, Beatrice Foods grew into a sprawling food, consumer, and industrial-products holding company with $9.19 billion in annual sales. It became a collection of 400 businesses selling 9,000 products ranging from taffy bars to steel tubing.

Its markets and its competitors were changing, but Beatrice remained the same. Problems were arising.

Most of its strong national brands, such as Samsonite luggage, had become successful without any help from their parent. Some units were competing with one another for supermarket shelf space; others, such as its three cheese companies, didn't talk to one another. The units were drifting without momentum or direction, and corporate management had isolated itself.

Then Dutt began his move. He started a two-year effort to reorganize the company into six operating groups. He got rid of fifty companies that were cyclical businesses or had small market shares. He consolidated units in smaller businesses for greater marketing clout, centralized some advertising and purchasing, moved research and development from the head office to the business-unit level, and reorganized management.

There have been successes and frustrations. Some units were acquired without consolidation in mind and are difficult to blend. Others, such as its two competing Mexican food operations, became stronger and their range of products broadened when they were combined.

There are still obstacles ahead, such as some very strong competition from entrenched national brands. But the changes are proceeding. Dutt summed up the moves in a speech to 450 of the company's managers. "We can't run this company tomorrow," he said, "with yesterday' game plan."

Source: "Beatrice Foods Moves to Centralize Business to Reverse its Decline," by Sue Shellenbarger, *The Wall Street Journal,* September 27, 1983, p. 1.

to get feedback, the degree of uncertainty about cause-and-effect relationships, and the extent to which tasks could be programmed.

2. *Organizational structures.* Unlike Woodward, who used measures derived from bureaucratic management theory, Lawrence and Lorsch used two principal indices of organizational structure: differentiation and integration. They defined **differentiation** as cognitive and emotional differences in formal structure, goal orientation, time orientation, and interpersonal orientation among units. **Integration** was defined as the process of achieving a unified effort among various organizational units.

3. *Organizational performance.* This variable included changes in profits and sales, the number of new products introduced, cost comparisons, and, for manufacturing firms, the manager's subjective appraisal of effectiveness. For the plastics firms, research laboratories were evaluated on the basis of how many books, scientific papers, and patents they generated, and the utility of the firms' research ideas.

The idea being tested was that successful firms adopt structures in line with the requirements of their environment (Fig. 5.11). The hypothesis was confirmed. Here are the findings:

1. *The more stable the environment, the fewer the requirements for differentiation and integration; the more unstable the environment, the greater the requirements for differentiation and integration.* If there is greater instability or uncertainty, a more flexible response to the environment arises. In plastics-manufacturing firms, which had to continuously develop new products in a rapidly changing environment, differentiated units with the skills to deal with their own subenvironments arose. A high degree of integration, or control, of these differential units was found. In food processing and metal-container firms, which faced more stable environments, the response was low-to-moderate levels of differentiation with a corresponding amount of control and coordination.

2. *More successful firms were able to develop organizational structures consistent with the demands of their environments.* Performance suffered when there were mismatches between company structure and the environment, and when differentiation and integration were not in proper proportion.

Firms with fairly complex structures and relatively certain or stable environments tended to spend more than necessary on maintenance requirements. In the metal-container industry, for example, an elaborate and costly integrative structure would make a firm less competitive. In contrast, firms that adopted relatively simple structures in the face of a rapidly changing environment would find themselves inflexible or less responsive to the changing demands of their customers. The added costs of maintaining a fairly differentiated organization and complex integration mechanisms are well justified, if not essential to ensuring success in operating in a fast-changing market.

Figure 5.11
The Most Successful Organizational Structures
for Two Types of Environments

CHARACTERISTICS OF THE ENVIRONMENT	HYPOTHESIZED ORGANIZATIONAL STRUCTURES	MEASURES OF SUCCESS
Stable Environment		
Clear information about environment	Mechanistic:	Change in profits and sales
Low rate of environmental change	Low levels of differentiation	Number of new products introduced
Shorter time of feedback	Low levels of integration	Cost comparisons
Certainty of cause-and-effect relationships		Subjective appraisal of effectiveness (manufacturing, food-processing, and metal-container industries)
Programmable tasks		
Unstable Environment		
Unclear information about environment	Organic:	Productivity
High rate of environmental change	High levels of differentiation	Patents
Longer time of feedback	High levels of integration	Subjective appraisal of effectiveness (research and plastics industries)
Uncertainty regarding cause-and-effect relationships		
Unprogrammable tasks		

Low levels of integration include such standardized and conventional methods as written rules, standard operating procedures, and simple decision rules. High levels of integration involve special skilled personnel or integrators, cross-functional teams, and ad hoc committees to mediate conflicts or differences that are not readily resolvable by more conventional and programmable efforts.

Size as a Contingency Variable. Much attention has been devoted to the effects of size on organizational structure, although size appears less significant a variable than technology or environment. Research has prompted considerable debate and controversy on the question.* We will present briefly three points of view that consider size to be a contingency variable.

* For a good discussion of the issues, see Kimberly, 1976.

Size causes structural differentiation. As the organization becomes larger, the number of levels and divisions must be increased to promote better coordination and to meet the demand for new personnel. Therefore, size is related to horizontal and vertical integration (Meyer, 1972; Blau, 1970).

Structural differentiation enlarges the administration. Demands for greater coordination and control mean the administrative staff must be enlarged to direct and administer the activities of the organization. This need is more apparent when growth includes geographical and functional dispersion (Hall and Tittle, 1966), which necessitates more effective control mechanisms. Increases in size are also thought to increase formalization and standardization (Pugh, Hickson, Hinings, and Turner, 1969).

Size moderates the effects of technology on structure. In smaller companies it has been suggested that unit technology, which exists within each major subunit, strongly influences organizational structure (Hickson, Pugh, and Pheysey, 1969). In such firms the entire organization is affected by activities at the work level. In larger companies the effect of unit technology on organizational structure is not as significant.

Implications for Organizational Design. Identifying situational or contingency variables that determine organizational structure is a central aspect of the contingency theory. Contingency variables such as environment, technology, and size are limits on organizational structures. Some claim that the contingency view represents an "it all depends" attitude instead of a universalistic "one best way" approach. But does it? In effect, contingency theory does prescribe a "best way," a particular approach, after different factors are analyzed.

The major contribution of contingency theory to organizational design is its premise that there are a number of ways to solve problems and that situational circumstances are important. By providing a comprehensive account of these circumstances, which include the changes in the environment, the rate of change, technological constraints, and the requirements of a growing organization, contingency theorists are able to help managers make better decisions on improving, if not changing, their organizational structures. Like all theories, contingency theory has its limitations. These are discussed in greater detail in the next section.

Neocontingency Theory: The Role of Strategic Choice

Contingency theory has been criticized by some researchers, notably Child (1972), for putting too much emphasis on the effects of the environment, technology, and size on structure. Child argues that structure does not automatically emerge or change when environmental conditions shift. Structure is the result of a **strategic choice** made by powerful managers within the organization. By neglecting strategic choices, contingency theorists may have overemphasized the ease with which organizational structures are developed to meet the requirements of new environmental and technological conditions.

If strategic choices are so important, why were they neglected in previous design theories? Partly because previous researchers examined the congruence, or fit, between patterns of environment, technology, and structure instead of studying managerial choices. The emphasis on strategic choices relating to structures and processes can be labeled **neocontingency design theory.**

Strategic choices determine both structure and organizational processes. Child (1977) lists some of the more fundamental choices:

1. Should jobs be broken down into narrow areas of work and responsibility to secure the benefits of specialization? Or should specialization be kept to a minimum to simplify communication and to give members of the organization greater scope and responsibility in their work?

2. Should the overall structure of an organization be "tall" rather than "flat" in its levels of management and spans of control? What are the implications for communication, motivation, and overhead costs of moving across these alternatives?

3. Should jobs and departments be grouped together by function, product, or geographical location?

4. Is it appropriate to aim for intensive integration among the different segments of an organization? What kind of integrating mechanisms are there to choose from?

5. How should management maintain adequate control over work done? Should it centralize or decentralize? Should there be extensive formalization? Should work be closely supervised?

6. What are the structural requirements for growth and development in an organization?

7. What pressures force management to change organizational structures, and what problems arise with reorganization? How can these be tackled?

8. In the light of contemporary social and industrial changes, what structural arrangements are we likely to see in the future? How will our present approaches to organization become inadequate or unacceptable?

Implications for Organizational Design. Neocontingency design theory improves on classic management theories and contingency theories by emphasizing the role of managerial discretion and strategic choice.* As a corollary, Child's theory is likewise sensitive to issues of power and organizational

---

* Two books provide excellent models of further development in neocontingency design theory: Miles and Snow, 1978, and Galbraith, 1973.

politics as these relate to organizational design. Organizational structure not only reflects the organization's response to contingencies, but may also indicate what management believes the organization can and cannot do. Recognizing this fact adds a more realistic perspective to the complexities of the organizational design problem.

Postscript. The contingency theory and strategic choice theory have been influential in directing organizational theory and design research. Considerable controversy has arisen over the years, partly because a number of replication studies have failed to confirm their findings. Much of the confusion, however, was generated by a vast array of studies that tested contingency relationships using a wide variety of conceptualizations, research instruments, and research samples. More somber appraisals (see Ford and Slocum, 1977) called for greater uniformity in research instruments and increased clarity in conceptualizations.

Overall Implications for the Design of Organizations

Organizational design involves choices concerning the most effective way to allocate tasks and responsibilities to employees in order to meet organizational goals and strategies. Our historical review has shown how theorists have looked at this problem at different times and under different circumstances. Despite all the studies, the research evidence does not provide enough specific prescriptions for management. This situation may reflect more on the growing complexity of the subject than on the abilities of the theorists who have tackled this problem. Nevertheless, some general implications for designing effective structures can be suggested.

Effective structures support corporate strategy. In 1969 Alfred Chandler published a thesis that held that organizational structure follows corporate strategy. The practical extension of this thesis is that organizational structures should be designed to support or accommodate the requirements of corporate strategy. An important reminder provided by neocontingency theorists is that the organizational design problem reflects fundamental choices made by managers. Structure should not be thought of as evolving in an ad hoc, haphazard fashion. Like many aspects of management, organizational structures are designed by managers to be responsive to corporate strategies.

Organizational design decisions are made repeatedly throughout the organization's history in response to the firm's changing strategies. As corporate strategies change and evolve, it becomes important to assess continuously the adaptability of the organizational structure of the firm. Miles and Snow (1978) have introduced the term **adaptive cycle** to describe how managers make conscious decisions on what strategies to adopt, which technologies are appropriate, and what structures accommodate the given strategies. It is important to recognize these key links among strategy, technology, and structure over time.

The choice of organizational structures cannot be made independently of the informal values and norms of the organization. The choice of structure should not be arbitrary and should involve careful consideration of the power structure and the needs of organizational members. Any adjustment will inevitably affect existing power relationships within the organization. One question that initially must be resolved is the effect of changes on power relationships. Proper attention also must be given to the needs, abilities, and ideologies of the people affected by the change effort. Successful adjustments result when the abilities of organizational members are considered in relation to the desired changes.

Summary

There are a number of ways in which organizational structures have been classified. These include emphases on formal structures, which include specialization, span of control, formalization, and authority; types of grouping, including functional, product management, divisional, geographic, and matrix groupings; and inertia (mechanistic and organic patterns).

Organizational design involves choices relating to the most effective way of allocating tasks and responsibilities to employees within an organization to meet organizational goals and strategies. Organizational design becomes a managerial concern because the needs and values of top management and its employees are not always consistent or reconcilable.

Historical approaches to the organizational design problem can be classified as universalistic approaches, attempts to find the one best way to organize, and contingency approaches, which try to define situational variables that make certain types of organizational structures appropriate. Universalistic approaches include bureaucratic management theory, scientific management theory, administrative theory, and human relations theory. Contingency approaches have been taken by researchers who have examined technology, environment, size, and strategic choice as determinants of organizational structure. The study of strategic choice is also called neocontingency theory in the research literature.

Questions for Discussion

1. What is the organizing function? Why is this function important for the manager today?
2. Describe the different perspectives from which organizational structures have been described. Provide an example of each of these perspectives.
3. What is organizational design? Why are organizational and individual needs said to be "constantly in conflict"?

4. Describe the following approaches to the organizational design problem:
   a. Universalistic theories
   b. Contingency theories
   c. Neocontingency theories
5. Compare and contrast the following approaches:
   a. Bureaucratic theory and scientific management theory.
   b. Bureaucratic theory and human relations theory.
   c. Contingency theory and neocontingency theory.

Exercise 5.1
Drawing an Organizational Chart

Fillmore National Bank has been a leading financial institution in Metropolis since its founding in 1882 by a grandnephew of President Millard Fillmore. When the law permitting bank holding companies was enacted five years ago, Fillmore National instituted an aggressive acquisition plan. To date twenty-three subsidiary banks have been added to the Fillmore Corporation. Although each subsidiary bank is encouraged to make full use of the numerous staff services at the parent bank, top management is firmly committed to a policy of decentralization. Even though such specialized departments as Gold Exchange are located only at the headquarters bank in Metropolis, each subsidiary bank offers a full range of services through its own professional staff. In keeping with the policy of decentralization, each subsidiary is operated as an autonomous profit center.

For the purposes of this exercise, *you* will assume the role of President of the Lawrence Security Bank. Lawrence Security was acquired by Fillmore National last year. Lawrence Security was previously owned by nine small-businessmen, and you have served as president for over seven years. Bob Evans is the executive vice-president.

Lawrence Security employs sixty-two people organized into four major departments: Operations, Loans, Accounting, and the newest department, Marketing. Each department is headed by a Vice-President of the Security Bank. Operations includes main bank tellers, motor banking, and maintenance. The loans department is divided into Mortgage, Auto and Personal, and Commercial. Accounting involves Bookkeeping, Data Processing, and the new Fillmore Management Information System (MIS). Marketing encompasses Customer Relations, New Accounts, and Advertising.

Joan Nolan is Vice-President of Marketing, Ken Baker is Vice-President of Operations, Jim Stevens is Vice-President of Accounting Services, and Larry Pate is Vice-President of Loans.

In the past, your organization has been small enough that you believed formal organization charts were unnecessary. However, your supervisor at Fillmore has asked you to formulate a chart for him. This is your immediate task: Draw the organization chart for Lawrence Security Bank.

(Hints: Use only the information given — no other information is available. When available, use both personal names and titles on your chart.)

Source: "Drawing an Organizational Chart," by Henry P. Sims. Reprinted by permission.

Case Study
Aikiki Electronics

Robert Waseda, President of Aikiki Electronics, contemplated his next organizational decision. He had just chaired a meeting in which a proposal for a new organizational structure was made. This proposal was debated at length, and emotional strains were evident at the conclusion of the meeting. Mr. Waseda wondered whether the "loosely linked, entrepreneurial" management team which he had assembled ten years ago was beginning to pull apart. In twenty-four hours, he had to make his decision.

In 1970, Aikiki Electronics was started in Cupertino, California, as the distributor of semiconductor laser chips manufactured by their parent company in Japan. These chips were unmatched in high quality and cost. Sales accelerated so rapidly that the products were sold out almost two years in advance. Growth averaged about 50 percent per year, although managers believed that the company could have grown even faster had the Japanese office provided more laser chips for sales and distribution.

The success of Aikiki was not unnoticed by United States semiconductor and laser chip manufacturers. The rapid ascent of Japan as the leader in the 64K memory chip had sent tremors of apprehension throughout the high tech community, and there were indications of intensifying lobbying activities in Congress. In an unprecedented move, to avoid any conflict with the United States government, Aikiki Japan decided that Aikiki Electronics be spun off as a separate, independent entity that would operate in the United States. To ensure that the quality of laser chips was maintained, three research and development scientists from Aikiki Japan were hired as part of a six-person management team.

The move was received favorably by Mr. Waseda and the rest of the management team. He said, "We can finally show our manufacturing and marketing capabilities. With or without Japan, we will be able to demonstrate our leadership in the laser chip market."

The team (shown in Exhibit 1) had functioned well. The members met frequently, discussed mutual problems, and often extended business activities to their social gatherings. In the words of Mr. Waseda, "The team was loosely linked and very entrepreneurial."

With soaring demand for laser chips, the company expanded from an 80-person unit to about 800 in 1983. At the advice of a well-known management consulting firm, the company tightened its overall operations: they added levels to the organization, developed a 200-page personnel manual, instituted a budget system, and formalized a review committee for resource allocation purposes. Bill Wynkoop, Senior Vice-President, said, "We enjoyed the fruits of a small, entrepreneurial firm in the past. With greater competition for a maturing product, however, we have to get better organized. I

Exhibit 1
Aikiki: Organizational Structure (1975)

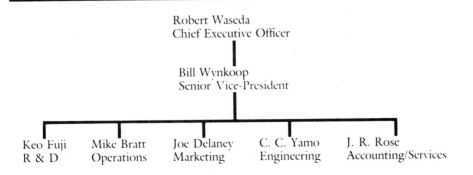

think that the systems we developed have resulted in greater consistency between our corporate goals and organizational activities. We are truly a well-oiled, 'battle-tested' organization."

It was not long, however, before organizational personnel experienced the strains of growing too fast. There were outright delays as proposals had to pass through different management echelons; research and development, engineering, and marketing had become embroiled in a daily battle of forecasts, schedules, and expectations. The situation had deteriorated to such a point that senior managers did not communicate with one another unless they had to. Future meetings were cancelled when two senior executives almost engaged in a fist fight. At this time, Mr. Waseda contracted the services of Richard Rivera, a professor of management in the Northwest. After a series of key interviews and a brief, one-week internship, Dr. Rivera proposed a "network" organization for Aikiki Electronics. Under this system, key units would be organized autonomously (limited to 400 persons), and communications would be structured in terms of a "loose network" (Exhibit 2).

The 400-person limit was done to retain the advantages of a small, flexible organization. Networking was intended to eliminate the almost militaristic chain of command. Control was to be effected by having research and development, engineering, and marketing meet frequently and develop common criteria for evaluation.

The proposal was met with mixed reviews. Keo Fuji, a Japanese-trained engineer with a business degree from Stanford University, said, "The new setup would bring us back to the innovative spirit we experienced when we were starting. I like the fact that we will be able to communicate with others, while retaining our autonomous stature." Mike Bratt of operations said, "In school, I learned about the perils of growth. I'm wondering why we did not realize this earlier. In the past, big companies were in vogue, perhaps because of scale economies. High-tech companies, however, should be small — I like the 400-person limit . . . I think that this is the way to go." The proposal was not endorsed by Bill Wynkoop, Joe Delaney, and J. J. Rose. Speaking for this group, Bill Wynkoop said, "People have to realize that we need control. As our product approaches

Exhibit 2
Proposed Aikiki Organizational Structure

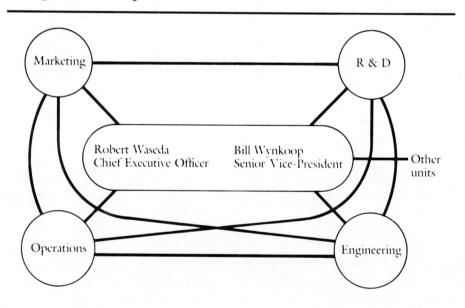

maturity, we will be facing more competition. As much as I enjoyed the early entrepreneurial years, we have to face the facts — our product is maturing and we need a more structured organization to deal with this problem. That's what I learned in my management theory class."

Mr. Waseda knew that the proposal had advantages and disadvantages. His options were: (1) retain the old organization; (2) adapt the proposed organization; or (3) develop a "hybrid" structure. Uncertainty had indeed characterized the activities of Aikiki in the past years. The only thing certain was that he had to make a decision the following day.

Case Question

What recommendation would you make for Mr. Waseda?

Source: This case was prepared by Professor Gerardo R. Ungson, University of Oregon, Eugene, Oregon, 1984.

Last year Jack Byrne's son Patrick gave him a copy of *The Tao of Pooh* by Benjamin Hoff. The book explains the ancient Chinese philosophy of the Tao (literally, the way) through A. A. Milne's beloved children's book character Winnie the Pooh. Patrick went on to study Oriental philosophy and religion at the University of Peking. Though the elder Byrne didn't go quite that far, he did find in Pooh Bear an exemplar of his own ideas about "muddle through" management.

"Pooh is an unlikely leader," says Byrne, "but his very unlikeliness puts him in the leadership role time after time. He's a relaxed realist who never thrusts himself forward, and it's surprising how often it works out." In one tale, for example, a baby kangaroo is in danger of drowning. Other onlookers are nonplussed, but Pooh finds a pole and uses it to save his friend. Though he's none too bright, Pooh Bear is sensible enough to notice an opportunity when he trips over it. Byrne, who doesn't think much of long-range planning or genius managers, believes that's usually enough to spell success.

Milne's Owl character, by contrast, shows very little aptitude for problem solving. He pre-

CHAPTER 6

Managerial Decision Making

tends to be the most educated animal in the forest, but Byrne, with unkind intent, compares him to the professional managers turned out by business schools. "Owl is a loser," Byrne says. "He's always first with a concept but he never makes things work. There are too many knowledge players in this game, and not enough people who know how to create a well-managed organization."

Byrne doesn't admire Rabbit either. Rabbit is an impetuous activist who, in Milne's words, "never let things come to him, but always went and fetched them." Good muddle-through management requires patience.

Basically, what brings Byrne and Pooh and Taoism together is a willingness to face and accept reality. That requires humility, an attribute rare in managers but always evident in Pooh. "I am a Bear," he readily admits, "of No Brain at All."

Source: Reprinted with permission from "Management Lessons from an Unlikely Leader," *Fortune,* September 5, 1983, p. 72.

Chapter Outline

- Problem Solving, Decisions, and Decision Making
- Defining the Problem
- The Individual Decision Maker
- Research on Individual Decision Making
- Group Influence on Decision Making
- Organizational Influences on Decision Making
- Improving Decision Making

Key Terms

- heuristics
- programmability
- rational decision making
- satisficing
- bounded rationality
- behavioral decision making
- normative decision making
- internal representation
- aspiration levels
- anchoring
- availability
- representativeness
- standard operating procedures
- mini-max strategy
- maxi-max strategy
- Hurwicz strategy
- decision trees

Chapter Objectives

After studying Chapter 6 you should be able to

1. Discuss the growing importance of managerial decision making.
2. Contrast rational, satisficing, and political decision making.
3. Explain how people solving problems resemble an information-processing system.
4. Understand some of the major information-processing strategies.
5. Recognize the dangers of the groupthink phenomenon.
6. Discuss some organizational influences on decision making.

Introduction

The 1978 Nobel Laureate Herbert Simon once said, "I shall find it convenient to take mild liberties with the English language by using 'decision making' as though it were synonymous with 'managing' " (1965, p. 53).

Indeed, management consists largely of making decisions. Much of what we have described in previous chapters about choosing which market to compete in, introducing new products, selecting organizational structures, and directing and motivating employees involves decisions that are the bedrock of management.

Bad decisions are costly. Ineffective decision makers spend most of their time dealing with ad hoc decisions and crises, trying to put out "fires" that never should have started. As a future manager, your decisions will affect your career and possibly the careers of others, so it is important that you learn the conceptual and technical skills to make better decisions.

Making good decisions has always been considered important, but there has been more interest recently in improving decision making. The growth of management consulting services, the popularity of decision-making courses, and the awarding of a Nobel Prize for work in decision making attest to growing interest in the subject. And recent research developments have made the study of decision making even more important for the practicing manager.

First, we saw in Chapter 4 that the turbulent environment has led to more complex managerial choices that are not easily resolved by past experience and intuition. For a long time people had faith that economists could predict the future and steer the economy. The past decade brought an abrupt end to that confidence. Predictions about prices, output, and interest rates proved to be embarrassingly off target. It has become clear that previous forecasting methods may no longer hold. The problems extend to businesses' strategic assessment of threats and opportunities. When Texas Instruments first moved into the digital watch market, the strategy was praised by experts who believed that the company's technology would give it a significant advantage over competitors. But the company never won a significant market share and has since deemphasized its role in the digital watch market.

A second reason for the growing importance of decision making is a new technology called decision-support systems, computer programs designed to help managers make better decisions. These systems often require input from managers on the major variables involved in specific problems. A descriptive framework — how managers make decisions — provides the basis for a prescriptive decision — how managers should make decisions. Thus, to improve decision making, the designers of these decision-support systems must understand the process they are attempting to improve: the decision-making process of managers.

A third reason for the growing emphasis on decision making is the discovery that decision makers are prone to several **heuristics** (i.e., "rules-of-thumb") and

Feature 6.1
Texas Instruments's Watch Problems

In the early 1970s, executives at Texas Instruments set a goal: to reach $3 million in annual sales before 1980 through sales of semiconductors, consumer electronics, and microcomputer systems. They reached the goal in 1979, but the record is mixed.

Industry analyst Benjamin Rosen said in his *Rosen Electronics Letter* that the company had only one proven winner, its line of "learning aids" designed to teach spelling, math, and reading, and one possible success, its home computer.

One of the company's problems is its approach to consumer products. Products have been treated as chips, offering the most performance at the lowest prices while paying little attention to fashion, styling, or cultivating of retailers.

A former member of the Texas Instruments digital watch group spoke of company president J. Fred Bucy and Mark Shepherd, its chairman and chief executive: "Fred and Mark kept pushing to slash the price to $9.95. That meant having a plastic case and band. We kept telling them consumers didn't want that, but they wouldn't listen."

Internal problems between the company's functional departments and product-customer centers have also hurt. Competing watch manufacturers, for example, introduced liquid-crystal displays, which are always visible, while Texas Instruments was still making light-emitting diode models, which give the time only after a button is pressed. The functional managers decided the market wasn't large enough to justify designing the new chips that were necessary for the liquid-crystal displays.

Source: "Texas Instruments Regroups," by Bro Uttal, *Fortune,* August 9, 1982, p. 42.

---

biases that impair their decision-making capabilities (Tversky and Kahneman, 1973). Thus, managers may make decisions they do not intend to make and then not recognize this because of systematic errors and biases. Research shows that these biases and heuristics are used by novices and experts alike in solving problems. To improve decision making, it is imperative to carefully examine the circumstances surrounding these biases and heuristics.

In this chapter we will examine the decision-making process and present selected research findings on how individuals make decisions in group and organizational contexts. First we will define problem solving and its relationship to decision making. By discussing attributes of a problem, we will relate problems to managerial decision making. Then we will discuss the contributions made by various schools of thought — human problem solving, behavioral decision making, and cognitive psychology — to defining how individuals make decisions. We will then examine group and organizational influences on individual decision making. A short discussion of improving managerial decision making on the individual, group, and organizational levels concludes this chapter.

Problem Solving, Decisions, and Decision Making

Many people use the terms *decision making* and *problem solving* interchangeably. Indeed, the differences between them tend to be more stylistic than substantive. A *problem* generally refers to the difference between an actual and a desired situation (Huber, 1980). For example, if you have to take four courses in a term to graduate and you discover that there are only three courses available, you have a problem. The department head might see the need to offer four courses but has enough faculty members to offer only three courses. In both cases a *gap* exists between what is desired and what is available. Problem solving is concerned with bridging this gap.

Decisions or choices can be thought of as specific and discrete actions taken to close this gap. You might decide, for example, to see the department head about the problem. If the outcome of this meeting were unsatisfactory, you might decide to petition your case to the proper parties. Similarly, the department head faces alternatives in solving his or her problem. One is to take no action; another is to increase the number of students for the three sections offered; a third is to obtain funds for a fourth course. Any ensuing action may be considered a *decision* on his or her part.

Decision making has been described as a process through which a decision or choice is made (Huber, 1980, p. 9). In making decisions we normally attend to the problem or task at hand and pay little attention to our manner of problem solving. If we were more attentive, we would see that decision making unfolds in a manner represented by the sequence shown in Figure 6.1.

It is generally agreed that the decision-making process involves the definition of the problem, the diagnosis of this problem, the development of alternate solutions, the selection of the best alternative, and implementation of the alternative. In practice the process can be much more complicated, with much backtracking. The process itself may even be reversed; that is, a solution is decided on and a search for a problem takes place. We will not get involved in such intricacies at this point. Instead we will accept the decision-making process just described and illustrate how it becomes complicated, to resemble actual managerial decision making.

The decision-making process has three fundamental elements, the *problem* itself, the *individual* faced with the problem, and the *context* in which the problem is to be solved by the individual. Herbert Simon (1965) has said, "Just as you need both sides of a pair of scissors to cut paper, you need to understand the elements of the tasks and those of the problem solver in order to understand problem solving." Simon was describing individuals solving puzzles and simple algebraic problems. To extend his observations to managerial problem solving, we need to add a third element to Simon's theory, the context in which the problem is solved. Managerial decision making normally occurs in groups and in organizational settings such as departments, committees, and quality-control groups. As a result, the goals, aspirations, and perceived reward structures of the

Figure 6.1
A Decision-Making Process

STAGE OF DECISION MAKING	PROBLEM AS FACED BY THE STUDENT	PROBLEM AS FACED BY THE DEPARTMENT HEAD
Problem definition	I need four courses in order to graduate, but I can take only three courses.	I need to offer four courses, but in view of present faculty load, I can offer only three.
Problem diagnosis	I need to graduate, but this will not be possible unless a new course is offered.	If I don't find a way to get a new course, some seniors will not be able to graduate.
Generation of alternate solutions	Should I talk to the department head? Should I petition my case to an appropriate committee? Should I try to substitute another course?	Should I talk to the dean? If I get funds, can I offer them to existing faculty, or should I hire from the outside?
Carrying out of the decision or choice	I will talk to the department head. If this does not work, I will petition.	I will talk to the dean and contact possible instructors.
Evaluation	Because I got into a new course, I regard my problem satisfactorily solved.	The dean came up with the funds to hire a new instructor. I consider the problem satisfactorily solved.

group are bound to affect the decision-making process. Politics and organizational structure are also likely to affect decision making at the organizational level. To gain a good understanding of decision making, it is essential to master the three elements: the problem, the individual, and the context.

Defining the Problem

Problems can be described in many ways: easy or complex, well defined or ill defined, well structured or ill structured. Balancing your checkbook against the bank's statements can be a relatively easy task if you faithfully record each transaction. But if you discover a significant discrepancy, you may be faced with a more complex problem: Did I record every transaction? Could the bank have made the error? If you visit your friendly banker only to find out that a new computer installation might have affected your banking transactions, you are now faced with an ill-structured problem. If the banker finally confesses that he does not know what went on, you have an ill-defined problem on your hands. By retracing this process we can make some conclusions on the attributes that define the nature of problems and problem solving (Fig. 6.2).

Problem-Related Information

In well-structured and well-defined problems, all information needed to solve the problem is complete, explicit, and clear. In other words, the initial and the desired states are clear and the programs or processes, i.e., **transformational rules,** needed to move from the initial to intermediate and then to the final, desired state are complete. Lack of clarity or incomplete information can easily transform an easy problem into a very difficult one. The game of chess is comprehensible only if you understand the rules.

Figure 6.2
Types of Problems and Their Attributes

| | TYPE OF PROBLEM | | |
ATTRIBUTE	*Simple and Well-Structured*	*Moderately Complex and Ill-Structured*	*Ill-Defined*
Completeness of problem-related information	Complete, specific, and clear	Incomplete, not as specific, and unclear	Incomplete; problem solver has to define goals, etc.
Number of informational items	Small to large	Moderate	Large
Programmability of outcomes and solutions	Can be programmed	Multiprograms for multiple solutions	Very difficult to program
Conditions defining decisional status	Certainty	Risk and uncertainty	Uncertainty
Number of decision makers	Single or dyad	Single, dyad, groups	Single, dyad, groups, and organizational

Number of Informational Items. Some problems, such as puzzles and board games, require relatively few informational items to solve. In contrast, problems in business and management generally have a large number of informational items. Calculating the internal rate of return for an investment when there are alternate ways of borrowing and paying back the money, for example, involves a large number of informational items. As a general rule, the more informational items, the more complex the problem. In the next sections we will specifically refer to the number of informational items in problems with multiple attributes.

Programmability of Outcomes and Solutions. Programmability refers to the relative ease with which transformational rules defining the solution to the problem can be specified. Solving an arithmetic problem, such as $12 + 8 = 20$, involves a simple program, $(10 + 2) + 8 \rightarrow 10 + (2 + 8) \rightarrow 10 + 10 = 20$. The game of chess, however, has a fairly complex program. In highly complex or ill-structured problems, the transformational rule might not even be specified. For example, the problem of introducing Sears dishwashers to Japan involves formulating complex market-entry strategies that are not defined at the start of the problem solving.

Problems that have more than one desirable outcome or solution are more difficult to program than those with single solutions. Linear programming models, for example, may involve situations that lead to more than one feasible and optimal solution.

Conditions Defining Decisional Status. Decision theorists have specified conditions under which the outcomes of decisions can be considered certain, risky, or uncertain (Raiffa, 1968). *Certainty* refers to the state of knowledge in which there is no question or equivocality about the outcome. In a chess game, for example, having your king checkmated is a virtual loss. *Risk* refers to the state of knowledge in which outcomes are not certain but can be represented in terms of probabilities. In flipping a coin you cannot be certain whether you will get heads or tails, but your chances of estimating correctly are 50 percent. *Uncertainty* refers to states of knowledge in which outcomes are not known and cannot be readily represented in terms of probabilities. For example, it is difficult to be certain that a presidential incumbent will run for reelection and that he will win the national elections. Generally speaking, ill-structured or ill-defined problems require decisions under uncertain conditions.

Single or Multiple Decision Makers. Typically, solving a problem alone is less complicated than solving the problem with others. Although group problem solving has led to better solutions, there is inevitably some conflict among the persons involved. The presence of different decision makers may also require compromises that may not meet the best interests of all parties.

Problem Situations
in Organizational Settings

Thompson (1967) has suggested that decision issues always have two major dimensions, beliefs about the relation of causes and effects and preferences about possible outcomes. Juxtaposing these two dimensions leads to a matrix that characterizes the types of idealized problem situations faced by managers in organizational settings (Fig. 6.3).

Thompson has suggested a strategy for resolving each particular situation. Well-structured problems occur when there is certainty about cause-and-effect relationships and there are preferences about possible outcomes. After repeated use, for example, the efficiency of machines with predetermined inputs can be fairly closely estimated. Thompson has called the strategy needed in this situation "computational" because the complexity of the problem centers on the amount of information that needs to be processed under repeated applications.

Ill-defined problems are likely to occur in situations in which there is disagreement on desired outcomes and cause-and-effect relationships are uncertain. This is a trying and rather unstable condition. Thompson perhaps jokingly

Figure 6.3
Problem Situations in Organizations

		Preferences Regarding Possible Outcomes	
		Certain	Uncertain
Beliefs about Cause-and-Effect Relations	Certain	Well-structured problems (example: machine applications; repeated purchase decisions) Strategy: Computational	Moderately-complex problems (example: new product applications) Strategy: Compromise
	Uncertain	Moderately-complex problems (example: hiring decisions; strategic decisions) Strategy: Judgmental	Ill-defined problems (example: strategic decisions in very uncertain environments) Strategy: Inspirational

Source: Thompson, 1967, p. 134. Adapted by permission.

suggested that the appropriate strategy for this particular situation is one of divine guidance or "inspiration." With better-grounded decision making, however, it is possible to develop a more solid basis for such inspiration.

The other two cells, in which outcome preferences are clear but cause-and-effect relationships are not, or the reverse, might characterize problem situations described earlier as moderately complex and ill-structured. Thompson has suggested the use of "judgmental" and "compromise" strategies for these situations. Future managers need to be well acquainted with these different situations and with how they can be adequately represented and resolved. The type of solution will depend largely on the type of individual solving the problem. We thus turn our attention to the second element in the decision-making process: the individual.

The Individual Decision Maker

It has become fashionable to describe people in terms of the particular orientations or models they use in decision making. The decision-making process, as well as methods of searching for information, hinge on these particular orientations and models.

Rational Decision Making

Prior to Simon's work (1947), the prevailing model of decision making described a **rational decision maker,** one assumed to have complete knowledge of all the relevant aspects of his or her environment, a well-organized and stable system of preferences, and almost infinite computational skills. Cast against our decision-making process, a rational person would

1. know the components of the problem
2. be able to diagnose the problem in accordance with well-established values and preferences
3. be able to plot all possible consequences of alternate solutions
4. be able to form a coherent judgment based on the merits of each alternate solution
5. select the alternative most likely to maximize his or her values and preferences

There is little evidence that people act and make decisions on this basis. In fact, this model is normally represented as the ideal, deviations from which have been used to study human decision making. Much of the work of March and Simon (1958) has been devoted to studying the limits of rationality in most people. Their theory forms the basis for the next model of individual decision making we will discuss.

Satisficing Decision Making

Simon (1947) criticized the rational model for failing to take into account the cognitive limitations of individuals. Incomplete knowledge, an unstable system of preferences, and limited computational skill seem to be characteristic of human problem solvers. Simon considered the problems in acquiring and utilizing information to result from limitations on the part of the problem solver as well as the external environment. He added that simplification tendencies, such as rule-of-thumb guidelines and heuristics, arise from the inability of problems solvers to consider all aspects of the problem.

According to Simon individuals are not rational, as most economists believed, but **intendedly rational,** or seeking to be rational in the face of incomplete information and limited computational abilities. In intendedly rational behavior, a person attempts to construct a simplified model of the real situation in order to deal with it. Within these limits the individual behaves rationally, demonstrating what is termed **bounded rationality.** In the terms of our decision-making process, the **satisficing decision maker** would

1. Settle for the most acceptable solution,
2. Not review all possible alternate solutions but, rather, use heuristics to cut down the search,
3. Form a coherent judgment based on limited alternatives,
4. Select not the alternative that is the best but one that is good enough.

There are a number of examples of bounded rationality in everyday life. Faced with great amounts of information, a customer choosing a pocket calculator will intentionally limit his or her search criteria to a few important factors, such as price, size, and functions. Instead of solving problems simultaneously, managers split them into small parts and solve the parts sequentially. Bounded rationality represents a trade-off between what economists and decision theorists call optionality, and the ease of decision making afforded by limited search and calculating efforts. In effect, people do not really optimize but **satisfice;** that is, they select the most acceptable solution.

Political Decision Making

The political model is characterized in Allison's analysis (1971) of the Cuban missile crisis. In contrast to the satisficing orientation, which is largely based on the limited cognitive processing capabilities of decision makers, the political orientation emphasizes the nature of power underlying the decision situation. Thus, a decision maker is influenced by the parochial interests of other parties affected by the decision, by the power of parties involved in the decision, and by explicit and implicit rules of conduct in resolving the problem.

In the context of the decision-making process we described earlier, the **political decision maker** would

1. Diagnose the problem in terms of the preferences, stands, and power of the other parties affected by the decision,
2. Assess the consequences of various alternatives in terms of their acceptance or resistance by other parties,
3. Make a judgment that represents some compromise among competing interests,
4. Implement the decision in a manner that recognizes the stakes and political position of each of the parties affected.

The political orientation emphasizes the diversity of goals and interests. This diversity reflects the pluralistic nature of organizations, reflected in organizational subunits, coalitions, and subcultures with different if not conflicting interests. Actions and decisions therefore result from bargaining and compromise, units with the greatest power receiving the greatest rewards.

The Bendix Case

The three models of individual decision making provide different perspectives for understanding decision making in organizations. A recent controversial event was the move by Bendix Corporation Chairman William Agee to acquire Martin Marietta Corporation, regarded as one of the country's fastest-growing defense contractors. Some observers would hold that the move was made to enhance Bendix's long-time strategy of diversifying from automotive products to defense-oriented goods. If so, it can be argued that the move was prompted by rational considerations consistent with rational decision making. Others have pointed out, however, that the obstinacy of the Marietta board toward this merger made it a poor choice for Bendix. Thus, Marietta might not have represented the optimal or best choice for Bendix but, rather, a choice that was considered good enough given the circumstances. Such a decision would be consistent with the satisficing orientation.

Finally, the pattern of events, which included Marietta's making a counterproposal to buy Bendix and seeking the aid of United Technologies, suggests that a fierce political struggle was going on among Agee, Martin Marietta's board of directors, and Harry Gray of United Technologies. These events can be explained by the political orientation.

All the models are helpful in illuminating the various phases of a decision. Regardless of the differences among the models, it is clear that understanding how people make decisions is crucial to appreciating managerial actions.

Research on Individual Decision Making

Individual decision making has been studied by researchers in a variety of disciplines: psychologists, economists, sociologists, mathematicians, and organizational theorists. Much of the discussion that follows emphasizes research on

Feature 6.2
Battles in the Bendix War

It was as if the law of the jungle had taken over the board room — eat or be eaten. Bendix tried to take over Martin Marietta. Martin Marietta spun around and went after Bendix. United Technologies stepped in to help Martin Marietta. Finally, Allied Corporation took over Bendix.

The affair all started conventionally enough. Bendix Chairman William Agee had been divesting his company's businesses to build up cash for future acquisitions. In August 1982, Bendix announced its offer to buy 45 percent of Martin Marietta's stock at $43 a share. Within days, Marietta's board decided it would be better to merge on their own terms, and announced that the company would buy up to 50.3 percent of Bendix at $75 a share.

Legal quirks meant the two companies could take control of each other simultaneously, a move that would create a monstrous corporate mutant with a $2.7 billion debt load on a $1.1 billion equity base. "It would not be a merger but an implosion of two companies," said one observer. The idea was so unthinkable that some people thought Marietta was bluffing.

In stepped Harry Gray, president of United Technologies and a friend of Marietta's President Thomas Pownall. The two men worked out an agreement to carve up Bendix, and Gray announced a backstop offer that matched Marietta's cash price.

In a last-ditch effort to convince Agee of their resolve, Marietta directors waived all but two conditions of their tender offer. They agreed to drop their bid if Agee walked away or if Bendix shareholders blocked Marietta. No deals. The sale went ahead. Bendix wound up with 70 percent of Marietta's stock. And then it was Marietta's turn.

With Marietta set to buy Bendix at midnight, Agee pulled Allied Corporation out of the hat. He hastily asked his board of directors to merge with Allied. Four board members resigned in dismay, but the merger went through and by nightfall Allied's brokers were ready to negotiate with Marietta for its Bendix stock. Marietta bought its independence.

Source: "Behind the Lines in the Bendix War," by Roy Rowan and Thomas Moore, *Fortune,* October 18, 1982, pp. 157–161.

behavioral decision making, or how people make decisions, rather than **normative decision making,** or how people should make decisions. The research findings of three schools are discussed: human problem solving, behavioral decision making, and cognitive psychology. The three schools provide different but complementary profiles of how individuals solve problems and make decisions.

Human Problem Solving

In their investigation of human problem solving in tasks such as chess, puzzles, and logic, Newell and Simon (1972) drew some conclusions about the characteristics of problem-solving behavior. One key premise of these researchers was that when solving problems individuals resemble an information-processing system (Fig. 6.4). The external environment is represented by the problem, which in their research consisted of tasks such as puzzles, algebraic problems, and cryptarithmetic (see question 5, p. 196). They found that the problem is encoded by the individual, who develops an internal representation of the problem called the task environment. The concept of **internal representation** is important for two reasons. First, the individual may represent the problem differently from the way he or she is instructed. We see this behavior often in cases in which instructions are not explained properly, causing the individual to misrepresent the problem. Second, different individuals may have different internal representations of the same problem. In such cases it is important to consider and specify individual differences. All these factors have a strong bearing on the subject of problem solving. It is important that the processes by which internal representations are made are well understood.

From this perspective, Simon and his associates presented several findings on how individuals solve problems and make decisions:

1. *Problem solvers are serial processors.* In essence, people solve problems by factoring and sequencing informational inputs one at a time. There is not much

Figure 6.4
Individual Problem Solving Represented as an Information-Processing System

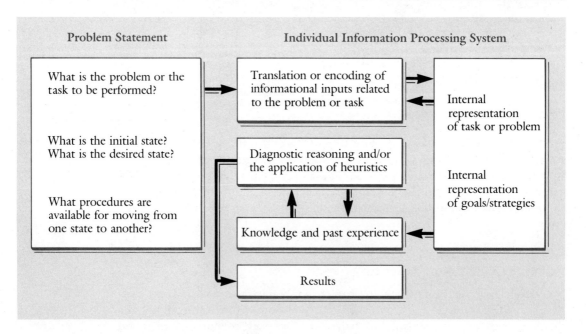

Source: Newell and Simon, 1972.

evidence that people attend to multiple items simultaneously when solving problems.

2. *Problem solvers use a number of heuristic methods to cut down highly selective searches and reduce enormous problems.* Various heuristic techniques were used in solving the cryptarithmetic problems, such as initially processing those columns that are most constrained. Managers use a number of such techniques to resolve complex problems. For example, a current ratio of two to one (assets/liabilities) often is considered a good gauge of the solvency of any particular firm. Also, the payoff criterion, or the length of time it takes for an investment to be paid off, often is preferred to more complex criteria because of its simplicity.

3. *Problem solvers make extensive use of previous experience and* **aspiration levels** *to solve present problems.* In solving present problems, people frequently rely on previous solutions and experiences. These experiences can be structured in terms of standard operating procedures. But although standard operating procedures may be appropriate for recurring and routine problems, they may not lead to good solutions for new and novel problems. Some implications of this finding will be discussed fully in the section dealing with organizational decision making.

Behavioral Decision Making: Modeling Human Judgment and Choice

In contrast to Simon's research, which developed the details of successive stages in decision making, behavioral decision researchers such as Coombs (1964), Dawes (1964), Tversky (1972), and Einhorn (1970) developed mathematical representations of the human judgmental process. Most of the problem-solving behavior they studied involved multiattributional problems, that is, problems with a number of well-defined characteristics or cues. Examples of these problems include:

- Evaluating job applicants for positions within an organization on the basis of college scores, recommendation letters, previous work experience, personality traits, and other criteria
- Selecting patented innovations for financial support, involving consideration of technical merit, feasibility, economic potential, and the track record of the innovator
- Determining which college football players would succeed in professional football, a process that considers the players' football skills, attitudes, league competition, and athletic ability

These problems involve assessing multiple attributes or cues. The assessment must translate these attributes into numerical scores in a way that makes them the most useful to the problem solver. Before reading further, you should conduct a self-experiment to see how you would solve the exercises presented in the Discussion Questions (questions 5–7, pp. 196–197). Pay close attention to your thought processes or the successive steps in solving the problems. After doing so, mentally respond to the following questions: Did you use *all* the cues? Did you weigh all the cues equally? If not, why?

In examining a number of problem solvers, behavioral decision theorists have come up with several information-processing strategies or models. These models assess the manner in which cues are weighted and combined.

Compensatory Processing, or the Linear Additive Model. In compensatory processing the individual is assumed to have assimilated cues along important dimensions. Cues can then be weighted equally or differentially. In using a weighted scheme an individual employs a summation or an averaging procedure to arrive at an *overall utility measure* for each alternative. Given this output, the common assumption in keeping with rational behavior is that the alternative with the highest overall utility measure will be selected.

Noncompensatory Processing. In compensatory processing, all the cues are utilized in such a way that the relative attractiveness of one cue compensates for the relative unattractiveness of another. For example, having a grade point average of 2.0 might still get you into business school if you had a (compensating) Graduate Management Admission Test score in the 99th percentile. In noncompensatory processing, only selected scores are used depending on the needs of the situation and the nature of other available cues. For example, a football team might select a person with the highest punting average and disregard other characteristics, such as intelligence, overall athletic ability, and individual motivation.

Conjunctive Processing. In this type of processing, an individual sets up cut-off points and rejects any alternative that falls below these points. For example, if a draftee for aerospace flights fails to meet the 20/20 eyesight requirement, he or she is automatically rejected regardless of other qualifications.

Disjunctive Processing. An individual using this strategy sets up cut-off points and accepts for further consideration alternatives that surpass these points. Typically, the alternative that scores highest on a given criterion is selected. For example, in drafting a potential football kicker, the one selected is the one who can accurately kick the ball the farthest most consistently.

Lexicographic Processing. According to this strategy, the individual rank orders the judgmental dimensions according to their relative importance and then evaluates all the alternatives against the most important judgmental dimension. The alternatives are then evaluated against the second most important cue. The same selection procedure is used until a choice is made. In buying a calculator, for example, a price of less than $15 may be considered the most crucial dimension. All calculators costing more than $15 are therefore eliminated. The rest are then examined against the next most crucial dimension, the number of mathematical functions. The same procedure is used until a selection is made.

Although the approach pursued by behavioral theorists differs significantly from the one used by Simon, the resulting picture of the problem solver is consistent with Simon's. First, in solving problems the individual is intendedly rational as he or she attends to a set of rules that leads to an acceptable choice or outcome. In addition, individuals seldom include *all* the possible cues or judgmental dimensions in a decision. Consistent with the argument of bonded rationality, individuals tend to develop a subset of cues and dimensions and employ finite rules that lead to resolution.

Studies of consumer behavior (Wright, 1975; Jacoby, 1975) have yielded a growing body of evidence that simplification strategies — conjunctive, disjunctive, and lexicographic — are extensively used in choice decisions. As a result, some studies in advertising have focused on the effective utilization of a few cues, rather than a large number of cues (Jacoby, 1975).

Cognitive Psychology: Heuristics and Biases

In the previous section we established that a person applies strain-reducing strategies to compensate for limited memory, attention, and reasoning abilities. In this section we will discuss the ramifications of this technique. Some researchers, notably Amos Tversky and Daniel Kahneman (1974), uncovered the use of systematic biases and heuristics by problem solvers that made their actions inconsistent with their true preferences and beliefs. The heuristics and biases explored arose out of having individuals solve well-structured probability statements and are relatively primitive and simple. These heuristics and biases, however, could significantly affect decisions made in broader situations, such as managerial or public policy decisions and even the declaration of war.

The Availability Heuristic.   When people are asked to judge the relative frequency or the likelihood of events, they are often influenced by events that are easy to imagine or to recall. Because more recent and frequent events are generally easier to recall, they become the basis for judging frequency and probability. Availability, however, is subject to factors unrelated to likelihood, such as ease of recall, recency, salience, and vividness, and thus relying on it may lead to systematic errors in judgment.

The problem used by Tversky and Kahneman (1974) to illustrate the **availability** heuristic was: Is the likelihood of an English word starting with the letter *R* greater or less than the likelihood of a word with *R* as its third letter? Most subjects responded that words starting with R are more common than words in which R is the third letter, yet surveys indicate that the opposite is the case. The difficulty arises from the inappropriate application of the availability heuristic. It is much easier to remember words that start with R *(really, remorse, recall, remember . . .)* than words with R as the third letter *(derail, care, street . . .).*

Availability bias is reflected in subsequent studies showing that people tend to overestimate the risks of nuclear war or the probable occurrence of well-publicized dangers such as botulism, tornadoes, and motor vehicle accidents but to underestimate the probabilities of less dramatic events such as asthma, diabetes, and emphysema (Lichtenstein, Slovic, Fischhoff, Layman, and Combs, 1976).

The Representativeness Heuristic. In making choices, people can rely on intuitive predictions and on normative principles of statistical prediction. The latter concept refers to *base rates,* which summarize what we know prior to receiving information or evidence about the case at hand. Kahneman and Tversky (1973) have shown that people seem to rely exclusively on specific information and neglect base rates. In effect, people attempt to match prediction with impression.

The problem Kahneman and Tversky used to illustrate the **representativeness** heuristic was: We have a friend who is a professor. He is rather shy, he likes to cook, and he is small in stature. Which of the following is his field: international studies or business administration? Most people matched the field of study with their impressions of the thumbnail description presented in the problem. No consideration was given to base rates or prior probabilities of international studies as opposed to business administration, that is, the fact that the likelihood of the professor being in business administration was greater than the likelihood of his being in international studies.

Surprisingly, the representative heuristic was observed in naive subjects as well as in those with statistical training. The statistically trained subjects used base rate information when no other information was given, yet when exposed to sketchy personality traits, which they recognized as invalid, they were unable to integrate their impressions with considerations of prior probabilities. Thus a case can be made that their judgments did not reflect their underlying beliefs (Slovic, 1976).

Anchoring Heuristic. In making decisions, people reduce cognitive strain by forming a *natural starting judgment* or anchor on the basis of limited information. The anchor is then adjusted to accommodate new information. Because this adjustment process is crude, its use often leads to disproportionate errors.

The problem used by Lichtenstein, Fischhoff, and Phillips (1977) to illustrate the **anchoring** heuristic was: How many foreign cars were imported into the United States in 1968? (1) Make a high estimate such that you feel the true answer would *exceed* your estimate only once in 100 times. (2) Make a low estimate such that you feel the true answer would be *below* this estimate only once in 100 times. Thus, subjects were asked to estimate a numerical value and to place upper and lower bounds so that the true value would fall between these bounds 98 percent of the time. Results indicated that the subjects set the bounds too narrowly. The true value exceeded the bounds 50 percent of the time! The bias existed even when the subjects were told that their initial confidence bounds were too narrow. Thus, when an initial anchor is reached, little can be done to correct it by way of process.

Overconfidence Bias. In the previous example it was noted that true value exceeded the bounds 50 percent of the time. These cases are referred to as *surprises*. The proportion of such surprises is related to the confidence a problem solver has in his or her ability to make correct predictions. Take the case of two salesmen attempting to forecast car sales for the next year. One estimates that there is only one chance in 100 that the firm will sell fewer than 5,000 cars and a probability of 99 percent that the firm will sell fewer than 50,000. The other estimates that there is one chance in 100 that the firm will sell fewer than 7,500 cars and a probability of 99 percent that the firm will sell fewer than 30,000. The second salesman has a narrower confidence interval, and this reflects a greater confidence on his part in his ability to predict car sales correctly.

Let us assume that actual sales at the end of the forecasted year were 35,000. This number would be a surprise for the second salesman but not for the first salesman. If this is reflective of the type of predictions made by the second salesman over a period of time or over a series of decisions, we would say that he is overconfident about his decision-making abilities.

Studying subjects in a variety of tasks, Fischhoff, Slovic, and Lichtenstein (1977) observed extreme overconfidence in people judging the odds that their answers to general questions were correct. There is also evidence that the degree of overconfidence increases with ignorance. Kahneman and Tversky (1979) found a 28 percent surprise rate in assessments of the air distance between New Delhi and Peking, with only 15 percent surprises for assessments of the distance between London and Tel Aviv. The two distances in fact are approximately equal. These researchers explained that overconfidence arises when people become insensitive to the quality of evidence, such as the availability of good information, and express high confidence in information based on unreliable data, such as small samples.

These findings present yet another picture of the individual problem solver. Some serious consequences arise from natural attempts to reduce cognitive-straining activities. Heuristics serve many useful purposes. If applied correctly, they produce more correct inferences than erroneous ones and enable managers to pursue activities with reasonable expenditures of time and effort. But if applied inappropriately, they can lead to significant biases and errors. "Forewarned is forearmed" is one popular maxim that may apply to this situation. As future managers, your task is to recognize the conditions that give rise to such errors and correct them whenever you can.

Group Influence on Decision Making

Advantages and Disadvantages of Group Decision Making

Much of the decision making in organizations takes place in groups: committees, panels, task forces, and special assignment teams. Working in groups can be helpful in many ways. First, in light of our previous discussion of the cognitive limitations of individuals, we can argue that different people may bring in ideas that will supplement those of others in a collaborative effort. There is enough evidence from laboratory studies and investigations to show that groups perform better than individuals on given tasks (Leavitt, 1975). Another reason for working in groups is that group members quite frequently will take part in implementing solutions decided by the group. Involving the appropriate people in the decision increases the likelihood of their support in the implementation. The Japanese system of *ringi-sei* provides a good example of how group decision making can be effective for all participating group members.

But working in groups has its drawbacks. First, the time consumed in group decision making normally is greater than the time it takes a person to solve the problem alone. Second, people with strong personalities may dominate group meetings, suppressing individual initiative. The third danger is that processes within the group may lead group members to delusions of infallibility and subsequent bad decisions. This pattern has been defined as groupthink (Janis, 1972) and will be discussed more closely.

The Groupthink Phenomenon

Studying mostly foreign policy decisions, Irving Janis (1972) formulated a theory that fiascoes may be explained by what he calls **groupthink,** or the "psychological drive for consensus at any cost that suppresses dissent and the appraisal of alternatives in cohesive decision making" (p. 9).

Janis (1972, p. 10) lists six major defects in group decision making that may result from groupthink:

1. The group's discussion is limited to a few alternatives (often only two) without the survey of the full range of options.

2. The group fails to reexamine the course of action initially preferred by the majority of members from the standpoint of nonobvious risks and drawbacks that had not been considered when it was originally evaluated.

3. The members neglect courses of action initially evaluated as unsatisfactory by the majority of the group.

4. Members make little or no attempt to obtain information from experts who can supply sound estimates of losses and gains to be expected from alternate courses of action.

5. Selective bias is shown in the way the group reacts to factual information and relevant judgments from experts, the mass media, and outside critics.

6. Members spend little time deliberating about how the chosen policy might be hindered by bureaucratic inertia, sabotaged by political opponents, or temporarily derailed by the common accidents that happen to the best-laid plans. Consequently, no contingency plans are formulated.

Janis discusses these deficiencies in the context of the Bay of Pigs invasion in 1961. The decision-making process involving President John F. Kennedy and his selected cabinet members was characterized by major miscalculations and shaky assumptions, enhanced by the groupthink phenomenon. In an effort to preserve what was thought to be the group's goal, different members of Kennedy's cabinet contributed, perhaps inadvertently, to suppressing doubts and reservations brought up by any member of the group. Janis cites the following symptoms of groupthink:

1. *Illusion of invulnerability.* Essentially, the members believed that if Kennedy was leading the group, nothing could go wrong.

2. *Illusion of unanimity.* Meetings were held in an atmosphere of assumed consensus on the Central Intelligence Agency plan.

3. *Suppression of personal doubts.* In meeting, doubts were entertained but never really discussed in detail. Eventually some members simply decided not to present their reservations to the group.

4. *Self-appointed mindguards.* Certain people placed pressure on other members whose points of view were different from theirs.

5. *Docility fostered by suave leadership.* President Kennedy's style of leadership made it difficult for group members to raise critical questions.

6. *Taboo against antagonizing valuable new members.* There was an informal group norm that one should not voice damaging criticisms of new members brought in as advisers to the Central Intelligence Agency plan.

Groups enhance or limit decision making. Groupthink illustrates ways in which groups impair the decision-making process. Future managers need to recognize the symptoms of groupthink, so we have provided guidelines for overcoming groupthink in the last section of this chapter. In the next section we will discuss some organizational influences on decision making. In doing so we will have delineated the full context in which managerial decisions are made.

Organizational Influences on Decision Making

One of our colleagues told a story about a consulting experience of interest to people concerned with managerial decision making. After a careful analysis of the client firm's external environment and forecasting procedures, he was able to develop a fail-safe method of economic forecasting, a method that would considerably improve the strategic planning of the firm. During the presentation, however, the vice-president of marketing and his staff voiced loud objections. The proposal was eventually rejected. In the postmortem session, the vice-president of marketing took him aside and confided, "I really liked your stuff. In fact, it is an excellent idea. But I had to kill it. Otherwise, those people in the meeting would have asked why I did not develop it, if it was so good."

Our colleague was introduced, perhaps rather rudely, to the realities of decision making in organizations. Organizational decision making is much more complex than individual and group decision making, in part because of the shifting multiple-goal coalitions of managers, workers, functional or staff specialists, and unions. All have some interest in the organization but have different goals, preferences, and beliefs about what should be done. This disagreement makes the task of reaching effective decisions more difficult, if not more challenging. In this section we will summarize some characteristics of organizations that facilitate or impede decision making. Recognizing these characteristics constitutes the first step in developing your skills as a complete decision maker.

Organizational Politics

Cyert and March (1963) have described an organization as a coalition of conflicting interests. The classic example is the uneasy relationship among marketing, production, and finance. The prime objective of marketing is to ensure that products are available when needed, which may at times necessitate quick response to customer orders. In contrast, it is in the best interests of production to cut down on set-up costs by setting long-term, predetermined schedules. Overall, the finance department has to ensure that all costs are within a specified budget. It is not hard to imagine how tempers can flare and get out of control in the event of an unprogrammed but massive demand for the product.

Organizations follow various procedures to maintain this uneasy alliance. First, conflict is never really resolved. Instead, each department deals with one set of problems, which it solves rationally within its bounds. If conflict arises between departments, the problem is solved not in one grand stroke but through a *sequential attention to goals*. An effort is made first to "smooth production," then to move in sequence to "smooth customer complaints," and so on. Still another approach is to accept a certain level of decision, satisfice, rather than try to make an optimal decision.

Problemistic Search and Uncertainty Avoidance

In organizations, search is not regular or programmed ("Every month we will collect competitor information.") but, rather, simple-minded and problem oriented. The occurrence of a problem ("Sales are falling.") prompts the search for a solution, but one that is anchored to previous solutions ("Jones must be spending more again."). Sometimes a solution ("Let's cut Jones's budget.") may induce a search for a problem ("Because sales are falling . . ."). Many of these decisions fall within the types of heuristics and judgmental biases discussed earlier. Because of the seemingly irrational way in which problems are defined, some theorists (March and Olsen, 1976) have referred to decisional processes in organizations as resembling a "garbage can model," in which solutions are almost randomly matched with problems.

Standard Operating Procedures

When faced with a recurring problem, organizations attempt to develop standardized responses called **standard operating procedures (SOPs).** Organizations also attempt to use existing SOPs to solve new problems. Only if these fail will they develop revised SOPs to deal with the new situations.

Because standard operating procedures are developed for standard scenarios, they are often ill suited to more novel problems. Allison (1971) provides an example in the December 7, 1941, attack on Pearl Harbor. When General Short was advised on November 27 to expect "hostile activities," which meant an external invasion, this was interpreted as a standard sabotage warning. Army Intelligence implemented SOPs for counterespionage instead of developing new procedures for an armed invasion.

Thus, organizational decision making draws on previous experience and organizational structure and processes. It should be recognized that organizational structure and processes are not always dysfunctional for decision making. In fact, for routine problems SOPs are quite appropriate and very efficient. Dysfunctionalities often occur when organizational decision makers face new problems, because attempts are made to solve these problems by forcing them to fit within the firm's limited problem-solving repertoire.

Improving Decision Making

We have discussed individual decision making in various contexts. Now let us turn to some of the recommendations for improving decision making. This last section will cover the improvement of decision making at three levels: individual, group, and organizational.

Improving Individual Decision Making

Because interest in individual heuristics and biases is so recent, procedures for correcting systematic biases are still rudimentary. We can examine some general guidelines, however, based on the work of Kahneman and Tversky (1979), Slovic (1976), and Nisbett and Ross (1980).

**Feature 6.3
Frustrations for Technologists**

American industry does not give engineers recognition and rewards equal to the contributions they make and their importance to business success, according to Ray Stata, president of Analog Devices Inc.

Traditional hierarchical organizational structures do not serve the needs of a knowledge-intensive company, he added. "Professional managers make most decisions, yet key technical professionals often have the best knowledge and experience regarding technology and products. The sharp edge of innovation can be dulled when important decisions have to be justified to managers and committees who do not understand the underlying issues."

Worse than that, Stata said, hard-driving engineers can be so frustrated by slow, complicated decision processes, which are often political in nature, that they may leave for a start-up environment in which their opinions are more important. Or if they stay with the larger company, they may move into management, where they can have more influence on decisions.

"We must find ways for very talented and experienced technologists to be recognized and rewarded and to extend their influence in the organization without having to assume significant administrative responsibilities," Stata said. "We need to learn how to delegate authority," he added, "and to respond to influence based as much on knowledge and proven competence as on position in the organizational hierarchy."

Source: "The Right Way to Strengthen U.S. Technology," by Ray Stata, *High Technology,* October 1983, pp. 18–21.

Know your limitations and work hard to correct them. As indicated in many of the research studies, judgmental errors are systematic in nature and not a result of random chance. Therefore, it is important to recognize the context in which a given heuristic promotes error. The task of making estimates generally is prone to anchoring biases. It is also more likely that people will make incorrect inferences about things or people with which they think they are more familiar. Finally, there are base rates for most questions. Make sure to check the base rates before making hasty generalizations.

Try to simplify the problem. When faced with a complex problem, it may be helpful to break the problem into more elementary parts. Raiffa (1968, p. 271) describes this procedure well:

> The spirit of decision analysis is divide and conquer: Decompose a complex problem into simpler problems, get your thinking straight in these simpler problems, paste these analyses together with a logical glue, and come out with a program of action for the complex problem. Experts are not asked complicated, fuzzy questions, but crystal clear, unambiguous, elemental hypothetical questions.

Because of time constraints and our limited motivational efforts, we are likely to continue to use our intuition to solve problems. With more training and greater awareness of judgmental decisional contexts, however, we can use our intuitive abilities to anticipate errors and biases.

Whenever possible, try to model your decision-making processes. At present, attention has been placed on developing a model of the decision-making process. The formal structure of a decision makes clear all the elements, their interrelationships, and modes of resolution. With such a structure, the location, extent, and importance of areas of disagreement can be identified. In addition, sources of inconsistency can be identified. Finally, an explicit model facilitates communication among people involved in the decision process.

Use of Decision Aids

Another way to improve individual decision making is through the use of decision aids. The examples presented in this section will not be highly detailed. We will instead present the underlying logic, indicating how these aids can help people solve more complex problems.

Decision Matrices. As adviser to some wood products firms in the Northwest, you are considering three particular strategic alternatives: to expand facilities to anticipate future demand, to cut back facilities to meet the requirements of declining demand, and to invest in a new line of business. Each alternative has different percentage rates of return depending on the possible states of the economy. A table such as that in Figure 6.5, relating strategic alternatives to future economic conditions and showing the values of these combinations, is called a *decisional matrix.*

There are three classic strategies:

1. **Mini-max strategy.** This strategy, developed by Von Neumann (Von Neumann and Morgenstern, 1944), is quite conservative and pessimistic. It assumes that the worst will happen and suggests minimizing losses by selecting the alternative with the least bad worst possible outcome. In such a case the strategy of investing elsewhere (MIN $= -2$) is preferred over cutting back (MIN $= -5$) and expanding (MIN $= -15$).

Figure 6.5
Percentage of Return on Three Investments
in Three States of the Economy

INVESTMENT	STATE OF THE ECONOMY		
	Better	*Same*	*Worse*
Expand	20	−10	−15
Cut back	5	15	−5
Invest elsewhere	10	10	−2

2. **Maxi-max strategy.** This strategy is the opposite of the mini-max in that it assumes the best possible outcome of the actions we choose. Thus, the strategy that yields the best possible outcome, expanding (MAX = 20), is preferred over the rest, cut back (MAX = 15) and invest elsewhere (MAX = 10).

3. **Hurwicz strategy.** This strategy (Hurwicz, 1953) is a compromise between the first two strategies. To apply this strategy, select a value between zero and 1, representing your coefficient of optimism (A). Low values are pessimistic; high values are optimistic. Assuming you select $A = 0.4$, your preferred strategy would be determined by computing $A (MAX) + (1 - A) (MIN)$ for each row. Thus,

Strategy 1 (expand): $(0.4)20 + (0.6)(-15) = 8.0 - 9.0 = -1.0$
Strategy 2 (cut back): $(0.4)15 + (0.6)(-5) = 6.0 - 3.0 = 3.0$
Strategy 3 (invest elsewhere): $(0.4)10 + (0.6)(-2) = 4.0 - 1.2 = 2.8$

On this basis, strategy 2 (cut back) is selected.

There are variations to these strategies, but the underlying logic is the same; that is, they represent your attitude toward risk. You may elect to be risk seeking or risk averse, but only after considering the data. It is important to remember that your judgment can only be as good as the validity of your data.

Decision Trees. **Decision trees** are graphic representations of the sequential decisions and events that constitute decision making. To illustrate their use, assume that you have been assigned to choose between two alternate processes, both with risks of relative success and failure. From design engineers you have been able to estimate such payoffs as the present value of contributions over the process lifetime, and such probabilities as relative success and failure. A simplified model of the decision tree is presented in Figure 6.6.

The net expected value (NEV) of each alternative can be computed by subtracting the cost from the sum of the possible outcome benefits, each multiplied by its probability (p in Fig. 6.6). The NEVs for the two process alternatives in our example can be computed as follows:

$$NEV_A = -35,000 + (0.65)(180,000) + (0.35)(25,000) = \$90,750$$

$$NEV_B = -55,000 + (0.55)(200,000) + (0.45)(40,000) = \$73,000$$

Based on this analysis, process A would be preferred. It is worth repeating that your decision is only as good as the quality of your data. In this example, the data include probability estimates (p), which may be difficult to arrive at. Perhaps the real value of this process is that it allows the decision makers to develop a broader understanding of the variables involved in the decision, which, in turn, may lead them to take any corrective action necessary — for example, to improve probabilities of success through additional research and development.

Monte Carlo Simulation. There are times when it is virtually impossible to estimate probabilities. On such occasions it will be difficult to use decisional

Figure 6.6
Decision Tree Problem

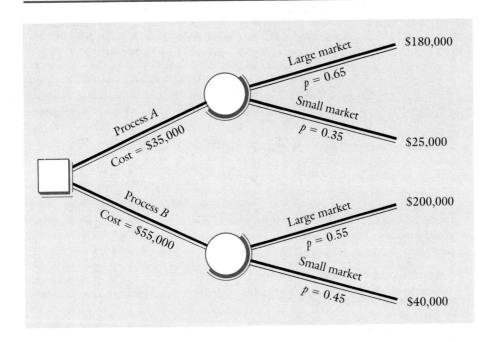

matrices or decision trees. One recourse is the use of simulations, or the genera-tion of sequences of events on a make-believe basis. Because of the enormous amount of data that can be generated, these simulations are normally done with a computer.

Simulations allow managers to examine the possible outcome of certain actions without having to incur the actual costs. Suppose we are analyzing the inventory needs of a new product and that circumstances do not allow an accu-rate estimate of the time to reorder, the lead time, and usage during lead time. In a simulation, the values for lead time and usage are randomly selected and a re-sulting distribution for a reorder point (reorder point = lead time × usage) can be developed. Based on this distribution, statistical tests can be made to develop the necessary safety stocks.

Improving Decision Making in Groups

Preventing groupthink is not an easy task, because some degree of con-sensus is required for groups to operate effectively. Techniques for preventing the premature closure of ideas include brainstorming, role playing, group scenarios, and the Delphi technique. In this section we will present Janis's own treatise on what groups can do to prevent the groupthink phenomenon.

Janis (1972) contrasted the Bay of Pigs invasion in 1961 with the Cuban missile crisis in 1962. The process of decision making was markedly different in these two foreign policy situations. Therefore, comparing the two demonstrates how groupthink can be prevented. The major features of the decision-making process in the Cuban missile crisis, according to Janis (1972, p. 148), were:

1. *A new definition of the participants' role.* Members of the policy-making group were given a new and much broader role. They were to function as skeptical *generalists* rather than consider themselves confined to their areas of expertise.

2. *Changes in group atmosphere.* Group meetings were more open-ended and freewheeling, resembling a brainstorming session in many respects. Also, the usual rules of protocol were suspended in these meetings and there was no predetermined agenda.

3. *Meetings of subgroups.* The meetings often involved splitting the executive committee into two subgroups to work independently on policy decisions and then debate in the reassembled group.

4. *Leaderless sessions.* President Kennedy at times left the meetings to allow his advisers full freedom to conceptualize a problem and discuss alternate solutions.

Improving Decision Making in Organizations

Perhaps the best way to improve decision making in organizations is to be aware of the overall *context* in which a decision is to be made. An effective decision maker is one who recognizes the opportunities and constraints presented by the organizational power structure, the limits to pursuing a specific solution, and the conditions that warrant a change in the SOPs of the organization.

The importance of context is illustrated in the next example, which involved one of our colleagues, a conscientious reader of the literature on decision making. In one of his lectures he cited an instance in which he spent a great amount of time preparing so he could get a good deal on a 1978 Honda Accord. After reading *Consumer Reports,* calling up various dealers in the country, and calculating a mental rate of return on his invested time, he confidently strode to his neighborhood dealer. After six hours of intense bargaining, he came away satisfied with his new car and happy with the bargain rate he had initially anticipated. At the end of the story, one student raised his hand and said, "It sounds too complex. . . . I simply see what girls like and buy the car. Today I have a [Datsun] 280Z Turbo." After some guffaws from the class, the professor quickly settled in and said, "That's one way of doing it."

In reflecting on what the student said, our colleague soon realized that the decision process used by the student was not irrational as he had originally thought but, rather, very rational. Because of a relatively tight budget, the professor had to be quite calculating in his purchasing strategy. For the student, who did not have the same budgetary constraints, the choice of a car was not as important. Furthermore, if he did not like the car, he could easily have changed it with one simple phone call. Obviously the contexts in which the decisions took place were quite different. Incidentally, the student called back a couple of weeks later, stating that he had shifted to a Mazda RX-7.

After cursory reading of the literature on organizational decision making, students are quick to point out that politics, problemistic search, and SOPs are illustrations of irrational decision behavior. What they fail to realize is that in some contexts such characteristics may in fact be functional for an organization. Quasiresolution of conflict in effect prevents costly personal confrontations, problemistic search limits the high costs of information search, and SOPs provide the necessary repertoire for solving the majority of organizational problems. Therefore, learn well the circumstances surrounding the decision. Context is important, and understanding that fact can make the difference between an effective and an ineffective decision maker.

Summary

The turbulent environment, the advent of decision support systems, and the discovery of the importance of heuristics and biases are behind the recent interest in improving managerial decision making. The decision-making process has three elements: the problem itself, the individual facing the problem, and the context in which it is to be solved. The goals, aspirations, and perceived reward structures of the group are also important.

The relative complexity of problems can be described in terms of the number of informational items; the programmability of outcomes and solutions; certainty, risk, and uncertainty regarding outcomes; and the multiplicity of problem solvers. Based on these attributes, one can define well- and ill-structured, or well- and ill-defined, problems.

Some decision aids to improve the representation of problems include decisional matrices, decision trees, and Monte Carlo simulations.

Individual problem solving can be characterized as "intendedly rational," or seeking to be rational in the face of incomplete information and limited computational abilities. Therefore, it can be argued that people satisfice, or seek an acceptable solution, rather than optimize, or seek the best solution.

In problem solving, people resemble information-processing systems, using internal representations of the problem, heuristic "rule-of-thumb" rules, and recent and more distant memories. On the basis of problem-solving research, problem solvers can be characterized as serial processors who use heuristic methods and other simplification techniques.

Behavioral decision theorists have developed mathematical representations of the judgmental process. Strategies include linear or compensatory processing and noncompensatory, conjunctive, disjunctive, and lexicographic processing.

There are a number of ways to combat the effects of groupthink, the psychological drive for consensus that suppresses dissent and appraisal of critical alternatives, among them brainstorming, role playing, group scenarios, and the use of the Delphi technique.

Organizational decision making is complex because decision makers must deal with organizational politics, simple-minded and problem-oriented search, and standard operating procedures that may be ill suited to novel problems. Understanding the context in which decisions are made is essential for effective decision making in organizations.

Questions for Discussion

1. Why has the study of decision making become important to the modern corporate executive?
2. Differentiate problem solving, decisions, and decision making. What are the generic phases of a decision-making process?
3. Define the importance of (a) the individual, (b) the problem, and (c) the context in understanding decision making.
4. What are the attributes of a problem? Differentiate well-structured, moderately structured, and ill-defined problems.
5. Consider the classic cryptarithmetic problem used by Bartlett (1958) and Newell, Shaw, and Simon (1958) in various experiments on human problem solving:

$$\begin{array}{r} D\ O\ N\ A\ L\ D \\ +\ G\ E\ R\ A\ L\ D \\ \hline R\ O\ B\ E\ R\ T \quad D = 5 \end{array}$$

Here each letter represents a digit (0, 1, 2, 3, 4, 5, 6, 7, 8, 9). For example, you know that D is 5. Each letter is distinct; that is, no letter other than D may equal 5. You are instructed to assign digits to letters such that, when the letters are replaced by their corresponding digits, the sum above is satisfied.
   a. Why is the problem well structured?
   b. Try your luck in solving this puzzle. In doing so, try to remember any heuristics used to solve this problem.
6. Let us consider a slightly different problem:
Here are some financial ratios for three imaginary firms, and industry ratios taken from *Dun's Review*. The data from *Dun's Review* are presented as they

are in the magazine: top figure is upper quartile, middle figure is median, and lower figure is lower quartile. Assume that all other financial factors for the three firms are relatively equal. Rank the three firms in terms of their apparent financial strength.

Ratio	Firm A	Firm B	Firm C	Industry Ratio
Total debts/equity (%)	55.0	83.5	75.6	47.4
				82.0
				123.9
Net profits/net sales (%)	4.78	5.06	4.86	5.66
				4.14
				2.77
Net profits/equity (%)	12.30	13.45	14.54	17.35
				12.30
				7.78
Current ratio	3.17	2.43	3.40	3.36
				2.58
				2.11

   a. How is this problem different from the one described in question 5?
   b. Solve the problem by: (i) assuming equal weights for the four performance ratios (debt/equity; profits/sales; profits/equity; current ratio) and (ii) assigning different weights to the four ratios. Some questions: (i) Would the selection of the strongest firm be the same? (ii) Which approach do you prefer, and why?

7. Now that you have solved two problems, try your skills on this third one:
You are advising the management committee of CBS-Columbia. They had been approached earlier by Akio Morita, chairman of the $5 billion Sony Corporation, about a license to produce a digital audiodisc system and software. Truly revolutionary, the compact disc will reduce the record to a small 4.7-inch disc that is tracked by a laser beam and sounds better than stereo. If successful, this innovation will render most existing stereo equipment obsolete. Thus far, twenty-four Japanese, five Korean, and eight European firms have signed up for licenses. No American firm has signed up. The management of CBS-Columbia is pondering their next strategic step, and is awaiting your advice.
   a. How is this problem different from the last two (questions 5 and 6)?
   b. Can this problem become even more complex if one considers the group and organizational factors that impinge on this decision? How so?

8. What are the main features of the rational, satisficing, and political models of decision making?

9. Describe the main contributions of the following schools of thought in helping us better understand individual decision making:
   a. Human problem solving
   b. Behavioral problem solving
   c. Cognitive psychology

10. Describe three heuristics and biases suggested by Tversky and Kahneman. How do these impair decision making?
11. What is groupthink? How can groupthink be prevented?
12. Why is it important to know the context of organizational decision making?

Exercise 6.1
"Blue-Collar Blues" Exercise

Introduction

It is 6:30 A.M. and just a few minutes ago you were awakened by a phone call from your boss, Harry Stoner. He is president of the Muddy Waters Pump Corporation, of which you are the industrial relations manager in charge of union negotiations.

When you answered the phone you hardly expected to hear Mr. Stoner's voice, and even less to have him start philosophizing about worker alienation and disenchantment! He said he'd been reading a book called *Work in America*, which talked about "blue-collar blues" and the dissatisfactions and frustrations of the blue-collar worker in America. According to Mr. Stoner, some sociologists claim that workers want more than good wages and fair treatment in a job. They want "to become masters of their immediate environments and to feel that their work and they themselves are important."

Mr. Stoner wanted to know your views and made it clear that you had better be ready to discuss this matter when you arrive at the breakfast meeting of the corporation's bargaining committee!

What do your company's employees want? Even though not highly educated they are fairly skilled, as they have to be to manufacture precision water pumps. Any they are almost all young, because in your employment area there are few skilled older workers. You know that the president of the national union recently said that this business of workers wanting to make decisions and have interesting work is so much bull! He said that the men want good pay and job security. "The time for fun and enjoyment comes after hours. The job is where you get the wherewithal to finance your recreation after working hours."

So later this morning you and the rest of the bargaining committee will have to reach a consensus on this question before you go into the negotiating meeting with the union at 10:30 A.M. But first you need to get your position clear. Just what would most of your workers want in their jobs? Your task is to rank order the following list of possible items Mr. Stoner read to you so you will be ready at the breakfast meeting to determine what is most important to your workers.

Rank order the attached list of fifteen items in their order of importance to the group of blue-collar workers in their early 20s, holding jobs requiring moderate skill and intelligence but only high school graduates. Place the number *1* beside the item that in your judgment the greatest number of employees would include in their list of things important in a job. Place the number *2* beside the item that the next largest number of employees would include in their list, and so on to number *15,* for the item the fewest number of employees would count as important. Be certain to number all items, and do not use the same number twice. (Further instructions on how you would extend this exercise to cover rankings for white-collar jobs will be provided by your instructor.)

THINGS WANTED IN A JOB BY YOUNG, NONCOLLEGE EMPLOYEES
18 TO 24 YEARS OLD — 1973

Blue Collar	White Collar	
_____	_____	Good chance for promotion.
_____	_____	Person in charge who is concerned about you.
_____	_____	Not being caught in a big, impersonal organization.
_____	_____	Job that doesn't involve hard physical work.
_____	_____	Freedom to decide how to do your work.
_____	_____	Good job security.
_____	_____	Good pay.
_____	_____	Chance to use your mind.
_____	_____	Interesting work.
_____	_____	No one standing over you/being your own boss.
_____	_____	Not being expected to do things not paid for.
_____	_____	Clearly defined responsibilities.
_____	_____	Friendly co-workers.
_____	_____	Time for outside interest.
_____	_____	Participation in decisions regarding job.

Sources: A. Cohen, R. Fink, and R. Willits, ''The Blue Collar Blues Exercise,'' *The Teaching of Organizational Behavior,* Vol. 1, No. 1 (1975), pp. 25–28; A. Cohen, ''Erring Around the Collar: Whitening the Blue Collar Blues Exercise,'' *EXCHANGE: The Organizational Behavior Teaching Journal,* Vol. 3, No. 4 (1978), pp. 44–45. Reprinted by permission.

Case Study
The Ringi System

The Ringi system of organizational decision making in the Japanese organization was used before the industrialization and modernization started in the middle of the nineteenth century. It is believed that the feudal political order in Japan gave birth to this system where the substantial job of policy making was left to the lower-upper or upper-middle level members of the hierarchy in order to make it possible for the top to escape from taking the responsibility by imputing it to those who made the drafts of the policies. The top leaders in the power structure holding the actual authority were thereby left untouched. The Ringi system was then nothing but a product of the totalitarian feudalism in the Tokugawa era, which lasted for more than two centuries before the Meiji restoration. When Japan started her modernization and industrialization in the Meiji era, the Ringi system was smoothly brought into the new bureaucracy of the Meiji government. In parallel with this, those public corporations and private companies established under the leadership of the government combined this system with the modern management system introduced from the West. What is important to note is that the introduction of the rational system from the West preceded the establishment of individualism which should be brought forth by way of spiritual revolution. The birth of individualism, even if being incomplete, had to wait for the end of World War II.

The word *ringi* means obtaining approval on a proposed matter through the vertical, and sometimes horizontal, circulation of documents to the concerned members in the organization. As an administrative procedure it consists of four steps; proposal, circulation, approval, and record. The typical procedure is such as described below.

In a section of a department middle management presents a good idea for a new sales campaign. The *Kacho*, the section chief, therefore calls a meeting of his section. Through discussion to boil down the factors of the idea, they judge that they will need the overall support of the firm. The *Kacho* reports this to his *Bucho*, the department head, and consults with him. The *Bucho* also agrees that it is a good idea. It is at this point that the time-consuming activity of getting a general consensus starts. Up to this point a local consensus in this section has been reached. Next, a wider agreement in the department is sought. Then an overall consensus in the firm is tried to be attained, possibly through meetings with other departments concerned arranged by the *Bucho*, as an information exchange process. Each department sends one *Bucho*, one *Kacho*, and perhaps two *Kakaricho*, subsection chiefs. If there are four departments involved, in all sixteen to twenty members will attend the meeting. If they need the opinion of specialists on the shop floor, they will invite engineers or sometimes foremen to their meetings. The initiator and his consonant colleagues, under the leadership of the *Kacho*, run about formally and informally from section to section and from department to department to prepare the necessary documents and materials. This prior coordination is vital for the Ringi system to be effective.

It is only after the moment when the department judges have attained an informal agreement from all of the other departments concerned that the formal procedure starts. This is the circulation of a formal document of request, the *Ringi-sho* (paper or document), for approval or authorization of the proposal. All of the responsible managers concerned affix their seals to it as a sign of agreement. (In Japan seals are used for signing instead of a signature.) The number of seals can reach ten or twelve. In order for this circulation to be carried out, the details of the plan are completed by the members of the original section. The *Ringi-sho* finally goes up to the top decision-making body for formal authorization and the final "go-ahead."

This is a somewhat simplified example of the Ringi system. There are other cases where the initiator is the head of a department or the *Kacho* of a section or an even higher echelon manager. But in most cases the initiator belongs to the middle management. Even if the initiator is a *Bucho* or a *Kacho*, however, in almost every case he will give his idea to his subordinate(s) and let him (them) propose it. What is important is that, unlike the feudal system, the responsibility is rarely imputed to the middle management. It keeps lying in the hands of the seniors.

After the War [World War II] as described later again, because of the purge of the older managers (over 40 or 50), younger members of the middle management had to take the responsibility of running the company. One after another they were sent to the United States to bring back the American way of management. As a result it became almost fashionable to "purge" the "feudal" system for the following reasons: the lack of leadership at the top; the inflexibility or narrowness of the drafts drawn by the middle management compared with those of the top management; the vagueness of the boundaries of authority and responsibility; the prior coordination, which takes into account as many comments, advice and opinions as possible from other departments concerned, may often make the final plan a product of compromise; the formality of the system is apt to be inefficient; the excess of *Ringi-sho* for the top management to check makes them only a stamping machine. Accordingly it is often said that the traditional Ringi system is now disappearing. Perhaps the use of the *Ringi-sho* is decreasing, but it is unlikely that the underlying spirit of the system is dying. It may be time consuming and politically delicate but it is very appropriate for the Japanese organization based on and protected by seniority. Here, like the feudal system, it is the middle management who take or are expected to take the initiative in making proposals and in making the substantial decisions, and the seniors manage the political affairs and arrangements to back them up. "To manage a seniority organization efficiently really needs a senior man." Under lifetime employment the seniors have stayed in a firm longer than the middle management; therefore, they know better what's what and who's who in their firm. Japanese organizations, where personal affairs and human relations should be paid due consideration, are not the place for the 1 percent of geniuses but for the 99 percent of ordinary people. Individual conspicuousness might destroy the harmony within the organization.

Ironically it was by Americans that the merits of the Ringi system were found. They were, for instance, J. C. Abbegglen, Peter Drucker and other managers who stayed some years in Japan on business. The biggest merit found was participation, in the Japanese way. Under the Ringi system many people including lower management automatically participate in the decision-making process. In addition to this, "there are four primary advantages: fewer aspects of the decision are overlooked; the trauma that accompanies change is reduced; participants feel committed to implementing a decision

they have helped to formulate; and far bolder decisions can be made."

When we measure the efficiency of management not only from the time needed for the decision but also from the time needed for implementation, the whole process, namely the former plus the latter, may be shorter for Japanese firms than for Western. This is due to the fact that in Japanese firms, after the thorough and overall discussion before decisions are made and after the consensus has been reached, no objection occurs in the implementation process.

Case Questions

1. How would the *Ringi* system be different from decision making in conventional organizational structures?
2. What are the advantages and disadvantages of the *Ringi* system?
3. How might the *Ringi* system help reduce some of the dysfunctional heuristics and biases discussed in this chapter?
4. Would the *Ringi* system work efficiently in United States organizations? Discuss.

Source: Case from Naoto Sasaki, *Management and Industrial Structure in Japan* (Oxford: Pergamon Press, 1981), pp. 56–59. Reprinted by permission.

*". . . and here to break the news to you gently
is our president, Lem Cauldworth."*

When times get hard, the double-talk starts.

Even in the best of times, the language of the business world is seldom lucid. But after a year of facing losses and layoffs, it can get downright murky. The letter to shareholders in the annual report is a prime place for organizations to sweeten or obscure adverse corporate information. A page or so of fifty-dollar words, some executives seem to feel, will keep the stockholders from looking at the numbers that follow.

A favorite ploy for business is to depict itself as a victim, so it is "impacted" by events that seem like acts of God. There are also other tacks. Mirro Corporation said it had a "mile-

stone year." It lost $1.2 million and is planning to sell more than half the company. Tennant Company's President Roger L. Hale has become more flexible. "A year ago I stated that 1981 was expected to be a year of transition from the slower growth of the 1970s," he said. "It has turned out to be a longer transition than expected."

Other companies don't seem to know which way to go. United Telecommunications Inc., Kimberly-Clark Corporation, and others are "cautiously optimistic." Ransburg Corporation is "optimistic, but proceeding with caution."

Ceco Corporation is included in the list of businesses looking at the world through rose-colored glasses. Rather than say its earnings fell

CHAPTER 7

Control Systems in Organizations

13 percent, it said it "enjoyed another good year" and had net income second only to its 1980 record. Similarly, Indianapolis Power and Light earnings "reached" $2.81 a share — reached downward from $3.68 a share the year before, that is.

Richard Mitchell, an English professor at Glassboro State College in New Jersey and publisher of a newsletter called *The Underground Grammarian,* calls this "the language of irresponsibility." "Everything is held away at arm's length to avoid accountability, or so the shareholders can't come back and say, 'But you said. . . .'"

Some investment advisers have said that this kind of double-talk is little more than a cover-up. "The amount of pontificating a company does varies in direct proportion to how screwed up it is," said David Bartlett, research director at Ladenburg, Thalman and Company.

Of course, there are always the refreshing exceptions, the companies who bare their souls. Iowa Public Service Company is one. "This industry," the shareholders' letter said, "faces every business problem known to exist."

Source: Excerpts from "Doubletalk Grips Business Reports as Firms Try to Sugarcoat Bad News," by Thomas Petzinger, Jr., *The Wall Street Journal,* March 31, 1982, p. 31. Reprinted by permission of *The Wall Street Journal,* © Dow Jones & Company, Inc. 1979. All Rights Reserved.

Chapter Outline

- The Concept of Control
- The Control Process: An Overview
- Types of Control
- Problems with Control Systems
- Characteristics of Effective Control Systems
- Budgets and Financial Controls
- Types of Budgets
- Special Approaches to Budgeting
- Financial Controls

Key Terms

- steering controls
- gatekeeper controls
- feedback controls
- cost centers
- revenue centers
- profit centers
- financing budgets
- cash budgets
- capital expenditure budgets
- balance sheet budgets
- PPBS
- zero-base budgets
- decision packages
- financial statement
- income statement
- cash flow statement
- external audit
- internal audit
- management audit

Chapter Objectives

After studying Chapter 7 you should be able to

1. See why control is necessary in organizations.
2. Discuss some problems of control systems.
3. Explain what constitutes an effective control system.
4. Discuss the stages in developing a budget.
5. Recognize the differences between operating and financial budgets.
6. Compare the PPBS and zero-base budgeting systems.
7. Contrast three types of auditing procedures.

Introduction

In this chapter we will begin to examine a theme that will emerge throughout much of the remainder of the book. We will introduce you to the concept of control and show you three general areas in which control systems are centrally important (Fig. 7.1).

Control systems frequently found in organizations, problems that accompany them, and mechanisms for improving their effectiveness will be discussed. We also will review the relationship of control systems to budgeting and financial controls.

Chapter 8 includes a discussion of operations and production control systems, and Chapter 14 focuses on employee performance control systems. Financial, production, and performance control systems are the heart of good management control in organizations.

Figure 7.1
Three Primary Control Systems in Organizations

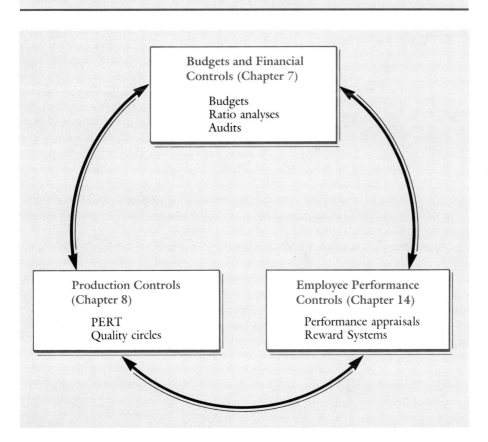

The Concept of Control

We will use Mockler's definition of **control** (1972, p. 2):

> Management control is a systematic effort to set performance standards with planning objectives, to design information feedback systems, to compare actual performance with these predetermined standards, to determine whether there are any deviations and to measure their significance, and to take any action required to assure that all corporate resources are being used in the most effective and efficient way possible in achieving corporate objectives.

Control is central to the effectiveness of managers and organizations. In fact, the control concept permeates any discussion of how managers can make their operations more successful. Whether financial issues, production problems, or employee performance is being discussed, the need for some form of control system must be recognized if the organization is to function effectively and achieve its goals.

Importance of Control in Organizations

Why is control necessary in organizations? There are several reasons. First, most organizations exist in turbulent environments. Control systems often enable managers to detect changes as they occur and to take action to cope with the changes. Without monitoring of changes in the external environment, it is quite likely that changes that can hurt the organization will go unnoticed. For example, organizations clearly need to monitor legislative activities that may affect organizational practices. Second, the growing complexity of today's organizations means that more controls are needed to coordinate departments and divisions. Without this control, there may be much wasted effort. Third, people make mistakes. Control systems often identify these mistakes before much damage is done — for example, by quality control checks on the production line. Finally, control systems often provide a way of monitoring subordinates who have been given tasks. Controls allow the unit manager to determine periodically how the unit is doing.

Many people consider control a bad thing. On the contrary, control systems are an essential aspect of organizational survival and productivity. Without control systems, there would be no viable mechanism to ensure that resources are allocated efficiently. If an organization is not efficient or effective, its survival and the well-being of its employees are jeopardized.

Newman (1975) advocates a more constructive view of control processes in organizations. He notes that:

1. Control is a normal, pervasive, and positive force in organizations. Everyone, individually or collectively, uses control systems to some degree.

2. Managerial control is effective only when it guides employee behavior. "Behavior, not measurements or reports, is the essence of control" (p. 4).

3. Successful control is future oriented and dynamic; it does not focus on the past.

4. Control relates to all sorts of human endeavors. Control systems are as important for charitable organizations as for major multinational corporations.

We can see that control systems are centrally important to the successful functioning of organizations. So it is useful to know how control systems work and how managers can use them to make their organizations more effective.

Relationship Between Planning and Control

In Chapter 4 we discussed the planning process in organizations. Planning and control are closely related. For instance, planning provides a sense of direction for attaining goals, and control focuses on guiding the activities designed to reach those goals. Planning determines how resources are allocated throughout the organization; control ensures that those allocations are made rationally and effectively. Whereas planning is an attempt to anticipate problems, controls try to correct them. Planning and control are two sides of the same coin; they should work together to make organizations more effective. This interrelationship will be evident throughout much of this book.

The Control Process: An Overview

Control systems vary in purpose and scope, but it is possible to describe the general control process. Most control systems consist of the following four sequential steps (Fig. 7.2):

1. *Setting objectives and performance standards.* Initially, managers must establish what they hope to accomplish. Standards might include sales goals per salesperson, passenger loads for airlines, or miles per gallon for automobiles. Whatever the objective, it is important first of all that it be clearly understandable and, second, that it set a reasonable or attainable standard of performance. These twin objectives of *clarity* and *reasonableness* help employees understand the performance standards and see them as fair and attainable.

2. *Measuring performance.* Using both quantitative and qualitative measures, managers next assess the actual performance within a given period: actual sales per salesperson, airline passenger loads, or miles per gallon. When objectives relate to both quantity and quality, people tend to emphasize quantity; it is more visible, more "countable." This tendency becomes very important in discussions of quality control, as we shall see in Chapter 8.

3. *Comparing actual performance to the standard.* Next, the actual performance is compared with the predetermined performance standards to determine

Figure 7.2
The Control Process

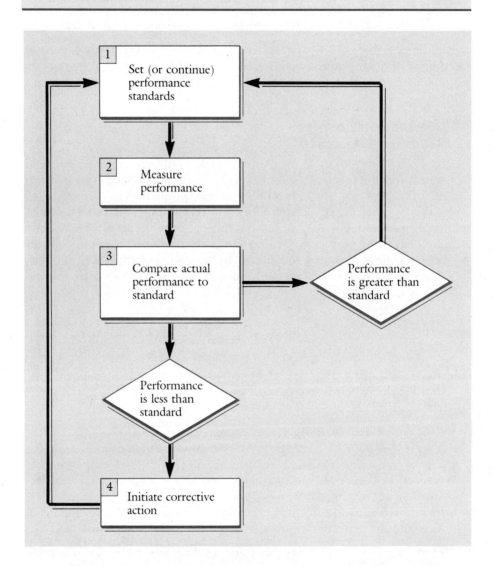

how well the goals and objectives have been met. In this way it is possible to identify performances that are unusually good, or well above standard, and unusually poor, or well below standard.

4. *Taking corrective action when necessary.* If actual performance does not meet the standard, managers may initiate corrective action. If sales figures fail to meet standards, the manager may invest in more advertising, change the in-

Feature 7.1
Rospatch's New System "Keeps Your Feet to the Fire"

Rospatch Corporation was progressive and profitable but just a little bit stodgy.

Directors of the Grand Rapids, Michigan, company could see from the balance sheet that something was wrong, but not why. The flexible packaging division, which accounted for nearly half of corporate sales from 1974 to 1978, was generating a progressively smaller percentage of corporate profits, and the cloth-label division was barely holding its own. Only the equipment division was doing well. Acquiring Jessco Inc., a particle-board laminator, boosted revenues but did not help improve corporate profit margins.

The company brought in a new number-two executive, Joe Parini, who soon moved up to president and chief executive officer. Parini began to make changes.

Research and development had taken place in corporate headquarters, and plant managers had often ignored the results. Parini returned the research and development responsibility and incentive to the divisions. He also dotted the solid-line reporting relationship between the divisional controllers and the corporate controller. The company's vice-president for finance still receives the same routine financial reports, but they come via the line managers, an arrangement that adds to their sense of responsibility.

Parini also created a climate in which managers were not only encouraged to ask the right questions but also to act on the answers themselves. He set up a formal but flexible system of reporting, forecasting, and evaluating the performance of each division and the four subgroups of each division as well as for the corporate totals.

The process begins at each product line. Managers there, and also at the division and group levels, forecast market size and growth and their own sales totals for three years. The refined figures Parini later takes to the board have been subjected to consensus judgments all the way up.

The process also takes place in the context of clearly stated, long-term, corporate financial goals: 5 percent return on sales, 10 percent return on assets, 15 percent return on equity, and 20 percent compound annual growth rate. The process "keeps your feet to the fire," said the label division's general manager, Cecil Jackson.

Source: "What Business are You Really In?" by Tom Richman, *INC.* Magazine, August 1983 pp. 77–80.

centive system for the salespersons, or reconsider the product mix. No remedies are needed when performance meets or exceeds standards.

Most control systems are far more complex than this basic model; nonetheless, it is useful for explaining the rudimentary aspects of control systems in organizations. This basic model can be used in a variety of control activities, including financial, human, and production controls.

Types of Control

Categorizing the many types of control systems in organizations is helpful in understanding the general strengths and limitations of such systems. We will identify three general types: steering controls, gatekeeper controls, and feedback controls (Fig. 7.3).

Steering (Feed-Forward) Controls

When **steering controls** are used, results are predicted and corrective actions are taken *before* the total operation is completed. For instance, shortly after an aircraft takes off, air traffic control systems accumulate such flight information as air speed, weather conditions, and fuel, and project an estimated time of arrival. This time is continually updated as factors such as weather change. Similar procedures are used in space flights, in which computer simulations project the likelihood of success based on initial flight information. If the initial information suggests problems, the flight can be aborted. The basic purpose of steering control systems, or **feed-forward controls,** is to anticipate problems as far in advance as possible so corrective actions can be taken.

Gatekeeper (Yes-No) Controls

Gatekeeper controls, also called **yes-no controls,** are primary checkpoints that must be passed before moving on to a new checkpoint in a production process. Many quality-control systems, which we will discuss in Chapter 8, use this technique: If a product is rejected at one checkpoint, it is returned for repair or reprocessing. Gatekeeper checkpoints are important because the sooner a mistake or error is discovered, the more easily and cheaply it can be rectified. It makes a great deal more sense to inspect parts of an automobile as it is being produced than after the entire car is built.

Feedback (Postaction) Controls

Feedback or **postaction controls** occur after the process is completed. For instance, most financial analyses consider annual financial performance after the year is over; management thus can look back and judge how the organization performed. Annual performance appraisals for employees are another such technique. Accurate postaction controls are also useful because they serve to document yearly performance. Long-term trends in profitability, employee performance, and so forth can be tracked over several years.

No one control process is innately superior to another. All three types of controls are useful, depending on the objectives of the organization and the specific purpose of the control system. Examples of all three systems can be found in contemporary organizations.

Problems with Control Systems

Like most things in life, control systems seldom work exactly the way they were intended to. We can identify a series of problems that permeate many control

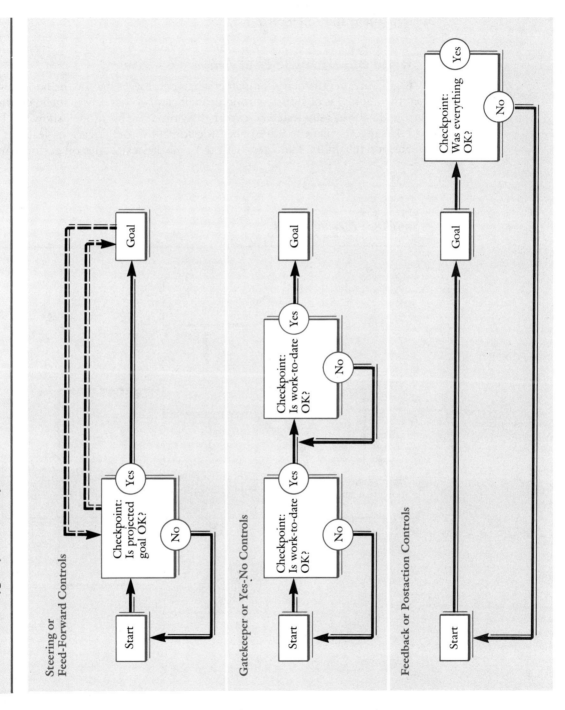

Figure 7.3
Three Basic Types of Control Systems

Steering or
Feed-Forward Controls

Checkpoint:
Is projected
goal OK?

Yes

No

Start

Goal

Gatekeeper or Yes-No Controls

Checkpoint:
Is work-to-date
OK?

Yes

No

Checkpoint:
Is work-to-date
OK?

Yes

No

Start

Goal

Feedback or Postaction Controls

Checkpoint:
Was everything
OK?

Yes

No

Start

Goal

systems. These include rigid bureaucratic behavior, strategic behavior, invalid data reporting, and employee resistance.

Rigid Bureaucratic Behavior

Rigid bureaucratic behavior occurs when employees "go by the book" even when the "book" is obviously wrong or inefficient. What causes such behavior? Merton (1940) has suggested an explanatory model. This model, shown in Figure 7.4, suggests that the initial need for control in organizations leads to an emphasis on reliability. Managers need to know they can count on getting some-

Figure 7.4
Simplified Merton Model

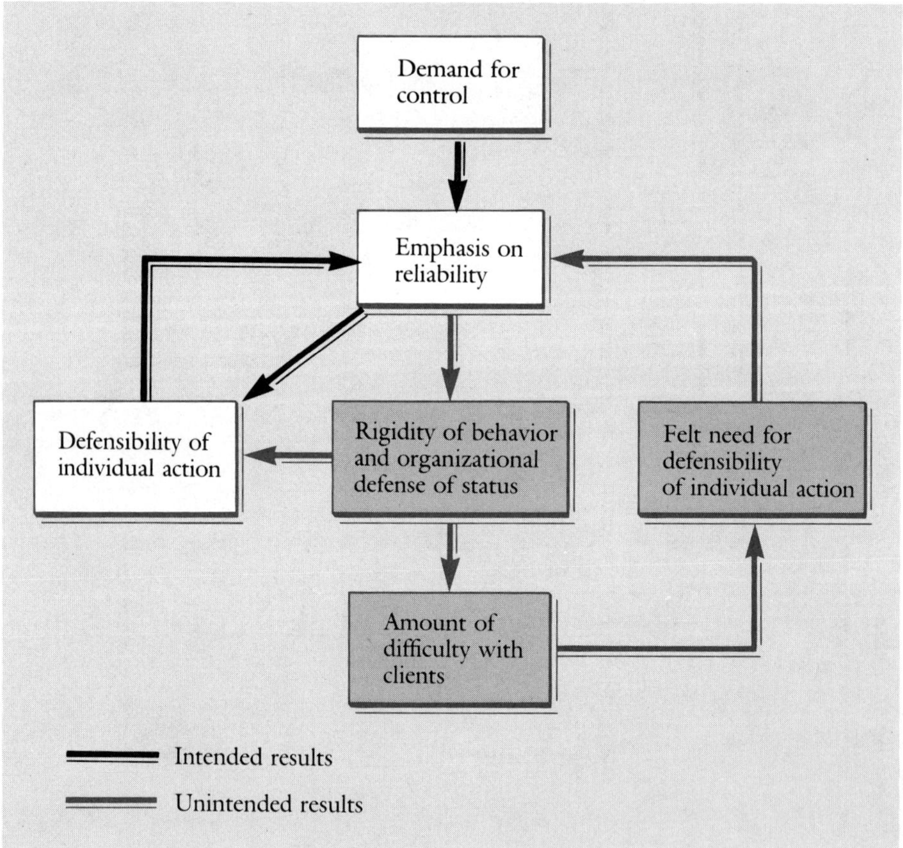

Source: Reprinted, by permission, from J. March and H. Simon, *Organizations,* p. 41. Copyright © 1958 by John Wiley & Sons, Inc.

thing done. This emphasis on reliability is intended to lead to the defensibility of individual action. In other words, each employee has a justifiable, or defensible, reason for the activities he or she carries out. These actions are sanctioned as proper by the organization.

As Figure 7.4 illustrates, however, there are also unintended and dysfunctional consequences of this emphasis on reliable, predictable behavior. It can lead to inflexibility in dealing with problems and, ultimately, to problems with clients. As a result, employees begin to feel a greater need to defend their actions and begin to do things by the book, largely for self-protection. This is a typical bureaucratic defense mechanism. It leads to even greater emphasis on reliability and predictability, which in turn reinforces the system.

An example from Lawler and Rhode (1976, pp. 84–85) illustrates this phenomenon in action:

> One of the authors recently tried to rent a car from a large car rental company only to be told that it would be thirty or sixty minutes before one would be ready. Further questioning revealed that there were cars available but they had to be washed because "we never rent cars that aren't washed." The author then asked that an exception be made because he was in a hurry and needed the car immediately. The salesperson, however, stuck to the rule despite the fact that it lost the company business and goodwill and failed to serve the need of the customer.

Lawler and Rhode note, however, that the car rental agency's rule may indeed be a good one, "since it probably does help business to rent clean cars" (p. 85). Put yourself in the awkward position of the employee in this example. Do you help the company financially by breaking a rule, and possibly lose your job, or do you adhere to company policy even if you lose a sale? In most situations an employee will go by the book and follow rigid bureaucratic behavior. It is clearly in the employee's self-interest.

Strategic Behavior

Often when employees try to make themselves look good in relation to the control system, their behavior is dysfunctional in terms of the organization's general goals. Such strategic behavior results when people "play the game" and manipulate their behavior to enhance the control indicators, regardless of the cost. For example, if a manufacturing employee is given the task of making twenty high-quality units of a certain product per hour and the quality level is unspecified or difficult to measure, it is likely that the employee will pay attention to the goal that is quantified: the number twenty. We may see the twenty units produced, but at the expense of quality. Etzioni (1964) noted that qualitative goals often are sacrificed to achieve quantitative goals, because quantitative goals are clear and measurable and qualitative goals often are not.

Strategic behavior occurs when control systems create situations in which employees feel compelled to take actions designed solely to influence their own performance indicators for a certain time period. This is not to say that false information is provided. Instead, the individual takes a short-term perspective, often at the expense of longer-term objectives. Departments may try to spend all funds before the end of a budget period for fear of losing what is left over, and sales representatives may push for quick, short-term sales during the last few days of a sales period instead of working for long-term and steady sales. It has been said, in reference to our current productivity and economic growth problems, that Japanese companies tend to focus on long-term results, whereas many firms in the United States emphasize immediate goals. Strategic behavior that results in short-term victories at the expense of long-term progress is one of the consequences of rigid control systems.

Invalid Data Reporting

A more extreme response to control systems is the reporting of invalid or distorted information. Employee responses to traditional time-and-motion studies on the shop floor frequently take this form. Gardner (1945, pp. 164–165) observes the following:

> In one case, a group who worked together in assembling a complicated and large-sized steel framework worked out a system to be used only when the rate setter was present. They found that by tightening certain bolts first, the frame would be slightly sprung and all the other bolts would bind and be very difficult to tighten. When the rate setter was not present, they followed a different sequence and the work went much faster.

One of the rationales often advanced for quality-of-working-life projects and participative management (see Chapter 19) is that game playing by employees will be reduced as managers and workers develop a more cooperative, rather than competitive, association. Still, control systems often make employees feel that they must provide false information or responses in order to survive and prosper in the system.

Employee Resistance

Control systems often lead to resistance. This resistance can take many forms, including sabotage, organized (perhaps union) resistance, foot dragging, and disregard of the system. Lawler and Rhode (1976) noted, however, that the important question is not whether resistance to control systems is likely; they suggest that we focus our attention on *why* resistance occurs. There are five main reasons for resistance to control systems:

1. *Control systems can automate expertise.* Highly sophisticated control systems often take the responsibility for successfully completing a task away from an employee and place it into the system. The employee is left with a less responsible position.

2. *Control systems often create new experts and give them power.* Implementing control systems (such as a management information system, discussed in Chapter 8) often requires new specialists to oversee them. These specialists gather considerable power and status in the organization, often at the expense of other employees.

3. *Control systems can often measure employee performance more accurately and completely.* As we become more precise in tracking performance, less discretion and autonomy are left to the employee. As a result, there often is a tendency to specify in more and more detail what employees are to do and how they are to do it. Emphasis is increasingly placed on results — the bottom line — at the expense of how the bottom line is achieved.

4. *Control systems can change the social structure of an organization.* Often, social relationships, such as people's responsibilities, interaction patterns, and opportunities to meet new people are altered by the introduction of control systems. The importance of such group processes in organizational dynamics is discussed in Chapter 11.

5. *Control systems can reduce opportunities for intrinsic need satisfaction.* As a result of the four factors just described, employees often find that there is less remaining in the job to satisfy their needs (see Chapter 9). Some control systems in many ways represent the antithesis of efforts to design work processes more effectively. When poorly implemented, they reduce employees to cogs in a wheel, thus making inefficient use of the organization's human resources.

Characteristics of Effective Control Systems

In view of all these problems, it is useful to ask what constitutes an effective control system. What attributes should we look for in evaluating the suitability of control systems? Stonner (1978) has suggested that effective control systems are:

1. *Accurate.* The information produced by the system must be correct.

2. *Timely.* Information must be generated in a timely fashion, so corrective actions can be taken when necessary.

3. *Objective and comprehensible.* Control systems must be clearly understood by people working under them.

4. *Focused on strategic control points.* Control systems should focus on points at which deviations from standards are most likely to occur or would do the greatest damage.

5. *Economically realistic.* The benefits of control costs must be realistically assessed (see Chapter 3).

6. *Organizationally realistic.* Is the system realistic for the organization? If a supervisor imposes unrealistically high standards, subordinates may begin to distort data reported to the supervisor.

7. *Coordinated with the organization's work flow.* To be effective, control systems must provide information that feeds back to the people who can take corrective action. If an organization is attempting to control absenteeism, daily absenteeism data must be reported back to first-line supervisors, not just to executives or the personnel department.

8. *Flexible.* Some flexibility should be built into the system to provide for unusual or unexpected events.

9. *Prescriptive and operational.* When performance standards are not met, an effective control system will indicate exactly what course of action is necessary. Some of the new navigational and guidance systems being installed in commercial aircrafts tell the pilot not only when another plane is getting too close, but also in which direction the pilot should turn.

10. *Acceptable to organizational members.* To be effective, control systems must have the general acceptance of the employees. If the system is not legitimate to them, it is unlikely to succeed. It is not necessary for the employees to like or approve of the system, but they must accept its right to exist.

A good example of an effective control system in action is the key performance area technique used by General Electric. *Key performance areas* are those areas of a unit that must function effectively if the entire organization is to prosper. General Electric identified eight key areas: profitability, market position, productivity, product leadership, personnel development, employee attitudes, public responsibility, and balance between short-range and long-range goals.

From the standpoint of the corporation, managers in each unit or department at General Electric have a responsibility to foster the achievement of all eight of these objectives if the organization is to attain its goals. As a result, these key performance areas form the basis for management performance appraisals (see Chapter 14). A manager must maintain a delicate balance if he or she is to score high on all fronts.

Budgets and Financial Controls

As we have stated, three general control systems operate in organizations: budgets and financial controls, operations and production controls, and employee performance controls. In the remainder of this chapter we will begin exploring budgets and financial controls.

First, what are budgets, and what role do they serve in organizations? We will examine different types of budgets, as well as two special approaches to budgeting, PPBS and zero-base budgeting. Next we will consider management information systems and how they work. Finally, financial controls will be discussed, including the role of financial statements, ratio analyses, and auditing procedures.

What Are Budgets?

We will define a **budget** as a statement of future expenditures and revenues that helps managers plan and control the use of financial and other resources. Budgets allow managers to quantify inputs and outputs in order to calculate whether the proper amount of a certain resource is expended or collected. A budget is a useful tool for both planning and control.

Anthony and Dearden (1980) have suggested that budgets typically:

1. Are stated in monetary terms,
2. Cover one-year periods, although quarterly and five-year budgets are also common,
3. Require a total commitment by management to achieve the budgeted objectives and goals,
4. Are prepared preliminarily by lower-level managers within given constraints and are then approved by higher-level managers,
5. Are modified only in extreme or special situations once set,
6. Are the basis for regular performance reviews to find and correct deviations.

Budgets serve several purposes (Welsch, 1976). First, budgets aid in the planning process by forcing managers to establish and communicate basic policies and objectives. Budgets also lead to periodic company self-analysis, forcing the company to take stock of itself and evaluate its progress. Budgets contribute to the efficient use of limited resources by prompting questions about how resources are spent (see Chapter 3). They also help to clarify specific areas of responsibility within the organization, explaining who is responsible for what. Finally, through resource allocation, well-designed budgets further the attainment of objectives by helping to implement corporate strategy.

In short, budgets are useful guidelines for managers, indicating how and at what rate limited resources should be used in order to make the organization more effective. Figure 7.5 shows the relationship between organizational objectives and budgets. As illustrated, the objectives of the organization lead to corporate strategies aimed at achieving those objectives. These strategies, in turn, lead to policy decisions that ultimately influence who gets what — in other words, a budget.

Steps in the Budgeting Process

The budgeting process is complex. The total amount of resources available for the coming year is often uncertain. Estimated expenses may be highly inaccurate because of unforeseen factors: inflation, competition, or union contracts, for example. Interdepartmental rivalry often enters the picture as each unit attempts to defend its territory or gain ground at the expense of others. Within this environment managers must somehow do the best they can to create budgets that will help the organization achieve its objectives. We are not saying that

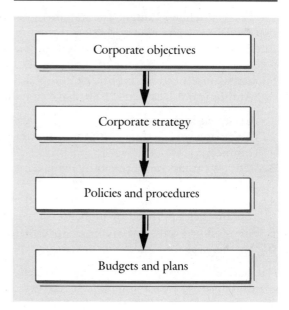

Figure 7.5
Relationship Between Budgets
and Organizational Objectives

budgets are highly scientific in nature, but only that they are necessary and important for the organization despite their inaccuracies.

What are the typical stages in the development of a budget? Here is a simplified view (Fig. 7.6):

1. *Top management initiates the budgeting process.* Top management tells departments what the primary corporate objectives are, how much is available, and under what assumptions the budgeting process should proceed.

2. *Each unit or department prepares a preliminary budget.* Given the goals and constraints of the first step, each unit head prepares a preliminary budget stating how he or she believes the available resources can best be used to achieve unit objectives. The previous year's budget often serves as a base for establishing the budget for the coming year.

3. *Preliminary budgets are reviewed, modified, and approved by upper management.* Upper management either approves or modifies the preliminary budgets of the various units. This is a crucial step, because it is usually here that coordination across the various diverse units is accomplished. It is important that all units and their resource allocations ultimately contribute to the same corporate objectives.

Figure 7.6
Steps in the Budget-Making Process

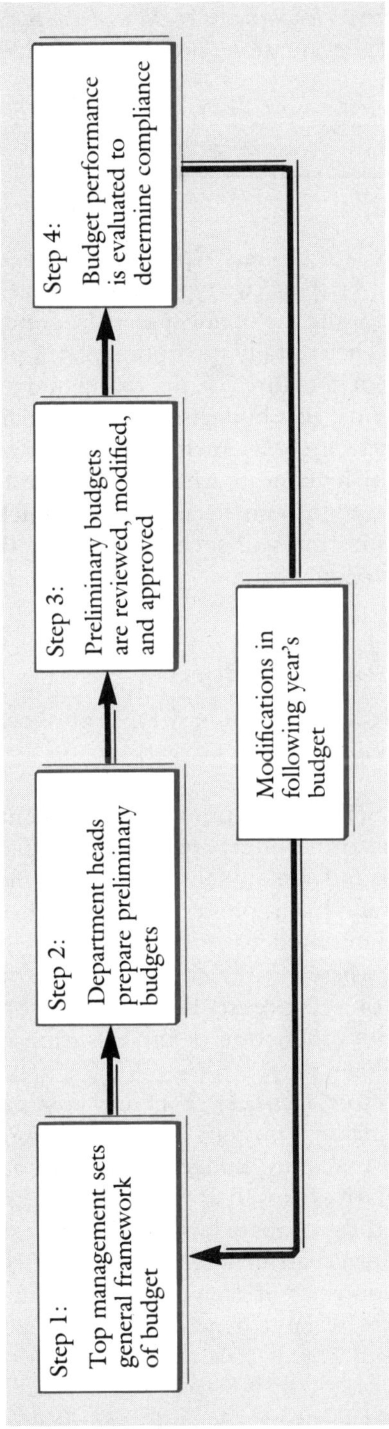

Step 1:
Top management sets
general framework
of budget

Step 2:
Department heads
prepare preliminary
budgets

Step 3:
Preliminary budgets
are reviewed, modified,
and approved

Step 4:
Budget performance
is evaluated to
determine compliance

Modifications in
following year's
budget

4. *Budget performance is evaluated during the year to determine compliance.* Based on this evaluation, problems are determined so corrective action can be taken.

Types of Budgets

There are two primary types of budgets, operating and financial. The relationship between these two types is shown in Figure 7.7. **Operating budgets** consist of plans for the use of raw materials, goods, and services for the specified period of time. They usually incorporate both physical quantities and cost figures. As can be seen in Figure 7.7, operating budgets can include action plans by various departments, cost budgets, and profit plans. Action plans lead to cost budgets, which deal with how much the action plans will cost. These in turn lead to profit plans, which delineate what revenues and expenses can be expected. Operating budgets feed into financial budgets, which spell out in considerable detail how the organization will spend money for the same period, as well as where the funds will come from.

Operating Budgets

There are three primary types of operating budget, based on the concept of responsibility.

Cost (Expense) Centers. **Cost centers** are units in the organization that have their own budgets relating to efficiency of operations. These budgets are usually found in manufacturing units, where attention is focused on the costs of material and labor, plus estimated overhead costs. Cost center budgets can also be found in staff departments, such as personnel, legal, and research and development, where it is difficult to measure output with any accuracy. The primary purpose of a cost center budget is to monitor closely and minimize costs associated with production or the provision of a particular service.

Revenue Centers. Whereas cost centers measure input costs, **revenue centers** measure outputs in monetary terms. Marketing and sales departments are good examples. Budgets or sales quotas are established for individual sales representatives as well as for departments. These are called *action plans*. Actual sales are then compared with estimated sales to determine how effective each individual or department is. Revenue centers typically have little control over the production costs of the products they market. Their focus instead is on maximizing the revenue generated by the sales and distribution of the product or service.

Profit Centers. A **profit center** is a unit of the organization designed to measure performance by comparing revenues with expenditures, assessing how

Figure 7.7
Types of Budgets

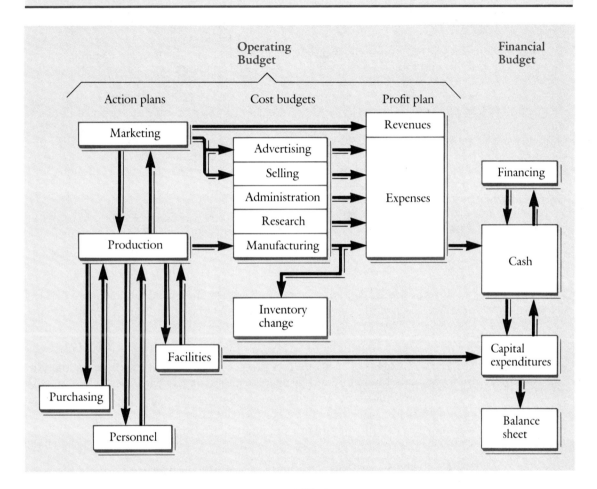

Source: From *Managerial Cost Accounting,* Fifth Edition, by G. Shillinglaw, p. 210. Copyright © 1982 by Richard D. Irwin, Inc.

well a unit has done with what it has. Profit centers often are used not only to evaluate the unit, but also to assess the manager's performance. The goal of such centers is obvious: maximize profits. Feature 7.2 describes profit centers in action in one organization.

Financial Budgets

The second major type of budget, the **financial budget,** focuses on how the organization intends to spend its financial resources during the year. Four types can be identified (see Fig. 7.7).

Feature 7.2
Profit Centers at the Bank of America

At the Bank of America, profit centers are a central aspect of the planning and control system. Under this system primary control over capital and major credit decisions is in the hands of the corporate leaders. All operating authority, however, is decentralized in about 150 profit centers around the world.

Based on the overall plan established by the top executives, managers at the various profit centers are asked to develop business plans that show how their own units will contribute to the objectives of the organization as a whole. This plan includes a very specific list of activities for the coming year in such

areas as new services, new market opportunities, and new strategies, and a more general list of activities for the next several years. Detailed financial plans are also prepared showing how available funds will be used.

The business plan and the financial plans are then combined and are used at year's end to assess the effectiveness of each profit center. As a result of this system, the Bank of America is considered one of the most efficient and effective financial institutions in the industry.

Source: "Banking's Aggressive Conservative," *Dun's Review,* December 1976, pp. 47 – 49.

Financing Budgets. **Financing budgets** are developed to ensure that the organization has sufficient funds to meet both short- and long-term borrowing obligations. They attempt to ensure that funds will be available when required.

Cash Budgets. **Cash budgets** project revenues and expenses for the year or appropriate budget period. They provide managers with useful data on cash flow in a particular unit, as well as on the pattern of cash receipts and disbursements. In many ways the cash budget provides day-to-day tracking of how well the manager is performing with the financial resources provided.

Capital Expenditure Budgets. **Capital expenditure budgets** focus on future investments in new buildings, property, equipment, or other physical assets. Decisions involving such investments are some of the most important managers must make, because of the sizable financial commitment usually required and the extreme difficulty of modifying the commitments once they are made.

Balance Sheet Budgets. **Balance sheet budgets** summarize and integrate all the operating and financial budgets, and project what the balance sheet will look like at the end of the year. As a result, projected results can be compared with original plans. In this way such budgets are a final check on the plans and objectives of the organization (see Fig. 7.3). These budgets are also called a *pro forma* balance sheet.

Special Approaches to Budgeting

The budgets we have just described can be found in almost every business organization. Less common are two rather recent budgetary approaches called PPBS and zero-base budgeting. Although more commonly found in public organizations such as state and federal bureaucracies, both techniques have found a following in business firms of various sizes.

PPBS

During the early 1960s the federal government introduced a new approach to developing budgets that was aimed at identifying and eliminating costly program duplications and producing a more efficient overall budget. The program was called the **planning-programming-budgeting system (PPBS).**

A PPBS program generally contains four steps. The organization first must clearly specify and analyze the basic goals and objectives of each program or activity. It must ask which programs are essential and which are expendable, given limited resources. Second, the success of each program in accomplishing its objectives is considered. Third, the costs of each program for the next several years, not just one year, are estimated. The question is, if the program is to go forward, how much will it cost over the long run? Finally, based on an analysis of the impact of each program on the total system, decisions are made about which programs should be continued and which should be curtailed. Throughout the process an attempt is made to determine which programs best serve the overall mission of the organization. In this way scarce human and financial resources can be applied where they can do the most good.

Although PPBS is a potentially useful budgeting technique, it has not been very successful in the federal bureaucracy. After its implementation PPBS encountered opposition that ultimately led to its being abandoned in most federal agencies. There were two reasons for the failure. First, many agencies resented having a program forced on them by President Lyndon Johnson without their consultation or consent. Second, implementation strategies were often incomplete or incorrect because PPBS was pushed so vigorously. Improper instructions were often issued, and poor communication prevailed between units. Because of a lack of managerial support and poor implementation procedures, PPBS was dropped from most United States government agencies. The Department of Defense still makes use of the technique, however.

Zero-Base Budgeting

As we have noted, the traditional budgeting process begins by using the prior year's budget as a basis for establishing the annual budget. Only minor additions and subtractions are made, because it is assumed that past expenditures are generally appropriate for each unit. In **zero-base budgeting (ZBB),** however, no such assumption is made; managers must justify each line item in a new budget from scratch, or from a "zero base." In a ZBB system, the manager must justify both new and current expenditure levels (Phyrr, 1970).

This new approach to budgeting allows the organization to consider resource allocation problems from a fresh vantage point each year. As a result, pet projects of various units must be either defended or omitted; they cannot go forward simply because they already exist. It is believed that ZBB allows greater control over the investment of limited resources.

The steps in a ZBB process are simple. First, activities of the various units and departments are broken down into **decision packages** that include information on the costs and benefits of each program. Each package also considers what would happen if the program were not implemented. The decision packages next are ranked according to their net benefits to the organization. Finally, based on the ranking, decisions are made concerning which packages and programs can be funded.

There are advantages and disadvantages to ZBB. Among the advantages is the fact that managers must quantify each program alternative, thereby providing useful means of comparison across programs. Low-priority programs are more easily identified and can be eliminated with more confidence. In addition, various alternate programs are presented more clearly, enabling managers to review periodically where their resources are, or should be, invested.

There are several disadvantages to ZBB, including the tendency of managers to resist submitting their programs, especially their pet programs, to scrutiny. They may inflate the importance of such programs. Considerable time also is required each year to reestablish budgets for activities that may be necessary to the organization. Another problem is the intentional or unintentional failure of managers to provide sufficient data with which to compare and make intelligent choices among packages.

Overall, these two relatively new budgeting techniques seem to facilitate the budgeting process. Although far from perfect, both PPBS and ZBB are analytical tools that managers can use to allocate and control scarce and valued resources.

Positive and Negative Consequences of Budgets

No one would deny that budgets are necessary in effective organizations. It is helpful for managers to have an idea of the primary positive and negative consequences of budgets. Irvine (1970) has noted nine *positive* aspects that result from the existence of budgets. In his view, budgets:

1. Motivate employees by bringing people together to pursue a common goal,
2. Facilitate work coordination across the entire organization,
3. Identify potential trouble spots, such as excessive spending, so corrective action can be taken,
4. Help people learn from past experiences (for example, to identify where overpayments continually occur),

5. Improve the allocation of resources by forcing a rational choice process in relevant decisions,
6. Improve communication by identifying who is responsible for what,
7. Help lower-level managers to see where they fit within the organization,
8. Help new employees see where the organization is going,
9. Help evaluation by tracking performance over time.

Irvine also identified several *negative* outcomes. Budgets may:

1. Assess results but be much less helpful in identifying the reasons for the failure to achieve goals,
2. Not allow for unusual events or opportunities by virtue of being too rigid and inflexible,
3. Involve so much paperwork that managers have little time for doing the rest of their job (as in the complaints of many sales representatives that the time they spend filling out reports interferes with their sales efforts),
4. Become an end in themselves instead of a means to the end or purpose of the organization,
5. Lead to distrust and restriction of information by employees when they are not openly shared with employees,
6. Backfire as a motivating factor when a unit fails to meet its budget or when standards are too high and employees simply stop trying.

There are other advantages and disadvantages as well. Although budgets must be recognized as a fact of organizational life, managers should not attempt to administer them without knowing both their advantages and their liabilities. With a clear recognition of such strengths and weaknesses, managers are in a better position to design and implement realistic budgets that will be taken seriously by employees and that will accurately reflect organizational activities. In this way, control is improved and organizational effectiveness can be enhanced.

Financial Controls

Budgets generally focus on input controls, controls on activities prior to the start of the operation. Financial controls focus on accounting during or after the operation. Financial control systems include financial statements and auditing procedures.

Financial Statements

Financial statements are designed to serve several crucial functions in organizations. They help determine the long- and short-term financial standing of the organization, they assist managers in analyzing how financial resources were used over a given period of time, and they help determine the liquidity of the organization, that is, its ability to convert its assets into cash to meet its current financial needs and obligations. Financial statements also help determine profitability.

Feature 7.3
Accounting Changes Cause Confusion

Nobody ever said that understanding corporate financial reports was easy. But when a company changes its accounting practices from one year to the next, all but the most diligent readers of annual reports can get lost.

The question for companies seems simple: to restate prior years' income statements or not to restate? That issue has been a long-simmering point of dispute among accountants, and a change in the way railroads account for track maintenance has restoked the fire. Last February the Interstate Commerce Commission decided that carriers could no longer expense track maintenance costs in their reports to the ICC. Instead, these costs should be depreciated over something like 30 years. Result: lower annual maintenance charges and higher reported earnings.

Naturally, that news has drawn huzzahs from the railroads, especially since most companies will now use the same technique on their public statements. Analysts estimate that this will add between 20 percent and 30 percent to the profits of many lines. . . .

But if this huge increase in earnings pops up . . ., won't that confuse readers of railroad annual reports? Investors looking quickly at the statements could be misled into thinking that all the good numbers stem from an industrywide boom. The obvious solution is to have railroads restate prior years' earnings using the new accounting method. Obvious, but ordinarily not allowed.

According to a rule enacted by the FASB's (Financial Accounting Standards Board) predecessor, the Accounting Principles Board, companies cannot restate earnings because of a voluntary accounting change. And everything is voluntary unless decreed by the FASB.

Now the FASB wants to create an exemption for the railroads — letting them change earlier results to conform with the more generous depreciation policy. That makes tons of sense. The problem, however, is that the rule against restatement is already riddled with exceptions. . . .

Some accountants, in fact, think too many exceptions spoil the rule. "The FASB is waffling again on how you make a change," says Joseph Connor, Price Waterhouse chairman and senior partner. "It seems to me that when you have as many exceptions as there are here, then maybe you had better take a look at which is the rule and which is the exception."

What's the defense for not allowing all companies to restate? . . . If companies were forever changing their earnings retroactively, investors would quickly lose whatever faith they once had in financial reports. . . .

The importance of the issue becomes even clearer when you see the alternative to restating earnings. . . . Companies that don't restate can't simply make a change on this year's income statements. Instead, they are forced to employ something called cumulative catch-up accounting. Here, a company calculates how much a new accounting method would have altered earnings to however many years the change was applicable. It then adds the cumulative change, all at once, into the current year's earnings.

Think about this. It is the worst of all worlds. Not only is the current year incompatible with past years, the change rips the current year's figures away from any link with reality. . . .

Of course, you can hardly blame the FASB for a rule that was implemented years before its time. But now that the board clearly sees the problems and has planned changes for railroads, why not stay on the track?

Source: Forbes, June 6, 1983, "Add a Dash of Cumulative Catch-Up," by Laura Rohmann, p. 98. Reprinted by permission. © Forbes Inc., 1983.

Understanding the three primary forms of financial statements is central to understanding financial control systems in organizations. The three are the balance sheet, income statement, and cash flow statement.

The **balance sheet** is a summary statement of what the organization owns and what it owes at any given time. These figures are stated in terms of *assets,* such as cash, land, inventories, structures, and accounts receivable, and *liabilities,* such as debts, leases, and accounts payable. A hypothetical balance sheet is presented in Figure 7.8. The difference between assets and liabilities represents

Figure 7.8
Hypothetical Balance Sheet

Assets

Current assets		
Cash, including time deposits	$ 630,000	
Marketable securities	940,000	
Accounts receivable	2,200,000	
Inventory	420,000	
Total current assets	4,190,000	
Investments and advances	150,000	
Long-term receivables	70,000	
Property, plant, and equipment	7,350,000	
Prepaid or deferred charges	85,000	
Total assets		$11,845,000

Liabilities

Current liabilities		
Notes payable	83,000	
Accounts payable	1,540,000	
Accrued taxes	430,000	
Total current liabilities	2,053,000	
Capital lease obligations	25,000	
Long-term debt	1,245,000	
Deferred credits and other liabilities		
Income taxes	515,000	
Employee pensions and benefits	185,000	
Total liabilities		$ 4,023,000

Stockholders' Equity

Preferred stock	660,000	
Common stock	1,192,000	
Capital surplus	2,220,000	
Retained earnings	3,750,000	
Total stockholders' equity		$ 7,822,000
Total liabilities and stockholders' equity		$11,845,000

the company's net worth in terms of stockholder equity. An income statement, shown in Figure 7.9, indicates how much money a company has made over a given time period, usually one year. An **income statement** shows both revenues earned and costs, expenses, and taxes. A net income statement shows the net difference between the two. It also indicates the amount of income not distributed to stockholders; this is referred to as *retained earnings*.

Finally, a **cash flow statement** indicates where funds come from — for example, sales, receivables, or sale of property — and where funds are spent, such as in paying dividends, purchasing equipment, or paying bills. Cash flow statements should not be confused with income statements, which show how much profit or loss was achieved. Cash flow statements show how available funds were used.

Auditing Procedures

Auditing plays an important role in financial controls by both verifying the fairness, accuracy, and honesty of financial statements and assisting in the critical assessment of managerial effectiveness. Three kinds of audits can be identified: external, internal, and management.

Figure 7.9
Hypothetical Statement of Income

Revenues

Sales and services	$22,375,000	
Interest and other income	1,467,000	
Total revenues		$23,842,000

Costs, Expenses, and Taxes

Costs and operating expenses	12,872,000	
Administrative expenses	1,967,000	
Depreciation, depletion, and amortization	705,000	
Interest and debt expenses	154,000	
Income and other taxes	6,023,000	
Total costs		$21,721,000

Net Income $ 2,121,000

Retained Earnings

Balance on January 1	3,975,000	
Dividends paid (on 21,327 shares)	225,000	
Balance on December 31		$ 3,750,000

Net income per share $ 99.45

Feature 7.4
Connecticut's Watchdogs

Businesses aren't the only organizations that have auditors. In Connecticut, auditors have been keeping watch over the taxpayers' money since the 1780s.

The audit office there — one of the oldest in the nation — has been served since 1967 by a Republican and a Democrat whose camaraderie has made their party differences unimportant and whose tough, hard-nosed attitude has made many a straying state employee quake.

Leo V. Donohue, the Democrat, and Henry J. Becker, the Republican, compare their operation with the work of the country's largest accounting companies. Middle-level pay and procedures are alike, but Donohue and Becker must labor under the restrictions of the state constitution and statutes on what a department may do. They also must deal with the tendency of state employees to be less concerned with keeping track of equipment and supplies than are their business counterparts.

In 80 to 85 percent of the 125 audits they do annually, Donohue and Becker find the department, agency, or elected official's financial house to be in order. "If we weren't coming in and doing these audits, you wonder what would happen," said Becker.

A lot has happened. The two have helped uncover the embezzlement of $100,000 from a community college, disclosed a construction contract scheme involving a state education employee, and reported the misuse of special auto marker plates for undercover investigators.

In 1981 their audit report cost the commandant of the state Veterans Home and Hospital his job for using state funds to buy a waterbed, bar stools, and other unauthorized items. The case was particularly tough for Donohue. The man was a fellow Democrat and good friend.

"That was a difficult time for us, particularly for me," said Donohue. "It was difficult because we were destroying a career. . . . We were impotent in our attempts to show that he was being unfairly treated."

The system works and is simpler than you'd think, Becker said. State law says that any auditor who fails to report financial abuses is subject to jail or a fine. But state law can't protect Donohue and Becker from the wrath of the officials they sting.

The fact that they had issued reports calling state housing department records chaotic and criticizing the Department of Human Resources for being slow in reclaiming $2.8 million in local grants drew a response from the state Commissioner of Administrative Services, Elisha C. Freedman. "An auditor," he said, "enters the battlefield after the war is over and attacks the wounded."

Source: "If We Weren't Doing Audits, You Wonder What Would Happen," by Dan Hall, *New England Business,* March 1, 1982, p. 48.

External Audits. An **external audit** consists of an appraisal of the firm's financial statements by a qualified independent agent, usually a certified public accounting firm. All financial documents are checked for accuracy and completeness. The purpose of these audits is not to prepare such statements but, rather, to verify that they accurately reflect the financial condition of the firm.

Internal Audits. **Internal audits,** like external audits, are intended to assess the accuracy and reliability of a firm's financial statement. Internal audits also evaluate the extent of operational efficiency in a firm. Such audits attempt to assess how well a firm's control procedures are doing what they were designed to do. Internal audits are carried out by staff personnel of the firm.

Management Audits. Management audits assess the general effectiveness of management in an organization. Rather than being limited to a study of financial controls, this analysis considers all aspects of management, including production efficiency, research and development investments, sales, service to stockholders, corporate structure, fiscal policies, and general executive effectiveness. Management audits are generally performed every three to five years instead of annually, as are financial audits, and are meant to indicate the overall health of the organization. To be effective, such audits are preferably done by outside professional staffs.

Summary

Control is central to the effectiveness of managers and organizations because of the turbulent environment and the growing complexity of organizations, and because it provides a means of checking on people's mistakes. Most control systems set objectives and performances standards, measure performance, compare the performance with the standard, and take corrective action when necessary.

There are several types of controls, including steering, gatekeeper, and postaction controls. Problems that can result are rigid bureaucratic behavior and invalid data reporting. Employees may also act solely to influence their own performance indicators or may resist the controls in a variety of ways.

Budgets aid in the planning process by forcing managers to establish and communicate basic policies and objectives. They lead to periodic company self-analysis, contribute to the efficient use of resources, clarify specific areas of responsibility, and help implement corporate strategy. Top management initiates the budgeting process, and then each unit prepares a preliminary budget that is reviewed, modified, and approved by top management. Performance is reviewed periodically.

There are two primary types of budgets, operating and financial. Operating budgets can be associated with cost (expense) centers, revenue centers, and profit centers. Financing, cash, capital expenditure, and balance sheet budgets are all types of financial budgets. Two recent approaches to budgeting are the planning-programming-budgeting system (PPBS) and zero-base budgeting (ZBB).

Financial statements help determine the long- and short-term financial standing of the organization. Three forms of financial statements are the balance sheet, income statement, and cash flow statement.

Auditing procedures are another kind of financial control; they verify the fairness, accuracy, and honesty of financial statements. There are three kinds of audits: external, internal, and management.

Questions for Discussion

1. Discuss what we mean by a control system and why such systems are important in organizations.
2. Describe the control process as a general model.
3. Identify the three primary types of control systems in organizations.
4. What are some of the more important problems with control systems?
5. How would you characterize an effective control system?
6. Describe the steps in the budgeting process.
7. Differentiate between operating budgets and financial budgets.
8. What is PPBS? How does it differ from zero-base budgeting?
9. Describe several positive and negative consequences of budgets.
10. Discuss the audit function in organizational planning and control.

Case Study
What Undid Jarman: Paperwork Paralysis

When Chairman Franklin M. Jarman wrested control of Genesco Inc. from his father, W. Maxey, to become chief executive officer four years ago, one of his primary goals was to impose a system of financial controls over the $1 billion retailing and apparel conglomerate. The 45-year-old Jarman did exactly that. His controls probably helped to save the company when it lost $52 million in 1973. But they were also chiefly responsible for his downfall last week.

Controls were an obsession with Jarman. According to insiders, he centralized management to the point of frustrating the company's executives and causing red tape and delay. Operations were virtually paralyzed by paperwork. One glaring example: Genesco's most recent annual report states that the company would spend $8 million this year to open 63 stores and renovate 124 others. Yet six months into the fiscal year, insiders report that little has been done because Jarman required more and more analysis for each project, postponing decisions.

Such delay and indecision can be particularly harmful in a company like Genesco, whose business is mostly in the fast-moving fields of apparel and retailing. Among its major product lines are Johnston & Murphy and Jarman Shoes, and its retail outlets include Bonwit Teller and S. H. Kress. "It was a classic case of the boss being in the way, and he had

to go," explains one Genesco insider, who was among the more than two dozen executives participating in the palace revolt last week when Jarman was stripped of his authority.

The Undoing

Two of Genesco's inside directors, Vice-Chairmen Ralph H. Bowles and Larry B. Shelton, had become alarmed by Genesco's inertia in October. At the same time many top managers complained to them that Jarman's management had been demoralizing. When Jarman seemed to be preparing to oust two key operating executives, Bowles and Shelton went to an outside director to explain how the company's fortunes were deteriorating. He in turn contacted other outside directors. Meantime, Bowles, Shelton, and several managers compiled for the directors a dossier of Jarman's managerial shortcomings.

Things all came together between Christmas and New Year's when Jarman was on vacation at Montego Bay. Bowles, Shelton, several managers, and four outside directors met in Washington. They called a special meeting of the board for the Monday after New Year's. With more than two dozen rank-and-file executives ready to quit if Jarman was not ousted — and waiting in the cafeteria next door on the second floor of the Genesco building in Nashville — the board did the next best thing. It took away Jarman's titles of president and chief executive officer and gave them to William M. Blackie, 72, a retired executive vice-president and former director, and told Jarman that he must take his orders from Blackie.

Jarman declined to be interviewed by *Business Week* for this article. But sources close to him and the company say that he was treated shabbily by the Genesco board and executives — many of whom owed their jobs to him. These sources say Jarman was the victim of a conspiracy, which they say started after word got out that he was looking for a new president with marketing experience, a job for which he had hired the New York search firm of Knight & Zabriskie. According to this scenario, Bowles, 46, and Shelton, 42, feared that if a new president were brought in they would lose standing. Jarman came back from vacation and just before the board meeting issued a statement saying that it would be "inappropriate and contrary to the interests of the stockholders of Genesco to make any radical change in the company's management. . . . With the approval of members of the board of directors, [Jarman has] been seeking to hire a new president." Bowles and Shelton maintain that they were not among those members, and that all they knew was that Jarman was looking for a senior marketing executive.

The Performance

In any case, Genesco's performance under Jarman was erratic. Although he pared many losing operations and improved the balance sheet, Genesco lost money in two of his four years as CEO. For example, last year earnings rebounded to $15.9 million, or about $1 a share, after a loss of $14.4 million the year before, but in the first quarter of this fiscal year ending October 31, earnings were off 61%, and Jarman had projected similarly disappointing results for the important second quarter, which includes Christmas.

Insiders are convinced there was a correlation between Genesco's earnings and the overcentralized and inflexible management style they say Jarman favored. Many criticisms of Jarman's management were chronicled by Genesco executives and by Bowles and Shelton in the form of internal memoranda. The memoranda were put in dossiers several

inches thick and given to each director. The board took its action last week largely on the basis of this material.

One Genesco director thinks that this approach was amateurish and unnecessary, although he voted to oust Jarman. He says the material in the dossier consisted principally of "record memoranda — written to the files after conversations with Jarman — that were very self-serving." The memoranda, he adds, contained many inconsistencies, such as that Jarman was too involved in detail or that he was not involved enough.

An insider who has read the material says that there are inconsistencies because Jarman was an inconsistent manager. He cites the example of a new shoe store under consideration. Jarman demanded a 75-page report on the $44,000 store dealing with such trifling details as whether it should have a water cooler and hot running water. On the other hand, this executive says that if a division executive had an overwhelming personality, he could push through decisions with "no checks, no balances, not even pro forma financial statements" — as was recently done with a proposal for a new Bonwit Teller store.

As a matter of course, insiders say, Jarman got bogged down in minutiae. He delegated little real authority to his managers, even the two vice-chairmen.

"Better run it by Frank" was the company watchword for the most routine, everyday matters. He spent a great deal of time insisting that reports be bound properly in notebooks.

An Aloofness

Another criticism is that Jarman isolated himself and avoided contact with company executives. Typically, he dealt only with the four other members of the management committee, of which he was chairman and which included Bowles, Shelton, and two operating executives. Jarman, an engineer educated at the Massachusetts Institute of Technology, had come up through the financial side of Genesco and, as a director notes, "has never been good at handling people."

One executive says that ever since Jarman had become CEO, top people in the company had been trying to get him to visit the company's many plants and offices. This executive says Jarman did it just once. Moreover, Jarman canceled the customary annual management breakfast meetings that brought all the top executives together with the chairman. Because of Jarman's isolation from other Genesco managers it is doubtless that the revolt against him was carried out so smoothly.

Jarman's style was to work from computer printouts, checking them for aberrations. He reportedly used to say that managing a corporation was like flying an airplane — his avocation. " 'You watched the dials to see if the plane deviated off course and when it did you nudged it back with the controls,' Jarman explained," the insider says. "At Genesco the computer printouts were the dials and Bowles and Shelton were the controls."

Sometimes, however, Jarman did not believe what the printouts said. He hired consultants to verify things, such as a division's overhead charges, or the quality and pricing of its products. The footwear division, which has been consistently profitable, got this treatment several times.

Still, a Surprise

Jarman's ouster, nevertheless, took many observers by surprise. To begin with, the board had recently granted him a $105,000 raise to $285,000 a year, even though Genesco pays no common stock dividend. (The board cut Jarman to $180,000 annually last week.)

Equally surprising was the fact that Genesco's board has been structured to Jarman's specifications in recent years. Over a four-year period, it was reduced from eighteen to ten members, and many of the father's supporters were replaced by the son's choices, such as Bowles, Shelton, and Wilson, with whom Frank Jarman served on several corporate and civic boards.

To insiders, however, things were different. First, after news broke of Jarman's 58 percent raise, Genesco employees signed petitions to protest. Moreover, there was overwhelming sentiment in middle management that Jarman had to go if Genesco was to survive. "You could count Jarman's supporters on the fingers of one hand," one executive said.

Last week the board started searching for an outsider to fill the presidency. Whoever lands the Genesco job will have a challenge not only to produce consistent earnings but also to gain the support of the managers, the vice-chairmen, and the board of directors. "It's a slippery perch," says one corporate recruiter.

Case Questions

1. Examine Jarman's motives in implementing his new control systems.
2. Why did the control systems fail to work? What could Jarman have done differently?
3. What can you learn from this case about implementing effective control systems in organizations? Explain.

Source: Reprinted from the January 24, 1977 issue of *Business Week* by special permission, © 1977 by McGraw-Hill, Inc.

Operations and Production Control

Kenneth D. Ramsing

"Whata you gonna make? What does it take to make it? Whata you got? Whata you gotta get?"

This is Oliver W. Wight's very successful translation of the material requirements planning inventory system. He repeats it several times an hour at educational seminars for purchasing agents and production chiefs and in presentations he videotapes in a studio near his New Hampshire home.

Wight probably picked up his no-nonsense manner in his days as an inventory clerk for Raybestos-Manhattan. It has served him well. Today he is one of the most successful of a group of consultants helping business learn to use computers to manage inventories. Wight was earning $25,000 a year as a manufacturing-education manager for International Business Machines when he quit in 1968 to start his own business. By 1981 the Wight companies were grossing more than $5 million annually.

He has also begun a consulting service that evaluates computer software packages available to companies unwilling or unable to develop their own inventory control systems. Now, because of the availability of these packages and increasingly inexpensive computers, "The small companies are doing better than the giants." Wight said.

He believes teaching top executives how to use material requirements planning is now his most important task. According to Wight, their insights will ultimately determine whether it lives up to its potential for improving productivity.

Source: Adapted with permission from "A Plain Teacher of a New Art," *Fortune,* July 27, 1981, p. 79.

Chapter Outline

- The Operations Management System
- Forecasting
- Scheduling
- Inventory Decisions
- Quality Control Systems
- Operations Information

Key Terms

- operations management
- transformation process
- moving averages
- exponential smoothing
- regression analysis
- inventory
- carrying costs
- shortage costs
- setup costs
- order costs
- material requirements planning
- *kanban* system
- quality circles
- management information systems
- decision support systems

Chapter Objectives

After studying Chapter 8 you should be able to

1. Discuss the basic inputs that have a direct and measurable influence on the operations manager.
2. Understand how trends, seasonal variations, and random occurrences can affect demand.
3. Explain how moving averages can mitigate the effects of random fluctuations in demand.
4. Understand the reasons for maintaining an inventory.
5. See how the computer revolution is helping managers by providing the data they need.

Introduction

It's easy to take our world for granted. We get accustomed to the convenience of having a car, a refrigerator, one or more television sets, and other luxuries. We seldom consider how these goods become part of our lives, and who makes them. It is easier, perhaps, to consider the services provided by supermarkets, travel agencies, insurance companies, banks, and many other organizations.

What do services and durable goods have in common? Both are available because of the efforts of labor and investment of capital. When you purchase something at a store or use the services of a bank, you are involved in the marketing segment of business. The production of goods and services is less easily observed.

Managing the production of goods and services, often called **operations management,** is vital to the international economic role of a country. It is not a new field of study, but it is regaining considerable interest as other nations become more competitive with the United States. Any discussion of management is incomplete if it does not consider operations and production control.

Operations management, production management, and manufacturing all describe the same basic discipline. The names have changed as the field has evolved from strictly the creation of goods to the provision of services as well. Today operations management is the process of obtaining and utilizing resources to produce goods and services that are consistent with the goals of the organization. This organization may be a manufacturer, a medical clinic or hospital, a university, or a department store.

The Operations Management System

The **transformation** or **conversion process,** or the process by which inputs are converted into desired goods or services, is the basis of the operations management system. The process, illustrated in Figure 8.1, is influenced by many environmental factors. For example, in June 1983 Pan American World Airways felt the pressure between China and the United States when it began to serve Taiwan from the United States. China demanded that the airline be removed as the carrier between the United States and China. Political pressures between nations can influence a company's actions.

But political influences are only a part of the environmental factors that can affect the operations management system. Another recent influence, the Japanese attitude toward industrial relations, is part of the reason for Japanese world market strength. It has been said that "there are no class barriers in [the] Japanese company, and inter-class mobility is high. Because of that, Japanese industrial relations are characterized by strong ties of faith and trust, and are also stable" (Takamiya, 1981).

Figure 8.1
Operations Management System

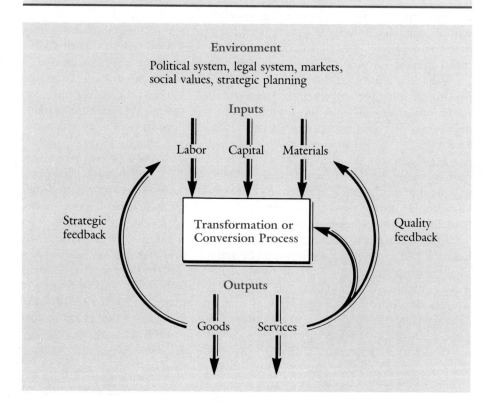

The influence of marketing is more obvious than that of most environmental factors. Elements such as consumer demand, prices, and competition are also important to the transformation system and strategic planning is another important consideration. Strategic planners determine both the types of products or services to be marketed and how they will be distributed to the consumer. In this way, their influence on the transformation system is crucial to the organization.

Inputs into the Operations Management System

It is important to be aware of the external factors that affect the operations management system. Keeping their influence in mind, we can turn to issues that have more direct and measurable influence on the operations manager. These basic inputs are labor, capital, and materials.

Labor is an organization's human resources — employees — who are involved in either making a product or providing a service. Some employees are not directly involved in the production of goods and services. These people, known as **support personnel,** may be responsible for accounting, record keeping, data processing, janitorial services, or maintenance. They may also include engineers, managers, and supervisors who are not directly involved in the production process.

Capital is the money, equipment, machinery, buildings, and other physical assets necessary to produce a product or provide a service. As has been the case during the past few years, in the next decade extremely large amounts of money will be needed to build new plants and equipment to improve productivity. Robots and other computer-controlled machines are expensive and require special facilities and personnel. A single robot may cost as much as half a million dollars; even the most simple robots may cost thousands of dollars. Nevertheless, these new production methods are necessary to increase productivity and competitiveness in the international marketplace.

Materials are the physical items directly used in producing a product or a service. When a car is made, the steel, plastic, aluminum, and fabric put into it account for a large proportion of the car's value. The materials involved in providing a service may include only paper, ink, or other incidental items. The amounts may be small per customer, but serving large numbers of customers or clients often requires tons of paper and forms. In a hospital, great numbers of disposable gowns, bed sheets, dressings, and other materials are used daily, even though the hospital, too, provides a service.

Conversion into Goods and Services

The transformation process is the conversion of labor, capital, and materials into goods and services through a production process. We can see the actual conversion of potatoes into chips, but it is hard to track mentally the production of gasoline from crude oil shipped from some distant country. Yet we know that with heat, catalysts, and additives, gasoline will flow from the refineries and be ready to fill up your car's fuel tank.

To provide a better understanding of the need for increased productivity in the transformation process, we will provide a look at the types of technology involved. We will describe the conversion process in terms of small batches or units of production, in-place production, mass production, and continuous production.

Unit (Small-Batch) Production. A unit (small-batch) production system, sometimes known as a *job shop,* manufactures small numbers of items or individual pieces, such as custom photographs, handmade pieces of furniture, or batches of cookies. This type of production includes a special form called **in-place production,** in which workers come to the job at a fixed construction site. We see this type of manufacturing when a house is constructed or a pipeline installed. In both unit and in-place production, it is necessary to have equipment with more than one function. For example, a hammer used to construct a house can pound nails, drive in a stake, or tap a board into place. This type of tool is termed **general purpose.**

Mass Production. In **mass production,** large volumes of identical or similar goods are produced. For example, the electric toaster you have in your kitchen was probably made on an assembly line on the same day as hundreds of others. That assembly line was probably capable of manufacturing several different models or styles with very little modification. The assembly line process uses special-purpose machines or tools capable of doing little more than one function. Computers, for example, have a special circuit board on which many small electronic parts must be soldered. On an assembly line these boards may be soldered on a specialized machine capable of doing only that one task. Although it is possible to change the size of the printed circuit board, and the number of electronic parts on the board may vary, the machine is still only soldering. It is in mass production that robots are being used today. Assembly line workers in mass production generally need a narrower range of skills than those working under the job shop system.

Continuous Flow System. The continuous flow system is different from the other forms of technology in that it involves only very limited human interaction with the transformation process. Most of the production is carried out by machines, and it is difficult to stop the flow in this system. A plant producing petrochemicals looks like a series of pipes and towers, with few people other than those in control booths monitoring visual display screens and dials. An electric generating plant is another type of continuous flow system. The workers in such a system are generally skilled but do not have a direct hand in creating the product. Instead, production is usually an automatic process that people monitor and maintain.

Output of Production Systems

What is the output of the transformation process? In the examples we have used, we can see some of the outputs: services and products. Transformation is going on all around us, in the offices and factories in our cities and on the farms and ranches of the countryside. Feeding and raising cattle or dairy cows is a production system just as is the processing of checks in a bank, and many of the same characteristics are present in the two. Service industries do not create a tangible product, but they use some of the same techniques and concepts as the factory.

How does this production system operate? In the rest of this chapter, some of the concepts and techniques used in operations management will be discussed. These techniques will shed light on the methods a manager can use to solve his or her problems in the transformation process. We will look at forecasting, scheduling, inventory, and quality control techniques used in operations management.

Forecasting

We all speculate on what the demands will be on our time in the next day or so. You may be looking forward to the weekend and considering how much homework you will have and whether you will have enough time to go water skiing or play tennis. In projecting your work load you are actually **forecasting.** In much the same manner, companies attempt to forecast the demand for their products and services so that they will be in a better position to plan the number of workers and the size of the facilities that will be needed in the future. It is this process of forecasting, or predicting future events through structured analysis, that we will investigate next.

    Demand has three basic components: trend, seasonal variation, and random occurrences. Over a longer period there may also be a cyclical variation in demand. These basic components are illustrated in Figure 8.2.

Figure 8.2
Market Demand

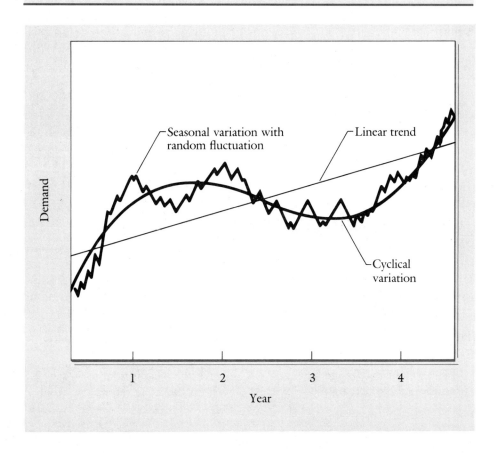

The term *trend* refers to the long-range change in demand for a product or service. Over a period of five or six years, for example, we may notice that demand is increasing slightly, as Figure 8.2 shows. The trend may continue to increase, remain at a constant level, or decrease.

Seasonal variation is a fluctuation in demand associated with the season of the year. For example, department stores rarely sell electric blankets during the hottest part of the summer. But when the weather cools a bit in the fall, the sale of blankets becomes brisk. Some industries, such as home construction, are highly seasonal, whereas the demand for milk, for example, is fairly constant and stable.

Random fluctuations are changes in demand that have no pattern and cannot be forecast. A highly fluctuating condition is usually removed from the forecast using a technique called *smoothing,* which is a part of the forecasting procedure.

Moving Averages

When there is a great deal of random fluctuation, it is difficult to visualize the demand for a service or product. One way of removing some effects of random fluctuation is by a simple process of moving averages. The **moving average** is illustrated in Figure 8.3. Let's see how the moving averages for four- and six-month periods were determined. The four-month moving average (MA) for electric blanket sales for April is calculated as

$$MA = \frac{662(\text{Jan.}) + 416(\text{Feb.}) + 265(\text{March}) + 105(\text{April})}{4} = 362.00$$

As you move from April to May, drop the oldest sales (January) and add the newest month's sales (May) but continue to divide by 4. If more smoothing is wanted, a larger denominator is used. Thus, the moving average for six periods is smoothed more than a four-period average.

Exponential Smoothing

When large numbers of data are used, the moving average of smoothing data is awkward. In addition, in the moving average all data points are given the same weight. A manager may want to give more weight to the most recent periods and less emphasis to the past. This can easily be done with a technique called **exponential smoothing,** which uses the following relationship:

Forecast = past period's forecast + [weight × (actual demand − past period's forecast)]

The weight may range from zero to 1. When the weight is large — say, 0.7 — considerably more emphasis will be placed on the most recent sales than if

Figure 8.3
Moving Average: Demand for Electric Blankets

MONTH	NO. OF ELECTRIC BLANKETS SOLD	FOUR-MONTH MOVING AVERAGE	SIX-MONTH MOVING AVERAGE
January	662		
February	416		
March	265		
April	105	362.00	
May	24	202.50	
June	93	121.75	260.83
July	14	59.00	152.83
August	63	48.50	94.00
September	75	61.25	62.33
October	326	119.50	99.17
November	786	312.50	226.17
December	1,211	599.50	412.50

the weight is small, such as 0.2. Let's consider an example of exponential forecasting. Suppose that the December sales for electric blankets were forecast as 1,127. Using the actual sales for December from Figure 8.1 and a weight of 0.25, we obtain the following:

$$\text{Forecast (Jan.)} = 1{,}127 + [0.25 \times (1{,}211 - 1{,}127)] = 1{,}148$$

Exponential forecasting can also be extended to adjust for seasonality and for trend.

Regression Analysis

Regression analysis is a more sophisticated method of dealing with sales forecasting. This method uses knowledge of the relationship of one variable, an independent variable such as time, to an estimate of a second, dependent variable, sales. In its simplest form, regression analysis develops a linear relationship from which a linear regression line may be determined. This is done with a series of statistical methods, resulting in an equation such as

$$Y = 116.575 + 33.86X$$

Y is the number of electric blankets sold. In Figure 8.4, the intercept, or point at which the straight line intersects the vertical axis (sales of electric blankets), is at 116.575 units. If we look at the slope of the line, we see that it increases at a rate of 33.86 blankets per month. (X in the preceding equation is the

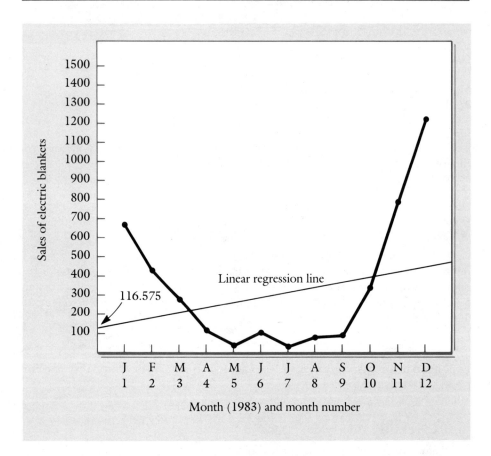

Figure 8.4
*Regression Analysis: Demand for Electric Blankets
(Based on Actual Sales)*

month number; e.g., January is 1 and October is 10.) Because this is difficult to see on the graph, it is more accurate to look at the change in slope over a ten-month period ($33.86 \times 10 = 338.6$). Thus, in month ten (October), we would expect the sales to be $116.575 + 338.6$, or 455.175.

The actual sales in October (326) are fairly close to this forecasted value. In November, however, the regression line understates the actual sales by a considerable amount. Such a finding is not uncommon when using regression, because the line is fitted to all the data points and does not adequately adjust itself to seasonality. There is a form of seasonal adjustment that can be used, however. Suppose that in November of the prior year the forecaster found that the ratio of actual sales to the regression forecast was 1.72. It is possible to multiply this ratio by the value from the regression line for November as follows:

Seasonally adjusted forecast = regression line forecast $\times$ seasonal adjustment

Our forecast, then, is:

$$\text{Blankets (Nov.)} = [116.575 + (11 \times 33.86)] \times 1.72 = 841.1$$

Scheduling

An important facet of the transformation process in operations management is the scheduling of work and people. **Scheduling** is the process of establishing the specific time when a job or some task is to be accomplished. One job usually must be considered as a part of many other jobs in the system. Thus, the scheduling of a particular order has an impact on all the other orders a company must process.

Let's consider what scheduling means. Imagine you are standing in line to cash a check at a bank in which only one teller's window is open. Normally, tellers take people as they arrive. (This is particularly evident in banks that require all their customers to form one line, the next customer in the line going to the next available teller.) Each person in the line is treated equally. This process is actually a form of scheduling called *first come, first served*. In a bank in which there is only one teller, however, the people in line may have to wait for some time if the customers ahead of them have lengthy transactions. A delay with the person being served will delay all those waiting.

To overcome this problem, another scheduling discipline may be used that is called *shortest processing time*. Suppose every person had some estimate of the amount of time he or she would require at the teller's window. The next person to be served by the teller would be the person requiring the shortest time to process his or her transactions.

You are no doubt thinking that this shortest processing time scheduling would be wonderful if you are the one with only a short transaction for the teller. If your business will require a long time with the teller, however, you may have a long wait before you are served, because others with briefer business will join the line. These people will go ahead of you and be waited on before you. Is this fair?

Normally, the shortest processing time rule is not used when there is a customer or client. It may, however, be used for processing forms or computer programs, or scheduling the manufacture or repair of equipment. The method is used in these areas because it actually results in a smaller average waiting time for jobs in the system than does the first come, first served rule. The shortest processing time rule does not work well with customers, because most of us feel annoyed or angry if someone goes ahead of us.

In some cases, scheduling is done with computer simulation models. The computer simulates the flow of orders into the system, considers different possible schedules, and then tests them. The computer simulation permits a manager to evaluate several types of schedules in the computer, changing the relationships among the variables without actually involving the workers and customers. Once a manager obtains the schedule that he or she feels is appropriate, the schedule from the computer can be used.

Inventory Decisions

It is common for us to read in the newspaper or in business periodicals that businesses are manufacturing for inventory or that business inventories are going up or down. We take it for granted when we go to the department or grocery store that we will be able to purchase what we want. We assume that the store will have what we want in stock or be able to obtain it in a matter of hours or days. But what about other aspects of inventory: having the goods when you want them, stabilizing the work force, reducing the problems associated with scheduling, and providing a smoother flow of goods in manufacturing?

Inventory is the amount of inputs or outputs that we keep on hand in an operations management system. Inventory may consist of raw materials, work-in-process goods, supplies, and finished materials in a production or service system. The supply of food that a restaurant must keep to meet its customers' varying tastes is an inventory. The extra gowns or bed sheets maintained in a hospital are inventory, items that must be available when needed. Let's look at some other reasons for maintaining inventories.

Benefits of Inventory Decisions

Perhaps the most important reasons for maintaining an inventory are to

1. Provide a buffer against fluctuation in the demand for goods,
2. Maintain independence between operations,
3. Protect against variation in raw material delivery times,
4. Allow flexibility in production schedules,
5. Take advantage of price breaks associated with large-quantity purchases of goods.

To provide a better understanding of each of these, let's discuss them in more detail.

Demand Buffer. It is nearly impossible for a store manager or a production superintendent to anticipate exactly the demand for a specific product at any one point. The inventory or stock of goods helps overcome the problem of random fluctuations in demand. Remember the random fluctuations in the sales of electric blankets we considered in our discussion of forecasting? A department store manager does have some notion that sales of electric blankets will increase when the weather begins to get chilly. But he or she does not know the *exact* demand for electric blankets. As a result, some extra blankets are prob-

Feature 8.1
LIFO Means Big Changes for Western Electric

Says Comptroller Kenneth Easter: "Western Electric is probably switching to LIFO for at least a part, and maybe all, of its inventories." Does that matter? You bet it does. The probable switch involves a jolt to AT&T's future earnings that could figure in the hundreds of millions of dollars. The jolt could hurt AT&T in the stock market. On the positive side, the change may also bring major increases in cash flow.

LIFO . . . stands for last in, first out, and is a method of accounting for inventories. It allows a firm to assume that the most recent goods manufactured are the most recent ones sold. FIFO (first in, first out), by contrast, assumes that you are selling the oldest goods first.

In times of high inflation the difference between these two methods can be major. Let's say you have two year's worth of inventory in your warehouse. You sell widgets today for $10. But are you selling the ones that cost you $9 to make last week or are you selling the ones you made two years ago that cost you $5 to make? If you claim you are selling the more recently manufactured ones, with higher related costs (last in, first out), reported earnings go down. But so do taxes. Result: higher cash flow.

While no one will part with exact estimates, Easter is willing to say that for Western Electric the change could bring in "tens of millions" in additional cash flow annually. Prior to the divestiture, of course, Western made up only 5 percent of AT&T's total income. After the spinoff is complete . . . , it will probably make up 30 percent. As a result, such a major change in Western is important to the company as a whole.

But though Western Electric will get this cash flow bonus for years to come, the first year on the new system is always painful. Investors are frequently thrown off by a sudden decline in earnings that results from a change to LIFO. . . .

How big will the earnings drop be at Western Electric? No one at AT&T is willing to discuss the matter, but with inventory at its current $3 billion level and an inflation rate of 5 percent, the figure could approach $150 million pretax, according to calculations provided by Lawrence Portnoy, at Price Waterhouse. If inflation is higher than 5 percent in . . . the first year Western (is) on LIFO, then the cost of the change will go up accordingly.

For example, when Du Pont switched to LIFO in 1974, general inflation was running at 11 percent. The change reduced the company's pretax earnings by $360 million, and aftertax earnings per share fell from $11.22 to $8.20. The effect at Western Electric could be similar. . . .

The change (to LIFO), however, puts Western in conflict with many of its competitors. Firms like ITT, Harris Corp. and Rolm Corp. do not use LIFO. They argue that it poses unnecessary risks in the volatile electronics business — where the cost of inventories is often as likely to go down as up.

Officials at Western accept that argument to a point: Easter says that the company may keep those product lines most likely to suffer inventory price declines on FIFO. That may be, but because of Western's use of LIFO elsewhere, its margins will probably appear slimmer than those of other firms. . . .

Source: Forbes, September 12, 1983, "Is It a Wrong Number?" by Laura Saunders, p. 98. Reprinted by permission. © Forbes Inc., 1983.

ably kept on the store shelves or in the warehouse. This is inventory kept to anticipate the random demand for the blankets, as it is for nearly every product that we use. Inventory is designed to absorb the variations in demand common to the marketplace. As in the case of the electric blankets, inventory also provides for the seasonal increase in demand.

Independent Operations. In processing work, one operator often depends on the completion of work by another person. In a cafeteria, as a plate is passed down the line from one server to another, the vegetable may be served first, then the potatoes, then the meat, and finally the ice cream. If only one plate is being served at a time, any delay by one person will delay all the subsequent operations. This is a simple example of how processing can be delayed in an assembly operation when there is sequential dependency of one operator on the preceding people or work stations. To overcome this problem, inventories may be maintained at each of the stations in the assembly line. This form of inventory is called *work-in-process inventory,* referring to partially completed goods. It provides workers in the assembly line with a store of products that can be drawn upon and sent down the rest of the line when there is a delay at a prior work station.

Delivery Time Buffer. The goods used in production or sold in stores in the United States often have been manufactured some distance away. They are transported by ship, truck, or rail from their point of manufacture to the place where they are sold or used. If there is no inventory and there is a delay in transporting the goods, there can be a delay in further assembly. Something like this may have happened to you when, for example, you saw an advertisement and went to a local store to buy the item in the ad. When you asked the clerk for the item, you may have been told, "I am sorry, but the truck did not come in last night as we expected. May I give you a raincheck?"

Inventory is maintained as a buffer to overcome the problems that arise when an item is out of stock. This form of inventory is also used when materials with different delivery times must be used to assemble a product.

Scheduling Flexibility. In the simplest form of this mechanism, a restaurant may use an inventory of hamburgers to make scheduling easier. The next time you go into a McDonald's restaurant, notice the inventory of hamburgers in the bins behind the counter. Observe what is happening. You will notice that eight to ten "Big Macs" are made and added to the bins at a time. Instead of assembling each hamburger as the order arrives, the person cooking and assembling normally puts together a group of one kind before moving to another type. This allows a faster and more efficient processing of hamburgers that will be in demand in a few minutes.

This example illustrates how the transformation process can be aided by using inventories to increase scheduling flexibility. By grouping orders or making a larger quantity in a single production run, there may be an increase in the time required between placing the order and the completion of the job. This period is called the **lead time.** Increasing the lead time often makes the scheduling smoother and permits more flexibility in the operations.

Economical Purchasing. It sometimes happens, particularly with industrial systems, that buying in larger quantities means a reduced price per unit for the purchaser. This is sometimes known as a *quantity discount* and means that the per-unit price becomes less if the order size increases. This approach does have some merit. Packaging, handling, and shipping costs are usually less per unit when large lots or orders are processed. Also, when an order is being placed, there is usually what is called *setup* time required to prepare for making the product. For example, it generally takes just as long to set up the toaster in the kitchen to prepare toast for one person as it does for four people. The actual time it takes to do the toasting changes, but the time it takes to take out the toaster from a cabinet is fixed. Thus, the setup time per slice is cut into fourths when four slices are made. In a similar manner, when considering the setup time for manufacturing, we may be prorating thousands of dollars over the production size of the particular order.

Costs Associated with Inventory Decisions

Merely keeping an inventory is not enough. Whenever inventory is held, capital is expended, and these costs must be considered. Even if a company does not have to borrow money for inventory, the capital could be used in other ways. In addition, inventory must be kept somewhere. Special rooms or buildings sometimes must be constructed and maintained for keeping goods in storage.

Managers have a tendency to carry more stock than is necessary, without realizing the costs of inventory. Such managers are concerned about *stock outages,* in which demand for an item goes beyond what is in inventory. When a company "stocks out," a sale or a customer may be lost.

There are four costs commonly associated with inventory: carrying, shortage, setup, and order costs. These are very important to consider when determining inventory size, and a manager who is involved with inventory decisions must understand their interplay.

Carrying Costs. There is a cost, although it is not always direct, of carrying inventory. Included are costs associated with obsolescence, depreciation, theft, maintenance of storage facilities, and breakage, as well as capital costs. **Carrying costs** can be quite high, as in the case of keeping green vegetables in the supermarket, or relatively low, as when sand or rock is stored in a vacant lot.

Shortage Costs. **Shortage costs** are more difficult to assess than are carrying costs, because they are associated with *not* selling an item. If an item is not in inventory, a customer may go elsewhere to purchase it or wait until it is in stock again. These costs, often called *opportunity costs,* are the difference between what is actually received and what could have been received had there been an item to sell.

Setup Costs. Getting the equipment ready for production also bears a cost. These **setup costs** may include obtaining raw materials, changing the equipment from one order to another, or cleaning out the machine. For example, changing from packaging white soap powder to blue powder requires a thorough cleaning of the packaging machine.

Order Costs. The managerial and clerical costs of placing an order for more goods to be added to the inventory are called **order costs.** These costs are generally small compared with the other costs we have discussed.

Relationships among Costs. Now that we have seen the costs associated with inventory, it is time to examine the relationships among them. Unless inventory is controlled, these costs can rise considerably. The cost of inventory is one topic that has been studied by the Japanese during the past decade. Companies in the United States also have been reassessing their inventory policies re-

---

Feature 8.2
At General Motors, Inventory is "Evil"

General Motors executives entered the 1980s thinking they had conquered their thorniest problem — radically redesigning their cars.

Sure, the cars were smaller, lighter, more fuel efficient, more radical in design, but the Japanese still maintained a $1,500 to $2,000 cost advantage for a subcompact car. And while American auto makers and their suppliers put 175 hours of management and labor into a typical car, the Japanese put in fewer than 100.

That gap — a result of organization and management — is General Motors's next target. The "just-in-time" inventory system is one phase of many changes planned by the company.

The Japanese say that "the goods flow like water" in their plants, and that quality and low cost go hand in hand. The just-in-time system minimizes inventory and expenses for handling materials, and also produces higher quality. Imperfect parts are revealed as soon as they are made instead of being hidden in among others.

Every General Motors assembly line uses some degree of the just-in-time system, and eventually the concept will govern all General Motors manufacturing.

"All the great warehousing methods will fall by the wayside now," said Robert D. Stone, the vice-president in charge of materials management, purchasing, and production control. "Inventory is evil."

The new system has trimmed General Motors's inventory to $8 billion, down $1.2 billion, in two years. Stone expected inventories to stay at this level in 1983 or even to drop as production rose.

Source: "Will Success Spoil General Motors?" by Charles G. Burck, *Fortune,* August 22, 1983, pp. 94–104.

cently in search of lower costs. In 1982 almost a third of General Motors Corporation's profit of $963 million was due to better management of inventories. General Motors, together with other auto manufacturing companies, has been shifting from large inventories to the Japanese concept of a *just-in-time* style, in which parts arrive as needed *(Eugene Register Guard,* 1983).

Figure 8.5 depicts the *fixed-order-quantity model,* the most common relationship among costs in inventory control. In this model, a manager places an order for the quantity that will minimize the total cost. This total cost, as shown in Figure 8.5, is the sum of the carrying costs and the order costs. The carrying costs increase as the quantity of the order increases; the larger the quantity, the more it will cost to hold the inventory. The order cost, in contrast, will become progressively smaller as the order quantity increases. These two cost trade-offs are important in determining the point at which the inventory levels will be maintained.

Figure 8.5
Cost Trade-off for Inventory Control

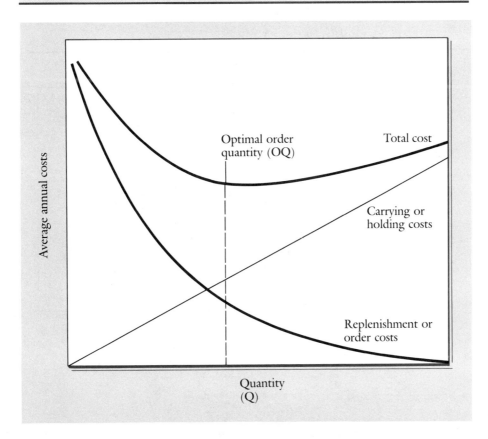

In the fixed-order-quantity model, the time between orders changes but the size of the order placed remains the same. This is illustrated in Figure 8.6. Under this system, an order will be placed for more goods to be shipped when the inventory is depleted to the point at which it crosses the dashed line (the reorder point). The reorder is generally placed before the inventory reaches zero to allow for the lead time usually required for processing an order and shipping the goods. Once the goods are replenished, the inventory will be back at the peak level. For this type of model, the optimal order quantity is determined by the following equation:

$$OQ = \sqrt{\frac{2\,DR}{C}}$$

where OQ = optimal order quantity (for the fixed-order-quantity model), D = average annual demand, R = reordering costs, and C = carrying costs.

The *fixed-order-period model* is similar only in appearance to the inventory system just discussed. In this model, goods are reordered at a specific time instead of when inventory reaches a particular point (Fig. 8.7). Orders are made

Figure 8.6
Fixed-Order-Quantity Inventory Model

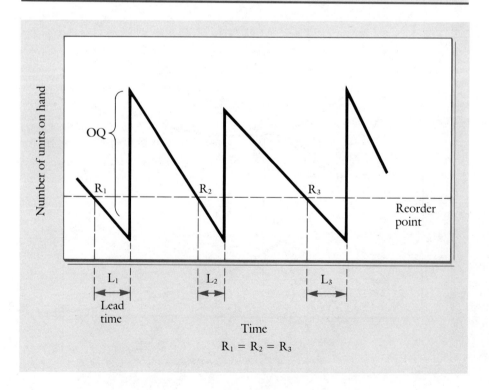

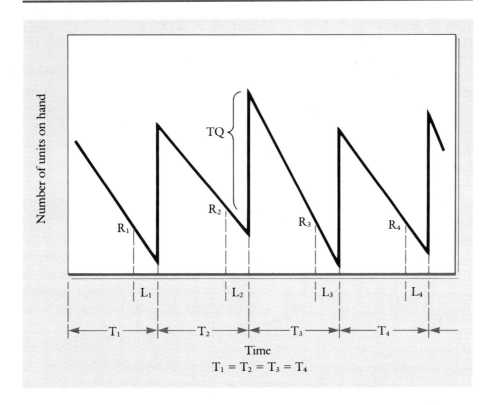

Figure 8.7
Fixed-Order-Period Inventory Model

on a given day of the month or at regular intervals of time. This means that if the demand changes from the average, the maximum inventory level will be greater in some periods than in others. The optimal quantity for reorder is given in the equation:

$$TQ = \sqrt{\frac{2R}{DC}}$$

where TQ = optimal quantity to order (at a particular time), R = reorder costs, D = average annual demand, and C = carrying costs.

Material Requirements Planning

Another form of inventory system has received some emphasis in recent years. This system is called **material requirements planning (MRP).**

As manufacturing has become more complex and the number of parts required for assembling a product has increased, it has become more important to keep better control of inventory and scheduling. This is the purpose of material requirements planning, which is a computerized data information system that performs scheduling and inventory functions for manufacturing. It takes an assembled product and "explodes" it into its components. Figure 8.8 illustrates such an "explosion." This is a simple illustration, but it does convey the same logic used to attack very complex systems with several thousand parts, such as a personal computer.

Material requirements planning uses the data provided by the inventory status file, the master production schedule, and the materials needed to generate information about releasing orders to insure they are received on time, rescheduling orders and planning for future orders. A schematic representation of the system is shown in Figure 8.9.

The *Kanban* System

Toyota Motor Company Ltd. has gained the attention of many companies with its **kanban** system. The objective of this system is to produce the necessary quantities at the required time. This objective appears deceptively simple.

Kanban gets its name from the Japanese word for "card." It is based on a concept of having a card for each item that indicates what has happened to that item. Whenever a part is needed, the operator goes to the storage area, removes the item, and places the *kanban* from that part into a bin for future processing, indicating that the item has been removed. He or she then attaches a new *kanban* to the part to indicate where it must go and how it is to be used. The use of

Figure 8.8
"Explosion" of a Picture Frame
(Material Requirements Planning)

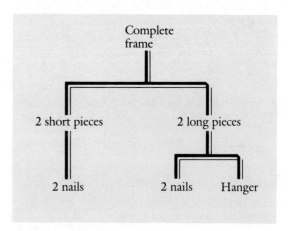

Figure 8.9
Material Requirements Planning (MRP) System

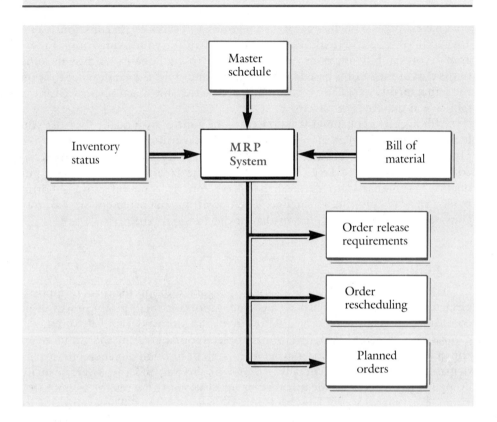

the "withdrawal" and "production-ordering" *kanbans* drives a system that tracks the needed parts and provides the lead time necessary to make new parts.

The *kanban* system was set up by Toyota to increase productivity by cutting production costs. Since that time it has been introduced into American manufacturing with considerable success. The system reduces and nearly eliminates unnecessary intermediate and finished-product inventories (Monden, 1981).

Quality Control Systems

Quality has become more of a concern in recent years to both the consumer and the manager. This may be partly a result of the Japanese emphasis on quality, which has made Japan's industrial system one of the best in the world.

Japanese companies have tried to make quality the personal concern of each worker. The Japanese worker is capable of reducing the rate of defects to an astounding 0.1 percent or even 0.01 percent, even though this may provide no economic benefit. The workers are generally so concerned about quality that they strive for perfection (Hayes, 1981, pp. 56–66).

Quality is important in producing goods and providing services, but quality does have a price. For this reason some goods and services are consciously created with low quality. If you purchase a new chair for your living room, for example, you can buy one of anywhere from low to high quality. Although some of the cost of the chair is based on brand name and style, a great deal depends on the actual quality of skill involved in its manufacture and assembly, as well as the fabrics and materials involved.

Although as a consumer you do have some control over quality because you have the option to buy a more expensive item, it is still the responsibility of the production system to ensure that the quality meets certain standards. This becomes an important strategic consideration. The Japanese generally have put quality at a higher strategic level than have American manufacturers. Fortunately, this is beginning to change. The operations management system now considers quality more important than it did in the recent past.

Quality Circles

The concept of quality is built into an organization in the form of **quality circles.** These quality circles have become important small group processes in companies in recent years. The quality circle is an almost deceptively simple organizational concept having the primary objective of increasing the productivity and quality of the operations management system through direct employee participation. The circle is generally a group of three to ten employees, usually doing related work, who meet at regular intervals (once a week for an hour, for example) to identify problems and discuss their solutions. The group and its leader are normally trained in problem solving, data analysis, quality control, and communications. Upon finding and solving a problem, the group will make a presentation, including cost estimates, to management. Management decides whether to implement all or part of the group's suggestions. Quality circles are finding the same success in American businesses that they have found in Japan.

Quality Control

Another aspect of the quality process in operations management is quality control. In **quality control,** items are normally sampled and compared with standards to determine their quality. Figure 8.1 illustrates the quality feedback loop originating in the outputs of the system and feeding into the transformation process as well as the inputs. This feedback is important to the entire concept of operations management as well as to maintaining the standards of goods and services.

For quality control to be possible, the characteristics of a product or service must be measurable. These measurements are then compared with expectations

Feature 8.3
Workers Run the Shop at Lawrence Cable

To Gino T. Strippoli, quality circles mean he can spend his time managing instead of putting out fires. "The teams," he says, "are putting out the fires way down in the organization."

Strippoli is the general manager of TRW's Lawrence Cable Division in Lawrence, Kansas. His plant makes cables for submersible oil well pumps and has been run by work teams since it opened its doors in 1976.

In 1981 it was one of about 750 corporations and government bodies using quality circles in the country. Unlike the rather narrow Japanese quality circles from which they originated, American quality circles have evolved into a variety of broad, participative systems. The American variety may deal with quality control and its technical details but also with factory lighting or seating, or even production processes or work schedule changes.

At Lawrence, the 130 nonunion members are grouped into ten teams of 5 to 28 members each. Most team members have no specified jobs and can handle most of the team's required functions. Workers may also take on indirectly related jobs such as driving a forklift or handling materials.

Strippoli loves that. Forklifts in traditional plants never have more than twenty or twenty-five hours of running time a week, he pointed out.

"So what are the operators doing with those other fifteen hours?" he asked. "Here we don't have that. The team members are doing whatever's needed — running machines, picking up scrap."

Management assigns output goals, but the teams set their own schedules and deal with other matters ranging from overtime to quality problems. The teams also train new members, appraise their performance, and recommend who should get raises. Workers have also merged overlapping teams and cut down teams that had grown too large.

Strippoli said it's harder to manage a system like the one at Lawrence than a conventional hierarchy. He has a whole plant full of workers ready to catch his mistakes. "I have to be right a hell of a lot more often than I used to be," he said.

Now, too, when something goes wrong, workers don't just stand around. They fix it. That means Strippoli can think less about minute-by-minute operations and more about improving future performances.

Norman St. Laurent, manager of manufacturing engineering at Lawrence, explains how decisions are made with an example about a problem with a machine.

"Since everybody is trained to have their own ideas, I had my idea, the first shift had their ideas, the second shift had theirs, and so on," he said. The answer to the problem came after St. Laurent called an intershift meeting and got group agreement to systematically try all the ideas.

At Lawrence, both workers and management understand the decision-making system. "The workers know that if I feel there's no payback to the company in the solution they arrive at, there will be a definite no," Strippoli said. "I'm not here to give away the store or run a country club."

Source: "What Happens When Workers Manage Themselves," by Charles G. Burck, *Fortune,* July 27, 1981, pp. 62–69.

to determine if the quality standard for the item has been maintained. For example, when we cook we frequently taste a bit of the food to determine if more spices or other additions are needed. In this case we are measuring the sampled food against our own standards, our perception of how it should taste. Quality control is more precise than the sampling of food in our kitchen. In complex industrial quality control, the standards may include pages of specifications with which the samples are compared.

Quality control does not measure merely the final service or product; rather, it starts with the input. Many companies, for example, take samples of the incoming materials to determine if they meet preset standards. Controls must be maintained whether we are dealing with raw materials, such as iron ore, or semifinished goods, such as electronic cables for computers.

It is more difficult to measure services than it is to measure and compare products, but there is a basis for determining the quality of services. The amount of time a person must stand in line waiting to mail a letter or cash a check may be measured, or the effectiveness of a surgical procedure in a hospital may be observed. Quality of service is just as important as quality of products.

Operations Information

The operations management system requires information in order to operate effectively. The owner of a small company may keep most of the information for running the operation in a few readily available journals and his or her own memory. As operations become larger and more complex, with more employees, however, a simple data source is no longer effective. There comes a point at which people are hired just to keep track of the information the organization needs. Even a relatively small firm of fewer than one hundred employees needs a great amount of information daily. Records of employee wage levels, days worked, sick leave accrued and taken, incentive and bonus programs, and other data must be kept. The firm also needs to maintain records of the costs of work centers, time standards, equipment maintenance, and productivity standards. The amount of information on which we base our decisions may increase substantially as the organization grows.

Management Information Systems

To cope with the increased data and information needs of a viable organization, computers are often used for mass data storage and high-speed calculations. This development has led to a field of study and use called **management information systems (MIS),** which is a method of providing management with timely and necessary reports.

The reports created by the computer are frequently the result of what the computer analysts perceive to be the kind of information management needs. Such reports may result from a manager's explaining his or her needs directly to the analyst, who then writes the program that creates the reports. The reports are created at regular intervals, daily, weekly, or monthly, depending on their anticipated use.

Decision Support Systems

The computer industry is undergoing a marked and rapid change. Machine size is being substantially reduced and speed and memory capabilities greatly enhanced. In addition, programs, known as software, are easier for the operator to use. This revolution has made the computer's power and the flexibility it allows available to even the smallest companies. Increased flexibility has led to an extension of MIS called **decision support systems (DSS).** Whereas MIS provides reports on a regular basis regardless of the decisions that need to be made, DSS is more responsive to the specific needs of managers. A manager who must make a decision concerning the output of his or her department can receive data on which to base the decision. There may be a need to find out what impact the marketing department's decisions will have on production in the next five days. The manager need not wait for a report that may not provide the necessary information. Instead, he or she may use a computer terminal or personal computer to call the necessary data base and begin to analyze the results when they are needed.

Whereas MIS deals with well-structured problems, DSS focuses on decisions in which it is not always clear what types of data are needed. This is an important area of decision making and will undoubtedly become an important field of data base management.

Summary

The basis of the operations management system is the transformation or conversion process, or the methods by which inputs are made into goods or services. Labor, capital, and materials all have an effect on operations management.

The types of technology used in the transformation process are unit or small-batch production, in-place production, mass production, and continuous flow systems.

Companies forecast demand so they will be in a better position to plan the number of workers and the size of facilities they will need. Moving averages and exponential smoothing take random fluctuations of demand into account in forecasting. Regression analysis is another way of forecasting sales.

First come, first served and shortest processing time are two methods of scheduling, which is another aspect of operations management.

Inventory decisions are also important. Inventory provides a buffer against fluctuations in demand for goods, helps maintain independence between operations, protects against variations in raw material delivery times, allows flexibility in production schedules, and helps the manufacturer take advantage of quantity-purchase price breaks.

Some of the costs associated with inventory are carrying, shortage, setup, and order costs. Two models that depict the relationship among costs in inventory are the fixed-order-quantity model and the fixed-order-period model.

The material requirements planning system keeps better control of inventory and scheduling. The *kanban* system is another inventory control system, pioneered by Toyota in Japan.

Quality recently has become of greater concern to both customers and managers. In quality circles, employees participate directly in operations management by identifying problems and discussing their solutions. Another aspect of the quality process is quality control.

To cope with the increased data and information needs of growing companies, management information systems, which provide managers with data on a regular basis, and decision support systems, which provide data when it is required, have been developed.

Questions for Discussion

1. This chapter views operations management as a system (see Fig. 8.1). For each of the following, describe the inputs, transformation, outputs, and environmental factors.
   a. An automobile assembly plant
   b. A hospital
   c. A fast-food hamburger restaurant
   d. A university
   e. A fishery

2. Name the businesses with which you are familiar that use some type of forecasting of sales or output.

3. Suppose that a company that makes sailboats has kept records on its boat sales and forecasted sales for eight periods. These data are shown below:

Period	Quarter	Actual Sales (no. of boats)	Forecast Sales (no. of boats)
1	1 '82	84	83
2	2 '82	71	75
3	3 '82	40	45
4	4 '82	49	47
5	1 '83	90	86
6	2 '83	79	82
7	3 '83	60	64
8	4 '83	71	74

   a. Determine a three-period moving average for the actual sales.
   b. Using the data from quarter 4, 1983, determine a forecast for quarter 1, 1984 (period 9), using a weight of 0.25 with exponential smoothing.
   c. The regression equation for these data has been found to be

$$Y = 67.36 + 0.1428\,X$$

   Plot the actual sales on graph paper. Using the equation, plot on this same graph the regression line. (Hint: Assume that quarter 1, 1982, is period 1 and that quarter 4, 1983, is period 8.)

    d. Using a seasonal adjustment from quarter 1, 1983, make a seasonally adjusted forecast for the same quarter, 1984, by extending the regression line you plotted in part c.

4. Just-in-time manufacturing focuses on achieving very low or zero inventories. Using the optimal order quantity formula, show how smaller lot sizes can be achieved by reducing the setup costs (which may be a function of time). Use your own values for the demand and costs for this problem.

5. Look around your home or apartment. What is your estimate of the life of such appliances as the refrigerator, range, and toaster? Is this long life a function of quality? What other attributes of quality do you consider when purchasing the following:

    a. A car

    b. Clothes

    c. Floppy disks for a computer

    d. Food

6. Personal computers are becoming very important in the lives of students and business people alike. Describe some of the types of decision making that are possible with the DSS concept supported by the software (programs) used with micro- or personal computers.

Exercise 8.1
American Ceramic and Glass Products Corporation

The American Ceramic and Glass Products Corporation employed a total of approximately 13,000 people, each of its three plants employing between 4,000 and 5,000 of this total. About three-quarters of its sales volume came from standard glass containers produced on highly automatic equipment; the balance of the company's sales were of specialized ceramic and glass items produced in batches on much less automated equipment. John Parr, production manager for American Ceramic and Glass Products, had just completed a trip that covered eight states, seven universities, and three major industrial centers. The purpose of his trip was to recruit personnel for American's three plants. He felt that his trip had been extremely successful and that he had made contacts that would, he hoped, result in his firm's acquiring some useful and needed personnel.

    Parr was anxious to secure a capable person to head up the inspection and quality control department of the largest of American's plants, located in Denver, Colorado. The position of chief of inspection and quality control had just been vacated by George Downs, who had taken an indefinite leave of absence due to a serious illness. There was little possibility that Downs would be capable of resuming any work duties within a year and a substantial probability that he would never be capable of working on a full-time basis. During the ten years that Downs held the position of chief of inspection and quality control, he had completely modernized the firm's inspection facilities and had developed a training program in the use of the most modern inspection equipment and techniques. The physical facilities of Downs's inspection department were a major attraction for visitors to the plant.

Thomas Calligan

During his trip, Parr interviewed two men whom he felt were qualified to fill Downs's position. Although each appeared more than qualified, Parr felt that a wrong choice could easily be made. Thomas Calligan, the first of the two men, was a graduate of a reputable trade school and had eight years of experience in the inspection department of a moderately large manufacturing firm (approximately 800 employees). He began working as a production inspector and was promoted to group leader within two years and chief inspector two years later. His work record as a production inspector, as a group leader, and as chief inspector was extremely good. His reason for wishing to leave the firm was ''to seek better opportunities.'' He felt that in his present firm he could not expect further promotions in the near future. His firm was known for its stability, low employee turnover, and slow but assured advancement opportunities. His superior, the head of quality control, was recently promoted to this position and was doing a more than satisfactory job. Further, he was a young man, only 32 years old.

James King

James King, the second of the two men being considered by Parr, was a graduate of a major southwestern university and had approximately five years of experience. King was currently employed as head of inspection and quality control in a small manufacturing firm employing approximately 300 people. His abilities exceeded the requirements of his job, and he had made arrangements with his employer to do a limited amount of consulting work for noncompeting firms. His major reason for wanting to secure a different position was a continuing conflict of interests between himself and his employer. King did not wish to make consulting his sole source of income, but he felt that his current position was equally unsatisfactory. He believed that by working for a large firm he would be able to fully utilize his talents within and thus resolve conflict occurring between his professional interests and the interests of his employer.

King's work record appeared to be good. This was evidenced by the fact that he had recently been granted a sizable pay increase. King, like Calligan, began his career as a bench inspector and was rapidly promoted to his current supervisory position. Unlike Calligan, King viewed his initial position of bench inspector primarily as a means of financing his education and not as the beginning of his lifetime career. King was 31 years old.

Role of Inspection and Quality Control

Major differences between these individuals centered on their philosophies regarding the role of inspection and quality control in a manufacturing organization. Calligan's philosophy was:

> Quality is an essential part of every product. . . . It is the product development engineer's function to specify what constitutes quality and the function of quality control to see that the manufacturing departments maintain these specifications. . . . Accurate and vigilant inspection is the key to controlled quality.

When asked how important process control was in the manufacture of quality products, he stated,

Process control is achieved primarily through the worker's attitude. If a firm pays high wages and provides good working conditions, they should be able to acquire highly capable workers. . . . A well-executed and efficient inspection program will, as it has done in my firm, impress the importance of quality on the employees and motivate high-quality production. In the few cases when quality lapses do occur, an efficient inspection program prevents defective products from leaving the plant. . . . Any valid quality control program must hold quality equal in importance to quantity. . . . Quality records must be maintained for each employee and be made known to both the employee and his immediate superiors. Superior quality should be a major consideration in recommending individuals for promotion or merit pay increases.

King's philosophy paralleled that of Calligan only to the extent that "quality was an essential part of every product." King made the following comments regarding his philosophy toward inspection and quality control:

If quality is properly controlled, inspection becomes a minor function. The more effective a quality control system becomes, the less inspection is required. . . . The key to quality control is process control, and inspection serves only as a check to assure that the process controls are being properly administered. . . . An effective inspection scheme should locate and pinpoint the cause of defects rather than place the blame on an often innocent individual. A good rejection report will include the seeds from which a solution to future rejections can be developed. . . . One sign of an unsatisfactory quality control system is a large, impressive inspection program.

King was asked what steps he would take to develop such a program if he were to be offered and accept the job of chief of inspection and quality control in the Denver plant. He answered,

I would design and install a completely automatic inspection and process control system throughout the plant. By automatic I do not mean a mechanical or computer-directed system, but rather a completely standardized procedure for making all decisions concerning inspection and process control. The procedures would be based on a theoretically sound statistical foundation translated into laymen's terminology. The core of the program would be a detailed inspection and quality control manual.

When asked how long this might take King continued,

I constructed a similar manual for my present employer in a period of less than twelve months and had the whole process operating smoothly within eighteen months after beginning work on the task. Since your firm is somewhat larger, and accounting for my added experience, I would estimate it to take no longer than two years and hopefully significantly less time. . . . As previously stated, I would place major emphasis on process control and would minimize inspection by applying appropriate sampling procedures wherever possible. . . . Employee quality performance should be rated on the basis of process control charts rather than on the basis of final inspection reports. The employee should be trained and encouraged to use these charts as his chief tool toward achieving quality output.

King further stated that one of the reasons for his desire to find a new employer was that he had developed the quality control program in his present firm to the point where it was no longer offering him any challenge. He further stated that he felt this situation would recur at American Ceramic and Glass Products but that, because of the size of the firm, he could direct his attention to bigger and more interesting problems rather than be required to seek outside consulting work to satisfy his need for professional growth.

When asked what his real interests were, King stated, "Application of statistical concepts to the nonroutine activities of a manufacturing organization." He cited worker training, supplier performance, and trouble shooting as areas of interest. King submitted several reports that summarized projects that he had successfully completed in these or related areas.

This was the extent of information that Parr had on each of the two individuals he felt might best fill the position vacated by Downs, the retiring chief of the inspection and quality control department.

Questions

1. What is quality, who determines it, how is it described, and how is it attained?
2. What should be the role of the chief of inspection and quality control?
3. What was Calligan's philosophy toward quality control?
4. What was King's philosophy toward quality control?
5. Under what conditions would you expect Calligan and King, respectively, to be most effective?
6. Excluding the differences in philosophies between King and Calligan, what other factors relative to each require consideration?
7. Which of the two candidates, if either, should be selected for the position of chief of the inspection and quality control department?
8. Where could each man be utilized outside of the area of inspection and quality control?

Source: Robert C. Meier, Richard A. Johnson, William T. Newell, and Albert N. Schrieber, *Cases in Production and Operations Management,* © 1982, pp. 8–12. Reprinted by permission of Prentice-Hall, Inc., Englewood Cliffs, New Jersey.

Case Study
AAA Farm Equipment Manufacturing Company

Background

AAA Farm Equipment Manufacturing Company (AAA) has been hard hit by current economic conditions. High interest rates and low farm prices have left the nation's farmer in an extremely poor financial situation with respect to capital investments. AAA manufactures various size augers and elevators that are used to transport grain.

In an effort to survive, AAA has diversified its product line and has entered the oil field equipment market with several new products. In addition to introducing a new product line, AAA's president, John Henderson, has required each department to operate with a minimum of personnel. Although these efforts have succeeded in reducing the magnitude of operating losses, the problem of returning the company to profitability still persists.

Tom Miller, Vice-President of Operations, hopes that the new MRP system AAA is currently implementing will have a material effect on the Company's bottom line.

AAA produces five basic sizes of augers and four types of grain elevators for the Farm Products product line. Each of these nine basic product groups or end items can vary based on customer or distributor specifications. Each end item is assembled from a variety of subassemblies called "bundles." There is wide bundle commonality amongst the various end items. In other words, many of the bundles are used on more than one end item. Because of the variable nature of the final product, the new MRP system will consider bundles as end items when scheduling production.

Tom Miller realizes that the success of the new MRP system will be highly dependent on how well AAA can forecast demand for bundles and major spare parts.

Current Forecasting Methodology

Currently, forecasting responsibility is divided at AAA between the Marketing Department and the Operations Department. Marketing is responsible for developing product group forecasts. Operations takes the product group forecasts and develops a bundle forecast for each bundle. In addition, Operations must predict demand for spare parts so that these items can be integrated into the production schedule.

To develop product group forecasts, Marketing uses a combination of grass-roots forecasting (aggregating forecasts from regional sales managers) and subjective forecasting at the corporate level where the two product line managers and the manager of marketing develop a consensus forecast. To aid in developing subjective product group forecasts AAA subscribes to several publications such as *Agricultural Outlook, Predicasts,* and *Midwest Unit Buying Intentions* to ascertain farm income, available grain storage capacity, total farm loans (Farm Credit Administration), and other information relevant to demand forecasting.

Operations takes the Product Group Forecast from Marketing and estimates the bundle demand using the estimated number of bundles of each type

for each end item or product group. For example, bundle 1235712-12 is used on two size augers — two on the 6-inch auger and one on the 8-inch auger. This means that if the 6-inch auger forecast is 75 units and the 8-inch auger forecast is for 50 units, Operations will have to manufacture 200 1235712-12 bundles.

Historically, spare parts forecasting has been a manual "eye ball" estimate. However, the new MRP software has the facility to forecast spare parts by using a simple exponential smoothing model.

Tom Miller has hired you as an external consultant to examine their forecasting procedure and make recommendations. Specifically, he has asked whether:

- There is a more scientific way of forecasting product group demand.
- The new MRP system should use the exponential smoothing model for forecasting spare parts.

Case Questions

1. What techniques might apply to the product group forecasting?
2. What steps would you take to develop an alternative to the existing product group forecasting methodology?
3. How would you evaluate your alternative product group forecasting methodology?
4. What models would you apply to the spare parts forecasting?
5. How would you set up a study to choose the best model?

Source: Thomas M. Cook and Robert A. Russell, *Contemporary Operations Management: Text and Cases,* 2nd edition, © 1984, pp. 530–532. Reprinted by permission of Prentice-Hall, Inc., Englewood Cliffs, New Jersey.

Behavioral Competencies of Management

CHAPTER 9

Motivation and Performance

"We read the papers. We're drunk, lazy, dopey," said Robert Valpredo, 43, with a thin crop of squared-off graying hair and a tired look because he's just put ten hours on the line at Ford Motor Co.'s Wayne, Michigan assembly plant. "How do you build 200,000 cars a year if you're lazy, drunk and dopey?" he asks. . . .

He's a relief inspector, which means he's filling in for others all day, checking on the headlight wiring, the wiper hoses, the power steering, the locks to make sure the keys work, the ceiling liner for smoothness, the windshield pillar and trunk molding for fits to prevent leaks. . . .

"If anything's wrong, you've got to catch it before it leaves your zone. The deeper it gets into the system (the assembly line), the worse it gets. Catch it quick. Once those panels are on, it becomes a major repair, and once they have to tear it down, that's where the quality goes."

Bob Valpredo doesn't sing the company song before the day starts, take a quick five for push-ups or sit cross-legged in any "Quality Circle," but this is his attitude: "If I don't do my job, I won't have a job. That's how I feel," he says. At 62.5 cars an hour, relaxing comes on the half-hour breaks (morning and afternoon) and lunch. There's no sitting down on the line. "It's hard on your feet. The legs are tired all the time. Eight hours are okay but ten hours beat you up." It's starting to warm up in the plant now. "If it's 90 outside, it will be 100 inside. We hump it through August. But if you want hot, go to the paint shop.

"I promised myself I'd never work in a factory, but here I am," he says smiling. Up at 5 a.m. and on the line at 6:30. . . .

Does he like it? "It's not a matter of liking it. It's what you've got to do, and you do the job right, like the Marines," says this ex-Marine. . . .

Source: *Forbes*, July 6, 1981. "The Myth of the Lazy American," by Jerry Flint. pp. 105–111. Reprinted by permission. © Forbes Inc., 1984.

Chapter Outline

- Behavioral Requirements of Organizations
- Managerial Assumptions About People
- Reasons for Low Productivity
- Individual Needs and Motivation
- Expectancy/Valence Theory
- Reinforcement Theory
- Techniques of Employee Motivation

Key Terms

- motivation
- expectancy/valence theory
- need for achievement
- need for affiliation
- need for power
- cognitive models of motivation
- acognitive models of motivation
- expectancy
- valence
- punishment
- reinforcement theory
- positive reinforcement
- avoidance learning
- extinction
- schedules of reinforcement
- work redesign

Chapter Objectives

After studying Chapter 9 you should be able to

1. Identify some of the reasons for low productivity among workers.
2. See how the need for power can predict managerial effectiveness.
3. Understand how reinforcement can change employee behavior.
5. Use guidelines for enriching jobs and redesigning work.
6. Describe the steps in implementing a behavior modification program.

Introduction

Employee motivation and leadership are popular topics among managers. "How do I motivate these people?" is a question often asked by managers. Motivation is closely related to leadership; both deal with how to create conditions that make employees willingly contribute to attaining organizational goals. The study of leadership focuses largely on managerial behavior, on what the manager can do, however, whereas the study of employee motivation concentrates on how employees determine their behavior in response to the work environment. The two topics are related, but they clearly address different aspects of the problem.

Our survey of motivational processes begins by considering the behavioral requirements of organizations — what organizations need from people. Next, we address several of the more common assumptions managers make about their employees, as well as factors often associated with low productivity. Following this, we present a formal definition of motivation and review the role of employee needs in organizational behavior. Two primary theories of work motivation, expectancy/valence theory and reinforcement theory, are compared. Finally, two techniques for improving motivation in the workplace are reviewed. We will try to show you that employee motivation is an important aspect of any discussion of how to manage effective organizations.

Behavioral Requirements of Organizations

Why do managers need to know about employee motivation? The easiest way to answer this question is to consider what types of behavior employers need from their employees to boost productivity and organizational effectiveness. Several years ago, Katz and Kahn (1978) suggested what they termed **behavioral requirements** for organizations. To be effective, it was thought, most organizations had to meet all three of these requirements.

First, people have to be attracted to join the organization and to remain with it. If an organization is to be successful, it must be able first of all to entice people to join and then maintain their membership. The second behavioral requirement focuses on employee performance. To be effective, an organization must get its people to perform their tasks in a dependable and predictable fashion. Without dependable performance, organizations would have trouble knowing who was doing what and when. Third, in many cases, employees must go beyond dependable performance to some form of creative or spontaneous behavior. An organization needs employees who will do more than what they are told to do, who will engage in innovative behavior, if it is to deal successfully with environmental uncertainty.

These three behavioral requirements all deal squarely with employee motivation. Organizations and their managers have to discover ways to encourage employees to join the organization and to remain with it, to perform their assigned tasks dependably, and to initiate innovative or creative behavior that takes advantage of the unique opportunities found in the work environment.

Managerial Assumptions About People

An interesting discovery in the study of management is that managers often have different views or assumptions about people who work under them. There have been several attempts to identify the models that managers employ. In one of the most useful, that of Raymond Miles (1965), managerial assumptions about the people who work under them are divided into three different models. Summarized in Figure 9.1, they are the traditional model, the human relations model, and the human resources model.

In the more *traditional managerial model,* it is assumed that work is inherently distasteful for most people and that money is a primary motivator. It is believed that few employees can handle work that requires considerable creativity, self-direction, or self-control. As a result managers focus on the need for close supervision and control of subordinates and the need to simplify tasks so that they can be easily learned by basically disinterested employees.

The *human relations model* gained prominence during the 1930s and still has a large following. It suggests that people want to feel useful and important and that they are highly motivated by social needs rather than economic needs. They have a strong desire to belong and to be recognized as individuals. The human relations manager focuses on how to make employees feel more useful and im-

---

Figure 9.1
Three Managerial Models of Motivation

TRADITIONAL MODEL	HUMAN RELATIONS MODEL	HUMAN RESOURCES MODEL
Assumptions		
1. Work is inherently distasteful to most people.	1. People want to feel useful and important.	1. Work is not inherently distasteful. People want to contribute to meaningful goals that they have helped establish.
2. What they do is less important than what they earn for doing it.	2. People desire to belong and to be recognized as individuals.	2. Most people can exercise far more creative, responsible self-direction, and self-control than their present jobs demand.
3. Few want or can handle work which requires creativity, self-direction, or self-control.	3. These needs are more important than money in motivating people to work.	

Figure 9.1 (continued)

TRADITIONAL MODEL	HUMAN RELATIONS MODEL	HUMAN RESOURCES MODEL

Policies

1. The manager's basic task is to closely supervise and control subordinates.	1. The manager's basic task is to make each worker feel useful and important.	1. The manager's basic task is to make use of "untapped" human resources.
2. He or she must break tasks down into simple, repetitive, easily learned operations.	2. He or she should keep subordinates informed and listen to their objections to managerial plans.	2. He or she must create an environment in which all members may contribute to the limits of their ability.
3. He or she must establish detailed work routines and procedures, and enforce these firmly but fairly.	3. The manager should allow subordinates to exercise some self-direction and self-control on routine matters.	3. He or she must encourage full participation on important matters, continually broadening subordinate self-direction and control.

Expectations

1. People can tolerate work if the pay is decent and the boss is fair.	1. Sharing information with subordinates and involving them in routine decisions will satisfy their basic needs to belong and to feel important.	1. Expanding subordinate influence, self-direction, and self-control will lead to direct improvements in operating efficiency.
2. If tasks are simple enough and people are closely controlled, they will produce up to standard.	2. Satisfying these needs will improve morale and reduce resistance to formal authority — subordinates will "willingly cooperate."	2. Work satisfaction may improve as a "by-product" of subordinates' making full use of their resources.

Source: Miles, Porter, and Craft, "Leadership Attitudes Among Public Health Officials," *American Journal of Public Health,* 56 (1966), pp. 1990–2005. Reprinted by permission.

portant. The manager should keep subordinates informed and attempt to listen to their objections to his or her plans.

The *human resources model* became popular more recently and generally represents the new wave in management. According to this model, managers generally believe that work does not have to be distasteful and that people really want to contribute to the goals of the organization in a meaningful way. The human resource manager typically believes that most people have the ability to exercise far more creative, responsible self-direction and self-control than their present jobs demand. Policy implications for the manager center around making use of the untapped human resources in the organization. The manager has a responsibility to create an environment in which employees can contribute to the limits of their ability. There is a need to encourage full participation on matters important to employees and to allow subordinate self-direction and control as much as possible.

Comparing these three models shows significant differences. The important point to note here is that managers who hold different assumptions about the people who work for them will likely behave differently toward those people as well. We cannot expect all managers to treat all people identically. The importance of these differences will become evident as we discuss the various approaches to motivation in the workplace.

Reasons for Low Productivity

We sometimes hear managers complain that employees simply don't work as hard as they used to. This opinion is fairly widespread among traditional managers, but the complaint also is heard among other managers. Unfortunately, although the complaints are frequent, much less often do managers seriously examine the causes for low productivity. If we look at the motivational factors behind high or low productivity, we see that many contemporary work situations simply do not motivate employees to perform on the job. There are at least five reasons for low productivity or restriction of output (Steers, 1977):

1. *Unappealing potential rewards.* Managers often assume that all employees want the same thing from their jobs. This is not the case. Whereas some employees desire higher earnings, others would prefer to have time off, for example. Consequently, there are managers who frequently offer rewards for good performance that are not highly prized by the employees. It is unlikely that employees will put forth maximum effort if the rewards offered do not appeal to them.

2. *Weak performance-reward linkages.* In many cases employees fail to see a strong link between increased job performance and the rewards they desire from the organization. When this linkage is not considered strong, it is unlikely that employees will perform at maximum levels.

3. *Distrust of management.* Sometimes employees simply do not trust managers. It is easy to see why employees, when this lack of trust exists, do not believe managers' promises that high productivity will cause positive outcomes. This distrust may result from previously unkept promises by management or from negative outcomes associated with high productivity, such as layoffs of unneeded employees that occur because workers have performed exceptionally well.

4. *Desire of employees to have greater control over their jobs.* One often overlooked cause of restricted output by employees is the desire to maintain some control over their own jobs. In today's work environment, many lower-level jobs are increasingly automated, often causing people to lose autonomy and personal discretion in their jobs. As a result, people try to convince themselves that they do have an important role to play at their workplace. To provide sufficient slack in their work schedule so that they can vary their work methods somewhat, and to maintain some control over their work behavior, people often will intentionally restrict their output. Knowing they can influence production sometimes convinces people that they count as individuals.

5. *Lack of job involvement.* People often just don't like the jobs they are asked to perform. When employees fail to identify with or are not involved with their jobs, they are not likely to devote the same energy that they would to jobs in which they were highly interested.

We have seen five reasons for low productivity. If managers are to remedy this situation, there must be significant efforts to understand the motives of employees and to find ways to show workers that there is a strong payoff if they perform well on the job. The Japanese have been highly successful at this endeavor but, unfortunately, attempts in the United States and Canada have met with far less success. Perhaps a better understanding of employee motivation would mean better results on the shop floor.

Individual Needs and Motivation

The term *motivation* is derived from the Latin *movere,* which means "to move." From this phrase we have developed a more comprehensive definition of **motivation:** it is that which energizes, directs, and sustains human behavior. Three distinct aspects of motivation can be identified in this definition. First, motivation represents an energetic force that drives people or causes them to behave in certain ways. Second, this drive is directed toward something; that is, motivation has a strong goal orientation. Finally, motivation serves to sustain motivational force over time.

The idea of motivation is perhaps best studied from a dynamic systems perspective. Therefore, to understand human behavior in work situations, it is important to consider what factors within both the individual and the work environment jointly cause behavior, and then to consider how that behavior is reinforced in the workplace.

Need Hierarchy Model

The best place to begin studying employee motivation is with individual needs. The most widely recognized expert in this area is Abraham Maslow, a clinical psychologist who did his early research among emotionally troubled children in the 1940s. Based on laboratory observations, Maslow tried to de-

Feature 9.1
Soviet Workers in for a Change

"We pretend to work and they pretend to pay us" ("Moscow Tries to Light a Fire," p. 44). This unofficial motto of the soviet worker may be in for some revisions as a result of a new labor reform law with just a hint of Western ideas, which was passed in August 1983 by the Kremlin. The new law will allow collectives, or brigades (the lowest unit in the Soviet factory system), to have a small voice in planning and management. The reform — the first since World War II — was passed for two reasons: to raise the country's abysmally low productivity rate and to slam the door on more radical reforms that have swept through Eastern European countries such as Poland and Yugoslavia.

A major cause of the Soviets' low productivity has been the system of wages. Salaries are low and are based on an incentive piecework plan that has resulted in too many of one item and not enough of another being produced. These incentive bonuses have even been paid to nonperformers, and very few workers are ever fired.

Under the new system, bonuses will be paid to brigades for production of finished products. In turn, the brigades will distribute wages and bonuses to the workers. The brigade leaders, now to be elected by the workers, will also be able to discipline nonperformers.

The Kremlin also passed new laws to combat absenteeism and alcoholism — two other factors that contribute to low productivity. Workers who are absent without a good excuse will lose one vacation day for each missed workday, and three hours of missed work will be considered a full lost day. A worker who is drunk on the job may be fired and is expected to pay for lost production and any damages. The Soviet news daily *Pravda*, in describing the new laws, said the workers were not the only ones at fault. *Pravda* also criticized managers who did not "set an example of discipline, proper organization of their work, or full use of their working time" ("Getting Everyone on the Wagon," p. 39).

Soviet economists hope that these new labor reforms and the laws against drinking and absenteeism will increase productivity, but Western experts are not as optimistic.

Sources: "Moscow Tries to Light a Fire Under Its Workers," *Business Week,* August 1, 1983, p. 44; "Getting Everyone on the Wagon," *Time,* August 22, 1983, pp. 39–40.

velop a model of how the healthy personality grows and develops over time, and the ways in which this personality manifests itself in motivated behavior. The result of his work is a theory called the **need hierarchy model** of employee motivation.

The model rests on two fundamental assumptions. First, people are motivated primarily by a desire to satisfy several types of specific needs. Second, these needs are arranged in a hierarchical form. People progress through this hierarchy as each of the lower needs is satisfied.

Maslow (1954) identified five general levels in the need hierarchy. The lowest level was termed *physiological* needs and represented the most basic needs of individuals, such as hunger. Following these were *safety* needs, those for a safe and secure physical and emotional environment. On the third level were *belongingness* needs, centering on the desire to be accepted by peers, to develop friendships, and to be loved. Fourth in the need hierarchy were what Maslow termed *esteem* needs. These focus on the desire for a worthy self-image, recognition, and appreciation from others. The highest level, *self-actualization* needs, involve development of the individual's fullest potential, becoming all that it is possible to become.

According to Maslow, individuals work their way up through this hierarchy by a process of deprivation and gratification as they grow and develop. He observed that when one particular need is unfilled, it emerges to dominate the individual's consciousness. As a result, the individual focuses primary attention on satisfying this particular need. When this need is gratified, however, the individual moves up one level in the hierarchy and begins to devote primary attention to the next need until it, too, is gratified. Maslow assumed that as individuals grow and mature, they work their way up through the hierarchy, ultimately approaching or achieving self-actualization.

Although Maslow's theory helps us considerably in understanding the growth processes of individuals from birth through maturity, the relevance of his model to the workplace seems somewhat questionable. By the time most employees begin working, many of their lower-order needs already have been fulfilled. Moreover, the nature of many jobs makes it almost impossible for many employees to achieve self-actualization, the highest need in the hierarchy, on the job.

Manifest Needs Model

A model developed by Henry Murray may be more relevant for studying employees at work. Murray's **manifest needs model** is distinct from Maslow's formulation, even though some similarities exist. Murray argued that individuals could be classified according to the strengths of their various needs. People were thought to have a variety of divergent and often conflicting needs at any one point. Murray defined a need as a "recurrent concern for a goal state" (McClelland, 1971, p. 13). He considered needs to be the primary motivating force for people. Unlike Maslow, Murray did not suggest that needs are arranged in a hierarchy.

Murray posited the existence of about two dozen needs. Later studies, however, have suggested that only three or four of these needs are germane to the workplace, mainly the needs for achievement, affiliation, and power. These needs were thought to be primarily learned, rather than inherited, and to be activated by cues from the external environment. If an employee has a high need for achievement, that need will become prominent (manifest) only if something in the external environment cues achievement-oriented behavior. Only when the need becomes manifest will the individual seek situations in which he or she can achieve.

Need for Achievement. The most important need from the standpoint of studying work behavior is the **need for achievement.** This need is defined by

McClelland (McClelland, Atkinson, Clark, and Lowell, 1953, p. 111) as "behavior toward competition with a standard of excellence." Following this definition, we can envision a person with a high need for achievement as someone characterized by (1) a strong desire to assume personal responsibility for discovering solutions to problems, (2) a tendency to set moderately difficult achievement goals and to take calculated risks, (3) a strong desire for concrete feedback on task performance, and (4) a single-minded preoccupation with the task and with accomplishing the task. In contrast, a person with a low need for achievement typically would prefer tasks with low risks, little feedback, and shared, rather than individual, responsibility.

Employee need for achievement has important implications for understanding human behavior in the work environment. Consider the example of job redesign, which will be discussed later in this chapter. If jobs are enriched by more variety, autonomy, and responsibility, employees are likely to perform positively if they have a high achievement need. The enriched job will then cue the achievement motivation, leading to greater effort and probably improved performance. In contrast, people with a low need for achievement probably would become increasingly frustrated by the greater personal responsibility and might perform even more poorly than they did before the task was enriched. As we can see in this example, a high need for achievement is not necessarily beneficial. It primarily benefits individuals whose jobs provide a challenge.

Need for Affiliation. The second of Murray's needs is the **need for affiliation,** defined as "an attraction to another organism in order to feel reassured from the other that the self is acceptable" (Birch and Veroff, 1966, p. 65). This need should not be confused with a sense of being sociable or popular. Rather, it is a need for human companionship and reassurance from those around us.

It has been suggested that people with a high need for affiliation typically are characterized by (1) a strong desire for approval and reassurance from others, (2) a tendency to conform to the wishes and norms of others when pressured by people whose friendship they value, and (3) a sincere interest in the feelings of others. We should therefore expect people with a high need for affiliation to take jobs characterized by a high degree of interpersonal contact, such as sales positions, teaching, public relations, or counseling. Whereas a high need for achievement is related to job performance, particularly when the achievement motive is cued, the affiliation need is not.

Some evidence does suggest that affiliation-oriented employees perform better in situations in which personal support and approval are strongly tied to performance. For example, the classic study by French (1958) found that whereas high achievement–oriented individuals performed better when given task-related feedback, high affiliation–oriented individuals performed better when given supportive feedback. Hence, the effort and performance of affiliation-oriented employees probably could be enhanced by the provision of a cooperative, rather than a competitive, work situation. Managers who supervise affiliation-oriented individuals should create to the extent possible a cooperative, supportive work environment in which positive feedback is fairly consistently tied to task performance. As a result, the individuals would be more aware that working harder could lead to the type of need satisfaction they desire most.

Need for Power. A third widely studied need in the workplace is the **need for power**. This need represents a desire to influence others and to control one's environment. People with a high need for power usually attempt to influence others fairly directly, either by making suggestions, by offering opinions, or by trying to talk others into accepting their own views. Such individuals typically seek positions of leadership in group activities. They are usually verbally fluent, often quite talkative, and sometimes even argumentative.

In his classic work on the need for power, McClelland (1976) has suggested that this need can take two forms among managers, that for personal power and that for institutionalized power. Employees with a *personal power* orientation attempt to dominate others almost for the sake of dominance itself. Personal conquest is very important to them. People with a high need for personal power also tend to reject institutional responsibilities. McClelland draws a parallel between personal power types and feudal chieftains or conquistadors, in the sense that they attempt to inspire subordinates to heroic performance but want them to be responsible to the leader, not to the organization.

In contrast, the individual with high *institutionalized power* needs is far more concerned with the problems of the organization and what he or she can do to help attain its goals. McClelland has described such individuals as follows: (1) they are organization-minded and feel personal responsibility for helping to develop the organization; (2) they enjoy work and getting things done in an orderly fashion; (3) they are often quite willing to sacrifice their own self-interest for the welfare of the organization; (4) they have a strong sense of justice and equity; and (5) they are more mature in the sense that they are less defensive and more willing to seek expert advice when necessary than those with a high need for personal power.

Needs as Predictors of Managerial Effectiveness. Which of these needs are the best predictors of managerial effectiveness? Again, we can look to McClelland (1976) for an answer. McClelland notes that managers who manifest a high need for achievement concentrate their efforts on personal accomplishments and improvements. They are rather independent individuals who want to assume primary responsibility and credit for accomplishing tasks, and they have a strong desire for short-term and concrete feedback on performance. These characteristics are most closely associated with entrepreneurial success and can be highly beneficial for individuals who are in business for themselves.

Many of these same characteristics, however, can be detrimental for managers attempting to supervise the work of others. For instance, in many complex organizations managers cannot perform all the tasks necessary to make sure that goals are accomplished; some form of teamwork is required. Moreover, feedback on the group's effort and performance is often vague and sometimes

Feature 9.2
For These Entrepreneurs, Experience Doesn't Necessarily Count

Picture an entrepreneur. Balding? Pin-striped suit with gold cuff links? Rolls-Royce? Alligator briefcase and a taste for power?

You may be in for a surprise. A 1980 survey of the 560,000 members of the National Federation of Independent Businesses, a Washington-based lobbying group, indicated that one of every three businesses in the United States in 1980 was started by someone aged thirty or younger. That's jeans, running shoes, and maybe a beat-up old car.

Despite their age, many of them are tasting real success. Brett Johnson, twenty-five, expected that his apparel marketing firm, Crowd Caps Inc., would earn as much as $2 million on sales of $10 million in 1983. Since he started the Minneapolis company in 1979, when he was twenty, he calculates it has grown at a compounded annual rate of 900 percent.

The Burch brothers of Malvern, Pennsylvania, twenty-nine-year-old Robert and thirty-year-old Christopher, started dealing in used cars and pinball machines when they were in their teens and then sold sweaters on college campuses. After they graduated in 1976, they built a ladies' and children's apparel company that expected revenues of $30 million and $1.8 million in earnings in 1983.

Then there's Debbi Fields, twenty-six, who expected to gross $30 million from selling freshly baked cookies in nearly one hundred stores, including Bloomingdale's in New York.

Purdue University economist William Dunkelberg explains the phenomenon by noting that business action today is centered in either high technology or services, areas in which young people have training. Starting your own business is also popular and is often the only way to go for someone who can't find work in the tight job market. It's also a result of college entrepreneurial departments, which teach students they don't have to wait to become entrepreneurs.

But the road is not always easy. Sometimes the young business people have trouble being taken seriously. Then there's the problem of attracting experienced management. There are big sacrifices, too.

Dirkan Bezjian, twenty-nine, is owner of Graphic Software Inc., a Cambridge, Massachusetts, company with $2 million in sales. "I put everything I've got into this thing," Bezjian said. "I moved back home and put all my money into it. I've hardly dated. My friends and family are all irked. But when you are totally immersed, you drop everything. It's like preparing for final exams."

Bezjian has some advice for budding young entrepreneurs. "Don't listen to the people who say you can't do it," he said. "You have to jump right in, go out there, and do it."

Source: "Young Entrepreneurs" by Lewis Beale, *Venture*, October 1983, pp. 40–48.

delayed or even nonexistent. The managerial environment that we find in most contemporary corporations is not totally suitable to cue the achievement motive within managers.

Similar problems exist with managers who demonstrate a high need for affiliation. Affiliative managers have a strong need for group acceptance and, as a result, often tend to be indecisive in decision making for fear of alienating one faction or another within the work group. In addition, affiliation-oriented managers have a strong concern for maintaining good interpersonal relationships, often at the expense of task performance. As a result, much of their effort is focused on keeping people happy rather than keeping people productive.

McClelland makes the argument that perhaps the best manager in many contemporary work situations is the individual who has a strong need for institutionalized power. Power-oriented managers who are truly concerned about the organization as a whole, instead of themselves, typically demonstrate the capacity to provide the structure, drive, and support necessary to facilitate goal-oriented group behavior. Such individuals fit very nicely into McClelland's definition of managerial success (1976, p. 102):

> a good manager is one who, among other things, helps subordinates feel strong and responsible, who rewards them properly for good performance, and who sees that things are organized in such a way that subordinates feel they know what they should be doing. Above all, managers should foster among subordinates a strong sense of team spirit, of pride of working as part of a particular team. If a manager creates and encourages this spirit, his subordinates certainly should perform better.

The institutionalized power-oriented manager clearly fits this definition of managerial success better than the manager with either a strong need for achievement or a strong need for affiliation.

Expectancy/Valence Theory

Although many complex theories of employee motivation and work behavior can be identified, most of these theories overlap to a considerable degree. It is not necessary for our purposes to examine each of these models in detail. Rather, we shall examine two diametrically opposed theories of employee motivation.

The first of the two, the **expectancy/valence theory,** is primarily a cognitive theory of motivation (Vroom, 1964; Porter and Lawler, 1968). The second model, to be discussed in the next section, is called *reinforcement theory* and is an acognitive theory of motivation. **Cognitive models of motivation** rest on the assumption that individuals often make conscious decisions concerning their behavior. It is assumed that prior to action some form of decision process takes place that must be clearly understood if we are to comprehend human behavior. Cognitive theories emphasize the how and the why of behavior by focusing on mechanisms inside the individual.

In contrast, **acognitive models of motivation** argue that it is possible to predict behavior without understanding internal processes. Acognitive models emphasize the relationship between behavior and external, environmental stimuli. People, it is thought, are reactive to such stimuli, so it is not necessary to examine internal processes. The distinction between cognitive and acognitive models will become clear as we further explore the differences between expectancy/valence theory and reinforcement theory.

Principles of Expectancy/Valence Theory

Perhaps the best way to understand expectancy theory is to divide the model into two sections. The first section attempts to answer the question "What causes motivation?" and the second section, "What causes job performance?" Motivation and performance are not considered equivalent in this model. To answer the first question, expectancy theory introduces two new terms. The first term, **expectancy,** is defined as a belief about the likelihood or probability that a particular behavioral act, such as working harder, will lead to a particular outcome, such as a pay raise or a promotion.

Expectancies are stated as probability statements ranging from zero, when the individual sees no chance that behavior will lead to a particular outcome, to 1.0, when an individual is absolutely certain that a particular behavior will lead to a certain outcome. Of course, most expectancies fall somewhere between these two extremes.

Expectancies can be divided into two types. The first type is termed an *effort-performance expectancy* (E→P expectancy) and represents the belief the individual holds that effort will in fact lead to performance. The second expectancy is a *performance-outcome expectancy* (P→O expectancy) and represents the belief that performance will lead to a certain outcome. This distinction between E→P expectancies and P→O expectancies highlights two related beliefs, or probability statements, that individuals formulate concerning the results of their behavior in the workplace.

The second term, **valence,** refers to the value an individual places on available outcomes or rewards. Valences are seen as varying from +1.0, when an individual places a very high positive value on a certain outcome or reward, to −1.0, when an individual places a strong negative value on a particular outcome or reward.

Putting these three variables together allows us to construct a general answer to the question concerning the causes of motivation. Figure 9.2 shows that motivation is a function of E→P expectancies, P→O expectancies, and valence. If an employee truly believes that high effort will lead to performance (E→P expectancy) and that such performance will lead to certain outcomes (P→O expectancy), and those outcomes are highly valued (valence), the employee is likely to be motivated to perform on the job.

As can be seen in Figure 9.2, job performance, the second aspect of the expectancy/valence theory, is influenced primarily by four important factors. First, employee *motivation to perform* should have a significant influence on job performance. But there are three other variables that need to be recognized. The first of the three is employee *abilities and traits*. To perform well, employees must have the capacity to perform, the abilities and traits to carry out the tasks assigned to them. In addition, it is important that employees clearly understand what is expected of them. They must have *role clarity,* and they must accept this particular role. Finally, they must be given the *opportunity to perform*. Poor job performance would probably be ensured by hiring highly motivated employees with the necessary abilities, traits, and a clear understanding of their roles and

Figure 9.2
Expectancy/Valence Model of Motivation

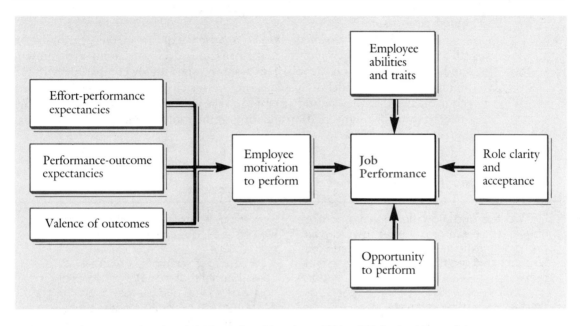

Source: Based on Porter and Lawler, 1968. Figure adapted from Steers, 1984, p. 179. Reprinted by permission.

then putting them into situations in which they are unable to perform effectively — for example, hiring an encyclopedia salesperson and then placing him or her in a low-income sales territory.

Implications for Management

As we can see, according to expectancy/valence theory, a myriad of factors from both the individual and the work situation influence employee motivation and job performance. When these factors are taken together, the model identifies several important managerial implications for the workplace.

Managers should clarify E→P expectancies. Managers have a responsibility to show employees how to increase their job performance. This can be achieved through training programs, coaching, support from the supervisor, and participation in job-related decisions. Through techniques such as these, employees can be made to feel that high levels of performance are within their reach.

Managers should clarify P→O expectancies. Managers have the responsibility to delineate the reward system clearly and show employees how job performance can lead to high levels of rewards.

Managers should match rewards to employee desires as much as possible. Different employees want different things from their jobs. Some attempts can be made, within the constraints existing in most organizations, to vary the rewards so employees are working for the things they want. One example is the cafeteria fringe benefit plan available in some organizations, in which employees can select from an array of rewards (e.g., more pay, more vacation) in exchange for good performance.

Managers should recognize conscious behavior. Expectancy theory is based on the proposition that employees make conscious decisions about their present and future behavior on the job. This assumption is highly compatible with the human resources model discussed earlier in this chapter. Moreover, it suggests to managers that they should attempt to take advantage of employees' willingness to think through situations relating to their jobs. If managers assume that

---

**Feature 9.3
Labor and Management Share Some Concerns**

Workers and management are coming up with some similar attitudes toward work and productivity that would make some old-time labor leaders and bosses roll over in their graves.

Surveys of workers' and managers' attitudes toward productivity done by the United States Chamber of Commerce indicate that four out of five workers and executives think that employees who are involved in decision making work harder and do a better job.

Both groups agree that workers' attitudes have been a cause of declining productivity in the United States, but both feel that workers are genuinely interested in producing top-quality goods.

The management survey was conducted in 1981 of 1,083 executives representing a cross section of business by industry, size of firm, and region. Results showed that many executives believe that explaining what productivity means for both the company and the employees will increase productivity. Asking workers for suggestions and clearly telling them what is expected of them were also considered important.

But when it came to how to encourage good ideas, management disagreed with workers, as indicated by the results from the workers' poll, done in 1979 by the chamber and Gallup.

The largest portion of workers, 42 percent, thought that monetary rewards are the best way to improve performance. Only 33 percent of the executives agreed, however.

Twenty-six percent of the workers favored personal recognition, a point advocated by 51 percent of the executives.

Promotions were favored by 51 percent of the workers but only 6 percent of the executives.

The chamber listed a rundown of company techniques to improve productivity:

- 56 percent: bonuses related to output or quality of work
- 52 percent: profit sharing, stock option, or employee stock ownership plans
- 14 percent: quality circles
- 13 percent: sharing of profits linked to productivity gains
- 1 percent: investment efficiency ratios to rank capital investment projects according to their expected return
- 18 percent: none of the above

Source: Adapted with permission from "Unlocking the Productivity Door," *Nation's Business,* December 1981, p. 55. Copyright: U.S. Chamber of Commerce.

their subordinates are thinking, reasoning individuals, it becomes far easier to tap those resources than if they subscribe to the traditional model of employee behavior.

Managers should select people who are equipped for the job. The role of employee abilities and traits in determining job performance should not be underemphasized. All too often employees are hired, promoted, transferred, or fired because of personality more than ability.

Managers should clarify role expectancies on the job. If managers expect high job performance, it is important that they are specific in delineating specific job responsibilities. In this way, employees receive a clearer idea of what is expected of them and can waste less effort.

Managers should provide employees with opportunities to perform. Placing employees in impossible situations or those in which the probability of success is minimal almost guarantees poor performance. A good example is the plight of bank branch managers. They often are held accountable for improving performance indicators such as the number of deposits, even though such indicators are determined more by the location of the branch than by the manager's own efforts. The message is clear: If we wish people to perform, it is only reasonable to place them in situations in which high performance is possible.

Thus, the expectancy/valence theory of motivation does point to several implications for managers interested in improving job performance. These are not suggestions to manipulate employees; rather, they are meant as guidelines for creating a work climate or work situation in which interested employees can pursue both their own self-interest and corporate objectives.

Reinforcement Theory

The second major theory of motivation to be considered in this chapter is **reinforcement theory.** As we have said, reinforcement theory is acognitive in that it presumes it is possible to predict behavior without understanding internal thought processes. The basis of reinforcement theory is the necessity to recognize external stimuli in the environment that affect behavior.

Reinforcement theory is based on the concept of learning. *Learning* can be defined as a relatively permanent change in behavior that occurs as a result of experience. In other words, something is learned if an individual consistently exhibits a new behavior over time. Thorndike's *law of effect* (1911) is basic to learning as it relates to reinforcement theory. This law states: "Of several responses made to the same situation, those which are accompanied or closely followed by satisfaction [reinforcement] will be more likely to occur; those which are accompanied or closely followed by discomfort [punishment] will be less likely to occur" (p. 244). In other words, behavior that leads to positive or pleasurable outcomes will tend to be repeated, whereas behavior that leads to negative outcomes or punishment will tend to be avoided. An example is the common practice of paying bonuses to sales representatives based on sales performance. Each time a sale is made, they are rewarded with a bonus. In this way the sales representatives learn the relationship or bond between certain behaviors, selling, and certain outcomes, the bonus.

Strategies for Behavioral Change

Related to the law of effect is the concept of **reinforcement.** Reinforcement is anything that causes certain behaviors to be repeated or inhibited. There are four basic strategies for reinforcing behavior: positive reinforcement, avoidance learning, extinction, and punishment.

Positive Reinforcement. **Positive reinforcement** is the practice of providing someone with a reward following a desired behavior. It is believed that this strengthens the probability that the desired behavior will be repeated. In Figure 9.3, one particular employee is consistently on time. This prompts the supervisor to praise the employee and perhaps to recommend a merit pay increase. In this case the praise or the recommended pay increase is a form of positive reinforcement to the employee. The hope is that the supervisor's actions

---

Figure 9.3
Strategies for Behavioral Change

SUPERVISOR'S GOAL: *To encourage employee to arrive at work on time.*

EMPLOYEE'S WORK BEHAVIOR	STRATEGY FOR CHANGING BEHAVIOR	SUPERVISOR'S ACTIONS TO IMPLEMENT STRATEGY	DESIRED RESULTING BEHAVIOR
Employee is consistently on time	**Positive Reinforcement**	Praise employee and recommend merit pay increase	Employee arrives at work on time
	Avoidance Learning	Avoid harassing or reprimanding employee	
Employee is consistently late	**Extinction**	Withhold praise and do not recommend merit pay	
	Punishment	Reprimand and harass employee	

Source: Adapted from Steers, 1984, p. 197. Reprinted by permission.

will reinforce the desired behavior and cause the employee to be on time for work repeatedly.

Hamner (1977) suggests that for positive reinforcement to be most effective in bringing about desired behavior, several important conditions have to be met. First, the reinforcement (in this case, praise) must be highly valued by the employee. If the employee is indifferent to the reward, the behavior probably will not be affected. Second, the reinforcement must be linked directly to performing the desired behavior. Finally, there must be ample occasion for the reinforcement to be administered when the employee exhibits the desired behavior. If the reinforcement is tied to a behavior that seldom occurs, such as exceedingly high performance, the employees probably will not associate this form of behavior with a reward. It is therefore of paramount importance that the performance-reward contingencies are relatively attainable by employees.

Avoidance Learning. When individuals seek to avoid an unpleasant condition or outcome by behaving in certain ways, avoidance learning, through negative reinforcement, occurs. For example, if an employee performs a certain task correctly or is continually prompt in coming to work (see Fig. 9.3), the employee may hope that the supervisor will not publicly reprimand or otherwise embarrass him or her. It is assumed in **avoidance learning** that the employee learns over time that correct behaviors diminish distasteful admonitions by the supervisor. To avoid these negative results, the employee probably will continue to behave as the supervisor desires.

Extinction. The concept of **extinction** rests on the assumption that if undesirable behavior is ignored or not followed by positive reinforcement, it will tend to decline over time. As noted in Figure 9.3, if a consistently tardy employee fails to receive supervisory praise or is bypassed for pay raises or promotions, this nonreinforcement should lead to an extinction of the tardiness. The employee will realize that being late is not leading to the desired outcome and may make efforts to come to work on time.

Punishment. The fourth type of reinforcement used by managers in work situations is **punishment,** unpleasant or adverse actions occurring in response to undesired behavior. A supervisor, for example, may publicly reprimand or harass an employee who is habitually tardy (see Fig. 9.3). As a result, the employee may refrain from being tardy in the future to avoid this undesirable outcome.

We can see that within reinforcement theory the supervisor has at least four different types of reinforcement available. Advocates of reinforcement theory would argue that positive reinforcement is by far the most effective. They also would argue that combining it with extinction gives the manager a very powerful mechanism to direct subordinates' behavior to organizationally desired outcomes. Punishment is considered a less desirable strategy, because it may cause the individual to become alienated from the work situation, reducing the chances to implement useful change. Moreover, avoidance learning should also be shunned, because it emphasizes the negative. Positive reinforcement and extinction in work situations are considered primarily positive control mechanisms, leading to fewer undesirable side effects than punishment or avoidance learning.

Schedules of Reinforcement

We have seen that several types of reinforcement exist within work organizations. It is also useful to examine the rather divergent ways in which these reinforcements can be administered, referred to as **schedules of reinforcements.** Costello and Zalkind (1963) note that both the rapidity with which learning takes place in organizations and the duration of the learning are largely determined by the timing of the reinforcements. A knowldge of reinforcement schedules is critical for managers in applying reinforcement theory.

We can distinguish two schedules of reinforcement: continuous and partial. A **continuous reinforcement schedule** rewards desired behavior each time it occurs. A manager may praise an employee each time that he or she performs a desired behavior. In view of the time and resource constraints on most managers, it is easy to see why continuous reinforcement schedules are difficult to implement. As a result most managers must rely on partial reinforcement schedules. **Partial reinforcement schedules** reward desired behavior at specific intervals rather than each time the desired behavior occurs. It is generally believed that partial schedules usually lead to strong retention of the desired behavior, but that the learning process is slower than with continuous schedules. Learning is generally considered more permanent under partial reinforcement schedules. There are four kinds of partial reinforcement schedules: fixed interval, fixed ratio, variable interval, and variable ratio. The four types are summarized in Figure 9.4.

Fixed Interval Schedule. The first schedule of reinforcement we will consider is the **fixed interval,** which provides individuals with rewards at prespecified times not based on performance. As a result, employees are paid even if they perform only marginally. This technique generally does not lead to high performance levels, because employees are aware that even marginal performance will usually lead to the same reward. There is little incentive for superior performance. Under this system, extinction of the desired behavior occurs rather quickly when rewards are withheld or suspended.

Fixed Ratio Schedule. Under a **fixed ratio schedule,** rewards are given when a certain number of desired results occur. Rewards are closely tied to performance in a ratio of rewards to results. The clearest example of a fixed ratio schedule is the piece-rate incentive program, in which employees are paid per

Figure 9.4
Schedules of Partial Reinforcement

SCHEDULE OF REINFORCEMENT	NATURE OF REINFORCEMENT	EFFECTS ON BEHAVIOR WHEN APPLIED	EFFECTS ON BEHAVIOR WHEN PERCEIVED	EXAMPLE
Fixed interval	Reward on fixed time basis	Leads to average and irregular performance	Quick extinction of behavior	Weekly paycheck
Fixed ratio	Reward consistently tied to output	Leads quickly to very high and stable performance	Quick extinction of behavior	Piece-rate pay system
Variable interval	Reward given at variable intervals around some average time	Leads to moderately high and stable performance	Slow extinction of behavior	Monthly performance appraisal and reward at random times each month
Variable ratio	Reward given at variable output levels around some average output	Leads to very high performance	Slow extinction of behavior	Sales bonus tied to selling X accounts, but X constantly changes around some mean

Source: Steers, 1984, p. 199. Reprinted by permission.

unit of output. Performance rapidly increases to high levels in this system. On the negative side, performance dramatically declines upon receipt of the reward.

Variable Interval Schedule. In contrast to the fixed reinforcement schedules, variable reinforcement schedules administer rewards at random times that cannot be predetermined or detected by the employee. The employee generally is unaware of when the next evaluation and reward period is coming. When the **variable interval schedule** of reinforcement is used, rewards generally are administered at time intervals based on an average. For instance, employees may be aware that, on the average, performance is assessed and rewarded once every two weeks, but they do not know when during this period the event will occur. Given this uncertainty it is not unusual to see relatively high effort and performance at a relatively stable rate. Employees are not aware of when the evaluation will occur and are consistently on guard to maintain high performance levels.

Variable Ratio Schedule. The fourth schedule of reinforcement is the **variable ratio schedule.** In this schedule rewards are administered only after employees have performed the desired behavior a number of times, the number changing from one reward period to the next but averaging over time to a certain ratio of performances to rewards. For example, an employer may establish a system in which sales representatives receive a bonus for every fifteen new accounts that are sold. But instead of administering a bonus every fifteenth sale, as would be the case in the fixed interval schedule, the manager varies the number of sales that are necessary for the bonus from perhaps ten for the first bonus to twenty for the second. On the average, however, the fifteen-to-one ratio prevails. Like the variable interval reinforcement schedule, the variable ratio schedule fairly consistently leads to high and rather stable performance. In addition, extinction of desired behavior is slow.

Research has shown that performance-contingent, or ratio reinforcement, schedules lead to higher performance than do time-contingent, or interval, schedules regardless of whether schedules are fixed or variable. This higher performance probably is largely due to the employee's uncertainty about when the assessment period or the reward will occur. Although the employee knows the reward is coming, he or she doesn't know when.

Implications of Reinforcement Theory for Management

Now let us consider what reinforcement theory can mean for management. Hamner and Hamner (1976) suggest six rules for management based on reinforcement theory research:

1. Do not give the same level of rewards to all employees.

2. The failure by an employer to respond to behavior should have reinforcing consequences. Superiors are bound to shape behavior of subordinates by the way in which they utilize the rewards at their disposal. As a result, it is important that managers carefully examine the consequences for performance of their nonactions as well as their actions.

3. Tell people what behaviors get reinforced.

4. Tell people what they are doing wrong when their behavior is inconsistent with managerial goals.

5. Don't punish employees in front of others.

6. Make the consequences equal to the behaviors. In other words, don't short-change workers when their performance justifiably should lead to significant rewards.

Techniques of Employee Motivation

So much for theory. What exactly can we learn from the discussion about motivation that will improve managerial techniques and organizational effectiveness? At least two divergent techniques directly follow from these theories. The first is work redesign, sometimes called job enrichment. The second is behavior modification.

Work Redesign

The concept behind **work redesign** directly follows cognitive theories of motivation, such as the expectancy/valence theory. This basic concept is that workers want a stronger voice in the decisions concerning their workplace and are willing to increase their involvement and productivity when given a chance to participate. In some ways work redesign, or job enrichment, represents a revolt against the early days of scientific management theory, when it was felt that jobs should be simplified as much as possible because workers were generally lazy and economically motivated. Scientific management argued that we should (1) increase the extent to which jobs are machine paced, (2) increase the repetitiveness of jobs, (3) reduce the required skill levels for jobs, (4) increase task specialization, (5) limit social interaction, and (6) clearly specify the tools and techniques to be used by employees. The characteristics of scientific management seem inconsistent with many of the assumptions prevailing about employees at work today. They clearly are incompatible with the theoretical foundations of expectancy/valence theory.

Many contemporary managers assume that employees want more control over resources, greater accountability for their own performance, and more feedback on how well they do their jobs. They also wish to control their work pace within certain limits, and they want achievement opportunities and the chance for personal growth and development. These assumptions indicate that work redesign is a possible solution to the problems of the contemporary workplace.

By far the most prominent model of work redesign is the job characteristics model proposed by Hackman and Oldham (1976). The model, shown in Figure 9.5, consists of four parts: core job dimensions, critical psychological states, personal and work outcomes, and employee growth need strength. Let us examine each of these.

Core job dimensions are the defining characteristics of an employee's job that have the potential to motivate effort and performance. The dimensions include the extent to which employees need a variety of skills; task identity, the extent to which an employee is doing a whole and identifiable piece of work; task significance, the extent to which the job has impact on the lives or work of other people; autonomy; and feedback. Based on these core job dimensions, Hackman and Oldham developed a questionnaire that calculates a *motivating potential score,* the extent to which employees see their jobs as motivating. The more jobs are characterized by skill variety, common-task identity, and so on, the greater the motivating potential score.

Core job dimensions are believed to influence *critical psychological states,* the employees' feelings about their jobs as influenced by job technology. Three psychological states are identified, including how meaningful employees feel their work is (with total meaninglessness equivalent to alienation), how much responsibility employees feel for the outcome of their work, and how much they know about the results of their work.

When critical psychological states are highly positive, it is suggested, *personal and work outcomes* will also be high. Figure 9.5 notes that personal and work outcomes include high internal work motivation, high quality of work performance, high job satisfaction, and, often, lower absenteeism and turnover.

Not all employees respond in the same way to work redesign, as manifested in the core job dimensions and critical psychological states. Remember our earlier discussion concerning employee need for achievement. Hackman and Oldham use the term *employee growth need strength* (GNS) to refer to a collection of higher-order needs, including achievement and affiliation, that are believed to moderate how employees react to their work environment. This influence emerges in two different ways, as can be seen in Figure 9.5. Employees with high GNS are believed more likely to experience desired psychological states when their jobs have been enriched than are those with lower GNS, because their high GNS is activated by the job characteristics. In addition, high-GNS employees also tend to respond more favorably to positive psychological states than do low-GNS employees, because these states are more likely to satisfy their higher-order needs. The model suggests that although work redesign does not necessarily lead to negative consequences among employees, its most beneficial effects are on employees whose growth needs, such as need for achievement, are strong.

Figure 9.5
The Job Characteristics Model of Work Motivation

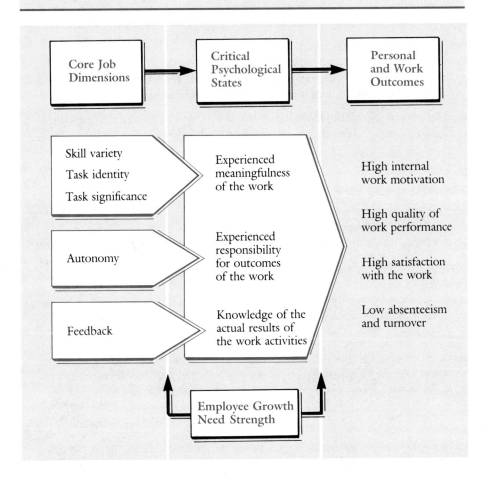

Source: J. R. Hackman and G. R. Oldham, "Motivation through the Design of Work: Test of a Theory," *Organizational Behavior and Human Performance 16,* 1976, 250–279. Reprinted by permission of the authors and the publisher.

An employer wishing to use the job characteristics model or a similar model to redesign work must formulate some principles that will lead to higher motivating potential scores. Hackman (1976b) has suggested five guidelines for enriching jobs and for redesigning work:

1. To the extent possible, form natural work units; that is work loads should be pieced together in a logical fashion. For instance, all the typing responsibilities for a person or department may be assigned to one typist instead of to a number of typists, who never see completed projects.

2. Similarly, enrich jobs by combining several of the related aspects that characterize the job. (E.g., a secretary might compose as well as type a letter for the boss.)

3. When possible, attempt to establish client relationships; that is, to the extent possible establish contact between the producer of the product and the client, rather than using a third party as a go-between.

4. Utilize vertical loading when possible. In other words, attempt to minimize the gap between the doing and the controlling aspects of work.

Feature 9.4
Encouraging Workers Makes a Difference

What's the worst thing management can do to low-producing employees who are locked into low-paying jobs with little chance for personal growth?

Give up on them.

The problem is one of the toughest management has to face. A study involving twelve low-producing sailors may provide some answers, however. Results of the study show that thinking well of subordinates and encouraging them to have high expectations does make a difference.

The navy chose twelve sailors who had been disciplinary problems before joining the navy and whose behavior was such a problem after joining that their fellow sailors labeled them with the onerous naval nickname ''dirt bags.'' Also involved in the study were their supervisors and special mentors, senior enlisted personnel who were to act as friends and supporters and who could reinforce positive changes in the sailors' attitudes and behavior.

The supervisors were involved in a brief motivation and leadership workshop designed to show them that their support was crucial in changing the sailors' behavior. Mentors also were given a short workshop in counseling and guidance. But the mentor program fell apart because the mentors derived no benefit from working with the sailors.

More intensive workshops were held for the sailors. Their superiors told them of their confidence that the sailors could improve their performance. Researchers showed the twelve that they had the power to determine their own future. The sailors developed realistic action plans that reinforced and rewarded their positive behavior.

The results were measured and compared with those of a control group. The twelve sailors in the program showed a significant increase in performance.

How do these results apply to business? Many jobs in business and industry cannot be enhanced. Many workers are locked into closely managed pay scales with little or no opportunity for merit pay. These jobs are comparable with those held by the low-producing sailors.

This research shows that thinking well of subordinates and encouraging them to have high expectations does make a difference.

Source: Adapted with permission from ''A Behavioral Science Approach,'' by Rodger D. Collons, *Best's Review,* October 1981, pp. 102–104. (Review of a study by Kent S. Crawford, Edmund D. Thomas, and Jeffrey J. Fink, ''Pygmalion at Sea: Improving the Work Effectiveness of Low Performers,'' *The Journal of Applied Behavioral Science,* Vol. 16, No. 4, 1980.)

5. Provide employees with as much feedback as possible on their job performance.

Other principles could be suggested. The five we have discussed are meant to illustrate the types of interventions that have been used successfully in organizations in work redesign attempts. Our point here is that managers interested in implementing work redesign have a responsibility to think carefully about the nature of the workplace, employees, and job technology and to consider ways to provide employees with more meaningful, challenging positions likely to lead to greater employee involvement.

Behavior Modification

The second prevalent technique for employee motivation is called **behavior modification,** a system that closely follows reinforcement theory. Whereas advocates of work redesign assume individuals want to be actively involved in their jobs, many advocates of behavior modification, such as B. F. Skinner (1971), argue that individuals are basically passive and reactive instead of proactive; that is, they tend to respond to stimuli rather than to assume responsibility for initiating behavior. (This distinction again highlights the differences between cognitive and acognitive theories discussed earlier in this chapter.) In addition, advocates of behavior modification emphasize that this technique focuses on observable and measurable behavior rather than unobserved needs, attitudes, or goals, another clear distinction between the two approaches. In addition, behavior modification emphasizes that permanent change can be caused only by reinforcement; this is the defining characteristic of behavior modification programs.

How do we implement a behavior modification program? Based on earlier efforts, it is possible to diagram and summarize a typical program. Such a program in the workplace would pass through five general stages (Fig. 9.6):

1. Management defines and clearly specifies what constitutes acceptable behavior. This behavior must be outlined in objective and measurable terms. Examples of behavioral criteria include promptness in arriving for work, completion of tasks on schedule, and good attendance.

2. Once the behavioral criteria have been identified, management initiates a performance audit. This is a technique that identifies areas in which behavioral criteria have been met and those in which they have not. It identifies potential trouble spots and targets for future action.

3. Managers set forth specific behavioral goals for each employee. The failure to identify concrete goals for employees is a primary reason for the failure of many behavior modification programs. Examples of specific goals include a decrease in absenteeism and an increase in productivity.

4. Employees keep a record of their own work. This record provides continuous feedback directly to the employees about whether they are on target in meeting their assigned goals.

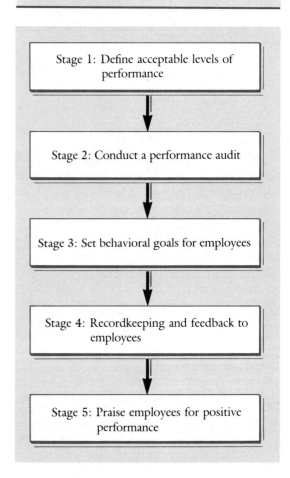

Figure 9.6
Stages in Implementing a Behavior
Modification Program

Stage 1: Define acceptable levels of performance

Stage 2: Conduct a performance audit

Stage 3: Set behavioral goals for employees

Stage 4: Recordkeeping and feedback to employees

Stage 5: Praise employees for positive performance

5. Supervisors examine each employee's record as well as other performance in-dicators and praise employees for the more positive aspects of their perform-ance. Praise or similar positive methods, combined with extinction, are believed to provide the employees with sufficient reinforcement to shape their behavior and keep them on target and working toward their assigned goals.

As we can see, several very practical things can be done to motivate em-ployees. We have explored two approaches, work redesign and behavior modifi-cation. Although the two are different, both aim to boost performance by changing the work environment in some way. The suitability of either approach depends on the specific motivational problem facing management, constraints on managerial action (such as union contracts), and the people and work situation. The real challenge to management lies in being able to assess the situation accurately and then to apply the most appropriate technique to achieve the desired results.

Summary

Motivation and performance are the subject of this chapter. Organizations and managers need to encourage employees to join and remain with the organization, to perform tasks dependably, and to initiate innovative behavior.

Many work situations do not motivate employees to perform. Reasons for low productivity include unappealing potential rewards, weak performance-reward linkages, distrust of management, employees' desire to have greater control over their jobs, and lack of job involvement.

Individual needs can be viewed in the terms of Maslow's need hierarchy model, which assumes that people are motivated primarily by a desire to satisfy specific hierarchical needs, and according to Murray's manifest needs model, which classifies individuals according to the strength of their needs. Later studies show that the needs for achievement, power, and affiliation are important in the study of the workplace. Power can be broken down into personal and institutionalized power.

The expectancy/valence theory of employee motivation is a cognitive theory that assumes that job performance is influenced by the employee's motivation to perform, abilities and traits, role clarity, and opportunity to perform. It divides expectancies into effort-performance expectancy ($E \rightarrow P$), the belief that an effort will lead to performance, and performance-outcome expectancy ($P \rightarrow O$), the belief that performance will lead to a certain outcome. Valence refers to the value an individual places on available outcomes or rewards.

Reinforcement theory is an acognitive theory of employee motivation that assumes that behavior leading to positive or pleasurable outcomes will tend to be repeated, whereas behavior that leads to negative outcomes or punishment will tend to be avoided. Strategies for behavioral change include positive reinforcement, avoidance learning, extinction of undesirable behavior, and punishment.

Reinforcements are administered through schedules of reinforcement, which may be continuous or partial. There are four kinds of partial reinforcement: fixed interval, fixed ratio, variable interval, and variable ratio.

The basic concept behind work redesign is that workers want a stronger voice in decisions concerning their workplace and are willing to increase their involvement and productivity when given a chance to participate. Work redesign may be a solution to some of the problems of the contemporary workplace.

The job characteristics model is the most prominent model of work redesign. In it core job dimensions, the defining characteristics of a job, influence critical psychological states, including how meaningful employees feel their work is, how much responsibilty employees feel for the outcome of their work, and how much they know about the results of their work. When critical psychological states are highly positive, personal and work outcomes will be high. Employee growth need strengths, higher-order needs including achievement and affiliation, influence how employees react to their work environment.

Another technique for motivating employees is behavior modification, which argues that individuals are basically passive and reactive. In a behavior modification program, management outlines objectives, initiates performance audits, and sets specific goals for each employee. Employees keep a record of their work, and supervisors examine the records and other indicators and shape employees' behavior with rewards and extinction techniques.

Questions for Discussion

1. What are the so-called behavioral requirements of organizations? What is their importance to management?
2. Describe three primary models concerning people at work that managers often use in dealing with people.
3. What are some of the reasons for low-productivity at work?
4. Define motivation.
5. What is the basic premise of the need hierarchy model of motivation? How does it differ from the manifest needs model?
6. Describe the basic tenets of expectancy/valence theory. Provide an example of how it works.
7. Describe reinforcement theory. Provide an example of how it works.
8. What is the law of effect?
9. Identify the major strategies for behavioral change.
10. Differentiate among the major schedules of reinforcement.
11. How can managers use behavior modification at work? What are some of the pitfalls of using such techniques?
12. Describe the basic assumptions underlying work-redesign efforts.
13. What is the job characteristics model? How does it work?

Exercise 9.1
Motivation Problems

Two motivational problems are presented here. For each case you are to analyze the nature of the problem and recommend solutions using need theory, expectancy/valence theory, and reinforcement theory. That is, each case should be analyzed three times. Make sure to follow strictly the guidelines from each theory. In your analysis, pay attention to the different management implications of each theory.

Problem 1

You are (high-paid) consultants to the manager of the shipping plant of a large airfreight company. Your drivers pick up freight shipments from customers and deliver them to your facility, where the appropriate paperwork is processed, and the packages are sent on conveyers to cargo loading docks, where they are routed for the appropriate flights. Each dock handles shipments for a particular destination. Because of the ease of handling, small shipments intended for the same destination fly at lower rates when shipped together in large, standard-sized boxes, called "bulk cargo containers," rather than separately as many small packages. Thus, the airfreight company can reduce its freight costs considerably simply by making more use of bulk cargo containers on the loading docks.

Managers responsible for the shipping dock were under the impression that bulk containers already were being used most of the time. A study showed, however, that bulk containers are being used for only 45 percent of all possible such shipments.

The employees on the shipping dock seem indifferent to using bulk containers. The amount of time and effort they have to expend is the same for either method. Relations between them and their supervisors are good.

Problem

How can the usage of bulk containers for small shipments be increased?

Problem 2

You are consultants to the district traffic manager of a telephone company. The traffic department is responsible for information service, long distance calls, and certain customer inquiries. Most of your employees are operators, both directory assistance (information) and long distance. About 85 percent are women, and most are in their late teens and early twenties.

Tardiness and absenteeism have been big problems in this district. As a result, the traffic manager has had to schedule 20 percent more operators than she needs for each shift, in order to have fully staffed boards. The personnel costs caused by this overstaffing are unbearable. Remedial action must be taken. If each operator would just show up for work each day, at the appointed time, personnel costs would drop back to their budgeted level.

Problem

Develop a plan that will motivate operators to come to work each day and to come on time.

Source: From *Experiences in Management and Organizational Behavior,* 2nd ed., by D. Hall, D. Bowen, R. Lewicki, and F. Hall, p. 82. Copyright © 1982 by John Wiley & Sons, Inc. Reprinted by permission of John Wiley & Sons, Inc.

Exercise 9.2
Annual Salary Evaluation

Instructions

You have to make salary increase recommendations for eight managers that you supervise. They have just completed their first year with the company and are now to be considered for their first annual raise. Keep in mind that you may be setting precedents and that you need to keep salary costs down. However, there are no formal company restrictions on the kind of raises that you can give. Please indicate the size of the raise that you would like to give each manager by writing a *percentage* amount next to his name.

_____% Abraham McGowan. Abe is not, as far as you can tell, a good performer. You have checked your view out with others, and they do not feel that he is too effective either. However, you happen to know he has one of the toughest work groups to manage. His subordinates have low skill levels, and the work is dirty and hard. If you lose him, you are frankly not sure who you could find to replace him.

_____% Beta Berger. Beta is single and seems to live the life of a carefree bachelor. In general, you feel that his job performance is not up to par, and some of his "goofs" on the job are well known to his fellow employees.

_____% Clyde Clod. You consider Clyde to be one of your best subordinates. However, it is quite apparent that other people don't consider him to be a very effective manager. Clyde has married a rich wife, and as far as you know he doesn't need additional money.

_____% David Doodle. You happen to know from your personal relationship with "Doodles" that he badly needs more money because of certain personal problems he is having. As far as you are concerned, he also happens to be one of the best of your subordinates. For some reason your enthusiasm for him is not shared by your other subordinates, and you have heard them make joking remarks about his performance.

_____% Elihu Yale. Elihu has been very successful so far in the things he has undertaken. You are particularly impressed by this since he has a hard job. He needs money more than many of the other fellows, and you are sure that they also respect him because of his good performance.

_____% Fred Framp. Fred has turned out to be a very pleasant surprise to you. He has done an excellent job, and it is generally accepted among the others that he is one of the best people. This surprises you because he is generally frivolous and doesn't seem to care very much about money and promotion.

_____% Greg Goose. Your own opinion is that Greg just isn't cutting the mustard. Surprisingly enough, however, when you check with others to see how they feel about him, you discover that his work is very highly regarded. You also know that he badly needs a raise. He has just gotten married, and his wife is putting a lot of pressure on him to buy a house and start a family.

_____% Harry Hungerford. You know Harry personally, and he just seems to squander his money continually. He has a fairly easy job assignment, and your own view is that he doesn't do it particularly well. You are, therefore, quite surprised to find that several of the other new managers think that he is the best of the new group.

Source: Exercise prepared by Professor Edward E. Lawler III, Center for Effective Organizations, University of Southern California. Reprinted by permission.

Case Study
Machinist

There is a production game that is played between workers and their supervisors. The supervisor or foreman almost always wants the people he [or she] is responsible for to produce more. Most workers seem to know instinctively that "more production" either leads to the challenging game of "you want more but I don't want to work harder" or to a bottomless pit. The challenge of the game can prove to be the most interesting part of the job. Workers are ingenious at this game.

I was talking with the Greek about how the foreman was catching up with our production innovations. "Look," I said, "we are in a double bind if we do the work as easily and as quickly as possible, maybe just to increase our schmooze* time. If the supervisor catches on and says we're real smart and incorporates our shortcuts, we end up doing more work for the same money. This requires that we hide our shortcut timesavers — and that will take our most creative effort." The Greek looked at me for a long time and then said, "Listen, the next time Ramirez is running far ahead of schedule, I am going to show you something you won't believe, Schrank."

A few weeks later on a summer night, the Greek came by and said, "Let's take a walk." We walked to the back end of the plant, out onto the loading platform. There I could not believe my eyes. I saw two guys burying a thirty-foot propeller shaft in the backyard. I burst out with, "What the hell are you guys doing?" They said, "Hey fellows, you watch us be heroes at the end of the month when the boss gives us that we-need-to-break-quota. . . ." I admit

that this was an extreme case, but if you can get a group of workers to tell work-banking stories, you will hear some fantastic tales.

Banking work in the sawdust, as was done in the furniture factory, or under benches, in machine shop lockers, under loose floor boards, even in car trunks, or by undercounting, are just a few of the ways I observed workers trying to monitor their own work pace to control the amount that they are asked to produce. I remember a typewriter plant where people would get ahead by taking the extra parts home, then on a day they wanted to take it easy, bring them in to be counted.

If you have not experienced a production line, it is very hard to understand the problem of work pacing. I remember doing things in an emergency, like turning out in seven hours a propeller shaft that normally took twelve or fourteen hours. Obviously I could never do that at a steady pace. It would surely end me up like Charlie Chaplin in *Modern Times*. To expect a production worker to work at his [or her] peak for a whole day is like asking a long-distance runner to sprint the whole race the way he does in the last 100 yards. It is simply impossible to do, yet some production-hungry industrial engineers expect that. The foreman at Vass would say, "After all, you produced thirty units this morning. How come you only made ten this afternoon?" I answered, "Because I wore myself out this morning." He did not seem to care about my explanation, just sort of shrugged and said, "If you can do it in the morning, you can do it in the afternoon."

I was learning that I might double or triple my productivity for a short, fixed period of time, but I could not possibly keep up that double or triple pace continuously without serious consequences to my health.

---
* "Schmooze time" is that time spent in social interaction with co-workers or friends rather than in performance of the required or assigned task.

Bennet Kremen, writing in the *New York Times* about the Lordstown, Ohio, General Motors assembly plant, told how workers doubled up (buddied) to relieve each other on the line. Some people in the Auto Workers Union were peeved at Kremen for suggesting that one employee on an assembly line could do the work of two; this surely could be seen as evidence that GM might be right when they complain that the workers are not giving a day's work. Workers on a production line may help each other by doing two jobs for a given period of time, but that certainly does not mean one person could do both jobs continuously. I can recall times when I did the work of two or even three men for short time periods. Can this possibly suggest that I could do that continuously and hope to survive? I think not. The problem that employees in manufacturing have is that supervisors continue to harass employees for increased production once the idea takes hold that workers can be more productive. They become extremely aggressive in constantly demanding more. That is how workers learn to pace the amount of work done for a day, a week, or a month. As Max said in the furniture factory, "We give just so much and no more."

A few years ago I visited the Volvo truck plant in Goteborg, Sweden. I spent a day observing work teams assembling trucks. In the afternoon, about three o'clock or three-fifteen, the place seemed to come to a halt as workers began to wipe their hands, wash up, and generally to appear as though the day's work was through. I figured my watch was wrong, because time-zone changes throw off my inner clock. Since quitting time was four o'clock, I asked one of the men what was happening. He looked at me quite surprised saying, "We made our thirty trucks today and that's it. Not even another bolt goes on today."

That example of production pacing is common in many parts of Europe. When I asked the Volvo management about it, they acknowledged the problem, yet they had no idea about what to do. As one manager put it, "What good is participation, team building, and all that stuff if I cannot get one more truck a week?"

Workers in manufacturing try to get some control over the work pace because they are fearful that if they do not, the speedup will kill them. Whether it is true or not is of little consequence because the tradition creates a fear that is real.

Case Questions

1. What limits does management put on performance? On schmoozing? What limits does the worker's group put on performance? On schmoozing? What effect do these limits have on individual worker's discretion?

2. Describe any experiences you have had where your (work) group put a limit on your individual performance.

3. Explore alternatives to the "production game" that can be used to reduce the negative effect of the worker's group on individual performance.

Source: From Robert Schrank, *Ten Thousand Working Days,* pp. 127–128. Copyright © 1978 by The MIT Press. All rights reserved.

CHAPTER 10

Leadership and Managerial Effectiveness

International Harvester, a leading manufacturer of farm equipment and heavy-duty trucks, was close to filing for bankruptcy in 1982. Its stock had fallen from a high of $45 per share in the fall of 1979 to a low of $3 in December of 1982. Then Donald D. Lennox took over as president.

Lennox has breathed new life into Harvester. He did it by cutting overhead by $1 billion, closing inefficient plants, laying off two-thirds of the work force, and selling off unprofitable subsidiaries. He also reduced inventories by basing manufacturing on customer orders only.

Although Harvester still has a long way to go and years of debts to pay off, investors are encouraged. They are impressed with Lennox and the way he operates.

When people who know Lennox talk about his style, they mention a poker game he once had with three other Harvester executives aboard the company plane. Lennox was losing, but his luck began to turn after the plane began its descent toward Midway airport in Chicago. He talked the pilot into slowing the plane's approach. By the time they landed, Lennox had recovered his losses and was $100 ahead. "Don," said one of the players, "absolutely can't stand to lose" ("Can Don Lennox Save Harvester?" p. 80).

Sources: "International Harvester Lives!" by Anne B. Fisher, *Fortune*, December 26, 1983, pp. 64–70; "Can Don Lennox Save Harvester?" *Business Week*, August 15, 1983, pp. 80–84.

Chapter Outline

- The Nature of Leadership
- Leadership Abilities and Skills
- The Contingency Theory of Leadership
- The Path-Goal Theory of Leadership
- The Normative Theory of Leadership
- Common Barriers to Leadership Effectiveness
- Overcoming Barriers to Effective Leadership

Key Terms

- leadership
- consideration
- initiating structure
- contingency theory
- least-preferred co-worker scale
- path-goal theory
- directive leadership
- achievement-oriented leadership
- participative leadership
- supportive leadership
- normative theory
- decision tree

Chapter Objectives

After studying Chapter 10 you should be able to

1. Describe the leadership patterns in the different levels in the managerial hierarchy.
2. Explain the role of consideration and initiating structure in group effectiveness.
3. Recognize the barriers to leadership effectiveness.
4. Present some ideas for overcoming barriers to effective leadership.
5. Understand the importance of managerial selection, placement, and training in effective leadership.

Introduction

In any discussion of managerial effectiveness, we invariably hear the word *leadership*. Promoting good leadership in organizations seems almost an obsession with many people. Leadership is believed to hold the key to solving many serious interpersonal problems on the job.

In this chapter we will examine the issue of leadership and begin to explore a series of topics related to the problems of managing effective work groups. In the next few chapters, we shall look at group processes, staffing and human resource management, and performance appraisal and reward systems. We will focus on how to develop and lead effective work groups so that they can contribute to organizational effectiveness.

Our discussion of leadership begins by defining the concept. The role of leadership in organizations and several of the more evident leadership abilities and skills are considered. Next, three prominent models of leadership are presented. We then address several common barriers to effective leadership, as well as mechanisms for overcoming these barriers. Attention throughout is focused on what the management student can learn to become a better leader in the contemporary organization.

The Nature of Leadership

Definition of Leadership

Let us consider the concept of **leadership** in organizational settings. Leadership can be viewed from three different perspectives. First, leadership is an attribute of a position. The president of a major corporation is considered a leader because of the position he or she holds, for example. Leadership is also a characteristic, a charismatic aspect of a person. We often hear, for instance, that a particular individual is a "natural-born leader." Finally, leadership is a category of behavior. This third definition is perhaps the most useful for our purposes, because it focuses on the ways in which people influence others in work settings.

Katz and Kahn (1978, p. 528) define leadership as "the influential increment over and above mechanical compliance with routine directives of the organization." This definition suggests that leadership occurs when one person in the organization influences others to do something of their own volition, not because it is required or because they fear the consequences of noncompliance. It is this voluntary aspect of leadership that sets it apart from other influence processes, such as power and authority. There are many instances in which a manager has the power or the authority to force compliance. Leadership exists when subordinates voluntarily comply because of something the leader has done.

Levels of Leadership

The nature of leadership is influenced greatly by the level in the hierarchy at which leadership attempts are made. Katz and Kahn (1978) suggest that there are three different leadership patterns, each specific to a different level in the managerial hierarchy:

1. *Origination,* introducing structural change or formulating policy.
2. *Interpolation,* piecing together various parts of the organization or making existing formal structure more complete.
3. *Administration,* using the organization's formal structure to keep it in motion and running smoothly.

Figure 10.1 shows that each of these types of leadership patterns is related to a different level in the organization's hierarchy; organization is typically done by executives, whereas interpolation is done by the intermediate levels and administration takes place at the lower levels. Managers in different levels of the hierarchy bear different leadership responsibilities. Some use leadership primarily as a vehicle for change and creation (origination); others use it to carry out the existing functions of the organization (administration).

Just as the reasons for leadership differ across hierarchical levels, so do the abilities and skills that managers must possess. Top-echelon managers using origination need the cognitive ability to look at the organization from a systems perspective. The rank and file sees its leaders as more charismatic, symbolizing

Figure 10.1
Leadership Patterns in Organizations

TYPE OF LEADERSHIP PROCESS	TYPICAL ORGANIZATIONAL LEVEL	ABILITIES AND SKILLS	
		Cognitive	*Affective*
Origination: change, creation, and elimination of structure	→ Top echelons	→ Systems perspective	→ Charisma
Interpolation: supplementing and piecing out of structure	→ Intermediate levels: pivotal roles	→ Subsystems perspective: two-way orientation	→ Integration of primary and secondary relations: human relations skills
Administration: use of existing structure	→ Lower levels	→ Technical knowledge and understanding of system of rules	→ Concern with equity in use of rewards and sanctions

Source: Reprinted, by permission, from D. Katz and R. Kahn, *The Social Psychology of Organizations,* 2nd ed., p. 539. Copyright © 1978 by John Wiley & Sons, Inc.

the organization and what it stands for. Middle-level managers, in contrast, are concerned primarily with subsystem decisions. They typically are responsible for a division or department and the activities of the people in it. They usually are not concerned with the day-to-day activities on the shop floor, although their focus is shorter term than that of high-level executives. A primary ingredient for success is good human relations skills, but these skills may be more impersonal and distant at this level than in lower-level management. Lower-level managers are supervisors and bear primary responsibility for the day-to-day operations of a single work group. To be successful, it is important that they have strong technical skills, understand the organizational reward systems, and ensure that the work is completed on time.

Although this three-way classification is crude, it does highlight the fact that managers at different levels bear distinct responsibilities and need different abilities and skills. This distinction will become clear as we further examine the nature of leadership in organizations.

Leadership Abilities and Skills

Attempts to Define the Basis of Leadership

The topic of leadership has been of interest to scientists and philosophers since the time of the ancient Greeks. During those early times it was assumed that great leaders were born rather than developed. This approach has been termed the **great man theory of leadership.** It was assumed that most great leaders were destined for positions of influence as a function of birth. This narrow view of leadership was popular throughout the nineteenth century. In 1869 Sir Francis Galton, in his book *Hereditary Genius,* argued that leadership qualities were primarily based on heredity.

As the twentieth century began, however, this narrow approach to leadership increasingly came under attack. There were efforts to make the study of leadership more scientific, focusing on the role of environment as well as heredity in the determination of leadership skills. The first early-twentieth-century development in this regard was an attempt to identify the abilities and skills that great leaders throughout history had in common. Much of this work has been summarized by Ralph Stogdill (1948) and Edwin Ghiselli (1966). In a review of 124 empirical studies of leader attributes, Stogdill identified three variables that seem to be consistently related to successful leaders:

1. *Height.* Leaders tend to be taller than their average followers.

2. *Intelligence.* Leaders tend to be rated higher on tests of intelligence, verbal fluency, originality, and overall knowledge.

3. *Initiative.* Leaders generally show higher levels of ambition, persistence, and energy than their followers.

In a separate study of leadership abilities and skills, Ghiselli examined twelve personality and motivational traits of various managers as they related to success on the job. The results of this study are summarized in Figure 10.2. As can be seen, the most important traits exhibited by successful leaders include supervisory ability, occupational achievement, intelligence, self-actualization, self-assurance, and decisiveness. Some overlap exists in the lists of Ghiselli and Stogdill. In particular, both studies found that highly successful managers exhibit high levels of intelligence and achievement orientation.

Successful Managerial Behavior

Another of Stogdill's conclusions (1948) is important because it began a new line of research into leader behavior. Stogdill found that in some instances the profile of a successful leader varied with the situation. In other words, different groups and different group activities sometimes required different types of leaders. Based on this finding, studies were initiated at Ohio State University and the University of Michigan that shifted the emphasis to the ways in which leaders interacted with groups under various conditions and whether these interactions succeeded or failed.

The Ohio State and Michigan studies concluded that it was necessary to go beyond studying leadership abilities and skills and to focus on the behavior of leaders and managers. Effective managerial behavior was perceived to be essentially multidimensional. Effective managers need to exhibit different types of behavior, depending on the situation. Two types of managerial behavior were identified.

The first, **consideration,** includes helping and doing favors for subordinates, looking after their welfare, explaining job-related activities, and being sociable, friendly, and generally available. The second, **initiating structure,** involves such managerial behavior as ensuring that subordinates follow rules and procedures, maintaining high performance standards, and clarifying leader and subordinate roles so that everyone understands his or her position.

Figure 10.2
Relative Importance of Leadership Traits to Managerial Effectiveness

VERY IMPORTANT TO SUCCESS	MODERATELY IMPORTANT TO SUCCESS	UNIMPORTANT TO SUCCESS
Supervisory ability	Low need for security	Low need for financial rewards
Occupational achievement	Working-class affinity	High need for power over others
Intelligence	Initiative	Masculinity-femininity
Self-actualization		
Self-assurance		
Decisiveness		

Feature 10.1
Ray Kroc's Standards Built McDonald's

He was called the Henry Ford of the service sector, one of the great marketers of modern times, but Ray Kroc had a simple explanation for the phenomenal success of McDonald's Corporation.

"We take the hamburger business more seriously than they do," he said. "We treat it as a regular business — and it *is* a regular business."

McDonald's is a "regular business" that also happens to be the world's largest restaurant chain, with annual revenues of $2.8 billion. It is the standard against which all others are judged.

Kroc won that position with an unbeatable combination of quality, speed, low prices, and cleanliness. He brought in assembly line techniques and automated every cooking function. His standards were rigid for every outlet. A littered McDonald's parking lot threw him into a rage. "The french fry would become almost sacrosanct for me," he said, "its preparation a ritual to be followed religiously."

Kroc, born in a Chicago suburb, quit school during World War I to become an ambulance driver. The war ended and he went back to school, only to quit again. After that he weaved his way through the world. He sold ribbon novelties, was a board marker for a Chicago brokerage firm, became a professional piano player for various bands, sold real estate in Florida and paper cups in Chicago. Then he became the exclusive distributor for a company that sold milk shake mixers.

The McDonald brothers used his mixers in their small chain of hamburger stands based in San Diego, California. Kroc was impressed. He became their agent in recruiting new franchises and bought them out in 1961 for $2.7 million at interest so high that the ultimate cost topped $14 million. When he died in 1984, Kroc's personal stake in McDonald's Corporation was worth nearly $500 million.

Source: Adapted with permission from "The Hall of Fame for U.S. Business Leadership," by Arthur M. Louis, *Fortune,* April 4, 1983, p. 147.

In the years since these original studies appeared, a steady stream of research has been carried out that focuses on leader behavior as it affects group performance. House and Baetz (1979) have summarized this research as it relates to consideration and initiating structure. They draw six general conclusions:

1. Task-oriented leadership or initiating structure is necessary for effective work-group performance in most situations.

2. For task-oriented leadership or initiating structure to be accepted, others must be allowed to respond by giving feedback, making objections, and asking questions.

3. Consideration-oriented leadership is required in addition to task-oriented leadership when groups are engaged in tasks that are not satisfying or ego involving.

4. Groups requiring both kinds of leadership will be more effective when these behaviors are performed by one person instead of being divided between two or among more persons.

5. When the leadership roles are differentiated, work groups generally will be more effective if the leaders are mutually supportive, and less effective when the leaders are in conflict with one another.

6. When formally appointed leaders fail in their group effectiveness, an informal leader typically will emerge and will perform the necessary leadership behaviors, provided group members want success.

Thus, research on leader behavior has suggested that both consideration and initiating structure are necessary at separate times for group effectiveness. If a manager does not successfully perform these two types of behavior, the group often finds a substitute from its own membership who will act as a surrogate leader to accommodate the needs of the group and ensure work effectiveness.

The Contingency Theory of Leadership

What generally is missing from these discussions of leadership abilities, skills, and behavior is a clear recognition of the importance of the situation in which leader–member interactions take place. Interactions between leaders and their followers do not occur in a vacuum. The behavior of leaders and followers, and the outcome, are often greatly influenced by the unique characteristics of the situation. We now turn to an examination of three different theories of leadership that attempt to account not only for the behavior of leaders and followers, but also for situational effects.

The **contingency theory,** proposed by Fred Fiedler (1967), rests on the assumption that group performance and effectiveness are a result of the interaction of leadership style and the "favorableness" of the situation. First we shall consider the situational factors, and then the ways in which leadership orientation interacts with the situation.

Situational Factors

Fiedler's model holds that a situation can be characterized by three distinct factors:

1. *Leader–member relations,* the degree of trust, confidence, and respect followers have for the leader; whether a leader is accepted by the group.

2. *Task structure,* the extent to which the task, goals, and role assignments are specified clearly so everyone knows exactly what he or she is supposed to do.

3. *Position power,* the extent to which power is distributed between the leader and the group. It generally is believed that the more rewards and punishments leaders have at their disposal, the more influence they possess.

Each of these three situational characteristics falls on a continuum ranging from very strong to very weak. Leader–member relations can be considered very good or very poor. Likewise, task structure can range from very high, such as that for an assembly line worker, to very low, such as that for a research scientist. Position power also can range from very strong, when the leader holds most or all of the power, to very weak, when group members hold most or all of the power. From these three divisions, a list of eight leadership situations can be developed. These situations are called *octants* by Fiedler and are shown in Figure 10.3. The figure shows that leader–member relations can be either good (octants 1 through 4) or bad (octants 5 through 8), whereas task structure can be either high (octants 1, 2, 5, and 6) or low (octants 3, 4, 7, and 8). Leader position power can be either strong (octants 1, 3, 5, and 7) or weak (octants 2, 4, 6, and 8).

Which of these eight different situational octants is the most desirable from the leader's position? Fiedler proposes that "situational favorableness" is highest from the leader's standpoint in octant 1 and lowest in octant 8. A leader or manager is in a far superior position when leader–member relations are good, when task structure is high, and when position power is strong, as is the case in octant 1. The reverse situation holds in octant 8.

Figure 10.3
Fiedler's Classification of Situation Favorableness

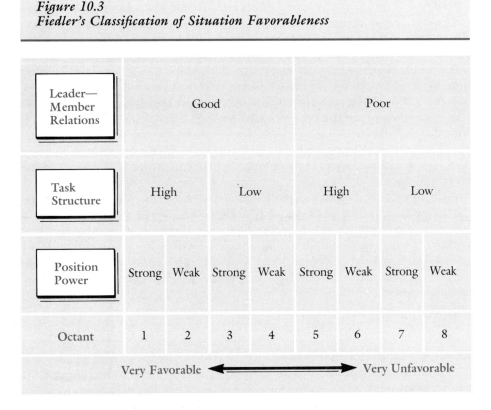

Source: F. Fiedler, *A Theory of Leadership Effectiveness*, p. 37. Copyright © 1967 by McGraw-Hill, Inc.

Leader Orientation

We now come to the second key variable in Fiedler's contingency theory. Based on his own research and closely following the Ohio State and Michigan studies, Fiedler argues that there are two basic leader orientations. The first, which he termed *relationship oriented,* is a more lenient or people-oriented style. The second is *task-oriented* leadership, which is characterized by an emphasis on task accomplishment. Fiedler uses a **least-preferred co-worker (LPC) scale** to predict and measure both of these leader orientations. This is a series of bipolar scales on which employees are asked to rate the least-preferred co-worker in their entire work experience. If they describe this "least desired" person favorably, it is believed that the person taking the test is generally relationship-oriented (called "high LPC"); that is, they generally like dealing with people. If, on the other hand, they describe the "least desired" person quite unfavorably, it is believed that the individual is more task-oriented (called "low LPC") than people-oriented (see Fiedler, 1967, for details).

We can now combine what we have learned about situational factors with the notion of leader orientation. In a series of laboratory experiments, Fiedler compared the statistical correlations between LPC scores and work-group effectiveness for each of the eight situational octants. These results are shown in Figure 10.4. In brief, negative correlations were found toward the middle of the continuum. Thus, high-LPC, or relationship-oriented, leaders were more effective in boosting group performance when the situation was moderately favorable or moderately unfavorable, toward the middle of the continuum. In this situation the leader is liked moderately and has some position power. In addition, the jobs carried out by the employees are vague but not terribly ambiguous. A leader with high interpersonal skills can exert the leadership necessary to clarify the task and remove job ambiguity through discussions and participation with the work force.

When the situation is highly unfavorable or highly favorable, at either end of the continuum, a more task-oriented leader with a low LPC appears to be more effective in aiding group performance. The logic of this argument is straightforward: In highly favorable situations, in which everyone gets along, the task is clear, and the leadership has all the power, all the manager must do is take charge and provide direction for employees. If the situation is highly unfavorable, the manager or leader is in a battle of wills with group members. In such a situation a strong leader with a low LPC is necessary to counterbalance the power of the group and to show some direction in an otherwise ambiguous task environment. Because leader–member relations are already poor, a strong task orientation will not make the manager less popular.

Thus, Fiedler's model defines leadership effectiveness in terms of group performance. (The two theories of leadership that follow employ different criteria for evaluating success.) Fiedler also argues that the two basic ingredients in a successful model of leadership are an understanding of the situation and an awareness of the leader's style. An effective work-group environment can be produced by matching the manager to the situation.

Figure 10.4
Results from Contingency Theory Research

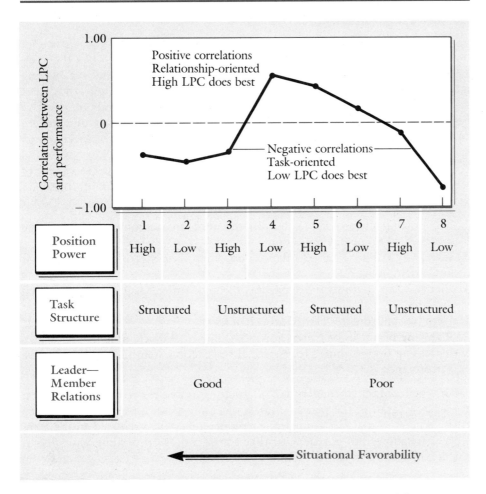

The Path-Goal Theory of Leadership

In contrast to Fiedler's contingency theory, the **path-goal theory** of leadership, espoused by Robert House (1971), emphasizes the ways in which leaders can facilitate performance by showing subordinates how performance can result in desired awards. In this way the path-goal model heavily builds on the expectancy/valence theory of work motivation discussed in Chapter 9. The model focuses on the ways in which the behavior of the leader motivates or satisfies subordinates. It suggests that such behavior is motivating or satisfying to the extent that it helps subordinates attain goals and clarifies the paths to these goals.

Basic Assumptions

The path-goal theory rests on two primary assumptions. First, it assumes that the behavior of a leader will be acceptable to subordinates when they perceive that it means immediate satisfaction or at least is instrumental in achieving future satisfaction. Second, it assumes that leaders are motivating to the extent that they make subordinates understand that satisfaction depends on effective performance and to the extent that they complement the subordinates' work environment by providing guidance, clear directions, and rewards for effective performance.

The theory suggests that leaders pursuing these two goals have a variety of techniques to increase the motivation of their subordinates. Among these are the following:

1. Recognizing and arousing subordinates' needs for outcomes over which the leaders have some degree of control.
2. Increasing the personal payoffs to subordinates for effective performance or goal attainment.
3. Clarifying the path to those payoffs, through either coaching or additional direction.
4. Helping subordinates clarify expectancies.
5. Reducing obstacles or frustrations that inhibit goal attainment.
6. Increasing opportunities for personal satisfaction stemming from effective performance.

It is believed that managers have a variety of strategies available for attaining goals by integrating the personal goals of employees with the organization's goals. When the goals are compatible, conflict generally is reduced and the employees are allowed to pursue what they consider most important while pursuing the organization's most desirable objectives.

Leader Behaviors

The path-goal theory recognizes four distinctive types of leader behavior. In **directive leadership,** the leader provides specific guidance, standards, schedules of work, and rules and regulations. The leader lets subordinates know exactly what is expected of them. When the leader shows concern for the status, well-being, and personal needs of subordinates, he or she is showing **supportive leadership.** This behavior style focuses on developing satisfactory interpersonal relationships between group members. In **achievement-oriented leadership,** the leader sets challenging goals, emphasizes improvement in performance, and establishes high expectations for subordinates. **Participative leadership** is exhibited when the leader attempts to consult with subordinates and solicits their suggestions and advice before making decisions relevant to the job.

Feature 10.2
Management Style Affects Evaluations

Employees who want to rise in their organization should look for supervisors with a democratic leadership style who are valued by the corporation.

If such a supervisor sees that an employee is self-motivated and can do a good job, the employee's chances of succeeding in the organization are excellent.

Research done by David Kipnis, Stuart Schmidt, Karl Price, and Christopher Stitt of Temple University reaffirms earlier findings that leadership has an important, measurable impact on performance evaluations. Democratic-style leaders tend to rate their followers higher than autocratic leaders, even when production is the same.

The research was done with 113 work groups from an undergraduate behavioral science class. The groups, which were composed of a leader and five followers, were given the job of constructing as many model airplanes as possible. Half the leaders were told to act in a highly autocratic manner, the other half in a highly democratic manner.

Decisions involved how many airplanes of each design to construct and how to divide production.

Both types of groups produced approximately the same number of model airplanes, but autocratic leaders rated their followers more harshly than the democratic leaders did. They evaluated their group members as poorly motivated, whereas democratic leaders tended to evaluate their followers as

self-motivated. Group members who were rated as self-motivated tended to receive higher performance evaluations than those rated the opposite.

It is important to look beyond performance to understand why the workers with democratic leaders fared better. One explanation is that the democratic leaders' style forced these leaders to rely on their group members to accomplish the task. The group did so without direct help, so the leaders had to give them credit.

Autocratic leaders had to rely on themselves. Because the leaders made the decisions and supervised the workers, the leaders could not consider the workers self-motivated and gave them low performance evaluations.

The findings indicate that workers with democratic leaders may receive higher performance evaluations, whereas workers with autocratic leaders may be overlooked for promotions or other rewards simply because of the management style of their leaders.

Organizations should intensify efforts to improve the objectivity of their performance evaluations and collect data on the leadership style of their managers.

Source: Adapted with permission from "The Influence of Leadership Style," by Rodger D. Collons, *Best's Review,* February 1983, pp. 100–102. (Review of a study by David Kipnis, Stuart Schmidt, Karl Price, and Christopher Stitt of Temple University, published in *The Journal of Applied Psychology,* 1981, Vol. 66, No. 3, pp. 324–328.)

In contrast to Fiedler's model, the path-goal theory generally asserts that these four styles can be practiced by the same manager at varying times and in varying situations. Fiedler, it will be remembered, argues that managers have great difficulty changing styles.

Contingency Factors

Like Fiedler's formulation, House's path-goal theory is a contingency model. It holds that effective leadership is a function of the interaction between the behavior of a leader and variables keyed to the situation. Two basic contingency factors are identified: subordinate characteristics and environmental factors. House's theory is summarized in Figure 10.5.

Subordinate Characteristics. The characteristics of subordinates can influence how they will react to the leader's behavior. For example, several personality characteristics have been found to be related to the way subordinates respond to influence attempts. One of these is an individual's *authoritarianism*. Highly authoritarian subordinates tend to be less receptive to a participative style of leadership and more responsive to a directive leadership style.

It also has been shown that an individual's *locus of control* can affect responses. Individuals who have an internal locus of control, who believe rewards are contingent upon their own efforts, are generally more satisfied with a participative leadership style. Individuals who have an external locus of control, who believe rewards are beyond their own control, generally are more satisfied with a directive style of leadership.

Environmental Factors. The path-goal model also suggests that at least three environmental factors moderate the impact of leader style on outcomes. These factors are (1) the nature of the task performed by subordinates, (2) the formal authority system of the organization, and (3) the primary work group, and they can have several effects. They may motivate individuals, as when a person performs an intrinsically satisfying job. They may constrain variability on the job, as on an assembly line, where behavior is prescribed by technology. Or they may clarify and provide rewards for satisfactory performance; for instance, group members may praise the individuals who most helped the group achieve its performance objectives.

Figure 10.5
Path-Goal Relationships

LEADER BEHAVIOR and CONTINGENCY FACTORS		CAUSE	SUBORDINATE ATTITUDES AND BEHAVIOR
Directive	Subordinate characteristics:		Job satisfaction:
	Authoritarianism	Personal	Job→Rewards
Supportive	Locus of control	perceptions	Acceptance of leader:
	Ability		Leader→Rewards
Achievement-oriented			
	Environmental factors:	Motivational	Motivational behavior:
	The task	stimuli	Effort→Performance
Participative	Formal authority system	Constraints	Performance→Rewards
	Primary work group	Rewards	

Source: House and Mitchell, 1974, p. 87. Reprinted by permission.

Such factors can influence an individual's response to a leader's behavior in a variety of ways. As House and Dressler (1974, p. 40) point out, "when goals, and paths to desired goals, are apparent because of the routine nature of the task, clear group norms, or objective controls of the formal authority system, attempts by the leader to clarify paths and goals would be redundant and would be seen by subordinates as an imposition of unnecessarily close control."

Subordinate Attitudes and Behavior

The last part of the model asks what the outcome is of this interaction between leader behavior and contingency factors. According to House, three possible outcomes exist. First, individual perceptions, which are influenced by subordinate characteristics, can lead an employee to determine that the job can result in rewards, increasing job satisfaction. Personal perceptions also can lead employees to conclude that the leader does, in fact, control many of the desired rewards, increasing leader acceptance. Finally, the motivational stimuli, constraints, and potential rewards can heighten motivational behavior. They can increase an employee's expectations that effort will lead to rewards. As such, the model points to several specific outcomes that are helpful in the pursuit of productivity and a high quality of work.

The Normative Theory of Leadership

It is debatable whether the model we will next discuss is a model of leadership or a model of decision making. In essence the model focuses on the extent to which subordinates should be allowed to participate in decisions affecting their jobs. In addition, the model examines how managers should behave in decision-making situations. The Vroom and Yetton model (1973) is a theory of how leaders should approach group-related decisions to facilitate performance.

In contrast to Fiedler and House, Vroom and Yetton present a **normative theory** of leadership. It attempts to prescribe correct leader behavior according to level of participation. The model rests on several assumptions. It assumes, as does Fiedler's theory, that there is no single leadership style that is appropriate for all situations. Rather, leaders must develop a repertoire of responses ranging from autocratic to consultative and employ the style that is most appropriate to the decision situation. Unlike Fiedler's, however, this model assumes that leaders must adapt their style to the situation. Fiedler argues that situations should be altered to match what he considers a relatively stable leader style (Fiedler's LPC).

Criteria for Leader Effectiveness

Whereas Fiedler uses group performance as the evaluation criterion to determine whether a leader is effective and House uses satisfaction and motivation, Vroom and Yetton use *decision effectiveness,* which is characterized by three factors:

Decision quality. This factor involves the extent to which decisions under consideration are important for facilitating group performance. For instance, a decision on where to place a water cooler in a plant requires low decision quality because it has little impact on group performance, whereas a decision on performance goals or on work assignments requires high decision quality.

Decision acceptance. This factor refers to the extent to which group members must accept decisions in order for them to be successfully implemented. Some decisions, such as what color to paint the walls in an office, do not require group acceptance to be executed successfully. Others, such as setting sales performance objectives, must be accepted by group members to be successful.

Time required to reach a decision. Decisions must be made in a timely fashion. Some decisions, such as the office-color choice, can be made slowly, whereas others, such as whether to invest in a particular stock, may require immediate action.

The model proposed by Vroom and Yetton suggests that a decision is effective to the extent that it satisfactorily accommodates these three factors. These criteria stand in stark contrast to Fiedler's, so much so that it has been suggested that the two models actually examine different areas of leader behavior. Whereas Vroom and Yetton consider how leaders make decisions, Fiedler examines how they achieve a satisfactory performance level in light of power considerations, co-worker relations, and task structure.

Leader Style in Decision Making

Based on the definition of what constitutes an effective decision, the normative model turns to how leaders may behave toward group members to arrive at these decisions. The model suggests that leaders have five decision-making styles available and that these five styles are arranged in a continuum from highly autocratic to highly participative. These five styles are summarized in Figure 10.6. As can be seen, the *A* style represents the more autocratic style of leadership. The *C* style is more consultative. The *G* represents a more consultative, group decision style. Hence we move from *A I,* in which the manager makes the decision alone, through the various styles to the most participative, *G II,* in which the manager and subordinates meet as a group to discuss the problem and the group makes the decision. Remember that Vroom and Yetton argue that each manager should be able to exhibit all five of these leader behaviors, depending on the particular situation.

Strategies for Decision Making.   To help select the appropriate decision strategy, the normative model suggests seven decision rules aimed at simplifying the process. By following these rules, managers can fairly easily discover the quickest and most acceptable way to arrive at a quality decision. The first three

Figure 10.6
Five Decision Styles of the
Vroom and Yetton Model

DECISION STYLE	DEFINITION
A I	Manager makes the decision alone.
A II	Manager asks for information from subordinates but makes the decision alone. Subordinates may or may not be informed about what the problem is.
C I	Manager shares the problems with subordinates and asks for information and evaluations. Meetings take place as dyads, not as a group, and the manager then goes off alone and makes the decision.
C II	Manager and subordinates meet as a group to discuss the problem, but the manager makes the decision.
G II	Manager and subordinates meet as a group to discuss the problem, and the group makes the decision.

A = autocratic; *C* = consultation; *G* = group.

Source: Adapted from *Leadership and Decision Making* by Victor H. Vroom and Phillip W. Yetton by permission of the University of Pittsburgh Press. © 1973 by University of Pittsburgh Press.

rules focus on assuring decision quality; the remaining four deal with the acceptance of the decision.

The leader information rule. If the quality of the decision is important and if the leader does not have sufficient information or expertise to solve the problem alone, the *A I* style is eliminated from consideration, because using it involves the risk of a low-quality decision.

The goal congruence rule. If the quality of the decision is important but the leader is not sure that subordinates share the goals of the organization — that is, they cannot be trusted to base their problem-solving efforts on these goals — the *G II* style is considered not feasible. In this case the leader cannot afford to allow the group to make the decision alone.

The unstructured problem rule. If the quality of the decision is important but the leader lacks sufficient information and expertise *and* the problem is unstructured — that is, it is not clear exactly what information is needed or where it is located — the *A I*, *A II*, and *C I* styles are eliminated. In such cases the ambiguity of the problem requires interaction between the leader and subordinates to clarify the problem and a possible solution.

The acceptance rule. If acceptance of the decision by subordinates is crucial to effective implementation, and if it is not certain that an autocratic decision made by the leader would receive acceptance, styles *A I* and *A II* are eliminated.

The conflict rule. If acceptance of the decision is crucial, an autocratic decision is not certain to be accepted, and subordinates are likely to be in conflict or disagreement over the appropriate solution, styles *A I*, *A II*, and *C I* are considered not feasible. Conflict is probably best resolved in this situation by allowing greater participation and interchange among group members.

The fairness rule. If the quality of the decision is unimportant but acceptance is critical and not certain to result from an autocratic decision, styles *A I*, *A II*, *C I*, and *C II* are eliminated. Because group acceptance is the only relevant consideration, a *G II* style is likely to generate acceptance more effectively than are less participative styles.

The acceptance priority rule. If acceptance is critical and not certain·to result from an autocratic decision, and if subordinates are motivated to pursue organizational goals, then methods that provide equal partnership in the decision-making process will lead to greater acceptance without risking decision quality. Because of this, *A I*, *A II*, *C I*, and *C II* are eliminated.

Although some of these rules may seem imposing, potentially they are of considerable value to managers as guidelines to action. The rules narrow the options open to managers and point to the most appropriate strategy.

Using the Model. Now that we are familiar with the five basic leader decision styles, we can consider how this model is put into practice. Vroom and Yetton (1973) suggest the use of a **decision tree** that aids in the selection of the appropriate decision strategy when one answers a series of questions. The decision tree and the related questions ae shown in Figure 10.7. An example should help explain how this decision tree can be put to use.

Consider that you are the supervisor of a group of twelve engineers. The formal training and work experience of these engineers are quite similar, and they can be used almost interchangeably in various projects. You have been informed by your superior that an overseas affiliate has requested that four of these engineers be sent abroad for six to eight months to help on a project. Your superior agreed to this request even though such overseas assignments generally are regarded as undesirable by engineers in your company. Your job assignment is to select the four persons who will go. All of your employees are capable of handling the assignment, and there is no reason why any particular engineer should be retained over the others.

How do you make this decision? Would you make it yourself, consult with the group, or let the group itself make the decision? Following the decision tree shown in Figure 10.7, the manager would ask himself or herself the following questions, starting from the left side of the figure ("State the Problem").

Figure 10.7
Decision Tree for Determining Appropriate Decision Strategy

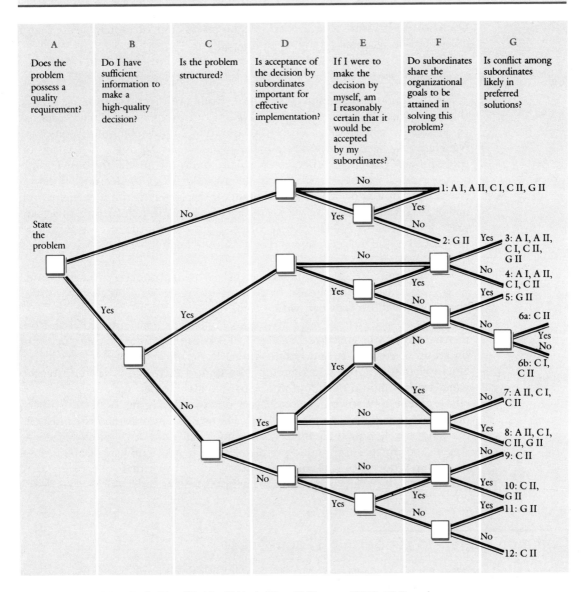

A	B	C	D	E	F	G
Does the problem possess a quality requirement?	Do I have sufficient information to make a high-quality decision?	Is the problem structured?	Is acceptance of the decision by subordinates important for effective implementation?	If I were to make the decision by myself, am I reasonably certain that it would be accepted by my subordinates?	Do subordinates share the organizational goals to be attained in solving this problem?	Is conflict among subordinates likely in preferred solutions?

1: A I, A II, C I, C II, G II

2: G II

3: A I, A II, C I, C II, G II

4: A I, A II, C I, C II

5: G II

6a: C II

6b: C I, C II

7: A II, C I, C II

8: A II, C I, C II, G II

9: C II

10: C II, G II

11: G II

12: C II

Source: Reprinted from *Leadership and Decision Making* by Victor H. Vroom and Phillip W. Yetton by permission of the University of Pittsburgh Press. © 1973 by University of Pittsburgh Press.

Question A: Does the problem possess a quality requirement?
Answer: No. The expected performance would be identical regardless of who goes on the assignment.

Question D: Is the acceptance of the decision by subordinates important for effective implementation?

Answer: Yes. It can be expected that the engineers will want to know that whoever was selected was chosen by open and equitable means.

Question E: If I were to make the decision myself, am I reasonably sure that it would be accepted by my subordinates?

Answer: No. Again, the absence of a group discussion could lead many engineers to assume that the manager's selection was capricious.

Following the answers in this example from Vroom and Yetton, we can see that we move from question *A* on the *No* line over to question *D*. Our response to question *D* is *Yes,* which takes us to question *E,* to which our response was *No.* Hence we have arrived at response *2,* which allows us as a feasible decision procedure only *G II.* In other words, according to this model the only feasible answer would be a highly participative or consultative group decision. If the answer to question *E,* dealing with acceptance by the group without participation, had been *Yes* instead of *No,* we would have had a wide set of feasible decision procedures, styles *A I* through *G II.* Because this was not the case on this particular decision, the model suggests that we should be highly consultative in making this decision.

Perhaps the best way to understand this particular model is to work through several cases using the decision tree shown in Figure 10.7. At the end of this chapter you will be provided with several case examples for this purpose.

It can be seen that the normative model of leadership is quite different from the two models discussed earlier. Fiedler looks at the effects of leader behavior on group performance, and House considers the effects of leader behavior on employee motivation and satisfaction. Vroom and Yetton consider the extent to which leaders should or should not be participative to be a function of the specific problem to be solved. No one theory of leadership is superior to the others, because each raises a separate question. The student of management must understand as well as possible the processes involved in any attempt by a leader to solicit subordinate support and performance. When we know more about these leadership processes, we are in a better position as future managers to achieve a desired level of performance and satisfaction.

Common Barriers to Leadership Effectiveness

Now that we have reviewed the nature of leadership, it is important to recognize certain constraints in the work environment that often hinder the effectiveness of leadership models. In this section we shall examine six common barriers to leadership effectiveness. Recognizing these constraints often can help managers overcome many of them. When constraints cannot be overcome, sometimes it is possible to apply alternate means to the end. The six common barriers to leadership effectiveness (Steers, 1977) are as follows:

1. In many cases management decisions or behaviors are preprogrammed because of precedent, structure, technological specificity, or the absence of familiarity with available alternatives. In such cases leaders and managers have little room to exercise what we normally consider leadership.

2. The skills and traits of the manager may represent a barrier to leader effectiveness. For example, research on leadership has indicated that effective leaders exhibit certain personal attributes, as discussed earlier in this chapter. A lack of these skills may preclude effective leader behavior in some instances.

3. The inability of managers to vary their leadership styles to suit the particular situation also may represent a constraint on leader effectiveness. For instance, rigid behavior patterns may be inappropriate in some situations and may trigger negative responses from subordinates.

4. The extent to which the manager has control over the reward system, such as pay raises or promotions, is another possible constraint. When such controls over rewards are absent, for example, much of the benefit of House's path-goal theory is diluted.

5. The characteristics of the work situation also can hinder the effectiveness of a leader. How much power does the leader really have? How important is a given decision or action? What is the quality of interpersonal relations between the manager and employees? These characteristics lie at the root of Fiedler's theory of leadership. Where these conditions are specified and are not subject to change, the ability to find a suitable leader is reduced considerably.

6. How open an organization is to variations in leader behavior also can influence the behavior's effectiveness. For example, in a military organization a highly participative leadership style may be discouraged or even prohibited. In such circumstances the freedom exercised by the manager is severely constrained.

We can see that managers do not attempt to exercise influence in a vacuum. There are several constraints that limit the success of influence attempts in organizations.

Overcoming Barriers to Effective Leadership

In view of the constraints just mentioned, what is the beleaguered manager supposed to do? There are several possible answers.

Substitutes for Leadership

Kerr and Jermier (1968) suggest that many constraints can be reduced by substitutes for leadership. They posit that many of the current theories or models of leadership implicitly assume that although leadership effectiveness may vary with the situation, at least one leadership style will be effective regardless of the situation. On the contrary, Kerr and Jermier argue, characteristics of the individual, task, and organization are often substitutes for leadership, negating the manager's formal authority to exert positive or negative influence over subordinates. In other words, they argue that many of these factors often act as a support structure for subordinates, thus making leader behavior at times irrelevant to subordinates' satisfaction. Several possible substitutes for leadership are suggested in Figure 10.8.

The conclusion to be drawn from this table is not that leadership efforts are in vain but, rather, that leadership is only one way to get things done through people. Other mechanisms for accomplishing tasks include structuring tasks with the characteristics of the individual's ability or experience in mind, and relying on the structure of the organization itself. Through a combination of leadership and its substitutes, it is thought that significant progress can be made toward task accomplishment and work-group cooperation.

Managerial Selection and Placement

A second approach to improving leader effectiveness focuses on the methods organizations use to select and place managers. Fiedler's model shows that an organization may wish to select a task-oriented, or low-LPC, manager to oversee a work group characterized by high task structure, centralized power, and distant or poor leader–member relations. A more relationship-oriented, or high-LPC, leader may be more appropriate for a group characterized by less task structuring, diffused power, and cordial leader–member relations. In other words, to some extent the problem of leadership effectiveness is one of matching people to leadership roles to make their own skills and abilities consistent with the characteristics and goals of the work group. This notion stands in stark contrast to the popular practice in many organizations of promoting employees to supervisory positions based on seniority or on good job performance. Although superior job performance may be a desirable trait for managers, it clearly does not by itself ensure good supervisory skills.

Leadership Training

Much has been written over the past several years on how organizations attempt to train and develop their people. With respect to leadership positions, one popular method is the extensive use of executive development or management development workshops and training programs to provide general management skills, human relations training, and problem-solving and decision-making skills for employees (Bass and Vaughn, 1966; Goldstein, 1975, 1980).

Figure 10.8
Substitutes for Leadership

CHARACTERISTIC	WILL TEND TO NEUTRALIZE	
	Relationship-oriented, Supportive, People-centered Leadership: Consideration, Support, and Interaction Facilitation	*Task-oriented, Instrumental, Job-centered Leadership: Initiating Structure, Goal Emphasis, and Work Facilitation*
Of the subordinate		
1. Ability, experience, training, knowledge		X
2. Need for independence	X	X
3. "Professional" orientation	X	X
4. Indifference toward organizational rewards	X	X
Of the task		
5. Unambiguous and routine		X
6. Methodologically invariant		X
7. Provides its own feedback concerning accomplishment		X
8. Intrinsically satisfying	X	
Of the organization		
9. Formatization (explicit plans, goals, and areas of responsibility)		X
10. Inflexibility (rigid, unbending rules and procedires)		X
11. Highly specified and active advisory and staff functions		X
12. Closely knit, cohesive work groups	X	X
13. Organizational rewards not within the leader's control	X	X
14. Spatial distance between superior and subordinates	X	X

Source: S. Kerr and J. Jermier, "Substitutes for Leadership: Their Meaning and Measurement," *Organizational Behavior and Human Performance,* Vol. 22 (1978), pp. 375–403. Reprinted by permission.

Rewarding Leader Behavior

Another technique for improving leadership effectiveness involves systems that amply reward leader behavior when it is effective for the organization. If pay and promotions are based on a manager's ability to get subordinates to perform well, managers may see it as in their best interests to draw out such

Feature 10.3.
Look for Napoleon, Not Hamlet

Hamlet, says consultant James B. Weitzul, wouldn't have made a very good executive.

"Very few, if any, top line executives are passive, contemplative, or 'sicklied o'er with the pale cast of thought,'" he adds. "There may be some contemporary Hamlets around, they may have key advisory or staff positions, they may possess significant authority, but they aren't holding the 'top job.'"

Weitzul, who is with Johnson and Higgins in New York, believes that the potential presidents are distinguished from the also-rans on the staff by several key characteristics. The best corporate officers have a great deal of drive and high energy expenditure and can do many things well simultaneously.

He said that Napoleon and Florence Nightingale could do seven things at once, and that one should look for such traits when hiring top executives.

He also believes that successful managers share the following subtle traits:

- *Discipline.* Weitzul calls this "just plain, sheer dedication and devotion."
- *Competitiveness.* Good executives, he adds, can't stand to lose. But they play by the rules, too. They don't waste their time with back stabbing and social maneuvering.
- *Honesty.* The best people are not likely to tell stories repeatedly about "the one that got away," he believes. They admit their shortcomings and move on to the next problem.
- *Realism.* Good executives look at how they're going to get where they want to be, Weitzul ways.
- *Maturity.* Good executives don't manipulate people, meddle in office politics, or accept the first solution that is offered. They are patient, and they bounce back.
- *Ability to handle pressure.* A good manager, he believes, is able to handle multiple pressures. "Anyone can do a good job if you give them one problem at a time and all the time they need to solve it. But when I see a person unwilling to pay attention to anything else until they get their one little problem solved, I worry," he said. "That kind of person will never know there's a fire next door until the whole company burns down."

Source: Adapted with permission from "Choosing and Keeping Potential Top Managers," by James B. Weitzul, *Best's Review,* November 1981, pp. 98–100.

performances in order to attain desired rewards. This performance–reward contingency should make managers more aware of the role of leadership in attaining organizational objectives and more likely to attempt to improve their capacity for effective leadership.

Rewarding Subordinate Behavior

It is possible to structure reward systems so that they stimulate rather than inhibit desired behavior of subordinates. When managers are given greater discretion in allocating rewards to subordinates, subordinates are more likely to follow managerial directives because doing so is important to attaining their personal goals. This basic argument is fundamental to House's path-goal theory.

Organizational Engineering

As Fiedler said, it sometimes is easier to make structural changes than behavioral changes to improve leadership effectiveness. Fiedler argues that rather than attempting to change people, organizations should attempt to "engineer the job to fit the manager." In other words, we should take people as they are, trying to restructure the work environment so managers can use their abilities to greatest advantage. For example, organizations that employ research scientists often discover that a scientist with managerial abilities is a rare commodity. Because they need the research scientist's intellectual skills, these organizations often attempt to redesign the work environment to capitalize on the scientist's skill and still get the necessary managerial work completed, perhaps through an administrative assistant.

Summary

The present chapter examines the issue of leadership and begins to explore the problems of managing effective work groups.

The nature of leadership is influenced by the level in the hierarchy at which leadership attempts are made. At each level leaders must introduce structural change or formulate policy, make existing formal structure more complete, and keep the organization in motion and running smoothly. The abilities and skills required at each level are different.

Research on leader behavior has suggested that showing consideration for subordinates and ensuring that they follow rules, as well as maintaining high performance standards and clarifying roles, is important for group effectiveness. If a manager is not successful in these areas, a group often will find a substitute leader from its own ranks.

Fiedler's contingency theory of leadership defines leader effectiveness in terms of group performance. He argues that the two basic ingredients in a successful model of leadership are an understanding of the situation and an awareness of the leader's style. Effective work-group environments are produced by matching the manager to the situation.

House's path-goal theory of leadership emphasizes that leaders can facilitate performance by showing subordinates that performance can result in desirable rewards. There are four types of leader behavior in this model: directive, achievement oriented, participative, and supportive.

The normative theory of leadership focuses on the extent to which subordinates should be allowed to participate in decisions affecting their jobs and the ways in which managers should behave in decision-making situations.

There are a number of constraints in the work environment that hinder effectiveness: preprogrammed behavior that restricts the manager, the skills and traits of the manager, the manager's inability to vary leadership style to suit the situation, the extent of the manager's control over the reward system, the characteristics of the work situation, and the organization's openness to variations.

The characteristics of the individual, task, and organization are often substitutes for leadership, providing a support structure for subordinates that at times makes the leader's behavior irrelevant to subordinates' satisfaction.

Leadership is only one way to get things done through people. Other mechanisms include structuring tasks with the personal characteristics of the individual in mind and relying on the structure of the organization itself. Matching the leader to the characteristics and goals of the work group also is important.

Techniques for improving the effectiveness of leaders include training, rewarding the behavior of leaders and subordinates, and engineering the job to fit the manager.

Questions for Discussion

1. Examine the nature and role of leadership at different levels in the management hierarchy.
2. Describe and evaluate the great man theory of leadership.
3. What was the major finding of the Ohio State/Michigan leadership studies?
4. What are the basic tenets of the contingency theory of leadership? What is its greatest contribution to the field of leadership?
5. Define LPC.
6. Contrast Fiedler's theory with the path-goal theory of leadership.
7. What is the normative theory of leadership? How does it differ from other theories?
8. Which of the three primary models of leadership discussed in this chapter do you prefer? Why?
9. Describe several common barriers to leader effectiveness. How can managers overcome these barriers?
10. What is meant by the term *substitutes for leadership*?

Exercise 10.1
Leadership and Decision Making

Review the decision tree in Figure 10.7. Your instructor will then form groups of four to five people to analyze each of the following three cases. Try to reach a group concensus on which decision style is best for the particular case. You are to select the best style based on use of the Vroom and Yetton model, available styles, and decision rules. Each case should take between 30 and 45 minutes to analyze as a group.

Case I

Setting: Corporate Headquarters
Your Position: Vice-President

As marketing vice-president, you frequently receive nonroutine requests from customers. One such request, from a relatively new customer, was for extended terms on a large purchase ($2,500,000) involving several of your product lines. The request is for extremely favorable terms that you would not normally consider except for the high inventory level of most product lines at the present time caused by the unanticipated slack period that the company has experienced over the last six months.

You realize that the request is probably a starting point for negotiations, and you have proven your abilities to negotiate the most favorable arrangements in the past. As preparation for this negotiation, you have familiarized yourself with the financial situation of the customer using various investment reports you regularly receive.

Reporting to you are four sales managers, each of whom has responsibility for a single product line. They know of the order and, like you, believe that it is important to negotiate terms with minimum risks and maximum return to the company. They are likely to differ on what constitutes an acceptable level of risk. The two younger managers have developed a reputation of being "risk takers," whereas the two more senior managers are substantially more conservative.

Case II

Setting: Toy Manufacturer
Your Position: Vice-President, Engineering and Design

You are a vice-president in a large toy manufacturing company with responsibilities that include the design of new products that will meet the changing demand in this uncertain and very competitive industry. Your design teams, each under the supervision of a department head, are therefore under constant pressure to produce novel, marketable ideas.

At the opposite end of the manufacturing process is the Quality Control Department, which is under the authority of the vice-president, Production. When Quality Control has encountered a serious problem that may be due to design features, their staff has consulted with one or more of your department heads to obtain their recommendations for any changes in the production process. In the wake of consumer concern over the safety of children's toys, however, Quality Control responsibilities have recently been expanded to insure not only the quality but the safety of your products. The first major problem in this area has arisen. A preliminary consumer report has "black listed" one of your new products without giving any specific reason or justification. This has upset you and others in the organization, since it was believed that this product would be one of the most profitable items in the coming Christmas season.

The consumer group has provided your company the opportunity to respond to the report before it is made public. The head of Quality Control has therefore consulted with your design people, but you are told that they became somewhat defensive and dismissed the report as "overreactive fanatic nonsense." Your people told Quality Control that, while freak accidents are always possible, the product is certainly safe as designed. They argued that the report should simply be ignored.

Since the issue is far from routine, you have decided to give it your personal attention. Because your design teams have been intimately involved in all aspects of the development of the item, you suspect that their response is itself extreme and perhaps governed more by their emotional reaction to the report than by the facts. You are not convinced that the consumer group is totally irresponsible, and you are anxious to explore the problem in detail and recommend to Quality Control any changes that may be required from a design standpoint. The firm's image as a producer of high-quality toys could suffer a serious blow if the report is made public and public confidence is lost as a result.

You will have to depend heavily on the background and experience of your design departments to help you in analyzing the problem. Even though Quality Control will be responsible for the decision to implement any changes you may ultimately recommend, your own subordinates have the background of design experience that could help set standards for what is "safe" and to suggest any design modifications that would meet these criteria.

Case III

Setting: Corporate Headquarters
Your Position: Vice-President

The sales executives in your home office spend a great deal of time visiting regional sales offices. As marketing vice-president, you are concerned that the expenses incurred on these trips are excessive — especially now when the economic outlook seems bleak and general belt-tightening measures are being carried out in every department.

Having recently been promoted from the ranks of your subordinates, you are keenly aware of some cost-saving measures that could be introduced. You have, in fact, asked the accounting department to review a sample of past expense reports, and they have agreed with your conclusion that several highly favored travel "luxuries" could be curtailed. Your executives, for example, could restrict first-class air travel to only those occasions when economy class is unavailable, airport limousine service to hotels could be used instead of taxis where possible, etc. Even more savings could be made if your personnel carefully planned trips so that multiple purposes could be achieved when possible.

The success of any cost-saving measures, however, depends on the commitment of your subordinates. You do not have the time (or the desire) to review closely the expense reports of these executives. You suspect, though, that they do not share your concerns over the matter. Having once been in their position, you know they feel themselves deserving of travel amenities.

The problem is to determine which changes, if any, are to be made in current travel and expense account practices in the light of the new economic conditions.

Exercise Procedures

Phase I: 10 to 15 minutes
 Individually read the case and select the proper decision style using the Vroom and Yetton model.

Phase II: 30 to 45 minutes
 Join the group indicated by the instructor and reach a group concensus.

Phase III: 20 minutes
 Each group spokesperson presents the group's response and rationale to other groups.

These phases should be used for each of the cases.

Questions

1. Discuss the applicability of this model/process to day-to-day decisions by a manager. How does this model help? Where does it fail?
2. Identify crucial and/or difficult decision points in the decision tree. What role does managerial judgment play in this process/model?
3. Describe a recent decision that you faced in terms of the decision tree model.

Source: Adapted from James Gibson, John Ivancevich, and James Donnelly, Jr., *Organizations: Behavior, Structure, Processes*, pp. 232–235. Copyright © 1979 by Business Publications, Plano, Texas. All rights reserved.

Exercise 10.2
Least-Preferred Co-worker (LPC) Scale

Purpose

This instrument was designed by Fred Fiedler to measure your LPC score, as described in our discussion of the contingency theory of leadership earlier in this chapter.

Instructions

Think of the person with whom you work *least well.* He or she may be someone you work with now, or may be someone you knew in the past. He or she does not have to be the person you like least well, but should be the person with whom you *have* or *have had* the *most difficulty* in *getting a job done.* Describe this person as he or she appears to you by circling the number between each pair of adjectives that you believe best describes that person. Do this for each pair of adjectives that you believe best describes that person. Do this for each pair of adjectives. Then transfer the numbers to the spaces provided at the right. Add up the numbers in this column and write the value in the box marked ''LPC Score.'' Your instructor will then explain the meaning of your score.

	LPC Scale (Circle one number for each line)	Transfer the numbers to these spaces	
Pleasant	: 8 : 7 : 6 : 5 : 4 : 3 : 2 : 1 :	Unpleasant	_____
Friendly	: 8 : 7 : 6 : 5 : 4 : 3 : 2 : 1 :	Unfriendly	_____
Rejecting	: 1 : 2 : 3 : 4 : 5 : 6 : 7 : 8 :	Accepting	_____
Helpful	: 8 : 7 : 6 : 5 : 4 : 3 : 2 : 1 :	Frustrating	_____
Unenthusiastic	: 1 : 2 : 3 : 4 : 5 : 6 : 7 : 8 :	Enthusiastic	_____
Tense	: 1 : 2 : 3 : 4 : 5 : 6 : 7 : 8 :	Relaxed	_____
Distant	: 1 : 2 : 3 : 4 : 5 : 6 : 7 : 8 :	Close	_____
Cold	: 1 : 2 : 3 : 4 : 5 : 6 : 7 : 8 :	Warm	_____
Cooperative	: 8 : 7 : 6 : 5 : 4 : 3 : 2 : 1 :	Uncooperative	_____
Supportive	: 8 : 7 : 6 : 5 : 4 : 3 : 2 : 1 :	Hostile	_____
Boring	: 1 : 2 : 3 : 4 : 5 : 6 : 7 : 8 :	Interesting	_____
Quarrelsome	: 1 : 2 : 3 : 4 : 5 : 6 : 7 : 8 :	Harmonious	_____
Self-assured	: 8 : 7 : 6 : 5 : 4 : 3 : 2 : 1 :	Hesitant	_____
Efficient	: 8 : 7 : 6 : 5 : 4 : 3 : 2 : 1 :	Inefficient	_____
Gloomy	: 1 : 2 : 3 : 4 : 5 : 6 : 7 : 8 :	Cheerful	_____
Open	: 8 : 7 : 6 : 5 : 4 : 3 : 2 : 1 :	Guarded	_____
		LPC Score =	_____

Source: F. Fiedler, *A Theory of Leadership Effectiveness*, p. 41. Copyright © 1967 by McGraw-Hill, Inc.

Case Study
The Brewster-Seaview Landscaping Company

NOTE: Do not read this case until directed to do so by your instructor. It has been set up as a Prediction Case so that you can test your analysis by answering questions before reading the entire case.

Part I

During the summer of my freshman year in college, I worked for a small private landscaping company planting shrubs, seeding new lawns, cutting grass, and tending flower gardens. The company was located in my home town of Seaview, N.J., which is a rural community on the coast about 80 miles from Philadelphia. The company was owned and run by Joe Brewster, a 45-year-old man who had lived in Seaview all his life. He had started the company some years ago and not only handled the paperwork (payroll, bills, estimates, and so on), but also worked along with the crew six days a week.

The crew consisted of five guys ranging in age from 17 to 20 years. We all lived in towns around Seaview and had gone to the regional high school, which was physically located in Seaview. Only two of us were attending college, but all had been hired personally by Joe following a short, informal interview. I can't be completely certain about the others, but I think all of us and several others sought the job because we needed work, enjoyed the outdoors, and had heard that Joe paid well and was an OK guy to work for. Working hours were from 8 A.M. to 4:30 P.M. with an hour off for lunch, Monday through Saturday. Once in a while we'd work overtime to help out some customer who had an urgent need. Each worker began at the same wage with the understanding that hard workers would be rehired the next summer at a higher wage. Several of the crew I was part of had been rehired under this policy.

Most of the customers we serviced lived in Seaview, knew Joe personally, and seemed to respect him.

Joe owned one truck which he used to transport all of us and necessary supplies and equipment from job to job. Each morning he would read off a list of houses that had to be completed that day. He would then leave it up to us to decide among ourselves who would do what task while at a particular house. We also were the ones who determined by our work pace how long we would spend at each house.

In doing the work itself, we were able to use our own ideas and methods. If we did a good job, Joe would always compliment us. If we lacked the necessary know-how or did a poor job, Joe was right there willing to help us.

At each house, Joe worked along with us doing basically the same work we did. He dressed the same as we did and was always very open and friendly towards us. He seldom "showed his authority," and treated us as equals. Although our workday was scheduled to begin at 8, Joe never became upset nor penalized us if we were 10 or 15 minutes late. Our lunch hour was usually an hour long starting anytime betwen 11:30 and 12:30 depending on what time we, the crew, felt like eating. Each member brought his own lunch to work and anytime during the day could take time off to go to the truck for a snack.

The crew itself became very well acquainted, and we were always free to talk and joke with each other at any time and did so. We enjoyed each other's company, although we did not socialize after hours.

We also became very friendly with the customers. They were always eager to talk to us as we worked, and Joe never objected. All in all, the job had a very relaxed, easygoing atmosphere. I for one felt little pressure to hurry and, like the others, respected and liked Joe very much.

Prediction Question

1. What will be the productivity in terms of quantity and quality of the work crew? Why?

Part II

The attitude we had toward the job was very high. We sometimes talked among ourselves about how we felt a sense of responsibility toward the job.

While we talked and joked a lot while working, little horseplay occurred; and the talking and joking did not interfere with the work. We were always working steadily and efficiently, seeking to keep ahead of schedule. The days seemed to go fairly quickly and a lot seemed to get done. I know Joe said that our output was 15 percent above that which other landscaping companies experienced with summer crews.

We also took a lot of pride in our work. Feeling responsible for the job we did, we were constantly checking and rechecking every job to be sure it was perfect. We were always willing to work overtime for Joe when he needed us to do so.

Case Question

1. What elements in the situation contributed to these positive results? Can you think of things which, if present, might have led to very different results? Explain how.

Part III

I returned the following summer to work for Joe because of the strong satisfaction I had with the job the summer before. So did the others. However, we were in for a surprise. Many things had changed. Joe had increased the number of workers to ten, bought another truck, and hired two young college graduates from Philadelphia as crew supervisors. His plan was to concentrate on the paperwork and on lining up new customers, leaving the direct guidance of the two work crews to the new supervisors.

Joe had hired the two supervisors during the early spring after interviewing a number of applicants. Both were young (23 and 24), from the city, and had degrees in agricultural management from Penn State, but had not known each other previously.

We "oldtimers" were assigned to one crew and five new workers were hired for the other crew. These new workers had little experience in landscaping. Except for the working hours, which were the same as during the previous summer, the two supervisors were told that they could run their crew in any manner they wished as long as they kept to the schedule prepared by Joe.

No one on the crew had known the supervisors before. Joe had found them through ads in the paper. The supervisors didn't dress quite as informally as Joe did, perhaps because they didn't do as much actual physical work, but they did dress casually in dungarees and shirts, the same as the crew. Though we called the supervisors by their first names, they did some nit-picky things. For example, Joe never cared who drove the truck or who did what job; sometimes a crew member would drive and Joe would talk with the rest of us. But the supervisors always drove the truck and decided when we would eat. Nor did the supervisors help us unload the tools as Joe had done. They stood around and watched us.

Both supervisors refused to tolerate tardiness in the morning and immediately set up a scheduled lunch hour which would remain the same throughout the summer. We were no longer allowed to go to the truck for a snack during the day and were constantly being watched over by our supervisor. The supervisors assigned us to specific tasks to be done at each job and told us how "they" wanted them to be completed. They also told us how much time we were to spend doing each job. They refused to let us talk to each other or to the customers (except about business) saying that it "only wasted time and interfered with our work." It was a more structured, more formal atmosphere than the summer before.

Prediction Questions

1. What kind of issues or problems are likely to develop during the second summer? Why?
2. How will productivity compare with that of the previous summer in terms of quantity and quality? Why?
3. What would have been your advice to the two supervisors about how they could best approach their new role?

Part IV

I was disappointed at the new setup and a little bit surprised that Joe hadn't hired one of the more experienced members of the old crew as supervisor. But I figured it was necessary because of the increased volume of business so I tried to make the best of it. However, very soon my attitude and that of the rest of the old crew fell significantly. We began to hate the new supervisors and soon developed a great disinterest in the work itself. While I'm a person who usually is very conscientious and responsible, I have to admit that before long I along with the others began to put little care or concern into my work. The supervisors soon found it very difficult to get anyone to work overtime.

The new employees didn't react as strongly as we did, but I could tell that they weren't working with much enthusiasm, either.

I thought about talking to the supervisors but didn't because I'd only worked there the one year and figured that it was not by place to. The others were older than I and had worked there longer so I figured that they should, but no one did. Instead, we talked among ourselves and individually griped to Joe.

Joe didn't seem to know how to deal with our complaints. He passed them off by saying "Oh . . . I'll talk to the supervisors and straighten it out with them." But nothing changed, and in fact they seemed to clamp down more and push even harder. This only made us madder. Our work rate continued to fall.

Incidentally, throughout this period we had little social interaction with the supervisors, but I noticed that they became more and more friendly with each other.

Meanwhile the new crew's difficulties increased. Being new and inexperienced, they couldn't do the work as easily as we could. Also the supervisors didn't, or couldn't, give them any adequate training. Their productivity went lower and lower. The supervisors were very upset and yelled at them, pushing them to get out their quota. We felt sorry for them and tried to help them; but we concentrated on reluctantly meeting our own quota.

I don't think Joe realized that the supervisors were not teaching the new crewmen. He was very busy and not around much, and I think he assumed that they were training the new men. I think he began to put pressure on the supervisors as the work rate fell, because things continued to get worse. We couldn't even accept drinks. Production lagged greatly as compared to the previous summer, and the two supervisors struggled to meet the schedule and deal with customer complaints about quality. By July 15th, the overall productivity of the company was 5 percent below "normal" and way below the previous summer.

As Joe became aware of this huge decrease in production, he became very concerned and wondered what to do about it.

Case Questions

1. What caused the poor production condition during the second summer?
2. How might this situation have been avoided from the beginning?
3. What should Joe do now?
4. Do you think the supervisors could have effectively adopted Joe's style of leadership? What kind of problems might they have had if they did? How should they have conducted themselves?

Source: Case from A. R. Cohen, S. L. Fink, H. Gadon, and R. D. Willits, *Effective Behavior in Organizations,* Third Edition, pp. 454–458. Copyright © 1984 by Richard D. Irwin, Inc. Reprinted by permission.

One morning during the Depression, a teenage freight handler in Roanoake, Virginia, watched some important-looking people boarding a private railroad car. He stared in awe as someone told him they were directors of the Norfolk and Western Railway headed for a business meeting.

"I didn't know what directors did," Carter Lane Burgess remembers today, "but it seemed like it had some importance to it. . . ."

Today Burgess knows what directors do. He is a former president of Trans World Airlines and a former president and chairman of AMF Inc.; he ran the National Corporation for Housing Partnerships and was head of the Foreign Policy Association. He now is retired and serves as a professional director on the boards of four companies: Ford Motor Company, J. P. Morgan and

Company, SmithKline Beckman Corporation, and Roanoake Electric Steel. The board of directors is probably the most important group in any organization.

His experience, humor, and diplomacy have served him well, according to managers of companies on whose boards he sits. Ford Chairman Philip Caldwell says Burgess brought common sense and good counsel to the difficult process of Henry Ford's slow, painful abdication. And he is grateful to Burgess for taking the long view in matters that came before the board in times of crisis.

Speaking of the political upheaval in Iran that touched off an energy crisis in 1979, Caldwell said, "We were modernizing our factories and changing our products, investing at twice the normal rate while the company was losing a

CHAPTER 11

Managing Effective Work Groups

great deal of money. Carter was right in the forefront, in the vanguard of those who continued to support us. If our board, and key members in particular, of which he is one, had insisted upon emphasizing the short run, it would have been difficult for us to resist."

Burgess recalls those days himself. "It's not the role of a director to panic just because business goes into a downslide," he said. "The bedrock of a company is that you don't let today's downswing kill tomorrow's upswing."

He does, however, speak up forcefully at meetings about mistakes he's seen before. "There are very few traps out there that he doesn't know about," said a fellow SmithKline Beckman director. "He has a real sensitivity about problems that arise in financing or personnel. He's wise about regulation and the rela-tionship of government to industry. And as one goes over the international business, he's been extremely helpful in pointing out situations that are developing in countries around the world."

Burgess has clashed with the management of other companies on whose boards he has sat. He left the board of Planning Research Corporation, an engineering and computer services company, at the request of the company's chief executive. Burgess believes he was considered "too insistent" in his proposals to management. He also became involved in a personnel matter with the following result: "I took the lead in this and discussed it like hell at the board meetings, but I didn't win."

Source: "How a Professional Director Earns his Keep," by Arthur M. Louis, *Fortune,* October 31, 1983, pp. 140–156.

Chapter Outline

- The Role of Groups
- A Model of Work Group Effectiveness
- Group Characteristics That Influence Effectiveness
- Making Work Groups More Effective

Key Terms

- group
- social loafing
- status differentiation
- internal status characteristics
- external status characteristics
- task specialization
- structural characteristics
- group norms
- return potential model

Chapter Objectives

After studying Chapter 11 you should be able to

1. Explain the value of groups in organizations.
2. Detect the major influences on a group's effectiveness.
3. Determine whether a group is effective.
4. See how the nature of the task determines what influences a group's effectiveness.
5. Understand the significance of group characteristics.
6. Relate group size and structure to effectiveness.
7. Describe how to make work groups more effective.

Introduction

Few people have neutral feelings about their experiences in groups; comments are either very positive or very negative, seldom moderate. In fact, there seems to be what Herold (1979) characterized as a "love–hate relationship" between individuals and groups.

Harlow ("Red") Curtis, former president and chief executive officer of General Motors, once observed that "the best committee is a committee of one" (Gray, 1980, p. 353). Many managers probably share Curtis's sentiments. Most of us know the standard jokes about decisions made by committees (What is a camel? A horse designed by a committee.), if not instances in which groups have made decisions with disastrous consequences. Moreover, the most frustrating organizational experiences often take place in group settings: the seemingly endless committee meetings that fail to make progress in solving problems. The reflections of one executive about the meetings he was required to attend as part of his job are presented in Feature 11.1. These meetings hardly seem to have been a positive feature of his career.

Many people find working alone on a project or decision vastly more enjoyable if not more effective than working in groups, where preferences and efforts must be coordinated with those of other people. Curtis didn't say so specifically, but we suspect that the "best" committee he had in mind was one in which *he* was the only member.

The Role of Groups

Despite the negative comments, it is increasingly common to read management articles suggesting that the use of groups is one way to improve both the quality of working life for employees and the overall effectiveness of organizations. Literature about Japanese management techniques, which stress group cohesiveness and consensus decision making, no doubt has contributed to the changing views about the role of groups in organizations (Hatvany and Pucik, 1981; Ouchi, 1981). Many corporations in the United States apparently are beginning to view the role of groups more favorably. A new teamwork approach to management at the J. C. Penney Company is described in Feature 11.2. Managers believe that group decision making and consensus management are partly responsible for Penney's success. The increasingly important role being given groups in organizations ranges from control over executive selection at Graphic Controls (Miller, 1980) to greater involvement of rank-and-file employees in solving production problems at Westinghouse (Main, 1981).

Managers' increased concern for the use of groups in organizations reflects more than just a passing interest in Japanese management; it indicates a growing recognition that groups can serve a more valuable role than they have in the past. In an article entitled "Suppose We Took Groups Seriously. . . . ," Harold Leavitt (1975) suggests several reasons why groups are valuable and should be more carefully considered by managers.

Feature 11.1
The Executive and the Group

Corporate managers and executives often spend more than 50 percent of their time in formally scheduled group meetings.

Calling together a group of high-priced executives for an hour-long meeting can be expensive for the organization, but these costs often are ignored. Instead, meetings are held to make decisions on unimportant or obvious questions, wasting valuable time and money.

One incident at General Motors illustrates this point. Top-level executives met on ten to twelve separate occasions for lengthy periods to resolve what might be considered a rather obvious problem. The problem was caused when a strike at one assembly plant left 400 cars on the line in various stages of completion between the 1971 and 1972 model years. Because the cars were technically 1971 models, they did not meet the more stringent pollution and safety standards that had gone into effect at the start of the 1972 model year. Without costly modification the 400 Chevrolet Camaros and Pontiac Firebirds in question could not be sold in 1972. In fact, there was even some question whether the cars could be made to conform to the new standards.

The options facing the company seemed obvious: The cars could be either scrapped for parts or donated to high school mechanics classes, with the corporation taking a tax deduction. Because the tax laws permitted the cars donated to be deducted at a price greater than actual production cost, the donation option appeared to have an economic advantage. In any event a $1 million problem was not exactly a "life-and-death" issue for a $35 billion corporation.

Even so, numerous meetings of top-level executives were called to deal with the problem. These meetings avoided the obvious and even managed to get the corporation into additional trouble. At one of the meetings, for example, someone suggested that the cars be sold in Canada, where pollution and safety requirements were less stringent. The question of whether Canadians would react favorably to receiving cars not considered safe or clean enough for the United States market was not considered. When word leaked out in Canada about the plan, the reaction was very negative. The image of General Motors in Canada was tarnished, and the plan had to be abandoned. In subsequent meetings opportunities to sell the cars overseas were explored, but these plans were abandoned when it was realized that 400 Camaros and Firebirds represented almost a lifetime supply of these models in most countries.

The company ultimately decided to donate the cars and take a $2 million tax write-off. Before this decision was reached, however, the problem had consumed many hours of executive time. The decision probably could have been made by a lower-level executive in consultation with his or her boss. Of course, there is no guarantee that a better decision would have been made further down in the corporate hierarchy. It is impossible to calculate the cost of the meetings held in terms of executive time, but it is likely that a decision made at a lower level would have been much less expensive to the corporation.

Source: On a Clear Day You Can See General Motors, by J. Patrick Wright, New York: Avon, 1979, pp. 28–31.

Groups appear good for people. Groups in organizations serve several valuable functions for their members, including the satisfaction of important social and affiliation needs. In addition, groups are often an important source of informa-

Feature 11.2
Consensus Management at J. C. Penney

When Donald V. Seibert retired as chairman and chief executive officer of the J. C. Penney Company in 1983, he left his successor a company run not by one all-powerful executive, but by consensus.

Modeled after a Japanese business concept, consensus management allows managers an equal voice in shaping policy and making major decisions. At J. C. Penney fourteen top executives comprise a management committee that discusses and makes major decisions ranging from strategy to personnel policies. In addition permanent subcommittees concentrate on specific, critical areas, and ad hoc committees often are established to address immediate issues, such as whether the company should divest its Treasury discount stores. All fourteen committee members are allowed to attend meetings of the board of directors.

Seibert also reorganized the office of the chairman into a four-person operation. One of the four, William R. Howell, became his successor as chairman and chief executive officer when Seibert retired. Howell, considered Seibert's right-hand man, was credited with implementing the company's plan to change its image by selling more expensive goods. When Seibert retired, the company also announced that the office of chairman was being expanded to five.

It was his own pending retirement and that of two other top executives that was partly responsible for Seibert's reorganization of the Penney management structure. He believed it is important to create developmental opportunities by helping people understand what is going on in different levels of the organization. "'If you have a conscience at all,' said Seibert, 'you have to involve the people who will have to live with the results.'" ("Teamwork Pays Off," 1982, p. 107).

Increasing the number of managers participating in important decisions helps expose them to all facets of the company's operations and prepares them for the day they will have to assume responsibility for the company. As a result, younger managers are able to take an active part in forming the policies that they will one day be implementing.

Whether or not you agree with the more philosophical reasoning underlying Seibert's decision, it's apparent that the move to create a strong management team is important at a time when the company faces increased uncertainty due to impending retirements. The question of whether this management stragegy persists and leads to continued organizational effectiveness in the future remains to be answered. Seibert appears convinced that it will.

Sources: "Teamwork Pays Off at Penney's," *Business Week,* April 12, 1982, pp. 107–108; "Penney Agrees to Buy a Bank in Delaware, Taps Howell to Succeed Seibert as Chief," *The Wall Street Journal,* April 28, 1983, p. 10; "J. C. Penney Appoints W. Howell and R. Gill to Vice Chairman Posts," *The Wall Street Journal,* April 29, 1982, p. 29.

tion for individual employees about appropriate behavior and effective ways to perform tasks. When people are confronted with new or ambiguous situations, they may turn to other group members for clues about appropriate reactions. Groups also can provide support for members in stressful situations, ranging from simple expressions of emptahy to assistance when work demands are excessive.

Groups are good problem-finding tools. In Japan, millions of employees formally participate in quality circles, voluntary groups that meet on company time to discuss production problems or ways to improve product quality. Quality circles reportedly have been quite effective in identifying problems and suggesting solutions, and often are credited with saving organizations thousands of dollars. The fact that many American corporations have implemented quality circles or similar groups is an indication of their potential value in identifying problems.

Groups frequently make better decisions than individuals. Although this assertion may fly in the face of popular wisdom about the quality of group decisions, the fact remains that groups often make more effective decisions than individuals. This is particularly true in the case of complex decisions that call for a broader range of skills and abilities than are likely to be possessed by any individual. As the environment and the decisions facing organizations become increasingly complex, it is likely that groups will play a more important role in decision making. Currently, the most important decisions facing organizations and society are made by groups, such as boards of directors.

Groups are good tools for implementing decisions. There is widespread agreement that groups can elicit from their members a high degree of commitment to group decisions. In fact, commitment to a decision made by a group is often greater than if the same decision had been made by an individual. Lawler and Hackman (1969), for example, found that a pay-incentive plan designed to reduce absenteeism was very successful among employees who had been allowed to participate in its development. The same plan failed to reduce absenteeism, however, when it was imposed on another group of employees. Participation by members in a group decision appears to enhance commitment to the effective implementation of the decision. Moreover, members who participate become more knowledgeable about the decision and thus better able to implement it effectively.

Groups more effectively control their members. Control systems in organizations often rely heavily on supervision of employees. Supervisors monitor the behavior and performance of employees, taking corrective action when problems are noted. Those who are responsible for large numbers of employees, however, may not become aware of problems until well after they have occurred. And supervisors do not always control the rewards that employees value. In contrast, groups often have a high degree of influence over the beliefs and behavior of their members. Groups establish norms that help regulate member behavior. Groups also are in a better position to observe deviations from these norms and take actions to control the individual's behavior effectively.

Groups help solve the problems of belonging to large, impersonal organizations. If you were employed by a large corporation like Exxon, you would be one of more than 100,000 people working for the company. Although there is a certain status attached to working for a large and powerful firm, individual employees may find it difficult psychologically to identify with a company this vast. Employees may feel that they are just minor cogs in a larger machine and that their individual contributions are relatively unimportant. Membership in subgroups of the larger organization provides employees with groups with which they can more easily identify. Within the group, individuals may find it easier to see how their contribution is important and that others take an interest in them as individuals. Groups can help overcome the problems associated with large organizations.

Leavitt (1975) cites another reason managers should be more concerned about the role of groups in organizations, although it is not related directly to the value of groups. The reason is simple: Groups are an inevitable feature of organizations. Whether we like them or not, groups always exist in organizations and must be dealt with. Some groups, such as a marketing department, result from the formal structure of the organization; others develop informally or cut across formal structural boundaries. As Leavitt (1975, p. 70) observed:

> Groups are natural phenomena, and facts of organizational life. They can be created but their spontaneous development cannot be prevented. The problem is not shall groups exist or not, but shall groups be planned or not. If not, the individualized organizational garden will sprout group weeds all over the place. By defining them as weeds instead of flowers, they shall continue, as in earlier days, to be treated as pests, forever fouling up the beauty of rationally designed individualized organizations, forever forming informally (and irrationally) to harass and outgame the planners.

Managerial effectiveness does not depend merely on the ability to manage individuals, but also on the ability to manage groups. Managers who are uncomfortable working in group situations or who find it difficult to manage employees working in groups will be at a disadvantage compared with those who have greater group skills.

Groups have the potential to play a very valuable role in organizations but often fall far short of the mark. Not all groups live up to their potential. An important question then is, Why are some groups more effective than others? The rest of this chapter will attempt to provide an answer to this question. First, a simple model will be presented. This model will direct our thinking about groups by identifying the major factors that can influence their effectiveness. Second, group characteristics that can enhance or impede the effectiveness of groups will be presented. Finally, we will examine the question of how managers can assess group effectiveness. We will consider steps in the assessment process and ways in which managers can intervene to increase group effectiveness.

A Model of Work Group Effectiveness

We now turn to a simple model of work group effectiveness that is based largely on the work of Richard Hackman of Yale University and his colleagues (Hackman, 1976a; Hackman and Morris, 1975; Nadler, Hackman, and Lawler, 1979). Such a model provides a summary of the different factors that can influence the effectiveness of a group. When one analyzes group effectiveness, whether in a work organization or in another setting, it is important to highlight the major influential factors. This also helps focus attention on the ways in which managers can intervene to improve the effectiveness of work groups, as we shall see in a later section.

Before describing the model, it is important to define what is meant by work groups. There are many definitions of **groups,** all of which tend to focus on one important group characteristic. We will use the definition provided by Cartwright and Zander (1968): "A group is a collection of individuals who have relations to one another that makes them interdependent to some significant degree" (p. 46). The critical component of this definition is the concept of *interdependence*. This defining characteristic of groups means that the actions of one member have implications or consequences for the other members. Consider a group engaged in the simple assembly of an electrical component. If the operation is organized as an assembly line, interdependence is sequential, because the ability of one person to perform his or her task depends on previous tasks being performed effectively. An employee, for example, cannot solder a connection unless a memory chip has been placed correctly in the unit. In other words, the ability of one person to perform a task depends on others' performance of their tasks. If an employee decides to take a break or skip a unit as it passes along the line, the work of others will be affected.

Work groups have either an assigned task or goal, or something else they wish to achieve. Work groups thus are distinguished from informal social groups, such as people who meet for coffee breaks, and other collections of individuals that come together without common purpose or goal. Many of the points made in this chapter will be relevant to groups outside the work setting. Our attention and most of the examples used, however, will focus on work-related groups.

The model of group effectiveness will be presented in three parts. First, we will explain what is meant when we say a group is effective in the performance of its task. Second, the major determinants of group effectiveness will be introduced. Finally, the nature of group tasks and how they influence the relationship between the determinants and effectiveness will be considered. The model of work group effectiveness we will be discussing is summarized in Figure 11.1.

Group Effectiveness

An effective group is one that accomplishes its goals or outperforms other groups doing similar tasks. A production group may be considered effective if it assembles its goal of fifty widgets, for example, and other groups manage to produce only forty-five. But effectiveness in groups, as in organizations, is more complex, because it can be evaluated along other dimensions besides actual output. Hackman (1976a) suggests that there are three critical dimensions to consider in determining the effectiveness of a group.

Productive output. The first and most familiar dimension of group effectiveness concerns whether the organization's standards are met or exceeded in terms

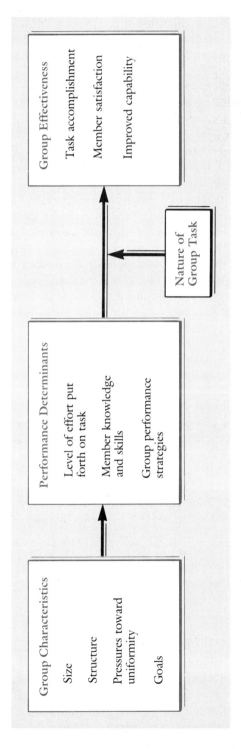

Figure 11.1
Model of Group Effectiveness

Source: Nadler, Hackman, and Lawler, 1979, p. 134–155.

of quality and quantity of production. Note that it is not just the number of units, or quantity, that is important. A production team that assembled fifty engines of which fifteen were defective would not be considered very effective. Effectiveness incorporates both how much is produced and how well it is produced. Also note that the reference point for determining effectiveness is some standard established by the group or organization, which also may contain comparisons with other groups. It is not sufficient that a group outperform other groups.

Member satisfaction. An effective group is one that provides satisfying experiences for its members while simultaneously attaining its goals. In the long run, groups that accomplish their goals in ways that are dissatisfying to members may risk disintegration. Dissatisfied members may seek to transfer to other groups or leave the organization, often threatening the future effectiveness of the group.

Enhanced group capability. In accomplishing tasks, groups apply the skills and abilities of their members. In many instances this is a relatively simple matter. In other instances groups can enhance the skills and abilities of members while performing a task. This is the case, for example, when individual members learn new skills through interaction with other members. Groups can also increase the effectiveness with which individual members interact with one another as a group. The result is enhanced overall capability of the group in the performance of subsequent tasks. This fact suggests that effective groups are characterized by growth and development, either in the skills and abilities of individual members or in the interaction processes that take place in task performance.

In viewing group effectiveness along these three dimensions, we see that a particular group may be high along one dimension but low on the others. For example, member satisfaction may be high in a group as a result of interaction in the performance of a task, but the group may never accomplish its production goals or increase its overall performance capability. In contrast, groups can accomplish or exceed their production goals, but they may create dissatisfaction among the members and diminish the ability of members to interact with one another in the future. The most effective groups are those that are high along all three of the dimensions mentioned.

It is important to recognize that effectiveness is multidimensional, because the strategies that are chosen to increase effectiveness depend on the particular area in which problems are evident. Strategies to increase member satisfaction may be different from those designed to increase production output.

Determinants of Group Effectiveness

It is commonly suggested that individual performance is a function of the individual's ability and motivation. At the group level of analysis, the determinants of performance are very similar, although things become a bit more complex because we are dealing with more than just one person. Three primary determinants of group effectiveness have been identified.

Level of effort applied to the group task. This factor reflects the motivation of individual members of the group. In general, groups with highly motivated members will be more effective than groups in which member motivation is low. High levels of member motivation may not always result in group effectiveness, however. Members may not have the ability required to perform the task, or they may direct their efforts in ways that are unlikely to ensure goal attainment.

It is also not always necessary for each member of a group to be highly motivated. To accomplish some tasks it may be necessary for only one group member to be highly motivated. For example, a group assigned the duty of developing a sales forecast for a new product can be successful if at least one member is motivated to gather the relevant marketing research data and perform the required calculations to predict future sales. Group success in this case is defined by an accurate sales forecast, and it does not matter whether it is the result of one member's efforts or the efforts of all members.

For other tasks, however, the distribution of motivation across members of the group can be quite important. For complex tasks that can be divided into subtasks for each group member, it is more critical that each member of the group be highly motivated. Unless each member is motivated, critical subtasks may not be performed and the group's overall effectiveness in performing the larger task may be threatened.

Amount of knowledge and skills applied to the task. Perhaps the most fundamental determinant of group effectiveness is the level of skills and abilities of the members. Unless members have the skill and ability to perform the task, even high levels of motivation may not be enough to ensure the success of the group. As with level of effort, the nature of the task determines whether it is important that all members of the group have high skill levels or if having at least one skilled member is sufficient.

Appropriateness of group performance strategies. The final determinant of group effectiveness reflects the choices that must be made about how a goal is to be accomplished. Groups must have a clear goal and then develop a plan for how to work toward the goal. Frequently there are multiple strategies for pursuing a goal, not all of which are equally effective or efficient. Consider a basketball team on offense. Even though the team is composed of motivated and skillful players, the ability to score a basket may depend on selecting and executing the right play. Teams that merely dribble the ball downcourt looking for an open shot usually are less effective than teams that create the open shot through the effective use of plays.

In work organizations it is also important for groups to have an effective strategy for the performance of tasks. Groups without an effective strategy may still accomplish their goals, but they often take longer and use more resources in the process; that is, the task is not performed efficiently. Research on group processes suggests that the strategy formulation step often is omitted by groups and that simply asking groups to think about their task performance strategy is one way to increase group effectiveness (Hackman and Morris, 1975).

Group Tasks

The nature of the task performed by a group has a major effect on the ways in which the three determinants of effectiveness influence group output. For example, as we mentioned, on some tasks the presence of at least one motivated and skilled member is sufficient for the group to be successful, whereas on other tasks it is important that all members have high levels of motivation and skill.

The nature of the task performed by a group also is important because it may make a determinant a more or less important influence on the group's ultimate effectiveness. For example, the level of motivation in the group may have little or no impact on the group's success in performing certain tasks. On machine-paced assembly line operations, putting forth additional effort cannot really increase performance because you can only work as fast as the speed of the assembly line. Other group tasks may be so routine and simplified that the knowledge and skills of members are relatively unimportant. Almost everyone, for example, can be assumed to have the skill necessary to perform the simple task.

The nature of the task to a large extent controls whether one, two, or all three determinants are influential in group effectiveness. We cannot truly understand what factors determine a group's effectiveness unless we have a good understanding of the requirements imposed by the group's task. Because the types of tasks performed by groups are so numerous, it is difficult to develop a task-classification scheme that will help us better understand the conditions under which the various determinants of group effectiveness are likely to be important.

Herold (1979), however, has developed a simple task-classification scheme. He begins by observing that group tasks impose both technical and social demands. The technical demands of a task relate to its programmability or routineness, difficulty, and skill and information requirements. Social demands are related to whether group members are likely to be invested in the group solution, whether members are likely to agree on goals, and what the preferred means to attain these goals are.

If we assume that all group tasks impose technical and social demands, and that these demands can be simple or complex, a fourfold classification of tasks results. This classification scheme and examples of tasks that are descriptive of each cell are presented in Figure 11.2. In general, we expect that the greater the technical demands imposed by a task, the more important member knowledge and skills will be in determining group effectiveness. Moreover, the question of member efforts can be important as well in technically demanding tasks, particularly when knowledge and skills are not distributed evenly among members. When the group's success depends on the knowledge and skills of only one member in performing a technically complex task, it is very important to ensure that this member is motivated to accomplish the group's goal. Performance strategies also can be very important, particularly when complex technical tasks must be subdivided and the efforts of many individuals working on separate subtasks coordinated.

Figure 11.2
Classification of Group Tasks

Technical Demands

	Simple	Complex
Simple	Maintenance of filing, record-keeping, or payroll systems	Preparation of marketing research or production planning reports
Complex	Budget allocation decisions	Strategic decision to divest a business

(left axis label: Social Demands)

Source: Herold, 1979.

When tasks impose complex social demands, the performance strategy chosen by the group may be crucial to effectiveness. When disagreement is likely over the group's goals or the means to attain these goals, the process used in performing the task is very important in determining how members later feel about their experience. In the making of difficult budget allocation decisions, for example, it is unlikely that all members will be satisfied with the outcome of group decisions. The extent of group-member dissatisfaction may be mitigated, however, if everyone agrees that the process of reaching an allocation decision was fair and effective. Tasks that impose complex social demands also require that members possess a certain degree of knowledge and skill, but of a different type than is required for technically demanding tasks. The knowledge and skills most likely to be important in this situation concern social interaction with others, including sensitivity to the feelings of others and the ability to communicate in a nonthreatening manner.

The general conclusion to be drawn from this discussion is that a careful analysis of the group's task must be conducted before we can understand which factors — member efforts, member knowledge and skills, and group performance strategy — are most important in influencing task effectiveness. Different tasks call on different resources from the group. It is not possible to develop a model of the determinants of group task effectiveness that suggests that each determinant will be equally important to members or equally important in all situations. Rather, the determinants of effectiveness must be considered in relation to the requirements imposed by the group's task.

Group Characteristics
That Influence Effectiveness

Our discussion has highlighted several important characteristics of groups that may determine their effectiveness in performing a task. A number of additional characteristics of groups have been identified that also may have implications for effectiveness. In the discussion that follows, an attempt will be made to show how these general group characteristics can influence the primary determinants of group effectiveness just discussed.

The Importance of Group Size

One of the most frequently discussed characteristics of groups is their size. Increasing group size often is blamed for inhibiting group effectiveness. For example, as groups grow larger, problems arise in coordinating the efforts of different members. Communication among members also becomes more difficult, and the participation of members in the group's activities may become limited to only a few people. Group size also can contribute positively to effectiveness, however. As group size increases, for example, the range of member skills and knowledge available to the group also should increase. The probability that at least one member will have the skills necessary for the group to perform its task will therefore increase with group size.

One area of current research suggests that group size can have a direct impact on the level of effort group members apply to the task. A series of experiments conducted by Latané and his colleagues (Latané, Harkins, and Williams, 1979) has identified a phenomenon they describe as **social loafing.** This is the tendency of individuals to work not quite as hard in a group. On simple tasks such as rope pulling and making noise by clapping, for example, they consistently found that individuals put forth less effort when working with others than when working alone (Fig. 11.3). As a result, groups performed consistently below the level that would be predicted by simply summing the performance of the individual members.

In large groups the temptation to rely on the efforts of others may be very great, particularly when individual contributions to the group's performance are difficult to identify. Individuals simply may not try as hard in a group setting as they would if working on the same task alone. Latané's research suggests that the social loafing effect can be overcome by making sure that each member's contributions can be identified, or that the individuals think they can. When the contributions of each member are apparent, reduced effort is less likely to result in group working situations, although group performance still may suffer because of coordination.

Group Structure

A major characteristic of groups is the differentiation of members along several different dimensions. Bales (1950) proposed that four kinds of differentia-

Figure 11.3
Noise Intensity as a Function of Group Size and Response Mode

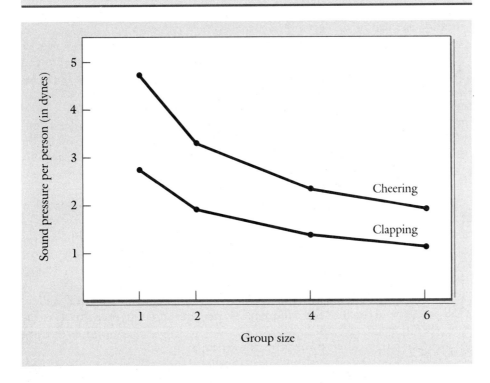

Source: Data from Latané, Harkins, and Williams, 1979.

tion typically take place in groups. First, members are differentiated in terms of their *access to resources needed by the group* to perform its task. Resources can be broadly defined to include information important to the group, knowledge necessary to perform successfully, and equipment and tools required for the task. Differences among members in terms of access to resources result primarily in differential power and influence within the group. There is general agreement that control over scarce and valuable resources is a major determinant of power in organizations (Pfeffer, 1981).

A second basis for differentiation within groups is the *legitimate ability* of individuals *to control the activities of others.* This difference refers to authority relations in the group and generally distinguishes the formally appointed group leader from other members. Organizations give group leaders the ability, within limits, to control the behavior of others on task-related matters. In some respects this factor is related to the first basis for differentiation, because leaders often have greater access to important resources. Access to resources is not limited to formally appointed leadership positions, however. It is common for informal leaders to emerge who have a great deal of power and influence over the group's activities. The *legitimate* right to control the behavior of others, in contrast, generally is bestowed only on the formal leader by the organization.

The *importance or prestige of individual members* is another dimension along which differences can emerge. Generally referred to as **status differentiation,** this dimension simply reflects the fact that some members are held in higher regard than others. The leadership position frequently carries higher status in groups, for example. Differences in importance or prestige of members can emerge from several sources. **Internal status characteristics** are based on an individual's position or contributions within the group. **External status characteristics,** in contrast, are derived from factors outside the group. Both can be important in determining the status of an individual. David Rockefeller's considerable status at Chase Manhattan Bank, for example, was based partially on his family name and background (external status characteristics) as well as on his position of chief executive officer and his performance in this role (internal status characteristics).

A fourth dimension along which group members can be differentiated is their *degree of identification and loyalty to the group.* Members differ in their level of commitment to the group's goals, their degree of identification based on membership in the group, and the value they place on membership. Identification with and loyalty to a group are based both on the individual's attraction to the group itself — its goals, activities, and members — and on the attractiveness of alternative group membership (Cartwright, 1968; Thibaut and Kelley, 1959). In general, members are more motivated and susceptible to group influence when they find the group attractive and when there are few opportunities for membership in other, more attractive groups.

Although not mentioned by Bales, another dimension along which differentiation can take place in groups concerns tasks. Frequently, not everyone in a work group performs the same task. Rather, it is common to find a high degree of **task specialization.** Task specialization is particularly common in groups performing complex and technologically sophisticated tasks, such as the National Aeronautics and Space Administration's space shuttle engineers. But it also may occur when tasks are less complex, such as on railroad train crews, when employees tend to specialize in one of several jobs and may be unlikely to perform the work of other crew members. Task specialization tends to produce skills and abilities within a narrow range of job duties. Many corporations in the United States are trying to encourage the development of broader skills and abilities by rotating employees among jobs or eliminating highly specialized job classification schemes.

Member Placement. The structure of a group is defined by the placement of members along these different dimensions. The total pattern of differentiation and relationships that develops among the parts of the group constitutes its **structural characteristics.** Groups can exhibit more or less differentiation among members, but it is unlikely that groups exist in which there are no such differences among members. Group structure has a very great influence on the experiences of group members. Individuals who are high in status and authority, for example, will have different experiences and thus react differently to their membership than will individuals low on these dimensions.

Structure and Effectiveness. The structure of the group also can have an important impact on group effectiveness. When groups include members of high status or authority, there is a tendency for other group members to defer to the judgment of those in leadership positions (Hoffman, 1965). Torrance (1954) gave a simple mathematical problem to bomber crews composed of a pilot, navigator, and gunner. Pilots solved the problem correctly less often than navigators, although they were more successful than the navigators in persuading others to accept their (incorrect) solution. High-status members of groups, such as the pilots in the bomber crews, often are successful in persuading others to accept their views even though their skills and abilities at the task may be lower. Low-status members with greater skills may not be motivated to make contributions, thus decreasing the overall knowledge and skills available to the group in accomplishing its task. In fact, the result may be a group performance strategy that simply looks to the leader or high-status member for guidance. This strategy may not be a problem if the leader also possesses the greatest knowledge and skills. Unfortunately, this is not always the case.

Differentiation in the tasks performed by members can increase the knowledge and skills within a group. As task specialization increases, members develop greater expertise in performing their particular duties. Unfortunately, this pattern can sometimes also have a disruptive effect. When there is turnover in group membership, for example, other members may not have the skills necessary to take over the position of the person who left. The greater the task specialization, the less flexibility there is in moving members around to different tasks. This relationship may make employee turnover and absenteeism potentially more disruptive than would otherwise be the case, although this disruption also depends on how easily members who leave can be replaced.

Differences in members' levels of identification and loyalty have obvious implications for the level of effort applied in pursuing the group's goals. Members with high levels of group commitment and loyalty would be expected to have much higher levels of motivation. Moreover, less committed members may tend to withdraw from participation, knowing they can rely on the more highly motivated members to get the job done. The social loafing phenomenon that can occur as groups grow in size may be caused in large part by the fact that members differ in their commitment to group goals and thus in their motivation level.

Most often, structural influences are viewed as detracting from the group's performance. Differences among members frequently result in unequal participation, deference to those in authority positions, and poor utilization of skills and abilities. It is important to recognize, however, that the influence of structure is not always negative. All things considered, groups are better off having at least a few members who are highly motivated and committed than none at all.

Feature 11.3
Life with Andre Meyer

He was considered the most creative financial genius of his time in the investment banking business, a man, it was said, who could "peel people like bananas" in negotiations.

But life with Andre Meyer at Lazard Frères was anything but easy. Besides being a genius, he was known as one of the country's most autocratic and dictatorial business leaders.

The extent of Meyer's power over the twenty or so partners at Lazard was enormous. The partnership agreement gave him the power to "hire, fire, allocate income, assets, and losses, and to do so without limit."

And he seldom hesitated to exercise this power, often treating the partners more as employees or clerks. He yelled at partners in public, telephoned them at all hours, and decided how much salary each was to receive. He even told one partner that the partner's wife should not be allowed to use the telephone at his home because it took Meyer more than an hour to get a call through to him.

At one point Meyer decided to hold regular meetings of the partners at 8:30 Monday mornings. They were short — only fifteen minutes long — but they must have seemed like an eternity to the partners.

Many of the partners were afraid to bring up information that had not been discussed personally with Meyer before the meeting. One participant said that anytime someone brought up something that he didn't want them to hear, he would cut off the man with, "We'll talk about that later."

Meyer's desire for secrecy often destroyed any value the meetings might have had. When new or important information was presented, Meyer frequently would engage in a cryptic conversation with a partner that the others could not understand.

One participant in the meetings remembered, "He would say to Howard Kniffin, 'How about that?' and Howard would say, 'Well, it looks pretty good, Mr. Meyer, but Jack thinks that we'll hear in two days.' What the hell, you didn't know who Jack was, you didn't know what the deal was, you just didn't know."

The partners survived by keeping quiet. Before long Meyer's experiment with meetings ended.

With this abrasive management style, why was Meyer able to attract and retain a group of the most talented people in banking and government? Why did they allow themselves to be treated this way?

Some were attracted by the challenge of working with some of the best deal makers and negotiators in the business. The reason for others was financial. They entered Lazard contributing little capital, and Meyer made them millionaires.

As one partner described it, "The bargain seemed a fair one: a child's security for a child's treatment."

Source: Financier: The Biography of Andre Meyer, by Cary Reich, New York: William Morrow, 1983, pp. 176–196.

Task specialization also can assist in the formulation of performance strategies. Recognized expertise often makes it easier to divide complex tasks and to ensure that members are matched correctly to subtasks according to their skills.

Pressures Toward Uniformity

At the same time that differences emerge among members of a group, there are strong pressures that tend to create standardization and uniformity (Cartwright and Zander, 1968). It has been suggested already that groups can have a strong influence on the beliefs and behavior of their members. In work groups, for example, members may share beliefs about important aspects of the work environment, such as whether the supervisor is considerate, and hold common values about appropriate behavior on the job, such as how hard people should work.

The ability of groups to influence their members derives from several sources. First, many of the objects of important beliefs are ambiguous and difficult to evaluate objectively. Questions such as whether a supervisor is considerate may be difficult to answer without reference to views held by others. *Socially defined reality,* therefore, may be more important in determining individual members' reactions to the workplace than are other factors. Second, some group members may lack confidence in their judgments and may look to other group members for clues about what is appropriate. Particularly for new members in organizations, groups are an important *reference point.* When we find ourselves in an ambiguous situation or are unsure of our own ability to judge the situation correctly, we naturally look to others to determine how to react. Third, the more members must rely on the group for important *rewards,* the more open they are to its influence. When members find the group highly attractive, when membership satisfies important needs, and when there are few attractive alternate group memberships available, the group's power over individual members increases. Finally, the continued *existence of the group* itself exerts a subtle pressure toward greater uniformity. Individuals who must work with one another over a period of time may hesitate to risk conflict in the group by dissenting or acting in ways others think inappropriate. Most people find conflict uncomfortable and will acquiesce to the group rather than risk a confrontation.

Group Norms. One important aspect of groups that increases uniformity is the existence of norms. **Group norms** are rules of conduct or behavior that regulate members (Nadler, Hackman, and Lawler, 1979). These unwritten group rules generally apply to overt behavior of group members and not to private beliefs. Moreover, norms tend to be established only for behavior that the group considers critical to its continued existence and effectiveness. The establishment of norms helps decrease the need for continued surveillance and monitoring of member behavior, which otherwise might be necessary to ensure comformity to important rules.

One of the best ways to understand the nature of group norms is in terms of the **return potential model** developed by Jackson (1965). This model can be used to graph a hypothetical norm for participation in discussion in a project group (Fig. 11.4). The horizontal axis of the model plots behaviors. In this case, behaviors reflect the number of times a person enters into the group discussion.

The vertical axis plots the amount of approval or disapproval associated with a specific level of behavior. The curve drawn in this example suggests a group norm in which either failing to participate or monopolizing the discussion results in the disapproval of other members. The norm is that each member should contribute to the group discussion, but not to the extent that others are prevented from participating. The range of behavior that is tolerated by the group is defined by the area of the curve that is above the neutral point on the approval/disapproval continuum. The highest point on the curve identifies the level of behavior associated with the highest approval.

What would happen to individuals in this example who either failed to contribute or talked too much? Generally, individuals who deviate from the established group norms become the objects of increasing attention from other group members in an effort to change their behavior (Shaw, 1981). If this effort is unsuccessful, a group may punish the offender by removing valued rewards or failing to include him or her in its activities. In the final stages, communication with the offender may cease entirely and the person may be excluded from all further group activities.

Groups often exert considerable pressure for uniformity among their members. This pressure can have several important implications for potential group effectiveness. In the workplace, groups commonly develop productivity norms. As demonstrated in the Hawthorne studies, groups can control their productivity by developing norms to regulate the performance of individuals

Figure 11.4
Group Norms Concerning Discussion Participation

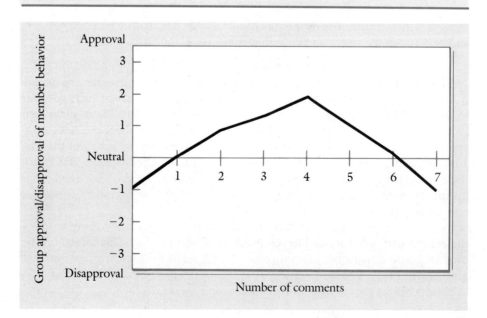

(Roethlisberger and Dickson, 1939). This may occur, for example, when groups fear that high performance levels may result in management's changing either production standards or the basis for performance bonuses. Thus, group norms can be used to influence the effort that members apply to the task.

Performance Strategies. Another area in which group pressures can influence effectiveness concerns performance strategies. Groups develop ways to perform tasks, and these gain member consensus as the appropriate strategy over time. For example, a management committee may begin a discussion about purchasing new equipment by sequentially evaluating each of the alternate pieces of equipment. This strategy may develop unconsciously in the group based on past experience from similar decisions. To the group members, this strategy is the most appropriate because things have always been done this way. Problems may occur when new or existing group members suggest alternate ways to approach the problem. A new member may feel that the group discussion would be more effective if the specific performance requirements of the new equipment were identified before the pros and cons of each alternative were discussed. The new member may be correct in suggesting a new strategy, although older group members may resist the suggestion. Because older members are comfortable with the way things have been done in the past, they may pressure the new member to conform to existing strategy. The result may be that the group continues to use a performance strategy that is not as effective as some others would be. The development of group norms and consensus about appropriate ways to perform the task may make the group very resistant to change. In fact, members may be hesitant to suggest change, fearing a negative reaction from others.

Group norms and pressures do not always result in less effective performance. Groups can develop norms that foster and encourage innovation and increased effectiveness. For example, group norms may encourage member participation by forbidding the expression of negative judgments, such as, "That was a stupid idea." Groups also can reward members for outstanding contributions and performance above and beyond the call of duty. When these types of norms develop in groups, effectiveness is likely to be enhanced.

The difficult task for managers is to ensure that the goals of the group and larger organization are compatible. When they are, group norms may emerge that encourage performance and contributions to organizational goals. Group-based incentive bonuses for performance often are developed, for example, in the hope that the group will view high individual performance as benefitting everyone. When high levels of performance directly benefit the group, individual performance is encouraged and it is more likely that group members will cooperate in performing their tasks.

Group Goals

One of the more important influences on the direction and level of group effort is the group's goals. On the individual level, there is overwhelming evidence that setting specific and challenging goals can enhance performance (Locke, Saari, Shaw, and Latham, 1981). There is little reason to believe that goals play a less important role in performance at the group level, although matters are made more complex by the fact that not all members share the same goals. In some groups, member disagreement over goals may inhibit performance until consensus is reached.

Group goals can influence performance in several ways. First, goals help direct the attention of group members and focus it on the task. Goals help clarify the task and provide a standard for measuring the group's achievements. Second, group goals can motivate members. When goals are challenging, members may become more highly motivated than when goals are unclear or unchallenging. Finally, group goals can lead to discussions of performance strategy. Once the group decides on a goal, it is natural for the group to discuss strategies for attaining the goal (although such discussions are not inevitable). In other words, once the group identifies where it wants to be, it can discuss the best way to get there.

Zander (1982) suggests that groups have a natural tendency to set more difficult goals. Achieving more difficult goals holds the promise of greater satisfaction. Failure to accomplish such goals also may prove less embarrassing to the group, because failure at a difficult task is easier to explain than failure at a simple one. In addition, there often are significant external pressures for the group to set loftier goals, particularly when other work groups are performing at a higher level. Competition among work groups can be a powerful motivator, and the knowledge of how others perform can be an important influence on the setting of a group's goal. When information is not readily available on how others are performing, groups may overestimate their own performance capabilities. When accurate information is not available about the group's potential performance, pressures may exist to set higher goals.

Zander suggests that the influence of group goals is more complex when members disagree on what the group should try to achieve and the best way to achieve it. When there is conflict over group goals, performance may be inhibited because not all members are working hard or in the same direction. Even when there is goal consensus, performance according to organizational criteria may not result unless the group's goals are consistent with those of management. Significant agreement on goals may help the group achieve its purposes, but they may not always be the same as management's. Thus, organizational performance can occur only when group members agree on goals and the goals are congruent with those of the larger organization. For this reason, many organizations have found it useful for managers and employees to set goals jointly.

Making Work Groups More Effective

We have discussed several determinants of group effectiveness: the efforts of members, the knowledge and skills available, group performance strategies, and group characteristics. Hundreds of group characteristics have been linked with effectiveness (see Shaw, 1981). Given such a large number, managers interested in improving work group effectiveness face a complex task. In this section we will suggest an approach managers can take in making work groups more effective.

Nadler, Hackman, and Lawler (1979) identified two important roles of managers in organizations that can help us focus our thinking about how to manage work group effectiveness. They suggest that the manager must serve as both a *diagnostician* and as a *change agent*.

Diagnosing Group Effectiveness

The *diagnostic* role of managers involves carefully assessing information about group functioning to determine if problems exist and what the specific causes of these problems are. Feature 11.4, a discussion of the effectiveness of the Joint Chiefs of Staff, points up a number of problems that relate to the determinants of group effectiveness we have discussed. The design of the group and its impact on performance strategies in decision making appear to be major factors contributing to ineffectiveness. Problems with member knowledge and skills or motivation levels are not apparent. After you have read the feature and the discussion of managerial interventions that follow in the next section, consider how the effectiveness of the Joint Chiefs could be increased.

Diagnostic activities can involve one of two different approaches. The *comprehensive* diagnostic approach identified by Nadler, Hackman, and Lawler (1979) is less problem centered and more concerned with assessing the appropriateness of work-group design and tasks to the organization's overall goals and strategy. This diagnostic approach is summarized in Figure 11.5. The process begins by identifying the critical goals and strategies of the organization. From this, the critical tasks facing each unit must be determined and the appropriateness of organizational structure for accomplishing these tasks assessed. Finally, managers must examine the patterns of individual and group behavior in the performance of these tasks.

In the comprehensive diagnostic approach, managers reflect upon the design and functioning of work groups based on a careful assessment of organizational goals and the critical tasks that must be performed to accomplish these goals. This approach begins with the big picture — goals and strategy — and progresses to more specific issues associated with the design of work groups. This approach may be most appropriate when organizations are being designed or when current organizational structures are evaluated. When faced with day-to-day demands, managers are less likely to engage in broad, comprehensive assessments of this type.

Most managers facing the daily pressures of managing work groups are more likely to engage in a second type of diagnostic activity identified by Nadler, Hackman, and Lawler (1979). *Symptom-based diagnosis* is problem centered. When managers detect problems in the functioning of work groups, both the problems and causes must be carefully assessed. The model of work-group

Feature 11.4
Evaluating Group Effectiveness: The Joint Chiefs of Staff

The Joint Chiefs of Staff is the highest level of military policy formulation and strategic decision making in the United States armed forces. Members include the army and air force chiefs of staff, the chief of naval operations, and the marine commandant. The fifth member, the chairman, is appointed by the president from one of the four service branches.

The Joint Chiefs' effectiveness as a policy- and decision-making group increasingly is being questioned. A former secretary of defense characterized their advice as "worse than nothing," and one of its own former chairmen has openly advocated its abolition.

Why are the Joint Chiefs ineffective? The problem is not that the individual members are untalented. They are intelligent, highly motivated, experienced, and supported by talented staffs.

Part of the problem lies with the design of the group itself. Each chief, but not the chairman, holds two positions. He, or maybe someday she, is a member of the group and also chief of staff of his respective service. Unfortunately, this may make it difficult to be truly impartial when difficult decisions have to be made on military strategy or the budget. Not surprisingly, Secretary of Defense Caspar Weinberger reportedly bypassed the Joint Chiefs completely on the question of what weapons system to sacrifice to avoid a military pay freeze. The current structure makes consensus on such issues difficult, if not impossible.

A similar problem exists at the staff level. Staff members work for the chiefs and return to their services after their tour. The individual services retain complete control over their future promotions. Those who become too impartial in their staff duties may be looked down upon by their respective service branches. Many staff officers are said to view a tour with the Joint Chiefs as having greater potential to harm their career than to help it, even though it would appear to be a prestige assignment.

The Joint Chiefs' performance strategies in policy making also may contribute to ineffectiveness. The group relies on the different services for basic information and analyses required to make decisions. Because the different services compete for scarce budget dollars, the information they provide may be biased. Obtaining good information for decision making is often difficult because of a practice one staff member compared to each service's "keeping two sets of books."

In addition, each service, represented by its chief, has the option of "nonconcurring" in reports or policy statements, effectively slowing down the process until consensus is reached. For example, the air force filed a nonconcurrence report after a report was prepared that was critical of tests comparing its B-1 bomber with the navy's cruise missile. This bought time for the air force to either kill the report or soften its conclusions. Because each service has its own high-priority projects, there is considerable room for negotiation on such issues.

When a group is ineffective, we most often focus attention on the skills or motivation levels of its members. But the group's design and performance strategies also can be significant barriers. Analyzing why the Joint Chiefs have become ineffective has proved easier than identifying acceptable solutions. Because the Joint Chiefs operate in a very political environment, reform is likely to remain a difficult issue for years to come.

Source: "Why the Generals Can't Command," by David C. Martin and Michael A. Lerner, *Newsweek.* February 14, 1983, pp. 22–24,

Figure 11.5
Steps in the Comprehensive Diagnostic Approach

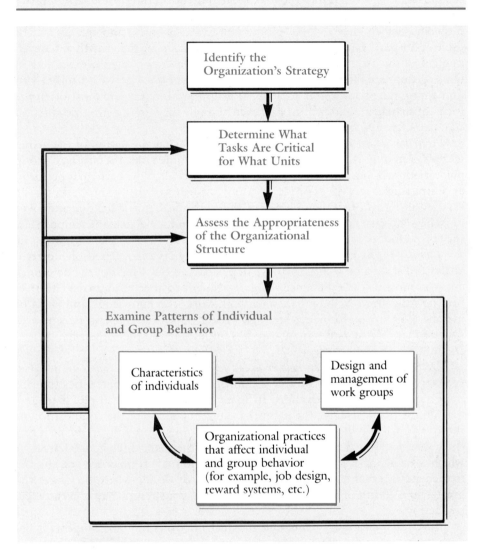

Source: From David A. Nadler, J. Richard Hackman, and Edward E. Lawler III, *Managing Organizational Behavior,* p. 268. Copyright © 1979 by David A. Nadler, J. Richard Hackman, and Edward E. Lawler III. Reprinted by permission of Little, Brown and Company.

effectiveness discussed earlier suggests how managers should go about conducting a symptom-based or problem-centered assessment. There are several important steps in such problem diagnosis.

Assess work group effectiveness. The first step is to determine whether problems actually exist. Perceived problems frequently prove unimportant on closer examination. At other times the manager's hunches about problems will prove correct. At this stage it is important to understand the specific nature of these problems, which may involve productivity (the quantity and quality of the group's output), satisfaction of group member needs, or the growth and development of the group in performing its task. Unless we know the exact area in which groups are failing to meet their effectiveness potential, we are unlikely to find appropriate solutions. Problems in group productivity are most often the focus of managerial attention. But even though they are meeting production standards, groups still may be ineffective.

Analyze the group's task. We suggested earlier that the nature of the group task plays an important role in performance. For some tasks, the efforts of group members may be less crucial to group performance than the particular performance strategies used, for example. It also was suggested that group tasks can be assessed in terms of the complexity of their technical and social demands. We must have a clear understanding of the technical and social demands imposed by the task before proceeding to the next step.

Identify the important determinants of group effectiveness. Based on a careful analysis of the group's task, the next step is to find out which of the determinants can most directly influence the group's performance. Can group effectiveness be influenced by how hard members work, the knowledge and skills of members, or the performance strategies the group uses? This assessment may suggest that certain determinants are less important and that others have a crucial influence on effectiveness.

Determine what interventions by managers to increase effectiveness are possible. Managers may not always be able to control the group characteristics that are important to group effectiveness. In many situations, for example, managers may not be free to change the nature of the group's task or the composition of the group. We will discuss the types of interventions more fully in the next section. At this point it is sufficient to note that there are three general areas in which managers can intervene: design factors, internal group processes, and the immediate external environment. Managers must decide where they have the greatest possibility of making changes and what constraints may prevent effective action.

Select an intervention. Once the manager uncovers the most important determinants of group effectiveness and assesses his or her ability to influence these determinants, some sort of intervention, or several, can be chosen. To put it simply, managers identify changes that need to be made and implement these changes.

Evaluate interventions. The final step in the process is for managers to assess the effectiveness of the changes that have been made. Has group effectiveness improved as a result of the actions taken by the manager? If not, the diagnostic process may be undertaken again to determine whether additional problems exist that were not identified previously. The important point here is that the process is not complete until managers assess the results of their actions. Unless managers can verify that the original problems have been solved and the effectiveness of the group has increased, additional work may be required.

These six steps are a systematic procedure for managers to follow in assessing the effectiveness of work groups. If problems exist and the diagnostic process is applied successfully, the nature of changes that need to be made should become apparent. The next step in the process involves the manager as a change agent. Even the most accurate diagnosis is unlikely to have an impact unless the manager is skilled at introducing and managing change. The next section will focus more specifically on how managers can act as change agents to improve group effectiveness.

Managerial Interventions to Improve Group Effectiveness

In discussing the ways in which managers can improve group effectiveness, it is useful to distinguish between two aspects of change. The *content of change* focuses on the specific aspects of the group or group processes that will be changed; the *process of change* involves the specific ways in which changes will be carried out within the group. Both are important considerations for managers interested in improving group effectiveness. The content of change strategies designed to enhance group effectiveness will be discussed first, followed by some general thoughts on the process through which change can be introduced effectively.

Content of Change. The procedure for assessing group effectiveness introduced in the previous section raises two important questions about change. First, analyzing the major determinants of group effectiveness leads one to ask in what aspects the manager should intervene: member efforts or knowledge and skills, group performance strategies, or any combination of these. The second question is, Where can an intervention be made most effectively? We have suggested that managers do not always control the factors that directly influence group effectiveness. Thus, managers need to determine what constraints exist in the situation that may limit their efforts. If it is impossible to change the composition of the group, for example, managers must think about other ways in which changes can be brought about to improve group effectiveness.

Nadler, Hackman, and Lawler (1979) suggest three general points at which interventions to improve group effectiveness can be made: design factors, internal group processes, and the immediate external environment. *Design factors* focus on the structure of the group and the tasks members perform. *Internal group processes* involve what happens when members interact within the group in performing their tasks. The *immediate external environment* includes factors outside the group that may play an important role in determining what happens within the group. For example, reward policies typically are established outside the group but can have a tremendous influence on the motivation of group members.

Specific interventions to improve group effectiveness become clearer if we combine the determinants of group effectiveness and the points at which managers can intervene into a matrix. Such a matrix, adapted from the work of Nadler, Hackman, and Lawler (1979), is presented in Figure 11.6. This matrix allows managers to focus on specific change strategies based on an assessment of the most critical determinants of effectiveness and the areas in which managers have some control and thus can intervene. For example, if we assume that the critical determinant of effectiveness in a managerial task is the knowledge and skills available within the group, we can find three possible ways to influence this determinant.

First, if the manager in charge of a task force has control over design factors, the most direct way to influence knowledge and skills within the group is to change the group composition. This simply means individuals with the critical skills should be added to the task force and those without these skills should be removed.

Second, if we examine knowledge and skills in relation to internal group processes, the matrix suggests that the sharing of knowledge and the weight given to member input are crucial areas that need to be examined. In discussing the influences on work-group effectiveness, we noted that problems often occur

---

Figure 11.6
Interventions to Improve Group Effectiveness

	INTERVENTION STRATEGIES		
PERFORMANCE DETERMINANT	*Design Factors*	*Internal Group Processes*	*Immediate External Environment*
Level of effort	Design group task to increase motivating potential	Coordinate member efforts and increase commitment	Design reward system for good group performance
Member knowledge and skills	Change composition of group	Focus on how member contributions to the group are received and whether knowledge is shared	Make task-relevant training or external consultants available to the group
Task performance strategies	Change group norms about appropriate performance strategies	Have group design and implement new performance strategies	Clarify group goals and performance constraints

Source: Nadler, Hackman, and Lawler, 1979.

when some members of the group do not participate and when the contributions of some members are dismissed or given more weight than others. Interventions designed to correct these problems generally focus on increasing participation and ensuring that the contributions of low-status members are evaluated on their merits and not according to their source. For example, nominal group technique and the Delphi approach to group decision making structure the process of individual contributions and provide for an evaluation-free period in which various ideas are recorded (Delbecq, Van de Ven, and Gustafson, 1975). These approaches are designed to ensure that each member participates and the contributions are not dismissed prematurely because of their source.

Third, the manager can influence the knowledge and skills of group members by intervening in several ways in the immediate external environment. For example, technical consultants can be hired to help the group with particularly complex or difficult problems. Alternately, group knowledge and skills can be enhanced through training and development. The use of outside consultants and training programs is common in organizations.

The specific nature of the intervention or change effort to be used is determined by assessing both the most important influences on group effectiveness and the areas in which managers can intervene directly. Depending on the outcome of these assessments, the strategies will differ. In most cases the assessment will lead to multiple changes, such as redesigning the group task and making outside consultants available.

Process of Change. We have been focusing on the content of changes made to improve group effectiveness, but it is also important to consider the process for introducing change. Unilateral changes imposed by management often are resisted by subordinates and thus are ineffective. The way in which change is introduced in groups therefore is very important. Three general approaches to managing the change process can be identified (Nadler, Hackman, and Lawler, 1979).

First, the group can be motivated to accept the change through the use of incentives. Revised reward systems that accompany changes in group processes, for example, may convince group members that it is in their best interests to adopt the new system. Second, and perhaps most effective of all, group members can be allowed to participate in the change process. Group members are more likely to recognize the need for change when they are allowed to identify problems and assess their causes, and are more committed to implementing a change when they have suggested and evaluated alternative solutions. We are not suggesting that groups should be the sole voice in selecting the appropriate change strategy, although in some cases this might be preferable (see Vroom and Yetton, 1973). What is being suggested is that group members be allowed to voice their opinions about a problem and have a meaningful say in their solution. Even when the solution that group members prefer is not chosen, participating in the process may enhance their commitment to implementing the ultimate solution successfully (Hoffman, 1979).

Finally, Nadler, Hackman, and Lawler (1979) suggest that powerful people in organizations can be useful in helping ensure that change efforts are successful. When a particular change is advocated or supported by a person in a position to reward and punish group members, the likelihood of compliance increases. This strategy still may result in subtle resistance to change, however, although group members may support the change verbally to the powerful person, they may act to ensure that it is not implemented effectively.

The choice of a strategy for change depends on several factors, and there is no one best approach for all situations. Managers should recognize, however, that group member resistance to changes designed to enhance group effectiveness may make even the most appropriate interventions ineffective. Therefore, it is important to consider the process for introducing change as well as the specific nature of the changes that need to be made. Failure to consider this fundamental point has frustrated many managerial efforts to improve effectiveness.

Summary

The present chapter explores the use of groups in organizations. Increasingly, groups are being used to improve the quality of employees' working life and organizational effectiveness. Groups appear to be good for people, and good problem-finding tools, frequently make better decisions than individuals, and are good at implementing decisions, controlling members, and solving the problems of belonging to large, impersonal organizations.

Hackman suggests three critical dimensions to consider in determining the effectiveness of a group: productive output, member satisfaction, and enhanced group capability. It is also important to look at the level of effort applied to the group task, the amount of knowledge and skill applied to the task, and the appropriateness of group performance strategies.

Group tasks and characteristics also influence effectiveness. Among the important characteristics are group size and structure. In large groups the tendency to rely on others may result in social loafing. Group members are differentiated by their access to needed resources, legitimate control over others, importance or prestige, degree of identification and loyalty to the group, and task specialization.

There are also pressures to create standardization and uniformity in groups. Group norms, goals, and performance strategies govern the behavior of individuals and the group.

Managers working with groups must act as diagnosticians and change agents. The comprehensive diagnostic approach is concerned with the group's design and tasks as they relate to the organization's overall goals and strategies. Symptom-based diagnosis is problem centered.

Managers diagnosing a problem must assess the group's effectiveness, analyze its task, identify the important determinants of group effectiveness, determine interventions, select an intervention, and evaluate the result. The content of change focuses on aspects of the group or its processes that will be changed. The process of change concentrates on how changes will be carried out in the group.

Questions for Discussion

1. What valuable roles can groups serve in organizations?
2. Why are groups generally more effective in controlling members than supervisors are?
3. What is the critical characteristic that defines a group?
4. Identify the different dimensions along which group effectiveness can be evaluated?
5. How is the nature of the task performed by the group related to the major determinants of group effectiveness? Give examples of different groups and tasks.
6. Size is often considered a sign of success in some groups (such as political parties), although along with increased size the group may experience some problems. What are the disadvantages of large size in groups?
7. How are groups likely to deal with members who continually deviate from norms the group considers important?
8. Are group norms likely to be established for all the activities in which groups engage, or only for some of them? What are the characteristics of activities that encourage the development of norms?
9. Describe the differences between the comprehensive and symptom-based approaches to diagnosis.
10. What steps should managers take in assessing group effectiveness and making changes to increase effectiveness?
11. Identify the three general points at which managers can intervene to influence group effectiveness.

Case Study
Clearview Institute of Science

Jonathan Leigh, a case writer from the Columbia Business School, met Professor Sam Morris of the Clearview Institute of Science on a flight from New York to Geneva. Morris was on his way to report to a special United Nations committee on the development of alternative energy sources. In speaking to Leigh about Clearview, Morris seemed frustrated.

> We always had such a great reputation — we did excellent research and published in the most prestigious scientific journals. We are always invited to major scientific conferences and always chair some of the sessions. Last year our department was awarded a United Nations grant for solar energy development. We are using solar energy to grow algae as a cheap source of protein and carbohydrates. We began working on this project several months ago, but somehow nothing has worked out. I'm on my way to Geneva now to report to the committee, but what can I tell them?

> We have talented graduate students — we only accept the best. We also have an extremely skilled technical staff; and unlike other research institutes, each professor in our department has his own technician. Take my technician Saul

Gardner. Even when I was working on the most complicated problems, I could count on him to carry out the daily experiments, and he learned to operate the equipment and report to me the next day. But now, everything is different. The technicians seem to have suddenly become incompetent, and the project is barely progressing.

The flight arrived before Leigh and Morris could discuss the problem; however, Leigh decided to spend some time at Clearview when he returned to New York.

Background

Clearview is a world-famous institute of scientific research founded by James D. Clearview in 1948. He strongly believed in the promotion of scientific research for the benefit of mankind. It was his specific wish that each professor be granted the utmost academic freedom and that individual research be facilitated in every way.

A relatively small number of scientists and technicians were employed at Clearview in the early 1950s. The institute was organized as a single unit with a very informal structure.

Milt Irving was one of the first Ph.D. students to graduate from Clearview. Charming and brilliant, his advance was unprecedented. His frequent trips and personal contacts with outstanding members of the scientific community increased the institute's prestige. His name attracted many scientists, several of whom joined Clearview solely to collaborate with him. As time went by the institute expanded, ultimately requiring its division into departments. Irving was appointed head of biophysics.

Among those who joined Clearview because of Irving were Sam Morris and Jack Burton. Both proved to be excellent scientists and teachers who devoted most of their time to teaching in the graduate program. This activity did not interfere with their personal research because most of the laboratory work was performed by their technicians.

Impressed by Burton's and Morris's success, Irving decided to delegate to them full authority to manage and supervise their subordinates. Irving maintained his position as active head of the department but limited other responsibilities to his own graduate students and technicians.

In time, Clearview gained international fame. A national survey of scientific research topics revealed that Clearview's competitors had diversified by undertaking numerous applied research projects. A limited number of researchers at Clearview considered similarly diversifying their personal research interests but refrained from doing so mainly because it demanded a change in institutional policy and the restructuring of most existing departments.

The recent snowballing effect of the energy crisis made Irving reevaluate his approach. About one year ago, although initially hesitant, Irving decided to deviate from institutional policy; he applied for and was awarded the solar energy development grant.

The funds made available in the first year were impressive, although the terms of the grant were rigid. While the United Nations committee did not insist on controlling the spending and allocation of its grant, it did require payback of all funds not spent during the first year. Extension of the grant was subject to a review of the initial success of the project.

Department of Biophysics

Walking into Irving's lab at 8:30 one morning, Jonathan Leigh was surprised to meet Ms. Smith, Irving's technician, preparing for an experiment.

Leigh: Are all of you such early birds!

Smith: No, only me! I come in around 7:00 and leave as soon as I finish. I've known Professor Irving since his first day as a graduate student here, twenty-five years ago! I work only for him. My hours are up to me, as long as I get the day's work done.

Ms. Smith's attitude reflects the strong position technicians enjoy at Clearview. Their union is very active, and firing a technician is unheard of. They receive tenure easily, and promotion is based on a seniority system. They are well paid, and many fringe benefits are provided by the local union. However, they do not receive rewards from their direct supervisors.

The scientific staff is comprised of graduate students, junior and senior scientists, and professors. Most graduate students leave the institute upon receiving their degrees.

The junior and senior scientists are promoted according to ability and performance. There are always a large number of applicants for junior staff positions even though their tenure rate is only 1 in 15. Because of this rate, the technicians are reluctant to work for the junior staff, since not only do they consider themselves superior but also they consider the juniors "temporary workers."

When Professor Irving arrived soon after 8:30, he told Leigh that he was very proud to have been awarded the grant. Despite his administrative load and his recent appointment as chairman of the board of directors, he was able to find sufficient time to spend in the laboratory. He loved the atmosphere and sometimes would work together with Ms. Smith. He relied fully upon Morris and Burton to carry out their share of the project. He did not believe in excessive interaction with those who were not his direct subordinates in the department; they were to report to Morris and Burton. The phone rang in Irving's office. When Irving hung up, he smiled and excused himself, explaining that an unexpected meeting of the board was to begin shortly.

Leigh's next stop was Morris's laboratory. Morris was still in Geneva, and Leigh found Gardner in Morris's recliner, reading the daily sports column. Leigh was not surprised by what he saw. He knew that the 10:00 A.M. coffee break was a well-established tradition at Clearview. The local union maintained a subsidized cafeteria that served mainly coffee and snacks. Each morning around 10:00 many of the technicians met in the relatively small lounge to exchange gossip and first-hand information on their research projects. A favorite topic for some time had been that some technicians had recently received a special bonus for their diligence during a recent project in the chemistry department.

The good news had raised the level of expectation among those employed in biophysics. They knew that working on the solar energy project would disrupt their established routine of the 10:00 o'clock break because they were expected to spend all day on the roof. However, they had confidence in their ability to perform well, and they had expected to receive a generous bonus in appreciation of their efforts. Their expectations had been disappointed, and technicians became discontented and hostile and lost all enthusiasm. Burton's and Morris's fre-

quent absences from the laboratory only encouraged the technicians' indifference. Lacking supervision, they showed up and left whenever they pleased. Gardner spoke:

> Ms. Smith told me you would be coming here. Let me show you our algae. We're growing them in containers on the roof. I find the whole thing rather stupid — last year our work was supposed to be free of traces of contamination, and now Morris is growing beasts on the roof! He must be out of his mind! I am really supposed to work all day on the roof, taking samples, etc., but it is actually Green who should be doing all this. He was appointed as my helper, but refuses to accept any orders from me. So for the time being he is doing nothing, and between you and me, neither am I. Morris never told us the real purpose of the whole project and never explained to us our specific tasks. A few days ago I found Ms. Smith taking samples from our containers. She seemed to be doing similar work to what we think we are supposed to be doing. If so, let her at least help us. She always refuses, and I know for a fact that she is hiding and locking all her equipment when she goes home. She belongs to Irving, so to whom can we complain?
>
> Morris never even shows up during the day. He has ordered me to leave the experimental results in his office, and in the morning I always find messages from him on my desk. Actually, even when Morris is in the lab he is hardly to be seen. If he thinks that I will be bullied around by the "baby" graduate students, he is in for a surprise. So, I am enjoying life, not working too hard, I am receiving my salary anyhow — I have tenure — who can fire me?

Gardner's monologue was interrupted by the entrance of Ms. White, Burton's technician.

> *White:* Saul, please help us with the vacuum pump. It's just come back from the workshop but something went wrong again!
>
> *Gardner:* Tell Burton to help you, we don't work for Burton's group. If you think that you can get away with monopolizing the lab you're mistaken. We all know that you double order from the warehouse, and nothing is left in stock when we get there. If you guys are so smart, you can surely fix a simple pump!
>
> *White:* So that's the way you see things. OK, there's nothing left for me to say!

Later in the cafeteria Leigh found himself seated next to Sue Cooper, one of Morris's graduate students. She told Leigh:

> It's not my business to interfere, but I know something is very wrong. I'm not personally involved with this project and all I know is what I see and hear day in and day out. This department has not had a routine staff meeting for months, everyone seems to be busy with the solar energy project, the way Irving wants to carry it out. One or another of the professors seems always to be out of town or even out of the country. None of the technicians seems to be motivated, and I don't blame them. Working on the roof, they have turned into the laughing stock of the whole building! They demand incentives and rewards for "hard labor." I tried to talk to them and to explain the importance of this project to the department and to the institute, but they will not pay attention to a female graduate student. When I discussed the matter with Morris, he told me not to interfere and stick to my own work. Personally, I feel that it would benefit both the department and the project if the whole department became equally involved. We should exchange information and help one another. The truth is that Burton and Morris have independently decided that the project was their baby. As for the graduate students, our work seems good enough for the professors to put their names on the papers we write, but our advice is never taken seriously.

Some weeks later Jonathan Leigh was talking to Morris, who had returned from Geneva. Morris said, "I'm very worried about the fate of this whole project. If we don't start coming up with results soon, our grant will not be extended. Something drastic has to be done immediately."

Case Questions

1. Analyze the effectiveness of the group working on the solar energy development project.
2. What steps should be taken to improve the effectiveness of this group?

Source: From David A. Nadler, Michael L. Tushman, and Nina G. Hatvany, *Managing Organizations: Readings and Cases,* pp. 538–541. Copyright © 1982 by David A. Nadler, Michael L. Tushman, and Nina G. Hatvany. Reprinted by permission of Little, Brown and Company.

CHAPTER 12

Effective Communication in Organizations

David Edwards learned about the importance of clear communication the hard
way.

Edwards is a former senior official in
Citibank's Paris office. One day the Citibank
trader at the Paris stock exchange, the Bourse,
called to inform Edwards that the dollar was
losing ground. Upset by the news, Edwards
yelled a rather common expletive into the
phone and slammed down the receiver so hard
it broke in his hand.

Although the expletive would have been
familiar to most Americans, particularly those
from Texas, where Edwards was raised, it
sounded very much like the French word meaning "to buy."

As the story goes, several moments later
the trader called back on another line to tell
Edwards he had bought dollars.

"You did what?" Edwards shouted.

"But you said *achète* (buy)," replied the
trader.

Later that evening, Edwards reportedly
walked into the office of his boss. "I've got a
funny story to tell you," he said, "but it's going
to cost you a quarter of a million dollars to hear
it."

Source: "The Maverick Who Yelled Foul at Citibank," by
R. Rowan, *Fortune,* January 10, 1983, pp. 46–56.

Chapter Outline

- Effective Communication
- The Communication Process
- Characteristics of Communication
- Barriers to Effective Communication
- Improving Communication Effectiveness

Key Terms

- noise
- feedback loop
- nonverbal communication
- technical communication
- interpersonal communication
- strategic communication
- distortion
- omission
- overload
- timeliness
- acceptance
- slack resources
- self-contained tasks
- gatekeeper
- liaison
- opinion leader
- cosmopolite

Chapter Objectives

After studying Chapter 12 you should be able to

1. Explain why effective communication is so important to managers.
2. Recognize what skills are important in the communications process.
3. Distinguish among the types of communication that take place in an organization.
4. Understand the importance of informal communication in an organization.
5. Recognize the barriers to effective communication and the influences on them.
6. Use several approaches to improving communication effectiveness.

Introduction

The failure to communicate clearly can make the job of the manager and his or her subordinates much more difficult. As we shall see, the ability to communicate effectively is often a major determinant of managerial effectiveness in organizations.

The settings in large organizations make effective communication difficult, however. It is important that managers understand the process of communication and the barriers to effective communication that frequently exist in organizations.

In this chapter we will discuss the nature and the problems of communication in organizations in order to help managers overcome these barriers and improve the effectiveness of communication. Many of the most effective corporations are aware of the importance of effective communication and are experimenting with ways to encourage better communication at all levels. Before discussing the communication process and the barriers that exist in organizations, however, we must consider what is meant by effective communication and why it is so important to managers.

Effective Communication

Definition of Effective Communication

Because it is such an important concept, let us consider what is meant by effective or ineffective communication. In the story about David Edwards at Citibank, the message he intended to convey was misunderstood by the trader. The ineffectiveness was the failure to convey the intended message clearly — which might be expected when someone with a Texas drawl speaks to a European. Thus, effective communication occurs when the message the sender intends to convey is understood accurately by the receiver.

We are not equating effective communication with clear communication in all management situations. Managers often find that there are times when purposely being vague and ambiguous — as distinguished from lying or being openly deceitful — is of some advantage. This may be the case, for example, in difficult negotiations with a supplier or in maintaining the element of surprise in strategic plans.

The importance of completely honest, open, and clear communication often is stressed in management literature and by managers themselves. But it is easy to find instances in which managers have counted on the fact that a message can be interpreted in more than one way. An incident illustrating this point involved General Motors and the United Auto Workers back in the 1930s. It is important to keep in mind that union–management relations were quite different fifty years ago. Moreover, General Motors currently is being praised for its cooperation with the union in introducing change in the organization. Relations between the company and union have not always been as cooperative as they are today, however, as suggested in Cray's history of the corporation (1980, pp. 293–294):

> When 2,000 workers at the Chevrolet transmission factory in (Toledo) . . . walked off in April, 1934, they effectively halted production of the automobile across the country. More than 35,000 workers in other Chevrolet plants were laid off until the Toledo strikers won a four-cents-an-hour wage increase and the unwritten agreement of the corporation not to form a rival company union.
>
> Five months after the workers went back and the flow of transmissions was resumed, the plant shut down, ostensibly for the 1935 model changeover. Plant manager Alfred Gulliver had assured the union that "as many men would be hired by the company as before." Instead, three-quarters of the machines in the plant were shipped to factories in other cities without unions and the Toledo plant dismantled. Gulliver followed his machines to Saginaw, explaining, "but I didn't say *where* the men would be hired."

Few managers would advocate such open deception in dealing with others, particularly their own employees — most managers would admit by their actions, if not their words, that being unclear often has its advantages. In practice, however, effectiveness may be more appropriately viewed as the ability to communicate the *intended* message. Few people would consider effective an executive who put a division of the company up for sale at $3 million and then let a prospective buyer know that the only other bid received was $1.5 million. The issue of deception in business communication is controversial and raises many ethical questions. It is not possible to go into this topic in depth here; those interested in pursuing it might benefit from a two-part series of articles published in the *Harvard Business Review* by Carr (1968) and Blodgett (1968). The second article in particular gives interesting insight into how practicing managers feel about this issue.

Importance of Effective Communication for Managers

Why is the ability to communicate effectively so important to managers? To a large extent, the job of managers *is* communication with others. The popular image of the manager may be one in which difficult decisions are made alone or long hours are spent planning the future strategy of the company. This picture, however, may not accurately reflect the way most managers spend their time. The point is made by Mintzberg (1973, p. 44) in reporting the results of a study of corporate chief executive officers:

> Unlike other workers, the manager does not leave the telephone or the meeting to get back to work. Rather, these contacts *are* his work. The ordinary work of the organization — producing a product, undertaking research, even conducting a study or writing a report — is seldom undertaken by its manager. The manager's productive output can be measured primarily in terms of verbally transmitted information.

Mintzberg (1973) analyzed the ways chief executive officers spent their time at work, which often extended beyond 5 P.M. to include social contacts with a business purpose. He found that 78 percent of their time was spent in communication-related activities that involved direct contact with others. These activities included scheduled meetings, (59 percent), unscheduled meetings (10 percent), telephone calls (6 percent), and tours of facilities (3 percent). Only 22 percent of the chief executive officer's time was spent on what Mintzberg called "desk-work," and much of this involved answering the mail and thus was communication related. Mintzberg found that managers appear to gravitate to activities involving direct communication with others, considering them of much greater value and interest than more routine activities.

Although Mintzberg's study was conducted among managers at the top of the corporation, it would be incorrect to assume that the activities of lower-level managers differ a great deal. Estimates of the amount of time spent in face-to-face communication vary from 59 percent for supervisors to 89 percent for middle managers (Mintzberg, 1973). Another description of what it is like to be a manager at a large corporation is summarized in Feature 12.1. Consistent with the findings of other studies, the activities of the typical manager were oriented heavily toward communication with others (Kanter 1977). The major conclusion that emerges from research on managerial activities is that managers at all levels of the corporation spend considerable time in communication. Moreover, time spent in these activities may be crucial to organizational effectiveness.

In a study of the best-managed companies in the United States, Peters and Waterman (1982) reported that the most effective firms were characterized by high levels of informal communication. In their words, "the intensity of communications is unmistakable in the excellent companies" (Peters and Waterman, 1982, p. 122). They also found that these companies consciously established management philosolphies that encouraged greater communication, or made changes in the physical layout of the workplace to increase opportunities for interaction. At Hewlett-Packard a philosophy of "management by walking around" encourages managers to leave their desks and talk with other managers, engineers, or shop floor employees. The Weyerhaeuser Company uses an open-space office design throughout its corporate headquarters, even on the executive floor where George Weyerhaeuser and his top managers work. Corning Glass designed its engineering building with escalators instead of elevators to increase chances for face-to-face interaction, and Intel designed its new buildings with many small conference rooms to encourage managers to get together for informal meetings. There is strong evidence that highly effective firms not only recognize the importance of increased comunication among their employees, but actually encourage it.

Although opportunities for communication are important, we must also consider *what* gets communicated — the quality of interaction. No matter how many times he or she comes into contact with others, even the most capable and innovative manager is unlikely to perform well without being able to communicate ideas effectively. Because managers are unlikely to take part in the routine daily activities of the organization, they must be able to communicate effectively

Feature 12.1
What's It Like to be a Manager in a Large Organization?

Folklore and myth surround the nature of the manager's role in organizations.

Although the manager is popularly portrayed as working alone in his or her office late at night, making hard decisions or planning for the future, reality often is quite different. Most managers do work long hours, but they are more likely to be in meetings with others than working alone. In an in-depth study of a major corporation, Rosabeth Moss Kanter observed that managers spent 30 to 55 percent of their time in meetings. This percentage does not include time spent talking with secretaries, on the telephone, or in routine communication around the office.

The managers she studied reported spending considerable time responding to superiors' demands for communication. They often felt that these demands were irritating and a distraction from more important tasks. Because the corporation was large and geographically dispersed, telegrams often were sent, sometimes to the manager's home.

In addition, time was spent entertaining higher-level managers on their periodic inspection trips. "You have to be there when these cats, the heavies, the dignitaries, fly through and say, 'I want to spend a day with your people at Blump-te-de-Blump.' And they come through and sit down in your office, from the corporate vice-president on down" (p. 57). One manager estimated that he spent nine days on entertainment, not including business lunches, during one quarter of the year.

Because of the demands on managers, Kanter found, communication with others had to be rapid. In addition, there was a great need for communication to be accurate, because others depended on the information being sent. Even so, managers frequently had to rely on impersonal means and communication channels that involved people they did not know. Thus, it was very important for managers to share a common language and understanding. Because managers simply did not have time to follow through on every communication, the element of trust played a large role in making the system work.

It is not surprising that Kanter found at this corporation, as one would at most, a high degree of homogeneity in the way managers thought and even dressed. Homogeneity facilitated the development of common understandings and predictability in behavior and thus fostered trust. "The structure of communication involved in managerial jobs generated a desire for smooth social relationships and a preference for selection of those people with whom communication would be easiest," observed Kanter (p. 57). She added, "One way to ensure acceptance and ease of communication was to limit managerial jobs to those who were socially homogeneous." The result was that communication often was avoided with those who were different, such as eccentrics or nonconformists. Such people included female managers, who represented a new development in the corporation at the time.

Source: Men and Women of the Corporation, by Rosabeth Moss Kanter, New York: Basic Books, 1977, pp. 55–59.

with people who perform these tasks. It is not sufficient for managers to understand how tasks are to be performed or what changes are needed to improve effectiveness; managers also must be able to communicate their knowledge and ideas to others.

The importance of communication skills in management increasingly is reflected in the number of master's programs in business administration that require coursework in verbal and written communication. The introduction of these courses into the curriculum has been influenced in part by reports from business executives that the technical training students receive seldom is sufficient to guarantee good performance on the job. In addition to technical skills, students must have the ability to communicate and work with others. This ability becomes more important as managers move up in the organization.

The next section of this chapter focuses attention on the communication process and how communication can be analyzed in organizations. Understanding communication and its process is fundamental to our later discussion of barriers to communication and the ways communication can be made more effective.

The Communication Process

Elements of the Process

Communication has been defined by O'Reilly and Pondy (1979, p. 121) as "the exchange of information between a sender and a receiver and the inference of meaning between organizational participants." Although this definition has a specific organizational reference, it could be generalized to a number of non-organizational settings as well. The definition points out that communication is a process through which information is transmitted from one party to another. The exchange of information between a *sender* and a *receiver* is essential for communication.

It is important to recognize, however, that a distinction is being drawn between the information exchanged and the interpretation of this information by the parties. For many reasons, the information the sender wishes to exchange may not be interpreted by the receiver in the manner intended. O'Reilly and Pondy's representation of the communication process (1979) may help to clarify what is involved when two people, or organizations, communicate, and the factors that can influence the interpretation of the message. This model is presented in Figure 12.1.

In discussing this model, it is useful to have an example to highlight various aspects of the process. An episode reported by John Kenneth Galbraith (1981) is appropriate. At the end of World War II, Galbraith was sent to Japan to help assess the impact of strategic bombing on the progress of the war. He had participated in a similar assessment earlier in Germany. While in Japan, Galbraith met with a senior executive of a Japanese business firm who was a prewar friend of a close colleague. The businessman asked Galbraith to intervene with General Douglas MacArthur so that he would be allowed to resume his business of manufacturing radios. When Galbraith pointed out that this might be difficult,

Figure 12.1
The Communication Process

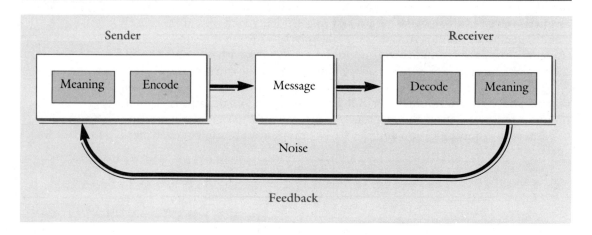

Source: Reprinted, by permission, from C. A. O'Reilly and L. R. Pondy, "Organizational Communication," in S. Kerr, ed., *Organizational Behavior,* p. 136. Copyright © 1979 by John Wiley & Sons, Inc.

in part because of the shortage of necessary materials, the businessman admitted he had been putting aside supplies that had been allocated to the war effort. "Does that mean you foresaw the defeat of Japan?" Galbraith asked. The businessman replied, "No, but we did observe that the victories of our glorious army and navy were occurring ever closer to our home islands" (Galbraith, 1981, p. 234).

The information being exchanged in response to Galbraith's question concerns the businessman's feelings about the likelihood of Japan's defeat in the war. Although it appears that he believed Japan would ultimately lose and that he held back needed war supplies in anticipation, the businessman did not consider it appropriate to say so directly. Thus, the businessman *encoded the meaning* he wished to convey (yes, it appeared the Japanese were losing) into a *message* ("No, but we did observe . . .") that transmitted his feelings in a way uncritical of the Japanese military (". . . the victories of our glorious army and navy . . ."), but made his point inescapable (". . . ever closer to our home islands"). Thus, the businessman created a message that transmitted the meaning he wished to convey in a carefully concealed fashion.

From Galbraith's perspective, this message required *decoding* to determine exactly what was being said. A more straightforward answer to his question would have required very little decoding (yes, things were going badly and it was only a matter of time). The nature of the message sent, however, necessitated some thought before the meaning could become clear. For example, the businessman said he didn't predict Japan's defeat but then pointed out that its "victories" were occurring increasingly close to home. Because successful armies generally advance rather than retreat, the victories would have taken place farther away from Japan if things were going well. Thus, the businessman must have recognized that the army and navy were in retreat, but he was too polite or frightened to say so.

An analysis of this episode suggests that in the communication process, the sender's meaning is encoded into a message that must be decoded by the receiver before the meaning of the message is inferred. Potential problems in the communication process become clear with this analysis. First, the meaning intended by the sender may be improperly encoded, resulting in a message that does not clearly convey the meaning. Second, even if the message is an accurate reflection of the sender's meaning, the receiver may not interpret it properly and thus receive a different message.

Third, the message itself may not be accurately received because of "noise" that exists at the time it is sent. **Noise** in communications is anything besides the message itself that can influence the meaning received. It can range from actual noise that makes the message difficult to hear by the receiver, as in a noisy factory environment, to contextual factors that can change the meaning of what is said. For example, co-workers may interpret an employee's comment about production problems in one way if it is made only to them and in another way if their boss is present. The presence of the boss changes the context of communication. The co-workers may interpret the comment less as an indication of a problem needing their attention and more as an attempt by the employee to impress the boss.

One check on the accuracy with which our messages are received is the **feedback loop** from receiver to sender. This feedback can come in the form of the receiver's behavior as a result of the message or the receiver's comments to the sender, who now reverses roles and serves as the receiver of the feedback. For instance, if in our example Galbraith had replied that Japan's surrender must have come as a terrible shock, the businessman would have received evidence that Galbraith had not really understood what he was trying to say.

Communication Skills

Our description of the communication process suggests that several skills are important for successful communications between individuals. First, the sender must be able to state his or her ideas in a fashion understandable to the receiver. These abilities involve primarily skill in verbal and written communication, but also an understanding of how the context of communication can influence the interpretation of messages. Second, it is important that receivers listen carefully to what is being said. Failure to concentrate fully when communicating with others can result in misunderstanding, because we may not hear all the important points.

Effective listening receives less attention than written and verbal communication skills, although it is clearly crucial if communication effectiveness is to be increased. Even the most carefully stated or written message can be ineffective if the receiver does not give it careful attention. For this reason, the Sperry Corporation has initiated a listening skills training program for its employees. More than 10,000 Sperry employees attended seven-hour seminars designed to enhance listening skills, including understanding, evaluating, interpreting, and responding to what is heard (DiGaentani, 1982).

Characteristics of Communication

It is possible to draw a number of important distinctions among the types of communication that can take place in organizations. Although there are a number of different ways to classify communication, five primary dimensions will be reviewed here. These include the level, method, content, direction, and purpose of the communication.

Level of Communication

Roberts, O'Reilly, Bretton, and Porter (1979) classified communication according to four levels at which it can occur.

Intraindividual. In an individual, messages are sent from sensory organs to the brain. For example, we observe two people sleeping on the job and record a message to initiate a personnel action to reprimand them. The ease with which we can be fooled by what we see suggests that this process is far from perfect. For example, in North Africa during World War II, the Germans often used tractors to drive back and forth across the desert, creating huge clouds of sand that were easily misinterpreted as the mass movement of tanks. While the Allies were concentrating on these clouds of sand and preparing for an attack, the main units of the German army were on the move elsewhere.

Interpersonal. Interpersonal communication takes place between or among two or more individuals. It is perhaps the most common form of communication in organizations, because it includes all communications among employees, including co-workers, and between management and employees. For example, when a manager asks an employee to prepare a report on projected sales for a new product, the request can be classified as an interpersonal communication.

Intraorganizational. These communications take place among different groups or subunits of an organization. The importance of communications among the different parts of the organization can be illustrated by an example. At General Motors in 1968 (Wright, 1979), at the same time that the sales staff was initiating a major promotion of the four-cylinder Chevrolet Nova engine, the manufacturing group had decided to deemphasize production of this model because of poor sales. In fact, machinery had been removed from production of this engine for use in other parts of the plant. When the sales promotion campaign was a success, manufacturing found it lacked the capacity to produce the engines being ordered. The result was that one part of the company could not meet the demand for engines that had been created by another part. Better communication between sales and manufacturing about the promotion campaign for the four-cylinder engine could easily have averted this problem.

Extraorganizational. A number of important types of communication take place among organizations or between an organization and important parts of its environment. For instance, organizations place orders with suppliers or send lobbyists to Washington to influence important legislation. Many types of communication are common among organizations, as when USAir announced that it would not be undersold on tickets. Other types are discouraged by law. When Robert Crandall, president of American Airlines, suggested in a conversation with Braniff President Howard Putnam that a pricing agreement might be considered in the Dallas–Fort Worth market, he clearly was treading on legal thin ice. Had Crandall known that Putnam was taping the telephone conversation, it is doubtful that he would have raised the issue ("Raise Your Fares," 1983).

Method of Communication

Communication among individuals and organizations can take place in a number of different ways, although verbal and written methods are the two most common. Both verbal and written communication are broad categories that include a large number of different vehicles, including the written memo and the company newsletter. A number of important messages are sent in organizations that do not fit easily within these two broad categories, however. A third important category concerns **nonverbal communication,** messages that can be inferred from the behavior or actions of others. A manager may perform a routine task, for example, to model and communicate to employees the correct way to perform on the job.

In the day-to-day operations of organizations, all three methods of communication can play an important role. This fact is illustrated by the events surrounding the firing of Lee Iacocca from the Ford Motor Company. Three important communications concerning this event, presented in chronological order, appear in Figure 12.2. The first message about Iacocca's position at Ford was a nonverbal message about a major reorganization of management. Even though Iacocca's position as president of Ford did not change, the reorganization resulted in his movement from second to fourth in the corporate hierarchy. Perhaps even more significant in its implications concerning Iacocca's future at Ford was the fact that Iacocca was not consulted about the reorganization or even informed that it would take place until shortly before it was to be announced publicly. At this point, Iacocca and many others within the company may have seen the handwriting on the wall. The second message confirmed the impression created by the first. Henry Ford II verbally informed Iacocca that he was fired after thirty-two years with the company. The final message was written and intended to reassure Ford's dealer network that the executives remaining at the company were fully capable of carrying out the company's policies — that is, that Iacocca was dispensable.

Figure 12.2
Examples of Different Methods of Communication

NONVERBAL

In June 1978, Henry Ford II announced a management realignment at the Ford Motor Company. Creating a new office of the chief executive, he named Philip Caldwell as deputy chief executive officer, reporting directly to Ford. William Clay Ford was named chairman of the executive committee, and Henry Ford retained his position as chief executive. Lee Iacocca, president of the Ford Motor Company and formerly Caldwell's superior, suddenly dropped from heir-apparent to fourth in the hierarchy. Iacocca was not informed of the management change until shortly before it was to be announced publicly.

VERBAL

In July 1978, Henry Ford II summoned his brother, William Clay Ford, and Lee Iacocca to his office. The purpose of the meeting was apparent to all parties, and Henry Ford came directly to the point. He told Iacocca, "You're fired." "But why me, Mr. Ford?" Iacocca asked. "I've been with the company for thirty-two years. What did I do wrong?" "Nothing," snapped Ford. "I just don't like you." For the short time he remained in the company, Iacocca was assigned a secluded office in a Ford warehouse.

WRITTEN

On the day Lee Iacocca's so-called resignation from the Ford Motor Company was announced, Henry Ford II sent a personal letter to each of the 6,500 Ford dealers. Because Iacocca had been very popular with the dealers, Ford sought to reassure them about the future. The letter stated: "The company has a strong and experienced management team. Our North American Automotive Operations are headed by talented executives who are well known to you and who are fully attuned to your needs of the retail market."

Source: Lasky, 1981, pp. 208–209, 211, 219.

The importance of nonverbal communication, particularly by those in important leadership positions, has not been fully recognized until recently. Pfeffer (1981), for example, has written about the importance of the symbolic actions of leaders in providing direction to others about the organization's top priorities. The important symbolism of leaders' actions can be seen in two examples involving Charles Revson of Revlon, which we present in Feature 12.2.

The first suggests the symbolic importance of how managers allocate the scarce resource of time. The fact that important managers within Revlon and other company executives found it difficult to reach Revson by phone, whereas ordinary customers got through with little difficulty, clearly signaled to others at Revlon that customer satisfaction was a high priority. Revson might have told his managers the same thing in written memos or at formal meetings, but his words might not have had the impact that his behavior did in making this message clear. The second incident also carries a message. Employees were not to

Feature 12.2
Working at Revlon under Charles Revson

What was it like to work at Revlon under its founder, Charles Revson? What were the important priorities within the company, and how were employees expected to behave?

These issues might have been discussed at employee orientation sessions, if these were conducted, or stated in the employee handbook. But two incidents associated with Revson's behavior communicated a more powerful impression to employees. Both incidents suggest how executives in organizations can communicate with employees through their actions.

Incident 1

One indication of the important priorities in a company can be found in the way busy executives allocate their scarce time. It was widely known at Revlon that bank presidents and advertising executives could not get through to Charles Revson on the phone. A woman having problems with one of the company's products, however, had no difficulty in reaching him.

To demonstrate this to some skeptical advertising executives, a Revlon manager arranged for a secretary to call Revson's office and explain that she had bought a Revlon lipstick that bled and was too soft. As predicted, Revson came right to the telephone, inquiring about the batch number of the lipstick and where it was purchased. Revson talked with her about the appropriate color dress to wear with that particular lipstick and arranged for the customer relations department to send her a sample of other Revlon products. For managers at Rev-

lon, there could be little question about the importance of customer satisfaction with the company's products.

Incident 2

Because Revson was concerned about employees' coming to work late, he required everyone to sign in when they arrived in the morning. One morning when Revlon was in the process of moving into its new offices in the General Motors Building, Revson walked into the building and looked at the sign-in sheet. The receptionist, who was new on the job, had been instructed that no one was to take the sheet. The following dialogue took place between the receptionist and Revson:

"I'm sorry, sir, you can't do that," the receptionist said.

"Yes, I can," replied Revson.

"No, sir," she said. "I have strict orders that no one is to remove the list. You'll have to put it back."

After several minutes of this, Revson finally asked, "Do you know who I am?"

"No, sir, I don't," she replied.

"Well, when you pick up your final paycheck this afternoon, ask 'em to tell ya."

The message to other employees about how to act toward Revson was clear. It is easy to imagine that the climate within Revlon at the time was not one in which employees felt comfortable confronting Revson or openly disagreeing with his decisions.

Source: Adapted from pp. 38–39, 98–99 in *Fire and Ice: The Story of Charles Revson,* by Andrew Tobias. Copyright © 1975, 1976 by Andrew Tobias. By permission of William Morrow & Company.

question Revson under any circumstances, even if they did so only in the process of effectively performing their jobs. It is imaginable that word of the receptionist's firing spread through the company quickly and that most employees clearly understood its implications for their own behavior. Because actions often speak louder than words, the force of this message was much greater than it would have been had it been communicated by other means.

Content of Communication

Another approach to analyzing communication is to draw distinctions based on its content or the nature of the message. Following the conceptual model presented in Chapter 1, communications can be classified according to type of content as technical, interpersonal (behavioral), and strategic. **Technical communication** refers primarily to instructions, policies, and procedures related to the performance of jobs in the organization. **Interpersonal communication** may or may not be directly job related. For example, interpersonal communication may range from praise from managers for a job well done to inquiries about the health of the employee's family. Finally, **strategic communications** involve the future direction and goals of the organization, as well as information relating to the external environment. Where is the company heading in the next five years, and how does it intend to get there? These three types of communication content are summarized in Figure 12.3, together with the different methods of communication discussed earlier. By superimposing different methods of communication on the three types of content, we can see that the same message can be communicated in several different ways.

Because organizations are goal directed, much of the formal and informal communication that takes place is related to work that needs to be performed. It is important to recognize, however, that many communications in organizations also are directed toward maintaining social relationships and may have less direct relevance to job performance. Employees in a work group, for example, may spend considerable time discussing the issues in elections or the outcomes of important sporting events. Although these communications are less directly

Figure 12.3
Common Forms and Types of Managerial Communication

NATURE OF MESSAGE	METHOD OF COMMUNICATION		
	Verbal	*Written*	*Behavioral*
Technical	Personally instructing employees in how to perform a task	Providing written job description or procedures	Modeling the correct way for employees to perform a task or interact with customers
Interpersonal	Stopping employees in the hall to tell them they have been doing a good job	Providing written commendation on employee performance for the personnel file	Inviting an employee to join a group of managers for lunch
Strategic	Addressing assembled managers to announce corporate goals and major changes	Providing a statement of goals and values in annual report or company newsletter	Allocating scarce time among competing activities and demands

relevant to work, it would be a mistake to underestimate their importance to the organization.

Social relationships help bind individuals to the organization, can be important in building organizational commitment, and may provide more effective communication channels when there is a need to transmit important job-related information. Although it is probably true that too much social communication can divert the employees' attention from the work that needs to be done, some communication of this type serves an important purpose in building more cohesive co-worker relations.

Direction of Communication

The hierarchical way in which most organizations are designed suggests that communication can flow in three directions: upward, downward, and laterally. Although each communication direction can serve multiple purposes, each has a primary function. **Horizontal communication** generally is used for coordinating efforts across employees or work groups in the performance of tasks. In the General Motors example we discussed earlier, horizontal communication between sales and manufacturing might have helped ensure that the engine being promoted by advertising would be available in sufficient quantity to meet customer demand, or at least that someone would be alerted that a potential problem existed.

Downward communication transmits information about the goals of the organization or specific directions about tasks to be performed. For instance, managers may inform their employees of the need to increase production of a certain product line. The primary purpose of **upward communication** in organizations is to provide feedback on the performance of the company's different operational parts. Production and sales reports may be communicated to upper-level managers, for example, to keep them informed about whether important goals are being met.

Downs (1967) has estimated that horizontal communication is the most frequent in organizations, partly because employees often feel more comfortable interacting with their peers than with either superiors or subordinates. Even so, there is evidence that individuals are more likely to initiate interaction with those of higher status (Bales, 1953). Upward communications, however, often are stressful and more formal. It also has been found that upward communication in organizations, because it often involves performance feedback, is frequently characterized by the distortion and omission of important information. Subordinates simply may fear the consequences of communicating negative information to superiors, although they probably wouldn't hesitate to offer positive information. Problems associated with upward communication often have disastrous consequences, a fact recognized by many managers.

When Michel Bergerac took over Revlon after Revson died, he initiated monthly meetings in which key operations managers give performance reports. An important part of the conference room in which these meetings are held is a

large screen used for projecting the financial information of the business being
discussed. As Bergerac suggests, "People who used to tell you how fantastically
they are doing change their tune rapidly when the numbers are right there. Now
the words match the music" (Morrison, 1981, p. 74).

Szilagyi (1981) ranked the effectiveness of different upward and downward
communication techniques based on a review of the literature. His rankings are
presented in Figure 12.4. The relative effectiveness of informal discussions and
small group meetings noted by Szilagyi is consistent with the results of the study
by Peters and Waterman (1982) of the most effective firms in the United States.
As discussed earlier in this chapter, they found that these firms took unusual
steps to encourage informal, small group meetings among employees. Szilagyi's
analysis also suggests that more impersonal and formal methods of communication, such as employee newsletters and annual reports, are less effective.

Purpose of Communication

The final basis on which we can classify communication in organizations is
its purpose. Scott and Mitchell (1976) identified several important purposes of
communication. First, communications can be intended to control the behavior
of others, to clarify duties, and to establish or reinforce authority relationships
within the organization. The management review meetings Bergerac has initiated at Revlon are probably viewed by managers as an attempt to exert tight
control over their activities and performance. Second, communications can
provide information on which to base important decisions. From Bergerac's
perspective, his meetings with managers may be intended less to control than to

Figure 12.4
Rankings of the Effectiveness of Upward and Downward
Communication Techniques

RANK	UPWARD COMMUNICATION TECHNIQUE	RANK	DOWNWARD COMMUNICATION TECHNIQUE
1	Informal discussions	1	Small group meetings
2	Meetings with supervisors	2	Direct organizational publication
3	Attitude surveys	3	Supervisory meetings
4	Grievance procedures	4	Mass meetings
5	Counselling	5	Letters to employees' homes
6	Exit interviews	6	Bulletin boards
7	Talks with union representatives	7	Pay envelope inserts
8	Formal meetings	8	Public address system
9	Suggestion boxes	9	Posters
10	Employee newsletter	10	Annual reports, manuals, media advertising

Source: Adapted from Szilagyi, 1981, p. 384. Reprinted by permission.

provide good information about operations. Third, communications can be used to motivate employees and elicit their cooperation and commitment. Corporations often assemble key managers to hear a speech by the chief executive officer. These meetings provide the chance to transmit important information about the corporation. They also can be used to motivate managers and secure their cooperation in pursuit of corporate objectives. Finally, communications often are used to express emotions or feelings about decisions or the actions of others inside and outside the company.

Because the specific purpose of a communication usually is unclear, misunderstanding can decrease its effectiveness. For example, a manager may mention an important product innovation made by a competitor because it represents information his or her subordinates should have. The subordinates receiving this information, however, may interpret the manager's message as a negative comment about their own performance. In the example used at the beginning of this chapter, Edwards's comment to the trader was merely intended to express an emotion about news that the dollar was declining. The trader thought the comment had a very different purpose, however.

Barriers to Effective Communication

A number of barriers to effective communication can exist in organizations. Their source lies in the characteristics of the organization and in individuals and their relationships. It is important to understand the immediate barriers to effective communication and how they arise in organizations. These relationships are summarized in Figure 12.5.

Types of Barriers

Steers (1981) identified five important barriers to effective communication in organizations which are representative of some of the problems that can occur.

Distortion. Communication **distortion** can be intended and unintended in organizations. The example from union–management relations at General Motors in the 1930s suggests that managers sometimes purposely distort communications. Distortion also can occur unintentionally, however, because messages are altered as they pass through communication channels. A message initiated at the level of the production supervisor, for example, may be quite different when it reaches a vice-president for production, because it has passed through a number of managers en route. Each manager receiving the message may interpret it differently or focus on different aspects before passing it along to a superior. Moreover, valuable content may be lost or subtle complexities may become less apparent as messages are condensed for transmission to others. The result is that messages sent may be quite different from messages received.

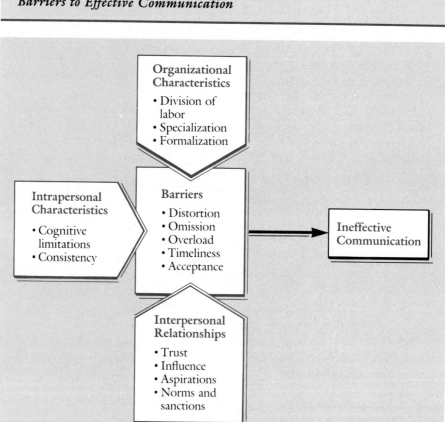

Figure 12.5
Barriers to Effective Communication

This problem becomes more pronounced when the initial message itself is unclear or imprecisely stated.

Omission. **Omission** is the transmission of only part of a larger message. When complex messages are condensed or summarized for transmission to others, for example, important parts of the original message may be eliminated. Omission also may occur when the information being sent is not entirely favorable. Because people fear punishment, they may omit information that reflects poorly on their own performance or that is likely to anger the receiver. Such an omission was evident in an incident that occurred when the Russian Tsar Peter III was deposed by his wife, who was to become Catherine the Great. When the young tsar first learned of his wife's intention to take the throne, he ordered his Holstein guards to set up their cannons for his personal protection. Although the guards did exactly as ordered, out of fear they neglected to mention that they

---

Feature 12.3
In Negotiation, Principle Is In

There's a new atmosphere in labor disputes called "principled negotiation." It replaces unprincipled skulduggery.

The new method is being applied by business, the government, and unions to other areas as well, including breach-of-contract allegations, patent infringement arguments, and even the location of waste disposal sites. The philosophy is simple: Instead of trying to defeat the other side, negotiators sit down with them, try to understand their needs, and deal fairly and openly. Instead of a win-lose situation, a win-win solution is the goal.

The Conflict Clinic in Cambridge, Massachusetts, a nonprofit mediation service set up by three universities, is helping a large foreign corporation and its union settle a seven-year dispute that centered on a round-the-clock shift schedule. The clinic got them to stop rehashing the old arguments and to talk about their common interests. After a while they discovered there were other ways for the company to achieve its productivity goals and for the union to gain work schedules that didn't disrupt family life.

Under this system, it's helpful if both sides use the same guidelines during negotiations. Before their contract talks, Dayton Power and Light Company and the Utility Workers of America called in Stephen Schlossberg, former general counsel of the United Auto Workers, to run seminars on how to negotiate.

The resulting negotiations were long and hard, but each side understood the other. Each also learned to catch the meaning of body language so people knew when it was time to ease up or take a break.

But principled negotiation is far from a "let it all hang out" system of total honesty. There's some disagreement about what the principles are.

"It's OK to mislead the other side as to your intentions," says Theodore Kheel, a veteran New York City labor negotiator. "You can say I'm not going to give in, and then give in five minutes later. But never give the other side misinformation about the facts."

Other negotiators use fatigue as a weapon to wear down the other side, or anger to shake them up. But fatigue and anger can backfire. Patience, however, is always a virtue.

If one side resorts to dirty tricks, the other should make it clear that the trick has been seen, but it should not strike back, say Roger Fisher, director of the Harvard Negotiation Project, and his colleague William Ury.

If your adversary puts you in a chair that leaves your chin at the table level so that you feel like a child, say, "I assume we're switching chairs tomorrow," according to Fisher and Ury.

Source: "How to be a Better Negotiator," by Jeremy Main, *Fortune*, September 19, 1983, pp. 141–146.

---

had no cannon balls (Lincoln, 1981). Catherine the Great had a long and illustrious reign.

Overload. When too much information is received, good decisions become more difficult. It becomes impossible to sort through and make sense of all the information available. Major issues may become lost in the process, and poorer decisions may result. Communication **overload** occurs when information intended for decision makers is merely passed along without being adequately condensed and summarized. Some managers insist that all memos submitted by subordinates be limited to one page. At Procter & Gamble, one brand manager submitted recommendations on strategy that ran to one-and-a-quarter pages. It was rejected as too long. The one-page memo has become a tradition at this company, as suggested by retired chairman Edward Harness: "A brief written presentation that winnows fact from opinion is the basis for decision making around here" (Peters and Waterman, 1982, p. 151).

Timeliness. A major problem occurs in organizations when critical information is not received in time to act on it. If communication channels are too slow and cumbersome, messages may take too long to travel from the sender to the receiver. The receiver is then left with insufficient time to act on the message, or the decisions are made before the information actually arrives. Steers (1981) suggests that messages sent too far in advance of an important decision or deadline also can pose problems; the importance of the information may become lost in the intervening time. Thus, the **timeliness** with which information is received can be critical for communication effectiveness.

Acceptance. The final potential communication barrier can be illustrated by an incident involving Henry Kissinger when he was secretary of state. He asked a bright new member of his staff to prepare a briefing paper. Because the staff member was new on the job, he labored day and night on the draft, which was submitted to Kissinger. The paper came back immediately with a note from Kissinger saying, in effect, "Can't you do better than this?" Because there were no other comments, the staff member was not sure what to do. He redrafted the paper and the process was repeated. When the staff member completed the third draft, he wrote a note that said he was sure the paper was not perfect, but it was the best job he could do. Back came a note from Kissinger saying, "If this is the best job you can do, now I'll read it."

The point of this incident is that a communication cannot be effective unless it is accepted and read by the receiver. Information often is disregarded because the source is considered noncredible or the topic unimportant at the time. Unless there is **acceptance,** there is little chance that the information will be acted on or that the message will have its intended effect.

Influences on Barriers

Barriers to effective communication in organizations are created for a wide variety of reasons. These influences will be summarized in terms of three general categories, organizational and intrapersonal characteristics and interpersonal relations (see Fig. 12.5). An extensive discussion of each category is not possible, because of the complexity of these issues, but we will highlight each in a brief discussion.

Organizational Characteristics. Several characteristics of organizational structure have important implications for communications between individuals and groups. Large organizations typically are highly specialized and formal. For example, their structure may be functional, grouping employees into areas such as marketing, production, and accounting. Structure affects the ease of communication; communication within subunits of the organization generally is easier, and communication between subunits more problematic. For instance, marketing employees may spend a great deal of time interacting with one another, if only because they are located in the same part of the company and they have common goals and problems. Communication between marketing and production employees may be more limited, however.

Identification with a particular functional area, such as marketing, also may cause employees to view the world differently, and they may even use a different jargon. So when organizational problems arise, marketing employees will interpret them from a marketing perspective, often with little thought to their implications for other areas (Dearborn and Simon, 1958). Because production people may have the same tendency, little consensus may be possible between the two areas about the cause or resolution of a problem.

Another aspect of organization structure with important implications for communication patterns is the degree of formalization. Organizations with highly formalized policies and procedures may specify the communication channels that employees are expected to use. Employees may be told not only to whom a specific piece of information should be communicated, but also how the communication should take place. For example, feedback on the performance of an operational unit may be required by the divisional manager in a formal report submitted through channels.

When organizations operate in a stable environment and operations generally are routine, formal communication channels may be sufficient to transmit information to higher-level decision makers. Formal channels may prove too slow and cumbersome, however, when problems requiring immediate action occur. Lengthy communication channels also increase the possibility that information will be distorted or important items omitted in successive review and summary. As suggested earlier, many managers find that they can be more effective by establishing informal lines of communication to supplement the more formal channels (Peters and Waterman, 1982).

The hierarchical structure of most organizations also creates status and authority differences that can influence communication patterns. Employees may be discouraged from communicating with those higher in status and authority because of infrequent contact or the necessity of getting through "closed doors" and past overly protective secretaries before appointments in the distant future can be scheduled. Busy managers always on the run from one meeting to the next often give the impression of not wanting to communicate with employees, even if this is not their intention. In addition to having access problems, employees may be very careful about what is communicated to superiors, particularly when reward systems are closely tied to performance. Status and authority differences, whether real or perceived, may boost the chances that communication distortion and omission will occur in organizations.

Organizational structure can have significant impact on communication among employees. It is important to keep the information processing needs of the organization in mind when considering different structural arrangements (Galbraith, 1973). Most organizations don't do this as well as they could.

Feature 12.4
Management Heads for the Shop Floor

Visitors to Apple Computer's headquarters are likely to wonder why many of the company's employees are wearing large badges labeled WAM. Code name for new computer? Hardly. The initials stand for Walk Around Management and reflect Chairman Steven Jobs' effort to preserve the entrepreneurial atmosphere that contributed to Apple's success.

With 4,500 employees on his payroll, Jobs no longer knows everyone on a first-name basis. That's why Jobs makes it a point to wander around, asking individuals about their work. "It's easy for technical companies to get hung up on technology and forget that people make things happen," explains Jay Elliot, the company's director of human resources.

There's nothing new about this. IBM's Tom Watson, Jr. and Hewlett-Packard's William Hewlett are legendary for walking plant floors. Edward Carlson, the retired chairman of United Air Lines and another proponent of being seen, calls the approach "visible management." H-P terms it Management By Wandering Around.

With today's emphasis on entrepreneurial skills and Japanese-style motivation, walk-around managers are more common than ever. Obviously, pressing the flesh with lower-level staffers can improve morale. Many floorwalkers also feel the practice prevents the growth of burdensome layers of bureaucracy.

But there may be a more important reason for breaking the conventional chain of command. "Management faces lots of problems if executives don't talk to and listen to employees," says Jack Reichert, chief executive of Brunswick Corp. "You learn a lot

more by getting out than you ever do by looking at numbers in your office."

Reichert, who recently broke off a tour of three Florida plants to play volleyball with employees, recalls a meeting at a Wisconsin plant where an assembly worker complained that it was too cold in the factory to do her job. A vice-president of manufacturing pooh-poohed the remark. Then Reichert showed up for an unannounced plant tour with the executive in charge. "We got to the area near a shipping dock where it was so cold you needed gloves," he recalls. "I said, 'Fix this right now.' It cost us a couple of thousand dollars. But all of a sudden productivity went up, and I was believable.". . .

Other executives believe it is so important to get out into the field that they do so on a scheduled basis. Greyhound Chairman John Teets tries to spend at least one day each week in the field. Sam Walton, Wal-Mart's founder and chairman, aims to visit up to a dozen stores weekly.

Stuart Buchalter, CEO at California-based Standard Brands Paint, takes this a step further. When he considers an acquisition, he asks managers below the executive level to look at the company he is about to buy. "Before we acquired a 22-store chain last year," he explains, "I had store managers and supervisors climb all over it. Many of their suggestions were implemented immediately, and it made the deal more of a 'we're doing it' than a 'they're doing it' proposition.". . .

Source: Forbes, August 29, 1983, "Where's the Boss? Taking a Walk," by John A. Byrne, p. 62. Reprinted by permission. © Forbes Inc., 1983.

Intrapersonal Characteristics. In addition to the characteristics of the organization, the characteristics of individual employees can influence communication barriers. People have limited capabilities when it comes to processing information and making decisions. Simon (1976) introduced the concept of "bounded" rationality in discussing the limitations placed on decision makers by their skills and intellectual abilities, value and belief systems, and knowledge of relevant information. These limitations mean that objectively rational decisions seldom are possible in organizations. From a communications perspective, the limitations are important because they suggest that managers do not always pay attention to a complete message, particularly when it is long and complex. Instead, managers may focus on what they consider several key points, ignoring other valuable information. Their general values and beliefs also may serve to filter information.

Research by Staw (1981) and his colleagues suggests another way in which the cognitive information-processing characteristics of managers can influence their judgments and their reactions to communications. This research focuses on the tendency of individuals to become committed to a course of action, persisting even after things do not work out as intended. For example, a manager who has invested considerable resources in a division may invest additional resources despite information that the investment is not paying off. Even though such behavior appears to be a case of throwing good money after bad, the manager may feel that reversing course may be an admission of earlier bad judgment. This tendency may be especially great when managers feel personally responsible for the earlier decision and their involvement is widely known to others. People generally strive for consistency in their actions and between their actions and beliefs. Thus, when information is communicated that is inconsistent with prior actions or beliefs, it may not receive the same attention as consistent information.

Interpersonal Relationships. The nature of the relationship between two parties to a communication also has the potential to create barriers to effectiveness. O'Reilly (1978) has identified four interpersonal variables that he believes are closely associated with the probability that accurate communication will take place. First, the level of trust between the sender and the receiver is important. When the sender does not trust the receiver, more sensitive information may be withheld. When the receiver does not entirely trust the sender, information received may be discounted or, in extreme cases, simply not believed. Second, the influence of the receiver over the sender or the sender over the receiver can have important implications. As suggested earlier, subordinates may be more careful about what is communicated to superiors in organizations. When those communicating are higher in status, there may be a greater tendency to believe the communication, and greater attention may be given to the information being transmitted. Third, *mobility aspirations* of the sender can cause information to be filtered. Employees who strongly desire promotion and advancement may hesitate to transmit negative information, or they may communicate it in such a way as to make it appear that others are at fault.

Finally, O'Reilly suggests that the norms and sanctions operating within the group may dictate how, when, and what information is communicated. Norms define what is considered appropriate communication behavior. Many organizations make a concerted effort to establish norms that foster open communication, such as the open-door policy for managers at Tandem Computers or the "management by wandering around" system at Hewlett-Packard. Moreover, some organizations have attempted to increase the entrepreneurial tendencies of their managers by creating an environment in which taking risks and failing are not associated with negative consequences. As Peters and Waterman (1982, p. 209) point out, "the only way of assuring more 'hits' is to increase the number of 'at bats.' " This is done by providing greater opportunities for individual initiative and showing a tolerance for failure. Managers then can feel free to transmit negative information without undue risk of punishment.

Improving Communication Effectiveness

At this point you may be wondering if it is possible to have an effective communication system in organizations. The answer, of course, is yes. A variety of suggestions have been made about how to improve effectiveness, ranging from general prescriptions about organizational design to more specific suggestions to improve transmission of messages between individuals. Strategies for improving communication effectiveness will be discussed at three levels. First, the broad implications of organizational design for effective communication will be considered. Second, the roles of individual organization members will be discussed from a communications perspective. Finally, some specific suggestions will be presented for transmitting messages more effectively in organizations.

Implications for Organizational Design

A number of factors are involved in decisions about organizational design. Galbraith (1973) has suggested that the information-processing needs of the organization are an important consideration that often is given insufficient attention. He looked at organizations in terms of the amount of information that must be processed and communicated to decision makers. Information-processing needs arise from the diversity of the organization's products or services, the diversity of inputs, the technological processes and technical skills required to produce these outputs, and the difficulty of achieving the organization's goals. All organizations need to process information in the performance of their tasks, and this need increases with the uncertainty of the organization's environment. For example, the rapidly changing nature of the computer industry suggests that a computer firm must process information in a more timely fashion than a company routinely manufacturing machine parts.

Faced with the need to process information, organizations can pursue one of two strategies. First, organizations can attempt to reduce the need to process information by creating slack resources or self-contained tasks. **Slack resources** are resources beyond those required to perform the task efficiently. The time scheduled to fill a customer's order can be increased, for example, to allow for problems that may arise. In **self-contained tasks,** all the resources required to perform the task are placed in a single unit. In the production of a car, units might be designed around major components, such as the engine, drive train, and chassis. Because all the required resources are centralized, the need to communicate with those outside the unit is minimized. Coordination among the units becomes important, however.

The second strategy organizations can pursue is to increase their capacity and ability to process information. Galbraith (1973) suggests that this can be done through improved vertical information systems and more effective lateral relations. The rapid development of computers and office automation has increased the availability of information and the speed with which it can be transmitted to decision makers. The creation of more effective lateral relations involves moving decisions down to the point at which the information exists rather than bringing them up to the level at which decisions usually are made in the organization. This can be done without taking the more extreme step of creating self-contained units. Instead, procedures can be instituted that increase the interaction among those who have a common problem to be solved. For example, task forces can be created that include representatives from different units, or individuals can be assigned the role of coordinating groups.

The important point here is that an organization's information-processing and communication needs must be assessed carefully when making decisions about organizational design. Rather than trying to discover how to circumvent cumbersome and awkward structures, organizations must be designed with increased attention to communications needs. This task involves careful assessment of what information is crucial to the effective performance of tasks, who in the organization needs access to this information, in what form the information is needed, and when it is needed to support important decisions. As a general design principle, it can be argued that those with the greatest need to communicate should be placed in the same units of the organization. Proximity greatly facilitates communication, and identifying the most crucial communication linkages in the organization can be valuable in deciding where individuals should be placed.

Implications for Communication Roles

An organization can be thought of as a system of interdependent roles filled by individuals. Most often, these roles are defined in terms of tasks to be performed, such as the role of accounts receivable clerk or shipping supervisor. Although the division of labor and task specialization are important considerations, it also is important to consider the different communication roles people play in organizations. Viewing organizational roles from a communications perspective can help identify important communication linkages and suggest ways to increase effectiveness.

Four primary communication roles suggested by Rogers and Agarwala-

Rogers (1976) are summarized in Figure 12.6. A **gatekeeper** in a communication network controls the flow of messages and information. The executive assistant to the chief executive officer of the corporation, for example, may decide which messages get passed along to him or her and which do not. The assistant also may condense and summarize messages before passing them along. Such individuals also may control the chief executive officer's calendar, deciding who gets an appointment and for how long. Gatekeepers therefore perform the important function of filtering and screening information.

The **liaison** provides a communication link between two or more groups and facilitates the exchange of information. The person acting in this role may not be a member of either group but, instead, encourages the flow of information and coordinates the actions of the groups involved. The **opinion leader** often serves in an informal capacity and has a highly influential position within a group. Opinion leaders may exert a great deal of influence over group decisions because others look to this person for advice. He or she may be very knowledgeable about the feelings of group members on important issues as a result of extensive communication with others. As a consequence, opinion leaders are an important source of information about the group and are in a strategic position to disseminate information coming into the group.

Finally, **cosmopolites** link the organization or group with its external environment. They interact extensively with people or groups outside the organization. They serve the valuable function of gathering important information from the environment and also may act as spokespersons for the organization to external groups. Corporate lobbyists, for example, keep executives informed about important legislation being considered by Congress and may communicate directly with members of Congress to influence legislation on the organization's behalf.

It is important to recognize that communication roles often exist in organizations without the specific intent of management. Informal group leaders emerge and become opinion leaders, with or without the organization's blessing. Recognizing the important role such individuals play in organizations, however, often can help the manager improve communication effectiveness. Managers who know the identity of opinion leaders may find them to be a valuable informal source of information about the attitudes and opinions of employees, as well as a credible route for disseminating information.

Some people who are strategically placed in communication networks may become gatekeepers to enhance their personal power and position in the organization. When this occurs, serious disruption of communication flow can result, and management must take corrective action. It is important for managers to be selective in placing people in strategic gatekeeping positions and to be sensitive to their acting as gatekeepers even when this is not their intended role. Because the communication roles of liaison and cosmopolite are so important for overall organizational effectiveness, managers must be sure that people in these positions have good communication skills. Individuals who have difficulty establishing good interpersonal relations should not be given these positions; they can do more harm than good.

Figure 12.6
Individual Communication Roles in Organizations

Gatekeeper

An individual who is located in a
communication structure so as to
control the messages flowing through
a communication channel

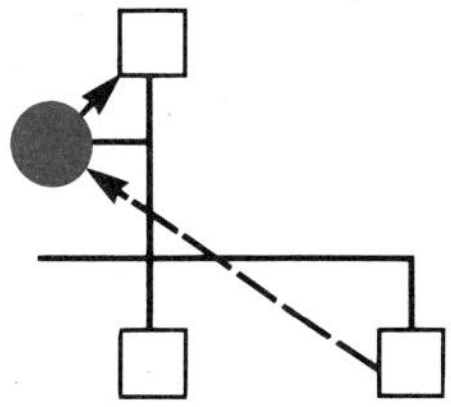

Liaison

An individual who interpersonally
connects two or more cliques within
a system, without himself belonging
to any clique

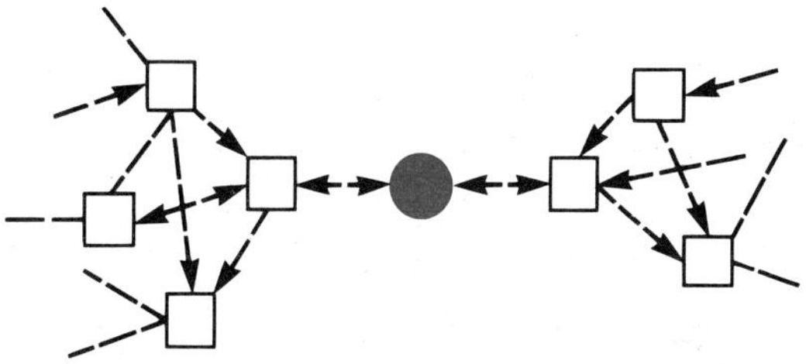

Opinion Leader

An individual able to informally
influence other individuals'
attitudes or overt behavior with
relative frequency

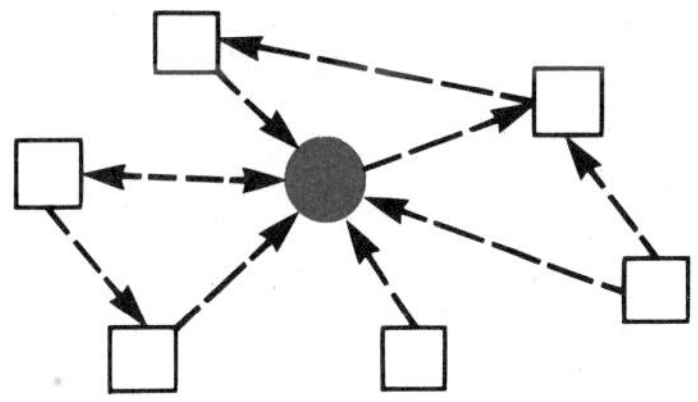

Cosmopolite

An individual who has a relatively
high degree of communication with
the system's environment

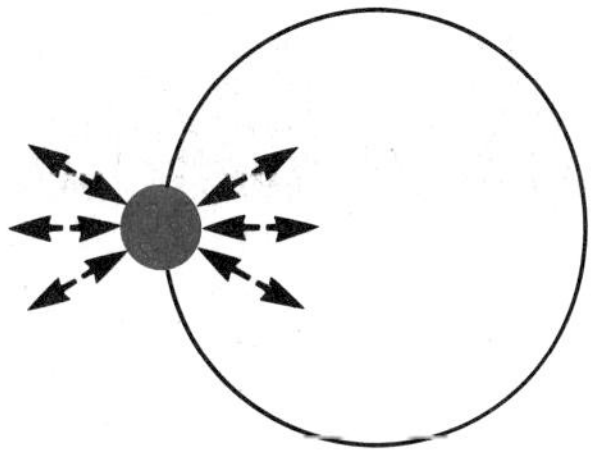

Source: Reprinted with permission of The Free Press, a division of Macmillan, Inc., from *Communication in
Organizations* by Everett M. Rogers and Rekka Agarwala-Rogers. Copyright © 1976 by The Free Press.

Managers assessing and improving communication must look at organizational roles from a communications perspective. Like other roles in an organiza-

Feature 12.5
Establishing Better Communication with Subordinates

The question of how to establish better communication between a manager and his or her subordinates is important but difficult to answer.

One suggestion comes from Andrew S. Grove, president of Intel Corporation, a company that sells computer memory devices and microprocessors. Grove has implemented regular "one-on-one" meetings with his immediate subordinates at Intel. These meetings are scheduled on a regular basis to exchange information. Problems may be discussed, but the meetings are designed to let him talk more generally with subordinates about their jobs and the business. Grove identified several guidelines that have proved useful to him in establishing these meetings.

How often should they be scheduled? This depends on the subordinate. New employees or those new to a particular job may benefit from weekly meetings. More experienced employees may require one every several weeks.

How long should the meeting last? Grove recommends a minimum of one hour. Less time may cause subordinates to stay away from difficult and complex issues.

Where should the meeting take place? Meetings take place in the subordinate's office. This provides the manager with valuable information about how subordinates work, such as whether they are organized.

Who controls the agenda? One-on-ones should be considered the subordinates's meeting. The subordinates prepare agendas and submit them to Grove in advance, forcing them to think through what will be covered and giving Grove advance warning about what is to be discussed. On a practical level, Grove points out that the practice saves the manager from preparing many agendas if he or she has many subordinates.

What should be discussed? Anything of managerial importance arising since the last meeting can be covered, including performance figures, hiring problems, and future plans. Time also should be available to dis-

tion, it is important to monitor communications roles to ensure that information is flowing effectively.

Improving Communication

A number of specific suggestions can be made to improve communication effectiveness in organizations. Several suggestions made by a leading corporate executive on improving superior – subordinate communications are summarized in Feature 12.5. This executive found that regular meetings scheduled between managers and their subordinates to discuss work-related problems help ensure better communication. A more comprehensive set of suggestions for improving communications has been offered by Steers (1977). His ideas for upward, downward, and lateral communications are summarized in Figure 12.7. Although many of these suggestions are self-evident, several specific techniques managers can use to improve their communication with others deserve further discussion.

Because communication within organizations is subject to distortion and

---

Feature 12.5 (continued)

---

cuss the subordinate's more personal concerns, such as job frustrations and dissatisfactions. Grove warns managers against leaving these issues to the end of the meeting, when sufficient time may not be available to discuss them. There also is a mechanism for carrying forward less crucial issues to future meetings.

Grove also takes careful outline notes in each meeting. This helps him concentrate on what is being discussed and organizes his thoughts. It also carries the symbolic message that what is being said is considered important. Grove admits that he rarely looks at these notes after the meetings, but subordinates may be more committed to following through on what is said if they think he does. He sees his role as not to lecture, but to encourage subordinates to talk about what is going on in their areas and what may be bothering them. He does this by careful listening and a technique called "Grove's principle of didactic management," which involves asking one additional question whenever a subordinate apparently has said everything he or she wants to about a particular subject.

The one-on-one meetings have been effective for Grove, but they may not work for all managers in every situation. For example, it is unclear how far down in the organization these meetings should go. Although some questions remain unanswered, one-on-one meetings are one approach to improving the quality of communication in organizations by initiating regular and continuing interaction. These meetings need not substitute for the more informal daily contacts between managers and subordinates, but they can supplement them.

Source: "How (and Why)to Run a Meeting," by Andrew S. Grove, *Fortune,* July 11, 1983, pp. 132–140.

---

misinterpretation, managers may wish to take additional steps in communicating particularly important information to ensure that it is received and accurately understood by others. Multiple communication channels can be used to enhance the chances that information reaches its intended audience. An announcement made in the company newsletter, for example, can be supplemented by posting of the announcement on the employee bulletin board.

Managers can follow up more formal communications with personal telephone calls to key individuals to determine whether they received and understood a particular message. These calls seek feedback about the communication itself: Did you receive it? What steps do you plan to take as a result? Rather than assuming that communications are clearly understood, it may be important to determine this firsthand when accuracy is crucial. The simple step of repeating messages also can help to ensure that they are received by others. The announcement of an important meeting may be made one month in advance, followed by a note reminding participants one week before the meeting.

Managers should choose their communication channels carefully, sometimes entirely bypassing formal channels when they are less likely to prove

Figure 12.7
Strategies for Improving Communication Effectiveness

DOWNWARD COMMUNICATIONS

1. Job instructions can be presented clearly to employees so they understand more precisely what is expected.
2. Efforts can be made to explain the rationale behind the required tasks to employees so they understand why they are being asked to do something.
3. Management can provide greater feedback concerning the nature and quality of performance, thereby keeping employees "on target."
4. Multiple communication channels can be used to increase the chances that the message is properly received.
5. Important messages can be repeated to ensure penetration.
6. In some cases, it is desirable to bypass formal communication channels and go directly to the intended receiver with the message.

UPWARD COMMUNICATIONS

1. Upward messages can be screened so only the more relevant aspects are received by top management.
2. Managers can attempt to change the organizational climate so subordinates feel freer to transmit negative as well as positive messages without fear of retribution.
3. Managers can sensitize themselves so they are better able to detect bias and distorted messages from their subordinates.
4. Sometimes it is possible to utilize "distortion-proof" messages (Downs, 1967), such as providing subordinates with report forms requiring quantified or standardized data.
5. Social distance and status barriers between employees on various levels can be reduced so messages will be more spontaneous.

HORIZONTAL COMMUNICATIONS

1. Efforts can be made to develop interpersonal skills between group members and departments so greater openness and trust exist.
2. Reward systems can be utilized which reward interdepartmental cooperation and minimize "zero-sum game" situations.
3. Interdepartmental meetings can be used to share information concerning what other departments are involved in.
4. In some cases, the actual design of the organization itself can be changed to provide greater opportunities for interdepartmental contacts (e.g., shifting from a traditional to a matrix organization design).

Source: Reprinted from Steers, 1977, p. 151.

effective. Some information can be communicated more effectively through direct interaction than through interoffice memos. Because communication channels in organizations may differ in terms of the speed and effectiveness with which messages are transmitted, managers should consider which channel will be best in a specific situation.

The suggestions in Figure 12.7, along with those discussed earlier, can help managers improve the effectiveness of communication in their organizations. As the study by Peters and Waterman (1982) suggests, the importance of effective communication is clearly recognized by the best-managed firms in the United States. These firms design management systems and work environments specifically to increase the amount and effectiveness of communication. Communication within organizations requires the careful attention of management, and improving communication systems within an organization may have important implications for its overall effectiveness.

Summary

The ability to communicate often is a major determinant of managerial effectiveness, but there are many barriers to effectiveness in organizations. The most effective firms in the United States are characterized by and even encourage high levels of informal communication.

In the communication process, the sender's meaning is encoded into a message, which must be decoded by the receiver. Problems occur when the meaning is improperly encoded, the receiver misinterprets the message, or the message is not accurately received because of noise at the time it is sent. The feedback loop is one check on the accuracy of the message that was received.

The sender must be able to state ideas clearly to the receiver, and the receiver must listen carefully to what is being said.

There are four levels of communication: intraindividual, interpersonal, intraorganizational, and extraorganizational. Communication can be verbal, written, or nonverbal.

Another approach to analyzing communication is to draw distinctions based on its content or the nature of its message. There are three types of content: technical, interpersonal, and strategic. The same message can be communicated in several ways.

The hierarchy in organizations suggests that communication can flow horizontally, upward, or downward. It is estimated that horizontal communication across employees or work groups is the most frequent in organizations.

Communications can be used to control the behavior of others, to clarify duties, and to establish or reinforce authority relationships. It also can provide information on which to base decisions and can motivate employees or elicit their cooperation and commitment.

The barriers to effective communication include distortion of the message, omission of information, an overload of information, problems with timeliness, and lack of acceptance by the receiver. Communication can be influenced by organizational structure, including the degree of formalization. Other influences are the characteristics of individual employees, the trust between the sender and the receiver, the influence of either the sender or the receiver over the other, the mobility aspirations of the sender, and group norms and sanctions.

Organizational design plays a significant role in effective communication.

The need to process information may be reduced by creating self-contained units or slack resources. Organizations also may increase their capacity and ability to process information.

Four primary communication roles are the gatekeeper, the liaison, the opinion leader, and the cosmopolite.

Some techniques for improving communication effectiveness are: opening up multiple communication channels, using personal telephone calls to follow up more formal communication, repeating messages, and carefully choosing communication channels.

Questions for Discussion

1. What is meant when a communication is said to be effective, and why is it important for managers to be concerned about communicating effectively?
2. What techniques have some of the more successful United States companies used to encourage greater informal communication among employees?
3. Describe the communication process and the major points at which communication can break down.
4. Describe the different types, methods, and directions of communications commonly found in organizations.
5. What important barriers to effective communication exist in organizations?
6. What important organizational characteristics encourage the emergence of communication barriers?
7. How can the different types of communications roles that exist in organizations be used by managers to improve communication?
8. What can organizations do when they are faced with a need to process a great deal of information, and how will their decisions influence communication processes?

Case Study
L. J. Summers Company

Jon Reese couldn't think of a time in the history of L. J. Summers Company when there had been as much anti-company sentiment among the workers as had emerged in the past few weeks. He knew that Mr. Summers would place the blame on him for the problems with the production workers because Jon was supposed to be helping Mr. Summer's son, Blaine, to become oriented to his new position. Blaine had only recently taken over as production manager of the company (see Exhibit 1, page 408). Blaine was unpopular with most of the workers, but

the events of the past weeks had caused him to be resented even more. This resentment had increased to the point that several of the male workers had quit and all the women in the assembly department had refused to work.

The programs that had caused the resentment among the workers were instituted by Blaine to reduce waste and lower production costs, but they had produced completely opposite results. Jon knew that on Monday morning he would have to explain to Mr. Summers why the workers had reacted as they did and that he would have to present a plan to resolve the employee problems, reduce waste, and decrease production costs.

Company History

L. J. Summers Company manufactured large sliding doors made of many narrow aluminum panels held together by thick rubber strips, which allowed the door to collapse as it was opened. Some of the doors were as high as eighteen feet and were used in buildings to section off large areas. The company had grown rapidly in its early years due mainly to the expansion of the building program of the firm's major customer, which accounted for nearly 90 percent of Summers' business.

When L. J. Summers began the business, his was the only firm that manufactured the large sliding doors. Recently, however, several other firms had begun to market similar doors. One firm in particular had been bidding to obtain business from Summers' major customer. Fearing that the competitor might be able to underbid his company, Mr. Summers began urging his assistant, Jon, to increase efficiency and cut production costs.

Conditions Before the Cost Reduction Programs

A family-type atmosphere had existed at Summers before the cost reduction programs were instituted. There was little direct supervision of the workers from the front office, and no pressure was put on them to meet production standards. Several of the employees worked overtime regularly without supervision. The foremen and workers often played cards together during lunchtime, and company parties after work were common and popular. Mr. Summers was generally on friendly terms with all the employees, although he was known to get angry if something displeased him. He also participated freely in the daily operations of the company.

As Mr. Summers's assistant, Jon was responsible for seeing to it that the company achieved the goals established by Mr. Summers. Jon was considered hard-working and persuasive by most of the employees and had a reputation of not giving in easily to employee complaints.

Blaine Summers had only recently become the production manager of Summers. He was in his early twenties, married, and had a good build. Several of the workers commented that Blaine liked to show off his strength in front of others. He was known to be very meticulous about keeping the shop orderly and neat, even to the point of making sure that packing crates were stacked "his way." It was often commented among the other employees how Blaine seemed to be trying to impress his father. Many workers voiced the opinion that the only reason Blaine was production manager was that his father owned the company. They also resented his using company employees and materials to build a swing set for his children and to repair his camper.

Blaine, commenting to Jon one day that the major problem with production was the workers, added that people of such caliber as the Summers' employees did not understand how important cost reduction was and that they would rather sit around and talk all day than work. Blaine rarely spoke to the workers but left most of the reprimanding and firing up to his assistant, Evelyn Brown.

Summers employed about seventy people to perform the warehousing, assembly, and door-jamb building, as well as the packing and shipping operations done on the doors. Each operation was supervised by a foreman, and crews ranged from three men in warehousing to twenty-five women in the assembly department. The foremen were usually employees with the most seniority and were responsible for quality and on-time production output. Most of the foremen had good relationships with the workers.

The majority of the work done at Summers consisted of repetitive assembly tasks requiring very little skill or training; for example, in the pinning department the workers operated a punch press, which made holes in the panels. The job consisted of punching the hole and then inserting a metal pin into it. Workers commented that it was very tiring and boring to stand at the press during the whole shift without frequent breaks.

Wages at Summers were considered to be low for the area. The workers griped about the low pay but said that they tried to compensate by taking frequent breaks, working overtime, and "taking small items home at night." Most of the workers who worked overtime were in the door-jamb department, the operation requiring the most skill. Several

Exhibit 1
L. J. Summers Company Organization Chart

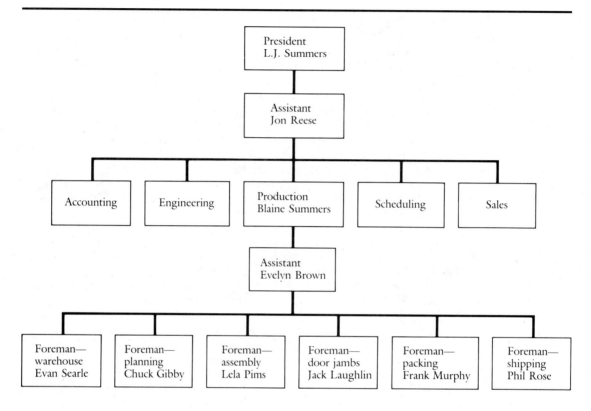

of these workers either worked very little or slept during overtime hours they reportedly worked.

The majority of the male employees were in their mid-twenties; about half of them were unmarried. There was a great turnover among the unmarried male workers. The female employees were either young and single or older married women. The twenty-five women who worked in production were all in the assembly department under Lela Pims.

The Cost Reduction Programs

Shortly after Mr. Summers began stressing the need to reduce waste and increase production, Blaine called the foremen together and told them that they would be responsible for stricter discipline among the employees. Unless each forman could reduce waste and improve production in his department, he would either be replaced or receive no pay increases.

The efforts of the foremen to make the workers eliminate wasteful activities and increase output brought immediate resistance and resentment. The employees' reactions were typified by the following comment: "What has gotten into Chuck lately? He's been chewing us out for the same old things we've always done. All he thinks about now is increasing production." Several of the foremen commented that they didn't like the front office making them the "bad guys" in the eyes of the workers. The workers didn't change their work habits as a result of the pressure put on them by the foremen, but a growing spirit of antagonism between the workers and the foremen was apparent.

After several weeks of no apparent improvement in production, Jon called a meeting with the workers to announce that the plant would go on a four-day, ten-hour-a-day work week in order to reduce operating costs. He stressed that the workers would enjoy having a three-day weekend. This was greeted with enthusiasm by some of the younger employees, but several of the older women complained that the schedule would be too tiring for them and that they would rather work five days a week. The proposal was voted on and passed by a two-to-one margin. Next Jon stated that there would be no more unsupervised overtime and that all overtime had to be approved in advance by Blaine. Overtime would be allowed only if some specific job had to be finished. Those who had been working overtime protested vigorously, saying that this would only result in lagging behind schedule, but Jon remained firm on this new rule.

Shortly after the meeting, several workers in the door-jamb department made plans to stage a work slowdown so that the department would fall behind schedule and they would have to work overtime to catch up. One of the workers, who had previously been the hardest working in the department, said, "We will tell them that we are working as fast as possible and that we just can't do as much as we used to in a five-day week. The only thing they could do would be to fire us, and they would never do that." Similar tactics were devised by workers in other departments. Some workers said that if they couldn't have overtime they would find a better paying job elsewhere.

Blaine, observing what was going on, told Jon, "They think I can't tell that they are staging a slowdown. Well, I simply won't approve any overtime, and after Jack's department gets way behind I'll let him have it for fouling up scheduling."

After a few weeks of continued slowdown, Blaine drew up a set of specific rules, which were posted on the company bulletin board early one Monday morning (see Exhibit 2). This brought immediate criticism from the workers. During the next week they continued to deliberately violate the posted rules. On Friday two of the male employees quit because they were penalized for arriving late to work and for "lounging around" during working

Exhibit 2
Production Shop Regulations

---

1. Anyone reporting late to work will lose one half hour's pay for each five minutes of lateness. The same applies to punching in after lunch.

2. No one is to leave the machine or post without the permission of the supervisor.

3. Anyone observed not working will be noted and if sufficient occurrences are counted the employee will be dismissed.

---

hours. As they left they said they would be waiting for their foreman after work to get even with him for turning them in.

That same day the entire assembly department (all women) staged a work stoppage to protest an action taken against Myrtle King, an employee of the company since the beginning. The action resulted from a run-in she had with Lela Pims, foreman of the assembly department. Myrtle was about 60 years old and had been turned in by Lela for resting too much. She became furious, saying she couldn't work ten hours a day. Several of her friends had organized the work stoppage after Myrtle had been sent home without pay credit for the day. The stoppage was also inspired by some talk among the workers of forming a union. The women seemed to favor this idea more than the men.

When Blaine found out about the incident he tried joking with the women and in jest threatened to fire them if they did not begin working again. When he saw he was getting nowhere he returned to the front office. One of the workers commented, "He thinks he can send us home and push us around and then all he has to do is tell us to go back to work and we will. Well, this place can't operate without us."

Jon soon appeared and called Lela into his office and began talking with her. Later he persuaded the women to go back to work and told them that there would be a meeting with all the female employees on Monday morning.

Jon wondered what steps he should take to solve the problems at L. J. Summers Company. The

efforts of management to increase efficiency and reduce production costs had definitely caused resentment among the workers. Even more disappointing
was the fact that the company accountant had just
announced that waste and costs had increased since
the new programs had been instituted, and the
company scheduler reported that Summers was farther behind on shipments than ever before.

Case Questions

1. Analyze the cause of the problem that led to the
   production slowdown by employees at the Summers Company.

2. How might management's concern about production costs and waste have been communicated to employees in a way that would have
   avoided the problems that occurred?
3. What steps should be taken now to address the
   actions taken by employees?

Source: Reprinted by permission from *Organization and People,* Second Edition, by J. B. Ritchie and Paul Thompson; Copyright ©
1976, 1980, 1984 by West Publishing Company. All rights reserved. Pp. 358–362.

"My whole career I've worked for a big, big desk. Now that I've got it, you know what I want, Hendricks? A big, big pen."

Sandra Kurtzig, founder and president of ASK Computer Systems Inc., was asked if she would serve on the board of another company. "I don't do boards," she said, "or windows."

Kurtzig is one of those executives who has a gift for the most admirable form of executive humor, the self-deprecating joke. That kind of humor is a gift whose importance is beginning to be recognized by managers.

Some companies look for executives who have a sense of humor because, as one recruiter said, "If a person can laugh, particularly at himself, he can probably step back and get the right perspective on things."

Humor has obvious benefits for the humorist. It's a way of reducing stress and getting rid of aggressive feelings acceptably. But there are other benefits as well. It can also be used to create rapport. In meetings between a company president and a clerk, if the president can mock himself or herself in a humorous way, status is momentarily wiped away and the two have a better chance of really talking.

CHAPTER 13

Conflict, Power, and Political Processes

Certain types of humor also can reduce rapport and stress status differences or even make the jokester seem more powerful. If the humor falls flat, however, the power dissipates too.

Humor can make difficult messages more agreeable, and it can avoid potentially troublesome situations. It's also the perfect way of building team cohesion or letting the staff know you're aware that something's up.

But the most important use of humor is to diffuse tense situations. When he was president of Chrysler, Eugene Cafiero met with workers at a troubled plant in England. He was escorted in to meet the union members.

A man stepped forward and loudly announced, "I'm Eddie McClusky and I'm a Communist." "How do you do," replied the Chrysler executive, extending his hand. "I'm Eugene Cafiero and I'm a Presbyterian."

Source: "Executives Ought to be Funnier," by Walter Kiechel III, *Fortune,* December 12, 1983, pp. 205–208.

Chapter Outline

- Power at General Motors
- A Political Perspective
- Conflict in Organizations
- Determinants of Organizational Conflict
- Conflict Resolution Through Power and Political Processes

Key Terms

- conflict
- pooled interdependence
- sequential interpendence
- reciprocal interdependence
- status inconsistencies
- jurisdictional ambiguities
- political processes
- power
- political activity
- reward power
- punishment power
- legitimate power
- expert power
- referent power

Chapter Objectives

After studying Chapter 13 you should be able to

1. See some of the positive outcomes of conflict.
2. Predict the areas in which conflict is likely to occur in an organization.
3. See how structural and design features in organizations and personal characteristics of key personnel can cause conflict.
4. Develop the proper attitude toward conflict.
5. Recognize the major influences on conflict.
6. Explain the importance and the use of power and political processes in conflict resolution.
7. Determine where the power lies in an organization.

Introduction

The purpose of this chapter is to explore the sources of conflict in organizations and the ways in which conflict typically is resolved. The discussion will focus primarily on conflict between groups and individuals rather than conflict that can arise within a person, as when an employee is given two important assignments that cannot both be completed on time.

We are not suggesting that intrapersonal conflict in unimportant. From a managerial perspective, however, greater time probably is spent managing conflict between groups and individuals. In some instances, managers will find themselves directly involved in conflict in their role as leaders of units or departments. Other times, managers will have to mediate or manage conflict between two parties. In either case, understanding how conflict arises in organizations and how it can be resolved is important if managers are to perform their jobs effectively.

We will pay particular attention to the development of power in organizations and its distribution among individuals and units. Power and political processes often are important in resolving conflict in organizations. Political processes frequently are neglected in the study of organizations, perhaps because they carry negative connotations. But positive or negative, power and politics exist in organizations and are important to understand. Not all groups or individuals in organizations are equally powerful, a fact with important implications for processes like resource allocation and the making of decisions about the organization's overall direction. As the following discussion of General Motors suggests, shifts in the distribution of power in organizations can have important implications for crucial decisions about what is produced and how it is produced.

We will also deal with the origin and resolution of conflict in organizations. The determinants of power in organizations will then be considered. The last section of the chapter will turn to the question of how power is exercised in organizations.

Power at General Motors

Many managers are becoming increasingly concerned about the competitive position of United States industry in world markets. In no industry have problems been more evident than among the major United States automobile manufacturing firms. The failure of American auto makers to compete effectively in the small car market have given imports an increasing portion of the market for new cars and have meant the loss of jobs for many Americans. Even though United States auto firms have for many years been the world's leading producers of cars, consumers are questioning more and more whether Detroit's products are as good as those from other countries.

How did the major auto makers get in this position? The question is very complex, and no one factor provides a satisfactory answer. The problem does not appear to be limited to poor planning or ineffective management, however. Pfeffer (1981) argued that the position of at least one auto maker — General Motors — may in part be the result of conflicting goals within the corporation and shifts in the balance of power among its major units.

To understand the changes that have taken place at General Motors, it is necessary to examine its history. Alfred P. Sloan, Jr., generally is credited with shaping General Motors into an enormously successful corporation that became the dominant firm in the auto industry and was at one time the largest corporation in the world. Sloan analyzed the General Motors organization and suggested several major changes in its management and structure. Perhaps the best known of his changes was a management approach that stressed decentralized operations and coordinated control. Sloan's management structure attempted to"preserve the best features of decentralized operations, while introducing a measure of financial control and interdivisional communication which would maximaze the efforts and efficiencies of this diverse and integrated company" (Wright, 1979, p. 223). In other words, divisions were given a great deal of operating discretion within a general framework provided by corporate policy and financial controls.

Under Sloan's plan, two dominant groups, operations and finance, formed the executive structure of the corporation. The chairman of the board was the chief financial officer. The position generally was held by a person who had worked up through the ranks on the financial side of the corporation. The president of General Motors, generally a person from operations — engineering and production — was the chief executive officer. Traditionally, the president was in charge of the day-to-day operations of the corporation. Operations was the dominant group, although it operated within the constraints imposed by the financial officers. The difference between the two positions and between operations and finance were reinforced by the fact that the president was located at corporate headquarters in Detroit, whereas the chairman worked in the New York office.

This balance of power within General Motors existed until 1958, when Frederick Donner was elected chairman and chief executive officer. Donner selected a person for president who reportedly was weak and not the obvious choice for the position, thus more clearly establishing the dominance of the financial side of the business. Many of the important duties were stripped from the position of president, including responsibility for international operations. The president in effect became an executive vice-president for North American operations, or, as described by another General Motors executive, the chief engineer.

The power shift from operations to the financial side had dramatic implications for General Motors. Cost considerations and profit implications replaced engineering considerations and consumer preferences as the heaviest influences on important production decisions. Pfeffer's analysis (1981) of the power shifts within General Motors helps explain why many of the corporation's actions appear unwise in retrospect. For example, General Motors was criticized for not being able to meet the consumer's increasing desire for smaller cars. The company continued to emphasize the production of large cars because of their cost and potential profit for the corporation. The Cadillac Coupe de Ville, for example, at one point cost roughly $300 to $400 more to produce than a mid-size Chevrolet but carried a sticker price $2,700 to $3,800 greater. A much greater profit could be made on large cars than on mid-size or compact car models.

Even when General Motors introduced models to compete in the small car market, problems resulting from an overemphasis on costs were evident. The Corvair, for example, introduced in the fall of 1959, developed dangerous steering problems at high speed. This problem, the fault of the suspension system, was evident to General Motors's engineers before the car was produced. The problem could have been corrected by adding a $15 stabilizing bar to the rear end of the car. But the addition of this part was rejected by the corporate executives as "too expensive," even after it became clear that Corvair owners were having many more accidents than expected (Wright, 1979, pp. 59–85). General Motors and other auto producers also stressed production of cars with expensive options because of the potential profit from these models. Cray (1980) reported that it cost General Motors $25 to add heavy-duty shock absorbers, bucket seats, and a chrome-plated gear shift knob to cars, options that were then sold for $400 as a "performance package." "New models" were created with a $300 higher price tag by adding $15 worth of chrome strips, larger tires, and upgraded upholstery. The economics of car production and sales favored larger, better equipped models, even if consumers preferred something else.

It is difficult to know if General Motors would be in a different position today if the balance of power within the corporation had not shifted from operations to finance. It is evident that the cost and profit concerns emphasized by financial officers may lead to decisions different from those favored by people with an engineering or production background. General Motors today is a very different corporation from the one Alfred Sloan envisioned. Centralized car design and production decisions have resulted in a more standardized product from each of the company's divisions. This may be a sound management strategy, because the automobile industry faces a period of increased competition.

The important point of Pfeffer's analysis, however, is that the strategic direction of corporations can be shaped by shifts in the balance of power among their major units, as well as by planned changes in strategy. Relationships among units in organizations, therefore, are important to consider if we are to understand corporate decisions fully.

A Political Perspective

Devoting attention to relationships among units is a departure from traditional approaches to the study of organizations. It is customary to think of organizations and their actions from a rational perspective (see Allison, 1971). This perspective views organizations as individuals and groups joined to pursue commonly accepted sets of goals and objectives. A definition of organizations provided by Porter, Lawler, and Hackman (1975) exemplifies this view: "Organizations are composed of individuals and groups in order to achieve certain goals and objectives by means of differentiated functions that are intended to be rationally coordinated and directed through time on a continuous basis" (p. 69).

The fact that this definition views rational coordination as "intended" implies that organizations may fall far short of the mark. As suggested by Pfeffer's analysis of General Motors (1981), a rational perspective may not always tell the whole story. Overall goals and objectives often are problematic. Also, the strategic decisions of organizations often can be better understood to be the outcome of the pursuit of narrowly defined goals by their individual units in competition with one another. An alternative to the rational view of organizations is provided by Pondy (1973): "The organization is a collection of interest groups who have goals which may be only partially consistent with those of other interest groups and with the superordinate goal of the organization" (p. 596). Pondy's view of organizations highlights the fact that conflict often exists between the goals of different units in organizations, as well as between unit goals and the objectives of the larger organization.

Conflict in Organizations

Positive and Negative Outcomes of Conflict

Conflict in organizations has been viewed as inherently negative and as a potential threat to overall effectiveness. As suggested by Schmidt and Kochan (1972), early definitions of conflict often reflected this view. Some called conflict "breaches in normally expected behavior" (Beals and Siegel, 1966), "a threat to cooperation" (Marek, 1966), and "antagonistic struggles" (Coser, 1956). Negative views of conflict follow from the stress placed on rational coordination of activities in organizations. Anything that threatens the ability to coordinate the efforts of different people and groups within an organization runs counter to the organization's primary goals and may impede its effectiveness.

More recently, writers have begun to view conflict in organizations in more balanced terms. This approach stresses the fact that conflict may have both positive and negative implications for effectiveness. The important issue is not to eliminate conflict but, rather, to *manage* conflict so that it can help groups and individuals perform better (Thomas, 1976). No one would question that conflict is sometimes very destructive in organizations. Managers increasingly are beginning to recognize that positive outcomes are a frequent result of conflict, however. Several positive outcomes of conflict can be cited (Miles, 1980; Thomas, 1976):

1. *Conflict between divergent views in the organization often results in higher-quality decisions or solutions to problems.* Conflict may cause the dominant viewpoint or favored position of a group to be questioned. Superior decisions often result when multiple alternatives are available and initially favored alternatives are reexamined in light of new evidence (Janis, 1972).

2. *Conflict among groups often increases their cohesiveness and strengthens them.* Members of groups in conflict often increase their identification and loyalty to the group.

3. *Conflict may make life more interesting in organizations.* Disagreements and divergent viewpoints stimulate and arouse organizational members. Conflict also provides the opportunity to test ideas and assess performance.

4. *Conflict can highlight important problems in an organization.* Disagreements between groups may bring problems to the surface and lead to changes that improve overall organizational functioning. Conflict also can lead to the design of methods for resolving conflict in the future.

5. *Conflict represents the aggressive pursuit of goals.* It may indicate that groups are motivated and that they want to achieve goals essential to their success even if they sometimes clash with other groups.

Conflict can have positive consequences in organizations, but it would be wrong to dwell too heavily on its functional aspects because often it has dysfunctional consequences. Conflict between groups or individuals can hinder cooperation and coordination of activities, for example, frequently at the expense of either party's ability to attain its goals. The important task for the manager is to channel conflict so that its consequences are more likely to enhance than to impede effectiveness. This is not always a simple task, however, because it is easy to become too personally involved and to lose sight of the larger goals when competing with others. In general, conflict that remains at the level of ideas is potentially less destructive and potentially more functional than conflict that becomes internalized at the personal level.

We will use Miles's definition of **conflict** (1980) as a condition that results when the goal-directed activities of one group or coalition of groups blocks or is thought to block the goal-directed activities of other groups. This definition suggests that the essence of conflict is the inability of two groups or individuals to achieve their goals simultaneously. When the actions of one group make it difficult or impossible for another group to pursue its goals, conflict is likely to result. It also is important to recognize that conflict can result when the incompatibility of goals is more apparent than real. In terms of the resulting conflict, actual barriers may be less important than perceived barriers. When groups believe that the actions of another group threaten their ability to accomplish a task, conflict may result whether they are right or not.

Basis of Conflict

Conflict can exist along so many different dimensions in organizations that it is impossible to mention them all. Alderfer (1977), however, has identified several major areas of conflict. Frequently, conflict in organizations has its roots in the different tasks performed by groups. For example, a production manager's goal of establishing a smooth manufacturing schedule may clash with the desire of sales personnel to respond quickly to customer orders. Conflicts of this type are fairly common. In addition to task-based conflict, disputes between management and labor also are common. Unlike other areas of potential conflict, however, elaborate rules and procedures have been established to govern the resolution of disagreements in labor relations, including collective bargaining, mediation, and arbitration. Conflict also can occur at the top levels of organizations or among subgroups. For example, differences among employees based on gender, ethnic group, and age are common areas of potential conflict (Alderfer, 1977).

Although it is useful to note the different areas of organizations in which conflict can emerge, it is more useful to approach the sources of conflict from a general perspective. In the next section a general model of the determinants of conflict in organizations will be presented. This model will help you understand why conflict occurs and will let you predict the areas in which conflict is most likely to emerge in an organization.

Determinants of Organizational Conflict

The model presented in Figure 13.1 is drawn from the work of Miles (1980) and is based on two important observations about conflict in organizations. First, most conflict is based on the structural characteristics of the organization rather than personal disputes. Second, there is a hierarchy of conditions that must be considered in understanding how conflict is created in organizations. For example, there may be conflict between division managers in one area of a corporation, but the conflict may actually originate in features of the organization that are far removed. To understand the sources of conflict, we must take a broader look at the organization and its environment, and how they work together with design features to cause conflict.

Antecedents of Conflict

As we noted in Chapter 5, the design and structure of an organization are influenced by several factors, including the nature of its environment, its size, and the characteristics of its technology. These factors lead to decisions about how the organization is to be structured, including whether it is to be subdivided into smaller units and how authority will be delegated among the units. These decisions lead to structural differentiation among the major units. For example, General Motors's major auto-producing divisions — Chevrolet, Pontiac, Cadillac, Oldsmobile, and Buick — historically have been semi-

Figure 13.1
Determinants of Organizational Conflict

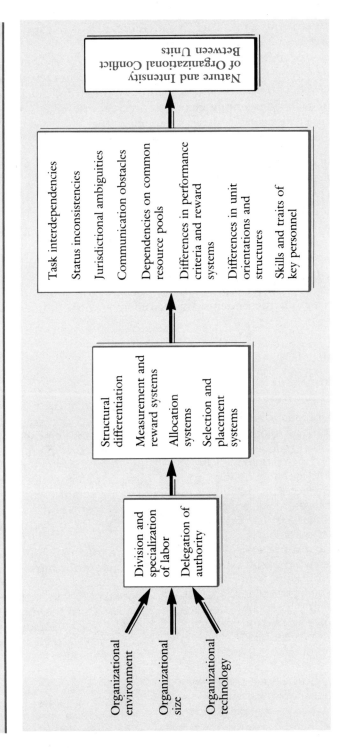

Source: From *Macro Organizational Behavior*, by Robert H. Miles. Copyright © 1980 by Scott, Foresman and Company. Reprinted by permission.

autonomous units. There is a division of labor and structural differentiation between units. Measurement systems must be developed to monitor the performance of units and to serve as the bases for distributing rewards. In addition, procedures for allocating budgetary resources to each unit and for selecting employees also must be established. From these decisions Miles (1980) identified the following eight immediate contextual antecedents of conflict, each of which will be discussed in detail separately:

1. Task interdependencies.
2. Status inconsistencies.
3. Jurisdictional ambiguities.
4. Communication obstacles.
5. Dependencies on common resource pools.
6. Differences in performance criteria and reward systems.
7. Differences in unit orientations and structures.
8. Skills and traits of key personnel.

Task Interdependencies. The division of labor in organizations often creates interdependence among different units. In the case of General Motors,

---

Feature 13.1
Conflict at Toyota

Japanese corporations have the reputation of fostering cooperation and harmonious relations among their employees. Despite this, conflict is as common in Japan as in the United States. Although the Japanese rarely resolve conflict harshly or suddenly, such tactics were apparently used in a management reshuffle at Toyota, Japan's largest producer of automobiles.

In 1949 the Bank of Japan ordered Toyota to split into two parts after the company nearly went bankrupt from producing more cars than its sales personnel could sell. The manufacturing company became Toyota Motor Company, and the sales company became Toyota Motor Sales Company, 43 percent of which is owned by Toyota Motor. For years differences between the two companies have been deepening — differences over model design, foreign investment, and market predictions.

Slumping domestic sales and reduced export quotas increased the friction, and in a very American-type of management power play Toyota Motor's president Eiji Toyoda ousted Toyota Motor Sales' president Sadazo Yamamoto and replaced him with Toyota Motor's vice president, Shoichiro Toyoda — Eiji's cousin and apparent successor.

The management reshuffle clearly puts the control back into the manufacturing side of Toyota and into the hands of the original founders of Toyota, the Toyoda family. Some speculate that this move is a step toward merger, which would ironically bring the company back a full circle to where it was over 30 years ago.

Sources: "Behind the Bloodletting Over Toyota's Sales," *Business Week,* June 1, 1981, p. 44; "One Times One," by James Cook, *Forbes,* July 6, 1981, p. 121.

the interdependence among the major auto divisions was minimized because each produced a line of cars largely independently. All the divisions were dependent on the Fisher Body Division, however, for auto bodies, and this interdependence was crucial to the effectiveness of the corporation: The assembly divisions could not complete their task unless Fisher Body first built and supplied the bodies. The nature of this interdependence may have been even more complex, however. Fisher Body may not have been able to manufacture the bodies until basic design and engineering work had been completed in the auto divisions. Recognizing the critical need for coordination among the different divisions, General Motors placed all Fisher Body and assembly plants under the common control of the General Motors Assembly Division in 1965 (Cray, 1980).

The interdependence of tasks in organizations can take a variety of different forms, ranging from very simple, additive effects to more complex, reciprocal relationships. Three different types of interdependence are illustrated in Figure 13.2. In **pooled interdependence,** the most simple form, the group or unit's product is the sum of the efforts of the individuals involved. More complex interdependence is involved when tasks are **sequential,** because the work of an individual cannot be undertaken until that of other employees has been completed. In **reciprocal interdependence** a complex interplay exists among the tasks of different individuals or groups. In planning a new product, for example, research and development may come up with an idea that is subsequently modified because of engineering considerations. The engineering plans also may be later modified as decisions are made about the best way to manufacture the product. Each step in the process may involve feedback to an earlier step that causes a previous decision to be changed.

Interdependence among units in organizations creates conditions under which conflict becomes possible or even probable. When one unit depends on another in the performance of its task, the accomplishment of goals can be impeded or blocked. This may be particularly true when the goals of each unit stress different aspects of the task as a whole. For example, if quality is the primary concern in manufacturing car bodies, supplies provided to the assembly plants may be slowed down, decreasing the ability to meet production quotas.

Status Inconsistencies. When tasks are divided among units in organizations, it is unlikely that each will be considered equally important or crucial to overall organizational effectiveness. Some functions or units come to be viewed as more important than others and therefore possess higher status. The basis for **status inconsistencies** will be discussed more fully later in the chapter. At this point it should be noted that people in low-status units may not always recognize the greater importance or contributions of higher-status units.

Jurisdictional Ambiguities. In differentiating among units of organizations, efforts often are made to define clear areas of task responsibility for each. But it is not always possible to define the boundaries between units in sufficient

Figure 13.2
Different Forms of Interdependency Among Tasks

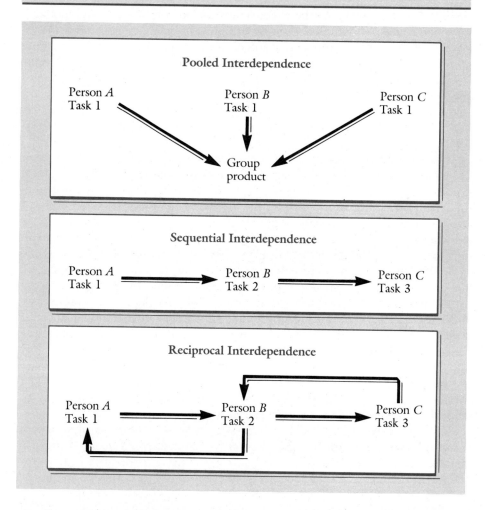

detail to prevent **jurisdictional ambiguities,** questions about who is responsible for a particular area. Moreover, changes in the environment may create new tasks that do not fall clearly within the boundaries of existing units. Disputes can arise within organizations about who has the responsibility for different tasks. These disputes often arise in organizations, as the example of the Vega's development by General Motors suggests:

> While the early announcement of the Vega was a break with GM tradition, so was the manner of its development. The guiding corporate precept of centralized policymaking and decentralized decision making was totally and purposefully ignored. GM tradition dictated that The Fourteenth Floor would decide

that a new market, such as small cars, should be developed (policy) and then would assign the responsibility for producing a car for that market to one of the five car divisions (operations). However, with the Vega, not only did corporate management make the decision to enter the mini-car market, it also decided to develop the car itself. This was to pave the way for many of the Vega's troubles. It was a corporate car, not a divisional car [Wright, 1979, p. 189].

Problems were created when recommendations made at the division level were ignored by the corporate staff. The general manager of the Chevrolet Division indicated that his most important problem with the Vega was motivating the divisional staff to put forth the effort to get the car in shape before its introduction.

Communication Obstacles. When employees are organized into separate units within the organization, communication among the units frequently becomes more difficult. This may be particularly true when the units are separated geographically, as often happens in large corporations. Many conflicts in organizations probably can be attributed to the failure of the parties involved to communicate effectively with each other. When communication is limited, chances increase that employees will misinterpret the goals and actions of others. Communication obstacles and the absence of shared information among units can create perceived conflicts when in fact no basis for actual conflict exists. For example, one of the problems reported in Koch Industries (Feature 13.2) is what the two brothers outside the corporation perceived to be the chairman's secrecy about the goals and activities of the company.

Dependencies on Common Resource Pools. One of the most commonly cited sources of conflict in organizations is the scarcity of resources. When different units rely on a common source of resources that is insufficient to supply all the demands, competition is likely to occur. Each unit may feel that the resources it requested are necessary to accomplish its goals. When resources become scarce because more resources are given to one unit, less can be given to another. It is common in organizations to find that the budget requests made by separate departments exceed the total resources available for allocation when added together. The budgetary process frequently results in difficult decisions about which units will have their requests met and which will not. Units that fail to receive their full budget request may believe that this is a result of greater allocations made to other units, whether this is the case or not.

Differences in Performance Criteria and Reward Systems. When interdependent tasks exist in organizations, the ability of one unit to perform its function depends on other units' performing their functions. Sales cannot sell products very well, for example, unless manufacturing makes high-quality products available in a timely way. When performance and reward systems are established separately for each unit, problems can arise. When sales personnel are rated on the number of products sold, for example, conflict can occur when

Feature 13.2
Feuding at Koch Industries

In their youth, Fred C. Koch wrote a letter to his sons about their inheritance. "If you choose to let this money destroy your initiative and independence, then it will be a curse to you . . .," he said. "Be kind and generous to one another."

The kindness and generosity the father sought for his sons has not materialized. Divisiveness and anger over the running of the family business, Koch Industries, has arisen instead.

The company founded by Fred Koch in 1928 has grown into a giant, with holdings in oil and gas services, exploration, production, and marketing; coal mining; cattle ranches; real estate; and manufacturing. Annual revenues were estimated at more than $14 billion in 1982, and assets appeared to approach $2 billion. But despite its size, the company is still privately held. Therein lies the rub, or at least part of it.

But first the cast of characters: Frederick, the eldest son, produces plays and operas, collects rare books, and lives in New York City; Charles, the second son, is chairman of Koch Industries, which is based in Wichita, Kansas; David, an executive vice-president of the company, runs its chemical technology group from New York; and his twin, William, is an investor and lives near Boston.

The disagreement began with Bill's worry about there being no way to establish a fair price for Koch shares. At the time, Bill was vice-president of corporate development

for the company. As one shareholder put it, "Koch is too large to remain a private company. If an owner dies, his family has to pay inheritance taxes and ends up with stock that can be readily sold only to the company or members of a shareholder's family for a fraction of its value." One proposal was to make 5 to 15 percent of the company's stock public to establish a fair market price.

Charles fired Bill. Each side began lining up support. Frederick aligned himself with Bill and claimed a board seat for his attorney, bumping one of Charles's supporters. Another ally installed a family-connected oil man. Bill's group tightened pressure on Charles.

The public–private issue is only part of the dispute. Charles's opponents also claim Charles is secretive about important company moves. In the early 1980s the company was convicted of conspiracy to misuse the federal oil and gas lease lottery. But board members didn't learn about it until after the indictment.

If the opposition wins, Charles may no longer be running the company. If that happens, according to one of his supporters, there will either be a splitting of assets in kind, a cash buyout, or a public offering for a small part of the company.

Source: "Family Feud at a Corporate Colossus," by Louis Kraar, *Fortune,* July 26, 1982, pp. 72–77.

manufactured products are not available and the number of sales therefore decreases. Interdependence in task performance also can result in interdependent reward systems. Unless performance criteria reflect this interdependence, conflict is more likely among units that must depend on each other.

Different problems can occur when units interpret their tasks and goals differently from the way those who make reward decisions do. Manufacturing personnel may believe that producing high-quality products is an important goal, whereas executives who make reward and resource allocation decisions are more concerned with the number of units produced. When manufacturing's efforts to reduce defects results in decreased production, the stage is set for conflict when reward decisions must be made based on performance assessments.

Differences in Unit Orientation and Structure. Perhaps the single most important source of conflict is the fact that people in different units tend to view the organization in different terms. An almost inevitable consequence of the division of labor and differentiation in organizations is a narrower orientation toward the goals and problems of the organization. As demonstrated in a study by Dearborn and Simon (1958), marketing people tend to view organizational problems in marketing terms, finance managers in financial terms, and so forth. Moreover, people in one unit may consider its goals and activities more important to the organization's overall effectiveness than the goals and activities of other units. It would be natural to find that marketing people believe the problem of declining profits in the auto industry can be solved best through increased sales efforts. Members of the financial staff, however, may approach this same problem by trying to control costs more effectively and to use resources efficiently. The problem generally can be considered a lack of consensus about what goals are important and what strategies will be most effective in achieving different goals (Pfeffer, 1981). Conflict is more likely in organizations when consensus about these two important issues does not exist.

Skills and Traits of Key Personnel. The seven sources of conflict we just mentioned can be traced to structural and design features in organizations. But the personal characteristics of key employees also are important in producing conflict. People differ with respect to how aggressively they pursue their unit's or their own best interests. Managers with high needs for power and dominance may find themselves in conflict with other managers more frequently than those with lower needs. People also differ with respect to their communication skills. The inability to articulate a position clearly to others may enhance the chances that motives and goals will be viewed with suspicion. As a result, the types of people in organizations partially determines whether conflict originating in structural features is minimized or made manifest. People themselves also can create conflict, whether or not the structural conditions for conflict are present.

Resolution of Conflict in Organizations

Conflict can have a number of sources in organizations. Because the potential for conflict lies in the organization's basic design and structural features, it is unlikely that conflict can ever be eliminated entirely. As a result, the way conflict is managed and resolved can have important implications for effectiveness. Unfortunately, many managers find it difficult or distasteful to deal with conflict. Rather than taking direct steps to intervene, managers may ignore it, letting it fester, often with potentially disastrous results. Other managers may try to minimize the likelihood of conflict by avoiding difficult decisions or becoming more secretive about decisions that are made.

It is not likely that any manager can avoid conflict entirely. Difficult decisions must be made, even at the risk of alienating some people in the organization. Moreover, avoiding potentially difficult decisions or increasing secrecy eventually may cause more problems than it solves. The best attitude that managers can have toward conflict is to recognize that it is inevitable and to understand the importance of resolving it effectively. The most effective strategies for resolving conflict in a particular instance depend on the issues involved and the situation. Several general approaches to the resolution of conflict, however, have been identified by Miles (1980).

Alter the context. Because many conflicts have their source in the structural arrangement of units, changes in structure are one way to reduce conflict. There are many specific methods of altering the context in which conflict occurs. For example, two conflicting units can be placed under a common superior, who can act as a mediator or arbitrator. Barriers to communication and coordination can be lessened by placing units in a closer working relationship. For example, at General Motors a project manager was given responsibility for specific Chevrolet products to help solve a problem:

> . . . In 1969 all of Chevy's car bodies were being designed in one department [and] all of the chassis and component work was done in another department. This was confusing because each car line was different in size, weight, style, performance characteristics and market. No department of engineers could be specialists in one car line. They had to be generalists for all of them. Furthermore, there was no coordination of engineering for each car line. It was quite common to have six different engineers working on the same car completely independent of each other and reporting to different department heads [Wright, 1979, p. 141].

Establishing a project manager for each major car line with jurisdiction over engineers working on different components helped clarify responsibility and achieve better coordination of activities. Although overt conflict was not responsible for this change, the potential for conflict was reduced in this situation.

Alter the issues in dispute. This approach involves changes in the issues over which there is disagreement. When conflict becomes too personalized, for example, the conflict may be moved away from personality to more substantive areas. Conflict over a complex issue often can be resolved more easily when the issue is broken down into its components; it may be easier to agree on smaller parts than on the larger issue. Sometimes, however, it may be necessary to expand the scope of a disagreement so that the conflicting parties recognize the larger goals involved.

Reducing the importance of an issue often can minimize the conflict. Miles (1980) suggests this can be done by making clear to the conflicting parties that a decision will not establish a principle or precedent to guide future actions. The less important the issue is perceived to be, the lower the motivation of different parties to pursue the conflict. In the design of the Chevrolet Vega, for example, the corporate engineering policy group overruled the divisional engineering staff on the design of the engine (Wright, 1979). This was perceived at the divisional level as a one-time decision and not a precedent for future design decisions, so conflict was minimized.

Alter relationships directly. Altering the relationship between two parties engaged in conflict can take one of two forms. First, the parties can be physically separated, reducing the likelihood of interaction and conflict. When two units are in conflict, for example, it is common for one unit to be moved to another part of the building or organization. Second, the interaction between the two units can be increased and guided toward resolution. Placing two managers in a conference room until they agree on an issue is one way of forcing a confrontation and, one hopes, resolving the dispute. A third party may foster resolution by facilitating interaction, particularly when he or she is skillful in clarifying the issues and channeling interaction into areas of possible agreement. One example of the resolution of conflict through the intensification of interaction can be found in Congress. When important issues generating intense disagreement come before the House, it is common for the Speaker to announce that he is locking the doors until agreement is reached. The announcement that the House will stay in session indefinitely often is reinforced by the order to move sleeping cots and food into cloakrooms. More often than not, this tactic works. It is unclear, however, whether a solution is reached because continuing interaction helps clarify the position of competing members or because the members simply grow tired. Sometimes the reason agreement is reached is less important than the simple fact that it is achieved.

Changing the individuals involved. Many conflicts can be resolved by simply changing the people. Perhaps the most straightforward approach is to fire one or both of the managers involved, although transferring individuals to other parts of the organization is less harsh and frequently can accomplish the same goal. More difficult is to train the managers to avoid conflict or resolve it more effectively when it occurs. For example, training in communication skills may help managers articulate their views and reduce the possibility that they will be misunderstood. Encounter or sensitivity training groups also have been used by organizations to make managers more sensitive to the feelings of others and to the impression they create. Trying to increase conflict resolution skills, however, does not directly address the source of the conflict. Disputes arising from the task interdependence between two units, for example, will still exist if the people are changed. Because it is not always possible to change the structural sources of conflict, however, strategies aimed at helping managers deal with conflict are important.

Individual Orientation to Conflict

In addition to the four approaches identified by Miles (1980), conflict resolution also can be considered from the perspective of the conflicting parties. Thomas (1976), for example, discussed five different orientations the parties can bring to a conflict situation and the conditions under which each is most prevalent. His model is presented in Figure 13.3. The major influences on the parties' orientations are their stakes in the relationship and whether the overlapping interests are mostly in conflict or mostly shared.

Competition between the parties is most likely, for example, when their stakes in the relationship are high and when their interests primarily conflict. Much is at stake in a situation such as this, and both parties can be expected to compete actively to resolve the conflict to their benefit. In contrast, avoidance may be most likely when the stakes are low and there are a number of disputed issues. Because each party's stake in the relationship is unimportant, conflicts simply may be avoided. When the stakes are high but the parties have a number of common interests, the stage is set for a collaborative approach. The groups may openly cooperate to resolve their differences. When interests are mostly

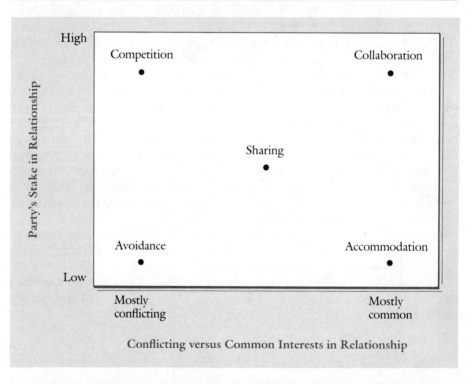

Figure 13.3
Orientations Toward Conflict Resolution

Source: Reprinted, by permission, from K. Thomas, "Conflict and Conflict Management," in M. Dunnette, ed., *Handbook of Industrial and Organizational Psychology,* p. 922. Copyright © 1976 by John Wiley & Sons, Inc.

Feature 13.3
Avoiding Conference Room Conflict

The conference room — it's the battleground of management.

Most important organizational decisions are reached in conferences, and sometimes the process is long and bloody. But there are techniques that can be used to minimize the conflict there, according to Joseph O. Roy, operations manager for Esso Eastern Inc. in Okinawa, Japan.

Imagine you are in a meeting with several colleagues and your manager, and someone makes an erroneous statement. Do you correct the colleague? First, says Roy, ask yourself if it is important to correct the mistake immediately. Waiting to talk to the person after the meeting will save him or her from looking bad in front of everyone else and could improve the relationship between the two of you.

What if you find yourself drawn into a conflict? Keep your composure and your sense of humor. Roy suggests using phrases like "Rather than take up more time here, why don't we get together after the meeting and talk about this further?" or "If it's OK with everyone, I'd suggest that we put off a decision on this item so I can have time to check some of my facts (files, notes, etc.)."

What if someone intentionally embarrasses you or your staff? A few seconds of silence will give you time to think and will cause the offender some discomfort, Roy

believes. Sometimes standing up for yourself is necessary, but most of the time demonstrating your ability to stay out of interpersonal conflicts is what impresses your superiors.

Roy suggests preselling your ideas or opinions to avoid conflict in meetings. Perhaps you need committee approval for a project that involves another department. Discuss the matter beforehand with the department head, so you know whether he or she agrees with you. Preselling also may be necessary if committee members have strong opinions about a point.

If you haven't done enough preselling and you encounter opposition during the meeting, see the dissenting person afterward. Give him or her time to cool off and think things over.

Don't bring up controversial subjects that haven't been presold, Roy cautions. Preselling takes time, but by doing it you'll avoid having everyone listen to a discussion between you and your adversary, which also takes time.

Source: "Avoiding Conflicts in Meetings," by Joseph O. Roy, *Personnel Journal,* September 1981, p. 677. Copyright Sepember 1981. Reprinted with the permission of *Personnel Journal,* Costa Mesa, California; all rights reserved.

shared but the stakes are low, one or the other party may give in on the issue to accommodate the other. Finally, compromise or sharing may be likely when the stakes and overlapping interests are both moderately high.

Collaboration and, to a lesser extent, sharing often are considered the most desirable approaches to conflict resolution, because each party is motivated to seek a jointly acceptable solution. Sharing, or **compromise,** implies that one or both parties give something up in order to reach a solution. **Collaboration** suggests that the parties seek a resolution that satisfies the goals of each party; that is, each party may attain its desired goal. Managers may want to influence the perceptions of conflicting parties to set the stage for collaboration. The par-

ties might be told how much they have in common and the importance of their
stake in the relationship, for example. By making these perceptions more salient,
the parties to a conflict might be encouraged to be more collaborative in resolving the conflict. Managers should recognize, however, that the perceptions of
the conflict may differ among the parties. One party may see its stake in the relationship as very important, whereas the other may not. As a result, a different
approach may be needed with each party.

Conflict Resolution Through Power and Political Processes

Many managers find that conflict is an undesirable part of their jobs. They may
hesitate to recognize that conflict exists, let alone actually intervene to resolve
it. As a result, many conflicts in organizations are resolved by means other than
those we have suggested. When the issues involved are important and power is
dispersed among units within the organization, Pfeffer (1981) suggests, conflict
is resolved by power and **political processes.** In other words, conflicting units
will compete in various ways to accomplish their goals. The unit that has the
most power and that exercises it effectively in competition with other units is
usually successful. When the issues are unimportant, it is unlikely that power
will be exercised in resolving a conflict, because the matter simply is not worth
fighting about. When power is centralized rather than dispersed, conflict is
most likely to be resolved by the individual or group with centralized decision-
making power. We will primarily be discussing situations in which issues are
considered important and power is dispersed throughout the organization.

Pfeffer (1981) suggests that power is a "relation among social actors in
which one social actor, *A,* can get another social actor, *B,* to do something that
B would not otherwise have done" (p. 3). **Power,** then, is force sufficient to
overcome others' resistance to complying with requested actions. The factor of
resistance is crucial to this definition; little power is involved when someone
would have complied without the exertion of force, although people often anticipate the desires of powerful people and act accordingly.

It also is important to recognize that power characterizes specific relationships between groups and people. An individual or group in an organization
may be more powerful than some but not all others. They also may be powerful
with respect to some but not all issues. It is important to consider power in
terms of specific groups and issues.

If power represents the ability to get others to comply with requested actions, **political activity** represents the actual process through which compliance
is gained. Pfeffer (1981) defines organizational politics as "those activities taken
within organizations to acquire, develop, and use power and other resources to
obtain one's preferred outcomes in a situation in which there is uncertainty or
dissensus about choices" (p. 7). Power represents the potential to gain compliance from others, whereas political activity represents the actual steps taken to

gain compliance. The distinction between power and politics is important, because those who are powerful are not politically active on every issue. Also, those who are politically active are not always the most powerful. Although we may tend to equate power and political processes when we think about organizations, it is important to recognize that one does not necessarily imply the other.

Power in Organizations

The sources of power in organizations are most commonly discussed in terms of five power bases identified by French and Raven (1959). The first three bases are most closely associated with a formal position in the organization. The last two are associated with the person occupying the position.

1. **Reward power** derives from the ability to reward others when they comply with requests, for example, with a pay raise or extra days off.

2. **Punishment power** is based on the ability to punish those who fail to comply.

3. **Legitimate power** is closely associated with the concept of authority and reflects the organizationally sanctioned ability to control others, such as the legitimate power of supervisors to request subordinates to perform different tasks.

4. **Expert power** reflects the power that derives from the possession of specialized skills or knowledge.

5. **Referent power** is the ability to influence others because they identify with you or want to be like you.

Although French and Raven's theory provides a useful way of thinking about the bases of power, it is necessary to take a somewhat broader perspective in understanding where power comes from in organizations. We must examine more fundamental sources of power, particularly when we focus on the question of why some groups are more powerful than others in organizations. Knowing that an individual has the power to reward others, for example, does not completely explain how he or she came to that powerful position in the first place.

On a very general level, Pfeffer (1981) suggests that "the power of organizational actors is fundamentally determined by two things, the importance of what they do in the organization and their skills in doing it" (p. 98). Organizations are characterized by specialization and a division of labor. Because all tasks do not make equally important contributions to accomplishing organizational goals, a particular task may be an important source of power. The fact that the chairman of General Motors generally has a financial background, for example, suggests that the task of providing financial resources to support the operations of the corporation is considered crucial. The mere fact of performing a task, however, does not enable one to derive power from it; the task must also be performed effectively. If chronic cash flow problems and the inability to obtain long-term financing were evident in General Motors, it is unlikely that the financial side of the corporation would have as much power as it appears to have.

Sources of Power

To develop a better understanding of what makes some groups and individuals more powerful in organizations, it is useful to look more deeply into the factors that create differentiated power. Pfeffer (1981) identified seven bases or sources of power in organizations.

Providing Resources. One of the most important sources of power derives from the ability to provide resources that are crucial to the organization's functioning. We tend to think of these resources in monetary terms. For example, profitable divisions of a corporation become more powerful because they provide the resources the less profitable divisions require to operate. Important resources in organizations are not limited to money, however; they also may include information, expertise, and prestige. In descriptions of International Telephone and Telegraph Corporation, for example, the lobbyists are portrayed as very influential largely because of their access to important people in government and information about contracts on which the corporation may bid.

Even when the resources are not absolutely necessary in operations, additional resources provide some measure of slack that can be allocated to activities that would otherwise be impossible. Slack resources often become an important way in which powerful individuals can reward those who support their efforts.

Creating Dependence. The ability to provide resources may not be enough to form a power base in an organization if these resources also are available from other sources. The concept of dependence thus becomes crucial. Dependence relations are created when an important resource is provided by a group and is unavailable from any other source. Consider two alternate financial policies that may exist in a very large corporation. In the first, major divisions are allowed to retain earnings and to secure loans, perhaps up to a specified amount, to support their operations. In the second situation, all retained earnings are controlled by corporate financial officers and individual divisions are not allowed to secure external financing. In the first situation, the divisions have a degree of autonomy in financing their operations that lessens their dependence on the corporate staff. In contrast, divisions are totally dependent on the corporate staff for resources in the second situation. The corporate financial staff would have much greater power over the operating divisions in the latter case.

In general, the more dependent others are upon you for a crucial resource that cannot be obtained by other means, the more power you will have over others. The division of labor in organizations and the resulting interdependence between units suggests that dependence is a very important source of power in organizations. It is important to recognize that crucial dependencies can be created in more than one area. Information, expertise, and task performance, as well as monetary resources, can be the basis upon which such dependence relations grow.

Coping with Uncertainty. A recent approach to the study of power in organizations highlights the importance of critical uncertainties and the power that is derived from the ability to cope with them. The capability to cope with uncertainty often is defined in terms of the ability to provide crucial resources. The organization's nature defines what resources are most important at the time. For example, the legal staff of American Telephone and Telegraph Company probably became much more influential as a result of government antitrust actions taken against the corporation. Cases such as this create major uncertainty that affects the survival of the organization. Power is likely to swing to those considered vital in dealing with the important problems that arise. The fact that outside legal services also could be obtained to fight the antitrust case, however, no doubt gave the corporate legal staff less influence than it might otherwise have had.

Power based on the ability to cope with uncertainty increases when other sources of coping are unavailable. A dependence relationship is created in which the organization must rely on one group or individual to solve major problems effectively. This pattern provides an important way to judge power relationships within organizations. Identifying the critical uncertainties facing an organization often can help indicate which units are influential. For example, the personnel department of a high-technology company faced with the task of recruiting trained engineers is likely to be more powerful than the personnel department of a manufacturing company hiring large numbers of unskilled employees.

Being Irreplaceable. The harder it is to replace a person or what they provide, the greater the power he or she will have. This factor is related to the concept of dependence. It is why engineers, who are difficult to recruit and in short supply, often receive better treatment than other employees. If an engineer leaves, it may be very difficult and expensive to recruit a replacement. Many people in organizations understand the relationship between power and irreplaceability. For example, the computer programmer who develops an important program for financial control but does not document any of the steps in development is probably following a strategy to make himself or herself irreplaceable. The airline executive with a good friend on the Civil Aeronautics Board may derive power from this friendship. In this instance, power would be based not on the fact that the executive is irreplaceable but, rather, on the fact that a replacement would be less likely to have such important contacts.

Controlling Decision Processes. A person in a strategic position to determine what decisions are to be made and the process that will be used to make them has an important source of power. Two aspects of decisions can be influenced. First, the goals and objectives the decision is designed to achieve often are subject to influence. In an equipment acquisition decision, for example, goals might involve the reliability and the cost of the equipment. Depending on which goal is considered more important, different decisions might result. Second, the constraints on the decision also can have a powerful influence on its outcome. Several alternatives in purchasing equipment might be eliminated if a ceiling were put on the cost and if goals were established for the production capacity of the equipment. It often is said that if the constraints can be specified, the outcome of the decision is a foregone conclusion; that is, if you can set the constraints, you shouldn't care who makes the decision.

Decision outcomes also can be influenced by the types of information available about each alternative. Those who collect information for a decision can have a powerful influence on the outcome by choosing what information to provide. Managers who establish the agenda for meetings in which decisions are made are in a very powerful position. They may be susceptible to influence, however, by staff members on whom they rely for information and expertise.

Developing Consensus. Pfeffer (1981) suggests that the consensus in a unit also can be a source of power in organizations. Units in which there is agreement over goals and how they should be attained can argue their positions much more forcefully than units with serious divisions. The strategy of divide and conquer reflects the fact that a lack of consensus can limit power. Coalitions on specific issues can also be a source of power. When consensus can be achieved between or among two or more units on an important decision, they will have greater influence than any would have had alone. In general, the more cohesion and homogeneity a group or collection of groups has on a particular issue, the greater its influence.

Having Political Skills. The sources of power just discussed are based primarily on the position of a person or group within an organization. Political skills reflect the ability of a person or group to use the power available. You may have the impression that powerful people or groups merely indicate their preferences in decisions, but this is seldom how it works in organizations. How well you play the game often can be as important as your power resources. Skillful organizational politicians often turn less powerful positions into positions of greater influence by effectively influencing decisions.

There is no set of rules for political behavior that will guarantee effective influence in all situations. The political process, however, involves several choices that must be made if power is to be translated into effective influence. The first choice is whether an attempt should be made to influence a decision. Unsuccessful attempts may accomplish little except to demonstrate to others your limited influence. As a result, managers often are careful to exert influence only in situations in which they have a reasonable chance of success. Successful influence on a decision can in itself be a source of power, whereas unsuccessful influence can detract from what power may be available.

A second important decision in the exercise of influence is the choice of whom to influence. This decision requires a knowledge of who will be important in shaping the decision outcome. Frequently, the person who can be most helpful in influencing the decision is the person with formal authority for the decision itself. Identifying an influence target can become a crucial step in the influence process.

A third important decision is to determine the best method of exercising influence, once an influence target is identified. Different people are best approached in different ways. One person may be open to persuasive arguments, for example, and another to an exchange of favors. Politically skilled managers in organizations are sensitive to the ways in which different people should be approached, and select their methods of influence accordingly.

Research on the influence people use in organizations suggests that this third decision greatly depends on the influencer's relationship with the target. Kipnis, Schmidt, and Wilkinson (1980) found, for example, that different methods of influence are likely to be used, depending on whether the person to be influenced is a subordinate, peer, or superior. Results of their research are summarized in Figure 13.4. For instance, rational arguments are more likely when dealing with superiors than when confronting subordinates. We are more likely to threaten sanctions or punishments for noncompliance when the person is a subordinate than when he or she is a superior. This research generally suggests that far more methods of influence are available for use with subordinates than with superiors. The greater power of superiors makes it less likely that threatening punishment will be credible and effective. In contrast, the relative power disadvantage of subordinates suggests that they can be influenced by a number of different methods, although research indicates that we may be less likely to appeal to their intellect through rational arguments.

A final decision in the influence process involves timing. Decisions in organizations generally are processes that take place over time and move from one level of the organization to another in a predictable fashion. For example, budget decisions may originate at the departmental level and move up the hierarchy. An important question becomes, at what stage of the decision process can influence best be exercised? There is a certain logic favoring the attempt to influence decisions at early stages, because failure early in the game may still leave later opportunities to exert influence. In some situations, however, it may be apparent that early attempts to exert influence are unlikely to be successful but later attempts may be possible. The department head may not be as sympathetic to your position as the division manager, for example.

The effectiveness with which power is used in organizations largely depends on political skills. Merely having a power base may not be sufficient to achieve one's goals in the organization. It also is important to consider the strategy through which power is exercised. While he was Senate majority leader, Lyndon Johnson turned a position of limited influence into a position of tremendous power (Evans and Novak, 1966). He did this through political skills and the careful use of the power he had. Effective political skills can increase a power base in an organization.

Figure 13.4
Methods of Influence and Their Targets

| | METHODS OF INFLUENCE | |
INFLUENCE TARGET	*Less Likely To Be Used*	*More Likely To Be Used*
Subordinate	Rational arguments	Ingratiation Assertiveness Threat of sanctions Exchange of favors Appeal based on higher influence of others
Co-worker	Rational arguments Assertiveness Threat of sanctions	Ingratiation Exchange of favors Appeal based on higher influence of others
Superior	Ingratiation Assertiveness Threat of sanctions Exchange of favors Appeal based on higher influence of others	Rational arguments

Source: Kipnis, Schmidt, and Wilkinson, 1980.

Assessing Power in Organizations

Power is an important determinant of how decisions are made in most organizations. We like to think that decisions in organizations are made rationally and are based on objective criteria. From all appearances, many decisions are made this way. If we probe a little deeper and determine how the objective criteria for the decision were selected, however, we often find that power and political processes played a role. What appears to be an objective decision often has actually resulted from powerful units or people imposing their own criteria.

Because power relationships are such an important influence on organizations, managers must have a good understanding of where the power lies in an organization and how it is used. Especially to those new to the organization, the distribution of power may not always be readily apparent. It is useful to consider how power can be assessed. How can we determine who has power in the organization? Our natural inclination is to look to the top of the organization, to the chairman of the board or chief executive officer. Although these usually are powerful positions, looking at only the top of the organization may not give a complete picture. Power typically is distributed across levels and areas. Several ways to assess power in organizations can be identified (see Pfeffer, 1981).

Assess by Determinants. Our previous discussion of the sources of power in organizations suggested that one useful strategy is to examine the determinants of power. This process involves identifying dependent relationships in the organization: Who provides crucial resources or who copes with the most critical uncertainties? If you clearly understand what causes groups or individuals to become powerful in organizations, you can determine the distribution of power in specific cases. But this understanding may not always be easy or yield an accurate answer. The perception of which resources or uncertainties are most crucial to the organization may be clouded, for example. The personnel staff commonly views human resources as the most crucial resource in the organization; marketing and sales personnel hold a different view. An analysis of the determinants of power in an organization, therefore, must take into account the fact that information often can be misleading. Those who think of themselves as irreplaceable may not be viewed in the same way by others.

Assess the Consequences of Power. If power often is used to determine important decisions in organizations, one way to assess power is to identify those who benefit most when these decisions are made. Because most units require financial resources, the budgetary process is one place to begin. The role of power in budget processes is particularly important during economic recessions or cutbacks in the organization. Because budgets typically are not cut equally across units, an indication of power comes from a determination of which units receive proportionally smaller budget cuts. (We assume here that most units try to influence the distribution of budgetary resources and that power plays a crucial role in how these decisions are made.)

Assess Power by Its Symbols. The description of the executive offices of the General Motors Corporation by their former vice-president, John DeLorean, suggests that power can be assessed by its *symbols* (Feature 13.4). The proximity of an office to the head of the corporation, the quality of the furnishings and decorations, and the view all have symbolic importance. These symbols may be jealously guarded in organizations, as DeLorean's failure to get his office redecorated suggests. Even if perquisites and symbols are not considered important by those who possess them, they may be interpreted by others as an indication of importance and power. That it is sometimes possible to misinterpret the importance of symbols is suggested in this story retold by Mirvis (1980):

> When visiting a friend's office (an aspiring manager climbing the corporate ladder in a New York bank), Nisberg spied a lush plant based in a rich wooden container. Upon commenting on the plant, he was urged to close the door and was informed, in a hushed voice, that the plant was new and sent from the Chairman of the bank himself. Such plants, he was told, were symbols that employees had

"made it" and were soon to be executives. Nisberg remained in his friend's office to do some paperwork that evening and while working was interrupted by a cleaning woman who scrupulously washed and tended to the plant. After introducing himself and inquiring about the woman's fastidious attention to the plant, Nisberg learned that she lavished care on all the plants in the area and — by the way — to lend some spice to the offices moved them annually from place to place [p. 436].

Symbols and perquisites are important in most organizations. People with greater power are likely to acquire better trappings than those with less power. But don't attach too much importance to these symbols, and take care in interpreting them.

Examine Reputational Indicators. Perhaps the most common method of determining power in organizations is to ask others their opinions. Most people know or believe they know who the most powerful groups and individuals are in organizations. Managers often acquire reputations based on their power, but the image of being powerful is not always the same as having power itself. People in powerful positions often influence important decisions in subtle and not easily observed ways; those with less power often may try to convince others that they are more powerful than actually is the case. The name dropper, for example, may be trying to convince others of a close relationship with powerful people. Reputational indicators of power, therefore, may be misleading in organizations. Powerful people frequently are secretive about their actions. Those who try to give others the impression that they are powerful are often substituting for the real thing.

Examine Representational Indicators. Another method of assessing power in organizations is to examine the representation of people or groups on important committees or decision-making bodies. For example, the boards of directors of major corporations generally are composed of outside members and managers in the organization. The fact that some vice-presidents serve on the board whereas others do not may be an indication of the relative power of various units in the organization. Membership on important subcommittees of the board, such as the executive committee, also may be an indication of power and importance. In many organizations, important decisions are made by groups or committees. Determining which areas of the organization are represented on these groups and which are not provides clues about the relative power of units and individuals.

There are a number of ways to assess power in organizations. Each of the methods, however, can give misleading information and may not be entirely accurate. As a result, Pfeffer (1981) argues that the most accurate assessment of power in organizations comes from using each of the methods. When more than one method of assessment is used, it is possible to look for convergence in the information that is gained. The group or individual who ranks high accord-

Feature 13.4
The Trappings of Power

One way to assess people's relative power in corporations is to compare the symbols of their position.

The most powerful managers are more likely to have private parking spaces, to be located in isolated areas protected from others, and to eat in a private dining room, and are likely to have larger and more nicely decorated offices than others. Before leaving his high-level positions in industry, John DeLorean witnessed this phenomenon at the executive offices at General Motors.

General Motors executives have offices on the fourteenth floor of the corporate headquarters. DeLorean calls the area "awesomely quiet." The hallways are usually deserted, and people speak in hushed tones. "The omnipresent quiet projects an aura of great power." The public can enter the executive offices only through an electronically locked door controlled by the receptionist. Executives themselves enter through their own private elevator. The offices are laid out on either side of an I-shaped hallway, with managerial rank increasing as one moves down the hall. Vice-presidents occupy offices along the long hallway; group vice-presidents are in the upper left and top executives in the upper right corner. According to DeLorean, there was great jealousy about how close one's office was to the chairman and president. Proximity was one indicator of importance in the corporation.

Executive offices are arranged in pairs, with the central office in between occupied by a private secretary for each executive. All offices are decorated in the same way. DeLorean describes the decor as "blue carpet, beige walls, faded oak paneling, and aged furniture." Top executives, however, were free to select their own decorating scheme. When DeLorean, then a group vice-president, asked that his carpet be replaced, the paneling be restained, and new, modern furniture ordered for his office, his request was refused. This might have upset the carefully maintained balance of symbols.

When DeLorean was in charge of the Chevrolet Division, however, he had complete freedom to redecorate his office on the second floor. On the fourteenth floor the best he could hope for was an extra table or lamp.

Not all corporations are characterized by such tightly controlled systems that are symbolic of power. George Weyerhaeuser, president of Weyerhaeuser Corporation, has his desk next to other executives in an open-space office. Some Japanese executives are said to share offices to facilitate communication. But in most large corporations, the symbols of power can tell you who's on top.

Source: On a Clear Day You Can See General Motors, by J. Patrick Wright, New York: Avon, 1979, pp. 20–22.

ing to each of the assessment methods is more likely to have actual power than those who rank high by one but not other methods.

Summary

The present chapter explores the sources of conflict in organizations and the ways in which it is resolved. The strategic direction of corporations can be shaped by shifts in the balance of power among their units as well as by planned strategy, as suggested by an analysis of events at General Motors.

Conflict may have both positive and negative implications for effectiveness. The important issue is to manage conflict so that it can help groups and individuals perform better. Conflict often results in higher-quality decisions, can strengthen groups, makes life interesting in organizations, can highlight important problems, and represents the aggressive pursuit of goals.

Most conflict is based on the structural characteristics of the organization rather than on personal disputes. A hierarchy of conditions must be considered to understand how conflict is created in organizations. Among the causes of conflict are task interdependencies, status inconsistencies, jurisdictional ambiguities, communication obstacles, dependencies of common resource pools, differences in performance criteria and reward systems, differences in unit orientation and structures, and the skills and personality of key personnel.

It is unlikely that a manager will be able to avoid conflict completely. Some approaches to resolving conflict, however, include altering the context or the issues in dispute, directly altering relationships between the parties involved or changing individuals by firing or transferring them, and instituting sensitivity and training programs. The individual's orientation to conflict also must be considered.

Pfeffer suggests that conflict often is resolved by power and political processes. Powerful groups and individuals in organizations are those who provide crucial resources, create dependence, can cope well with uncertainty, are difficult to replace, control decision processes, or have consensus or political skills. In political behavior, decisions must be made concerning whether to exercise influence, whom to influence, and in what way to exert influence. Timing also is important.

Studying power in an organization involves assessing its determinants, the consequences of power, its symbols, and reputational and representational indicators.

Questions for Discussion

1. What are the implications of taking either a rational or a political approach to understanding organizations? What different characteristics of organizations does each approach tend to highlight?
2. What positive and negative outcomes are likely to be associated with conflict in organizations?
3. What are the important antecedent conditions for conflict in organizations?
4. How can the development of interdependent tasks create the potential for conflict? How can this potential for conflict be minimized?
5. Describe the general strategies that managers can use to resolve conflict.
6. Describe the distinction between power and politics in organizations. Why is it important to make this distinction?
7. What are the major sources of power in organizations?

8. What are the important steps managers take in exercising power?

9. How can power in organizations be assessed, and what important limitations are associated with each approach?

Case Study
Ranch Supplies Company

John Watson, executive vice-president and general manager of Ranch Supplies Company (RSC), sat at his desk mulling over the events of the past few months, which had just climaxed in a serious clash between two of his key employees — George Cox and Dale Johnson. When John hired Dale, he had expected that a marketing team combining George's long-time field sales experience with Dale's recent UCLA business school training would result in great benefits to RSC. However, almost since the day Dale came to work, his relationship with George had deteriorated. And now George had just stormed into John's office and stated that he didn't want Dale to work with him on any more projects. John wondered what, if anything, he could do to help resolve the conflict between Dale and George.

Background

Ranch Supplies was an international company that annually grossed close to 4 million dollars worth of cattle tags, bull semen, and other herd management supplies. RSC was a subsidiary of Jones Enterprises, which was owned by Bill Jones. Bill had convinced John less than a year before to leave a prominent Chicago consulting firm to come to work for him at the head office of both companies, in Grand Junction, Colorado. John was promoted quickly from assistant to the president of Jones Enterprises to General Manager of RSC (see Exhibit 1).

When John came into the RSC organization, he turned to George Cox to teach him the ropes of the cattle industry and RSC's part in it. George did not have a college education but had worked his way up through RSC's organization from one of the original salesmen to his present position as director of marketing. He was one of the old-timers in the organization, having been with RSC since before it was acquired by Jones Enterprises. He was responsible for setting up the original marketing distribu-

tion system for the Big Green Tag (considered the "Cadillac" of the cattle ear tag industry) and for organizing the company's A.I. (artificial insemination) program. George was considered by many at RSC to be one of the most valuable people in the organization because of his close involvement with the Big Green Tag and bull semen, the two major items distributed by the company.

In spite of George's long-time service with the company, however, Bill Jones had voiced the opinion that George was not vital to the organization. He recognized that George had great ability as a salesman and that he had successfully persuaded many of the owners of famous bulls to sign contracts granting RSC exclusive distributorship of their bulls' semen, but he did not think of George as a good administrator because he was hard headed in many ways and didn't like to delegate authority.

John voiced similar impressions about George's lack of administrative ability. He commented that George not only lacked administrative skill in keeping up on all the detail work that went along with the deals and commitments he made, but also liked to "feel as if he had total control over the company's marketing and distribution system." According to John, it seemed that George didn't like to have his operations subject to the approval of either John or Bill and that "he wants to be in my position as executive vice-president."

Unlike George, Dale Johnson had considerable formal business training. He and John had been classmates in the MBA program at UCLA. Dale was much more theoretical in his approach to solving problems than was George.

Dale originally came to work with the understanding that he would devote half of his time to Jones Enterprises and half to RSC; but because John had hired him and there was a greater need for him to help solve some of RSC's problems, he spent most of his time at RSC and had his office in the

Exhibit 1
Organization Chart: Ranch Supplies Company

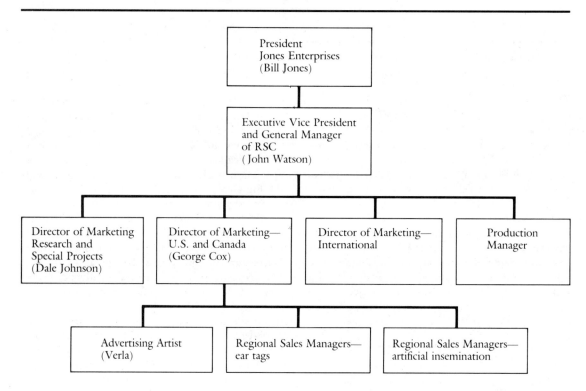

RSC building. John said that Dale was extremely creative in thinking of new ideas and ways to approach a problem but that he constantly hopped from one project to another, so that his work was disorganized. He often dreamed up projects on his own and started working on them. John also noted that Dale lacked the patience and skill needed to promote his ideas effectively within the organization. He added, however, that Dale was considered an important asset to the company because he had developed a point-of-purchase display that had proved successful in promoting RSC's new line of ear tag, the upright tag. RSC was planning to distribute another new tag in the near future, the stay-fast tag, which they hoped would be competitive in price with the "Fords and Chevrolets" of the industry and, at the same time, would not affect the sales of RSC's other ear tags. Dale was thought to be the person best qualified to develop a quality advertising and promotion campaign for the stay-fast tag.

The Conflict

It was during the development of the promotion for the stay-fast tag that the clash between Dale and George first became evident. In deciding who would work on the project, John saw great potential in putting George and Dale together so that George's experience and Dale's training could be utilized. Dale and George were considered to be the best marketing men employed by RSC, and it was expected that they would cooperate with each other and coordinate their marketing efforts. However, even in the early stages of the project it was apparent that the relationship between the two was not cordial. It seemed that neither man was willing to compromise his own ideas. Soon the conflict became apparent to everybody in the office, for not only had George and Dale failed to present a unified proposal on the new marketing strategy, but George visibly shunned Dale each time they passed each other in the hallway.

John felt that there was little organizational pressure to make Dale and George work together: both reported to John directly, and there was no superior-subordinate relationship between the two (see Exhibit 1). The fact that Dale was considered staff and George was a line manager seemed to add to their unwillingness to cooperate.

John made the following observations about the two men:

> Dale likes to be a one-man show. He does not desire to be a leader in a large organization, but he likes to be in charge of his projects. He doesn't like too many people under him. Dale is extremely creative, but many of his ideas are impractical. He has not yet learned to screen himself. For example, he has sometimes come to me for advice; and then, after I have advised him to do something a certain way, he has ignored my advice and done it his way.
>
> George, on the other hand, is resentful of Dale because I hired him, and he doesn't want someone who is working for me to be a success. He also has difficulty in accepting people's weaknesses as well as their strengths, and, because Dale's impulsive nature annoyed him, he refused to work with him.

The growing tension between Dale and George came to a head when Dale was assigned to design a new box for the Big Green Tag.

Dale developed a box that seemed to bring approval from a good number of people in the company. After a prototype was approved, several hundred thousand boxes were ordered from an outside firm. During the development of the new box, Verla, the company artist with whom Dale had been working on the new design, complained several times to George (her boss) that Dale was finicky and that he changed his mind too much.

After the newly designed box had been approved and ordered, Dale announced his decision that not only should the box graphics be changed, but all of RSC's products should be promoted under the acronym "RSC Tags," and new colors should be used in the graphics scheme. Dale took it upon himself to hire an outside advertising agency to come up with a new logo. When George found out about Dale's new project he nearly exploded. He stormed into John's office and told him that he flatly refused to work with Dale on any more projects. George refused to talk to Dale about the matter, but news of the problem soon got around to the rest of the office staff. John wondered what he could do to help resolve the conflict and get Dale and George to work together.

Case Questions

1. Analyze the sources of conflict between Dale Johnson and George Cox.
2. What steps should John Watson take to resolve the conflict?

Source: Reprinted by permission from *Organization and People,* Second Edition by J. B. Ritchie and Paul Thompson; Copyright © 1976, 1980 by West Publishing Company. All rights reserved. Pp. 219–222.

Do people have the right to get sick? It sounds like a foolish question, yet it may emerge as the key issue in occupational health in the years ahead. That's because, increasingly, doctors are discovering that many diseases are not simply the result of germs, chemicals, or hazardous substances but, at least in part, a result of the genetic composition of the person who gets sick. And, as scientists have learned to identify which genes are linked to which illnesses, genetic screening has become a hotly debated jobs issue.

The reasons are simple. If people vary in their genetic susceptibility to a disease, the theory goes, then some will have a higher probability of getting ill from exposure to chemicals and dust in the workplace. Screen out those workers and you cut occupational illness. The benefits could be large. In 1981 alone, doctors diagnosed over 126,000 cases of work-related disease, and industry spent an estimated $5 billion on employee safety and health.

But organized labor is leery of genetic screening, which the unions think will create genetic untouchables, workers who cannot get jobs because of their heredity.

"The issues under discussion are social and not scientific," says Sheldon Samuels, director of health, safety, and environment for the AFL-CIO's Industrial Union Department. Samuels and other labor officials worry that screening will encourage industry to use such tests as a legal defense against cleaning up the workplace and against compensating any sick workers. . . .

. . . (W)hen genetic screening is fully developed, industrial workers aren't the only ones who may have to wrestle with the problem. What about the young corporate executive

CHAPTER 14

Managing Human Resources

who has a gene linked to a high incidence of heart disease? Or the brand-new M.B.A. who carries the gene for Huntington's disease, a neurological illness that doesn't appear until middle age? Will a company hire him, knowing there is a high probability that he will become fatally ill at the height of his career?

Screening also hits on several tricky legal issues. If tests did accurately predict future illness, an employer who placed susceptible workers in a high-risk environment might be charged with negligence. Yet employers whose screening tests only affect one race — and genetic diseases, by their very nature, tend to concentrate within ethnic groups — may be guilty of discrimination under the Civil Rights Act. And how about this — does a genetic predisposition to illness constitute a handicap? If so, will screened workers be protected by stat-

utes barring discrimination against the handicapped? Under any of these laws, it's likely that an employer would have to demonstrate that screening is the only safe, effective way of eliminating exposure risks.

Still, despite all the controversy, there's no denying the benefits that could come from screening. No one knows how many will be affected, or even how widespread screening will be. But by the end of the decade, scientists, in all likelihood, will be able to warn many people away from jobs that endanger their health. . . .

Source: Forbes, April 11, 1983, "The Bad Seed," by Jane Sasseen, pp. 160–162. Reprinted by permission. © Forbes Inc., 1983.

Chapter Outline

- The Changing Nature of Personnel
- Influences on Human Resource Management
- Human Resource Management

Key Terms

- human resource management
- human resource planning
- forecasting
- personnel objectives
- recruiting
- inside recruitment
- outside recruitment
- job analysis
- unfair discrimination
- false positive error
- false negative error
- halo error
- external equity
- internal equity
- comparable worth
- Scanlon plan

Chapter Objectives

After studying Chapter 14 you should be able to

1. Understand the organizational and external influences on human resource management.
2. See why most organizations engage in human resource planning.
3. Forecast, plan, monitor, and control an organization's human resource needs.
4. Use the job interview more effectively.
5. Discuss the use of different recruiting techniques.
6. Understand the difference between discrimination and unfair discrimination.

Introduction

Traditionally, personnel departments have not been held in the highest esteem. Herbert Meyer (1976) called them the "orphan box" in the organizational chart, "one that came from nowhere and didn't seem to fit anywhere" (p. 84). The staffs themselves sometimes have been regarded as "a bunch of drones whose apparent missions in life were to create paperwork, recruit secretaries who couldn't type, and send around memos whose impertinence was exceeded only by their irrelevance" (Meyer, 1976, p. 84).

The relative importance of the department can be judged by counting the corporate chief executive officers who reached the top by working their way up through the personnel ranks. The exact number is unknown, but it cannot be large compared with the numbers from other areas like production and finance. In the past, managers with their eye on the top position in corporations often went to great lengths to avoid personnel assignments, and with good reason. Personnel careers frequently dead-ended well below the executive level. People who reached executive positions in personnel, such as executive vice-president, seldom were given important roles in organizational decision making. It is common to find vice-presidents for finance and production on the boards of directors of major corporations, but it is rare for a seat to be given to a personnel executive. Worse still, in many organizations late-career transfers into personnel from a functional area such as production often were regarded as a charitable substitute for dismissal, and in fact they often were just that. There is some truth to the old joke that poorly performing corporate executives never die, they just go into personnel (where if they did die, presumably few would ever know).

Despite the historical perception of personnel, there is growing evidence that managers are beginning to recognize the important contribution this department can make to the overall effectiveness of the organization. This growing importance is partially reflected in the fact that many organizations have changed the name of their personnel departments to human resources management. This may seem like an innocuous change, but the new name reflects the fact that employees are *resources* that need to be managed effectively if organizations are to be successful. In addition, several major corporations have begun to rotate upwardly mobile managers through human resource management in preparation for higher-level executive positions (Meyer, 1976). What once was avoided is increasingly recognized as an important component in developing executives.

This chapter discusses the major aspects of human resource management in organizations and suggests how such management can be performed more effectively. Factors that can influence decision making in these areas also will be discussed.

To organize the discussion, it will be useful for us to have a conceptual model of human resource management. Such a model is provided in Figure 14.1. The model presents human resource management in terms of four broad, interrelated functions: staffing and personnel planning, recruitment and selection, employee training and development, and performance assessment and reward systems. The model indicates that each function exists in an environment consisting of both organizational and external influences. Because factors in the environment can influence how decisions are made with respect to each function, it is important to consider the nature of these environments.

The Changing Nature of Personnel

There are several reasons organizations have changed the way they view the contribution of effectively managed human resources. One of the most frequently cited concerns the increasing federal and state regulation of the relationship between workers and their employers. The financial impact of effective human resource management policies is evident in the large judgments handed down against several organizations found to have practiced systematic discrimination. American Telephone and Telegraph, for example, agreed to pay $15 million in back wages to female and minority employees who had been discriminated against. It has become increasingly common in the last ten years for employees to sue major companies successfully for a variety of discriminatory practices. The legal implications of what once were considered routine management and personnel decisions have jolted many organizations into taking a closer look at their human resource management practices.

There also is growing evidence that because of the changing nature of industry in the United States, employees are now making a more direct contribution to the effectiveness of their organizations. In the past, the American economy was dominated by semiautomated, mass-production manufacturing, such as that in the automobile and steel industries. Employees most often performed relatively simple, routine jobs requiring a low skill level. When an employee quit or economic conditions forced layoffs, there was little concern about finding replacements.

In the past twenty years there has been a dramatic shift in the labor force toward high technology and service jobs. Organizations in these new industries may depend more on the skills and motivation of their employees to be successful. The need for service-sector employees with human relations skills has been apparent for a long time, because of the direct contact these employees have with customers. A major airline, for example, cannot afford to have customers greeted by a service representative who is alienated, discourteous, or unmotivated. Policies concerning human resource management can help determine how employees feel about their jobs and whether they are motivated to work, which makes these policies crucial in the service sector.

In the high-technology industry, the most important need is for employees with a high level of expertise and knowledge. The ability of computer companies such as International Business Machines to attract and retain employees with sophisticated technical and engineering skills is crucial. These skills often are in short supply, and companies find themselves in direct competition for the best

Figure 14.1
Human Resource Management

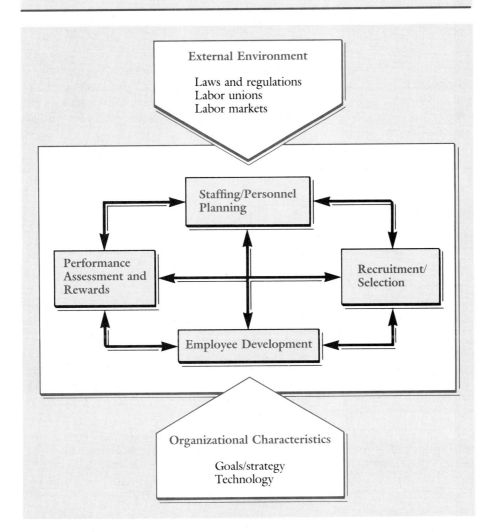

employees. The stakes in this competition are very high. When companies find it difficult or impossible to recruit employees with the expertise they require, serious disruption can occur in product development. As organizations become increasingly dependent on the intellectual rather than the physical efforts of their employees, the importance of effective human resource management increases. It is not a coincidence that some of the most innovative and best human resource management policies are found in high-technology firms (Peters and Waterman, 1982). Perhaps Meyer (1976) was correct when he suggested that personnel managers have become the "new corporate heroes."

Influences on Human Resource Management

Decisions about human resource management are influenced by a number of different factors. Some factors are related to the nature of the organization, and others to outside sources. In both cases, these environmental influences are the context within which specific personnel decisions are made. Influences may range from legal constraints that dictate organizational actions, such as the requirement to pay minimum wage, to those that simply shape actions that organizations were planning to take. For example, an organization planning to recruit on a college campus may make a special effort to contact minority student groups. Because these influences often shape or constrain personnel decisions, they are important for managers to understand.

Organizational Influences

Perhaps the most important influence on human resource management is the nature of the organization itself. The purpose and goals of the organization to a large extent determine the types of human resources that will be required, the number of employees needed, and the time at which the need will be greatest. A steel manufacturer, for instance, has different human resource requirements than does a firm developing computer software. Both companies need good employees, but the average level of education required of employees in the computer software firm will be much higher than that needed for steel-industry employees.

The nature of the industry the firm is part of influences the nature of the human resource problems confronting it. For example, the steel industry has been declining for a number of years, in part because of increased competition from lower-priced imports. As a result, human resource managers in steel companies are likely to face problems associated with a shrinking work force. Issues concerning employee layoffs, early retirement, helping to place excess employees in other organizations, and retraining are probably more salient to a personnel manager at United States Steel Corporation than are recruiting and selection issues. In contrast, the computer software industry has been characterized by rapid growth and expanding market opportunities. Personnel managers in computer software firms may spend a majority of their time on strategies to recruit and retain technically sophisticated employees.

The level of technology of an organization also has an important impact on human resource requirements. To a certain extent, technology is related to the industry in which an organization operates. Within industries, however, organizations may differ in their degree of technological sophistication, and technology may change as organizations follow different acquisition or merger strategies. Changes in the level of technological sophistication are currently evident in the automobile industry. Computer-assisted car design and the growing importance of electronic components in the operation of cars have created a need for a new category of technically sophisticated employees. The increasing use of industrial robots in auto manufacturing has changed the emphasis from semiskilled assemblers to specially trained technicians who can monitor and maintain this equipment.

A final organizational characteristic that may have an important influence on the human resource requirements of organizations is long-range strategy. Human resource policies are shaped not only by what organizations are, but also by what they want to become. The long-range plans and strategy of a corporation can have important implications for the mix of human resources necessary to manage the company effectively.

The actions of the Bendix Corporation prior to its acquisition by Allied, illustrate this point. Historically, Bendix drew most of its revenues and profits from automotive products. More recently the Bendix strategy has been to decrease its reliance on the automotive industry and increase its investment in such diverse areas as forest products and aerospace technology. Thus, the mix of managers appropriate for the corporation has changed. The importance of having managers with skills and ability in the automotive industry has decreased, whereas managers with skills in high technology and natural resources have become more important.

The way Bendix chose to move into new industries also has had implications for human resource planning. Rather than starting its own companies, which would have created an immediate need to hire large numbers of employees with different skills, Bendix chose to diversify by acquisition and investment in existing firms. As a result, the strategic changes in human resource requirements have been much smaller than if Bendix had chosen a different strategy. The important point is that the organization's long-range strategic plan creates a need for human resource planning. Human resources that currently exist may become less important in the future. The organization may need to recruit employees with backgrounds more closely related to future needs.

External Environmental Influences

Perhaps the most important influence on changes in human resource management in recent years has come from the external environment. Increasing federal regulations and laws governing employment have fundamentally altered the way personnel decisions are made. Government regulation of labor–management relations and income maintenance in the form of Social Security has existed for a number of years. More recently, the federal government has become much more active in regulating health and safety in the workplace and ensuring equal employment opportunity. Organizations have had to make important changes in their personnel practices to guard against systematic discrimination with respect to sex, religion, race, color, national origin, and age. Many organizations have had to evaluate traditional personnel practices to determine whether they discriminate in ways prohibited by law. Organizations doing business with the federal government also have had to change recruiting and hiring strategies to ensure that greater numbers of women and minority group members are employed. Federal employment regulations have had important implications for human resource management in organizations and have contributed to its importance.

A second aspect of the external environment that can have important implications for human resource management is the labor market organizations draw on. Organizations compete for the best employees in a labor market composed of people with differing skills, experience, educational backgrounds, and motivation. Competition for employees with specific skills and abilities may be fierce. The phenomenal growth in the computer industry, for example, has created a shortage of employees with computer backgrounds and high-technology skills. Failure to compete effectively in recruiting these people may doom firms with opportunities for market expansion to grow at a slower rate. Tandem Computers, for instance, would find it impossible to continue growth at past rates (100 percent) if it were unsuccessful in recruiting new employees. Organizations may also be forced to hire new employees with less than the desired skill level and provide extensive training programs.

Organizations also must make efforts to retain valued employees who are likely to be recruited by other firms. Such efforts can lead to changes in compensation and benefit packages designed both to facilitate recruitment and to increase the employee's desire to remain in the organization. For example, the Lockheed Engineering and Management Services Company recently changed from a pension plan that became vested after ten years of employment to one that guarantees immediate vesting and portability of pension contributions ("Pension Plans," 1982). The president, Robert B. Young, Jr., thinks the plan will make it easier to recruit engineers and computer programmers and to retain employees to whom retirement benefits are important. Even though immediate vesting decreases the costs associated with leaving Lockheed, the company had experienced complete turnover of the nonunion work force every five years under the old system. Therefore, turnover was already a problem. Under the new system, Young expects, more employees will want to remain with Lockheed.

Conditions in the labor market can be ignored only at considerable risk to the organization. Labor market conditions, like federal employment regulations, can have important implications for how personnel decisions are made. The incident described in Feature 14.1 suggests that factors in the external labor market — in this case, unions — can even affect the organization's survival.

Human Resource Management

Within the context of the organization's nature and external environment, **human resource management** involves several important functions in organizations. We will highlight four that are crucial: planning, recruiting and selecting employees, training and development, and performance assessment and

Feature 14.1
Labor Troubles Plague Nation's Airlines

The nation's airlines are facing rough going.

Federal deregulation of the industry prompted many of them to lure passengers with costly price wars, and the prolonged recession hurt air travel. A number of airlines have asked their employees to take wage cuts to remain financially viable.

Many employees have accepted the cuts, but the employees represented by the International Association of Machinists and the Teamsters generally have been dragging their heels. These employees, including mechanics, inspectors, baggage handlers, and aircraft cleaners, have called strikes against several major carriers.

Golden West Airlines, one of the nation's largest commuter carriers, was one of their victims. Golden West gave its employees a choice between a 10 percent wage cut or unemployment. The Teamsters and the Air Line Pilots Association, representing the pilots, rejected the wage cut. The company invited the unions to audit its books in an attempt to convince them of the airline's serious financial plight. Instead, the unions chose to "call the carrier's bluff." Unable to meet its next payroll, Golden West declared bankruptcy.

Eastern Airlines did win wage concessions from its flight attendants and pilots but not from employees who were members of the International Association of Machinists. The company warned the machinists that pay increases might mean massive layoffs. There was an impasse in negotiations, but a strike was averted when Eastern agreed to a 32 percent wage increase over three years.

The same day the union ratified the contract, Eastern furloughed 1,600 employees, including 1,200 members of the machinists' union. The action caused a furor. The union charged the airline with retaliation. There was concern that the flight attendants would hold out for a costly new contract and the pilots would cancel their wage-concession agreement. The airline's 16,000 nonunion employees were angry about the wage settlement, raising the prospect that their pay would have to be increased as well.

Although Eastern had a history of cooperative relations with employees, it looks as if they'll be plagued with labor troubles for some time to come.

Source: "The Airlines' Invisible Warlords," *Frequent Flyer,* August 1983, pp. 36–39.

compensation systems. From a managerial perspective, these functions correspond to four important personnel questions: How do we determine our hiring and staffing needs? How do we ensure that high-quality employees are brought into the organization? How do we ensure that employees have the necessary skills required to perform their jobs? How do we determine which employees are performing well and then reward them?

Human Resource Planning

In some organizations, human resource planning may be virtually nonexistent. Vacancies are filled as they occur, and new employees are hired as jobs are created. Most large organizations have recognized, however, that this can be a very ineffective method of human resource management. Because it often takes considerable time to recruit good replacements, for example, there can be severe disruption when organizations do not adequately plan ahead for human resource needs. Although the sophistication level of planning systems varies widely, most large organizations engage in some form of human resource planning.

Human resource planning has been defined by Glueck (1982, p. 85) as "the process by which management determines how the organization should move from its current (human resource) position to its desired (human resource) position." More specifically, it involves translating organizational goals and objectives into specific human resource objectives. The nature of the planning process may differ, but generally it involves three major activities (Glueck, 1982; Heneman, Schwab, Fossum, and Dyer, 1980): forecasting, programming, and evaluation and control.

Forecasting. The first stage of the planning process involves **forecasting,** a careful assessment of future human resource needs in relation to present capabilities. Organizational goals and anticipated changes in organizational structure, jobs, and productivity must be assessed to evaluate future requirements. For example, planned expansion or reduction in specific parts of the organization will place demands on human resources, as will changes in production methods and reorganization of departments. Heneman and colleagues (1980) provide a simplified illustration of this process:

> Assume that an organization has determined that there is a direct relationship between its dollar sales (corrected for inflation) and the number of salespeople it requires. Historically, this relationship has been $40,000:1. The sales projection for next year is $400,000 (in constant dollars). Thus, an initial estimate of the demand for salespeople is ten. It is also known, however, that a new sales technique will be introduced. It is predicted to increase the productivity of salespeople by 10 percent. Thus sales per person will increase to $44,000, and the demand for salespeople will be only nine [p. 177].

In this example, the process begins by translating organizational goals — projected sales — into specific personnel requirements needed to achieve these goals.

The next step involves assessing current human resources to determine whether they are sufficient to meet anticipated needs, or whether they will be greater than needed. If the hypothetical company in the illustration already has nine full-time salespeople, for example, it appears that current human resources are consistent with anticipated needs. What makes this process more complicated is that other changes also must be anticipated. For example, employees may leave the organization, retire, die, or take leaves of absence. It would be important to know whether any of the current salespeople are close to retirement or have applied for transfers to other parts of the company. Because many unanticipated changes can take place among employees, it is difficult to assess precisely the organization's future capability. Historical information on turnover rates, however, and information from other sources, such as the knowledge that a competitor may attempt to recruit some of your employees, can be taken into consideration to improve estimates.

Assessment of the organization's human resource capability should not be limited to current resources. When additional employees must be brought into the organization, it is important to evaluate the labor market carefully to determine whether they can be recruited. For certain highly technical positions, there may not be enough trained people available to meet the organization's needs. In a sales position, however, it is more likely that the labor pool will be sufficient. Depending on the background and experience of the individuals, extensive training programs may become a necessity.

Thus, the first step in the human resource planning process reconciles the demand for human resources with the available supply, both inside and outside the organization. When discrepancies are found between anticipated demand and supply, some form of action is called for. The nature of this action is determined in the next stage of the planning process.

Programming. Once human resource needs become clear, they must be translated into specific **personnel objectives** and goals. Following the earlier illustration, objectives may be as straightforward as the acquisition of three additional salespeople. There are likely to be a number of alternate ways, however, to achieve any personnel objective. For example, additional salespeople can be hired from outside or transferred from other parts of the organization. Similarly, the work force can be reduced through firing, layoffs, transfers to other jobs, natural attrition, or plans that encourage early retirement. Because different strategies are likely to be available for achieving each goal, it is important to identify and evaluate clearly the feasibility, costs, and benefits of the alternatives.

The importance of comprehensive planning is underscored by the fact that problems in one part of the organization may provide solutions to problems in another area. Reducing the marketing staff in one division, for example, may provide a pool of talent for increasing the sales force in another division. It is useful to prepare a chart to compare projected human resource needs with capabilities for each major unit and job category in an organization. Comparing the discrepancies among major areas can help identify creative solutions that might otherwise go unnoticed. These solutions may even suggest cost savings. For example, transferring employees from an overstaffed department to another that needs additional people avoids difficult and potentially disruptive problems associated with firing employees and eliminates recruiting and hiring costs.

When personnel objectives have been set and the alternate methods of achieving these objectives evaluated, specific action plans must be developed. These plans are the specific steps to be taken to achieve each objective. Again, the importance of developing a comprehensive and integrated action plan must be stressed. It would be wasteful, for example, if an organization sent two re-

cruiters to universities to hire people for two different positions when one recruiter could have handled both jobs. Because human resource functions are
interdependent, actions in one area may create demands in another area that
must be planned for. Hiring a large number of additional employees may create
a need for additional personnel to conduct orientation sessions and training
programs. Similarly, changes in certain personnel practices, such as compensation systems, may be required if action plans for recruiting new employees are to
be accomplished effectively. The ultimate goal is to identify a set of action strategies that simultaneously maximizes the likelihood of success and minimizes the
costs involved in achieving the organization's goals.

Personnel objectives provide direction for specific actions needed to manage human resources effectively. They also provide standards for judging success
in achieving these objectives. The final step in the planning process involves
carefully evaluating human resource activities that have been undertaken to
achieve important objectives.

Evaluation and Control. After action plans have been implemented,
their progress must be monitored and their success evaluated. Unanticipated
events during implementation may necessitate a change in direction or the ini-
tiation of new plans, and therefore it is important to monitor plans continually
during implementation as well as after they are established and achieving their
results. For example, a large retailing corporation recently implemented an early
retirement plan to overcome obstacles to promotion for younger managers. The
corporation found that it had a large number of older managers at the middle
and top levels. Because of poor promotion opportunities, some younger employees were leaving. An early retirement plan was established and presented to
about 2,100 management personnel, about 700 of whom were expected to take
advantage of it. To the corporation's surprise, however, 1,400 managers, twice
the expected number, chose early retirement. This created not only a drain on
resources that were an enticement for managers to retire early, but also a shortage of senior managers. The corporation possibly lost many people it never
thought would leave and whom it had wished to retain.

Evaluating this personnel action would raise questions about whether future actions should be changed. The inducement for early retirement was
greater than that needed by the organization to achieve its goal of reducing the
number of managers by 700. In addition, during monitoring of the plan it probably became clear that people were leaving in greater numbers than had been
anticipated. Once this became obvious, the organization could have started
training programs to prepare younger managers for promotion to more responsible positions. When crucial vacancies were created, experienced managers
might have been recruited from other companies. It is not always possible to
predict the consequences of human resource policies with complete confidence.
As a result it is particularly important to monitor their outcome and, when necessary, to take corrective action before problems become too great.

When properly conducted, human resource planning sets the agenda for
what needs to be done in each of the important functional areas.

Recruiting and Selection

Recruiting and selection are probably the most visible human resource activities in organizations, if only because these areas are often the first in which those outside the company, such as students, come into contact with organizational representatives. **Recruiting** is a process with which all of you will become familiar. It is most often viewed from the perspective of either the individual job seeker or the organization attempting to hire new employees. It is best, however, to consider the process as one that matches the preferences and goals of individuals with the needs and preferences of organizations. The nature of the process suggests that conflict exists within and between the two parties (Porter, Lawler, and Hackman, 1975). The potential areas of conflict are depicted in Figure 14.2.

First, let us take the perspective of the job seeker. People often try to make themselves attractive to potential employers, but they also need to gather information to make a good job choice. Organizations also need to make themselves attractive to potential employees. At the same time, they must gather information to be used in the selection process. The potential for conflict in this situation is apparent. The more unrealistically people describe themselves to become more attractive, the most frustrated organizations will become in gathering ac-

Figure 14.2
Potential Conflict in Recruiting and Selection

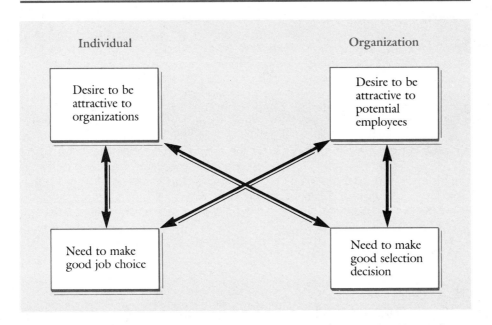

Source: L. W. Porter, E. E. Lawler, and J. R. Hackman, *Behavior in Organizations,* p. 134. Copyright ©
1975 by McGraw-Hill, Inc.

curate information for selection. Similarly, organizations that describe their jobs in unrealistically positive terms are not providing job seekers with accurate information for judging whether the job is right for them.

Labor market conditions will influence the motivation of each party in the recruiting process and thus the potential nature of conflict. In a *buyer's market,* in which the supply of candidates exceeds available jobs, organizations will be less motivated to be unrealistically positive in their recruiting. In a *seller's market,* in which the supply of candidates is much smaller than the number of jobs available, job seekers need not be as motivated to make themselves attractive. They can focus on gathering good information about available positions, for example, by asking difficult questions of recruiters.

If it is assumed that the goal of both individuals and organizations is to ensure the best possible match between employees and jobs, it is in the best interests of each party to be as candid and honest as possible. Inaccurate or fraudulent job descriptions and resumés will hamper the recruiting process (Feature 14.2). When erroneous information of this type is exchanged, it is more likely that individuals will be dissatisfied with their jobs or that organizations will be dissatisfied with individual employees. A poor match between em-

---

Feature 14.2
Stopping Resumé Fraud

Four out of every five resumes contain false job history information, and about 30 percent misrepresent educational background.

These startling charges come from Thomas Camden, president of Camden and Associates Inc. He says that the most common misdeeds are exaggerating job responsibilities, making up job titles, inflating salary levels, covering up employment gaps, and listing college degrees that don't exist. People also lie about their height, weight, and marital status.

"Resumé fraud is so widespread today because of intense competition in the job market and severe economic pressures to secure better-paying jobs," he said. Job candidates also apparently believe that employers won't read the resume carefully and verify the information.

Camden noted that many interviewers are untrained and uncomfortable. As a result, they don't closely examine and verify the applicant's credentials. This is especially true if the appearance and personality of the job seeker please the interviewer.

He encourages employers to catch fraud by studying the resumé before the interview and making notes on questions to ask. Interviewers also should inform applicants that all personal information is subject to routine verification, which is a condition of employment.

Interviewers also should ask open-ended questions to get more information and to resolve discrepancies or gaps that may appear. Incongruities must be sought out: Would a twenty-five-year-old be a bank vice-president?

And finally, if the candidate is viable, check the past employment history and educational credentials before making the job offer.

ployees and jobs — which may result in dissatisfaction, poor performance, or turnover — is ultimately in the best interests of neither individuals nor organizations.

Recruiting Activities. Large organizations typically engage in a wide variety of recruiting activities, ranging from job postings at state employment offices to the use of executive recruiting consultants. The nature of organizational recruiting activities depends on a number of factors. The influence of labor market conditions on recruiting has already been mentioned. Organizations facing tight labor markets must use more intensive recruiting to ensure an adequate number of good applicants. The nature of the recruiting process also depends on the types of positions open and the budget available for this purpose. Different recruiting activities are illustrated in Figure 14.3

For entry-level positions that are unskilled or that require few skills, recruiting generally is confined to the local area. Organizations may rely heavily on unsolicited applications to the personnel department, advertisements in local trade journals or newspapers, job postings at employment offices or union halls, or referrals from current employees. The more skill the positions require, the more regional in scope recruiting may become. For example, advertisements may be

Figure 14.3
Organizational Recruiting Activities

TYPE OF POSITION	SCOPE OF RECRUITING	PROBABLE RECRUITING METHODS	COST

Unskilled or entry level	Local	Unsolicited applications
		Advertisements in local
		  newspaper
		Posting at state
		  employment office
		Employee referral
			Low

Semiskilled	Regional	Advertisements in
		  newspapers in
		  surrounding cities
		Recruiting at vocational
		  or technical schools
		Employment agencies
			Moderate

Skilled and management/ executive	National	College recruiting
		Recruiting at professional
		  or technical society
		  meetings
		Executive recruiting
		  firms
			High

placed in newspapers in nearby cities, recruiters may visit technical or vocational schools in the area, and employment agencies in several different cities may be contacted. For executive and highly technical positions, nationwide recruiting may be undertaken. Visiting a large number of college campuses across the country, as well as attending meetings of professional and technical societies, may be more common recruiting activities.

Inside and Outside Recruitment. Another important decision organizations must make about recruiting concerns whether efforts will be directed inside or outside the company, or both. Many large organizations have established policies of **inside recruitment,** which permit current employees to bid on job openings. Promotion from within provides greater career opportunities for employees and reduces the time and money required to fill a position. In addition, better selection decisions often can be made, because more is known about the performance of people already in the organization. Some personnel departments maintain detailed skill inventories of current employees to assist in determining whether qualified candidates already exist in the organization. When individuals with the relevant skills or potential do not exist inside the company, **outside recruitment** may be the only alternative. External recruiting may be most likely at the lowest and highest levels of the organization, with internal promotion policies used to fill positions in between.

The goal of all recruiting efforts is to ensure that an adequate number of qualified applicants is available from which to select. For many lower-level, unskilled positions, one applicant may be sufficient. For other positions it is usually in the organization's best interest to generate a large applicant pool. The larger the number of applicants, the greater the probability that one or more will have the skills required to perform the job effectively. Knowing just what skills are required for the effective performance of a job and then determining which applicants possess these skills are the two most difficult problems in selection.

Job Analysis. The recruiting and selection process typically is preceded by a careful analysis of the skill requirements of a job. Generally termed **job analysis,** this process involves analyzing the component tasks required in a job and the skills necessary for effective performance of each task. For example, a receptionist may be required to greet visitors to the organization and send them to appropriate locations, type routine correspondence, and file memos and correspondence. A general knowledge of the organization (so he or she will know where to send visitors), interpersonal skills, typing ability, and a knowledge of filing procedures would be important in performing the job.

Once the relevant skills for a particular job are identified, methods must be devised to determine whether they are possessed by applicants. This process is illustrated in a somewhat unique situation in Feature 14.3. When Renaldo Nehemiah decided to enter professional football, there was agreement on the skills required to become a good wide receiver. The most important questions about his suitability — whether he could catch a pass and take a hit — could be an-

Feature 14.3
The Recruiting of Nehemiah

Renaldo Nehemiah was a world-class track superstar. The holder of several world records in sprint hurdle events, he was virtually unbeatable. His time of 12.93 seconds in the 110-meter high hurdles was a record some experts predicted would stand until the end of the century.

But it wasn't until Nehemiah won television's "Superstars" competition two years in a row that people began to notice his other athletic abilities. One year he finished second in weight lifting to Mark Gastineau, a 6-foot, 5-inch, 250-pound defensive end for the New York Jets. Gastineau pressed 300 pounds in the competition; the 6-foot, 1-inch, 177-pound Nehemiah lifted 265 pounds. Why, asked some of the people in the competition, aren't you in professional football?

The idea intrigued Nehemiah. Although he hadn't played football since he was a high school quarterback, he qualified as a free agent, which meant he was not subject to the National Football League draft and could negotiate with any team in the league. When his lawyer, Ron Stanko, began contacting teams, however, a very strange recruiting and selecting process began.

Most of the teams had Nehemiah demonstrate that he could catch a football. But when Stanko suggested that the Philadelphia Eagles suit up their three biggest defensive linemen to see whether Nehemiah could take a hit, the player personnel director asked, "What if he gets hurt?"

The Dallas Cowboys gave Nehemiah a personality test with such questions as, "If a car goes 9 miles in thirty minutes, how many miles per hour is the car traveling?"

Apparently forgetting he was a world-class track star, the Eagles administered a test to measure leg strength and the San Diego Chargers gave him a physical. Almost incredibly, the Pittsburgh Steelers insisted that Nehemiah be timed in the 40-yard dash. The team considered a time of 4.1 seconds fast, apparently unaware that Nehemiah had run the same distance in 4.5 seconds *over hurdles.*

The teams showed the same lack of reality in salary negotiations. Perhaps believing the image of the poor amateur track athlete, Philadelphia initially offered him $35,000 for the first year. At the time Nehemiah was earning more than $100,000 a year, independent of a lucrative endorsement and consulting agreement with a shoe company.

The whole process led Nehemiah to conclude that football front-office personnel "were naive, narrow-minded, and not very bright as a group."

Nehemiah eventually signed a contract with the San Francisco 49'ers, a team that recognized his body strength, athletic ability, and football potential from the very beginning.

Source: "... But Can He Take a Hit?" by John Papanek, *Sports Illustrated,* April 26, 1982, pp. 30–36.

swered, at least in part, by simulation tests such as pass-catching drills. Interestingly, no team was ultimately willing to test realistically whether he could take a hit. In this example, a number of selection devices did not seem necessary. Although there may be some justification for a physical examination, it seems safe to assume that the world's fastest sprint hurdler could run the 40-yard dash in a time acceptable to most teams.

In the case of job skills such as typing and filing, the process of assessing the potential of applicants is relatively straightforward. Standard tests that measure the ability to perform both these tasks can be administered. When tests are administered beyond those necessary to establish the applicant's ability to perform the job, problems may arise for the organization. Unless screening devices can be shown to be job related, charges of discrimination are possible.

For many jobs there are no agreed-upon standards to determine what skills are necessary, or the skills themselves may be very difficult to measure and evaluate. Good interpersonal skills are important in most management positions, for example, but it may be difficult for people to agree on what constitutes "good" interpersonal behavior. A person you believe is interpersonally skilled may not be viewed the same way by others. Even if it is possible to agree on a definition, measuring such skills in applicants may prove very difficult. When job skills are not easily defined or not objectively measurable, the recruiter often must make subjective judgments. Previous employers may be contacted to determine how the applicant has performed in similar positions, and interviews may be held to evaluate these skills more directly.

Discrimination Laws. When job-related skills are difficult to define and measure or when selection devices are not job related, organizations frequently encounter major problems. A number of laws designed to end unfair discrimination govern selection processes and employment policies in organizations (Arvey, 1979). It is important to recognize that the intent of these laws is not to end all discrimination in the selection process but, rather, to stop discrimination that can be viewed as unfair. Arvey (1979, p. 7) defines **unfair discrimination** in selection as follows: "Unfair discrimination or bias is said to exist when members of a minority group have lower probabilities of being selected for a job when, in fact, if they had been selected, their probabilities of performing successfully in a job would have been equal to those of nonminority group members."

Federal and state laws prohibit organizations from discriminating against employees on the basis of race, age, color, religion, sex, or national origin. Exceptions are made only when employers can establish that one or more of these attributes are directly related to the individual's ability to perform the job. Most organizations have found this to be a formidable task. For example, Northwest Airlines was recently ordered to pay $52.5 million in back pay to 3,364 female flight attendants who were paid less than their male counterparts for performing what a judge determined was essentially the same work ("Northwest's Bias," 1982). The airline argued that paying men more than women was justifiable given the nature of their jobs, but it found it difficult to convince others of the merits of this view.

Fair Discrimination. We have mentioned that laws governing employment practices are designed to end unfair discrimination. Implicit in this statement is the recognition that some discrimination is fair. It is important to recognize that the primary intent of selection procedures in organizations is to discriminate those applicants who can successfully perform the job from those who cannot. Organizations typically use a number of selection criteria to predict whether applicants can effectively perform a job. These include tests such as work sample tests, interviews, recommendations from prior employers, and the information provided on employment applications on such matters as training and educational background. The goal is to predict subsequent job performance from information collected during the selection process. Because job skills are often difficult to identify and even harder to measure, and individual motivation on the job is hard to predict, selection is an imperfect process.

As Figure 14.4 shows, four different types of outcomes can result from this process. Correct selection decisions are made when, based on information collected in the selection process, an organization predicts either that individuals would perform well on the job and they ultimately do, or that individuals would perform poorly on the job and they ultimately fail. Errors in the selection process occur when a person is predicted to succeed and he or she ultimately fails (a **false positive error**) and when a person is predicted to fail and he or she ultimately succeeds (a **false negative error**). The relative seriousness of these two errors depends on several factors. You may have noticed that the definition of unfair discrimination provided earlier basically describes a false negative error. In other words, the selection process predicts that an individual within a protected class, a minority, will fail when in fact he or she would have performed the job very well. In view of the monetary judgments being levied against corporations for discriminatory practices, this is a very serious error. When dealing with members of minority groups, many organizations have decided it is in their best interests to minimize the false negative error even if this means increasing the

Figure 14.4
Outcomes of Selection Decisions

	HOW INDIVIDUAL WOULD HAVE ACTUALLY PERFORMED ON JOB	
PREDICTED PERFORMANCE BASED ON SELECTION INFORMATION	*Low*	*High*
Low	True negative	False negative (error)
High	False positive (error)	True positive

number of false positive errors that are made; that is, applicants should be given the benefit of the doubt.

Labor market conditions also are likely to be an important factor in judging the relative seriousness of each type of error. In very tight labor markets in which there are few qualified candidates, organizations want to avoid rejecting candidates who have even a remote chance of being successful. With few applicants from which to choose, organizations can afford to reject only the most obviously unqualified. In contrast, in job markets in which there are many applicants, organizations can afford to be a little more choosy. Even if an applicant who would have performed well is passed up in the selection process, there are likely to be many other qualified applicants from which to choose. In this situation, the costs of passing up someone who might have performed the job well are minimal.

The recruiting and selection process is one of the most crucial functions of human resource departments. To be effective, organizations must ensure that they can attract high-quality employees. In addition to being extremely important, the recruiting and selection process has proved to be one of the more difficult functions to perform well. Predicting job performance from information collected in the selection process is at best an imperfect endeavor. In addition, the costs to organizations of making poor selection decisions have increased as some labor markets have tightened and government agencies have increased their regulation in this area.

Even when selection processes work well, the important functions performed by human resource departments do not end. Not all applicants for a position may possess the necessary skills or know how to perform the job in a way the organization considers appropriate. As a result, organizations frequently must offer extensive training programs for newly hired employees. In addition, the need to train and develop employees does not end with their first positions. Organizations need to ensure an adequate supply of employees to move into higher-level slots. People must not just be trained for their current jobs, but also be developed so they can advance in the organization. Training and development activities, therefore, are an important component of human resource management. We will discuss them in the next section.

Training and Development

Large organizations typically spend millions of dollars on employee training and development. Training programs can range from sessions on safety awareness for production employees to thirteen-week executive development programs such as Harvard's Advanced Management Program, which has tuition fees in excess of $15,000. Because of the costs involved, organizations must carefully plan their training and development efforts. Heneman and colleagues (1980) suggest a four-step planning process for employee training and development (Fig. 14.5).

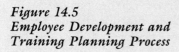

Figure 14.5
Employee Development and
Training Planning Process

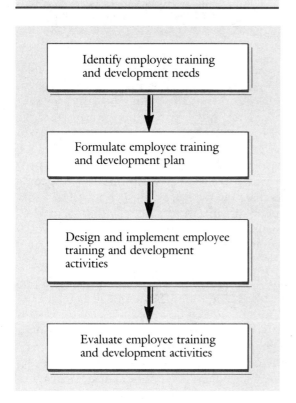

Source: Heneman, Schwab, Fossum, and Dyer, 1980.

Identifying Training Needs. The first step in the process involves identifying employee training and development needs. Training needs can be assessed in many different ways, ranging from surveys of line managers about the perceived needs of their employees to identification of specific areas in which actual performance falls below the desired level, as when there is a higher-than-expected number of industrial accidents in a department. Although a clear distinction is rarely drawn, employee *training* efforts appear to be directed toward increasing skills and abilities relating to the performance of the current job. In contrast, employee *development* efforts are directed toward increasing the level of an employee's knowledge and skill so that advancement is possible.

When performance discrepancies are noted, it is important to determine whether they interfere with effectiveness. Discrepancies that are relatively minor or that relate to peripheral areas of the job may not justify the costs associated with a training program. In addition, training existing employees is not the only way such problems can be solved. If present employees do not possess the skills and abilities to perform a job or are unlikely to be motivated to attain these skills, hiring new employees may be a more cost-effective solution. Organizations may assess whether training needs are widespread or isolated in one or two individuals. If they are isolated, the organization is more likely to transfer or dismiss than to train the employees.

Formulating a Plan. After specific training needs are assessed throughout the organization, the second step involves formulating a training plan to satisfy these needs. Organizations frequently find that training needs exceed the resources available for this purpose. Therefore, organizations must determine which training needs are most vital to overall effectiveness. A development plan then can be prepared that specifies exactly who is to be trained, in what areas, and when. What may appear to be isolated training needs in any one department may be major training needs across departments, as when one or two people from twenty different departments share the same need. In such a case, developing a comprehensive training program, organization-wide or within major divisions, is valuable. A comprehensive development plan also facilitates coordination and greater efficiency in training.

Designing and Implementing a Plan. Once a development plan is prepared, more specific decisions must be made about the design and conduct of specific training activities. The nature of the training objectives has an important influence on how these decisions are made. For example, one decision involves whether training should be conducted in-house by staff personnel or by an external organization that provides such services. The American Management Association, for instance, offers an extensive series of management training programs. Frequently, sending managers to these programs is more effective than trying to duplicate the programs internally. If training is to be offered within the organization, a decision must be made about whether on-the-job training or special sessions conducted away from the job would be more effective. For example, certain types of employee development are better achieved by job rotation or special assignments than by training lectures. When training objectives include the transmission of a great deal of standardized knowledge, lectures or films may be most appropriate. When making these decisions, organizations should always have as their goal selecting a training method that will be most effective in attaining the specific objective.

Evaluating Effectiveness. After training programs have been designed and initiated, their effectiveness must be evaluated. Has the training program accomplished the stated objectives? In many organizations, training efforts are never carefully evaluated. At best, members of the training staff survey participants to determine if they were satisfied and thought the experience worthwhile. As Main (1982) has noted, however, "executives who have attended almost any sort of management training usually recall the experience warmly. Of course, no one is likely to come back from Aspen and admit that he has just wasted two weeks" (p. 235). Although the feelings of participants in the training program are important to determine, they are perhaps not the most unbiased source of information.

Because most training and development efforts consider changes in behavior and improved job performance their ultimate goal, it is important to determine whether this goal has been met. For training programs with relatively straightforward objectives, this may not be overly difficult. The number of accidents among employees who attend a safety awareness program could be examined, for example. Other programs, such as those involving executive development, may be much more difficult to assess in concrete terms, because training objectives are less tangible and results may not be expected for several years. It is still important, however, to determine whether the organization's resources were spent usefully.

Employee training and development activities represent an important organizational attempt to ensure that adequate human resources are available. Although selection practices have the same end, they are seldom enough. Organizations must continually develop their employees, both to ensure that job skills remain current and to prepare employees for advancement. In the next section, attention will be directed at how organizations assess the performance of employees and establish reward systems.

Performance Assessment and Compensation

After selection and training, most organizations face the crucial problem of retaining their best employees. Hiring and training good employees may have limited utility if most leave shortly after joining the organization. Organizational effectiveness often is influenced by the ability to retain a core of high-quality employees on a long-term basis. If high-quality new workers leave shortly after joining or if the best longer-tenure employees are likely to quit, organizational effectiveness may suffer.

The issue of retaining high-quality employees has two components. First, it must be possible to determine which employees are of high quality. To be effective, retention efforts must distinguish between high- and low-performing employees, for the simple reason that not all employees are worth retaining. In fact, Porter and colleagues (1975) suggest that the effectiveness of human resource management can be judged in part by the extent to which high performers are encouraged to remain and low performers are encouraged to leave. The ability to assess employees' performance accurately, therefore, may be crucial.

Second, once high-performing employees are identified, methods must be designed to encourage them to remain with the organization. Organizational reward practices will be a heavy influence on the desirability of remaining in the organization, as well as on the likelihood that those who remain continue to perform at a high level. Reward practices in organizations encompass a number of specific policies, including pay, fringe benefits, promotions, job assignments, opportunities for travel and development, and what often are known as **perks** (perquisites), such as a private corner office or a company car. To the majority of employees, however, pay is probably the most important reward an organization can offer. When compensation practices in organizations are inadequate, such as when pay levels are below those of competitors, the other rewards that can be given to high performers may not be sufficient to encourage them to remain. But not everyone is motivated by pay or has a need for a higher salary. Some employees may even state that pay is of secondary importance in their value systems. Even so, most practicing managers will tell you that few employees will turn down a pay raise or fail to become concerned when others are given raises and they are not. Because performance assessment and compensation practices are central to effective human resources management, they will be given special attention in this section.

Performance Evaluation. Evaluations of employee performance take place in all organizations, whether or not formal performance appraisal systems exist. Managers are continually making judgments about the relative performance of their employees. The presence of formal appraisal systems indicates only the extent to which these judgments are standardized and systematic.

In assessing the desirability of developing formal *performance appraisal* systems, Stone (1982) suggests that organizations must answer several important questions.

First, a decision must be made about why performance is to be evaluated. Performance evaluation systems can serve a number of important purposes in organizations. They can be the basis for pay raise decisions, provide feedback to employees on ways to improve their performance, be used in assessing employee training and development needs, and validate selection practices. Depending on the evaluation system's purpose, different performance assessment techniques will be appropriate. Global ratings or comparative rankings of overall employee performance may be appropriate for pay raise decisions. If the goal is the provision of feedback to improve performance or the assessment of training needs, however, evaluations must be conducted on specific aspects of job performance.

Second, organizations have to decide which employees are to be evaluated. Formal performance appraisal may not be equally appropriate for all types of employees. For instance, production employees in assembly-line or continuous-production operations may exhibit very little variance in performance. Because employee performance often is machine paced or largely controlled by the technology, little may be gained by assessing performance. When union contracts limit the basis on which personnel decisions can be made, performance assessment beyond extreme judgments may be unimportant. In addition, when people work in groups or production teams, it may be very difficult to assess individual performance. Not only will it be difficult to assess the individual's contribution to the overall group product, but the individual's ability to contribute may be controlled by the performance of others. Formal performance evaluation systems may not always be appropriate or worth the expense of development and administration.

But for many jobs in organizations, if not the majority, the assessment of performance is both feasible and desirable. For example, it is important for organizations to know whether managers are accomplishing important objectives, such as sales or production goals. The important point is that organizations must decide where it is most appropriate to evaluate employee performance and how to use the information from the evaluations for more effective human resource management.

Third, the organization must select specific criteria to be used in judging performance. Typical criteria range from employee traits (such as whether they are conscientious and cooperative) to behaviors on the job (such as whether they come to work on time) to actual results (those relating to the sales level, for example). The appropriateness of any one of these types of criteria may depend on the specific nature of the task performed. For example, for many production employees it is possible to measure results in terms of the actual numbers of units produced. In contrast, the results of efforts of employees in staff positions may not be apparent for many years. An employee engaged in long-range strategic planning, for instance, may have to be evaluated on behaviors thought to lead to good performance rather than on actual results. The nature of the employee's work has an important influence on his or her evaluation criteria.

In addition to the three general issues suggested by Stone (1982), organizations must make other, more specific decisions in developing performance assessment systems. The first concerns the *format of the rating.* Rating scales for purposes of evaluating employee performance have received considerable research attention (Kane and Lawler, 1979). Two general approaches to performance rating can be identified. These, and the specific techniques that fall within each, are summarized in Figure 14.6.

Comparative performance evaluation techniques involve the direct comparison of the performance levels of two or more employees. For example, if you were asked to rank your employees in terms of overall performance, this would involve comparative judgments. Comparative approaches to performance evaluation have the advantage of forcing supervisors to make difficult judgments. Whereas some supervisors tend to be overly lenient in their performance assessments, rating every employee high, comparative techniques force them to make distinctions among employees. One disadvantage of this approach is that rankings, by their nature, cannot tell us *how much* difference exists between the performance levels of employees ranked high and those ranked low. The difference between the highest- and lowest-ranked employees may be very small, but the ranking approach would force a distinction. In addition, comparative approaches provide limited information that can be used for feedback to employees on areas of performance deficiency. Thus, comparative approaches may be more useful in making pay raise decisions than in assessing training needs or providing feedback.

Absolute Standards is the second general approach to rating performance. In

Figure 14.6
Approaches to Employee Performance Evaluation

APPROACH AND TECHNIQUE	BRIEF DESCRIPTION
Comparative Approaches	
Straight ranking	Employees ranked from high to low on performance dimension
Alternative ranking	Employees ranked beginning with highest, then lowest, then second highest, and so forth
Paired comparison	All possible pairs of employees compared, and better performer of pair chosen
Forced distribution	Employees distributed into performance categories according to set distribution, e.g., only 10% can be in highest category
Absolute Standards	
Graphic rating scales	Employee performance rated on 5- to 7-point scale ranging from "very poor" to "very good"
Mixed standards scale	Behavioral descriptions of good, average, and poor performance are written; rater indicates whether employee fits the description, is better than the description, or is worse than the description
Behaviorally anchored rating scales	Rating scale is anchored by actual descriptions of job behavior indicating different levels of performance

Source: Porter, Lawler, and Hackman, 1975.

this format, employees are rated against a set of standards that depict varying levels of performance. For example, an employee's performance level might be rated on a 5-point scale anchored at the ends by descriptive terms such as "unacceptable performance" and "outstanding performance." One advantage of these techniques is that they facilitate rating employees on a number of different performance dimensions, such as quality, quantity, and cooperation with co-workers. Unfortunately, this approach has a number of faults. As suggested earlier, some supervisors make the mistake of being too lenient in rating employees. Less common but also possible with rating approaches are errors of strictness, in which everyone is rated too low, and of central tendency, in which everyone is rated average. In addition, supervisors may fail to make distinctions across different rating scales in evaluating individual employees. In the **halo error,** supervisors generalize from one important performance dimension to all other performance dimensions even though important differences may exist. An employee who produces a large quantity of items, for example, may be rated high in quality as well, even though the items produced vary greatly in quality.

Considerable research has been devoted to finding ways of improving the performance evaluation process. Unfortunately, the perfect system of evaluating employee performance has yet to be discovered. It generally is believed, however, that more valid and reliable evaluations can be achieved when anchor points on the rating scales describe specific behaviors. A rating scale anchor point of "excellent," for example, may be replaced by one that gives an example of excellent behavior, such as "processes orders for shipping the day they are received." Called **behaviorally anchored rating scales,** these tools are complex and difficult to develop. They promise to increase the accuracy of performance ratings, however, by focusing the supervisor's attention on specific examples of good and bad performance.

A second question that must be addressed in designing performance evaluation systems concerns who conducts the evaluation. In most organizations performance is evaluated by the employee's immediate supervisor. It is important to recognize, however, that others in the workplace often are in a good position to provide information for evaluation. An employee's performance also can be evaluated by co-workers, for example, who often are in a better position than the supervisor to observe work on a day-to-day basis. In addition, employees can rate themselves. Each particular source of information may have a unique problem. Self-ratings may be biased, for example. In combination, however, information collected from several different sources may be superior to information from any one source alone.

Compensation Systems. Perhaps the most important influence on employee decisions to remain in organizations is the rewards or compensation offered for membership. The way rewards are distributed to employees is crucial to how well employees perform while in the organization. Compensation systems therefore serve the dual purpose of encouraging employee retention and encouraging high levels of performance.

Overall compensation levels must be high enough to encourage employees to join and remain, but not so high as to waste scarce resources. In evaluating overall compensation systems, the concept of equity is useful. Equity can be evaluated along two separate dimensions. **External equity** is maintained when compensation is comparable to that employees might earn in other organizations for performing the same work. When overall compensation levels are low relative to those of other organizations, an incentive exists for employees to leave. When compensation is relatively high, the costs of leaving will be greater for employees, including poor performers whom organizations may wish to get rid of.

Compensation systems in organizations are composed of both salary and fringe benefits. Most organizations conduct periodic surveys of other organizations to determine whether the basic level of salary and fringe benefits they offer for different types of jobs is competitive. When employees are represented by a union, the collective bargaining agreement is crucial in determining overall compensation. Unions also may be very concerned about external equity, although they may be less sensitive to this issue when average compensation levels are above those offered by other organizations rather than below.

Within organizations the concept of **internal equity** becomes very important. Decisions have to be made about the value of specific jobs to an organization and the relative compensation to be offered employees in different positions. It would make little sense, for example, to offer the same level of salary and fringe benefits to a shipping clerk as to an executive. In theory, it should be possible to rank jobs in terms of their overall contribution and importance to organizational effectiveness. In practice, this is very difficult. This problem is overcome partly by conditions in the labor market. When the supply of potential employees in a job category is great, lower compensation is required than when a severe shortage exists. The fact that assistant professors of computer science may earn more than full professors of English may seem unfair, particularly to English professors, but it reflects the conditions in the labor markets for the two disciplines.

It is safe to assume that employees will compare their compensation levels with those of other employees. When discrepancies exist and they are felt to be unfair, motivation problems and turnover may result. Thus, it is important for organizations to design their compensation systems on a sound basis. Recently, discriminatory practices in compensation systems have come under increasing attention. The most blatant form of discrimination exists when men and women, or minority and nonminority employees, are compensated differently for performing the same job. The concept of **comparable worth** also suggests that comparisons between *different* jobs are important. Comparable worth reflects the contribution of different jobs to the organization and suggests that equal wages be paid to men and women performing tasks of equal value. In the past, certain positions dominated by female employees have paid lower wages than positions dominated by male employees. If these positions are of comparable value to the organization, there is little justification for differences in pay and a discriminatory practice may be involved. Although comparable worth is likely to become an increasingly important topic in coming years, there currently is no objective standard on which different jobs can be compared (Stone, 1982).

The effectiveness of compensation in motivating employees may depend less on the level of rewards given than on the basis on which they are distributed. If organizations want to encourage job performance, for example, rewards should be given to those who perform well and withheld from those who do not. This conclusion follows directly from current motivation theory and seems like such common sense that one would assume all organizations do this as a matter of course. Although many organizations say they relate rewards to job performance, however, particularly for managers, research often finds only a limited relationship between the two.

Even for chief executive officers with ultimate responsibility for the performance of the firm, which is easily measured, little relationship often is found between the bonus earned and overall organizational performance (Loomis, 1982). For instance, the chairman of Union Oil was paid $1.3 million in 1981, including $800,000 in incentive pay, and return on stockholders' equity was about 19 percent for the year. In contrast, the chairman of Standard Oil of Ohio (Sohio) achieved a return on stockholders' equity greater than 32 percent but was paid less than $800,000. In periods when organizational performance is poor, it is difficult to justify paying large bonuses to executives. A recent analysis in *Fortune* (Loomis, 1982), however, suggests that this is precisely what has happened in many companies.

It is easy to suggest that pay be tied to job performance to increase employee motivation. But in practice this may not be an easy suggestion to implement. Nadler, Hackman, and Lawler (1979) suggest that unless certain conditions are present, the disadvantages associated with using pay to motivate performance may outweigh the advantages. The conditions they identified as particularly important are:

1. Important rewards can be given.

2. Rewards can be varied depending on performance.

3. Performance can be validly and inclusively measured.

4. Information can be made public about how the rewards are given.

5. Trust is high.

6. Superiors are willing to explain and support the reward system in discussion with subordinates.

Many managers find it difficult to reward their high-performing employees. In some instances resources may not be available to provide them with meaningful rewards. Organizational policies such as across-the-board pay raises or union contracts may limit managers' discretion in how raises are given. Managers may find it difficult to measure the actual performance of individual employees and may not have accurate information on which to base their reward decisions.

Because individual performance often is difficult to measure and conflict results when pay raises are tied to performance at the individual level, some organizations have adopted plant- or organization-wide bonus systems. Systems like the **Scanlon plan** directly tie bonuses to organization-wide or plantwide performance standards (Lawler, 1981). People are paid bonuses that are calculated as a percentage of their salary under this system. By tying rewards to organizational performance, a situation is created in which it is in the best interests of all employees to perform well. In isolated instances in which an employee fails to carry his or her fair share of the workload, peer pressure may be more effective in changing the situation than supervisory actions. One example of an extremely successful organizational reward system based on performance bonuses is found at Lincoln Electric (Feautre 14.4).

Feature 14.4
Compensation System Boosts Productivity

A drive along the Cuyahoga River, past Cleveland's broken factory windows and abandoned steel mills, might convince you that America's older industries are dying. But continue just beyond the city limits, to East 222nd Street, and you will come upon a thriving 87-year-old manufacturer that disproves all the stories about lazy American workers. It's Lincoln Electric Co., little known outside its field of arc-welding equipment and induction motors.

(In 1981) it paid its 2,624 workers an average of about $44,000. Many of the production workers, who are paid on piecework, did even better. The company hasn't had a layoff in over 30 years. But this is Cleveland, not Japan. Whoever heard of guaranteed employment in Cleveland?

With their more liberal fringe benefits, U.S. steel and auto workers come close to matching the pay of Lincoln's factory workers. But they have done so at the cost of pricing themselves out of jobs. That isn't about to happen at Lincoln. In arc-welding equipment, where Lincoln is world market leader and does 93 percent of its sales, U.S. exports outnumber imports 3-to-1. The main reason for that is Lincoln's extraordinary productivity gains. In 1915 Lincoln was selling one of its earliest arc welders for $1,550. The price of a comparable model today is $996. In the intervening 67 years, Lincoln's average factory pay has climbed 100-fold, to about $21 an hour, including a year-end bonus that effectively doubles base pay.

Quite simply, Lincoln workers are turning out their machines faster and faster. They have run General Electric out of the arc-welding business and squeezed Westinghouse into a small corner of it, leaving several privately held firms as the chief competition. . . .

And they toil. "They don't give anything away. You work for it," says a 16-year veteran at Lincoln. Unlike the tonnage bonuses common in the steel industry, Lincoln piece rates are not a supplement to base pay, they *are* the base pay. If a worker calls in sick, he doesn't get anything. If he lets a defective machine through, he fixes it on his own time. . . .

In the Lincoln system of "incentive management," the worker is expected to be self-motivated. If he can rearrange his work space or tasks to get a job done faster, he is free to do so — and will pocket more money. The company doesn't object if someone figures out a way to beat the times figured into the piecework rates, since the higher volume will spread overhead costs over more pieces. The worker will get rich, but so will the company. . . .

The employees, for their part, are constantly reminded that there is no free lunch. They once voted down a dental insurance plan, fearing it would cut too deeply into profits and thus their bonus checks. For the same reason they don't challenge the lack of air-conditioning. In peak years, like 1981, overtime is mandatory. When orders are slack or machines broken, workers accept arbitrary job reassignments. Sometimes the substitute assignment pays worse than the regular one. There are no seniority rights. . . .

In its reclusive, iconoclastic way, Lincoln Electric remains one of the best-managed companies in the U.S. and is probably as good as anything across the Pacific. . . .

Source: Forbes, July 5, 1982 "This is the Answer," by William Baldwin, pp. 50–52. Reprinted by permission. © Forbes Inc., 1983

Organizational reward practices are important in retaining good employees and in encouraging high job performance. As a general rule, people engage in those behaviors that they believe will lead to the rewards they value (Kerr, 1975). When problem behavior or poor employee performance is observed in organizations, therefore, it is important to consider whether an inappropriate reward system is at the heart of the problem. Should we be surprised if professors neglect their students and teaching duties if promotion and tenure decisions are based largely on research and publication? In order for rewards to be used effectively, however, it first is necessary to be able to measure performance accurately. An effective performance appraisal system provides the required foundation upon which reward systems can be built. Without an effective way to measure desired behaviors — performance — it is difficult to see how good decisions can be made concerning the use of rewards in encouraging these behaviors.

Summary

The present chapter discusses human resource management in organizations and how it can be made more efficient.

The growing importance of the personnel department is partially reflected in the fact that many corporations are changing the department name to human resources management. Increased federal and state regulation of employment has prompted employers to look more closely at the way they manage their human resources. More direct employee involvement in organizational effectiveness and the greater need for highly skilled and motivated employees in high technology and the service sector also are behind the growing importance of human resource management.

The purposes and goals of an organization largely determine the types of human resources needed, the number of employees required, and the time at which the need will be greatest. The external environment, however, has been perhaps the biggest influence on changes in human resource management. Government regulations and laws and the nature of the labor market are two external influences.

Forecasting human resource needs is the first step of the planning process. Once needs become clear, they must be programmed into specific personnel goals and objectives. After the plans are implemented, their progress must be monitored and their success evaluated.

Recruiting matches the preferences and goals of the individual with the needs and preferences of the organization. The nature of the recruiting process depends on labor market conditions and the type of position open. Recruiting typically is preceded by a job analysis that evaluates the component tasks and skills necessary in a job.

A number of laws govern unfair discrimination in employment. Some discrimination, however, is fair. The primary intent of selection procedures in organizations is to discriminate between applicants who can successfully perform the job and those who cannot. Work sample tests, interviews, recommendations from prior employers, and the application information are among the criteria used to screen employees.

Two different types of errors can occur in the selection process: a false positive error, in which a person is predicted to succeed and ultimately fails, and a false negative error, in which failure is predicted but the person ultimately succeeds.

Organizations must carefully plan their training and development efforts. The first step in the process involves identifying employee needs in this area. Then a development plan must be designed and initiated, and its effectiveness must be evaluated.

Organizational effectiveness often is influenced by the ability to retain a core of high-quality employees. Performance assessment and compensation are essential to effective human resource management. Organizations must decide why they are evaluating performance, which employees to evaluate, and what criteria to use. Two performance evaluation techniques can be used: comparative and absolute.

The concept of equity is useful in evaluating overall compensation systems. Equity can be evaluated along two separate dimensions, external and internal. The concept of comparable worth states that equal wages should be paid to men and women performing tasks of equal value.

Questions for Discussion

1. Human resource management departments appear to be growing more important in organizations. What are the reasons for this growing importance?
2. Describe several instances in which important human resource management practices within organizations have been influenced by events in the external environment.
3. What are the major activities involved in human resource planning?
4. How might the nature of recruiting efforts change depending on the position being recruited for and the nature of the labor market?
5. When does unfair discrimination or bias exist in the selection process? Describe unfair discrimination in terms of an error in selection.
6. What are the major goals and activities involved in job analysis?
7. In a labor market characterized by many firms seeking few individuals, what selection error would an organization be most likely to minimize?
8. Describe the steps that must be taken in planning employee training and development programs.
9. Relate the appropriateness of comparative versus absolute standards per-

formance assessment approaches to the different purposes performance evaluation can serve in organizations.

10. Distinguish between external and internal equity in designing organizational compensation systems.

11. What are the implications of the comparable worth doctrine for the ways organizations design their compensation systems?

12. Under what conditions should organizations consider reward systems that link pay to performance?

Case Study
Derco United Corporation

"I just wonder how to make a Bonus Award Program really effective in this company," thought Jerry Barker, Assistant to the President of Derco United Corporation as he sat in his Menlo Park office late one afternoon in September 1975. "The concept of rewarding 'singular, outstanding achievements that significantly contribute to the success of the company' makes so much sense — but it is not at all easy to translate this concept into a program that will work here in this plant."

Barker, with a background in finance, had recently joined Derco upon completion of the MBA program at Stanford. A job prior to his graduate work had given Barker some exposure to the compensation area, and the President of Derco, Robert James, had asked him to take part in designing the Bonus Award program. Barker had been involved in the several top management discussions about the Program. In two days, he was to present a proposal that would capture the philosophy of top management and address the need for effective shop-floor implementation.

The Company

Derco United Corporation (DU) was a publicly held corporation with two divisions — nonunion Derco Engineering (the focus of this case) in Menlo Park, California, and unionized Derco Systems in Chicago. Corporate offices were with Derco Engineering in Menlo Park.

DU had been founded in 1950 to develop and manufacture highly technical equipment. By 1975,

Derco Engineering products ranged from small, standardized devices manufactured in modest quantities (up to 5,000 per year) to large, one-of-a-kind pieces of gas-process equipment. These products comprised four main groups: military, industrial, advanced technology and gas-process. The Division marketed its products worldwide using its own marketing group and selected sales representatives. In 1975, approximately 20% of total sales were outside the United States, a slight drop from 1974. Sales under government contracts or subcontracts were approximately 40% of the 1975 total. The company had been facing strong competition at home and abroad.

The year 1974 had been a record breaker for DU. Corporate sales had reached $23 million, a 34% increase over 1973. Net income had doubled to $730,931 or 44¢ per share (Exhibit 1). Similar growth had occurred during the first two quarters of 1975.

In September 1975, Derco Engineering employed 315 people. The Division actively sought skilled, well-educated workers and generally found them locally for all but the most specialized jobs. Turnover was low and wages good, relative to other local high-technology companies.

The Chicago-based Derco Systems Division was smaller (125 people). Its 100 production workers were members of the United Automobile, Aerospace and Agricultural Implement Workers of America (UAW). The Division had never experienced any work stoppage due to labor problems.

Derco United had four corporate officers and a

Exhibit 1
Sales and Income before Taxes — Five-Year Summary ($000's)

	DERCO ENGINEERING	DERCO SYSTEMS	TOTAL
1974			
Sales	$17,672	$5,557	$123,229
Income before taxes	1,427	20	1,447
1973			
Sales	15,538	1,772	17,310
Income before taxes	565	(368)	197
1972			
Sales	14,233	476	14,709
Income before taxes	870	(68)	802
1971			
Sales	9,706	359	10,065
Income before taxes	638	(59)	579
1970			
Sales	7,298	34	7,332
Income before taxes	584	—	584

seven-person Board of Directors (Exhibit 2). Robert James, 41, had been promoted from Vice-President to President in 1970; he had come to Derco in 1966 with a business-oriented education and with management experience in manufacturing. John Williams, 45, had joined Derco in 1974 as Corporate Vice-President and President of Derco Engineering; he had a background in engineering and had worked for a consulting firm. Kurt Shaeffer, 42, had held various management positions in another company before joining Derco in 1975 as a Corporate Vice-President and President of Derco Systems. Ben Burdoe, 41, had joined Derco in 1972 as Corporate Vice-President and Secretary-Treasurer, had had an accounting background, and had previously been the Controller of an electronics firm.

**The Product Line
and Production Process**

Derco Engineering's four product groups — military, industrial, advanced technology, and gas-process — fell along a spectrum with a wide range of product size, unit volume, worker skill, and process characteristics. A worker was assigned to a specific

product group and, to a large extent, was identified with that group; nonetheless, the small size of the plant ensured some daily social contact among most of the workers. In general, Derco Engineering both designed and manufactured its products. Except for the gas-process line, most manufacturing was assembly work; fabrication of components was subcontracted. All manufacturing was supervised by Joseph Moore, Manager of Operations, who had been with the company since 1961.

The military products were small (about the size of a coffee mug) and standardized. The work consisted of routine, repetitious assembly operations performed at benches; the product was carried from one worker to the next. Unit volume numbered in the hundreds per month, and these products represented about 25% of the Division's business in 1975. Cost was the most significant competitive factor. This product group, while at the low end of Derco's skill and quality spectrum, had good growth potential and the workers derived a certain intra-divisional prestige from this fact.

The industrial products were larger (about the size of a portable TV), although still standardized. An individual unit was typically placed on a cart,

Exhibit 2
Organizational Chart

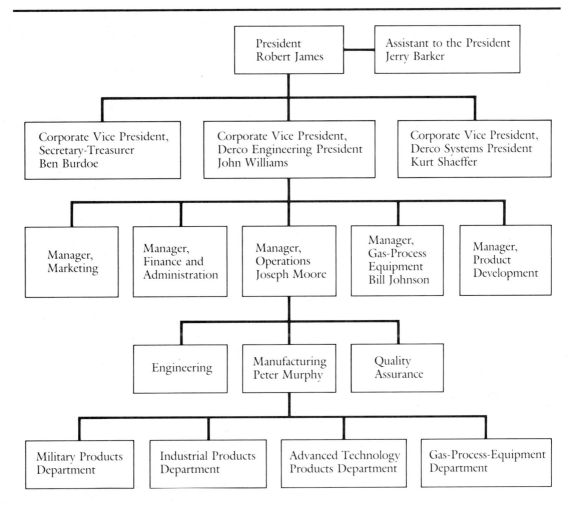

and a group of workers was assigned to assemble each particular model. Worker skill levels were higher than in the military products department, reflecting the greater complexity of the assembly work. Unit volumes were 20 to 100 per month per model, and production was scheduled in batches. Industrial products, as a whole, represented about 45% of the Division's business. Both cost and quality were important, with the emphasis depending upon the individual model. New-product development was constant in a market environment in which the major portion of business in any one year might be in a market that had not existed three years before. The workers shared this sense of newness and quick pace.

The advanced technology products were large units (refrigerator-sized) for educational and research laboratories. In contrast to the military and industrial departments, a unit in this department remained in one spot during the one-month assembly period, and the group of skilled workers came to it. Typically, three units were in process at any one time. Output from this department was about 20% of the Division's business. Quality was paramount, not only for the customer but also for Derco, as the products typically could not be tested until they were complete. The market for these products was relatively stable, and the workers reflected this with a generally slower, more painstaking pace of work.

The gas-process products were huge (box-car-sized), one-of-a-kind pieces of equipment. Usually state-of-the-art, these projects ran in the million dollar range and took six months to a year to complete. The department had been formed in 1973; in 1975 it accounted for about 10% of the Division's business. While actual manufacturing work was under the direction of Joseph Moore, the gas-process line had a program manager, Bill Johnson, who coordinated each project from sales through engineering to manufacturing. On the shop floor, a core team (a lead person, two assembly technicians, and a welder) typically was appointed for each project and carried the primary responsibility for fabrication and assembly. This team, however, was supported by other workers and departments, and as many as 15 to 20 people often contributed to any one project.

Compensation

Production workers were paid a straight hourly rate with no formal incentive or bonus pay system, although the Division President, from time to time and without publicity, presented an individual worker with a bonus check for an outstanding accomplishment.

In January 1971, DU had set up a formal Management Incentive Compensation Plan for key executives and employees. Payments were made when the Corporation or the Division met or exceeded annual financial goals; a payment represented a percentage of the individual's total standard compensation. Originally, about 20 people had been involved in this Plan.

In a series of meetings earlier in 1975, James, Williams, Shaeffer, and Burdoe had decided that this Plan had accumulated too many participants (some three times the original 20). In addition, they felt that the Plan did not provide the specific accountability they believed necessary in an incentive program appropriate to the company's size and continued rapid growth. In particular, the Plan did not reward the achievement of individual goals nor did it include a "down-side" risk for the participant who did not meet these goals. Thus, incentive awards, originally viewed as extra compensation paid in addition to fair and competitive wages, were increasingly seen by management as the basis of a variable annual pay system.

The old Plan had been revised to reflect these concerns. The revision, which had not yet been announced, included corporate officers and five or six key people in each Division. These "contract participants" were to receive variable compensation based on their success (or failure) in meeting specific goals and upon the achievement by the Division (or the company, for corporate officers) of specified financial goals.

The Bonus Award Program Discussion

In 1975 top management had also discussed a formal Bonus Award Program. Top management philosophy at Derco saw the typical worker performing at a normal level punctuated by intermittent peaks and troughs. A worker whose performance consistently improved could expect increased responsibility and higher pay. However, management also wanted to recognize and reward the employee whose performance was at a short-term peak. The company-wide Bonus Award Program was an attempt to expand and formalize the informal bonus system that had been developed by the Division Presidents.

Jerry Barker had attended the several discussions among James, Williams, Shaeffer and Burdoe. Barker's notes, excerpted below, illustrated the issues discussed and the viewpoints represented.

On Program Rationale

James felt that it was moral and useful to have a Bonus Program for both motivational and reward purposes. Existence of such a Program:

. . . Should motivate all employees to increase their contribution to Derco, and

. . . Should be a means of strengthening the "psychological contract" between management and the employee by demonstrating management concern for the worker.

James had worked extremely hard to build a successful company, and expected all other employees to contribute their utmost, too. He would like to find a way to reward those who do outstanding work: "In any organization, 5 to 10% of the people are typically truly outstanding. They make the organization go, and their contributions should be recognized." He suggested a small "Nobel Prize" type of program.

On Criteria

Williams wanted to reward "the extra measure of resourcefulness." Shaeffer sought "an unusual commitment" and "extraordinary on-the-job performance." James looked for "stand-alone-effort." All agreed that it is an important managerial skill to be able to identify such superior performance.

Burdoe felt that care should be taken to insure that performance selected for recognition was viewed as worthy of such attention by other employees as well as by management.

On Nomination and Decision

James felt that recommendations should come from an employee's immediate supervisor, or perhaps from one level above that. Williams and Shaeffer both felt the Division President should make the final decision on an award in his Division.

On the Amount of the Award

All felt that the award should be "significant," and should depend upon both the achievement and the recipient's salary. James suggested the $500 to $1,500 range as appropriate.

On Announcement and Presentation

James felt that an award should be publicized within the company to enhance the Program's power as a motivator and to increase the recognition given to the recipient. Williams suggested that the company newspaper would be the appropriate medium. Both liked the idea of a special presentation ceremony in the President's office.

Shaeffer expressed hesitation about surrounding an award with much publicity. He would prefer to post a brief notice on the department bulletin board and enclose the award check within the recipient's regular pay envelope.

On Administration

Williams and Shaeffer both felt that the Program should be administrered separately by each Division, with each President determining the appropriate Pool of Bonus money to establish (an absolute $ amount? a percent of payroll? a percent of profits?), the recipients, and size of an award.

Burdoe would like to review the size of any Pool set up.

On Implementation

All agreed that the circulation of a clear statement of the Program would be sufficient, and that formal training of supervisors would not be necessary.

A Brief Visit from the President

As Barker sat at his desk late on that September afternoon, Robert James dropped in and voiced his expectations:

> Jerry, I'm really looking forward to seeing your Program proposal on Wednesday. I'm proud of what we have been able to accomplish here at Derco, and I'm eager to build into our policies a means of really recognizing and rewarding the people who make the outstanding contributions that continue to spark our growth and success.

Case Questions

1. If you were Jerry Barker, what would you recommend? Why?
2. If you were John Williams, what would you do? Why?
3. What should John Williams do? Why?

Source: 9-678-149 Derco United Corp. Copyright © 1978 by the President and Fellows of Harvard College. This case was prepared by Donna Hale under the direction of Fred K. Foulkes as a basis for class discussion rather than to illustrate either effective or ineffective handling of an administrative situation. Reprinted by permission of the Harvard Business School.

Strategic Competencies of Management

CHAPTER 15

Strategic Adaptation to the Environment

In the game of business, the best managers, like the best quarterbacks, have always had some notion of what their game plan should be. But nowadays managers, like quarterbacks, are increasingly looking for expert advice from the sidelines. To be sure, businessmen haven't really relinquished the strategic-planning function to management consultants. . . . But corporations are finding that the tools devised by the consulting industry can help in some aspects of strategic planning — specifically when it comes to scouting out and understanding competitors' strengths and weaknesses and in figuring out how best to deploy their own corporate assets.

The rapid growth of a relatively new industry — strategy consulting — is testimony to the potent appeal of the various conceptual tools. In 1979 companies paid management consultants well over $100 million for work labeled "corporate strategy." And talk of new "strategic planning" systems is cropping up in more and more annual reports.

The efflorescence of interest in strategy has been attributed in part of the increased uncertainty that businessmen feel these days when they contemplate the future — what will government intrusion, roaring inflation, or the sudden appearance of competition from abroad do to them next? If their businesses are going to be buffeted by uncontrollable forces, better to have a systematic plan for dealing with the aspects that *can* be predicted. . . .

Source: From "Playing by the Rules of the Corporate Strategy Game," by Walter Kiechel III, *Fortune,* September 24, 1979, pp. 110–115. © 1979 Time Inc. All rights reserved.

Chapter Outline

- The Importance of Strategic Management
- Understanding the Industry Life Cycle

Key Terms

- strategic management
- input-throughput-output
- economies of scale
- substitute products
- bargaining power
- overcapacity
- industry life cycle
- emerging introductory industries
- growth industries
- mature industries
- declining industries

Chapter Objectives

After studying Chapter 15 you should be able to

1. Compare strategic management with traditional and contemporary management.
2. Relate strategic management to the state of the United States economy and foreign competition.
3. Discuss the factors that determine industry profitability.
4. Understand the role of change and evolution in competition and the requirements for success in an industry.
5. See the implications for management in the life cycle of an industry.

Introduction

Strategic management concepts have been growing in popularity in the United States and the rest of the world. This growth attests to the importance of systematically relating a company's resources and capabilities to its changing environment. Traditional management tended to emphasize the internal affairs of organizations. Contemporary management extends this approach to take into consideration external changes and developments. Strategic management has evolved from modest extensions of the planning function (see Chapter 4) to more analytical and complex representations of organizational–environmental interaction (Schendel and Hofer, 1979; Porter, 1980).

Strategic management has become increasingly important among top executives whose major responsibility involves maintaining and improving their firm's performance by providing guidance and direction. This responsibility is particularly acute since the precipitous decline in industrial performance in the United States (see Chapter 1) has placed an enormous burden on the modern executive. He or she must respond in a manner that not only will improve the performance of the organization, but also will contribute to the revitalization of our industrial economy.

This chapter begins with a statement on the importance of strategic management. We then discuss the relationship between strategic management and industrial revitalization. An explicit proposition offered is that understanding the structure of industry and the dynamics of its evolution is essential to meeting the needs of industrial revitalization. In this context, a framework to analyze the structure of an industry, proposed originally by Porter (1980), is presented.

Industrial evolution is discussed in the context of the development of an industry life cycle. Specific proposals for managing introductory or emerging, growing, maturing, and declining industries are then discussed. This chapter provides an introduction to materials that are more comprehensively covered in courses in business policy and strategy.

The Importance of Strategic Management

Jemison (1981) describes **strategic management** as the process by which general managers of complex organizations develop and utilize a strategy to coalign their organizations' competences with the opportunities and constraints in their environments. Prasad (1983) views it as a process that identifies present and future critical issues for the organization and develops ways to resolve them within the organization's resources and external constraints. A synthesis of the two definitions suggests that strategic management is (1) a process and therefore *dynamic* and *adaptive,* and (2) a *systematic* way of relating the company's resources to its environment.

Organizations are products of their environments. For some time organizations have been described as **input-throughput-output** systems, with inputs and outputs coming from and going to the environment. Over time the environment has become more complex, more unpredictable, and more turbulent. Inputs become more scarce and the sale of outputs more unpredictable because of greater domestic and international competition. Industries such as steel, automobiles, tires and rubber, and metal, which flourished in the past, have either matured in the 1970s or are expected to mature in the 1980s. These changes have made the environment more complex and difficult to predict.

In response to the growing complexity of the environment, many firms in the United States have started to use strategic management concepts. The ex-

---

Feature 15.1
Responding to Threats: The Timex Case

Timex, the world's largest maker of mechanical and electric wrist watches, wasn't ready for the world's new digital watches. Timex has lived in a world of its own since its founding by two Norwegians shortly after World War II. Joakim Lehmkuhl ran the company and mass-produced the low-cost watches, and Thomas Olsen was the major shareholder. The company was so successful that by the late sixties 50 percent of the watches sold in the United States were Timexes.

Thomas Olsen's son, Fred Olsen, replaced Lehmkuhl in 1973 when it became apparent that Lehmkuhl was becoming eccentric due to failing health. This change in leadership, however, was just the beginning of Timex's problems. The management team that carried on spent most of its time engaging in fierce in-fighting and in the seventies seemed unable to meet the challenge presented by the introduction of low-cost digital watches. Timex couldn't match the price or the technology. In fact, the one digital watch the company did finally produce was so large and awkward that it was dubbed by Timex employees as the "quarter-pounder."

Timex's mistake was in not taking solid-state technology seriously. Management thought digital watches were a fad that soon would wear thin. When the company finally realized that digital watches were here to stay, it hired a new breed of high-tech designers to get Timex into the digital market. These people were unable to coexist with the mechanical watch employees. The two groups saw little to admire in one another, and tended to stay at odds. Management was unable to bridge the gap. Instead, Timex executives fought among themselves over how to play catch-up in the industry. The result was watches that were outdated by the time they were produced. Even worse, the mechanical watch-making line was neglected. Said one former employee, "We allowed our *only* product to die" ("Timex Takes the Torture Test," p. 115).

By 1980, Fred Olsen decided to clean house. He fired his top executives and took over himself. Since then, Timex has produced more marketable digital watches. It has also moved into computers and the health-care field, with a digital scale, thermometer, and blood-pressure kit. Olsen is a barrel of energy who spends two weeks in America followed by two weeks in Oslo, his home. It is going to take energy, however, if Timex is ever going to regain its former status. Olsen has lots of futuristic ideas but at the same time lots of day-to-day problems before he can get Timex "ticking" again.

Source: "Timex Takes the Torture Test," by Myron Magnet, *Fortune*, June 27, 1983, pp. 112–120.

plosion of consulting services in strategic management provides additional testimony to the importance of strategy. In 1979 companies paid management consultants about $100 million for their "corporate strategy" services. During the same year the Boston Consulting Group, the forerunner of strategic management consulting, had consultants in seven offices around the world generating revenues of about $35 million (Kiechel, 1979). It has been documented that many successful firms employ strategic analysis in their operations (Thune and House, 1970; Herold, 1972). In addition to providing financial benefits, strategic analysis can help a firm prevent problems and make the contributions of employees more effective (Pearce and Robinson, 1982).

Perhaps the most important reasons for developing strategic management concepts, however, are the consequences of failing to do so in our present complex environment. The demise of the *Saturday Evening Post, Life* magazine, W. T. Grant, and the Penn Central Railroad, to name a few, resulted in part from their inability to recognize and capitalize on numerous opportunities in their environments. Timex, once the pioneer in the mechanical watch market, missed out on digital watches and solid-state technology because it initially considered digitals a fad or a specialty watch (Feature 15.1). In contrast, McDonald's emerged as a leader in the fast-food business by quickly responding to changing consumer needs and eating habits.

Strategic Management and Reindustrialization

In June 1980, *Business Week* devoted an entire issue to the revitalization of the United States economy. The editors noted:

> The U.S. economy must undergo a fundamental change if it is to retain a measure of its economic viability, let alone its leadership, in the remaining twenty years of this century. The goal must be nothing less than the reindustrialization of America. A conscious effort to rebuild American productive capacity is the only real alternative to the precipitous loss of competitiveness of the last fifteen years, of which this year's wave of plant closings across the continent is only the most vivid manifestation [p. 56].

Understanding the economy of the United States and the impact of foreign competition is the first step in the study of strategic management. A proper understanding of these factors will aid the strategist in identifying key trends in the environment (see Chapter 1) and in discerning their impact on a particular organization.

The United States economy has been evolving and changing in fundamental ways over the last five years. Historically, we have been accustomed to representing the economy in terms of basic industries such as automobiles, textiles, steel, appliances, tires and rubber, and heavy machinery. In an issue of *Business Week* ("America's Restructured Economy," 1981), the editors suggested that the economy can best be described in terms of five, not one, separate economies:

1. *Old-line industry*. This consists of the basic manufacturing industries that have long been the conventional strength of the United States: automobiles, textiles, steel, appliances, and so on. A number of these industries have matured or will mature shortly and also face serious international competition.

2. *Energy*. This economy includes coal mining, natural gas, electric utilities, and petroleum. Demand for energy will continue to be great and will be affected by world requirements, the limitation of supply, and the uncertainty of policies of the Organization of Petroleum Exporting Countries. Capital requirements of this industry will squeeze financing of other industries.

3. *High technology*. Including electronics, semiconductors, and integrated circuits, these industries have tremendous growth potential but also face heavy international competition.

4. *Agriculture*. The demand for American foodstuffs will grow as the world population grows. The *Business Week* editors, however, note that the pace of production growth will slacken and lead to inflation.

5. *Services*. This area includes financial, personnel, communications, and information processing. Services also have strong growth potential, particularly in the international market.

The key participants in these five economies are presented in Figure 15.1.

It has become crucial for managers to recognize the structural complexity of the United States economy and to deal with this complexity in strategic terms. Managers in fast-growing industries such as high technology, semiconductors, and integrated circuits face different demands than do those in slower-growing or maturing industries, such as steel and textiles. The demands also are different for managers in declining industries, such as baby foods, electronic tubes, and tobacco. Overall, future managers have to be prepared to deal with growth, maturity, and declining industries. In doing so, the challenge to renew our economic viability by improving the strength and competitiveness of our industrial sector will be directly and effectively addressed. As a first step in examining the different requirements imposed by industries at different stages of growth, we will examine the factors that determine industrial profitability.

Industrial Profitability

A cursory reading of business periodicals will indicate that some industries are more profitable than others and that certain firms within an industry outperform others. For example, the automobile industry remains more profitable than the airline industry. In addition, General Motors has consistently outperformed its traditional rivals, Ford, Chrysler, and American Motors. In its 35th annual report on American industry, *Forbes* listed the most and least profitable industries (Fig. 15.2).

What accounts for such variations in industrial profitability? Porter (1980) suggests that the structure of an industry determines competitive patterns or

Figure 15.1
Key Participants in the Five Economies

WHO'S WHO IN THE FIVE SECTORS

For this special issue, BUSINESS WEEK worked with Data Resources Inc. to classify all production in the private economy (excluding wholesale and retail trade) into five key sectors and to measure their output, employment, and prices.

These data were supplemented by data on profits and investment from the Commerce Dept. More than 400 industrial classifications were identified. Here are the component industries of each sector:

Energy

Coal mining
Petroleum refining and related products

Gas utilities
Crude petroleum and natural gas

Electric utilities

Agriculture

Dairy products
Livestock
Food grains

Tobacco
Vegetables
Oil-bearing crops

Miscellaneous crops
Poultry and eggs
Cotton

Feed grains and grass seed
Fruits and nuts
Forestry and fishery products

High Technology

Complete guided missiles
Calculating and accounting machinery
Scales and balances
Industrial controls
Telephone and telegraph equipment
Electron tubes
ᵃ Electronic components
ᵃ Aircraft

Aircraft parts and equipment
Aircraft engines and engine parts
Engineering and scientific instruments
Dental equipment and supplies
Optical instruments and lenses
Photographic equipment and supplies
Electronic computing equipment
Typewriters

ᵃ Office machines
Radio and TV receiving sets
Radio and TV communication equipment
Semiconductors
Measuring and control instruments
Surgical appliances and supplies
Watches and clocks
Ophthalmic goods

(continued)

Figure 15.1 (continued)

Services

Hotels and lodging places
Beauty and barber shops
Advertising
Eating and drinking places
Motion pictures
Doctors and dentists
Other medical and health services
Nonprofit organizations and miscellaneous professional services
Railroads and rail-related services
Motor freight

Air carriers and related services
[a] Transportation services
Radio and TV broadcasting
Communications other than radio and TV
Banking
Insurance carriers and agents
Real estate
[a] Miscellaneous personal services
Miscellaneous business services
Automobile repair and services
Amusement and recreation services

Hospitals
Educational services
[a] Social services
[a] Passenger transportation
Water transportation and related services
Pipelines, except natural gas
Water and sewer services
Credit agencies and securities brokers
Owner-occupied dwellings

Old-Line Industry

The 19 basic industry groups include:

Food and tobacco manufacturers
Textiles and textile products
Lumber and wood products

Paper and paper products
Chemicals and allied products
Stone, clay, and glass products
Construction

Metal mining
Metals and metal products
Electrical and nonelectrical machinery and equipment

[a] Not classified elsewhere.

Source: Reprinted from the June 1, 1981 issue of *Business Week* by special permission, © 1981 by McGraw-Hill, Inc.

Figure 15.2
Who's Who in Industrial Profitability

INDUSTRY	RETURN ON EQUITY(%)	
	1977–1981 Avg.	*1982 Avg.*
The Ten Most Profitable Industries		
1. Oil field drillers and services	21.9	23.0
2. Tobacco	21.7	19.7
3. Publishing	20.5	19.5
4. Health care	20.4	19.4
5. Broadcasting	20.3	16.7
6. Drugs	20.2	16.8
7. Office equipment and services	19.7	15.0
8. Toiletries/cosmetics	19.1	17.7
9. Energy	18.8	12.1
10. Electrical equipment	18.6	15.9
The Ten Least Profitable Industries		
1. Airlines	2.8	Deficit
2. Thrifts	3.7	Deficit
3. Automobiles and trucks	8.6	Deficit
4. Steel	9.0	1.7
5. Railroads	11.0	9.5
6. Apparel	11.0	10.0
7. Nonferrous metals	11.2	Deficit
8. Building materials	11.4	3.1
9. Packaging	11.8	8.3
10. Retailers	12.0	9.7
Industry median	15.9	12.7

Source: Data from "Who's Where in the Industry Groups," 1983.

forces within it. Competition within an industry in turn is shaped by five basic competitive forces, as shown in Figure 15.3. The profit potential in each industry is determined by the collective strength of these forces. In industries in which competition is intense or cut-throat, such as airlines, the profit potential tends to be low. Conversely, when competition is relatively mild, as it is in oil field drillers or cosmetics, the returns are much higher. Porter also identifies some of the structural determinants of the intensity of competition: entry, threat of substitution, the bargaining power of buyers, the bargaining power of suppliers, and rivalry among existing firms. We will discuss each in turn.

New Entrants. High profits in an industry often attract new entrants. As newcomers move into an industry, capacity is increased and prices are driven down, reducing profitability. Firms may hesitate to enter the industry, however,

Figure 15.3
Forces Driving Industry Competition

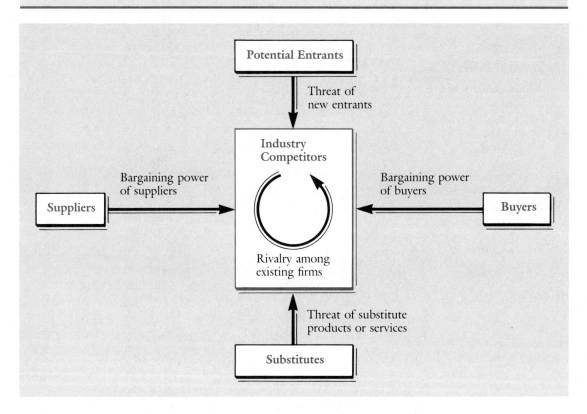

Source: Reprinted with permission of The Free Press, a division of Macmillan, Inc., from *Competitive Strategy* by Michael E. Porter. Copyright © 1980 by The Free Press.

if entry barriers are high and if the retaliation expected from incumbent firms is particularly adverse.

Barriers to entry arise from economies of scale, capital requirements, product differentiation, absolute cost disadvantages, and government policy. **Economies of scale** refers to the decline in unit costs as the volume of the product increases over a time period. Entrants risk severe retaliation from incumbents who enjoy advantages from such economies, if they come in on a large scale, but suffer cost disadvantages if they come in on a small scale. Additionally, the entrant may face tremendous capital costs for new plant construction, for example, to come into the industry at a competitive level. If incumbent firms have established brand identification and loyalty, such as product differentiation, entrants will need to spend heavily on advertising to overcome these disadvantages. Absolute cost advantages are the proprietary product technology, favorable access to raw materials, favorable locations, and government subsidies that incumbents may enjoy (Porter, 1980; pp. 10–13). Finally, government policy can limit entry by imposing licensing requirements and restricting access to raw materials. The role of government is presented in more detail in Chapter 17.

Threat of Substitutes. Manufacturers of coaxial copper wires, such as Phelps Dodge, look with apprehension at the steady development of a **substitute product,** such as the fiber optics produced by Corning Glass Works. The profits of sugar producers have been limited by the ready availability of high-fructose corn syrup and, recently, other sugar substitutes. Airlines fear that their low profit potential will be reduced further by the development of teleconferencing, which would drastically reduce the demand for travel. In all these examples, the threat of substitute products limits the potential returns of an industry.

Feature 15.2
Army of Competitors Stuns Atari

For five years it seemed nothing could stop Atari. Between 1977 and 1981, sales went from less than $200 million to $1 billion. Earnings zoomed from a $300 million loss to a profit of almost $300 million. In 1982 sales were $2 billion and profits $320 million.

Then the bubble burst.

In the fourth quarter of 1982, retailers began cancelling orders for the company's video game software cartridges. Profits plummeted. In the first half of 1983, Atari was expected to report a loss of more than $100 million. The company was trying to dump millions of unsold 1982 cartridges and was fighting losses in its home computer division that were a result of competitive price cutting.

A major reason for the company's fall was that it lost its competitive position in what is becoming a ruthless business. Atari's share of the software sold for its own video game player dropped from more than 80 percent in 1981 to 56 percent in 1982. Its share of the home computer market went from 30 percent to 18 percent in 1982 alone. Coin-operated games suffered too. A formidable competitor, Bally Midway Manufacturing Company, came along and for a while even moved ahead of Atari in market share.

An army of competitors suddenly arose in video game software, including such giants as CBS and Twentieth Century-Fox. In video game players Coleco Industries snatched a chunk of Atari's market.

Coleco and a string of other competitors are fighting it out with Atari in the $200-to-$800 home computer area too. Atari is depending on its software to attract buyers, whereas Coleco and the others are offering computers with larger capacity. On the upper end of the computer price scale, Atari faces a major challenge from Apple Computer Inc. and International Business Machines Corporation.

Atari's success was built on its video computer system. Some observers believe lower-priced home computers will spell the end of such units, which provided a major portion of Atari's profits.

Warner Communications Inc., which was Atari's parent company at the time, responded to the company's troubles by making major shifts in management. But whether Atari has the technological power to survive against all the competition remains to be seen.

Source: "Atari's New Game Plan" by Gary Hector, *Fortune,* August 8, 1983, pp. 46–52.

When substitute firms have high profits, the threat is even stronger. Conversely, in industries in which substitutes do not pose a threat, such as securities and health care, profits of major manufacturers tend to be higher.

Bargaining Power of Buyers and Suppliers. Buyers exert pressure on an industry by forcing down prices and by using the threat of backward integration to demanded better bargaining concessions. In **backward integration** a buyer enters its supplier's business and directly competes with the supplier. Porter (1980, p. 25) describes how General Motors and Ford have used the threat of self-manufacture to enhance their **bargaining power** to their suppliers. By producing some of their components in-house, they make such a threat credible and also obtain a detailed knowledge of costs to aid them in negotiation processes. Other buyers, such as Sears, Roebuck and Company, use volume purchases, such as purchases of dishwashers from Design and Manufacturing, to reduce their prices. Through standardization and economies of scale, Design and Manufacturing in turn is able to provide Sears with lower prices, an advantage not shared by many suppliers.*

Suppliers exert pressure on an industry by forcing up prices and encouraging forward integration to limit the profitability of their buyers. In **forward integration** a supplier enters the business of its buyers and competes directly with them. Perhaps the most dramatic example of supplier power is the case of the Organization of Petroleum Exporting Countries. Oil price increases in the mid-1970s triggered a worldwide recession and forced even the most industrialized countries, such as the United States and Japan, to reassess their energy requirements and to consider alternatives for oil. On a less dramatic scale, the continuous threat of forward integration by aerosol can manufacturers has neutralized the power and potential profitability of the companies they supply.

Intensity of Rivalry. Porter (1980, p. 17) describes rivalry among existing competitors as a jockeying for competitive position through the use of tactics such as pricing, new product introduction, advertising, and customer service. The pattern of competition — whether it is best described as "warlike," as with the airlines, or "polite," as among oil drillers — is determined by interrelated factors. Let us examine some of the most important factors.

Concentration. Industries with many firms of about equal strength, such as the electronic component distribution industry, tend to be more competitive than those that are concentrated or dominated by a few firms, such as the automobile industry. When firms are numerous and fragmented, no one firm can establish control over pricing decisions. In highly concentrated industries, however, the leaders can impose discipline through price leadership, thereby reducing competition.

---

* For a more thorough report, the student is referred to the Notes on the Home Appliance Industry (6-372-349); Tappan (6-372-159); Sears, Roebuck and Company (6-373-010); and Design and Manufacturing (6-372-343). All these cases are available from the HBS Case Services, Harvard Business School, Boston, MA 02163.

Industry growth. Rapid growth tends to mask strategic errors and may even allow inefficient firms to be profitable. As industry growth slows, however, firms become more competitive and gain market share at the expense of others. Slow growth and recessionary periods reveal which firms have managed to grow with the expanding industry and which managed their resources strategically.

Overcapacity. The balance between demand and supply is critical to maintaining the existing level of price competition. As industrial supply increases through added capacity, the balance between demand and supply is disrupted. In cases of **overcapacity,** firms resort to lower prices to cover their costs. Such was the case in the manufacture of chlorine, vinyl chloride, and ammonium fertilizer. Overcapacity and extreme price cutting act to depress the profitability of an industry.

Personalities of competitors. Historically, industries develop standard rules for competing. Yet mavericks or others who do not conform to these rules may benefit the initiating firm. For example, when Philip Morris Inc. acquired Miller Beer in 1980, it immediately transformed the staid brewing company into an aggressive, consumer-oriented company. Philip Morris brought in John A. Murphy, the executive vice-president of Philip Morris's international operations, to head Miller. Murphy, whose background was in marketing tobacco, quickly applied marketing strategies that had worked in the tobacco industry. While the leading brewer, Anheuser-Busch, was embarking on a strategy to improve product quality and increase plant capacity, Miller emphasized advertising and introduced new products: a seven-ounce pony tester, Lite beer, and Lowenbrau beer. From 1970 to 1975, Miller rose from seventh to fourth in national sales; it surpassed Pabst to become number two in the industry in 1976.

Industry profitability is determined by the five competitive forces described in the previous section. Variations in profitability across industries can be understood by carefully examining how these five forces interact and shape competitive patterns in each. For example, the personal computer industry is relatively new and has experienced phenomenal growth, from a modest beginning in 1977 to a $1.5 to $2 billion industry in 1981.* As the personal computer industry has grown, so have its different markets. In 1981 the personal computer had three distinct markets: business, consumers, and education. Figure 15.4 provides information on each of these markets, using the Porter framework discussed in the previous section.

Understanding the Industry Life Cycle

In addition to knowing the structural determinants of industrial profitability, the manager also needs to understand the dynamics of an industry's evolution and change. Identifying the particular phase of an industry's evolution can reveal changing competitive patterns and requirements for success. To a large ex-

* See "Apple Computer, Inc." by Steve Gauthier. In James M. Higgins *Organizational Policy and Strategic Management: Text and Cases.* New York: Dryden Press, 1983, pp. 599–632.

Figure 15.4
Strategy Determinants for Personal Computer Manufacturers

	BUSINESS MARKET	CONSUMER MARKET	EDUCATION MARKET
Threat of new entrants	Greatest here because: 1. Market is most active personal computer segment now, and 2. Large computer manufacturers already sell into much of this market and can exploit existing distribution channels to enter the market.	Not as great here because: 1. Market has not developed as fully yet, and 2. It is more difficult to cultivate; specialized software is required and price limits are restrictive.	It is necessary to work with schools on bids and payment schedules; therefore, this market may not attract smaller or more specialized manufacturers. Tandy, Commodore, Apple, and Atari appear to be strongest in this market and all have corporate involvement in facilitating sales to schools.
Jockeying among current contestants	Centers on advertising campaigns, price, service, and capability comparisons (especially software support); some manufacturers seek specialized clientele (scientists, engineers, and at least one company has a portable unit designed for salesmen).	Centers on reliability, price, software, and "friendly" image computer.	Schools are expected to be large continuing buyers of software, so manufacturers are willing to sell hardware at low prices to ensure an installed base which will be continuing software consumers.

Threat of substitute services	Substitute services exist:
	    Time sharing
	    Data processing services
	    Large computers
		There is currently no viable substitute for the home market.	There is no good substitute for teaching computer literacy, but there are alternatives to using personal computers for other educational purposes (remedial work or teaching math, etc.).

tent, the five competitive factors mentioned in our earlier section may account for change in an industry: Newcomers may enter or incumbent firms may leave, the bargaining power of buyers and suppliers may increase or decrease, or firms with substitute products may exert pressure or become an insignificant force. In

	BUSINESS MARKET	CONSUMER MARKET	EDUCATION MARKET
Figure 15.4 (continued)			
Strength of buyers	Potential multiple purchases by large corporations give those buyers some leverage.	No collective forces are operative within the buyer population.	Since most school purchases are done on the local level, buyer groups are not strong; however, manufacturers perceive educational exposure as very important for security, brand loyalty, which will be carried over into the consumer market.
Strength of suppliers	Those manufacturers which have office product distribution channels already in place can offer more complete office product service (e.g., IBM, Xerox); those manufacturers which have large installed bases can offer better software support immediately, as well as established service channels.	Those manufacturers whose visibility is highest (through advertising or through educational and job site penetration) come to be identified by consumers as generic.	Computer literacy: Schools are more likely to choose a variety of machines so suppliers are not as strong. Teaching aids: Schools may choose the machine with the software that serves their needs best. Administrative: Software is an important determinant.

Source: "Basic Analysis, Personal Computers," by Barbara S. Isgur, Paine Webber Mitchell Hutchins, Inc. (October 28, 1981), p. 10. Reprinted by permission.

addition, structural changes such as overcapacity, increased concentration, and different styles of competition could fundamentally alter the competitive pattern among firms in the industry.

Figure 15.5 indicates the fastest- and the slowest-growing industries in the United States from 1977 to 1981. Those in the fast-growing category include brokerage services, oil field drillers, computer manufacturers, natural gas suppliers, and banking services. The slowest-growing category includes apparel, steel, automobiles and trucks, building materials, and automobile supplies. As we said before, managerial requirements differ in fast-growing and slow-growing industries. To obtain a better perspective of these requirements, it is neces-

Figure 15.5
Who's Who in Industry Growth

INDUSTRY	5-YEAR RANK	5-YEAR SALES GROWTH AVG. (%)[a]
The Ten Fastest Growing Industries		
Brokerage	1	33.8
Oil field drillers	2	22.8
Computers	3	22.7
Natural gas	4	20.7
Banks	5	20.5
Office equipment	6	19.9
Energy	7	19.7
Thrifts	8	18.6
Broadcasting	9	18.2
Specialty retailers	10	17.0
The Ten Slowest-Growing Industries		
Apparel	46	7.3
Steel	45	8.7
Automobiles and trucks	44	9.3
Building materials	43	9.5
Automobile supplies	42	9.6
Construction, mining, and rail equipment	41	10.2
Conglomerates	40	10.4
Food processors	39	10.5
Household goods	38	10.7
Packaging	37	10.8
Industry median		13.3

[a] Editors used ten years to calculate the five-year rate of sales growth. They compared average sales for the company's most recent five years against the average for the preceding five years, and expressed the change in terms of a five-year compounded annual growth rate.

Source: Data from "Who's Where in the Industry Groups," 1983.

sary to examine the characteristics of these industries more carefully in the context of change and evolution.

One way of conceptualizing these changes is to consider the industry in terms of a life cycle (Fig. 15.6). Like its precursor, the product life cycle, the **industry life cycle** has distinct phases: emerging, growing, maturing, and declining. As with product life-cycle analysis, it has been common to ascribe particular characteristics to different stages of growth (Fig. 15.7). We will review these options briefly and present some implications for management.

Figure 15.6
Stages of Industry Life Cycle

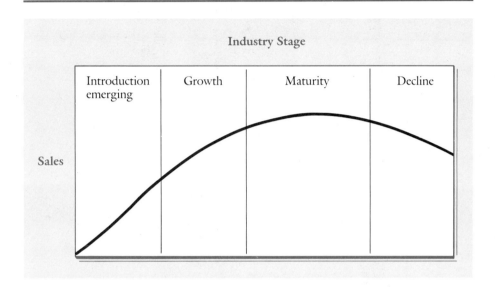

Industry Stage

| Introduction emerging | Growth | Maturity | Decline |

Sales

Managing Emerging
Introductory Industries

The **emerging introductory industry** is characterized by uncertainty. No clear product differentiation has been developed; there is no "right" strategy with which to compete; and there is a lack of technological know-how to arrive at good estimates of costs (Porter, 1980). Emerging companies also face problems related to raw material supply, raw material prices, and consumer confusion. In view of these problems, McNichols (1983) and Porter (1980) have suggested several strategies.

Assess strengths and weaknesses. Given the general uncertainty surrounding an emerging industry, it is important for the management to develop a deep understanding of the firm's competitive strengths and weaknesses. A thorough assessment should not be confined to financial resources but should explicitly address the level of commitment in the industry. Within its resources and capabilities, the firm then should attempt to set the "rules of the game." Early leadership in areas of product policy, marketing approach, and pricing may well enable the leading firm to retain its leadership in the growth stages.

Distinguish the firm from its competitors. It is good to develop a "distinctive competence" from the start. In the battle for the 64K computer chip market, the Japanese conquered all competitors with their low-price, high-quality chip made possible by superior manufacturing methods. This advantage enabled Japanese manufacturers to overcome many of the American semiconductor manufacturers who had key market positions when the competition began.

Figure 15.7
Selected Characteristics of Industry Growth Stages

	INTRODUCTION/ EMERGING	GROWTH	MATURITY	DECLINE
Key signals	Great uncertainty; learning and development in product and market	Demand exceeds supply; high profit potential; competition enters market	Sales saturation; high price competition; lower product differentiation	Differing patterns of decline; competitors leave the market
Buyer and buyer behavior	Buyer inertia; buyers need to be convinced to try the product	Widening buyer group; greater learning between buyer and industry	Mass market; repeat buying; emphasis on price	Buyers are sophisticated customers of the product
Suppliers and supplier behavior	Uncertainty surrounding source of supplies	Widening supplier group; growth in supplier industry	More selectivity in supplier	Declining supplier market
Rivalry	Few companies; some overcapacity due to uncertainty; specialized channels	Many competitors; some undercapacity; scramble for distribution; good acquisition climate	Shakeout among competitors; more price competition; some overcapacity; stable manufacturing processes; pared-down channels	Exits and less competition; substantial overcapacity; specialty channels
Representative examples	Solar heating; video games; fiber optics; bioseparation media	Personal computers; brokerage; banks	Automobiles; steel; apparel; building materials	Tobacco; electronic tubes; baby foods

Sources: Porter, 1980, pp. 160–161; Metzner, Watt, and Glueck, 1975, pp. 61–63.

Be flexible. An emerging industry is prone to constant changes, particularly in the choice of suppliers and distribution channels. A dilemma confronting fledgling firms in this stage is balancing strategic decisiveness ("Let's develop this channel in order to differentiate ourselves from competitors") and strategic flexibility ("What do we do if we have to change channels in the future?"). To recognize the various contingencies, Porter (1980) suggests the use of scenarios portraying the "optimistic" and "pessimistic" outcomes of particular strategic alternatives.

Managing Growth Industries

Growth industries are characterized by widespread demand for the product, a wider buyer group, an influx of competitors, and greater uncertainty about the technological characteristics of the product. Because industry supply of the product is likely to be met by a strong demand, most firms in the industry will survive financially, if not prosper economically. Still, there are numerous strategies to employ at the growth stage.

Build market share. One key finding of the profit-impact-on-market-share study (PIMS) (see Chapter 4, pp. 108–111) was that building market share ultimately may lead to profitability. This is particularly true in fast-growing industries. A common strategy is to increase capacity to take advantage of scale economies and to penetrate the market at a price lower than competitors, as Texas Instruments did in consumer electronics, the Japanese did in television, motorcycles, and consumer electronics, and Design and Manufacturing did in dishwashers. It is important to establish a broad market front or become a market leader in a special market segment.

Secure buyers with a differentiated product or service. A related strategy is to promote brand and customer loyalties through advertising, innovations, image building, and judicious expenditures for research and development. Advertising programs can enhance product and brand identification, if not instill customer loyalty. In the home appliance industry, General Electric was noted for its dual strategy of capitalizing on scale economies by building capacity ahead of demand and developing its reputation as a high-quality, innovative manufacturer. Similarly, in attacking the world motorcycle industry, the Japanese took advantage of scale economies and modernized equipment to produce a high-quality, low-cost vehicle that they aggressively promoted with substantial advertising expenditures. A low-cost product coupled with a highly differentiated image is a combination that often is very difficult to beat.

Fill a vacant niche. In growth industries there are excellent opportunities to service a particular niche or segment that might not be served effectively by the leading firms. To achieve this end, firms must carefully scan the market and identify lucrative niches. When Anheuser-Busch was busy selling beer to the general population, the Miller Brewing Company had already segmented the market and was concentrating on the eighteen-to-thirty-six-year-old age group. Specialty manufacturers such as Raytheon and Tappan are successful in pene-

Feature 15.3
Apple Computer Matures

Once a child prodigy in the personal computer market, Apple Computer Inc. is growing up.

Founded in 1976 in a California garage, the company has become a legend on the verge of becoming a $1 billion operation as well. It made millionaires of 300 people, most of them under age forty. But with the growth have come growing pains. Earnings and stock prices are sliding. A stock price drop in 1983 represented a decline of almost $278 million in the stock owned by its co-founder and chairman, Steven Jobs. Jobs is twenty-eight years old.

Apple is not about to throw in the towel, however. The company is cutting costs, centralizing marketing and manufacturing, and becoming a disciplined, aggressive marketer. The company believes an industry shakeout is under way and that 1984 will be strategically crucial.

"We are absolutely prepared to sacrifice short-term profits to emerge from the shakeout," Jobs said. "It's a reality check for Apple to see that even a company that has broken all the rules and grown faster than all the others really needs to have internal disciplines," said the company's president and chief executive officer, John Sculley.

Sculley was Pepsi-Cola Company's president in the spring of 1983 when he was hired to make Apple a more mature company. But although seeking maturity, Apple also is trying to preserve its youthful, "jeans-and-open-shirt" image.

The company has been phenomenally successful with that character. Since 1978 sales growth has averaged 228 percent a year. But the success may have blinded it to competitive threats. In-house deadlines weren't met, and the company didn't protect its flanks.

"With so much success surrounding you a note of failure gets lost in the applause," Jobs said.

Former employee Trip Hawkins put it another way: "When you do things that have never been done before and they work, you start thinking that you have answers that other people don't have. It makes it hard to listen to others. Apple didn't recognize the competitive climate. They waited too long to get tough."

Apple has more than 150 competitors, the most threatening of which at the moment is International Business Machines Corporation. Apple is preparing for battle armed with what Sculley says is focus, discipline, and a defined marketing strategy. He also is trying to open up internal communications and improve relations with dealers by keeping them better informed.

Dealers say the change is evident. Whereas the dealers used to find things out via the grapevine or in the newspapers, they now find Apple more responsive.

"They used to be a very egotistical company, especially during the last year (1982)," said one dealer. "They thought, not unjustifiably, that they were the best."

Source: "Growing Pains: Once All Alone in Field, Apple Computer Girds for Industry Shakeout," by Erik Larson and Carrie Dolan, *The Wall Street Journal,* October 4, 1983, p. 1, 16.

---

trating the high-income appliance market because they fill a niche too small for the major manufacturers to bother with.

A growing industry offers industry participants opportunities to become financially secure and may even be highly profitable. But growth also masks strategic errors that may prove detrimental when the industry reaches maturity.

Good strategic planning is essential to managing well in a growth industry. As is the case in a military battle, it is important to secure that first critical position from which future sorties can be launched.

Managing Mature Industries

The transition from growth to maturity often is characterized by the following signals: a slowing of industry growth, a strengthened hold on repeat buyers, an emphasis on cost and service rather than on product differentiation and promotion, a decrease in product and technological innovation, a decrease in industry profits, and greater international competition.

The **mature industry** presents a number of strategic problems for the manager. Unlike periods of rapid growth, during which strategic errors can be masked, maturity reveals key weaknesses of a particular company, such as incorrect pricing structure, inadequate cost structure, and positioning that is ineffective in defending market share. A number of theorists (Porter, 1980, McNichols, 1983, Hamermesh and Silk, 1979) have proposed the following strategies.

Identify, create, and exploit growth segments in the industry. Industry growth as a whole may slow while different segments within it are still growing. The growth in women's cosmetic sales has slackened, for example, but there are great growth opportunities for men's cosmetics. Another example involves General Cinema, whose management was able to recognize that the shopping center theater was growing in popularity despite the decline in the number of motion pictures over a twenty-year period. By moving into this segment, General Cinema avoided the pitfalls of a declining market.

Systematically and consistently improve the efficiency of production and distribution systems. When an industry matures, its products become commodities with no distinctive product or market features. This has occurred in the cases of wheat, chalk, farm products, and appliances such as room air conditioners. In such instances, competition shifts from product differentiation to costs and services. It therefore becomes imperative that the firm maintain a low cost position. This is achieved in part by improving the efficiency of production and distribution systems. The Japanese have successfully utilized this strategy in competing in the automobile, camera, steel, and motorcycle industries.

Engage in product development activities. Managers need to improve the quality of their products to create some demand within certain niches. Despite the slow growth in the coffee industry, General Foods's innovative freeze-dried coffee continued to be a big money maker. The management of Levi Strauss and Company responded to the saturating market for jeans by introducing an entire line of moderately priced casual and semiformal apparel. Levi Strauss labels also are evident in shoes, wallets, luggage, briefcases, and other items.

Diversify or pursue new market opportunities. A popular strategy among firms facing stagnant markets is to seek new markets through diversification. International Telephone and Telegraph Corporation, originally an operator of telephone systems, has diversified into hotels and motor inns, rental cars, homes, and heating and air-conditioning equipment. In response to the slackening market in consumer retailing, Sears, Roebuck and Company pursued a highly diversified strategy involving entry into real estate and financial services.

It is important to recognize, however, that diversification can lead to strategic pitfalls. Clark Equipment Company targeted a 20 percent growth rate through diversification only to realize that there were tremendous managerial problems associated with managing acquired companies. Clark sold off its diversification venture and has concentrated on its basic business, lift trucks and construction (Murdick, Eckhouse, Moor, and Zimmerer, 1980). The experience of American Can is described in Feature 15.4.

Thus, industry maturity provides the real test of sound strategic manage-

---

Feature 15.4
The Ups and Downs of Diversification

Styles change. Once the American Can Company hewed closely to its original business lines and bragged about such accomplishments as inventing the beer-can opener.

When William C. Stolk was president of American Can, he made the following remarks concerning diversification at a gathering in 1960 of the American Newcomen Society, a business historical society: "People sometimes ask why we didn't diversify more widely. Well, we did diversify—in the past—completely out of the container business. And frankly, we didn't do so well. In the 1920's we tried our hand at making bodies for the old 'Tin Lizzie,' and then took a flyer at adding machines. We lost $3 million in these two ventures, and since then we have appreciated the green of our own pastures."

The company now sees its pastures sullied by double-digit inflation, high interest rates, and expenses that curb manufacturing profits, and it is eyeing the apparent greener grass in the service and distribution industries. It will still have one capital-intensive business—cans—left when it sheds its paper operation, and it says one is enough. Here is a breakdown of some of the company's current business lines:

• Container and packaging: International operations were a bright spot in 1980,
with income up 9 percent. Domestic operations posted a decline in net income of $36 million, down to $84 million. Metal container operations were hurt, with decreasing demand for the older-style three-piece can. Seven plants making those cans were phased out last year, leaving 36 can facilities.

• Consumer products/distribution: Fingerhut direct-mail merchandising (which sells a variety of items including women's clothing and hand-crafted imports) posted income gains. Pickwick (specializing in home entertainment products) lost money with a weak market for records and tapes. Dixie (paper) products showed profits. Towel and tissue operations—under such brand names as Northern, Brawny, and Gala—were under margin pressure and showed a drop in income.

• Resource recover/chemicals: The drop in domestic auto sales hurt the business for recycled metals, with operating profits down. Lower sales of polyethylene hurt profit at the Complex Company, owned jointly by American Can and Getty Oil.

ment. Those firms that prospered in the growth phase without benefit of strategic management are likely to be exposed in the maturity phase. Managers who do well in the maturity phase are those who are well trained in the fundamentals of management: those who can plan, organize, and motivate well. A successful company typically is one that is the most cost efficient and consequently the most productive.

Managing Declining Industries

Harrigan (1980) suggests that industries decline in many ways. The industry may decline quickly (rubber baby panties), diminish slowly (cigars), plummet to a lower level and plateau (baby food), or decline to zero (millinery equipment for ladies' hats). The different rates and patterns of decline suggest that there are different ways to respond to declining demand. Some firms exit quickly, such as E. I. DuPont de Nemours and Company in rayon. Others are "milked"; that is, their cash is taken out and invested in another organization with better prospects for growth. PPG Industries milked the investment in its synthetic soda ash operation. Others stick it out to the very end, as did Regal Ware in percolator coffee makers. Harrigan tested eight industries to determine if there are effective strategies for managing **declining industries.** Her conclusions can be reformulated in terms of several contingency prescriptions.

The first two strategies cover the ends of the favorable-unfavorable spectrum. The last three strategies relate to the middle of the road, when the declining environment is not totally favorable or unfavorable and the position of the firm in the industry is at a medium or intermediate level.

Increase the firm's investment to dominate or get a good competitive position. Investment should be increased if there is a long-term advantage in doing so. Long-term advantage arises from: (1) a "favorable" rate of decline, a slow, predictable decline in demand in which there are several niches for firms to capitalize on; and (2) the relative competitive strength of the firm in financial resources, managerial talent, and degree of commitment. Gerber Products, a strong competitor in baby food, and Dow Chemical Company, a strong competitor in acetylene, increased their investment because they faced excellent opportunities for profitability.

Exit quickly. Quick divestment is recommended for firms facing "unfavorable" rates of decline, such as a rapid, unpredictable decline in demand in which there are no clearly identifiable niches, and if the relative position of the company in the industry is poor. Raytheon Company and DuPont divested their electronic receiving tube and acetylene businesses, respectively, when they saw opportunities to cut their losses.

Milk the investment. PPG Industries and DuPont milked their investments in synthetic soda ash and acetate, respectively. This was done after their analyses indicated that little profit could be gained by staying in the business.

Hold the investment level constant. This strategy is particularly appropriate when there is unresolved uncertainty about the industry. Courtaulds and Havatampa Cigar adopted this strategy when faced with the uncertainty of demand in cigar consumption. When demand patterns become clearer, the firm can either increase its investment if the rate of decline is slow and predictable, for example, or milk its investment and leave the industry if the rate of decline becomes rapid and erratic.

Shrink selectively. In this strategy, the firm decreases its investment in segments that it deems unprofitable and increases its investment in more lucrative niches. Mead-Johnson and Sunbeam Appliances reduced their investments in baby foods and percolator coffee makers, respectively, after they realized that these segments were unprofitable.

The different patterns of declining industries provide many strategic opportunities for industry participants. Successful managers are those who are adept at recognizing and analyzing these patterns. Harrigan's contingency model is an invaluable aid for managers in deciding which strategy to adopt after having identified patterns in the industry.

Summary

Strategic management, which has become increasingly important to top-level executives, systematically relates a firm's resources and capabilities to its changing environment. Understanding the economy of the United States and the impact of its foreign competition is the first step in the study of strategic management.

The United States economy has been evolving and changing over the last five years. The economy can best be described in terms of five economies: old-line industry, energy, high technology, agriculture, and services. Each has its own growth and profitability cycles.

Porter identified the structural determinants of the intensity of competition, including the effect of newcomers to an industry, the threat of substitute products, the bargaining power of buyers and suppliers, and the intensity of rivalry. Factors affecting rivalry include the concentration of firms in an industry, industry growth, overcapacity, and the personalities of competitors.

Managers also must understand the dynamics of an industry's change and evolution. In the emerging stage, managers must assess competitors' strengths and weaknesses, distinguish the new firm from the competition, and be flexible. In the growth stage of an industry, managers must concentrate on building a market share, securing buyers with a differentiated product or service, and filling a vacant niche.

Managers in mature industries should identify, create, and exploit growth segments in the industry, systematically and consistently improve the efficiency of production and distribution systems, engage in product development, and diversify or pursue new market opportunities. Managers in declining industries can increase the firm's investment to dominate or achieve a good competitive position, exit quickly, or milk the investment.

Questions for Discussion

1. What are the major concerns of strategic management? How does strategic management differ from traditional theories of management?
2. Discuss the importance of strategic management for the modern corporate executive.
3. How can a lack of a "strategic mentality" lead to organizational failure? Provide some examples.
4. Why is strategic management critical to our needs for economic reindustrialization?
5. Discuss the five sectors of the economy as suggested by *Business Week*. Provide some idea of the growth and profitability of each of these sectors.
6. What are the five competitive forces that determine industry profitability? Select one industry with which you are familiar. Discuss how each of the five factors act to increase or decrease industry profitability.
7. What is the industry life cycle? Discuss the implications of emerging/introductory, growing, maturing, and declining industries for the practice of management.
8. Present some characteristics of the following:
   a. Emerging/introductory industry
   b. Growth industry
   c. Maturing industry
   d. Declining industry
9. Assume the role of a management consultant who has been requested to counsel *one* of the following industries. Prepare a detailed list of questions to ask in the introductory meeting. Justify your selection of questions.
   a. Emerging/introductory (fiber optics)
   b. Growth (personal computers)
   c. Maturing (automobiles)
   d. Declining (tobacco)
10. What is diversification? Discuss some advantages and disadvantages of this strategic option.

Exercise 15.1
Using Scenarios to Analyze Strategic Situations

Purpose

The objective is to illustrate the use of scenarios for better understanding of strategic situations.

Instructions

1. Before the actual exercise, read one or two of the most recent issues of *Business Week,* paying close attention to the companies featured in the "Corpo-

rate Strategies'' section. Make some notes on these companies for class discussion.

2. Read through the three scenarios presented here.

Most Likely Scenario

There was sufficient stability in personal disposable income during the 1982 to 1992 period. Monetary and fiscal policy, while not perfectly coordinated, was carried out by the federal government in a more cohesive fashion than was characteristic of the prior decade. The basic trend in the rate of inflation has remained upward, although at a diminished rate.

In terms of demographics, the 20 to 32 age group declined, the 33 to 50 age group showed increases, and the 51 to 80 age group provided a significant increase. Expenditures for consumer durable goods remained generally strong, particularly for the first two age groups. Changing life-style trends produced demand for newer models, styles, and types of consumer goods, including electronics. Some softness in demand was experienced in the Northeast and other depressed geographical areas.

Pessimistic Scenario

United States monetary and fiscal policy was severely strained during most of this period. The declining productivity trends in the United States remained unchecked. Several new attempts to bolster productivity and check inflation were ineffective — or minimally effective, at best.

Consumer expenditures for durable goods and other noncash types of purchases were dramatically slowed. All purchasing groups — families, singles, single-parent families, and so on — experienced dramatic reductions in real purchasing power. Expenditures for discretionary purchases of all types showed negative real growth during the 1982 to 1992 period.

Further eruptions in the Mideast raised oil prices again, producing a ripple effect in the economy. In general, manufacturers were unable to pass these price effects on to the consumer because of softness in demand.

Optimistic Scenario

New approaches to United States monetary and fiscal policy begun in the early 1980s achieved a higher degree of success than even their most enthusiastic supporters would have thought. In particular, the 1985 to 1992 period experienced robust growth.

Continued investment in research and development and capital expenditures began to produce synergistic benefits throughout the economy. The resiliency in the United States economy contributed to a generally strong demand for all types of consumer goods. Demand for personal computers, home electronic communication devices (videophones, etc.) experienced a strong growth over the decade.

Changes in educational processes brought about new industries, since traditional classroom education was gradually shifted to an electronic classroom approach, with students and teacher connected by means of new videoscopes and other devices. Such decentralization was typical of work patterns that began to emerge on a large scale in this period.

3. Describe the implications of each of the scenarios for the one or two companies you selected.

Sources: The exercise was designed for class use by Professor Gerardo R. Ungson, University of Oregon, Eugene, Oregon, 1984. Descriptions of the three scenarios were adapted from Alan J. Rowe, Richard O. Mason, and Karl E. Dickel, *Strategic Management and Business Policy: A Methodological Approach,* © 1982, Addison-Wesley, Reading, Massachusetts. Pgs. 123–124. Reprinted with permission.

Case Study
The Fast-Food War: Big Mac Under Attack

"Competitors can hit me with a left jab, but unless they've got a knockout punch, sooner or later they're going down," warns Michael R. Quinlan, the 39-year-old president and chief operating officer of McDonald's Corp. "We have more money and more dedication — and we'll be there as long as we don't go off half-cocked."

Quinlan and other executives at the Oak Brook (Ill.) company are riled at spreading talk of cracks in the "golden arches." This experience is a new and unsettling one for McDonald's, which from the time the late Ray A. Kroc took over and began expanding two McDonald brothers' hamburger stands in 1955, has both dominated and defined the fast-food industry. Last year, McDonald's laid claim to nearly 18% of the industry's total sales of $38 billion and accounted for a staggering 42% of the $18 billion hamburger segment.

Critics say, however, that the chain's high-quality image is slipping, its advertising strategy is confused, and it has lost touch with the consumer. They note that growth in sales per unit slowed to only 5.3% in 1983, down from 9.9% in 1978. "They are the slowest-growing, most boring fast-food company," asserts Michael Culp, a restaurant analyst at Prudential-Bache Securities Inc.

Much of the criticism stems from the way McDonald's is proceeding on a business-as-usual basis in the face of the sharpening competition. The company plans few changes in its menu even though a slew of upstart chains offering ethnic fare as well as dishes for the health-conscious are winning over an aging population of fast-food junkies. Meanwhile, McDonald's direct competitors, Wendy's International Inc. and Burger King Corp., are going after the adult market with a vengeance. Wendy's is diversifying beyond burgers, while Burger King, having learned the pitfalls of menu expansion, is staking its future on the all-American staple and adult-oriented advertising.

Burger King has become a constant irritant for McDonald's over the past 16 months. A new and pugnacious management team drew blood with its "battle of the burgers" campaign, which claimed that Whoppers are bigger and better than Big Macs, because they are broiled while the rival product is fried. Kyle T. Craig, Burger King's executive vice-president, says McDonald's response shows that it "has the twitches. They've made moves in the last year that are only made by a nervous management."

Stock Slide

One mistake was suing Burger King over last year's "battle" ads before they even appeared. The No. 2 chain claims the suit, which was settled out of court, gave it prominence and an estimated $30 million in free publicity. "It was the best thing that ever happened to us," says a cocky J. Jeffrey Campbell, 39, who became Burger King's chairman and CEO last June.

The two are currently locked in combat over a 39¢ hamburger promotion. Early in January, McDonald's announced its program, which matches Burger King's nationwide offering in selected markets. Within two days, McDonald's stock dropped more than three points when investors feared that the limited-time program could escalate into a costly price war. Campbell found the situation "considerably less amusing" when shares of Pillsbury Co. — Burger King's parent — slid as well.

The price-cutting program has raised eyebrows on other fronts. Since McDonald's concedes it has a problem with perception of its burgers' quality, observers wonder how selling them cheaper will enhance the chain's image. "We do suffer from negative quality perceptions," says Paul D. Schrage, McDonald's executive vice-president for marketing. "People think if you can buy it for less [than a competitor's product], then how good can it be?" McDonald's, which hasn't raised prices in its company-owned stores since November, 1982, and still boasts operating margins in the 18% range, wants to spend more of its $300 million ad budget on harder-hitting, product-oriented spots to correct the misconception.

Marketing Tightrope

Leo Burnett Co., the Chicago ad agency that has handled the account for the past two years, however, still seems to favor ads emphasizing a "good-feeling" image. An attempt to tackle the quality issue head-on resulted in a spot that cast the aristocratic actor John Houseman in the unlikely role of a McDonald's customer. "I didn't like the ad; it was overkill," says Fred L. Turner, McDonald's chairman. "There has been, or is, a learning curve on McDonald's for Burnett."

The real difficulty for the company though, is that it is walking a marketing tightrope. Its mammoth size—6,000 domestic units and about 1,500 overseas, more than twice that of Burger King — has become a double-edged sword. It means a huge advantage in a business where consumers choose eateries based upon how easy they are to reach. But at the same time, McDonald's can't introduce a raft of new products without diluting its best-in-the-industry service and efficiency record. Says Quinlan: "We are mainstream America and can't be all things to all people unless we want to take a shot at ruining our business."

McDonald's is not a business to tamper with. The company has never had a down quarter and has a return on equity of more than 20%. Most analysts are predicting 12%-to-15% earnings gains for the next few years, which, while down from the 20%-to-25% growth McDonald's realized in the 1970s, is hardly shabby. For the first nine months of 1983, sales rose 10%, to $6.4 billion, while net income spurted 13%, to $263 million.

International Focus

The company has come to grips with the fact that its geographical expansion in the U.S. — 350 stores a year — will be slowing by the end of the decade as first-rate sites become harder to find. Hence, it will accelerate its development of the international market, where it has been adding 150 units a year. Overseas units may account for as much as 80% of McDonald's yearly store additions by 1990. It already has a nearly insurmountable lead over domestic foes in the overseas arena.

The trick will be to shift to an international focus without jeopardizing its standing at home. McDonald's says it is moving to stay abreast, if not ahead, of the domestic market. It is testing smaller, limited-menu stores, dubbed McSnacks, and looking at barely tapped distribution outlets such as schools, parks, and military installations. Subtle changes include more-contemporary decors and the use of energy-efficient clamshell-shaped grills that cook hamburgers on both sides simultaneously.

McDonald's straddles the fence, however, when it comes to the major challenges: developing new products, getting dinner business, and advertising. The company's first successful new entry since 1977 is Chicken McNuggets, deep-fried morsels of white meat chicken. It has had embarrassing failures with its McChicken and McRib sandwiches. In the third quarter of 1983, McNuggets rang up 12% of company sales, with 60% of that purely incremental volume.

Chairman Turner declares: "If it's a half-reasonable [new product] idea, I say try it." But it remains unlikely that McNuggets will soon be joined nationally by any other new product. Items ranging from a low-calorie Big Mac, a McFeast sandwich, a Mexican product, caramel rolls, and biscuits are under review, but Quinlan says: "If we add another product in the next five years, that would be a lot. We might even drop a few." He asserts loftily: "One of our strengths is that we've never been too quick on the trigger to react to an alleged trend."

Not surprisingly, such complacency has been a source of frustration to McDonald's marketing department. It has lost four high-ranking members in the past 10 months. "McDonald's is operations-driven, while the market has become consumer-driven," says a former marketing executive. "And they still equate advertising with marketing."

Upscale Outlets

McDonald's No. 1 mentality could prove to be its biggest handicap as scores of new and established chains begin to take bites out of the company's consumer base. With the population growing older and with two-paycheck families on the rise, "the dining customer has become more sophisticated," says Roger Lipton of Ladenburg, Thalmann & Co. "He used to be content with a clean place, reliable quality, and courteous service. But that's not enough these days. People are willing to pay more to get more." Lipton adds: "The best place to invest is in companies that are providing more of a dining experience and better food." Indeed, while McDonald's stock has been selling at a low price-earnings ratio of 12, shares of the relatively inexperienced Chi-Chi's Inc., a Mexican-food chain, have fetched multiples of 44.

The Mexican-food segment scored the biggest gains overall last year, moving up 20.7% to become a $1.6 billion market, and upscale Chi-Chi's has become the star performer. "Baby boomers are tired of eating in a plastic environment," declares Shelly Frank, who founded the Midwest-based dinner-house six years ago. With an average check running about $7.20 — 35% coming from high-margin margaritas and Acapulco coolers — the 116-unit chain saw earnings surge 81% to $8 million on sales of $74.3 million in its first fiscal six months ended in October.

Other segments are also doing well. Gourmet hamburger chains such as Chili's Inc., which offers $3.25 burgers cooked to order as well as beer to slosh it down, are proliferating. D'Lites of America Inc., an innovative, Atlanta-based chain specializing in low-calorie food, is undergoing an expansion from 5 units to 50 this year. Barbecue and pizza chains are enjoying strong growth, and many predict that Japanese fast food is poised to take off.

One of the best-performing categories, chicken chains, saw growth of 19.7% last year to become a $4 billion segment. Here, too, the upscale outlets have been among the strongest gainers. Grandy's, a unit of Saga Corp., and Tennessee-based Mrs. Winner's Chicken & Biscuits, have found niches by serving meals in homey surroundings.

Attracted by the potential of the chicken market, Wendy's launched its Sisters Chicken & Biscuits chain in 1980. With sales per unit running about $850,000 a year, Wendy's plans to add about 40 stores in 1984 to its base of 50. "Sisters is another trump card," says Robert L. Barney, chairman

and CEO of Wendy's. Burger King is hinting that it, too, may try its hand at a new chain. "We don't believe we need solely to be in the burger business," says Campbell.

McDonald's says it isn't interested in starting any other operation and predicts failure for most of the new chains that are sticking to a regional expansion strategy. "You need the geographical spread to offer convenience," argues the 51-year-old Turner, a Kroc protege. "And with the demand for higher volume and higher breakeven points, you need a national advertising presence." A blunter Jack M. Greenberg, McDonald's chief financial officer, says: "Very few of these newcomers will make it. It won't be because the concepts aren't good, it will be because there is less interest in running the business than there is in selling franchises."

Strategy Flip-Flops

At the moment, it is the competition from Burger King that is causing McDonald's the most discomfort. Although Campbell concedes that "McDonald's is still the best-operated fast-food hamburger restaurant," he expects that to change. "Five years from now, we'd like to see ourselves with an equal or better volume per store than McDonald's, better-operated, better-looking stores and happier franchisees," he says. "I'm convinced it's achievable."

Burger King was nearly on the ropes in the late 1970s after a rash of management changes, flip-flops in strategy, and a disastrous expansion into items such as veal parmigiana sandwiches and pizza. Campbell, who rose through the advertising ranks, is focusing again on burgers and tightening quality controls. The plan has been gathering momentum since the "battle" ads broke. Dean Witter Reynolds Inc. estimates that for the two years ending in May, 1984, Burger King sales will have increased 40%, to $1.2 billion, while pretax operating earnings will shoot up 59%, to $115 million.

Since it is outspent $3 to $1 by McDonald's in advertising, the Miami chain's spots are deliberately combative. Says Campbell: "If we only have 30 seconds to tell the consumer who is not passionately involved in our business why he should come to us and drive past three McDonald's along the way, we better have something compelling to say."

Taco Salad

Wendy's, by necessity, has also become tougher. "It used to be that a plain vanilla, generic message would bring people in," sighs Chairman Barney. "But now there are so many messages out there you have to break through the clutter." The nine-year-old chain is moving away from burgers to appeal to adults whose palates crave something different. In 1979, Wendy's became the first chain with a salad bar, a move it credits with boosting its female customer base 10%, to 50% of the total. Since then it has added products such as chicken sandwiches, taco salads — which it markets as a complete meal of less than 400 calories — and stuffed baked potatoes.

The Dublin (Ohio) chain is trying to crack the breakfast market by attacking McDonald's lack of variety. It is testing made-to-order omelets and French toast with toppings. But the biggest push is to develop a dinner trade with entrées such as chicken parmigiana, fish filets, and chopped beef with mushrooms. "Our biggest obstacle is getting people to think of us as a fast-service restaurant that offers a superior dining experience," says William M. Welter, senior vice-president for marketing.

McDonald's is also eager to cultivate a dinner business. But like its rivals, the chain may have a tough time persuading the customer who was in earlier for a quick lunch to come back for the evening meal. Its close association with the children's market could be an additional handicap. Ronald McDonald mascots are ubiquitous, and its vast number of playgrounds have made McDonald's the favorite of the sandbox set. Quinlan speculates that modified table service at dinner might help and insists that "we want to move toward the adult user. In fact, the appeal to adults was one of the things that attracted us to McNuggets."

Yet some observers think McDonald's has not gotten sufficient mileage out of McNuggets. They point out that the company failed to emphasize its low calorie count — 310 for six pieces — or to go after the female audience, which often favors chicken over beef. "The McNugget campaign didn't capture the difference in the product, and that's a crime," says a source close to the company.

For their part, McDonald's franchisees are pushing headquarters for some kind of regionalized marketing strategy, and they place the chain's wan-

ing quality reputation at the top of their list of concerns. "I don't care if McDonald's doesn't want to sell a biscuit at the national level, but I need it," contends James G. Devlin, a franchisee in Tullahoma, Tenn. Four years ago, Devlin felt the impact of Hardee's Food Systems Inc.'s made-from-scratch biscuit on his breakfast business but couldn't get the home office excited enough to develop one. They finally acquiesced with a prebaked, frozen biscuit that Devlin says "turned customers off fast." After further badgering, McDonald's came up with a recipe for a biscuit to be made on the premises, and Devlin happily reports that his morning business has shot up 60%.

Cash Cushion

"One of the disappointments over the years is that the public doesn't understand McDonald's attention to quality," says Irving H. Klein, a McDonald franchisee in New York and a former president of its national advertising council. Along with others, he feels that the tug-at-the-heartstrings ads are not suitable in today's cynical marketplace. "We've been trying to sell an intangible," agrees an operator in the South. "The focus should be food."

In a study last fall by Video Storyboard Test Inc., a company ad agencies hire to assess the pull of commercials, only 6% of those surveyed mentioned McDonald's food after viewing several of its spots. Instead they commented on its characters, music, and the family orientation. In a similar Burger King test, 22% said the food looked appetizing.

McDonald's may be under attack at home, but it is operating without peer overseas. The company has outlets in 32 countries and is awaiting approval to open stores in several others. Meanwhile, Burger King will not begin rapid international expansion until 1986.

Clearly, McDonald's has no financial problems. Between now and 1990, it is expected to accumulate an excess cash flow of $1 billion. And while Turner says the strategy is to "concentrate on McDonald's and plow the cash back," there are suggestions that management is starting to look at life beyond the golden arches. To speculation that McDonald's could be interested in companies such as Walt Disney Productions or Holiday Inns Inc., Turner says: "We don't want to be in the booze or bed business. We might consider acquiring some-

How the Three Hamburger
Giants Slice the Market

Market Share
Percent

(Percentage point change
in market share since 1981)

Estimated 1983 sales
Billions of dollars

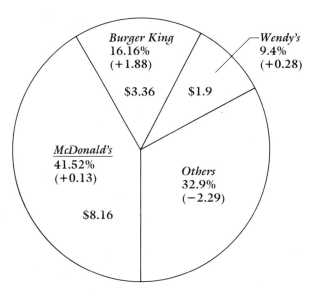

Fiscal years ended December, 1983, for McDonald's and
Wendy's; May, 1984, for Burger King.

Data: Montgomery Securities, Dean Witter Reynolds,
Business Week estimates.

thing in the food-service area." Says Greenberg: "Because we've got enormous financial resources and talented management, we've got to start thinking about what we could do with all that if we're careful and smart. And once we get beyond the next few years, all things are possible."

Case Questions

1. How might you describe the nature of competitive rivalry in the fast-food market?
2. What structural factors have influenced this type of competition?

3. What strategic adjustments are necessary as firms such as McDonald's, Burger King, and Wendy's move from the introductory/emerging stage of industry development to that of growth and development?
4. Evaluate the strategies developed by McDonald's, Burger King, and Wendy's.
5. What advice might you give to the management of McDonald's, Burger King, and Wendy's as these firms move closer to a mature industry?

Source: Reprinted from the January 30, 1984 issue of *Business Week* by special permission, © 1984 by McGraw-Hill, Inc.

"Use the right tool for the right job." That bit of handyman's wisdom once worked beautifully for Black & Decker. During the Seventies do-it-yourself boom, homeowners couldn't get enough electric drills, saws, routers, sanders and grinders. B&D dominated this multibillion-dollar market with 14 percent plus returns on equity, an average 19 percent annual sales growth and a price/earnings multiple that approached 50.

But now, Maryland-based B&D seems to be hammering nails with the butt end of a screwdriver. Basements and garages are chock-full of tools. Roughly 80 percent of U.S. homes now have electric drills, so most future sales must come from replacement and trade-ups. The situation is almost as bad in Europe and elsewhere overseas, where B&D now gets over half of its $1.2 billion annual revenues. "Unit growth in the power tool market is very flat," explains Chief Executive Laurence Farley.

That is an important admission. And a change from the thinking that prevailed before Farley took over from the current chairman, Francis Lucier (in January of 1983). "Prior management could not accept the fact that the company is mature," says Merrill Lynch's William Genco. "Larry Farley is more return-on-investment oriented."

Indeed he is. Farley was a force behind B&D's painful unloading of its McCulloch division, a move that brought a $94 million writeoff (in 1982). McCulloch, which makes gasoline-powered chain saws, had overexpanded to meet the stampede of would-be lumberjacks who were cutting heating bills by burning logs. Then the market choked, and B&D was struck by losses of $29 million during 1981 and 1982.

Getting rid of McCulloch, however, doesn't bring B&D out of the woods. Competition in the professional power tool market (21 percent of sales) is intense. The Japanese, led by Makita

CHAPTER 16

Managing Organizational Change and Development

Electric Works, now have a solid 20 percent share worldwide, a block about as big as B&D's. . . .

Meanwhile, the consumer business (40 percent of sales) is changing. Handymen today prefer more sophisticated tools. That should benefit B&D because of its growing competitive capability in professional equipment. But foreigners are grinding away here, too. . . .

Farley's mature businesses spin off considerable profits — an estimated $35 million companywide last year. But new growth? B&D expects it to come largely from diversification into household products, now only 10 percent of revenues. The company hopes to use its well-known name, proven merchandising capability and a worldwide distribution system to expand its customer base beyond homeowners. . . .

Thus far, B&D's household ventures have worked well. Popular items include . . . a rechargeable hand-held vacuum cleaner, . . . a high-powered flashlight, . . . and a rotary cleaner for floor tiles and carpets. . . .

What's next? Farley is interested in home security and energy saving devices, possibly even small robots. He is also considering blenders and toasters — if B&D can find a cost advantage.

The strategy won't be easy. "Typically, new household products have short life cycles, so B&D will have to keep coming up with new ideas," says Genco. . . .

Farley, however, seems to be making all the right moves. Rather than shopping for a showy acquisition, he wants to diversify on the basis of his company's proven strengths. That won't be easy, and B&D may never be a red-hot growth stock again. But the important thing is that Farley knows he must change.

Source: Forbes, June 6, 1983, "Splinters," by Jeff Blyskal, p. 161. Reprinted by permission. © Forbes Inc., 1983.

Chapter Outline

- Forces for Organizational Change
- Resistance to Organizational Change
- Planned Change in Organizations
- Strategies for Planned Organizational Change
- Organization Development: An Integrative Approach

Key Terms

- performance gap
- structural change
- technological change
- individual change
- achievement motivation
- organization development
- non-zero-sum games
- survey feedback
- process consultation
- team building
- Grid organization development

Chapter Objectives

After studying Chapter 16 you should be able to

1. Recognize the internal and external forces for organizational change.
2. Understand personal and organizational resistance to change.
3. Compare structural, technological, and human approaches to change.
4. Explain the assumptions behind organization development.
5. Trace the steps in the organization development process and the different techniques available to change agents.

Introduction

Throughout this book we have been showing you that the ability to adapt successfully to a changing environment is a primary characteristic of effective organizations. Such adaptation is no easy task in view of the often conflicting demands of employees and the complex environment facing an organization, including various markets, economic conditions, and government regulations. Nevertheless, organizational change must not be random or initiated merely for the sake of change. Management has a responsibility to balance the need for adaptation and innovation with the equally important need for stability and continuity. As noted by Kast and Rosenzweig:

> Management is charged with the responsibility for maintaining a dynamic equilibrium by diagnosing situations and designing adjustments that are most appropriate for coping with current conditions. A dynamic equilibrium for an organization would include the following dimensions:
>
> 1. Enough stability to facilitate achievement of current goals,
> 2. Enough continuity to ensure orderly change in either ends or means,
> 3. Enough adaptability to react appropriately to external opportunities and demands as well as changing internal conditions,
> 4. Enough innovativeness to allow the organization to be proactive [initiate changes] when conditions warrant [1974; pp. 574–575].

The ability of managers to meet these four conditions simultaneously will largely determine whether an organization can survive and how well it can grow in a turbulent environment.

Our discussion of organizational change and development will examine several related topics. First, we will consider several forces for change in organizations. Next, resistance to change will be discussed, followed by a description of the planned change process in organizations. Strategies for planned change then will be covered. Finally, organization development as a technique for planned change will be discussed.

Forces for Organizational Change

The need for change becomes apparent when managers sense that an organization's activities, goals, or values are deficient in some way. When there is a noticeable gap between what an organization is trying to do and what it actually is accomplishing, management must take positive steps to reduce this disparity. For instance, several years ago many scientists and mathematicians — and a great number of college students — considered a slide rule essential for their required computations. Almost overnight, however, the advent of inexpensive, electronic pocket calculators made the slide rule a thing of the past. One company alone watched its slide rule sales drop 75 percent in just two years. The technology of calculating instruments changed radically, necessitating change in organizations that produced such instruments. Only companies that were aware of future trends and began planning early were able to maintain their positions in the market. Other companies either disappeared or moved on to other fields of endeavor, leaving behind a lucrative market.

The reasons for **performance gaps** that necessitate organizational change can be found both within and outside organizations. If managers are to take a comprehensive view of innovation and adaptation, they must be aware of both types of forces and be able to account for both in their actions (Fig. 16.1).

External Forces

There are a wide variety of external forces for organizational change that require managerial action. These include (1) changes in economic or market conditions, such as a sudden decline in demand for a company's products; (2) changes in product or manufacturing technology, such as the discovery of a less expensive manufacturing process by a competitor; (3) changes in the legal or political situation, such as a new consumer protection law that affects current products or practices; and (4) changes in resource availability, such as an increase in cost or sudden unavailability of a major input such as oil.

These forces create gaps in performance that can lead to severe threats to organizational stability and survival if not remedied. For instance, the oil shortage of the mid-1970s and resulting corporate distribution policies led to the demise of many independently owned service stations that lacked the resources necessary to survive and compete with company-owned stations. Simply put, the independent stations did not have the capacity to respond adequately to external forces for change and were forced out of business as a result.

Figure 16.1
External and Internal Forces for Organizational Change

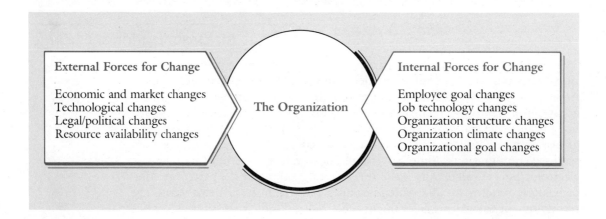

External Forces for Change

Economic and market changes
Technological changes
Legal/political changes
Resource availability changes

The Organization

Internal Forces for Change

Employee goal changes
Job technology changes
Organization structure changes
Organization climate changes
Organizational goal changes

Internal Forces

Several factors within an organization also can be important forces for organizational change. These factors include (1) changes in the composition or personal goals of employees, such as the hiring of newer or younger employees with a work ethic different from that of more senior employees; (2) changes in job technology, such as the replacement of craft-type jobs by automated equipment; (3) changes in organization structure, such as new divisions necessitated by company growth; (4) changes in organizational climate, such as the creation of a climate of distrust, hostility, and insecurity as a result of mass layoffs; and (5) changes in organizational goals, such as those caused by goal succession. Goals may change because management realizes its initial expectations were too high, too low, or misdirected.

These forces create unstable conditions within organizations and jeopardize goal-directed efforts. When stability and continuity are threatened, organizations must attempt to adapt their structure or behavior to ensure long-term growth and survival. Before considering such change processes, however, it is useful to discuss several reasons why change in organizational settings often is difficult.

Resistance to Organizational Change

An important lesson learned by most managers who are set on introducing changes is that resistance to change can be found throughout an organization. The sources of resistance can be either personal (individual) or organizational. Some of the more prominent personal and organizational sources of resistance are listed in Figure 16.2.

Personal Sources of Resistance

As seen in Figure 16.2, employees may resist the introduction of new techniques or methods on a personal level because they feel secure under existing conditions and fear that the changes will destroy interpersonal relationships that have developed through the years. Some employees may not fully understand the reasons behind a change or how it will affect their own particular situations. Group norms may operate to resist any change in work procedures for fear it will lead to higher output without commensurate rewards or compensation.

Employees simply may not identify with the proposed changes, often creating passive resistance and dragging their feet in implementation. This reaction often has been cited as a reason for the failure of many affirmative action programs that attempt to increase minority hiring. Current nonminority employees often are simply indifferent to the goals of affirmative action. It is important to realize that most personal reasons for resisting change are not the result of any overt intention to interfere with goal attainment. Instead, such resistance often

Figure 16.2
Personal and Organizational Sources of Resistance to Change

PERSONAL SOURCES	ORGANIZATIONAL SOURCES
1. Misunderstanding of purpose, mechanics, or consequences of change	1. Reward system may reinforce status quo
2. Failure to see need for change	2. Interdepartmental rivalry or conflict, leading to an unwillingness to cooperate
3. Fear of unknown	3. Sunk costs in past decisions and actions
4. Fear of loss of status, security, power, etc., resulting from change	4. Fear that change will upset current balance of power between groups and departments
5. Lack of identification or involvement with change	5. Prevailing organizational climate
6. Habit	6. Poor choice of method of introducing change
7. Vested interests in status quo	7. Past history of unsuccessful change attempts and their consequences
8. Group norms and role prescriptions	8. Structural rigidity
9. Threat to existing social relationships	
10. Conflicting personal and organizational objectives	

Source: Reprinted from Steers, 1977, p. 167.

results largely from a fear of the consequences of change and a preference for the known over the unknown.

Organizational Sources of Resistance

The nature and character of the organization itself also can influence the extent to which change is accepted. For instance, the prevailing reward structure may be designed to favor existing behavior, as when an organization pays salespeople solely on the basis of total sales and ignores effort and time spent in developing new customers. When various departments see one another as rivals, they may subvert cooperative efforts aimed at change for fear of encroachment on their territory. Managers may consider themselves bound by past decisions and actions because of large investments made previously in a particular product or technology. It sometimes is easier to live with past decisions than to admit that a mistake was made or that conditions have changed. In addition, previous organizational attempts at change may have been ill conceived and unsuccessful, leading to a lack of confidence in the success of any new change efforts.

Additional reasons could be identified, but the important point is that management must be aware of the various sources of resistance to change in organizations and be able to act to minimize them. Managers have an obligation to assess accurately the nature of and need for change. Then they must lay the groundwork for implementing change by examining and dealing with the possible sources of resistance. The manner in which change is implemented is at least as important for success as the actual change itself. With this fact in mind, we now turn to a consideration of the change process in organizations.

Planned Change in Organizations

The change process in its ideal form is a series of fairly distinct, sequential steps leading from the recognition of the problem to the introduction and assessment of the change strategy. Although actual change may be far more complex, a simplified flow diagram can highlight some of the more important steps in the process. The steps in a simplified change process are represented in Figure 16.3.

Performance gaps initially emerge because of changes in the environment, structure, technology, or membership of an organization. These gaps may take the form of a loss of sales revenue, reduced productivity, or increased absenteeism and turnover. Once managers recognize such gaps, they can try to create a climate that is conducive to change. If sufficient time and effort are invested initially in eliminating the causes for resistance, a more open approach to the change process can be taken. Next the manager diagnoses the extent of the problem. Based on this analysis, he or she makes recommendations for appropriate adjustments that it is hoped will remedy the situation and eliminate or reduce the performance gaps. After the implications, costs, and benefits of the alternatives are considered, a decision on a particular change strategy is made and implemented. Once implementation is complete, management can assess how successful the strategy is in reducing the performance gap. The manager then can take steps to reinforce and maintain the new program to the extent that it serves the needs of the organization, its members, and its shareholders.

To see how this process works, consider the following true example. For twenty years, a major United States research laboratory specializing in valves and gauges spent most of its time and effort designing hardware for aerospace projects. Most of its income came from government contracts. As government funds became scarce, however, the laboratory was faced with a performance gap. Because it could see no further contracts coming, management recognized the need for change and began laying the groundwork for a shift from aerospace engineering. After diagnosing the situation, management concluded that the laboratory's technical expertise could be applied with minimal organizational disturbance to hardware problems in the automotive industry. Thus, management shifted the laboratory's goals to providing precision valves and gauges for automobiles instead of space vehicles. An assessment of the change revealed that the process had been carried out with minimal loss of personnel and that the laboratory had sufficient revenues to continue operations in an area in which it had ample expertise. The organization responded to environmental changes by adapting its goals to maintain stability and continuity, thereby enhancing its chances for survival and growth.

Figure 16.3
Basic Change Processes in Organizations

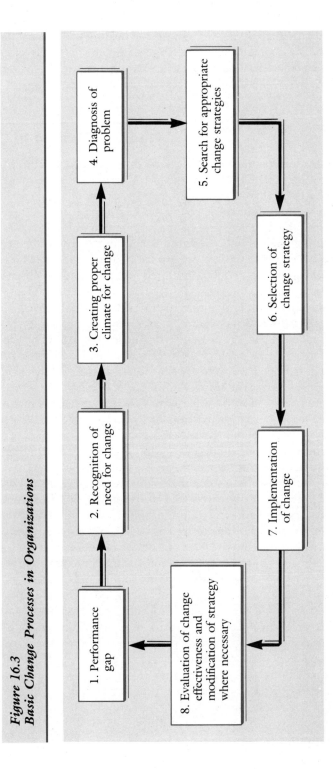

Source: Reprinted from Steers, 1977, p. 169.

Strategies for Planned Organizational Change

The success or failure of organizational change rests not only on accurately identifying the problem and successfully reducing resistance to change, but also on the degree of appropriateness of the selected strategy for implementing change. Understanding the problem is not enough, nor is having employees

---

Feature 16.1
New Corning Chairman Gets Tough

For years the management style at the Corning Glass Works was so laid back that it spawned a Wall Street joke. The company's management training program, so the joke went, consists of three weeks of polo, three weeks of squash, and three weeks of platform tennis.

Some observers believe the management style was behind the company's 41 percent drop in net income between 1979 and 1983. Management was accused of being unwilling to make the necessary tough decisions on cost cutting, divestitures, and acquisitions.

But all that is changing. Amory Houghton, Jr., chairman and chief executive of the Corning, New York, company for nearly twenty years, was replaced by his brother, James R. Houghton. The tough new boss is the architect of a new strategy that the company hopes will revive it.

James Houghton divided the company into three groups—electronics and communications, consumer and industry, and health and science—and designated a president for each group reporting directly to him. Houghton named the three presidents to a six-member advisory committee that will help make operating decisions. The new chairman said he put the three presidents on the committee to create peer pressure and to force them to think in terms of the entire company.

Houghton also has made it clear which divisions will grow. He combined most of Corning's traditional businesses, such as television tubes and Corelle dinnerware, into the consumer and industry group. He plans to make cuts there because, he said, "there are some questionable businesses where we have very high market share, a lot of competition, and margins are eroding a bit." The company also is pulling out of the light bulb and European laboratory glassware businesses.

Instead, corporate resources are being directed into biotechnology and fiber optics. The company also has reordered priorities for its research budget, which in 1983 totaled about $90 million. Now operating units will decide what the research division will work on, and costs will be charged to the individual units.

Eighty percent of the research money will remain in glass and ceramics, however. "We're number one in the world in glass and ceramics, and if we ever lose that we're stupid," Houghton said.

His general idea is to move faster. "We used to be in a position where we could be pretty sleepy," he said. "We could come up with a development and nurse it along and take our time and whenever we got ready the marketplace would accept it. That's gone."

Source: "With New Chairman, Corning Tries to Get Tough and Revive Earnings," by Ann Hughey, *The Wall Street Journal,* April 22, 1983, p. 31.

who are willing to change. Managers have to make the right selection among a wide variety of strategies or techniques of change. Three general strategies can be identified: efforts to change structure, technology, and people. As noted by Leavitt (1964), these three key ingredients interact with more general organizational activities to create conditions that make it easier for organizations to be more effective (Fig. 16.4). We shall consider each of these three approaches briefly.

Structural Approaches to Change

Changes in an organization's structure can take several forms. Glueck (1980, p. 427) has summarized some of the more common techniques:

- Effecting changes in job design that permit more specialization or enrichment.
- Clarifying job descriptions.
- Altering the basis of departmentation (changing from a functional organization to a department system based on products, for example).
- Increasing or decreasing the span of control and therefore the height of the hierarchy.

Figure 16.4
Interdependence of Three Strategies for Organizational Change

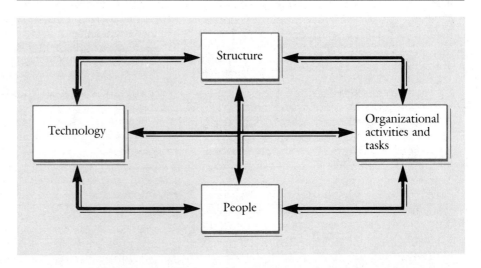

Source: H. J. Leavitt, "Applied Organization Change in Industry: Structural, Technical, and Human Approaches," in W. W. Cooper, H. J. Leavitt, and M. W. Shelly (eds.), *New Perspectives in Organization Research* (New York: John Wiley, 1964), p. 56. Reprinted by permission.

- Modifying the organization manual and its description of policies and procedures.
- Clarifying coordination mechanisms, such as policies and procedures.
- Changing the power structure (moving from a centralized to a decentralized authority, for example).

Structural changes are very common in organizations. In fact, one study found that two-thirds of the major firms make substantive structural changes at least once every two years (Daniel, 1966). The larger the firm, the greater the likelihood of change.

A major purpose of **structural change** is to create conditions in an organization that facilitate and reward goal-directed efforts. For example, a matrix organization (discussed in Chapter 5) may be introduced in a situation in which divergent areas of expertise must be integrated and coordinated for a particular product or project, such as a space satellite. The underlying assumption of this approach is that behavior, performance, and effectiveness are largely determined by the way an organization or work group is structured. An example of this theory in action can be seen in the Chase Manhattan Bank's efforts to change its prevailing reward system and culture (Feature 16.2).

Technological Approaches to Change

A second major approach to change involves alterations in the prevailing technology. Research has shown consistently that when the nature of job technology — how we do our jobs — changes, the work environment also changes, although not necessarily for the better. Examples of technological approaches to change include:

- Altering the techniques used for doing work, such as using human factors engineering to change worker-machine relations,
- Changing the equipment used in work, through the introduction of robots on an assembly line, for example,
- Modifying production methods, such as shifting from an assembly line method to an autonomous work-group method,
- Changing engineering processes, through the introduction of microprocessors or chips into a product to replace more cumbersome or less reliable mechanical equipment, for example.

The principal assumption underlying **technological change** is that improved technology or work methods can lead to more efficient operations and either increased productivity or improved working conditions, perhaps by relieving workers of the more tedious tasks. A good example can be seen in discussions surrounding the introduction of word processors in offices. It is argued that word processors allow typists to become more efficient and productive, thereby saving the company money and presumably offsetting the cost of the equipment. Unfortunately, in many situations no one bothers to ask the typists for *their* opinions on such changes. The consequence is often diminished results,

Feature 16.2
Changing Corporate Culture at Chase Manhattan

You can't see it or feel it, but one of the most important aspects of an organization is its culture. A "culture" is a pattern of beliefs and expectations shared by the members of an organization that establish the norms and rules governing acceptable employee behavior. The culture of an organization can have a profound effect on behavior in it. Many people believe that serious efforts to change an organization can only succeed if managers are successful in changing its culture first.

Consider the example of the Chase Manhattan Bank. David Rockefeller, the youngest of John D. Rockefeller's six grandchildren, became president of the Chase Manhattan in 1961, having risen to the top the easy way. Once there, he ran the nation's third-largest bank like a "club." Bank officers tended to worry more about how many oils from the Chase art collection they had on their walls than about profits," said one Wall Street analyst ("The Change at David's Bank," p. 49).

By 1977 profits had plummeted. Return on assets fell to $.33 per $100, and bad debts totaled $1.9 billion. Numerous poor business decisions had been made, and many of the bank's most experienced executives had resigned.

It was David Rockefeller himself who decided at last to change the culture from one that rewarded people for appearance to one that would reward them for performance. He set himself a goal of making the

three years until his mandatory retirement "the most productive of my career" ("The Change at David's Bank," p. 49).

The first thing Rockefeller and a group of his top executives did was to draw up a three-page statement of the bank's goals. "We will only do those things we can do extremely well and with the highest level of integrity," the statement said ("Corporate Cultures," p. 149). Those things included closing 50 unprofitable branches in New York, turning away risky loans, replacing about 600 executives with new young talent, and updating the bank's customer services. In addition, the bank made efforts to increase communication both up and down in the hierarchy — a marked change from the past top-down approach.

The results speak for themselves. Three years later assets had risen from $45 billion to $65 billion, while bad debts had declined from $269 million to $93 million, and net income had risen from $116 million to $303 million. Chase Manhattan had created a new culture. David Rockefeller proudly took his share of the credit when he told a financial correspondent for *Time* magazine, "I helped to create a climate that has finally produced a really professional management team, which was essential to our success" ("The Change at David's Bank," p. 49).

Sources: "The Change at David's Bank," *Time*, September 1, 1980, p. 49; "Corporate Culture," *Business Week*, October 27, 1980, pp. 148–160.

negative attitudes, or, at the very least, misunderstandings. It is most important to consult and involve the employees concerned when attempting to introduce technological change.

People Approaches to Change

The third category of change techniques focuses on attempts to change individuals. Strategies aimed at changing people tend to emphasize improving employee skills, attitudes, or motivation. These approaches assume that behavior in organizations — and ultimately organizational effectiveness — are largely determined by the characteristics and actions of the members of the organization. If these people can be changed in some way, it is believed that they will work harder to achieve the organization's goals.

Individual change strategies take many forms, including a wide variety of personnel training programs, such as skills training, communication effectiveness, and decision-making training; attitude motivation training; and socialization efforts to develop a "company man" or "company woman." An example of attitude motivation training is offered in Feature 16.3, which describes a technique used to increase **achievement motivation.**

Most such strategies rely on a basic model of individual change that was first advanced by Kurt Lewin (1947) and later developed by Ed Schein (1961). The model consists of four basic steps, as shown in Figure 16.5.

1. *Desire for change.* Before change can occur, the individual must feel a need for it. This need can result from a perceived deficiency, actual dissatisfaction, or a desire for improvement.

2. *Unfreezing.* As Schein (1961, p. 62) notes, unfreezing involves "an alteration of the forces acting on the individual, such that his stable equilibrium is disturbed sufficiently to motivate him and to make him ready for change; this can be accomplished either by increasing the pressure to change or by reducing some of the threats or resistance to change."

Feature 16.3
Training Employees in Achievement Motivation

How can achievement motivation be developed in employees?

The primary researcher on this subject has been David McClelland, who believes that achievement motivation can be taught to adults with moderate success. His approach to training consists of four steps. First, participants are taught how to think, talk, and act like a person with a high need for achievement. Second, participants are taught how to set higher but carefully planned and realistic work goals for themselves. Third, participants are given considerable feedback about both their behavior and their performance on work-related goals. Finally, efforts are made to create an *ésprit de corps* among the participants so

that a support group is established to help encourage and reinforce achievement-oriented efforts.

McClelland claims that such a program can work. With few exceptions, managers from various countries who attended these programs received more rapid promotions, earned more money, and expanded their businesses more quickly after the course than did control groups. Hence, in at least some instances, achievement motivation training has been used as an effective individual change strategy.

Source: "Toward a Theory of Motive Acquisition," by D. C. McClelland, *American Psychologist, 20,* 1965, pp. 321 – 333.

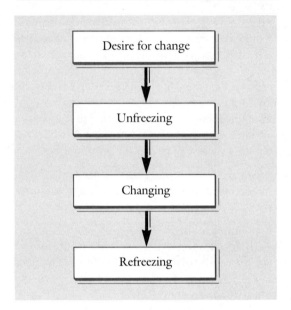

Figure 16.5
The Lewin/Schein Model
of Individual Change

Sources: Lewin, 1947, and Schein, 1961.

3. *Changing*. According to Schein (1961, p. 62), changing involves "the presentation of a direction of change and the actual process of learning new attitudes. This process occurs basically by one of two mechanisms: (a) *identification* — the person learns new attitudes by identifying with and emulating some other person who holds those attitudes; or (b) *internalization* — the person learns new attitudes by being placed in a situation where new attitudes are demanded of him as a way of solving problems which confront him and which he cannot avoid."

4. *Refreezing*. In refreezing, the changed attitudes are integrated into the individual's personality in such a way that they become part of the person's way of thinking.

Although the model is simple, it highlights the basic processes involved in attempts to change people. If managers are aware of this process, they stand a far greater chance of succeeding with planned change atttempts than they would if they ignored the people involved.

In summary, the selection of an appropriate change technique depends largely on the nature and character of the problem, the goals of the change, the orientations of the people implementing the change, and the resources available. For instance, if poor communication is seen as a barrier to effective performance, management may decide to make structural changes, such as using a matrix design, to remedy the situation. With changes in reporting procedures, lines of authority, and so forth, more interaction and exhanges of views may occur, thereby improving communications. Management may also institute communications training programs to improve both interpersonal competence and communications skills. Both approaches may reduce barriers to effective communications, although the techniques and underlying assumptions are quite different. The important point is that it is the primary responsibility of managers to recognize the need for change in organizations, to diagnose the nature and extent of the problem, and to implement what they consider to be the most effective change strategy given the circumstances. Without such leadership, an organization's ability to respond to both internal and external threats to stability and continuity is greatly diminished, which in turn reduces the likelihood that the organization can maintain an effective level of operation over time.

Organization Development: An Integrative Approach

We have examined three primary strategies for planned organizational change involving structure, technology, and people. Each of these approaches usually is aimed at attaining a fairly specific goal within the organization, such as improving employees' achievement motivation through training or improving job efficiency through job redesign. We now come to an integrated approach to change that focuses not on one aspect or problem within the organization but, rather, on long-term, global change and development throughout the organization. **Organization development,** as we shall see, is an ongoing and systemwide developmental approach. It seeks to improve both productivity and efficiency on one hand and the quality of working life on the other.

The field of organization development is broad and involves many different and often conflicting approaches (see, for example, the discussion in Beer, 1980, p. 198). Even so, it is possible to suggest a definition for organization development broad enough to encompass most of the different activities. We will use the definition presented by French and Bell (1973):

> [Organization development is] a long-range effort to improve an organization's problem-solving and renewal processes, particularly through a more effective and collaborative management or organization culture — with special emphasis on the culture of formal work teams — with the assistance of a change agent, or catalyst, and the use of the theory and technology of applied behavioral science, including action research.

Several dimensions emerge from this definition. First, organization development is a *problem-solving* process aimed at alleviating threats to organizational survival or well-being, or at capitalizing on a unique opportunity. Second, it is aimed at helping the organization *renew* itself and recapture some of its vitality. Third, *collaborative management* is stressed; that is, change efforts are undertaken only with the active participation of all parties involved. Fourth, major organization development efforts are attempts to change an organization's *culture* and *work climate*. Finally, *action research* represents a central aspect of many organization development efforts. Action research is the process by which behavioral research findings are collected and then fed back to participants, who discuss the results and use them as a foundation for planned change.

In essence, organization development is a mechanism for change that is highly participatory, broad in scope, and evolutionary in design. As such, it truly represents an integrative approach to planned change in organizations.

Assumptions Underlying Organization Development

Any change technology rests on certain assumptions and values espoused by its advocates, and organization development practitioners tend to hold certain values and assumptions about what life in organizations should be like and how change should occur. Although they are not universal, it is possible to summarize some of the more general assumptions. These assumptions relate to individual employees, group relationships, and organizational relationships (French and Bell, 1973; Wexley and Yukl, 1977).

Assumptions about Individuals. Organization development advocates often assume that employees want and need personal growth and that they need fulfillment on the job. It also is assumed that people generally have a capacity to contribute more to the organization than they are typically encouraged or allowed to. In other words, organization development assumes that most people are "premotivated" to perform at high levels. Its purpose, then, is to develop a work environment that encourages this motivation and allows employees to realize their full potential on the job.

Assumptions about Groups. Organization development practitioners also hold several assumptions concerning the nature of group relations. It often is assumed, for example, that there is less interpersonal trust and mutual support among group members than is desirable for maximum effectiveness. It is believed that leadership responsibilities (see Chapter 10) can be shared more among group members, instead of being concentrated in one person. The emphasis is on facilitating group activities and group cooperation, such as that found in autonomous work groups. Open communication is stressed as a means to secure the active participation of everyone and to root out potential problems or conflicts. Finally, advocates believe that it is important to develop an *ésprit de corps* among group members so that they have positive feelings about one another and are genuinely interested in the welfare of group members.

Assumptions about Organizations. The final set of assumptions underlying many organization development activities focuses on the organization as a whole. It is largely assumed, for example, the change in one part of an organization, such as the marketing department, will of necessity influence and be influenced by other parts, such as engineering or production. As we have said, organization development is a systemwide change effort. In addition, it must be recognized that the members of an organization not only are involved in their own groups, but also must interact with other groups — hence the emphasis on developing intergroup relations. Efforts to reduce conflict emphasize **non-zero-sum games;** that is, efforts are made to avoid situations in which someone wins entirely and someone loses entirely. Instead, a search is made for a solution to the conflict that will satisfy all parties. Finally, if organization development is to succeed, it must have the full and active support of top management.

Although there may be minor variations in these assumptions, the major thrust of organization development activities can succeed only in environments characterized largely by the values and norms just presented. Organization development is as much a philosophy of change as a technology of change. It assumes that people are open to change and that organizations and their managers are willing to change. Without this willingness, most organization development efforts cannot succeed.

The Organization Development Process

The basic change process used in organization development follows the steps shown in Figure 16.3. As a change technology, however, it adds or emphasizes several features not typically found in more focused or narrow efforts. Organization development as a process consists of seven distinct steps (Glueck, 1980):

1. *Initial diagnosis.* At this stage, fundamental questions are asked: What is the basic problem? Can the problem be solved using organization development techniques?

2. *Data collection.* Data are collected through interviews and questionnaires to verify the initial diagnosis and suggest possible solutions.

3. *Feedback and confrontation.* The findings from the survey are fed back to the participants, discussed, and examined as they relate to the group. Priorities for change are identified.

4. *Planning and problem solving.* Problem-solving groups are established to tackle major problem areas and goals.

5. *Team building.* Conscious efforts are made to develop work groups into cohesive teams rather than isolated individuals who happen to work together.

6. *Intergroup development.* Efforts are made to build and solidify good working relationships among the various teams.

**Feature 16.4
At Action Instruments, Workers Are Capitalists**

At first glance Action Instruments Inc. looks ordinary. The San Diego, California, company is eleven years old, it manufactures electronic measurement and control devices, and in 1982 it had a modest $530,000 pretax profit on sales of $15 million. It is private, and it has never produced a major product innovation.

But look again. Action Instruments's strength lies not in the bottom line but in its people. "We are building capitalism with a heart," said president and founder Jim Pinto. "Our competitors don't have people on their balance sheet. Ours does, and they're at the very heart of our growth."

The company Pinto founded in 1972 has succeeded in blurring the distinction between employees and owners.

"The future of this company is to eliminate the differences between workers, managers, and owners by making them all capitalists," said the India-born Pinto. "If you own a piece, if you feel a part of this, you do everything to increase productivity. The whole ethos is based on the idea that love is a better motivator than compulsion. We don't have 'yes, sahib, no, sahib' relationships around here."

Pinto encourages his employees to invest as much as 10 percent of their gross income in the company. In 1983 almost half the company's 285 employees controlled about 20 percent of the company and its independent field representatives another 18 percent.

Action employees are expected to take an active interest in their company. An information center provides them with weekly statements about profits, shipments, bookings, and bottlenecks, details usually reserved for the top management in an organization.

There also are extensive training ses-

sions. Two series of seminars deal with basic attitudes, such as trying to be 2 percent better than other companies, avoiding procrastination, and being dedicated to the company's long-range growth strategy. Also covered are basic communication, human relations skills, and the "barrier," the company's strict screening process for potential employees, which is aimed at selecting only the most dedicated people.

There is a distaste for formal symbols of power at the company as well. There are no personal secretaries and no reserved parking spaces, and dress is casual. There are few private offices. Pinto has one, but the sign on the door reads, "Miscellaneous."

In 1983 the company's top manufacturing personnel burned their business cards and eliminated their titles. Instead they formed a system called OCTA — for Orchestration, Concept, Task, and Analysis — moved into a large, common "nerve center," and began working as a team.

One of Action's outstanding aspects is the freedom it gives to assembly line workers. They have a minimum of supervision and are expected to carry out their tasks on their own. They're also personally consulted on procedures and new techniques. As a result, the turnover rate is less than half what is expected for electronics manufacturing businesses.

"Compared to every place I've worked, this is paradise," said assembly line supervisor Ruth Valentini. "People feel at ease and do a better job. It's like I'm self-employed — everybody is. I tell people what to do, but then I leave them alone. It's like everybody has their own little business — yet we all work together."

Source: "A Call to Action" by Joel Kotkin, *INC.* Magazine, November 1983, pp. 85–96.

7. *Follow-up and evaluation.* Results are compared against initial goals, and steps are identified to ensure that resulting change "sticks." New change goals are established when necessary.

The result of this process should be a more cohesive organization with highly integrated work teams, good intergroup relations, less conflict, and greater focus and consensus on organizational goals. An ideal world is not created. Nevertheless, organization development has been credited in many situations with contributing to substantial improvements in organizational functioning. It is because of this, perhaps, that a good number of the top Fortune 500 companies have adopted some form of organization development.

Types of Organization Development Activities

A variety of techniques are available to change agents interested in organization development.

Survey Feedback. Survey feedback is a relatively straightforward technique in which employees are surveyed with a questionnaire or interview and the results are given back to them in an aggregate or summarized form. Next, there is group discussion concerning the meaning of the results. Topics commonly surveyed include the general level of job satisfaction, perceptions of leadership styles, openness of communication, and conflict actually experienced. As a result of the discussions, training and development activities are initiated to solve the problems the survey has pointed out.

Process Consultation. In process consultation a change agent is brought in to observe a group at work. Observations are made about such things as leadership styles, communication, conflict and cooperation, and decision-making processes. The change agent's observations then are shared with group members and serve as the basis for a discussion concerning ways to improve the situation. The change agent may discover, for example, that decisions are highly centralized — made by the general sales manager, perhaps — but that people far down in the hierarchy who are seldom consulted, such as sales representatives, have important information bearing on the decision. As a result, useful information is ignored. Such a conclusion and possible remedies would be discussed.

Team Building. This approach attempts to analyze the effectiveness of a work group and help it discover how to work more effectively as an integrated and cohesive team. Techniques of team building include discussions with group members about possible barriers to developing cohesiveness, and behavioral techniques such as sensitivity training that increase awareness of how other people respond to an individual's behavior.

Grid₀ Organization Development. An approach that has received considerable attention in recent years is Grid organization development. This approach was developed by Blake and Mouton (1969, 1978) and represents one of the more comprehensive and systematic approaches to change. The technique is based on Blake and Mouton's managerial grid, which suggests that two key outcome variables are important to organizations: a concern for people and a concern for production. The Grid, shown in Figure 16.6, identifies the possible combinations of these two concerns.

In Figure 16.6, concern for people is plotted on the vertical axis of the Grid and concern for production is plotted on the horizontal axis. Five major intersections between these two concerns are shown, beginning with what is called a "1,1" management style, in which managers show little concern for either people or production. In "1,9" and "9,1" management styles, managers emphasize one concern, either people or production, at the expense of the other. A "5,5" style exists when managers attempt to compromise and show "sufficient" attention to both. The ideal form — a "9,9" management style — emerges when managers are successful in developing highly committed, cohesive, and satisfied work teams that are dedicated to maximum production and organizational effectiveness.

Change agents help managers locate themselves on the Grid. Ideally, this self-evaluation will serve as a starting point for development of a "9,9" manager. The program through which such managers are developed consists of six steps. They are:

Phase 1: Training. After top management has concluded that grid organization development may help solve the organization's problem, key managers attend a week-long seminar to learn the basic concepts of the program. They assess their own managerial styles and work to improve their communication, group problem-solving, and team-development skills. Following this seminar, each key manager returns to the organization and attempts to put the program into effect.

Phase 2: Team development. Managers and their subordinates next attempt to work together to improve their interrelationship and to develop cohesive teams capable of operating on a "9,9" level.

Phase 3: Intergroup development. Efforts are made to shift the nature of intergroup relations from conflict to cooperation. The basic idea is for the entire organization to work together and for individual members to help one another work toward achieving the organization's goals.

Phase 4: Organizational goal setting. Once intergroup cooperation is achieved, the organization as a whole can consider what changes are needed in long-term corporate goals. Active participation at all levels is encouraged in the attempt to define what the organization will or should look like in the future.

Phase 5: Goal attainment. Effort is directed toward making the ideal organi-

Figure 16.6
The Managerial Grid

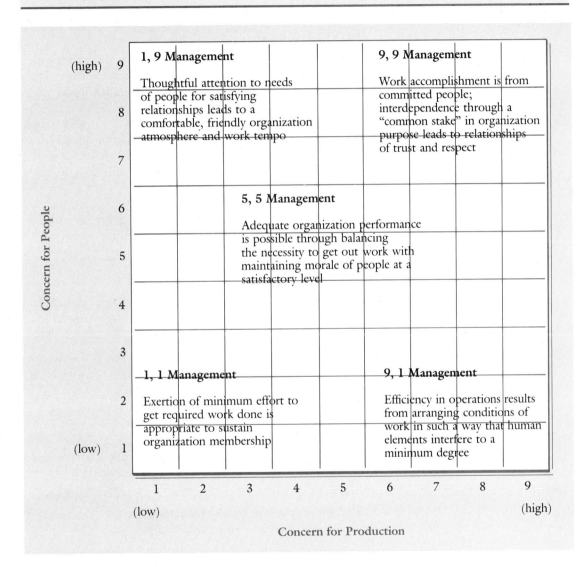

		1, 9 Management		9, 9 Management
(high)	9	Thoughtful attention to needs of people for satisfying relationships leads to a comfortable, friendly organization atmosphere and work tempo		Work accomplishment is from committed people; interdependence through a "common stake" in organization purpose leads to relationships of trust and respect
			5, 5 Management	
	6		Adequate organization performance is possible through balancing the necessity to get out work with maintaining morale of people at a satisfactory level	
		1, 1 Management		9, 1 Management
(low)	1	Exertion of minimum effort to get required work done is appropriate to sustain organization membership		Efficiency in operations results from arranging conditions of work in such a way that human elements interfere to a minimum degree

Concern for People

Concern for Production

(low)   (high)

zation a real one. Concern focuses on how to reduce obstacles to achieving organizational objectives.

Phase 6: Stabilization. The entire program is evaluated to determine where success has been achieved and where more effort is needed. When necessary, new improvement goals are set to remedy past failures. Finally, efforts are made to stabilize and secure the positive outcomes that have been achieved.

Successful Interventions

The history of organization development interventions is difficult to interpret. Most of the research carried out to evaluate the effectiveness of such interventions has been done by organization development consultants, who have an obvious interest in positive results. Moreover, as Strauss (1976) notes, "As a rapidly evolving field, organization development presents a moving target, making it difficult to define or criticize." Even so, organization development remains a popular form of change among managers who feel that some form of change is necessary. In other words, many managers feel that although organization development is not perfect, it does represent one of the better approaches to planned change in organizations.

Efforts can be made to enhance the likelihood of success in organization development interventions. French and Bell (1973) have listed eleven factors:

1. Recognize that the organization has problems. Without this recognition, no change effort can succeed.

2. Make use of an *external* change agent. Internal change agents usually lack the necessary experience or expertise and typically have greater political problems in orchestrating serious change.

3. Elicit strong support from top managers for the organization development intervention efforts. Such support is necessary if the efforts are to succeed.

4. Make use of action research. Decisions should be guided by facts, not opinions.

5. Ideally, if a small success in some part of the organization can be achieved, employees will be more likely to be motivated to participate actively in the program. A small success indicates that the program can work.

6. Make sure that employees understand what organization development is and is not and that they are aware of why it is being used. In this way, apprehension and resistance to the unknown are reduced.

7. Ensure that change agents do not condescend to managers or employees.

8. Ensure that managers from the personnel department are actively involved. Internal expertise concerning an organization's human resources can be incorporated into the change efforts.

9. Begin to develop internal expertise in organization development. In this way the internal facilitators can assume responsibility from the external change agents in time and assure the continuity of the program.

10. Monitor the results continuously and be sensitive to deviations from the program or to weakening support for the program.

11. Ensure that valid and reliable measures are taken before and after the intervention to provide an accurate indicator of actual change. Without such data it becomes virtually impossible to determine whether the efforts were of any value.

Summary

The need for change becomes apparent when there is a noticeable gap between what an organization is trying to do and what it actually is accomplishing. The reasons for these performance gaps can be found both within and outside the organization.

External forces for change include changes in economic or market conditions, product or manufacturing technology, the legal or political situation, and resource availability. Unless remedied, they can lead to threats to organizational stability and survival.

Internal forces for change include changes in the composition or personal goals of employees, job technology, organizational structure, and organizational goals. When stability and continuity are threatened, organizations must attempt to adapt their structure or behavior to ensure long-term growth and survival.

Resistance to change can be personal or may stem from the nature and character of the organization itself.

The change process ideally is a series of distinct, sequential steps leading from recognition of the problem to the introduction and assessment of the change strategy. Three general strategies for change are structural change, including alterations in job design, job descriptions, and the power structure; technological change, altering the techniques or equipment used; and personal change, in which people are changed in some way by improving their skills, attitudes, or motivation. The technique used depends on the nature of the problem, the goals of the change, the orientation of the people implementing the change, and the available resources.

Organization development is a long-range, problem-solving process aimed at helping the organization renew itself. It stresses collaborative management in an attempt to change an organization's culture and work climate. Action research is a central aspect of many organization development efforts.

Organization development consists of seven steps: the initial diagnosis, data collection, feedback and confrontation, planning and problem solving, team building, intergroup development, and follow-up and evaluation. Several of the more common techniques available to change agents are survey feedback, process consultation, team building, and grid organization development, which stresses a concern for people and production. The likelihood of success in organization development interventions can be enhanced by the actions of management and the change agent.

Questions for Discussion

1. Identify several external and internal forces for change in organizations. How would such factors be expected to change across organizations?
2. What are some of the more important sources of resistance to change in organizations?
3. What are performance gaps? How do they emerge?
4. Outline a basic change process. What is the role of management at each stage of the process?
5. Distinguish a structural approach to change from a technological approach. Where would each approach be most effective?
6. What is meant by a "people approach" to change? How is it unique?
7. Define "unfreezing."
8. What is organization development? How does it differ from the approaches described earlier?
9. Outline the organization development approach to change.
10. Define and provide examples of (a) survey feedback, (b) process consultation, and (c) team building.
11. Describe how grid organization development works.

Exercise 16.1
Job Analysis and Design

Jerry Taylor has been involved with the administrative functions of the National Insurance Company for almost twenty years. About three months ago, Jerry was appointed group manager of the Policyholder Service and Accounting Departments at the home office. Before he actually assumed the job, Jerry was able to get away for a three week management development program at the State University College of Business. One of the topics covered in the program was the concept of job enrichment, or, job redesign. Jerry had read about job enrichment in several of his trade journals, but the program was his first opportunity to think about the concept in some detail. In addition, several of the program participants had had some experience (both positive and negative) with job redesign projects.

Jerry was intrigued with the idea. He knew how boring routine administrative tasks could become, and he knew from his previous supervisory work that turnover of clerical personnel was a real problem. In addition, his conversations with the Administrative Vice-President and Joe Bellows, the Personnel Manager, led him to believe that some trials with redesigning the work would be supported and favorably regarded.

Description of the Work

Group Policyholder Service Department

The principal activities undertaken in this department are the sorting and opening of incoming mail and then matching to accounting files; reviewing of Group Insurance Bills from policy holders; and coding required changes to policies (e.g., new employees and terminations). These activities are carried out by approximately 28 people, 53 percent of whom are over age 35, 82 percent female, 89 percent high school graduates, and 53 percent with less than two years' experience in their current job.

Organizationally, the department is headed by a manager. The employees are grouped into the four functional categories of clerical support, senior technician, change coder, and special clerk. The general work flow and a more specific list of the tasks carried out within each functional category are shown in Exhibit 1.

The Group Policyholder Service Department shares the same physical working area as the Accounting Department. The people within Policyholder Service who work in the different functional categories are in very close proximity to one another, frequently just one desk away. The files for the department are located at one corner of the work area and the supervisors have offices along one side (see Exhibit 2).

In the last few months, Jerry has observed that the functional breakdown and the accompanying physical arrangement of people and files leads to a number of problems. Since work is assigned or selected on a random basis, there is no personal accountability for it. Files are at one corner of the work area where they can be retrieved by the clerical group and distributed to a senior technician who randomly distributes them to be processed. After a file is coded, it is placed in a holding area for processing by the Accounting Department. Here, assignment of work is also done on a random basis. It is difficult to respond to phone calls or written requests for information promptly, because it is frequently difficult to find a file. In fact, several people are kept busy doing nothing but looking for files.

The typical employee performs a job which consisted of two tasks on approximately an eleven-minute cycle. All work is cross checked. The training for the job is minimal and there are a number of individuals performing the same set of tasks on files randomly issued. A clerk occasionally corresponds with a policyholder, but all correspondence goes out with the manager's signature on it. The manager thus receives all phone calls and correspondence from policyholders.

Because of the random distribution of work, individual performance is difficult to measure. There are spot checks on some completed work by someone other than the doer, but it is difficult or impossible to determine the specific individual who was responsible. Consequently, it is not possible to provide specific information to individuals at regular intervals about their work performance.

Accounting Department

The Accounting Department processes the files, bills, and checks received from the Group Policyholder Service. Premiums are posted on IBM cards and worksheets. Necessary adjustments are made to accounts and the checks, cards, and worksheets are balanced. Approximately 28 people are employed at any one time performing these tasks. Seventy-seven percent of the work force are under 35 years of age. Everyone has at least a high school degree and 54 percent have less than two years' experience in the job they were performing.

Exhibit 1
Policyholder Service Department Work Flow and Tasks

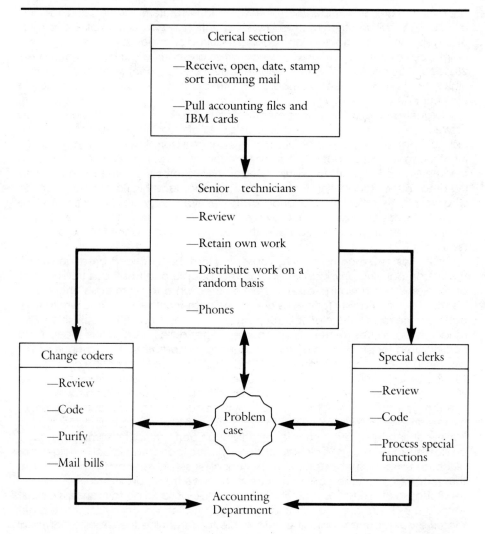

The department has both a manager and a supervisor. The employees are divided into senior technicians, premium posters, and special clerks. The general work flow and tasks carried out in each of these functional areas are shown in Exhibit 3. As shown in Exhibit 2, the Accounting Department shares its work and files with Policyholder Service.

Work is selected on a random basis. Clerks go to a bookcase file and choose the cases they wish to do. Occasionally, correspondence with a policyholder is necessary, and is signed by the manager.

Exhibit 2
Policyholder Service Department and Accounting Department
Physical Layout[a]

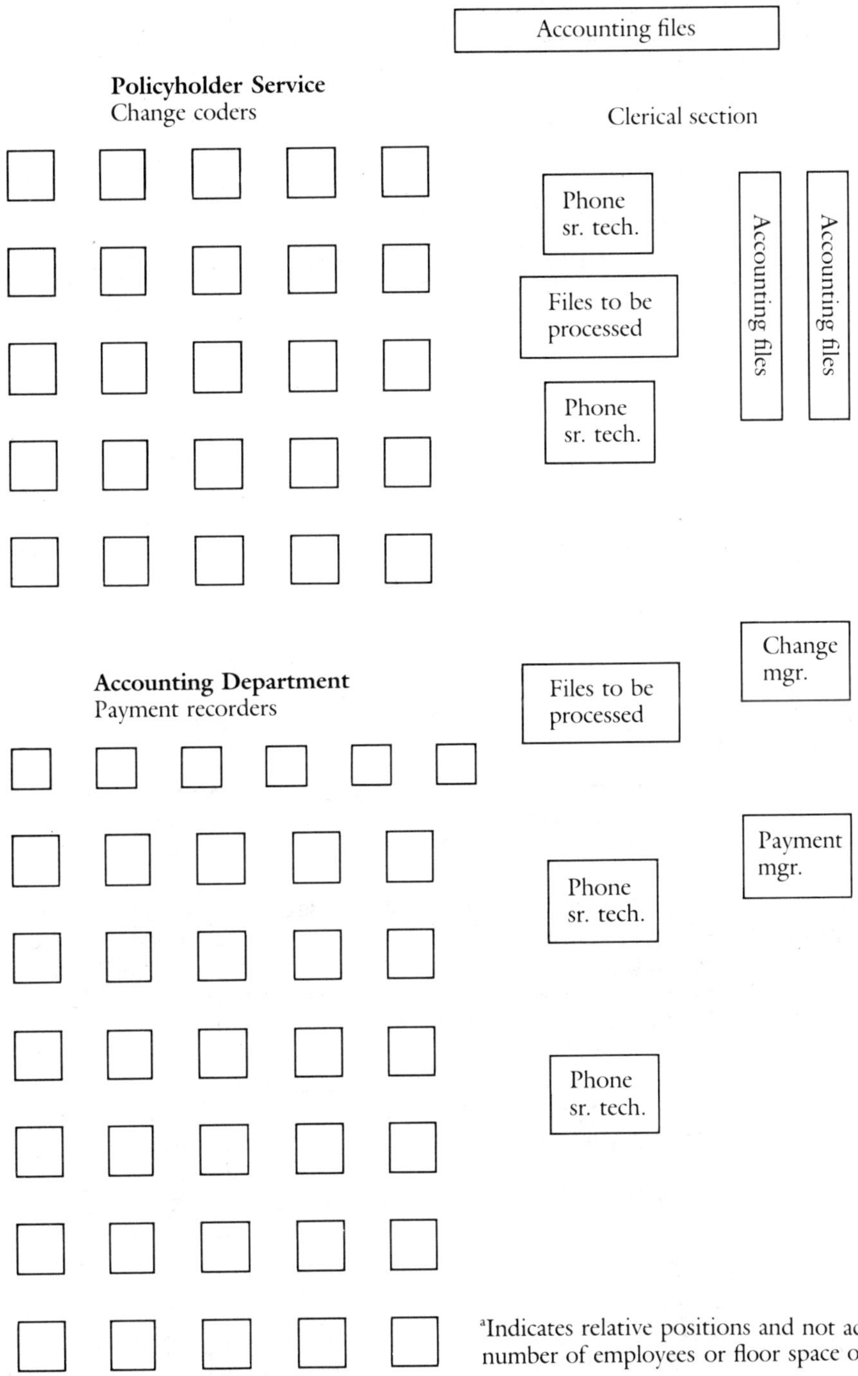

Accounting files

Policyholder Service
Change coders

Clerical section

Phone
sr. tech.

Accounting files

Accounting files

Files to be
processed

Phone
sr. tech.

Change
mgr.

Accounting Department
Payment recorders

Files to be
processed

Payment
mgr.

Phone
sr. tech.

Phone
sr. tech.

[a]Indicates relative positions and not actual
number of employees or floor space occupied.

Exhibit 3
Accounting Department Work Flow and Tasks

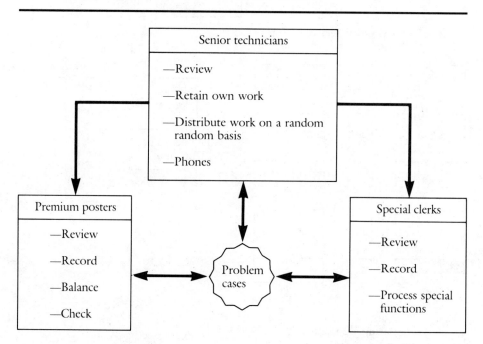

The Problem of Change

Jerry believes that if the work in his department can be *properly* redesigned, then departmental effectiveness can be improved. In addition, he believes that substantial improvements can be made in terms of individual employee work satisfaction.

In thinking about redesigning the work, Jerry has separated the problem into two parts. First, he is concerned about the *process* of change. How can he best accomplish a job redesign project? Second, Jerry has been concerned with the *arrangement* of the tasks themselves. Before he begins such a project, Jerry hopes to have at least some preliminary ideas about the feasibility of such a change.

First, *as an individual,* write down your thoughts about how Jerry should implement the process of change.

Then, as a group, can you agree on the *process* that Jerry should use to bring about the change?

Next, still *as an individual,* how would you actually redesign the work in Jerry's department?

Finally, *as a group,* how would you redesign the work in Jerry's department?

Source: "Job Analysis and Design," by A. Alber, Henry P. Sims, and Andrew D. Szilzgyi in Antone F. Alber, *An Exploratory Study of the Benefits and Costs of Job Enrichment.* Ph.D. dissertation, The Pennsylvania State University, 1977. Reprinted by permission.

Case Study
The Case of the MSWD

Changing the culture of an organization is a difficult, time-consuming, often gut-wrenching process. This is as true in public corporations as it is in the private domain. In fact, effecting such change in a public institution is, if anything, more difficult because of the number of legitimate constituencies — the public, legislators, unions, employees, special-interest groups — that can raise barriers to change. But change can be accomplished if a sufficient level of commitment is applied to the process for a long enough time. One example will reveal all the expenditures — of time, money, and morale — that are involved.

Metropolitan Sewer & Water District (MSWD — a major public wholesaler of these essential services to a large American city) is a public-sector corporation. It employs 2,500 people, has an annual budget of $75 million and spends $200 million a year on capital improvements. MSWD is one of the oldest public agencies of its kind in the country.

Throughout the years, the MSWD carried out its mandate in fine fashion. Its accomplishments were not achieved without difficulty and controversy, however. At times in the history of MSWD, senior officials were charged and convicted of misuse of public funds.

A second problem MSWD faced both internally and in the eyes of the public was patronage. Over the years, administration after administration had found ways to plant favorite sons on MSWD's modest operating-budget payroll.

The third problem MSWD faced was one of rampant bureaucracy — a problem that organization theorist Henry Mintzberg suggests affects all older organizations. The average contract required seventy-two separate signatures and took close to nine months to wind its way through the bureaucracy before being let. Even a minor contract involved a foot-high pile of forms.

Despite the presence of a modern computer system, there were at least six separate manual personnel record systems operating in MSWD. And even with these systems, no one could say with certainty how many people were on the payroll at any time.

All business was conducted by memo, and usually in a prescribed official format rather than face-to-face. Everything was done by the book. If it wasn't on paper, it wouldn't get done. A classic case of the process culture gone awry.

Still, this bureaucracy would not have been a serious problem except for some issues that surfaced in the late 1970s. Water usage continued to rise and gradually began to exceed the design capacity of the system. Moreover, federal EPA regulations that were enacted required MSWD to upgrade its facilities. Confronted with these problems, the state secretary of the environment was determined to "bring the MSWD into the twentieth century." He recognized that it would be almost irresponsible to launch the MSWD into these major capital expenditures with the organization in its current state of apparent bureaucratic ineptitude. He knew, however, that revitalizing this moribund culture would be difficult and would have to be accomplished without major infusions of new management talent. Nevertheless, he and his new general manager, Ken Dillon (not his real name), were determined to take on the challenge.

Ken Dillon was a key figure in changing MSWD. Dillon was in his mid-fifties, semi-retired, and a successful entrepreneur when he took over the reins at MSWD. He was used to getting things done and making things happen. When he brought this attitude to the career-oriented bureaucratic environment of MSWD, it was like a breath of fresh air.

During the first several months in revitalizing MSWD, Dillon familiarized himself with the organization. What he found was not encouraging. The MSWD's extremely cumbersome superstructure made Dillon officially responsible for running the organization, but most major and many minor decisions were subject to the review of an advisory committee. Decisions required a majority vote of the committee although Dillon did have veto power.

Further crimping his style was the fact that this highly centralized organization reported to a chief operating officer — a career civil servant. Originally this post was intended to help insulate MSWD from self-serving initiatives by politically minded general managers. In practical terms, it meant that Dillon had little direct authority in the day-to-day management of MSWD, since everyone else reported to the chief operating officer who could, in turn, go over Dillon's head to the advisory committee.

In terms of the MSWD's people, there were grounds for encouragement and disappointment. The biggest problem was the average age of the staff: fifty-five or older. The people in the agency had, for the most part, joined right after the war and spent their whole careers with it. The threat of impending retirements and the accompanying loss of the knowledge and skills of those who retired was a serious long-term problem for Dillon to deal with. On the positive side, the loyalty and motivation of the vast majority of the staff was remarkable. Despite public perceptions of a patronage-ridden bureaucracy, these people were dedicated public servants who were sincerely interested in making the MSWD work as well as possible.

Dillon's objective in this change was nothing short of changing MSWD from a reactive, bureaucratic culture to the proactive can-do attitude he was familiar with in his own company — a shift from a process culture to a work hard/play hard culture.

After six months of study, Dillon decided the time had come to act. To reshape the culture, he began by taking two major steps: he engaged consultants to supplement his staff in an aggressive change process, and he announced in a memo to MSWD's permanent complement of 2,500 employees that there would be no firings or layoffs as a result of the process he was launching. His objective, he said, was to work with the talented people of MSWD to improve its effectiveness. This second step turned out to be very significant later in the process since it helped buy time for some basic changes to take hold.

The Change Process

The team of four consultants spent its first six weeks learning about MSWD. In a meeting at the end of this period, the first gesture in the change process was decided on — to set up three major task forces of MSWD employees to work with the consultants on three commonly agreed-upon problem areas. The three areas selected were:

- *Contracting.* Everyone generally agreed something should be done to speed up contract processing.
- *Operations and Maintenance (O & M).* Over the objections of the chief operating officer's functional managers, a second task force was assigned responsibility for O & M.
- *Personnel.* All managers in MSWD used personnel constraints as their argument for why things couldn't be done differently no matter what the issue. The chief operating officer, for example, was convinced this task force would prove that nothing could be done.

In all, twenty-five professionals and/or middle managers were assigned to these task forces full-time for their indeterminate duration — a gesture that in itself caused great consternation in the agency. Reservations aside, people in the MSWD were used to following orders, so all twenty-five members dutifully showed up for the initial group meeting that launched their efforts.

Meanwhile, Dillon initiated a weekly series of staff meetings with the chief operating officer, functional officer, functional managers, and their assistants. He specifically excluded these people from membership on the task forces; he would work with them himself.

During their first week of work, the task forces accomplished little. Members were not used to working in this fashion; many of them felt uncomfortable in this new role. By the second week the members began to open up in their meetings. For example, engineers on the contracting task force admitted disappointment when projects they had worked on were not received warmly by operations personnel. They were astonished to learn that the operations people were often distressed when the engineers didn't consult them about projects they were working on and when they delivered equipment that was hard to operate and maintain. Both sides agreed that better communications on projects between the two sides was definitely called for. In the other task forces, similar revelations were occurring — to everyone's amazement.

By the third week, all three task forces were hard at work trying to formulate recommendations to deal with the problems they had identified. Their recommendations — delivered during the seventh week — were reviewed by Dillon, senior management, and the advisory committee.

Awaiting management's response, the task forces had gone back to work on their recommendations. A half dozen more members were added to the task forces. Everyone seemed more and more committed to the change process as time went on.

Six weeks later, the task forces presented their final recommendations — essentially offering details on their original plans. Senior management raised some objections, and modifications were discussed. Then attention turned toward the consultants' recommendations for significant streamlining and decentralization of MSWD. They suggested (1) the elimination of the job of chief operating officer, (2) elimination of the jobs of the assistant functional managers, (3) establishment of a line-of-business (in other words, sewer and water structure), (4) a reassignment of the staffs of major functions such as engineering and environmental planning to create the nucleus of real engineering functions within both the sewer and water divisions, (5) creation of a new director of planning position to run the new planning system, and (6) creation of an office of contract administration to run the new project-management and contracting systems. After some review the package was finally endorsed.

The Implementation of Change

With the endorsement in hand, Dillon moved quickly. True to his original pledge, no member of the organization was fired; all were slotted into new jobs. The reorganization was comprehensive enough that, in effect, a new management team was put in place.

Offices were moved on a Monday. On Tuesday, Dillon launched the new planning process that was designed to get the new management groups of each division working together as a team.

The planning process was designed to dovetail with the state budget process, thus creating very tight scheduling. However, despite weekend and late evening flurries, both divisions made it under the wire. The head of the sewer division, exhausted by the process, said to one of the consultants just after the advisory committee had approved his proposed budget: "This is the best thing that ever happened to the MSWD . . . and the most exhilarating experience I have ever had. We'll never go back to the old way again."

Six months later, no one could doubt that the MSWD was significantly different. There was still too much paper and too much conformance to the book, but there was also a clear set of agreed-upon priorities, a sense of real urgency in pursuing these priorities, and the beginnings of a "we can make it happen" mentality. Dillon believed that with one more year of operation in this new mode, the new culture would really take hold.

The secretary of the environment, the person who launched the whole process, claims it is the greatest organization turnaround he has witnessed in his twenty-five years as a public-sector manager.

Case Questions

1. Describe the role of Dillon in the change effort.
2. What internal and external threats existed in the change process?
3. What role did training play in the change effort?
4. What potential problems do you see down the road as the change process takes hold?

Source: Terrence Deal and Allan Kennedy, *Corporate Cultures,* © 1982, Addison-Wesley, Reading, Massachusetts. Pgs. 169–174. Reprinted with permission. This case is based on a real consulting assignment carried out by the authors. Names, titles, and a few facts have been changed in the interest of respecting the confidential interests of the client.

Your Hamburger: 41,000 Regulations

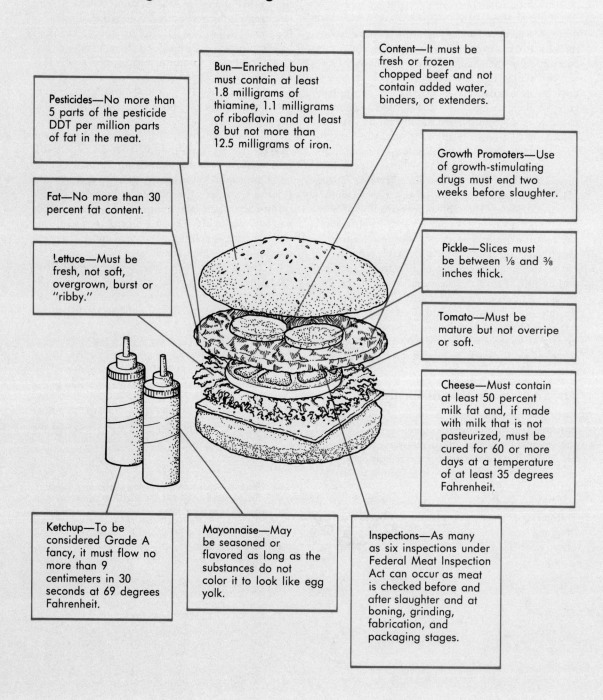

Pesticides—No more than 5 parts of the pesticide DDT per million parts of fat in the meat.

Bun—Enriched bun must contain at least 1.8 milligrams of thiamine, 1.1 milligrams of riboflavin and at least 8 but not more than 12.5 milligrams of iron.

Content—It must be fresh or frozen chopped beef and not contain added water, binders, or extenders.

Growth Promoters—Use of growth-stimulating drugs must end two weeks before slaughter.

Fat—No more than 30 percent fat content.

Lettuce—Must be fresh, not soft, overgrown, burst or "ribby."

Pickle—Slices must be between 1/8 and 3/8 inches thick.

Tomato—Must be mature but not overripe or soft.

Cheese—Must contain at least 50 percent milk fat and, if made with milk that is not pasteurized, must be cured for 60 or more days at a temperature of at least 35 degrees Fahrenheit.

Ketchup—To be considered Grade A fancy, it must flow no more than 9 centimeters in 30 seconds at 69 degrees Fahrenheit.

Mayonnaise—May be seasoned or flavored as long as the substances do not color it to look like egg yolk.

Inspections—As many as six inspections under Federal Meat Inspection Act can occur as meat is checked before and after slaughter and at boning, grinding, fabrication, and packaging stages.

CHAPTER 17

Understanding the Role of Government

Deregulation was supposed to reform the myriad of federal rules and regulations that for years have frustrated business and industry. The Reagan administration claimed to have achieved that goal in 1983 when it disbanded the President's Task Force on Regulatory Relief, chaired by Vice-President George Bush. Claiming to have gotten rid of enough red tape to save consumers $150 billion over the next ten years, Bush stated that "these savings will continue to make an important contribution to the economic recovery ... without jeopardizing the environment, job or consumer safety, or other regulatory goals" ("Three Steps Forward," p. 12).

Many disagreed, among them consumer advocates, environmentalists, and public interest groups. While the public generally favors deregulation, a Harris survey in 1983 showed that 88 percent of Americans prefer tougher standards for clean air, and 91 percent want stiff or stiffer regulations for safety in the workplace. In industry, deregulation has caused such stiff competition that many businesses have folded.

New state and local agencies have helped increase the red tape that deregulation was supposed to lessen. In August 1983 New Jersey enacted a tough chemical-labeling law; soon after New York began enforcing a new "lemon law" to protect car buyers; and California is giving local governments more responsibility for monitoring pollution and coastal development.

Some industry officials wonder if federal regulation is less of a hassel than a multitude of state regulations. One representative of the Chemical Manufacturers Association said, "Most of our companies ship across state lines. We would prefer to see a reasonable federal regulation that lets us do business, rather than put a different label on a product every time you cross a state line" ("Deregulation Drive," p. 82). While this is the view of those who favor re-regulation, most industry officials continue to favor deregulation, but with modifications.

Sources: "Deregulation Drive Runs into Roadblocks," by Clemens P. Work, U.S. News & World Report, December 12, 1983, pp. 81–82; "Three Steps Forward, Two Back," by Ed Magnuson, Time, August 29, 1983, pp. 12–14; "State Regulators Rush in Where Washington No Longer Treads," Business Week, September 19, 1983, pp. 124–131.

Chapter Outline

- Regulation and Management
- History of the Regulatory Movement
- Impetus for Regulatory Reform
- Recent Trends for Reform and Deregulation
- Managing the Impact of Government Regulations
- Managing the Transition to Deregulation
- The Quest for a National Industrial Policy

Key Terms

- regulations
- economic regulations
- social regulations
- laissez-faire
- natural monopolies
- destructive competition
- externalities
- regulatory-review programs
- regulatory budgets
- sunset laws
- deregulation
- regulatory costs
- regulatory inefficiencies
- industrial policy

Chapter Objectives

After studying Chapter 17 you should be able to

1. Recognize the importance of government to management.
2. Identify some problems that have resulted in government regulation.
3. Trace the history of government regulation of business.
4. Understand the costs, inefficiencies, and burdens of regulation.
5. Discuss moves toward regulatory reform.
6. Better manage an organization strongly affected by government regulations.
7. Understand the issues in the debate over a national industrial policy for the United States.

Introduction

In the past twenty years, there has been a massive expansion of government involvement in business, particularly in worker health and safety, environmental protection, and consumer product safety.

In a typical business corporation, selection procedures follow standards set by the Equal Employment Opportunity Commission, work practices are governed by Labor Department regulations, new and existing products must comply with standards set by product safety agencies, and expansion plans must be made in accordance with numerous zoning restrictions and statutes. Government influence on business is so pervasive that Murray Weidenbaum (1981) has described a "shadow" organizational chart of government regulatory agencies that matches the organizational structure of private organizations.

The shift from private to government control of our natural resources reflects the government's dominant role in our society. Virtually every industry in the United States is affected by the growing involvement of government. For a number of years, the government controlled the prices and conditions of entry in the transportation, communications, and financial sectors of the economy. Economic regulation has diminished over the years, however, with efforts to deregulate airlines, trucking, natural gas, common-carrier telecommunications, broadcasting, and banks. Nevertheless, business and government again are at a crossroads. The deep recession in the early 1980s, coupled with the declining competitiveness of the United States in the world market, has prompted considerable debate about the appropriateness of the government's role in developing a national industrial policy.

The message to the manager in the 1980s is clear: To be successful, firms must learn to anticipate and adapt to changes in government, and deal skillfully with government officials and policy makers. To do this, managers need to understand the complex role of government in the private sector and to deal with this complexity in strategic terms.

This chapter provides the manager with the perspective to understand the role of government more fully. The chapter begins by elaborating the growing importance of government in the management of private affairs. Then the involvement of government is discussed against the backdrop of regulation, deregulation, and industrial policy making. Strategies for firms in heavily regulated industries are discussed to provide a framework for comparing strategies for deregulated firms. Finally, the presently contested role of government in developing a national industrial policy is examined.

Regulation and Management*

Managers have not developed adequate responses to the increasing role of government. Too many managers complain about the abundance of paperwork, the high cost of capital compliance, and the loss of entrepreneurial spirit govern-

* This section was adapted from Lindholm *et al.*, 1981.

ment regulations engender. But these managers have done little to anticipate new regulations and monitor their effects on organizations. In the past, several reasons have been given for the importance of government to management:

1. *Government regulations can be very costly.* Capital compliance can be expensive for a large firm and disastrous for a small firm. In addition, the paperwork required to comply with the myriad government regulations can waste top managers' time and raise administrative costs. Finally, the costs of mitigation — the legal fees involved if a firm challenges a ruling made by a government regulatory agency — not only can be expensive, but also can result in lost opportunities, since the time expended for regulatory issues could well have been spent elsewhere.

2. *Government regulations can lead to frustration, stress, and the loss of entrepreneurial spirit.* In one study (Cole and Tegeler, 1979), managers of small organizations reported that the "psychological costs of compliance," or feelings of frustration, stress, and the loss of entrepreneurial spirit, were even more significant than the actual costs of compliance.

3. *Monitoring regulatory costs can save money.* Most businesses are unaware of their regulatory costs because they are not monitored as easily as labor or suppliers' costs, for example. The Dow Chemical Program, however, was able to save about $20 to $30 million a year, primarily because people in the company became more aware of the impact of new regulations and decided to track and manage regulatory costs more effectively.

4. *New government regulations may lead to opportunities.* With the arrival of a regulatory-reform era, much emphasis has been placed on the adverse effects of government regulations. Regulations can lead to new market opportunities, however. For example, the requirements for better instrument calibration in the health and entertainment appliance industries provided market opportunities for high-technology firms involved in manufacturing test instruments.

5. *Changes in the United States economic structure may be the occasion for more government involvement in managing organizations.* The changing base of the United States economy (see Chapter 15) suggests that government will become involved in encouraging emerging industries and protecting our maturing and declining industries. The current debate is fueled by popular comparisons of the United States with other countries, such as Japan and West Germany, that have national policies to facilitate economic growth and to make them strong international competitors. These are strong signals that a manager cannot ignore. The development and implementation of a United States industrial policy are bound to have an impact on the way strategic management is practiced today.

Definition of Regulations

Defining regulations is not easy. President Gerald Ford once asked for a list of government regulatory services. After extensive investigation and interviews, it was concluded that virtually every Cabinet department except the State Department was engaged in regulation of one kind or another. This study estimated the number of federal regulations alone to be about 100,000.

We define **government regulatory agencies** as those with statutory power to issue rules and standards. They are distinguished from other government agencies by their rule-making capability. **Regulations** are an agency's written statements, designed to interpret law, policy, and the intent of legislation, that have the force of law within the authority given to the agency by the legislature (Bervirt, 1978).

Regulations are broadly differentiated into economic regulations and social regulations. **Economic regulations** relate to the control of prices and the conditions for entry in certain industries. Such regulatory agencies include the Federal Communications Commission, the Civil Aeronautics Board, and the Interstate Commerce Commission. **Social regulations** cover situations in which unregulated activity may pose significant threats to public health, safety, or the environment. Agencies formulating such regulations include the Occupational Safety and Health Administration, the Environmental Protection Agency, and the Consumer Product Safety Commission.

Regulation can be accomplished in a variety of ways, including rate making, licensing, setting standards, and requiring informational disclosure. Two approaches to the setting of standards are popular. First, regulatory agencies can set *specification standards,* which detail the means of achieving a desired end. The second way is to set *performance standards,* which specify the desired goal but do not specify the means by which firms must meet the goal. Performance standards have been used in the automobile industry, particularly in the reduction of automobile emissions.

Why Regulations?

You may wonder why regulations exist in the first place. Economic regulations date back as far as the Babylonian Code of Hammurabi, which established uniform weights and measures, and to ancient Rome, where imperial edicts were used to fix the price of goods. With the publication of Adam Smith's *Wealth of Nations,* much attention was focused on the merits of **laissez-faire** competition, in which it was argued that every individual, if led to pursue his or her own individual desires, would achieve the best results for all. It is argued that competition in nineteenth-century America and Great Britain was close to a laissez-faire system (Healy, 1979). In America the states were primarily agricultural and the federal government was more interested in encouraging the exploitation of natural resources. This period of great economic prosperity also was a time of business crises, economic waste, and social inequities. The existing legal framework — statutes enforced by the courts — was inadequate to cope with the growing complexities of economic industrialization.

Natural Monopolies. Given these conditions, government regulations seemed reasonable and prudent. In fact, the first of such economic regulations was developed to protect competition and to ensure that large firms operating in **natural monopolies,** such as public utilities, did not drive out competitors by their lower costs. Because their greater volume of production leads to lower costs, natural monopolies can restrict their output and charge higher-than-competitive prices. In practice, however, natural monopolies are hard to identify. One reason is that the introduction of new technologies may lead to the erosion of their power. For example, the development of the trucking industry gave railroads intense competition. Similarly, the development of microwave transmission led to the decline in the natural monopoly conditions in long-distance telephone service (Waverman, 1975).

Destructive Competition. Government regulations may also be enacted when **destructive competition** occurs: when a dominant firm sets prices low enough to drive out its competitors and then raises prices before new firms can move in. If prices fall too far below costs and firms are subsequently squeezed out of business, the products may end up costing much more than their initial prices. Such predatory pricing can be disastrous for the economy as a whole.

Inadequate Information. Consumers need adequate and correct information to make purchase decisions consistent with their preferences. Yet consumers are not always well-enough informed to make correct decisions. Information may be costly or unavailable or may be too complex to be used by consumers.

Two types of regulations can correct such shortcomings. The first requires accurate labeling and disclosure information concerning product characteristics. Examples are the Federal Trade Commission's truth-in-advertising programs and the Food and Drug Administration's labeling requirements. A second type of regulation enforces product standards, particularly when consumers may have difficulty interpreting technical information provided to them. An example is the specification of building codes. Because consumers are not usually sophisticated enough to evaluate the quality and safety of materials used in construction, government standards ensure that the design and materials are sound. Also, worker health and safety regulations correct for the worker's inability to evaluate the risks associated with various jobs.

Externalities. The problems of **externalities,** or external costs, also have been used to justify the enactment of regulations. External costs occur whenever the total cost of producing or consuming a product is not covered either by the producer or by the customer. In the case of environmental protection, for example, firms that pollute the environment do not normally price their products to include the costs of spills or pollution. Government regulation in this instance is designed to make individuals or firms aware of the external costs they impose and to make them behave as though these external costs are direct production costs. Similarly, the risk of injury and illness associated with a job may not be fully reflected in the wage rate, necessitating worker health and safety regulations. Government regulations to account for externalities can include more stringent negligence laws, taxes and subsidies, and mandatory insurance.

Interdependence in Resource Extraction. Without government regulations, poor conservation can exist. If the coastal fishing industry were unregulated, for example, each fisherman would have no incentive to conserve, because anything he or she left would be taken by other fishermen. Fishing then might occur at a rate that exhausted the resource for future generations. Government

---

Feature 17.1
Energy Standards Plague Manufacturers

After three years in office, President Reagan found getting government off the backs of American business harder than he thought.

The administration's efforts to eliminate costly and complicated federal regulations waned after countless confrontations with consumer groups, activists, bureaucrats, and judges.

In one case conservationist groups and their congressional allies were pushing for strong minimum-performance standards for major home appliances. Free-market advocates in the Reagan administration dug in their heels, however, and in the summer of 1983 the Department of Energy advocated standards only for the blatant energy guzzlers — central air conditioners. Such leniency countered the Energy Policy and Conservation Act of 1975, which was passed after the oil-price increases and called for the government to set energy-efficient standards for appliances.

Citizen groups such as the Natural Resources Defense Council said strong standards for everything from refrigerators to furnaces could save consumers billions of dollars on their electric bills.

Officials in the home-appliance industry argued that products had become more efficient without federal rules and that appliance standards were an idea that had come and gone.

Home builders and developers, who buy up to half of the new appliances, have no reason to pay attention to efficiency or operating costs. "Standards aren't going to drive people to buy the most efficient appliances," said Howard Geller, a researcher at the American Council for an Energy-Efficient Economy, "but they will help get the dogs off the market" ("Will Regulators Switch," 1983, p. 80E).

Some states have taken regulation into their own hands. California, Kansas, Wisconsin, and New York have acted on their own to stop the sale of certain appliances, much to the annoyance of the appliance makers. The Department of Energy's ruling is intended to wipe out these regulations.

Representative Richard L. Ottinger from New York countered by sponsoring federal legislation to give the states the right to set such regulations. And the National Resources Defense Council took the Energy Department to court to challenge its findings that the standards are not needed. More suits are likely to follow; clearly the struggle is not over.

Sources: "Will Regulators Switch Off Efficiency Standards?" *Business Week,* August 1, 1983, p. 80E; "Deregulation: Dream Deferred," *Nation's Business,* February, 1984, pp. 24–25.

regulations have taken the form of allocating output to various producers in such cases.

Equity. The reasons for government regulations generally have been economic. This economic orientation has been referred to as the *market failure hypothesis,* in which government intervention is posited as necessary to ensure the efficient allocation of resources. Other justifications for government intervention are based on equity considerations. For instance, government regulations have been enacted in a number of instances to encourage the provision of services to small, rural communities. This is true for telephone, airline, and trucking services in small communities. In addition, regulations pertaining to equal opportunity in employment are justified on the basis of equity rather than efficiency.

The conditions for regulation we are discussing here are not intended to be exhaustive. They can, however, provide some perspective on the reasons for the enactment of regulations through the years. In practice, most regulation is motivated by a combination of factors. In financial institutions, for example, regulations have been justified on the basis of inadequate consumer information (for examination), externalities (for examination and deposit insurance), and equity (usury laws).

History of the Regulatory Movement

In early court decisions, principally the 1877 case of *Munn* v. *Illinois,* the right of states to practice regulation was upheld. With these decisions as a precedent, Congress established the first federal regulatory agency, the Interstate Commerce Commission, to regulate the railroads, which the states were unable to regulate at the time. The commission's authority over the railroads grew steadily until World War I. From 1913 on, Congress created a series of new agencies, such as the Federal Reserve System (in 1913) and the Federal Trade Commission (in 1914). Other major regulatory agencies were established in the 1930s under the administration of President Franklin D. Roosevelt.

In the 1970s new types of regulatory agencies, including the Environmental Protection Agency, the Consumer Product Safety Commission, and the Occupational Safety and Health Administration, came into being. During this period these regulatory agencies dramatically increased in size and in scope of operations. At the federal level, it is estimated that regulatory expenditures increased from $1.2 billion in 1971 to about $6 billion in 1980 (Weidenbaum, 1981). The number of pages in the *Federal Register* grew from 20,036 in 1970 to 42,422 in 1974; in March 1979, the office of the *Federal Register* reported that 61,000 pages of government regulations had been issued in 1978. A list of regulatory agencies showing their dates of establishment, their jurisdiction, and the 1980 budgets is presented in Figure 17.1.

Figure 17.1
Major Federal Regulatory Agencies,
Their Jurisdictions, and 1980 Budgets

AGENCY	DATE ESTABLISHED	JURISDICTION	1980 BUDGET (MILLIONS OF DOLLARS)
Economic Regulation			
Interstate Commerce Commission (ICC)	1887	Interstate railroads (1887) Interstate trucks (1935) Interstate water carriers (1940) Interstate telephone (1910–1934) Interstate oil pipelines (1906–1977)	80.0
State regulatory commissions	35 states 1907–1920; 50 states by 1973	Local electricity (46 states in 1973) Local gas (47 states in 1973) Local telephone (48 states in 1973)	148.0
Federal Communications Commission (FCC)	1934	Interstate telephone (1934) Broadcasting (1934) Cable television (1968)	77.2
Federal Power Commission (FPC)	1935 ⎱	Interstate wholesale electricity (1935) Interstate natural gas pipelines (1938) Field price of natural gas sold in interstate commerce (1954) Oil pipelines (1977) Intrastate gas and gas pipelines (1978)	72.3
Federal Energy Regulatory Commission (FERC)	1977 ⎰		
Civil Aeronautics Board (CAB)	1938	Interstate airlines (1938)	29.7
Federal Maritime Commission (FMC)	1936	Ocean shipping (1936)	11.7
Federal Energy Administration (FEA)	1973 ⎱	Petroleum prices and allocations (1973)	155.4
Changed to Economic Regulatory Administration (ERA)	1977 ⎰		

(continued)

Figure 17.1 (continued)

AGENCY	DATE ESTABLISHED	JURISDICTION	1980 BUDGET (MILLIONS OF DOLLARS)
Environmental, Safety, and Health Regulation			
Food and Drug Administration (FDA)	1906	Safety of food, drugs (1906), and cosmetics (1938); effectiveness of drugs (1962)	324.2
Animal and Plant Health Inspection Service	1907	Meat and poultry packing plants (1907)	258.6
Federal Trade Commission (FTC)	1914	False and misleading advertising (mainly after 1938)	31.0
Securities and Exchange Commission (SEC)	1934	Public security issues and security exchanges (1934) Public utility holding companies (1935)	72.9
Civil Aeronautics Board (CAB)	1938	Airline safety (1938) (flight standards program only)	227.9
Federal Aviation Administration (FAA)	1958		
Atomic Energy Commission (AEC)	1947 ⎫	Licensing of nuclear power plants (1947)	368.2
Nuclear Regulatory Commission (NRC)	1975 ⎭		
National Highway Traffic Safety Administration (NHTSA, pronounced *Neetsa*)	1970	Automobile safety (1970), automobile fuel economy (1975)	58.9
Environmental Protection Agency (EPA)	1963–1972	Air, water, and noise pollution	420.0
Occupational Safety and Health Administration (OSHA)	1971	Industrial safety and health (1971)	187.2
Mine Enforcement Safety Administration (MESA)	1973 ⎫	Safety and health in mining, especially coal mines (1973)	144.1
Mine Safety and Health Administration	1978 ⎭		
Consumer Product Safety Commission	1972	Safety of consumer products (1972)	40.2

Source: Data from Fritschler and Ross, 1980, pp. 4–5.

Impetus for Regulatory Reform

The first signs of a regulatory-reform effort occurred after World War II, when there was widespread criticism of anticompetitive characteristics of the Interstate Commerce Commission, the Civil Aeronautics Board's policies toward airlines, and the Federal Communications Commission's regulation of broadcasting and cable television. In the past, reform efforts had centered on improving the internal management of the regulatory agency and making it more accountable to the legislature and governor or president. At present, reform movements are concentrating on reducing the regulatory cost burden and improving the administration of the regulatory process.

Cost of Regulations

How much do regulations cost? What are the benefits associated with particular regulations? Are the benefits sufficient to justify the costs? These questions have occupied center stage in the hotly contested area of regulation. Although measuring the cost of regulatory compliance has proven to be difficult, recent studies indicate that the costs can be substantial.

- In a report prepared by Murray Weidenbaum for Congress's Joint Economic Subcommittee on Growth and Stabilization, it was estimated that the total cost of regulation was about $102.7 billion in 1979, including $4.8 billion for administration and $97.9 billion for compliance.
- From 1978 to 1979, the Business Roundtable retained Arthur Anderson and Company to measure the direct cost of regulation and to determine the costs of specific regulations to forty-eight participating member companies. For the study year 1977, the forty-eight companies reported a total of $2.6 billion in extra costs to comply with specific regulations. Much of the overall compliance cost was considered wasteful because of (1) excessive and unintended costs caused by regulatory programs, (2) conflicting regulations, and (3) inflexibilities in regulatory requirements.
- In 1978 Dow Chemical Company presented findings indicating that federal regulations cost the company $186 million. The study classified $69 million of the cost as excessive.
- The University of Pennsylvania found that the cost of complying with twelve federal programs jumped from $350,000 in 1972 to $3.2 million in 1977.

Inefficiency

Accompanying compliance costs is the feeling that businesses are not given opportunities to comply with regulations in a less costly, more efficient manner. Previous criticisms were directed at the length of time it took regulatory agencies to decide cases. For example, it took thirteen years for the Federal Communications Commission to decide on one major case and about five years to decide between competing applicants for a television channel. Healy (1979, p. 19) presents an example in which the Federal Power Commission in 1960 estimated "that it would take thirteen years with its present staff to clear up its pending 2,313 producer rate cases pending as of July 1, 1960, and that with the contemplated 6,500 cases that would be filed during the thirteen-year period it could not become current until A.D. 2043 even if its staff were tripled."

Another emerging source of inefficiency is overlapping jurisdiction of agencies, which has led to confusing and conflicting requirements. For example, the Occupational Safety and Health Administration requirement that butcher shops have grated floors to reduce the risk of employee slippage contradicts Department of Agriculture standards that floors must be smooth because grates increase contamination hazards. Standards of the Environmental Protection Agency for reducing auto and air pollution contribute to inflation, which impairs mandated fuel efficiency (Healy, 1979).

Burden on Small Business

Another impetus for regulatory reform has been the increasing burden of regulations on small business. In a White House conference on small business, it was estimated that about 60 percent of the roughly $100 billion in annual compliance cost is borne by small business. This problem is worsened by the fact that small businesses generally are unable to pass along cost increases to customers. In a survey of 168 companies made by Charleswater Associates Inc. (1975), it was reported that only 25 percent were able to pass along more than 75 percent of cost increases to customers. In addition, 63 percent reported little or no ability to pass along cuts.

Recent Trends for Reform and Deregulation

Although there seems to be a growing sentiment for regulatory reform, there is less agreement on how to reform the system. This difficulty is reflected in a speech by Charles H. Percy, senator from Illinois, in March 1976 (quoted in Healy, 1979, p. 52):

> Often when I talk to business leaders, they tell me that too stringent environmental, health and safety regulations are ruining them. But they gloss over the widespread waste caused by much of today's economic regulation. When I talk to labor leaders, they complain about the anti-competitive regulation of certain industries, but overlook the effects of OSHA [the Occupational Safety and Health Administration]. When I talk to consumer leaders, they decry the effects of a good deal of economic regulation but imply "hands off" when it comes to health and safety.

What should be reformed? How should reform be done? These are pressing questions faced by lawmakers. Among the various reform agendas presented, most attention has been focused on regulatory-review programs, regulatory budgets, and sunset legislation. **Regulatory-review programs** require regulatory agencies to analyze the costs and benefits of particular regulatory programs and to examine the feasibility of alternate methods of achieving the objectives. Despite their popularity, they contain no mechanisms to ensure that costs and benefits are systematically considered and hence lack the potency to change current regulatory practices.

Because they establish limits on the amount of compliance required, **regulatory budgets** are an improvement over regulatory-review programs. Advocates of the regulatory budget have suggested that the state or federal government set a budget figure for regulatory agencies, providing an incentive for the agencies to adopt cost-effective regulations. But the problem of measuring costs remains and has hindered the adoption of regulatory budgets.

Sunset laws require a regular legislative review of the effectiveness of government agencies. For example, Colorado and Florida have laws requiring state agencies to justify their existence every six years. A number of other states have considered the adoption of some form of sunset legislation.

Deregulation is a more substantive reform mechanism. Industries such as motor freight, long-distance telephone service, electric-power generation, and rail freight have been considered targets for deregulation. The airline industry and commercial banking have been subject to some forms of deregulation. At present, most deregulation is directed at economic rather than social regulations in an effort to improve the efficiency of the process. Some of it has brought about disturbing results (Feature 17.2).

Managing the Impact of Government Regulations

With this general background, let us now examine the task of managing an organization strongly affected by government regulations. Central to this task is identifying and managing the costs of such regulations. An underlying assumption is that managers can deal with regulatory agencies effectively if they are sufficiently aware of the potentially adverse or favorable effects of regulations.

As with any part of the external environment, the actions of government regulatory agencies have to be monitored and carefully analyzed. Murray Weidenbaum (1979) argued that firms often have deemphasized the impact of government regulations in the strategic planning process, resulting in mostly ad hoc and reactive responses to existing and new regulatory requirements. In this section we will set some guidelines that managers can use in developing more adequate responses to government regulatory agencies.

Monitoring the Costs of Regulations

As discussed in the previous sections, regulatory costs are one of the direct effects of government regulations. We must distinguish, however, between regulatory costs and the costs of regulatory inefficiencies. **Regulatory costs** are all

Feature 17.2
Deregulation and the Airline Industry

In the past, life was relatively simple for airline management.

Prior to deregulation they simply projected the growth in traffic and determined their requirements for acquiring and scheduling aircraft. This type of planning suited the old, regulated environment. There was certainty about the route structure of domestic and international competitors, and there were stable fare and cargo rates, predictable cost increases, and, most important, a growing demand.

Deregulation brought about sweeping changes. First, the new market freedom allowed firms to enter and duck out of existing route schedules. It also allowed some of them to offer incredibly low rates as a result of the use of nonunion labor.

Second, the changes put more pressure on the airlines to have their own sources of capital in the event they decided to de-velop a new route. The Civil Aeronautics Board had protected the airlines from bankruptcy, but the free market changed the rules of the game.

Third, as a result of the Carter administration's efforts to implement its domestic regulatory policies internationally, more carriers offered service to previously protected routes.

Some knowledge of the effects of deregulation could have helped the strategic planners in the airline industry and might have prevented the predatory prices that almost brought the industry to the brink of disaster. The events in the airline industry provide a good example of the importance of knowing the effects of government regulations.

Source: Airline Planning, by Newal Tanega, Lexington, Mass.: Lexington Books, 1982.

costs attibutable to regulations or resulting from adherence to regulations. Regulations impose costs on a firm if they require the firm to alter its behavior and cause it to consume more resources than it would in the normal course of doing business. These resources could have been redirected to other productive uses in the absence of regulation. One type of regulatory costs is direct compliance costs, such as those involved in changing machine or product specifications or adding a special railing for handicapped people — that is, all labor and nonlabor costs of a capital and operating nature. Administrative costs are associated with obtaining information about regulations and with housekeeping functions such as accounting, record keeping, and reporting. Mitigation and noncompliance costs result either from legal, political, or public relations actions taken to mitigate the impact of regulations on the firm, or from a failure to comply with regulations.

A specific example may help to differentiate these costs. Suppose a major capital project was completed in 1977 to meet new requirements of worker health and safety in a plant. The capital project represented an expenditure of $100,000 to reduce worker exposure to a particular air contaminant from an eight-hour average of one hundred parts per million to seventy parts per million. Prior to the new regulations, management had desired a level of eighty parts per million, which would have cost about $80,000. Additional administrative costs resulting from this major project amounted to $25,000. The company also hired legal counsel for an estimated $15,000 to appear in the Occupational Safety and Health Administration hearings. In this example, total costs were $140,000, of which $60,000 would be regulatory costs ($20,000 in incremental costs resulting from regulations, plus $25,000 in additional administrative costs, plus $15,000 in additional legal costs).

Regulatory inefficiencies are defined as that portion of regulatory costs that result from (1) conflict or unnecessary duplication among regulatory requirements and (2) regulatory requirements that do not permit the firm to comply in the most efficient, least costly manner. If it has specific and detailed knowledge of the impact of regulations on the firm, management is in a good position to make judgments about these forms of regulatory inefficiencies.

Consider again the capital project we just described. The purpose of the project was to reduce worker exposure to a particular air contaminant over an eight-hour period from one hundred parts per million to seventy parts per million. Assume management believed it could obtain the level of air quality mandated by regulatory standards — seventy parts per million — at a lower cost by better sanitary controls. The estimated savings if the firm had been allowed to use these sanitary controls would have been $15,000. This represents a cost of regulatory inefficiency as perceived by management.

In practice, regulatory costs are not so easily retrievable, because current accounting methods are not designed to record the costs of regulations. Therefore, it becomes necessary to develop a system to track down and monitor regulatory costs. Monitoring actual compliance costs as they are incurred, particularly when significant changes in regulations are made, is the essential feature of such a program.

Adverse Characteristics of Regulatory Agencies

Costs represent only one way in which regulations have an impact on organizations. The relationship between government regulatory agencies and organizations can be described as adversarial. Many managers complain more about the way inspections are conducted than about the actual regulatory costs. A study by Lindholm, Cole, Brown, James, Ramsing, Smith, Spicer, and Ungson (1981) identified some of the characteristics that have a negative impact on organizations:

1. *Frequency of inspections or contact with the firm.* Government inspections are considered time-consuming and demanding of company resources. Often, key organization officers have to spend significant time with government inspectors during the process.

2. *Harmful effects on management and worker morale.* In the Cole and Tegeler (1979) study, small firms reported that government regulatory agencies

caused extreme frustration to the point of impairing the entrepreneurial spirit of managers.

3. *Noncooperative attitude of inspectors.* Problems with government inspections are exacerbated if inspectors are perceived as incompetent, unreasonable, and generally hostile.

4. *Difficulty in obtaining regulatory information.* Regulatory information may be difficult to obtain, possibly leading to project delays and cost overruns. This problem is particularly evident in start-up operations in new industrial zones.

As one example, respondents from two industries, wood products and high technology, were asked to rate the negative impact of these four characteristics (Lindholm et al., 1981). For the wood products sample, "harmful effects on management morale" was rated as the most severe effect, with the cost of record keeping next in severity. In contrast, the high-technology sample considered the difficulty in obtaining regulatory information the characteristic most severely affecting their organization. Like the wood products industry, they indicated that the cost of record keeping and the harmful effects on management morale also adversely affected their organizations. From the preceding discussion, it is clear that industries may be affected differently by government regulatory agencies. Knowing how different government regulatory agencies affect an organization is essential for developing corrective procedures.

Adjustments to Changing Regulations

Firms respond differently to changing regulatory requirements. For the most part, firms adapt by hiring or firing employees, making process adjustments, and adding or eliminating sections and departments.

An important adjustment mechanism is the ability of an organization to pass along the costs of regulatory compliance to its customers. Studies of this problem (Charleswater Associates, 1975; Lindholm et al., 1981) indicate that differences in the ability to pass along costs occur not only between industries, but also between firms operating in the same industry. For policy considerations, therefore, it is worthwhile to examine the ability of firms of varying sizes to pass along costs. Regulatory costs have a large fixed component, so they have a greater impact on smaller firms. Smaller businesses generally have greater difficulty than larger firms in passing along this cost to customers. This documentation is useful in evaluating the impact of such legislation as the Small Business Regulatory Flexibility Act and the Miscellaneous Revenue Act, which are designed to establish different compliance requirements for small firms.

Regulations and Performance Measures

Ultimately, the effects of regulation are reflected in such performance outcomes as the management of regulatory costs, profitability and market prices, and management morale and entrepreneurship. Although regulatory benefits may be difficult to compute, the strategic benefits of regulation may be reflected in lower regulatory costs, higher profits and market prices resulting from better products and redistributive or transfer effects, and better management morale. Thus, it may be important to refine the performance criteria just listed to improve our assessment of both regulatory costs and benefits.

One direct outcome of better regulatory management is lower regulatory costs. The Dow Chemical Program (Bervirt, 1978) reported that it made a net profit by recovering wastes whose control was mandated. It also indicated that the knowledge and conscious monitoring of regulatory costs eventually led to lower costs through better regulatory management. Finally, by providing employees with incentives to improve safety, the program also reportedly led to lower costs.

Because better regulatory management implies lower costs, it can lead to higher profits. Regulatory management, however, also involves choosing product lines and markets in which the management of regulatory costs will most effectively improve profits. This in turn requires selecting product lines and markets in which there is the least ability to pass along regulatory costs. Regulatory management requires identification of the areas in which regulatory costs are the greatest, as well as those products and markets in which regulatory costs have the worst impact on the firm's profitability.

Good morale is crucial to effective management. One objective in managing the regulatory process in organizations is to enhance management morale. Along with reform efforts directed at small business, it is important to maintain or even enhance entrepreneurial spirit.

Action Programs for Dealing with Regulations

In *The Future of Business Regulation,* Murray Weidenbaum (1979) offers four prescriptions for business: (1) make sure that the needs of customers are met, (2) exercise self-restraint in prerequisites for officers and directors, (3) help the public better understand the full impact of government involvement in business, and (4) actively participate in joint activities with government regulatory agencies and other constituents to improve appreciation of the regulatory process.

Communication is the critical factor underlying the relationship among the firm, government regulatory agencies, and the public. Firms should not passively agree to every demand made by the government. It is equally ineffective, however, for firms to be combative or to undertake lavish public relations programs to highlight their accomplishments. A more prudent strategy for firms is to be sensitive to the demands of government and other interest groups.

Thus, regulated firms must determine the impact of government regulations and develop appropriate responses. Central to this effort is the implementation of an accounting system that accurately monitors regulatory costs and regulatory inefficiencies. Understanding these impacts will allow managers greater latitude in controlling regulatory costs and will permit them to lobby more effectively in their dealings with government regulators.

Managing the Transition to Deregulation

As with any fundamental change in the external environment, the transition to deregulation is likely to provoke a period of uncertainty and considerable disequilibrium. New competitors enter the market, new products are introduced, new pricing schemes are offered, and new strategies are put into effect. For example, in the wake of deregulation, the airline industry suddenly faced new competitors in People Express Airlines, Air Florida, Muse Air, and Midway Airlines. With lower costs resulting from the absence of unions and more efficient aircraft, these entrants use a cost-leadership strategy to capture market share in the high-volume market segments. The decision by New York Air to challenge the shuttle service between New York and Washington, D.C., that was traditionally provided by Eastern Airlines exemplifies this particular strategy.

Many regulated industries have viewed new competition with apprehension and have lobbied against deregulation. Even so, it would appear that regulatory reform is currently headed toward the loosening, if not the abandonment, of regulations. Therefore, it is important for managers to be adequately prepared for the transition. One way to understand the way this transition must be managed is to compare what Robertson, Ward, and Caldwell (1982) term the "regulation mentality" with the "market-oriented mentality" (Fig. 17.2). A comparison of these mentalities suggests the following prescriptions for management.

Focus on the ultimate customer, rather than the regulators. Regulated firms generally focus on the regulator, becoming more concerned with dealing with government than monitoring customer needs and the competition. Robertson, Ward, and Caldwell (1982) cite two cases in which regulated firms lost market opportunities because of this focus. First, Rolm Corporation and Mitel Corporation succeeded because American Telephone and Telegraph Company focused exclusively on the small telephone switchboard segment. Second, the emphasis in commercial banks on limited portfolios of checking and savings paved the way for money market funds to capture a significant market share. From these examples, it is clear that deregulated companies have to develop marketing skills if they are to survive and prosper in a market-oriented economy.

Be more concerned with systematic growth. Assured of a "fair" rate of return, many regulated firms are not as concerned with growth. Also, regulated industries tend to downplay growth for fear of criticism by the public, as did American Telephone and Telegraph Company, for instance. Eventually, deregulated firms must be more concerned with systematic growth that is determined not only by service needs, but by market opportunities as well.

Be more concerned with costs. Managers in regulated firms are not as adept at

Figure 17.2
Regulation Versus Market-Oriented Mentalities

FOCUS	REGULATION MENTALITY	MARKET-ORIENTED MENTALITY
The customer	The regulatory agency may be viewed as the most important customer	The ultimate customer is the focal point of the company's direction
Objectives	Generally slow, manageable growth	Moderate or high growth
Costs	Cross-subsidization of products and services, and often a lack of sensitivity to costs	Costs kept up by product and (often) markets served
Accountability	Managers feel a lack of accountability because regulators may have the final decision power	Managers are responsible for their own actions
Employees	Paternalistic orientation	Results orientation
Competition	Regulation limits competition	Product superiority and cost efficiency are used competitively

Source: Reprinted by permission of Harvard Business Review. Exhibit from "Deregulation: Surviving the Transition," by Thomas S. Robertson, Scott Ward and William M. Caldwell IV (July–August 1982). Copyright © 1982 by the President and Fellows of Harvard College; all rights reserved.

cost estimation, joint-cost analyses, and **cross-elasticities** as managers in unregulated industries (Robertson, Ward, and Caldwell, 1982). Because regulated firms often can pass along cost increases for such things as raw materials to customers, knowledge of these costs is not considered crucial by management. It is hardly surprising, therefore, that newly deregulated firms face stiff competition from entrants that have a better understanding of costs. Such a situation was observed in New York Air's battle with Eastern Airlines for the shuttle market. Aware of Eastern's high labor costs, New York Air quickly penetrated the shuttle market by introducing low fares and good service. Throughout the battle New York Air continued to hold down costs by resisting unionization and controlling overhead.

Design systems that reflect accountability for results. Managers in regulated firms often lack a sensitivity for personal accountability because they believe regulators have the final decision power. These managers often attribute corporate outcomes to uncontrollable events, such as the regulators' decision, rather than their own discretionary efforts. Deregulation shifts the emphasis from uncontrollable to controllable decisions that more accurately reflect managerial responsibilities. In the face of competition, deregulated firms must quickly develop incentive systems that reward results based on personal decisions.

Develop strategic programs. Under regulation, firms frequently are not actual rivals. Because of the exclusivity of franchises or market divisions, supposedly competing firms tend to have a mutually cooperative attitude (Robertson, Ward, and Caldwell, 1982). Until the late 1970s, the Civil Aeronautics Board regulated the airline industry by allocating interstate routes among the airlines and controlling airline fares on these routes. Through the control of air routes, the board also restrained entry into the industry. It is understandable, therefore, that competition among the airlines was based primarily on service and flight frequency. This lack of price competition differs qualitatively from the situation in the automobile industry, in which firms competed on the basis of price, service, dealership, and product differentiation.

Deregulation in the airline industry brought sweeping changes that fundamentally altered the pattern of competition. From 1978 to 1981, the number of certified airlines in the United States more than doubled, from thirty-six to eighty-six. Aircraft departures from large, medium, small, and nonhub cities increased substantially over the two years following deregulation in 1977. The prospect of the entry into the market of rival carriers creates pressures for close-to-competitive air fares (*Economic Report to the President,* 1983). These changes call for better strategic planning and competitor analyses on the part of industry firms. Those that are most likely to succeed in the future will have developed strategic programs that are appropriate for this new competitive order.

Newly deregulated firms face an environment fraught with uncertainties and disequilibrium. To prepare adequately for this transition, firms need to move from a regulatory-oriented to a market-oriented mentality. An early recognition of the customer and the need for corporate objectives, monitoring of costs, and accountability, as well as the adoption of a strategic program, would hasten this transition.

The Quest for a National Industrial Policy

For a long time there has been debate on the proper role of government in economic affairs. As early as 1791 Alexander Hamilton argued for strong government measures that included protectionist tariffs, bounties, and premiums for infant industries. Opponents of this point of view cited the government's inadequacy in directing business affairs and the merits of a free enterprise system.

A decade of recession, high inflation, mounting unemployment, and declining competitiveness once again has raised the question of whether a national industrial policy is appropriate. The need for such a policy is heightened by the fact that our international competitors have adopted such strategies, raising the possibility that a competitor soon will dislodge the United States as the world's leading economic power. This section summarizes the issues under debate and the arguments for and against a national industrial policy. Because any development is likely to have a strong impact on business in general, all future managers must develop a good understanding of these complex issues.

What Is an Industrial Policy?

The following four countries have something in common that is not shared by the United States: a well-conceived national industrial policy.

- **Japan.** *Industrial Policy Vision of the 1980s,* a publication of Japan's Ministry of International Trade and Industry, is regarded by Japanese businessmen as an authoritative statement of industrial policy. For years the ministry has helped formulate a national policy that has been instrumental in Japan's success. In the 1980s the ministry will back high technology (ultra-high-speed computers, space development, ocean development), energy, and new products (optical fibers, high-efficiency resins) to accelerate its quest for more economic leadership in the next decade.
- **West Germany.** A key to West Germany's high investment rate is the financial structure that forges strong links between industrial companies and banks and encourages companies to invest in long-term growth. West German bankers typically sit on the boards of companies to which they regularly loan money. They also actively consult with labor unions and have had success in avoiding inflationary wage outbursts ("What We Can Learn from Our Rivals," 1980).
- **France.** France has shifted from a macro model of industrial development to strategic planning, in which the government considers select areas of industry for concrete investment proposals. In these sectors the government negotiates with individual companies in setting goals for sales, exports, and jobs. In return, companies receive tax incentives, subsidized loans, and other official aid "What We Can Learn from Our Rivals," 1980).
- **Singapore.** Under the leadership of Prime Minister Lee Kuan Yew, Singapore is plotting its "second industrial revolution." Its industry, which was highly labor intensive, has faced increased competition from South Korea, Taiwan, and Hong Kong. The new goal is to build a different economic base resting on high technology. To do this, industry and government have identified twelve industries that will be supported by the government to compete effectively in the world market. Japan has been selected as a model and a standard for this development (Heenan, 1983).

Leone and Bradley (1981) define **industrial policy** as

> ... the sum of a nation's effort to shape business activity and influence economic growth. Its proper concern is not transitory issues of industrial well-being but the long-term structural integrity of a nation's industrial base. It is government's version of a company's long-term strategy [p. 92].

In broad terms, an industrial policy can be anything from a plan to aid particular industries with subsidies, tariffs, and tax breaks, to more centralized planning that attempts to identify growth areas for development. Robert B. Reich, one of the principal advocates of an industrial policy, has argued for one that responds to the changing industrial base of the country. He believes that the industrial base is changing from less profitable industries based on raw materials to more profitable, high-technology industries (see Chapter 15, pp. 491–492). With an industrial policy, Reich argues, the government can hasten the transition and make the country more competitive on the international front (Magaziner and Reich, 1983).

An industrial policy as prescribed by Magaziner and Reich (1983) would include measures of two principal types:

1. Measures that would assist workers and regions facing industrial displacement, such as those affected by the misfortunes of the automobile, steel, and textile industries. Such measures would include government-funded job-training programs, business tax credits for company-run job-retraining programs, and special employee educational vouchers to enable them to obtain new skills.

2. Measures that would encourage productive investment and growth. Promising industries would receive low interest rates, price premiums, and an array of government subsidies.

Arguments for an Industrial Policy

The principal argument for an industrial policy is that it would improve the competitiveness of the United States in international markets by expanding and rationalizing the role of government in promoting productive investment. There are two supplementary reasons as well. The first is that our principal competitors — Japan, West Germany, and France — already have industrial policies. The absence of a well-conceived industrial policy, therefore, places the United States at a significant strategic disadvantage.

If the United States must compete against these and newly industrializing, developing countries, some type of policy must be adopted. Steel and automobiles often are cited as examples of United States industries that have been at a disadvantage because of the lack of organized government support. Proponents of an industrial policy also cite the case of Japan's Ministry of International Trade and Industry as an example of an agency that has effectively directed industrial growth and development.

Another argument maintains that we already have an industrial policy, but it needs to be more explicit and better coordinated to be effective. The United States does have a policy composed of voluntary restrictions on imports, occasional bailouts for major companies close to bankruptcy, money for job training and job relocation, and a huge program directed at defense procurement and research (Magaziner and Reich, 1983). The problem is that these policies often are irrational, haphazard, and not coordinated with the goal of international competitiveness. They must be molded into a coherent framework that has as its goal international competitiveness. The industrial policies of Japan, West Germany, and France have been more successful than that of the United States because they have been explicitly oriented to this goal.

Arguments Against an Industrial Policy

Most arguments against an industrial policy are based on the difficulty of implementing a rational policy such as this in the United States, which has a different ideological and cultural base than its international competitors. Four supplementary arguments have been advanced. The first is that industrial policy making as practiced abroad cannot readily be transplanted to the United States. Effective industrial policy making must be carried out by an elite bureaucracy. Historically, Japan, France, and West Germany have been blessed with a well-educated and trained bureaucracy. Most officials of Japan's Ministry of International Trade and Industry, for example, come from the prestigious University of Tokyo Law School. There is no counterpart in the United States, in which a career in law and business generally is preferred to one in the civil service.

Second, the outcome of previous government efforts to protect industries has not been encouraging. The United States began to regulate trucking in the 1930s to shelter the railroads from cut-throat competition. It is acknowledged by economists that price protection weakened the railroads instead of strengthening them ("Industrial Policy — Yes or No," 1983). The Economic Development Administration guaranteed loans to the Seatrain Shipbuilding Corporation for building large tankers. Cost overruns continued to mount, and so did the infusions of guaranteed credit. Seatrain finally filed for bankruptcy in 1981, leaving the Economic Development Administration with $60 million in debts (Reuss, 1981).

A third argument against an industrial policy notes that strategic errors, not the lack of government support, are the cause of failures in the steel and automobile industries. There is little evidence to suggest that foreign subsidies caused the decline in these industries. The decision of the steel companies not to upgrade, together with high labor costs, makes them noncompetitive in the world market. Similarly, the reluctance of United States auto makers to invest in the production of small cars soon enough may be the principal cause of their declining sales.

Another argument maintains that the role of industrial policy making abroad often is misconstrued and exaggerated. The Japanese succeeded in the world market because they happened to be good strategists. The industrial policy formulated by Japan's Ministry of International Trade and Industry unquestionably was instrumental in carrying out this strategy, but opponents of industrial policy argue that the ministry's role has been exaggerated. Various industries, such as the automobile industry, have resisted the ministry's proposals. The ministry also has had failures, specifically over its protection of agriculture and banking, which have not achieved any success in the world market ("Industrial Policy — Yes or No," 1983).

Summary

The growing involvement of government in the private sector is a strong signal to future managers of the need to monitor the impact of government systematically.

There are several reasons why government is important to management: government regulations can be costly; they can lead to frustration, stress, and the loss of entrepreneurial spirit; and monitoring regulatory costs can save money. New regulations may lead to new opportunities, but changes in the United States economic structure may prompt more government involvement.

Government regulations generally have been economic rather than social. They arise because of natural monopolies, destructive competition such as predatory pricing, the consumer's need for adequate information, the problems of externalities or external costs, interdependence in resource extraction, and the need for equity.

The impetus for regulatory reform, which began after World War II, is currently concentrating on reducing the cost burden and improving the administrative process. Another reason for reform has been the increasing burden of regulations on small business.

Among the various suggestions for regulatory reform are regulatory-review programs, regulatory budgets, and sunset laws. Deregulation is a more substantive reform mechanism.

It is important for managers to monitor the costs of regulations, including direct compliance costs, administrative costs, and mitigation and noncompliance costs. Regulatory costs are not easily retrievable, because current accounting methods are not designed to record these costs. A system to track and monitor regulatory costs must be developed, a system that will monitor compliance costs as they are incurred.

Costs are only one adverse effect of regulations. Others are the frequency of inspections/contact with the firm, harmful effects on worker morale, noncooperative inspectors, and the difficulty in obtaining regulatory information. Other strategies for dealing with government regulations include evaluating the impact of regulators on organizational adjustments and performance measures, and developing an action program.

Deregulation brings about sweeping changes in the nature of competition, as well as considerable uncertainty and disequilibrium. To manage this period of transition, managers are encouraged to focus on the ultimate customer rather than the regulators, to be more concerned with systematic growth and costs, to design systems that reflect accountability for results, and to develop strategic programs.

A decade of recessions, inflation, unemployment, and declining competitiveness has prompted debate over whether the United States should have a national industrial policy. Proponents argue that a policy is necessary to overcome our inadequacies in international competition. They claim that the gap between the United States and its rivals may widen because Japan, West Germany, and other countries already have industrial policies.

Opponents cite the difficulty of transplanting such policies to the United States because of ideological and cultural differences. They add that the outcome of previous government efforts to protect industries has not been encouraging, and that strategic errors, not lack of government support, have been the cause of failures in the past.

Questions for Discussion

1. Why has the growing involvement of government in the private sector become a strategic problem for managers?
2. Differentiate between economic and social regulations. Why are both types of regulations needed?
3. Select a newly deregulated industry, such as airlines, trucking, depository institutions, or energy. Review the six reasons for government regulations. Develop a case showing why your selected industry should be deregulated, based on the six reasons.
4. Provide three reasons for deregulation.
5. What are some strategies for dealing with government regulations?
6. What are some strategies for managing a deregulated environment?
7. What is a national industrial policy?
8. Why would a national industrial policy work in the United States? What factors militate against the adoption of a national industrial policy in the United States?

Exercise 17.1
Field Assignment: Government Regulatory Agencies: An Interview Exercise

Purpose
To study how different employees might perceive the effects of government regulatory agencies.

Instructions
Contact and interview one or two employees holding various jobs in each of several different types of organizations. It would be helpful if the sample included managers and workers, public and private employees, and minorities. For each employee, note his or her answers to the following questions:

1. In what ways do you deal with government regulations (or government regulatory agencies) in your job?
2. What are some major problems associated with government regulations? What are some of the major benefits?

Note the answers during each interview and summarize the results for presentation in class.

Case Study
Preparing for Deregulation:
The Experience of the Trucking Industry

As Congress moves closer to enacting legislation to lessen the government's economic regulation of the trucking industry, the organized opposition of that industry grows more intense. But meanwhile, many trucking companies are quietly positioning themselves so that they can leap from the starting gate if Congress throws the industry open to competition.

"There are a number of closet deregulationists out there," says Thomas F. Herman, president of Delta California Industries, Inc., which owns two truck lines, both of which are preparing for a new environment. "We've begun doing a lot of work in management information, costing, and market research."

Commonplace although those terms may be in other industries, they are relatively new in trucking. Freight rates today are jointly set by company representatives meeting under the auspices of regional "rate bureaus," with immunity from antitrust prosecution. And the regulated trucking industry has always predicted that chaos would ensue if Congress were to do away with that system of rate-making and with the Interstate Commerce Commission's route-and-rate authority. The American Trucking Association has warned insistently that under deregulation, service would deteriorate while prices would rise. More to the point, some companies might go out of business, and thus the ATA has fought deregulation long and hard on Capitol Hill and at the ICC [Interstate Commerce Commission].

Quiet Preparation

But the ATA is losing. The Senate Commerce Committee on March 11 sent to the full Senate a bill that would remove much of the ICC's authority, and hearings are almost completed on a weaker House version. Although no major trucking company has formally broken ranks with the ATA as yet — as did several airlines with their trade association in similar conditions three years ago — what one analyst calls "a vast minority" of firms have begun strategic planning for deregulation.

"If we're forced to publish an individual tariff, we don't plan to be sitting around on our hands," says one trucking executive. Consolidated Freightways, Inc. has been working on pricing strategy options for more than a year, and other industry giants, including Yellow Freight System Inc. and Roadway Express, Inc., are doing the same.

The Senate bill, sponsored by Senator Howard Cannon (Democrat–Nevada), would make it easier to enter new markets, a provision the ATA also opposes strongly. Yet many carriers are looking at new expansion. "A lot of companies are seriously determining what markets they should be in," says Michael P. McGee, director of economic and market research for IU International Corp.

Eager to Grow

ICC restrictions clearly have held down expansion in the past. The commission began granting new routes more freely two years ago, and the number of formal applications since then has jumped sharply. Moreover, since the ICC offered to give any trucker authority to carry government freight in January — a step the ATA opposed — it has been flooded with queries about how to apply for the business.

A recent trend in trucking may be partly responsible for the shift in some companies' attitudes toward deregulation. More and more, nontransportation companies are buying general-freight and other carriers. In the last few years, such companies as American Natural Resources Co., PepsiCo, Sun Oil, and ARA Services have bought trucking companies despite the considerable uncertainty in the industry over deregulation. "Although there could be some dislocations [due to deregulation], we feel in the long-term this was a good investment," says David D. Dayton, vice-president-financial of ARA, which last year bought Smith's Transfer Corp.

There is another, paradoxical reason why companies are beginning to think they can live with more competition. It, too, is reminiscent of the reasons airlines finally switched positions. Some ICC members now use 12 percent as an interim desirable rate of return in deciding truck rate cases, while the ICC debates what a permanent standard ought to be — should rate regulation continue. That figure scares truckers, many of whose returns are as high as 20 percent. "That 12 percent return standard makes regulation look so awful, people are screaming about it," says Herman of Delta California Industries, Inc. "Anything is better than going back to the ICC."

Case Questions

1. Discuss the advantages and disadvantages of deregulating the trucking industry.

2. Using Figure 17.2 as a guide, evaluate the strategic responses made by trucking firms in anticipation of a more deregulated environment.

3. Based on your information about the airline industry (see Feature 17.2), what practical advice might you provide to corporate executives in the trucking industry as they prepare for a deregulated environment?

Source: Reprinted from the March 24, 1980 issue of *Business Week* by special permission, © 1980 by McGraw-Hill, Inc.

Brazil has long been an attractive country for foreign investors. However, in recent years the Brazilian government has not been receptive to foreign multinationals in the high-tech industry. Ford, which has several auto plants in Brazil, and IBM, which has been manufacturing in Brazil since 1939, have both experienced problems in this area.

In 1979, Ford joined forces with RCA to set up a Brazilian subsidiary to manufacture computer chips for cars and radios. Although Ford started with analog chips, plans called for a switchover to digital chips, needed for second-generation integrated circuits. In 1980, the Special Secretariate for Information (SEI), the agency in control of Brazil's high-tech development, announced that foreign companies could not manufacture digital chips.

At first Ford paid little heed to the announcement, feeling confident that the company would be granted an exemption because of the huge investment it had already made and because its digital chips were not going to be used in microcomputers. But the SEI stood firm. Ford next tried to find Brazilian buyers for its subsidiary, but no one was willing to take over the plant without government backing. Ford finally had little choice but to close its chips subsidiary.

IBM Brazil, which is managed and staffed by

CHAPTER 18

International Considerations in Management

George S. Vozikis

Brazilian nationals, has had its own problems. After years of making computers to the point where IBM ranked eighth among Brazil's exporting companies, IBM was informed that the government is prohibiting foreign companies from manufacturing or selling small computers in the country. Brazil is trying to protect its own small computer makers in the hopes that eventually the computer industry will no longer be dominated by foreign manufacturers.

IBM has participated in an annual high-tech fair in Brazil at which they have exhibited industrial robots, microchip technology, and IBM microcomputers. At the same time, the company has conducted an advertising campaign stressing their contribution to Brazil's national goals through exports, employment, technology transfer, and increased business opportunities for local suppliers and contractors.

Through these measures, as well as through direct dialogue, IBM Brazil wants to convince the Brazilian government that its market restrictions are depriving the country of the capital and technology required to nurture a viable domestic computer industry.

Sources: "IBM Mounts Publicity Drive in Brazil, Hoping Computer Restrictions Will End," *The Wall Street Journal,* January 13, 1984, p. 27; "Tough Choices in Brazil: As the Junta Squeezes High-Tech Multinationals . . . ," *Business Week,* December 19, 1983, p. 44.

Chapter Outline

- The Nature of International Business
- Theories of International Trade
- Restrictions on International Trade
- International Trade Vehicles:
  Multinational Corporations
- Strategic Management in Multinationals
- Guidelines for Multinational Corporations

Key Terms

- dynamic equilibrium
- portfolio investment
- multinational corporation
- contract manufacturing
- licensing
- franchising
- turnkey project
- joint venture
- wholly owned subsidiary
- mercantilism
- absolute advantage
- countervailing duties
- antidumping duties
- protectionism
- global enterprise
- tariffs

Chapter Objectives

After studying Chapter 18 you should be able to

1. Understand the scope and duties of international management.
2. Describe the main categories of international business.
3. Explain what is meant by a multinational company.
4. Define "new globalism" and relate it to international management.
5. Discuss several international trade theories.
6. Understand the range of government restrictions on international trade.
7. Analyze risk for an international firm.

Introduction

On August 20, 1982, at a meeting at the Federal Reserve Bank in New York, Mexico's finance minister told more than one hundred bankers that his country could not repay its loans (Witcher and Rout, 1983, p. 1).

Three months later the Banco do Brasil, the commercial arm of the Brazilian central bank, was short more than $50 million on its debt obligations for the day. South America's economic giant was saved from default on $80 billion of debt by a short-term loan put together by three American banks after frantic wires and phone calls (Anderson, Ma, Lampert, and Cane, 1983, p. 34).

Since 1982 thirty-five nations, including Nigeria, Poland, Argentina, and Zaire, have had difficulty repaying hundreds of billions of dollars in debt to international banks. Some United States banks have more in loans outstanding to Third World countries than they have in equity: Manufacturers Hanover with $6.7 billion in loans, or 245 percent of its capital; Chase Manhattan with $6 billion, or 217 percent of its capital; and Citicorp with $9.8 billion, or 203 percent of its capital.

How do these items relate to management? Why should a manager be concerned about less-developed countries, international debt, or the economic growth and output of foreign countries? Aren't domestic problems complex enough? Can't we raise walls and insulate ourselves from the influences of foreign governments and events?

The answer to the last of these questions is no. If the big debtors of the Third World defaulted, they would put the big banks into immediate bankruptcy, because their remaining assets would not be enough to cover existing deposits. Panic would spread among depositors, who would scramble to move as much of their money as they could to safer places. The bankrupt banks could neither roll over old loans nor make new domestic loans, and the economy would crumble (Thurow, 1983).

Defaults of countries are unlikely, mainly because defaulting nations run the risk of having their export goods and foreign-based assets seized by foreign creditors. And even in the case of default, the Federal Reserve Bank and foreign central banks would energize a "safety rescue net" that would most likely prevent a global chain reaction of private bank failures and insulate the world's banking system. Nevertheless, the United States and other countries would suffer substantial financial hardship even if the banks did muddle through the crisis. The debt will not manage itself; it must *be* managed.

This chapter illustrates the importance of international business and its influence on domestic business and organizational affairs. The discussion focuses primarily on the manager's awareness and knowledge of the international environment. Such awareness can result in better-balanced decision making. The chapter will explore the essence of international business and management, the economic theories of international trade, and the protectionist realm of trade barriers. We also will discuss the evolution of the multinational corporations and their relationship with their home and host countries, and strategic management in an international setting.

Feature 18.1
Banks Urged to Prepare for More Loan Problems

Federal bank regulators are warning the banking industry to start warning its shareholders about the pending crisis that may result from less developed countries not meeting their debt obligations. The Federal Reserve Board and the Comptroller of the Currency are pressuring banks to increase their reserves, which, of course, will come out of shareholders' profits. The banks, understandably, have been reluctant to frighten their shareholders. Some have even been including IOUs from the troubled countries as income when preparing their earnings reports.

The problem is that less developed countries, particularly those in Latin America, are having problems repaying their debts. Many of them are borrowing just to pay the interest on their loans. Some countries are pressuring U.S. banks to offer longer payment schedules and lower interest rates. Argentina even stopped payment of interest for several months while it studied its debt repayment problems.

If all less developed countries in Latin America stopped payment on their interest and loans, as many observers fear could happen, U.S. banks could lose almost $10 billion a year in interest earnings, according to David Wyss of Data Resources Inc. (DRI). Such a loss in earnings would cause banks to cut back on their loans. Interest rates would rise, and the U.S. economy would suffer substantially. A full default on loan repayment would be a far worse problem. Analysts at DRI estimate that if all of Latin America were to default, the U.S. gross national product could fall by $70 billion, 1 million Americans could lose their jobs, and the federal deficit could increase by $26 billion.

Most analysts are quite sure that the Latin American countries will not default, although many expect that the debt moratorium that took place in Argentina could occur in several other countries as well. The optimists among the analysts believe that U.S. economy can survive if any of the less developed countries stop payment. Financial deregulation would allow customers to secure loans from other financial institutions such as brokerage houses and savings and loan associations if the banks were forced to cut back on their loan funds. The optimists also place their faith in the Federal Reserve's past success in dealing with bank crises. Says C. Fred Bergsten, director of the Institute for International Economics in Washington, "I think the Fed is on top of it" ("How an LDC Default Would Hit the U.S. Economy," p. 118).

Sources: "How an LDC Default Would Hit the U.S. Economy," *Business Week,* November 7, 1983, pp. 118–121; "The True Face of Bank Earnings," *Fortune,* April 16, 1984, pp. 82–86.

The Nature of International Business

The world has become so complicated and unpredictable that managers must raise their level of attention and understanding about world problems. Unfortunately, public attitudes have not changed much from the days when international trade was a relatively insignificant portion of the United States gross national product. During the last decade, however, foreign trade of goods and services has doubled and still is expanding rapidly (Fig. 18.1). World trade volume has increased more than threefold since 1961.

Figure 18.1
Portion of United States Economy Involved in Foreign Trade

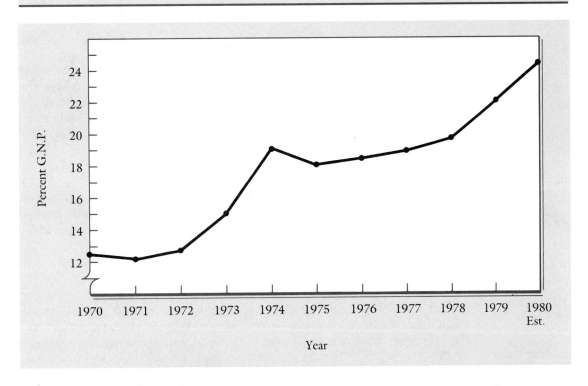

Source: Data from U.S. Commerce Department.

What Is International Business?

There are many different definitions of international business. Richard Robinson calls it a "field of study and practice that encompasses that public and private business activity affecting the persons and institutions of more than one national state, territory, or colony . . . convictions, skills, or knowledge" (1978, p. 17).

Others note that it involves the movement of goods, services, capital, technology, or data, or the supervision of employees, across national boundaries (Robock and Simmonds, 1983, p. 3). Kolde (1982, p. 6) believes international business polarizes around "intercountry" links, creating an international business system with no fixed geographical boundaries.

For our purposes, we will define **international business** as a multifaceted system linking countries, governments, firms, and people that is less encumbered by national borders than political processes are. International business includes all kinds of public and private business activities and transactions involving goods and services, skills and technology, raw materials, and information. It also includes sociocultural, political, and legal processes stemming mainly from the activities of multinational corporations.

International Management

We have seen that international business involves a wide range of activities and processes. Even though management principles are considered to have universal application, a new type of thinking is necessary when dealing with the international dimensions of business. Very subtle international influences sometimes may be devastating. Unique problems may require unique management strategies to ensure the survival and growth of an organization.

International management is defined as the process of accomplishing the international and global objectives of an organization (Phatak, 1983, p. 3). International management involves maintaining a state of **dynamic equilibrium** for the organization within the framework of the multifaceted international system. The organization is affected by the international environment, which may involve such things as overlapping jurisdictions or different tax laws. The organization in turn affects the international environment through its products, cultural innovations, conflicts with national interests, and so on. Because the international environment may have both positive and negative effects, an organization must maintain a dynamic and fragile state of equilibrium. This will result in either positive outputs — for example, when a business contributes to the economic development of a less-developed country as well as making a profit — or negative outputs, as when a company resorts to bribes to increase sales and profits.

The process also involves managing international practices such as foreign licensing, export and import documentation, multinational production, and marketing. In addition, the manager must coordinate international business activities by procuring, allocating, transferring, and utilizing the organization's physical and human resources as well as technical, managerial, and entrepreneurial skills and methods. The scope and variety of international business environments and the diversity of the institutions that must be dealt with, such as labor unions, capital markets, and market distribution channels, necessitate careful coordination.

The manager in a multinational corporation also must maintain *flexibility* in the sociocultural, political, and legal interaction between the home country and the host country or countries. The international manager must monitor developments in this area to help foster timely and conflict-free interactions. The sociocultural environment includes such elements as:

- Customs, values, beliefs
- Attitudes
- Status symbols

- Language
- Religion
- Social class structure
- Social institutions
- Motivating hierarchy of needs
- Status of managers

Political and legal elements requiring a flexible management approach include:

- Form of government
- Political ideology
- Stability of government
- Foreign policy
- Treaties with foreign nations
- Membership in regional integration blocks (EEC, Comecon, etc.)
- Social unrest
- Political unrest and/or insurgency
- Legal tradition
- Effectiveness and/or efficiency of the legal system
- Patent and trademark laws
- Laws affecting business firms
- Government attitude toward business firms
- Government attitude toward foreign business firms
- Monetary and fiscal policies
- Taxation policies

By maintaining flexibility the international manager can adapt to the special managerial requirements of various countries.

Figure 18.2 provides a general outline of the elements of international management. In the center lies the ultimate objective of international management, maintaining a dynamic equilibrium among the three areas that surround it: management of international practices, the coordination of international business activities, and flexibility in the management of home and host country sociocultural, political, and legal processes. All three aspects must be dealt with equally or the equilibrium will be upset and problems will arise for the firm. For example, if greater emphasis is placed on foreign profits, the firm may face a conflict with the host country's national interests. If the company disregards international business practices and resorts to bribes to win foreign contracts, it risks conflicts with other multinational corporations as well as with the nationalism of the home and host nations.

Types of International Businesses

International business is composed of four main categories: international trade (imports and exports), portfolio investment, direct investment, and multinational enterprises.

Figure 18.2
The Scope and Composition of International Management

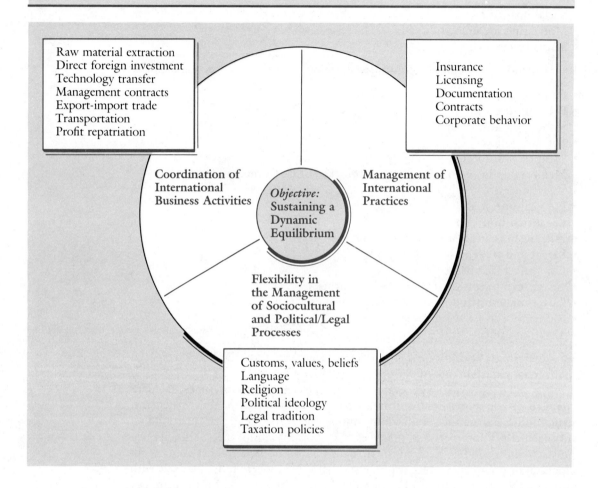

Raw material extraction
Direct foreign investment
Technology transfer
Management contracts
Export-import trade
Transportation
Profit repatriation

Insurance
Licensing
Documentation
Contracts
Corporate behavior

Coordination of
International
Business Activities

Objective:
Sustaining a
Dynamic
Equilibrium

Management of
International
Practices

Flexibility in
the Management
of Sociocultural
and Political/Legal
Processes

Customs, values, beliefs
Language
Religion
Political ideology
Legal tradition
Taxation policies

Imports and Exports. The trading of merchandise, the buying and selling of goods by residents of different countries, is the oldest form of international business. Most of the world trade today is among the industrialized countries. One-third of the world's exports originate in Europe even though more than half of this trade is among the European Economic Community's ten member countries, as Figure 18.3 shows. Most of world trade is made up of manufactured goods.

World trade is always balanced, but this does not hold true for individual countries. In the United States the trade gap between exports and imports — the gap between what the United States sells to other countries and what foreign

Figure 18.3
The Ten Major Exporting Nations: 1980

COUNTRY	EXPORTS (U.S. $ BILLIONS)	EXPORTS AS PERCENTAGE OF GROSS NATIONAL PRODUCT
1. United States	217	10
2. West Germany	193	23
3. Japan	130	11
4. France	116	19
5. United Kingdom	115	26
6. Italy	78	21
7. USSR	77	6
8. The Netherlands	74	46
9. Saudi Arabia	103	102
10. Canada	64	26

Source: Export data from General Agreement on Tariffs and Trade, *International Trade 1980/81* (Geneva, 1981); GNP data from *1981 World Bank Atlas* (Washington, D.C., 1982).

producers sell here — has remained at a deficit since 1975, as Figure 18.4 shows.

The primary reasons for the United States trade deficit are the worldwide recession of 1981 to 1983 and the continuing strength of the dollar, which has kept the price of American exports high. Economists believe another reason is that although the United States trade problem is real, the data on our current account deficit are flawed and inaccurate. Even though the total of deficits and surpluses of all nations in the world should equal zero, in 1982 there was a residual deficit of $80 to $100 billion. If the American figures are as flawed as those of other nations, the United States deficit could be overstated by as much as $20 billion, according to Morgan Guaranty Bank estimates (Cook, 1983; p. 10).

The strong dollar hurts exports, because it takes more deutsch marks or yen to buy products carrying the same dollar price tag. C. Fred Bergsten, director of the Institute for International Economics, estimates that for each percentage-point rise in the value of the dollar, United States net exports are reduced by about $3 billion (Fierman, 1982, p. 68). Indeed, the strong dollar has caused United States exports to fall by 6.8 percent, from $63 billion in 1981 to $59 billion in 1982. The United States trade deficit would have been much more severe if not for the persistent growth of international trade in such services as international licensing agreements, tourism, and so on. This service trade amounted to slightly more than 40 percent of the trade in goods (Fig. 18.5). In the long run, however, gains in service exports to some degree come at the expense of the merchandise sector (Malabre, 1982, p. 48).

Export business is beneficial for a country not only in terms of trade, but also because it creates export-related jobs. A report of the Office of Trade and

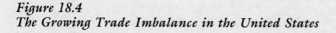

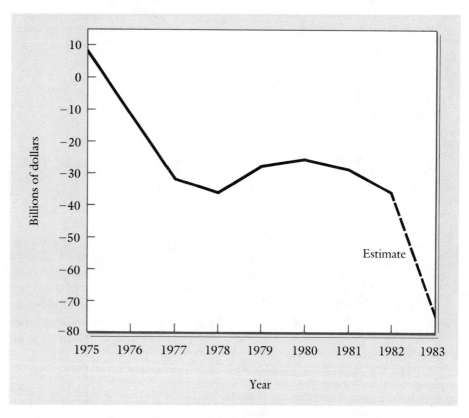

Figure 18.4
The Growing Trade Imbalance in the United States

Source: Data from the U.S. Commerce Department and Harris Bank.

Investment Analysis of the International Trade Administration of the federal Commerce Department noted the extent of the benefit:

- In 1980 more than 6 million United States workers owed their jobs to exports. By 1982 the number dropped to 5 million, mainly because of the drop in export volume.
- Changes in export volume have had a far greater than proportionate impact on total United States employment. Export growth between 1977 and 1980 accounted for 30 percent of the increase in private-sector employment in the United States. Yet when export volume decreased during 1980 to 1982, this decrease accounted for 40 percent of the rise in unemployment.
- The estimated number of jobs generated per billion dollars of United States exports has been decreasing annually, primarily because of inflation and improved productivity. The job rate for total exports dropped from 30,300 to 25,200 between 1980 and 1982. In 1982 export-related employment ac-

Figure 18.5
The United States Balance of Trade

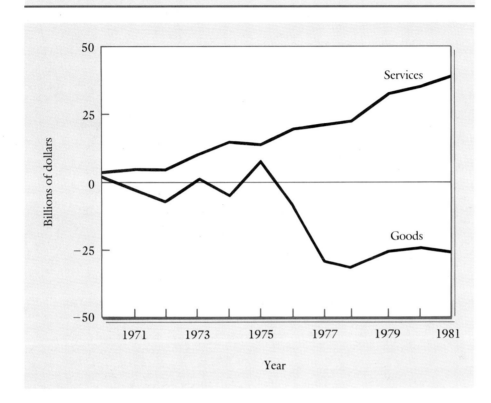

Source: Data from the U.S. Commerce Department.

counted for one in eight jobs in manufacturing (down from one in seven in 1980), one in six jobs in nonmanufactured goods, and one in twenty-four jobs in services.

The future of United States exports looks grim. The pattern after most recessions has been an export trade decline, as Figure 18.6 shows, but the decline after the most recent recession has been steeper than usual. Figure 18.6 also demonstrates that the trade balance shows a tendency to improve in the latter stages of an economic expansion. If recessions follow one another in a relatively short period, however, as they did in 1980 and 1981 to 1982, the trade balance worsens before it improves (Malabre, 1983, p. 60). The offsetting effect of export services on the trade deficit is diminishing, mainly because of the strong dollar. The point to remember is that lagging foreign demand can slow business activity at home at the rate of one percentage point of gross national product growth, according to some estimates (Malabre, 1983).

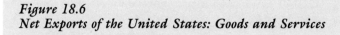

Figure 18.6
Net Exports of the United States: Goods and Services

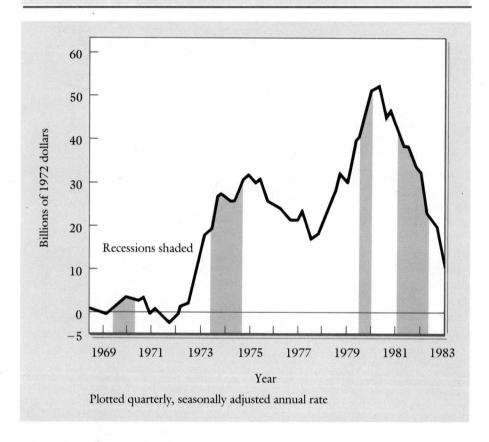

Source: Data from the U.S. Commerce Department.

Portfolio Investment. International **portfolio investment,** or indirect foreign investment, is the second main type of international business. It is the purchase of foreign securities in the form of stocks, bonds, or commercial paper to obtain a return on that investment in the form of dividends, interest, or capital gains. A United States Treasury Department study showed that people residing outside the United States hold stocks and bonds of American firms valued at nearly $100 billion. Five countries, Canada, France, the Netherlands, Switzerland, and the United Kingdom, accounted for more than three-fourths of the holdings (Ball and McCulloch, 1982; p. 26).

Acquiring foreign stocks and bonds does not confer managerial control of a foreign enterprise on the buyer. Rather, the international portfolio investor is a creditor whose main concern is a decent return on his or her investment. This capital flow therefore is greatly affected by relative interest rates and strong currency values that produce high yields.

Direct Foreign Investment. Long-term capital flows, **direct foreign investment,** involves longer-term considerations of political stability and profitability than portfolio investment. It involves acquisitions by domestic firms of foreign-based operating facilities such as plants, factories, warehouses, and hotels. The investor effectively has managerial control over the assets of the acquired firm.

Direct investment may be financed in a number of ways other than through capital movements. Foreign investments may be financed by borrowing locally, by reinvesting foreign earnings, by the sale to the foreign affiliate of nonfinancial assets such as technology, or through funds generated by licensing fees and payments for management services to the parent company. Essentially, direct foreign investment is not so much international capital movement as capital formation abroad (Robock and Simmonds, 1983, p. 6).

Earnings from direct foreign investment by the United States have skyrocketed since the early sixties, representing a very big boost for the American balance of payments. Figure 18.7 (page 594) shows that income from foreign companies in which a United States firm has a direct stake of 10 percent or more reached about $41 billion in 1981. In addition to such things as dividends paid to the United States companies, the $41 billion includes amounts the American firms reinvested in the foreign units. This often accounts for about half the income total.

In 1981 there was a 5.5 percent increase in direct United States investment overseas over the year before, reaching a level of $447.34 billion. Foreign direct investment in the United States increased to $89.76 billion in 1981, a record 31.3 percent growth over 1980. For the first time since the Second World War the dollar amount of the rise in foreign investments in the United States surpassed the increase in United States investments abroad.

A Commerce Department study has shown that foreign investment in acquisitions and start-ups in the United States far outpaced the overall spending increase, surging 57 percent to $19.2 billion in 1982. Canada and Europe provided $13.5 billion of this investment; slightly more than $3 billion came from the oil-producing states in the Middle East. Although the dollar volume of the investment surged, the number of companies that were started or underwent at least a 10 percent acquisition by foreign interests shrank from 1,659 to 875 from 1980 to 1981.

This trend of reduced overseas investments by United States firms could have a detrimental effect on domestic employment, according to an independent study. For years American companies that invested abroad have been charged by critics with "exporting" jobs, reducing exports, weakening the dollar, and neglecting developments at home.

In a survey of overseas investments made by eighty-one companies between 1970 and 1980, however, the research firm Business International Corporation

Feature 18.2
Are Foreign Governments Easing Up on Investors?

When the dollar was weak, countries that once courted U.S. investments cracked down, tightening up compliance and deductions. But with today's strong dollar, a little tax on the subsidiary of a U.S. company goes a long way indeed. As a result, foreign tax collectors are getting very friendly — in some cases, perhaps, too friendly for their own good.

Sounds great for the U.S. businessman, doesn't it? Unfortunately, incentives for foreign investment can be a trap for the unwary as well as an opportunity for the alert. International tax policy is a cyclical affair, and many governments grant concessions "provisionally" — that is, when it suits their purposes. Companies caught in a change of policy can be in real trouble.

Here, some of the more interesting developments on this increasingly significant front.

France . . . the socialist Mitterrand government is granting tax concessions to Americans in hopes of keeping dollars in the country. Prominent among these concessions is a five-year exemption for Americans from France's two-year-old "wealth tax," a claim of up to 1.5 percent on real and personal property in excess of 3.2 million francs (about $400,000) whether in France or outside it. . . .

Beware of socialists bearing gifts, however. The exemption is an act of desperation by a government that has promised the voters more than it can deliver. . . .

France is also offering . . . a research and development tax credit. Assuming a company spends more for R&D in 1983 than it did in 1982, it can deduct 25 percent of the difference up to 3 million francs.

China The People's Republic charges a 20 percent withholding tax on "dividends, interest, rentals, royalties and other sources in China by foreign companies, enterprises and other economic organizations which have no establishments in China." . . . however, the Ministry of Finance cut the withholding tax to 10 percent. . . .

Foreign banks are already more enthusiastic about lending to companies doing business in China. Previously this has been a break-even proposition at best. But the tax cut is a sign that China is ready to come into the world market. . . .

Saudi Arabia The Saudis have never made it easy for a foreign company to make money in their kingdom. But the sheikhs now

found that the investments had a positive effect on the United States economy. The study concluded that the more a company invests abroad, the greater its exports and employment at home. The study reports, for example, that the sample of companies active in overseas investments showed a 9.7 percent increase in their United States payrolls, while United States manufacturers overall reported a 0.7 percent rise. The most active overseas investors reported a 26 percent increase in payrolls, whereas those less active exhibited a 14 percent rise. In addition, companies active in overseas investments showed a substantial increase in their own balance-of-trade surplus during the decade, whereas the overall United States balance of trade went from a surplus to a deficit ("Pace of Overseas Investments, 1982).

Feature 18.2 (continued)

seem to be taking some small steps to modify their tough policies. . . . For the first time, accounting books and records of non-Saudi companies must be maintained in the kingdom — in Arabic — and audited by Saudi-licensed accountants. Also, standardized forms will replace a mishmash of tax rulings. . . . These laws will tend to make tax assessments less arbitrary.

Sweden . . . A new law . . . would require Swedish companies to put 20 percent of their aftertax profits (adjusted for inflation) into five funds. The funds would invest only in Swedish stocks, with voting control resting with the unions. Proceeds would go into workers' pension funds.

This bit of economic arrogance could, among other things, siphon off capital that companies could plow back into the business. Furthermore, the funds managers could and probably will use some of the money to support failing companies as a means of protecting jobs. . . .

But what's bad for Swedish business, however, is not as bad for American and other foreign companies doing business in Sweden. Swedish subsidiaries of foreign corporations will have to contribute to the profit-sharing funds, but the managers can't

buy foreign stocks — which removes the threat that the Swedish workers could one day control non-Swedish firms. Foreign-owned subsidiaries, in addition, will benefit from the reduced corporate tax rate — if the latter goes through.

But won't all this make Swedish business anticompetitive? "It might," shrugs Ernst & Whinney partner Nils von Koch. "The government doesn't really know what it is doing."

Canada . . . A U.S. corporation can set up a Canadian subsidiary to lend money to other Canadian subsidiaries. The lender, however, must pay Canadian withholding tax on the interest received, while the borrower can deduct interest paid from ordinary income. In addition, Canadian assets repatriated to establish the new subsidiary may be exempt from Canadian withholding tax.

Maybe there has been a change of heart among governments. Maybe they are learning the benefits of foreign investment and the perils of treating it badly. But what man giveth, man can take away.

Source: Forbes, October 10, 1983, "But Will It Last?" by Anne Bagamery, pp. 154–156. Reprinted by permission. © Forbes Inc., 1983.

Multinational Companies. Direct foreign investment is the vehicle for the birth and growth of the fourth type of international business, the multinational company. A corporation that has a worldwide approach to foreign markets and an integrated global philosophy, the **multinational corporation** encompasses both domestic and overseas operations (Daniels, Ogram, and Radebaugh, 1982, p. 9). It includes all components of the definition of international business discussed earlier. It is a multifaceted system of domestic and foreign operating facilities called affiliates, operating across national boundaries. The multinational corporation's international business also involves sociocultural, political, and legal processes that stem from the range of problems associated with operating in many different countries.

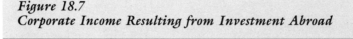

Figure 18.7
Corporate Income Resulting from Investment Abroad

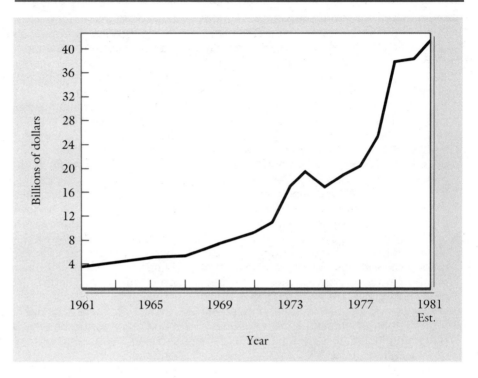

Source: Data from U.S. Commerce Department.

These companies also engage in all kinds of business activities and transactions with different degrees of international involvement, including *indirect exporting,* mainly through export merchants and agents such as export-management companies, and *direct exporting,* setting up an export organization within the firm. Other activities include portfolio investment, transferring funds across national boundaries for the purpose of buying stocks, bonds, or commercial paper issued by a foreign company or a foreign government, and direct foreign investment. The latter is done in a number of ways, including:

1. **Contract manufacturing,** in which a foreign producer manufactures the company's product for sale in the foreign market.

2. **Licensing,** in which the international company, the licensor, agrees to provide access to its patents and trademarks to another company abroad, the licensee. In exchange for the use of these trade secrets, the foreign company pays the licensor a royalty or other form of fee.

3. **Franchising,** a form of licensing in which the supplier of a product or serv-

ice, the franchisor, grants a dealer, the franchisee, the right to sell this product or service in exchange for a fee. Some examples of international franchises are Avis, Hilton, and McDonald's.

4. **Turnkey projects,** in which a firm sets up an operation abroad involving the design and construction of an entire project, such as a dam or refinery, in exchange for a fee. Upon completion of the project, the international company turns over the operation to local personnel.

5. **Joint venture** with a foreign firm or government, in a manufacturing facility abroad to meet local demand or to be used as an "export platform" to boost that country's export sales.

6. **Wholly owned subsidiary,** in which the company owns 100 percent of a foreign affiliate.

Typically a multinational corporation engages in all the preceding types of international activities simultaneously to various degrees in different parts of the world.

Multinationalism is no longer the eminent domain of one particular country or firm. The international marketplace has passed the point at which any single multinational corporation or nation can expect to dominate the world market. As Walter F. O'Connor, vice-chairman-international of Peat, Marwick, Mitchell and Company puts it, we have entered an era that might be called the "new globalism," characterized by an interesting political and economic interdependence of nation-states and innovation in technology and organizational structures. Only the multinational corporations can generate the cooperation and innovation needed in this new era (O'Connor, 1983, p. 29).

Theories of International Trade

The world's explorers, such as Columbus, Marco Polo, and Captain James Cook, were brave men seeking adventure in new lands. But they also were seeking exotic products, natural resources, and new ideas. This section will explore some fundamental questions: Why do nations trade? Why do businesses cross national boundaries? What are the motivational factors determining international trade? What are the purposes of protectionist barriers such as tariffs?

Mercantilism was the prevailing philosophy of international trade during the seventeenth and eighteenth centuries. It is the product of the reemergence of strong national entities. One of the major advocates of mercantilism was Colbert, the finance minister of King Louis XIV. The discovery of new lands and new products created an international market almost overnight.

The central idea of mercantilism was that more goods had to be exported

Feature 18.3
Mexico Seeks Foreign Investors

A Mexican law passed in 1973 sought to restrict foreign investment by putting a 49 percent ceiling on foreign holdings in any local company. Now the country is easing the restriction in the hope of drawing in more currency to help pay off the interest of its staggering debt. Although the law remains on the books, the government is interpreting it with more flexibility.

One Mexican economist said, "Allowing more foreign investment is the only way Mexico can get hold of large amounts of money without getting on its knees and begging to the banks" ("Mexico Eases Foreign Investment," 1983, p. 31). The country's debt stands at more than $80 billion.

Apple Computer Inc. is one American company hoping to take advantage of the government's relaxed rules. The company had been suffering from restrictive Mexican import quotas and heavy duties that have made the Apple IIe three times more expensive in Mexico than in the United States.

At the time the new government policy was announced, Apple was seeking permission to begin assembling computers in the country either through a licensing arrangement or a joint venture with its distributor, Computadores Personales. Apple favored a licensing deal because it would eliminate the problem of shared control and would re-

quire a smaller cash outlay. The company reportedly was considering the Mexican move a model for similar ventures in other Third World nations, such as Brazil, China, and South Korea, that have strongly protected markets.

A Mexican government official said the country now will permit more than 50 percent foreign ownership in any nonrestricted areas if there are no local companies to compete in the area, if the foreign firms agree to use chiefly Mexican-produced raw materials, and if the companies export the products. Restricted areas include petroleum and petrochemicals, mining, and communications. Majority ownership also may be granted when local companies are unable to satisfy the internal demand for a product.

In the past the restriction has been applied loosely to companies the Mexican government didn't want to lose, such as Ford Motor Company and Volkswagenwerk AG of West Germany who own 100 percent of their Mexican subsidiaries.

Source: "Why Apple Wants a Mexican Branch," *Business Week*, June 13, 1983, p. 51; "Mexico Eases Foreign Investment Rules, But Investors Still May Be Hard to Attract," by Lynda Schuster, *The Wall Street Journal*, June 20, 1983, p. 31.

than imported so that the surplus would benefit the nation. This economic chauvinism put the government into a central role in the production, consumption, and trade of goods. Mercantilists had the notion that a country's wealth consists only of precious metals, and enterprises that were bringing in gold through their exports had to be kept alive even if they were inefficient. Mercantilism curbed private initiative, built elaborate bureaucratic controls, and fostered wars and trade rivalries among nations, finally destroying the very markets it was trying to create (Wren, 1979, pp. 37–38). Present-day arguments for protection of domestic "smokestack" industries tend to advance the notion that mercantilism may be old, but it is not dead (Ball and McCulloch, 1982a, p. 51).

The Physiocratic School of Economic Thought

François Quesnay, the founder of the physiocratic school of economic thought, challenged the mercantilistic preoccupation with the state, central planning, and precious metals. He advocated instead a natural order and harmony in economics, with the government practicing a laissez-faire capitalism. Quesnay maintained that wealth did not lie in gold and silver but, instead, in agricultural production.

A more famous Scottish political economist, Adam Smith, was influenced by Quesnay's writings even though he was not a pure physiocrat. Smith's book, *The Wealth of Nations,* established the classic school of liberal economics. Smith brought the Age of Enlightenment that was sweeping the arts and politics of the time into the market and economic activities. The "invisible hand" of the market would ensure the best allocation of resources for production, he said, based on the best economic self-interest of each person and the nation. Smith also thought that the protectionist tariff policies of mercantilism were destructive and that, rather than protecting industries, they penalized efficiency and consequently misallocated the nation's resources (Wren, 1979, pp. 38–39).

The Theory of Absolute Advantage

Under Adam Smith's free-trade conditions, an explanation of why nations engage in international trade was developed: A country can gain most by allocating its productive resources to the production of those goods that it is most efficient at producing, in which the country has **absolute advantage** over other countries.* Whenever one country can supply a given product at a lower absolute cost than another country because of a better climate, a unique mix of natural resources, or an acquired advantage in management training and technology, it has an absolute advantage over other countries that may attempt to produce the same product. The surplus quantity of this product not absorbed by domestic consumption can then be traded with other countries for products in which *they* have an absolute advantage. In this way, both countries benefit from the trade. For example, for countries X and Y and for the commodities of wheat and cloth we have the following facts:

OUTPUT		LABOR INPUT REQUIRED	
	X		Y
20 tons of wheat	1 day	2 days	
10 tons of cloth	2 days	1 day	

* One fundamental assumption of economics is that multinational business is to be limited to foreign trade and payments, even though this is not the full story of international business. Still, trade constitutes a large share of multinational business, and therefore economic, theoretical explanations are quite useful.

With no trading, in three days country X can produce twenty tons of wheat and ten tons of cloth, country Y ten tons of wheat and twenty tons of cloth. The combined output for both countries would be sixty tons of wheat and cloth.

If X and Y specialize and concentrate their production on the goods in which they have an absolute advantage, something amazing happens: In three days country X produces sixty tons of wheat and country Y thirty tons of cloth, for a combined output of ninety tons. This is thirty tons more than before specialization. Each country benefits from trading with the other. But what would happen if country X had an absolute advantage in both wheat and cloth? Would no trade at all take place?

The Theory of Comparative Advantage

In 1817 Ricardo used the labor theory of value to construct his theory of comparative advantage. He claimed that because the value of any product is equal to the value of the labor time required to produce it, a country will produce and export products that use the lowest amount of labor time relative to foreign countries and import those products that use the greatest amount of labor time relative to foreign countries. Only *relative costs* matter, because the more efficient country with an absolute advantage in both goods is not more efficient to the same extent in both goods (Magee, 1980, p. 18). Therefore, this country will specialize in the production of the goods that can be produced more efficiently, that is, those in which it has a *comparative* or relative advantage. The result is that the nation with an absolute advantage in both goods still will trade, because more goods can be produced by specialization in the goods with the comparative advantage, and both countries will benefit with a higher level of consumption.

The Heckscher-Ohlin Theory of Factor Endowments

Despite the logic of Ricardo's model, it is unrealistic to believe that labor is the only factor of production that can explain international trade. Eli Heckscher and Bertil Ohlin argued that differences in national production-factor endowments — land, capital, and labor — explain the differences in factor costs and production possibilities. The production possibilities for the People's Republic of China, a country with an abundant labor supply and low labor costs but little capital, should favor labor-intensive goods. The reverse holds true for the United States, whose production possibilities should concentrate on capital-intensive goods.

The Heckscher-Ohlin theory assumed that the proportion of different factors producing each commodity in every country is exactly the same, with identical productivity. This assumption was a major flaw of the theory of factor endowments, as demonstrated by the famous Leontief's paradox. In 1953 Professor Wassily Leontief of Harvard analyzed United States exports and imports in terms of their actual labor and capital contents. He anticipated that the United States, a capital-rich country, would export only capital-intensive goods and import only labor-intensive goods. The results showed that not only was the United States importing and exporting both kinds of goods but that, taken as a whole, United States exports were actually less capital intensive — that is, more labor-intensive — than import-competing goods (Leontief, 1954).

New Theories

Until the 1950s the Heckscher-Ohlin theory of factor endowments was considered accurate, especially because commodity trade and portfolio investment dominated the international scene. With the growth of multinational corporations and direct foreign investments, however, certain inconsistencies developed with theories of international trade (Kolde, 1982, p. 188). Since then other theories have arisen.

The Head-Start Theory. This theory postulates that firms will trade and invest internationally to gain a head start over their competition in a particular product. Economies of scale and the experience curve will lead to successive shifts in the production-cost curve for the product. Also, growing consumer acceptance will cause the head-start firm's demand curve to shift to the right, and at the same time become more inelastic, as the product becomes the standard for the industry and widely accepted by consumers all around the world. The gap between the head-start firm and its competitors will not start closing until some other firm decides on foreign involvement and starts to catch up, or some indigenous competition emerges (Kolde, 1982, pp. 193–194).

The Product Life-Cycle Theory. Based on a study of the historical development of 187 major United States multinational corporations, Vernon (1966) advanced the concept of the product life cycle in international trade, as shown in Figure 18.8. According to this theory, products pass through four stages.

The first stage simply is the normal process whereby a domestic business develops a new product for the domestic market without consideration of international sales. In the second stage the firm starts exporting to foreign markets whose demand was considered too small before and then grew. As the domestic position of the firm erodes and the volume of sales abroad increases, the third stage — foreign production — starts, taking advantage of market proximity and the gains from the experience curve. The fourth stage shifts production to low-cost plants from which the firm exports into the domestic and other high-cost markets. Eventually, Vernon hypothesized, the competitive status of the multinational corporation abroad will diminish and local producers will emerge (Vernon, 1966).

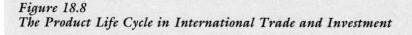

Figure 18.8
The Product Life Cycle in International Trade and Investment

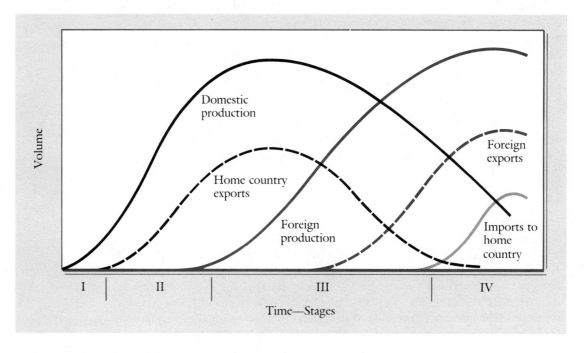

Source: Reprinted with permission from Fayerweather's *International Business Strategy and Administration,* copyright 1978, Ballinger Publishing Company.

In a seminal work, *Sovereignty at Bay,* Vernon (1971) observed that the product life-cycle theory was not very appropriate to explain the later stages:

> By 1970, the product cycle model was beginning in some respects to be inadequate as a way of looking at the U.S.-controlled multinational enterprise. The assumption of the product cycle model — that innovations were generally transmitted from the U.S. market for production and marketing in overseas areas — was beginning to be challenged by illustrations that did not fit this pattern. The new pattern that these illustrations suggested was one in which stimulation to the system could come from the exposure of any element in the system to its local environment, and response could come from any part of the system that was appropriate for the purpose [p. 108].

There is not as yet an integrated body of international trade theory to explain all aspects of international business operations. There are, however, three known factors that create the commercial incentives for international business transactions: economic differentials, the relative advantages of each nation in supply and demand; the influence of government actions in the pursuit of national interests, including tariffs and controlled exchange rates; and the capabilities of the multinational corporations to transmit capital, labor, and natural resources, as well as technological, managerial, and entrepreneurial know-how (Fayerweather, 1978, p. 6).

Restrictions on International Trade

There are some strong arguments in favor of free trade without government restrictions and barriers. Each nation is a sovereign state, however, and each sovereign state formulates its own foreign policy according to its national interests. Foreign policy covers such matters as national security and defense, cultural exchanges, and foreign economic policy. The Constitution forbids the imposition of trade barriers for trade within the United States, but international trade is a different matter. There is a broad range of commercial or foreign trade policy choices between the two extremes of **autarky,** or national economic self-sufficiency, and absolute free trade, the economic interdependence of nations. Trade policy directly affects and influences a nation's business environment as well as its relations with other countries. **Protectionism** influences the formulation of policy and strategy within a corporation by affecting the availability of markets for its goods and services. In general, the effects of protectionist trade barriers touch practically every sector of the international business community.

Types of Trade Barriers

Trade barriers can be classified into tariff and nontariff barriers. **Tariffs,** or duties, are the oldest and the most widely used trade control device. If collected by the exporting country, they are known as *export tariffs*. They are common among less-developed countries that depend on a single commodity for export and tax revenues. If the tariff is imposed by a country through which the cargo must travel en route to its destination, the tariff is known as a *transit duty*. The United States imposes only the most common type, the *import tariff*.

Import duties can be levied as a fixed amount per physical unit, called a *specific duty;* as a percentage of the value of the imported goods, an *ad valorem* duty; or as a combination of both, a *compound duty*. Tariff schedules are classified into a hierarchy of groups and subgroups of products, with higher tariffs imposed on finished goods than on raw materials.

Nontariff barriers are less visible than tariffs but are extremely effective in restraining free trade. There are several types of nontariff barriers:

1. *Surtaxes.* Placed on international cargo, these are temporary measures designed to correct a serious short-term balance-of-payments deficit. With a surtax, imports are restrained for a few months.

2. *Government participation in trade.* This participation occurs in the form of direct export subsidies in cash to stimulate the export of certain goods. The government also may discriminate in procurement by favoring domestic manufacturers, or it may impose indirect export subsidies in the form of low

freight rates, reduced domestic taxation, government-guaranteed, low-interest loans, or government grants for research and development.

3. *Corrective duties.* These duties are imposed on imported goods suspected of having been export subsidized by their country of origin. They can take the form of (1) **countervailing duties,** which normally are set at the amount of the suspected export subsidy, or (2) **antidumping duties.** The latter are imposed when imported goods have a price lower than they command in their country of origin because the foreign exporter (1) wants to profit from the economies of scale resulting from operating at full capacity or (2) wants to gain early monopolistic control of the export market and later profit by charging substantially higher prices. This is called *predatory dumping.*

4. *Quantitative limitations.* These are quotas that specify the quantity of certain products that can be imported or exported. When the quota limit is reached, no more goods can be imported regardless of the demand. Because quotas set absolute limits, they can impose far more effective trade restrictions than tariffs, which, depending on the elasticity of demand, can be absorbed by consumers. Recently Japan has agreed to "voluntary" quotas in automobiles, electronics, and other items to avoid probably harsher import restrictions.

5. *Customs and entry procedures.* Government control also may take the form of regulations covering valuation methods, classification, documentation, and health and safety. In May 1983, *The Wall Street Journal* reported that during 1982 United States officials estimated that about 60 percent of American exports of manufactured goods to Japan, valued at $9.8 billion, were subjected to costly dockside inspection required by Japanese law.

6. *Standards.* Government standards for products, packaging, labeling, and translation, may be required.

7. *Monetary or exchange controls and quotas.* These barriers control the amount of foreign exchange allocated to importers, thus preventing them from importing greater quantities.

8. *Import charges.* These charges may be levied as prior import deposits, special duties, or variable levies, or in other forms.

This list provides some idea of the complexity of foreign trade policy. But to understand the policy formulation process, it is even more important to be familiar with arguments in favor of protectionism through trade barriers.

Arguments for Protectionism

To understand the controversial issue of whether a nation should impose tariff or nontariff barriers to international trade, we should see how these barriers affect different segments of society and what role they play in shaping a nation's commercial policy.

Feature 18.4
Japanese Car Companies Profiting from Quotas

Import quotas on Japanese-made cars were supposed to give U.S. auto manufacturers time to retool for the production of smaller cars. The three-year quota was extended to a fourth year in 1984 and supposedly was set at 1.85 million vehicles. In actuality, the figure is more like 2.6 million if it includes four-wheel drive vehicles, station wagons, cars shipped to the U.S. via Puerto Rico, and the 100,000 cars made at the Honda plant in Ohio.

Indeed, what has happened is that the Japanese auto makers and their U.S. dealers have benefited from the quotas while the U.S. buyer has lost. Because the quotas have limited the supply of cars for sale in the United States, the prices have gone way up. For example, a Honda that would sell for $7,500 in Japan sells for $11,000 in the States. Although the dealer claims to be throwing in a few extras, most of the difference is going straight into the dealer's pocket.

But do American buyers think they are really losing? Most of them do not. The Honda that Americans wait in line to reserve, that may take three months to arrive, and for which they are willing to pay hundreds of dollars over the sticker price is in their eyes a better car. These same people, according to one dealer in Chicago, would not pay more than the sticker price for a Chevy. Whether or not Japanese cars are any better than American cars is an issue that Detroit has never dealt with successfully. Another factor helping the Japanese auto makers is the American public's desire for luxurious cars. The Japanese manufacturers have loaded their cars with options.

Imports from Japan now account for 21 percent of the U.S. automobile market. Some predict that once the quotas are lifted the Japanese will gain 30 percent of the market and as much as 40 percent within five years if the climate is fully competitive.

Few Japanese analysts believe that American car manufacturers will derive any long-term benefit from the quota system, which has failed to stop Japanese domination of the small-car market in the United States. Japanese auto makers also warn that the restraints could become a crutch that will lessen American auto makers' competitiveness if they continue. Instead, the Americans should work out a system to restore more competitiveness in the U.S. market, said one auto executive in Tokyo.

Sources: "U.S. Car Quotas: How Less Is More for Japan," *Business Week*, November 7, 1983, pp. 61–62; "Import Quotas: The Honda Dealer's Best Friend," by Anne McGrath, *Forbes*, December 5, 1983, pp. 43–44.

Government. Government imposes trade restrictions to control the direction of foreign trade, to provide public revenue, and for national security. Control of the direction of foreign trade discriminates against consumers whose needs are better met by imported than by domestic goods. Protectionism also imposes huge costs on business and results in lost tax revenues for government. The costs charted in Figure 18.9 cover tariffs on apparel and sugar, and quotas and tariffs on footwear. What consumers must pay in higher prices generally is gained by companies and workers in the protected industries. But nobody benefits from losses in production and consumption, which occur when protected companies produce inefficiently and high prices discourage some buyers.

Trade restrictions for national security reasons also have been assailed, especially for smaller countries that cannot afford to subsidize expensive defense

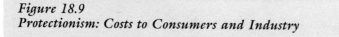

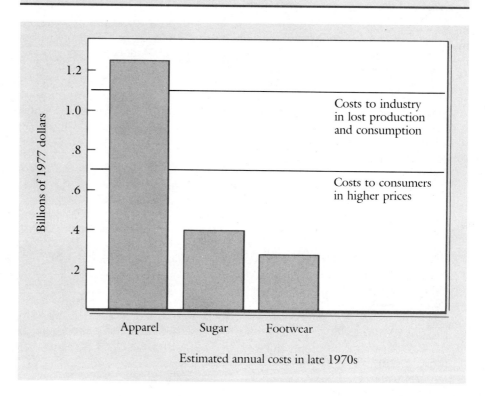

Figure 18.9
Protectionism: Costs to Consumers and Industry

Source: Data from Morris E. Morkre and David Tarr of the FTC, as cited in Guzzardi, 1983, p. 86.

industries (Kolde, 1982, p. 72). In their article "The Incidence of Trade Restriction," Canto and Laffer (1982) examine the effects of the United States embargo on Occidental Petroleum Corporation's export of superphosphoric acid to the Soviet Union following the Soviet invasion of Afghanistan. Their analysis illustrates that the embargo had little or no effect on the Soviet Union, but it imposed a significant cost on Occidental and affected the United States economy in general.

Another argument in favor of protectionism is the "infant-industry" argument first advanced by Alexander Hamilton as early as 1792. The logic goes that new industries require protection against foreign competition because initial output costs for these young industries may be too high to make them competitive in world or even domestic markets. In time, however, the costs will decrease enough to achieve lower per-unit cost production and a comparative advantage. Policy makers, who can only hope that tariffs will help develop the infant industry, run the risk of protecting the wrong industry at the same time (Kolde, 1982, pp. 75–76).

Business. In business, attitudes toward tariffs vary according to whether a firm depends on foreign materials for its survival, as Boeing Company does, or is threatened by competition from imports, as is United States Steel Corporation. It is wrong to believe that the business community is united in supporting high, protectionist tariffs. Industries that neither depend on nor compete with imports lie in the *indifference zone,* even though they too may be indirectly influenced if their customers are import dependent or import competing (Kolde, 1982, p. 72).

Consumers. Looking again at Figure 18.9, we can see that tariffs mean higher prices for consumers. Although universal, however, consumer interest usually is secondary to professional interest and therefore has very little impact on the national scene.

Labor. Labor's stand on national commercial policy is generally protectionist, aimed at safeguarding jobs and wage standards. The central argument is that imports take jobs away from domestic labor and contribute to unemployment, which is a valid argument up to a point. Labor also contends that their own high wages must be protected by high tariffs against imports from low-wage countries. Wage rates are not production costs, however. Moreover, if productivity rates differ between two countries, wage-rate comparisons do not reveal the true picture. Figure 18.10 shows the costs to the national economy per job during the 1970s in three protected industries: apparel, sugar, and footwear. Dividing the loss in production and consumption resulting from inefficient production and high consumer prices by the number of jobs saved gives

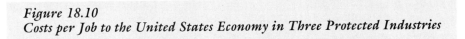

Figure 18.10
Costs per Job to the United States Economy in Three Protected Industries

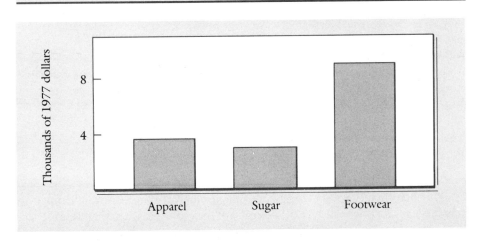

Source: Data from Morris E. Morkre and David Tarr of the FTC, as cited in Guzzardi, 1983, p. 86.

the cost to the economy of saving each job. In footwear this figure is $9,333 a year, 47 percent higher than the industry's average wage. Figure 18.11 presents labor's point of view.

Proliferating protectionism could seriously inhibit international commerce, the vast expansion of which has contributed mightily to post–World War II prosperity. In the past twenty-five years, the volume of goods traded among nations has increased more than tenfold, from less than $100 billion in terms of the dollar's 1975 buying power to more than $1 trillion. This growth, which serves to allocate economic resources more efficiently, far outstrips domestic expansion in most economies. In the 1930s, in contrast, world trade shriveled and protectionism was rampant. It is widely held that this factor seriously aggravated the Great Depression (Malabre, 1981, p. 1).

International Trade Vehicles: Multinational Corporations

Moving a product into the international market involves entering a new environment in which the basic cultural, political, legal, and monetary assumptions are different and in which a company must communicate with people inside and outside the organization with different motivations and behaviors.

The Conference Board Research Association declared that "the multinational corporation has been recognized as one of the key institutions that will influence the nature of the twentieth century" (Duerr and Roach, 1973, p. iii). The economic, social, and political effects of these multinationals are becoming more vast every day. Managers must examine these effects carefully and determine the underlying causes. Using these analyses, leaders of potential multinationals may devise workable strategies and policies for use in organizing and operating an international corporation.

Corporations that formerly were strictly domestic, providing goods for the United States and occasionally for foreign customers that sought out their products, have developed overseas distribution networks, built worldwide production facilities, and developed operational plans for competing on a multinational level. Great changes in strategies and organizational structures are helping companies compete more effectively in foreign markets. Strategic management is crucial in the development and operation of these multinationals. Rational planning and decision making are the only answer to the difficult problems posed by the internationalization process.

Evolution of Multinational Corporations

Multinational business is not a new phenomenon. The East India Company managed a subcontinent. The Phoenicians not only traded throughout the known world, but also established manufacturing centers and facilitated the transfer of technology.

Figure 18.11
The United Steelworkers' Opinion of Imports

"The British Are Coming, The British Are Coming"

AND AMERICA'S STEEL INDEPENDENCE IS GOING

A Message Especially for Stockholders Of American Steel Companies

As Independence Day approaches this year, Paul Revere's warning takes on a new and dangerous meaning.

If a deal struck by the U.S. Steel Corporation and the government-owned British Steel Corporation goes through as planned, it could be the beginning of the end for America's steel independence. As the union representing America's steelworkers, we find that prospect extremely disturbing, and for reasons that go beyond our self-interest. It is, for example, contrary to the best interests of stockholders of other American steel companies.

Here's what is involved.

U.S. Steel wants to quit making steel at its Fairless Hills plant in Pennsylvania, but continue to operate the Fairless finishing facilities. It wants to accomplish this by importing millions of tons of semi-finished steel "slabs" from the British Steel Corporation's Ravenscraig plant in Scotland.

U.S. Steel says it would be cheaper to do this than to modernize the steel-making facilities at Fairless. To make the deal more palatable for Americans, the British say they will create a so-called "private corporation" just to operate Ravenscraig.

That's supposed to take the sting out of U.S. Steel's importation of subsidized foreign steel. Of course it ignores the fact that the Ravenscraig technology is a direct result of subsidized investment. The same is true for the entire money-losing British steel operation.

The fact is that Ravenscraig would not exist but for this subsidy.

It is indeed ironic that in the past, even U.S. Steel has charged that government subsidies saved British steel from bankruptcy and allowed it to install new technology while encountering huge operating losses.

The logical, fair and reasonable thing for U.S. Steel to do is to forget the British deal and modernize Fairless. Earlier this year, our union negotiated a new contract that will save the steel industry some $3 billion. As the largest steel company, U.S. Steel will realize the largest share of those savings. Our one condition was that these savings be plowed back into existing facilities.

Certainly this is consistent with the industry's long-stated objective of modernizing its facilities to sharpen its competitive edge.

If U.S. Steel is allowed to consummate this unlikely match, it can make other deals with the Europeans, Brazilians, Nigerians, Taiwanese and others who have the capacity to flood the American market with subsidized steel. Then, one by one, other American steel companies will be forced to follow suit to remain competitive. If they don't, they'll be priced out of the marketplace.

The losers in such a scenario would be the thousands of new unemployed American steelworkers, the stockholders of other, smaller American steel companies, and the American people, who would find themselves dependent on foreign producers for our steel needs, including steel for defense purposes.

Smaller steel companies are especially vulnerable. One half or more of their investment in steel properties is tied up in iron and coal mines, and the ovens and furnaces that produce steel. If these facilities are made useless by a national shift to imported raw steel, all of that will have to be written off. The effect on balance sheets and the market value of investments is obvious.

The United Steelworkers of America is determined that this will not happen. We have committed the resources of our union to this total effort. We will employ every legal means at our disposal to block this dangerous precedent.

★ Within recent days, we have engaged counsel to file on our behalf a petition charging that the proposed transaction is illegal under U.S. trade laws.

★ We will press fully our rights under existing collective bargaining agreements with U.S. Steel, as well as our rights under the National Labor Relations Act.

★ We will call for a Congressional investigation of the entire proposed U.S. Steel-British Steel arrangement—including the issuance of subpoenas to examine all documents and notes exchanged by the parties and the relative costs of producing steel at Ravenscraig and the extent of subsidization.

★ We will carry out an extensive information program to provide the public with the facts about this important case.

On April 28, the President of our union, Lloyd McBride, testified before the Steel Caucus of the U.S. House of Representatives about this matter. He closed with these words:

"We may be witnessing here the beginning—for the U.S.—of the internationalization of American steel production. And when steel companies engage in what is essentially unfair trade for the purpose of shifting their production base out of steel for the advantage of their shareholders, then our union and its members are being severely injured and sorely used. Our steel communities are severely impacted. And, I submit to you, our nation is the worse for it. When private decisions have such widespread, devastating consequences on the private and public sectors, those decisions should not be made unilaterally without a thorough investigation of the consequences.

The consequences of U.S. Steel's proposed joint venture with the British Steel Corporation are indeed great. An entire industry as we have come to know it is at

stake. U.S. Steel is single-handedly attempting to forge a new national steel policy for America.

The Steelworkers of America are prepared to fight this dangerous proposal at every juncture. And we want your help.

We invite others who share our views on this important matter—especially steel company stockholders—to join us. We'll be glad to provide you with additional information.

United Steelworkers of America
Lloyd McBride, President
Five Gateway Center
Pittsburgh, Pennsylvania 15222

Source: Reprinted by permission of the United Steelworkers of America.

During the colonial era, firms such as the Dutch East India Company and the Hudson's Bay Company focused each colony's exports and imports on the home country, suppressing any colonial production that competed with the products of the mother country. This colonial-type company has been extinct since the 1960s. In contrast, contemporary manufacturing multinational corporations are much less inclined to assume the exploitive colonial company role.

The early international ventures of United States business abroad were mainly a result of technical inventions or products that conformed to the head-start model discussed earlier. Singer obtained a patent on his sewing machine in 1851, and fifteen years later his company built its first overseas factory in England.

Another impetus to internationalize was the Sherman Antitrust Act of 1890, which prohibited collusion among business firms in restraint of domestic trade but was indifferent about market sharing, price fixing, and competitive retaliation in foreign markets. The result was a rush to acquire foreign firms, with the most systematic expansion occurring during the 1950s. In the 1970s the patterns changed, and other nations' businesses found the United States a safe haven for direct foreign investment (Kolde, 1982, pp. 176–177). As a result, multinational corporations are a global phenomenon. Even communist nations and less-developed countries have established their own multinational corporations or at least a semblance of them to participate in this universal development.

Multinational and Global Corporations

What is a multinational and what is a global corporation? *Multinational* describes a firm that views each of its businesses around the world as virtually independent in serving the national market in which it is situated. The company may be a pasta operation in Brazil, a chocolate business in Europe, or a dog food subsidiary in Australia. Each enterprise is a separate subsidiary, and the subsidiaries do not necessarily work together (Kiechel, 1981, p. 111).

A **global enterprise** sells a fairly uniform product in all markets in which it participates; thus, every section of the organization is coordinated to work together. For example, a global corporation may buy components on three continents, ship them to a country with cheap labor to be partially assembled, and then put on the finishing touches in factories close to the customer. The result might be a Honda motor scooter, which is basically the same product worldwide, a Sony shortwave radio, or an International Business Machines mainframe computer. One part of the organization could not exist without the others. Figure 18.12 shows an example of a multinational firm and Figure 18.13 a global firm.

Not only firms but also industries, become international. To keep up with the competition, an individual firm must adopt a global strategy if others within its industry are planning similar actions. (Kiechel, 1981, p. 114).

Figure 18.12
Structure of a Multinational Corporation

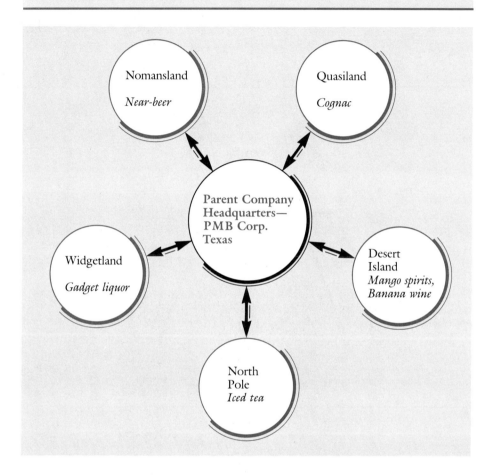

What causes an industry to go international? The industry generally is led by an individual firm attempting to get a step up on its competitors. That firm may expand abroad by exploiting low labor costs or cheaper raw materials. Or it may find that to achieve maximum economies of scale, it must sell more than its home market can absorb. Innovative firms may go international when impediments such as trade barriers or high transportation costs are removed.

When a corporation goes international, it must change its strategy to long-term planning, because the payback in foreign investments may take many years. There also will be a considerable financial drain on a company, because the corporation often has to start from scratch to build a whole new industry within a country. This is one reason why large firms have an advantage with internationalization.

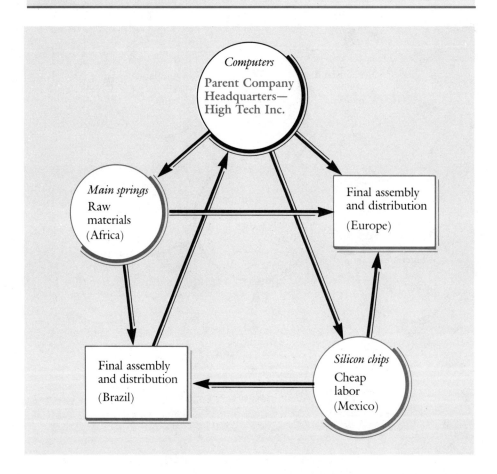

Figure 18.13
Structure of a Global Corporation

Political Risk and Environmental Scanning

International organizations face a major political risk that domestic organizations face only indirectly: A company's investment value in a foreign nation may drop from $100 million to zero in a matter of days for various reasons.

There are more common and subtle political risks also, including repatriation of income law changes, sabotage, and nationalization. A multinational corporation's structure is better able to withstand this risk than that of a global corporation. The multinational loses only what it had in that particular nation, but the global corporation can lose its supply line, which feeds the whole company. This is the main reason for the structure of multinational corporations. A multinational can allow a single subsidiary to take great risk without fear of damage to the total organization. A global firm does not have this advantage and must take this risk into account when choosing locations for its production plants or other supply lines (Rummel and Heenan, 1978, p. 67).

At the same time, multinational managers have discovered that they no longer have the great powers that they once held over other nations. Schemes to manipulate or even destroy foreign governments to control trade no longer have the same chance to succeed as United Fruit had in Central America, for example (Kraar, 1980, p. 86). The United States Foreign Corrupt Practices Act also has limited corporate payoffs for contracts or special treatment. The age has come when business can no longer "buy or rent governments" (Kraar, 1980).

This atmosphere, as well as foreign hostility to possible exploitation of the host countries by foreign investors, has caused a greater need for strategic management during the internationalization process (Vernon, 1972, p. 166). Firms must be compatible with the people with whom they have surrounded themselves, as well as being economically efficient and competitive in both domestic and foreign markets. Long-term survival is not possible without some form of strategic environmental scanning.

Analysis of Political Risk. How do international firms analyze political risk? There are four basic methods for an executive to judge this danger, besides analyzing available news reports (Rummel and Heenan, 1978, pp. 68–71).

1. *Grand tours.* An executive or team of executives can visit the host nation after some preliminary market research. The information from these trips often is selective, chosen by the local government. Even with the limited information, it is beneficial to have the executives get a feel for the political climate in person.

2. *Old hands.* The firm can acquire area or country expertise from seasoned educators, diplomats, journalists, or businessmen hired as consultants. The quality of the information varies with the individual. The danger of this technique is that the firm is putting implicit faith in the judgment of outsiders. These "old hands" can be wrong.

3. *Delphi technique.* Strategists can attempt to identify selective elements influencing a nation's political destiny: the size and composition of armed forces, delays experienced by foreign industries, and political kidnappings. Next, experts weigh the importance of these factors and put them into a checklist. This checklist often is transformed into an index so nations can be compared. Corporations like this method because it can be both quantitative and qualitative, but it is meaningless unless the mechanics are carried out properly, a difficult and time-consuming procedure. For this reason, many firms do not use this technique.

4. *Quantitative methods.* Tools and techniques can be employed that involve multivariate analysis, which uses a number of mathematical variables. This type of analysis can be used to predict trends using historical data or to understand more fully the underlying relationships affecting a nation. Like the

Delphi technique, this method can be of great benefit if the mechanics are done properly.

The best analysis technique is a combination of all four methods. But multinationals have developed a method of handling political risk that is even better. They spread out risk through structure and diversification so that one failure will not overly damage the company.

One extreme risk is that of political changes or upheavals, revolutions, and expropriation. The political atmosphere must be monitored constantly and with a critical eye. In this way, if elements change in the political environment, a firm will have ample time to deal with the situation through retrenchment or some other means. If a firm is considering investing in a country that is likely to experience drastic political changes, this possibility must be weighed in the overall analysis. Political change also may be an opportunity. If a firm can keep abreast of a potentially stable situation, it may capitalize on a market not considered by others. For example, in 1975 Gulf Oil Corporation considered the group emerging from a civil war in Angola to be stable even though the United States government opposed it as a Soviet tool. The group supported the liberation of Angola. Later, because of the firm's timely involvement, Angola became one of Gulf's largest production sources (Kraar, 1980, p. 88).

Environmental Scanning. Several specialized areas must be considered when conducting a thorough examination of the environment with an eye to foreign investment. One area of possible threat or opportunity is government regulation. A country that holds a negative view of foreign investment may find endless ways to limit production and sales. Many countries discriminate against business, unlike the United States. In contrast, countries that encourage foreign investment because of internal needs for economic or social advancement may provide land and capital grants, low-interest loans, training and reconversion allowances, tax holidays, and government purchase orders (Kapoor and Boddewyn, 1973, p. 7).

A final area of importance concerns misinformation. When more than one nation or group of cultures become business partners, the communication process becomes exceedingly complex. Misleading information or gaps in information may cause conflict in such things as jurisdictional boundaries, and clashes between varying cultures. Problems may arise in labor, production, marketing, and all other phases of the business (Hagen, 1966, pp. 147–155). The only way multinational corporations can expect to survive is to have a complete, up-to-date, accurate perception of the host country.

Guidelines for Operations of Multinationals

Michael Duerr and John Roach (1973) believe that firms must not consider foreign countries as just an additional region for production or marketing. General guidelines must be formulated to fit an individual firm's framework and organizational structure. The underlying strategy should be the transition to a totally internationalized enterprise. A group of guidelines covers the ground rules that a firm must have to organize and operate internationally.

The firm's safety and survival depend on information it receives. A second set of guidelines concerns this area:

1. *Establish what types of information are needed* (Beauvois, 1966, p. 71). The information should cover the basic strengths and weaknesses of a country's economy, provide an interpretive analysis of the local business structure, and analyze the investment climate of the country. It also should analyze the main factors affecting business operations, namely, energy, labor, resources, and market size.

2. *Establish specific guidelines concerning the methods of information gathering.* Special consultants may be hired. Bechtel Corporation employs Richard Helms, a former director of the Central Intelligence Agency and ambassador to Iran. Advisory councils of prominent foreign businessmen and retired government officials may be formed, such as those used by General Motors and Caterpillar Tractor. Private intelligence systems such as those used by Gulf may be established. In addition, local management may be given the responsibility for maintaining information within the business community. Performance should be tied directly with compensation (Kraar, 1980, pp. 86–92).

3. *Purchase political risk insurance.* These policies may cost from 1 percent to 6 percent of the total investment, depending on the safety of the region.

4. *Use a different method of accounting for risk* by adding from 1 percent to 5 percent to the firm's required rate of return for investments in risky areas. Exxon Corporation does this.

Managerial Audit

A *managerial audit* is an internal evaluation of the policies, major programs, and managerial effectiveness of overseas affiliates, major divisions, and the overall company. The audit should pinpoint management's success at all levels in implementing the company's strategies and policies, and its contributions to profitability. The audit also must evaluate the effectiveness of past strategies and major programs. This evaluation points out the strengths and weaknesses of all major international units and ways to improve past policies and management. Major changes in strategies, organization, and personnel may be called for.

The managerial audit begins with an analysis of the past profitability of each affiliate in national and regional markets in relation to that of the entire company. After this analysis, each management group investigates its strengths and weaknesses in marketing, finance, production, personnel, labor relations, and other areas or major product lines.

First, each national subsidiary and then each division analyzes strengths and weaknesses. Then corporate headquarters reviews the audits conducted by each overseas affiliate and division and makes its own assessment of their performance. Top management compares and assesses not only functional strengths and weaknesses, but also the overall effectiveness of the management of each affiliate and division in view of special environmental and competitive restraints.

Strategic Management in Multinationals

The guidelines for multinational corporations discussed in the previous section will help management identify environmental strengths and opportunities, and organizational strengths and weaknesses. The management audit is important in establishing realistic objectives for each affiliate, allocating the company's resources, and adjusting company activities in different countries. When analyzing a firm's ability to transmit resources, it is important to consider economic differentials, government actions, relationships with the host country, and national interests (Fayerweather, 1978, pp. 149–150).

Once the manager has come to understand the capabilities and limitations of the firm, the second step in the strategic management process can be more easily accomplished: the establishment of a framework for policies and actions. From this framework, consistent policies for production, research and development, marketing, personnel, and financing can be formed. These policies and the actions that implement them come together to form a *united global strategy* (Fayerweather, 1978, p. 8). The third step in the strategic management process is the development of an organizational structure. This structure should satisfy the characteristics of the firm and its environment.

As companies grow larger and increase their foreign sales, they must adapt their organizational structure to new demands and be constantly aware of new challenges. As multinational corporations grow, they must not only come to terms with their new size and strength, but also manage an array of diversified product lines in geographically dispersed markets.

A multinational corporation must answer two major questions involving its structure, needs, and goals (Drake and Caudill, 1981, p. 83): How much autonomy should be given to individual geographic operations? How can an organization develop strategic guidelines and allocate resources efficiently on a worldwide basis?

The need to maintain central control and the need for flexibility create key problems for multinational corporations trying to manage growth in major international markets. The company headquarters must be willing to give up some of its power to allow its subsidiaries to adapt to their particular climates. There are hundreds of ways to balance flexibility and control, including the use of separate international divisions, regionalized divisions, a global-regional organization coordinated by a world headquarters group (such as that used by the Dow Chemical Company), and independent local units (Duerr and Roach, 1973, pp. 6–15).

Drake and Caudill (1981, p. 84) argue that the way in which a company finds the appropriate balance between central control and flexibility depends on four main factors: (1) the company's stage of development abroad, (2) the nature of its product lines, (3) the size and significance of its foreign markets, and (4) the particular managerial style and competencies of its foreign-based management teams.

The multinational corporation's organizational structure must be both varied and flexible because of the changing and diverse nature of the relationship between the parent company and its foreign subsidiaries. Accordingly, the *matrix form* of organization is widely used. The matrix structure is adaptable and well suited to stress and change. Every matrix pattern is different, but each involves a mix of product and geography. When the power rests with the product divisions, as it does with American Cyanamid Company, the company tends to be highly centralized. The opposite is true of companies such as Nestlé, which give the power to geographic regions. The trend recently has been geographic, toward decentralization and flexibility (Drake and Caudill, 1981, p. 87).

Fayerweather (1978, p. 487) gives the multinational manager three basic guidelines for selecting or devising the optimal operations structure:

1. Create a structure in which planning and decision making in each area of operations may be performed by people with the necessary responsibility for a unified strategy in that area.

2. Make the decision and the information channels as direct, short, and structured as possible to encourage communication.

3. People having specialized international knowledge and experience in solving communication problems should be able to go where they are needed in the organization.

The complexity of multinational operations has forced international firms to adopt a more sophisticated strategic management approach than their domestic counterparts. For an international organization to be effective, it must be able to operate well in a wide range of environments that can be, and usually are, substantially different from home. To operate effectively in these varying environments, each affiliate must be able to meet immediate needs based on its own outlook without depending on answers from home. Strategy must be planned on a regional basis, because an overall organization strategy cannot encompass all the needs or situations of every affiliate. Blanket strategies limit the efficiency and possibly the effectiveness of the organization.

Even so, the parent must maintain some control to prevent its subsidiaries from becoming disjointed. This trade-off between centralization and flexibility is a major problem, the solution to which depends on the structure of the particular organization. The greater the subsidiary's flexibility, the greater its potential to exploit fully its particular market, almost to the point at which its geographic region, not organizational headquarters, becomes home. Instead of an international organization viewing itself as a United States–based or Swiss-based corporation, it should think of itself as a world-based organization.

> A global economy is no idealistic pipe-dream but a hard-headed prediction; it is a role into which we are being pushed by the imperatives of our own technology. Because the global corporation rests its claim of efficiency on its ability to view the planet as a single economic unit and to shift money, resources, and people freely from one continent to another it has transcended the nation-state and in the process, is transforming it [Gotcher, 1981, p. 27].

Guidelines for Multinational Corporations

The world economic system today cannot be explained by static economic models, despite their statistical sophistication. We live in an interdependent world with enormously complicated, interlocking domestic and international problems. The late Charles W. Yost, an editorial writer for *The Christian Science Monitor,* stated:

> What will be required of leaders everywhere will be much more bold, comprehensive, and coordinated economic planning, national and international, than they have dared apply in the past. What will be required of citizens in both rich and poor countries will be much more sympathetic understanding of each other's needs. If these qualities prevail, the problems are soluble. If they do not, the situation a decade from now will certainly be much worse than it is today [1976, p. 39].

The multinational corporation should exhibit social responsibility in its functions and its management as a company-wide commitment to a contract between business and society. The multinational corporation must change its philosophical view of the world, especially with respect to the developing countries, to continue operating in a balanced and symmetrical manner.

Finally, the multinational corporation must continue to seek the participation and the assistance of the international, political, and economic organizations that are attempting to integrate the world economic system and avoid a confrontation between the haves and the have-nots of the world.

Summary

In the present chapter the importance of international business and its influence on domestic business and organizational affairs are discussed. The complicated nature and unpredictability of the world, together with increasing foreign trade, make it important for managers to be more aware of world problems.

International management must maintain a state of dynamic equilibrium in an organization within the international system, balancing the effects of the external environment with the company's effect on its environment. Managers also must oversee international practices, coordinate international business activities, and maintain flexibility in sociocultural, political, and legal problems.

There are four main categories of international business: imports and exports, portfolio investment, direct investment, and multinational enterprises. Multinational corporations engage in all kinds of business activities with different degrees of international involvement, including direct and indirect exporting, portfolio investment, and direct foreign investment.

Direct investment is accomplished through contract manufacturing, licensing, franchising, turnkey projects, joint ventures, and wholly owned subsidiaries. Typically a multinational corporation engages in all these activities simultaneously in different degrees in various parts of the world.

Trade barriers can be classified as tariff or nontariff. Tariffs, or duties, are the oldest and most widely used trade control devices and include export, transit, and import duties. Import duties may be specific, *ad valorem,* or compound. Nontariff barriers are extremely effective in restraining free trade. There are several types, including surtaxes; government participation in trade, providing direct export subsidies in cash; corrective duties; quantitative limitations, or quotas; customs and entry regulations; standards for products; monetary or exchange controls and quotas; and import charges.

The economic, social, and political effects of multinational corporations are growing daily. International organizations face major political risks, including repatriation, sabotage, and nationalization. These risks, as well as foreign hostility toward possible exploitation of the host country, have created a greater need for strategic management.

There are several basic ways in which firms can analyze political risks. Executives may visit the host country to get a feel for the political climate; they may rely on the expertise of seasoned educators, diplomats, journalists, or businessmen hired as consultants; or they may use the Delphi technique or other quantitative methods to predict trends or understand the underlying relationships affecting a nation.

The type of information a company receives is crucial. A firm must establish what kind of information is needed and set guidelines concerning the ways in which it will be gathered. A firm may also minimize risk by purchasing political risk insurance or using a different method of accounting.

Managerial audits evaluate the policies, major programs, and managerial effectiveness of overseas operations and the overall company.

The need to maintain central control and the need for flexibility create problems for multinational corporations. This balance may be achieved through the use of separate international divisions, regionalized divisions, a global-regional organization, or independent local units. Recent trends have been toward decentralization and flexibility.

Multinational corporations should exhibit social responsibility, become accustomed to unpredictability, operate in a balanced and symmetrical manner, and continue to seek the participation of organizations that are trying to integrate the world economic systems to avoid confrontations between the rich and the poor of the world.

Questions for Discussion

1. What is the difference between international business and international management? Explain.
2. Distinguish several types of international businesses.
3. How does portfolio investment differ from direct foreign investment?
4. Summarize the primary managerial problems facing multinational corporations, in contrast to one-nation companies.
5. Define the term *turnkey project*.
6. Describe the basic tenets of mercantilism. What problems can you identify with the concept?
7. Describe the theory of absolute advantage. Provide an example. How does it differ from the theory of competitive advantage?
8. Identify some restrictions on international trade that relate to management practice.
9. Differentiate a multinational corporation from a global corporation.
10. What is the role of environmental scanning in international management?
11. Discuss the role of organizational structure in the effective management of multinational corporations.

Case Study
Trans-Europa Business Credit

Trans-Europa Business Credit (TEBC), a commercial finance company, was acquired as a wholly owned subsidiary by a large conglomerate holding company 10 years ago. It is headquartered in New York and has 30 branches, most of them located in North America and Europe, and a few in the Middle East. The branches have always operated separately and autonomously.

TEBC's primary business is accounts receivable financing, but it also books loans secured by inventory or other collateral when a borrower needs more money than can be secured by accounts receivable alone. The minimum loan is $100,000 and the average is $250,000. The District Manager, who usually has four or five Branch Managers reporting to him, has authority to approve all loans.

When TEBC was acquired, the management of Trans-Europa Corporation decided it wanted more control over the subsidiary. There was an overall concentration of loans in a few business areas that could become dangerous should the world economy change and undermine one of those business areas. To reduce the risk, Paul Bergonzi, the President of the finance company, hired George Praeger, an experienced loan executive, as Vice President of Commercial Finance Lending. Praeger was to reorganize the branch system and diversify the loan portfolio. Bergonzi assigned Tom Baldwin as Praeger's assistant. Over the years, Baldwin had worked in several areas of TEBC and knew most of the Branch Managers personally.

One of Praeger's first decisions was to centralize the loan approval process by requiring that head office be notified of all loans over $250,000 and that head office make final approval of all loans over $350,000. This would include any increases in existing accommodations that would bring the loan line over $350,000.

Praeger discussed this idea with Bergonzi who presented it to the conglomerate management. They approved the plan.

Praeger then drafted the following letter to the Branch Managers:

Dear _____.:

Paul Bergonzi and the directors of the Trans-Europa Corporation have authorized a change in our loan approval procedures. Hereafter, all Branch Managers will notify the Vice President of Commercial Finance Lending of any loans in excess of $250,000 before the preliminary approval and before TEBC's auditors conduct the survey. In addition, final approval of all loans for more than $350,000 will come from the New York office. This includes new accommodations and increases in the loan line which brings the limit up to $350,000 or more.

By centralizing loan approval, we can ensure that our monies are not concentrated in only a few areas and we can broaden our base of operation. I am sure you will understand that this step is necessary in such times of increasing economic uncertainty. By effecting this change, the interests of each branch and the company as a whole will best be served.

Yours very truly,

George Prager

George Prager
Vice President of
Commercial Finance Lending

Praeger showed the letter to Tom Baldwin and asked for his opinion. Baldwin said he liked the letter but suggested that since Praeger was new to TEBC, he might visit the branches and meet the managers to talk to them in person about the new procedure. Praeger decided that there was so much to do at the head office that he could not take the time to go to each branch. He sent the letter instead.

In the next 2 weeks, most of the branches responded. Although some managers wrote more, the following is a characteristic reply:

Dear Mr. Praeger:

We have received your recent letter about notifying the head office about negotiations of loans of $250,000 and the change in the approval process for loans in excess of $350,000. This suggestion seems a most practical one, and we want to assure you that you can depend on our cooperation.

Sincerely yours,

Jack Foster

Jack Foster
Branch Manager

For the next 10 weeks, the head office received no information about negotiations of loan agreements from any of the branch offices.

Executives who made frequent trips to the field reported that the offices were busy making somewhat more loans than usual.

Case Questions

1. How do you explain the branch managers' response to George Praeger's memo? Draw on the material in the chapter in your answer.
2. In view of cross-cultural problems and problems with multinational firms, what could Praeger have done differently?

Source: From David A. Nadler, Michael L. Tushman, and Nina G. Hatvany, *Managing Organizations: Readings and Cases,* pp. 538–541. Copyright © 1982 by David A. Nadler, Michael L. Tushman, and Nina G. Hatvany. Reprinted by permission of Little, Brown and Company.

CHAPTER 19

Social Issues in Management

What is the value of a letter of recommendation? What would result if such a letter said, in effect: "Dear XYZ Company: About your applicant, Joe Jones — Save yourself a headache. Sincerely . . ."? If XYZ Company believed the contents of the letter, such information would be most helpful in making their hiring decision.

Companies seldom receive such letters, however. Instead, they receive letters crammed with a series of nonspecific, affirmative adjectives that invariably lead to the conclusion: "I therefore strongly recommend this individual. . . ." As a result, companies (and universities) are increasingly treating such letters lightly and relying instead on other (presumably more valid) information.

The moral and legal obligations of the letter writer are becoming the subject of growing concern. Does a college professor or former employer have an obligation to describe the job applicant accurately? Does responsibility for discovering the truth about an individual's strengths and weaknesses rest exclusively with the company, or does the letter writer have a duty to be candid in the appraisal process? If letter writers are forthcoming, what happens to them? Will they lose a friend or colleague? Will they be sued for libel? In short, how does the letter writer resolve the ethical dilemma of balancing objectivity with the potential negative personal consequences that may result?

Unfortunately, there are no clear solutions to these and other similar problems that people in business encounter every day. As a result, it has often been said that ethical behavior is one of the most important attributes of an effective manager.

Chapter Outline

- Managerial Ethics
- A Model of Corporate Social Responsibility
- Areas of Social Responsibility

Key Terms

- managerial ethics
- value programming
- code of ethics
- stakeholder

Chapter Objectives

After studying Chapter 19 you should be able to

1. Understand how internal values and external guidelines influence the ethical behavior of managers.
2. List the requirements for an effective code of corporate ethics.
3. Evaluate an organization in terms of what it does to society and what it does for society.
4. Discuss corporate responsibility to consumers, investors, employees, and society.
5. Explain the provisions of several laws and regulations dealing with equal employment opportunity and worker safety and health.

Introduction

With alarming frequency we read newspaper reports about corporations involved in questionable or frankly illegal affairs. Whether these involve illegal payoffs, discrimination against employees, or unfounded claims about products, they reduce the credibility of business organizations and business people in the eyes of the public and often create pressures for increased regulation. In short, actions such as these only create additional constraints and further problems for all business organizations.

Because of the importance of the related issues of managerial ethics and corporate social responsibility, we shall deal with these issues in considerable detail in this chapter. First we examine the nature of managerial ethics, focusing on the causes of unethical behavior and what can be done about it. Next we turn to the somewhat larger issue of corporate social responsibility. A model is presented that ties together the various aspects of the problem. As will be seen, this is a thorny issue and one in which sometimes there are no easily identified "right" answers. Throughout our discussion we emphasize the role of management in ensuring the adherence to at least minimally acceptable codes of conduct and guiding the corporation to assume responsibility for being a good citizen in society. It will be argued throughout that if organizations are to continue to exist in a relatively free society, they must contribute to that society.

Managerial Ethics

Often lip service is given to the importance of ethical behavior among managers, but seldom do we see a serious examination of the topic. Recent examples of the adverse consequences of unethical behavior for both individuals and organizations suggest that the subject deserves greater attention. Consider the following examples (Glueck, 1980):

- The Schlitz Brewing Company was charged with 3 felony and 743 misdemeanor counts for making illegal payoffs and kickbacks to retailers. The amount of these payoffs was estimated to be more than $3 million. In a settlement, the company agreed to pay $750,000 in civil and $110,000 in misdemeanor penalties.
- The founder of Mattel Corporation pleaded no contest to charges that between 1969 and 1974 she falsified ten company reports to create the impression that corporate growth was higher than it actually was.
- The Danion Corporation, a major clinical laboratory, was accused of paying kickbacks to physicians in exchange for the doctors' use of their laboratory services.
- The chief purchasing agent of Frito Lay was accused of making a sizable profit — estimated to be several million dollars — by ordering corn from a company he owned.

• Executives from the REA Express Company were indicted for conspiracy to use false invoices, fictitious bills of lading, and dummy corporations to make a million dollars in secret profit for themselves at the same time that the company was going bankrupt.

Each of these examples involves a question of **managerial ethics.** We shall consider several aspects of the problem. First, however, exactly what do we mean by managerial ethics? For our purposes, **ethics** will be defined as an individual's personal code concerning what constitutes acceptable behavior. It deals with a person's beliefs concerning what is right and wrong. As we would expect, there are considerable differences in the specific aspects of acceptable behavior.

Influences on Managerial Ethics

Influences on the ethical behavior of managers are diverse. There are, however, two general areas of influence: (1) internal values and (2) external guidelines. Internal values result largely from such factors as religious beliefs, innate values that individuals hold to be self-evident "truths," and value programming. **Value programming** is the formation of values as the result of observing and imitating role models, particularly during the ages of ten to twenty years. Role models may include parents, friends, and national heroes. It is believed that our major foundation of ethics is formed as a result of these influences.

Added to these internalized values, particularly in later life, are various external influences. These external influences in the work situation include the behavior of a supervisor or peers on the job, the climate created in the work place, and pressures for money and achievement. A study of factors influencing unethical decisions asked executives to rank five major influences (Brenner and Molander, 1977). Data were collected in both 1961 and 1976. As shown in Figure 19.1, the behavior of one's supervisor was considered the most significant

Figure 19.1
Factors Influencing Unethical Decisions

	RANK	
FACTOR	*1961*	*1976*
Supervisor behavior	1	1
Industrial climate — common practice	2	3
Behavior of peers	3	4
Lack of formal policy	4	2
Personal financial needs	5	5

Source: Reprinted by permission of the *Harvard Business Review.* An exhibit from "Is the Ethics of Business Changing?" by Steven Brenner and Earl Molander (January/February 1977). Copyright © 1977 by the President and Fellows of Harvard College; all rights reserved.

influence in both years. Common practices or climate and an absence of formal policies governing such behavior were cited next. A good example of the effects of external pressures on ethical behavior can be seen in Feature 19.1, which describes the plight of Lockheed Aircraft Corporation.

Corporate Codes of Ethics

To overcome such pressures, many corporations have attempted to provide corporate **codes of ethics** to constrain behavior and to provide guidelines for acceptable practices. One example can be seen in Figure 19.2.

Feature 19.1
The Lockheed Scandal

"The bribes and the payoffs associated with doing business abroad represent a pattern of crookedness that would make . . . crookedness in politics look like a Sunday school picnic by comparison."

Those remarks were in Senator Frank Church's opening speech of the Congressional investigation of bribery and kickbacks in the aircraft industry. Several aircraft companies were accused of misconduct, but the brunt of the scandal fell on the Lockheed Aircraft Corporation and its chairman, Daniel J. Haughton.

The Senator from Idaho went on to charge that "foreign agents or consultants are hired not for their local expertise or their technical knowledge but for their connections in influential government circles, and they are paid huge fees on this. . . . "

The Congressional inquiry revealed that over many years Lockheed and others had systematically paid millions of dollars in kickbacks and bribes to foreign officials and dignitaries in an effort to secure sales of its aircraft. Included among those receiving the payments were the prime minister of Japan, a Saudi prince, a general in the Italian air force, and the prince consort of the Netherlands. Moreover, the company went to great lengths to cover up such payments.

When the scandal began to break, Lockheed President Carl Kotchian defended the payoffs, saying in the case of the Japanese incident, "These payments are made in connection with our marketing efforts. This man has connections. If you want to sell airplanes in Japan this is the way you do it. It is the normal practice outside the United States."

Evidence seems to support what Kotchian said. A British Broadcasting Corporation poll of twenty of Great Britain's largest exporting companies revealed that ten had special payments built into their foreign contracts for such purposes. French, German, and Japanese companies follow similar practices.

Lockheed was held accountable for its "corrupt" practices and was made to initiate actions aimed at eliminating payoffs for overseas sales. But for other companies in other countries it was business as usual. Who is at fault then? And more important, what should be done to remedy the situation?

Source: The Lockheed Papers, by David Boulton, London: Johnathon Cape, 1978.

Figure 19.2
An Example of a Corporate Code of Ethics

- TO PROVIDE our employees a stimulating work environment that will attract and challenge effective people and provide rewarding employment opportunities.

- TO DETERMINE consumer wants or needs and to fulfill these with quality products or services.

- TO IDENTIFY with appropriate local issues and to contribute to the economic and social development of the community involved.

- TO HOLD a single standard of integrity everywhere.

- TO INSURE the highest level of objectivity in our procurement practices.

- TO REQUIRE that our employees refrain from actions that constitute a conflict of interest.

Source: From Grover Starling, *The Changing Environment of Business,* Second Edition (Boston: Kent Publishing Company, 1984), p. 429. © 1980 by Wadsworth, Inc. Reprinted by permission of Kent Publishing Company, a division of Wadsworth, Inc.

To be effective, a code must specify what constitutes acceptable behavior. It also must be clearly written, be widely circulated among employees, and receive the strong endorsement of top management. A well-written code that is lost in an employee's manual or that is largely ignored by top management cannot be expected to have a major influence on ethical behavior. If we are serious about curtailing unethical behavior by employees, it is importat that top managers set an example in their own conduct.

Beyond the issue of managerial ethics is the related topic of corporate social responsibility. Here our concern goes beyond individual behavior and focuses on collective action by the corporation in society. In other words, is the organization a good corporate citizen? It is to this topic that we now turn.

A Model of Corporate Social Responsibility

Corporate **social responsibility** deals with two central concerns. First, it focuses on what an organization does *to* society. Here we are concerned with the legal limits of corporate behavior, such as whether the firm is acting within the law. Second, it focuses on what an organization does *for* society. This deals with the extent to which the organization is acting in a responsible fashion. Whereas the first concern is determined largely by society through its laws and social dictates, the second function is fulfilled largely at the discretion of the company. A major corporation may be barred from discriminating against minorities or women — a legal issue — but it is free to choose whether to make charitable contributions to the United Way — a social responsibility issue.

Feature 19.2
The Business of Charity

Every year American business hands over millions of dollars to a vast array of charities — hospitals, housing for the poor, the Boy Scouts, colleges, the Red Cross, and many more.

Doubtless, thousands and thousands of people are helped by the corporate givers. But is it all given in the spirit of love and kindness? Not quite. A good measure of self-interest is usually thrown in.

A company might give money to the hospital that will treat workers injured in an explosion in one of its plants. Another might contribute to the United States Olympic Committee because the son of a prominent customer is a member of the team. To cultivate community goodwill, Xerox Corporation lends money for housing for the poor in its headquarters town of Stamford, Connecticut, and Atlantic Richfield, the largest oil producer on the North Slope, supports native artisans in Alaska.

Take the example of Interpace Corporation, a Parsippany, New Jersey, manufacturer of plumbing and electrical fixtures and building projects. The company had a simple, passive contribution program until 1978, annually giving the United Way about $150,000, or 0.5 percent of its pretax earnings.

Then a consultant inspired Interpace Chairman William Hartman to create a distinctive program using a moderate amount of money. Under the new program the company allows its individual plants to allocate their share however they would like. One bought a kidney dialysis machine for a local hospital.

In addition, Interpace spends an extra $150,000 on sculpture, primarily backing shows at New York City museums. There are two goals. The company wants its name to be familiar on Wall Street. It needs credit to acquire other companies, and investment bankers often sit on museum boards. The company also wants to give its managers and employees a sense of Interpace's commitment to quality. About 80 percent of the company's employees work with such materials as clay, steel, and aluminum. Interpace officials think sculpture is something they can understand.

Dayton-Hudson Corporation began giving the legal maximum of 5 percent of its taxable income in 1945, directing most of it to cultural and welfare programs in cities in which it has stores. The reason? Because stores can't survive in devastated cities. But, said Kenneth N. Dayton, chairman of its executive committee, social conscience is also important. Dayton is one of a number of executives pushing corporations to give 5 percent in direct payments to charities.

"I totally reject the view that the only business of business is business," he said. "The purpose of business is to serve society."

Source: "The Unsentimental Corporate Giver" by Lee Smith, *Fortune*, September 21, 1981, pp. 121–140.

A model has been created to highlight this distinction (Dalton and Cosier, 1982). Shown in Figure 19.3, the model allows us to evaluate both these dimensions and generally determine which quadrant best describes a particular organization. Let us briefly examine each of these four quadrants.

Illegal and nonresponsible. In quadrant *A* we are concerned with a firm that violates prevailing laws and at the same time does little for society. Examples of companies caught bribing officials, breaking pollution or employee safety standards, or dumping unsafe products appear regularly in newspapers and maga-

Figure 19.3
The Four Faces of Social Responsibility

	Illegal	Legal
Nonresponsible	A	C
Responsible	B	D

Source: Dalton and Cosier, 1982, p. 20. Reprinted by permission.

zines. In many cases these companies also seem unconcerned about their role in improving society. Because the behavior of such companies reinforces the "robber baron" image of corporations, it damages the impression created by all companies.

Illegal and responsible. The strategy shown in quadrant *B* is more common than you might think. The organization here is attempting to do the right thing and be socially responsible but in doing so violates either the letter or the spirit of the law. Sometimes the illegal behavior is intentional, as when a company wishes to test the constitutionality of a law it deems unfair. Other times, however, the tangle of conflicting laws ensnares the company. An example is American Telephone and Telegraph Company, which was indicted and convicted of discriminating against women. As a result of the affirmative action programs subsequently introduced, American Telephone and Telegraph was sued successfully by men for discrimination. American Telephone and Telegraph stood convicted of sex discrimination against its entire work force! All the while, the company was making what it considered sincere efforts to improve opportunities at all levels for its workers.

Legal and Nonresponsible. An organization that obeys the law yet does little else exemplifies this approach. This strategy is shown in quadrant *C*. Note that "nonresponsible" as used here is different from "irresponsible"; *irresponsible* implies a failure to comply with one's responsibilities, whereas *nonresponsible* implies that one has no such responsibilities. Companies that follow this strategy basically feel that although they are bound to obey prevailing laws, it is not appropriate to use shareholders' money for social causes. This strategy may bring accusations that a company is unfeeling. It also reinforces calls for government to step in and do what private enterprise has failed to do.

Legal and Responsible. Quadrant *D* represents the strategy of being both legal and responsible. This is the preferred, socially desirable strategy in the Dalton and Cosier (1982) model. The position taken is that corporations have a responsibility not only to abide by legal constraints, but also to take a proactive stance and support social causes or institutions that they believe represent a positive force, after allowing for a reasonable profit. Figure 19.4 shows the major reasons for corporate participation in philanthropic activities, based on a survey of corporate executives. Note the primary reason organizations get involved and assume responsibility for such things as the United Way campaign, higher education, and the fine arts: It is a belief that corporations have a responsibility to be good citizens in the community and to protect and improve the environment in which their people live, work, and do business.

Figure 19.4
Corporate Management's Most Important Reasons
for Undertaking Philanthropic Activities[a]

POSSIBLE REASONS FOR UNDERTAKING CONTRIBUTION ACTIVITIES	SPECIFIC ACTIVITIES		
	United Funds	*Higher Education*	*The Arts*
Corporate citizenship: Practice good corporate citizenship	74%	49%	48%
Business environment: Protect and improve environment in which to live, work, and do business	68	46	43
Employee benefits: Realize benefits for company employees (normally in areas where company operates)	47	31	31
Public relations: Realize good public relations value	34	20	32
Pluralism: Preserve a pluralistic society by maintaining choices between government and private-sector alternatives	28	40	10
Commitment: Of directors or senior officers to particular causes, involvement	23	31	28
Pressure: From business peers, or customers and/or suppliers	12	8	17
Altruism: Practice altruism with little or no direct or indirect company self-interest	10	8	15
Worker supply: Increase the pool of trained or untrained workers or access to minority recruiting	5	63	2
No contributions or activities in this area	2	2	7

[a] Based on responses of 417 chairmen and presidents; adds to more than 100% because multiple responses were requested.

Source: Data from Harris and Klepper, 1977, as cited in Starling, 1980, p. 342.

Although the model suggested here is simplistic, it highlights some of the fundamental issues involved in corporate social responsibility. Beyond simple adherence to state and federal laws, for what exactly is an organization responsible? Does it have a responsibility to its employees, consumers, or community, or is it responsible solely to its shareholders?

Areas of Social Responsibility

We have just considered four different strategies of corporate social responsibility. In this section we address the areas of such responsibility. Contemporary organizations, as members of society, have clear and distinct responsibilities to various groups and entities that have a stake in the organization. These **stakeholders** may not own a financial share of the company. Even so, they have a claim on the organization, requiring it to act responsibly toward them (Feature 19.3). We will examine four areas in which corporate social responsibility is most evident. These include responsibilities to consumers, investors, employees, and society (Fig. 19.5). This list is not meant to be exhaustive, but it does focus attention on several important areas.

Feature 19.3
Social Responsibility at Honeywell

For several years, Honeywell Corporation has been attempting to systematize its social responsibility efforts. The company has four primary goals in this area: (1) community improvement, or "doing our share to help"; (2) impact on profits, including offsetting regulatory action by instituting better methods of their own volition; (3) maintenance and improvement of employee pride and confidence in the company, including its impact on motivation, performance, and recruitment; and (4) maintenance and improvement of public confidence in the company.

Since their establishment in 1975, these objectives and their degree of fulfillment have been reviewed annually by top management. Every general manager specifies his or her community relations objectives for the unit and takes an active part in encouraging employee interest and participation.

Honeywell makes available about $3 million per year, which is allocated to various projects based on perceived importance and need. In the past, projects have included urban and community development efforts, rehabilitation programs for ex-prisoners and juvenile delinquents, and environmental conservation programs.

In addition to money, Honeywell makes available technical assistance, equipment, general office and factory facilities, and opportunities for sponsorship. Results of the various divisional programs are monitored both in the division and in the executive branch to assess the impact of each program. In this way Honeywell feels it makes maximum use of its limited resources to enhance the quality of life for everyone.

Source: How to be a Good Corporate Citizen by D. Clutterbuck. London: McGraw-Hill, 1981.

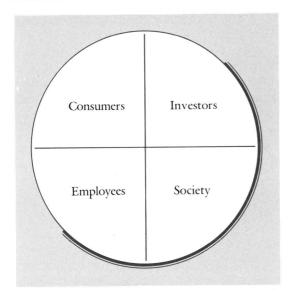

Figure 19.5
Stakeholders in an Organization

Consumers | Investors

Employees | Society

Responsibilities to Consumers

Product Promotion. Contemporary organizations have a responsibility to use good judgment and honesty in the claims they make about their products and services. As Starling (1980, p. 445) puts it, "Nobody really believes . . . that United Airlines flies 'the friendly skies' while other airlines are daily strafed by Zeros, Messerschmitts, MIG-15s, and unfriendly UFOs." There is a clear need for responsibility in this area. Customers have a right to know the truth about what they are buying.

Product Safety. According to the National Commission on Product Safety, it is estimated that about twenty million people injure themselves in their homes each year using various consumer products. In fact, more than 30,000 Americans are killed, 110,000 permanently disabled, and 585,000 hospitalized each year as a result of accidents while using consumer products (Starling, 1980). The major culprits for these injuries are listed in Figure 19.6, which ranks the most hazardous products based on the frequency and severity of accidents. Although it is not possible to protect all people from all accidents, honest efforts must be made to produce safe products and to warn users of potential dangers.

Product Reliability. We hear a great deal about "planned obsolescence," or intentionally designing and manufacturing goods to become obsolete sooner than they should. A study by Lund (1977) found that most appliances, for example, easily could be made to last longer. There remains some doubt, however, concerning the extent to which consumers are willing to pay for such improvements. As Benjamin (1978) notes, "No one has ever documented a case in which firms refused to produce goods of greater durability when customers were willing to pay the costs of added durability." Even so, corporations have a responsibility to ensure product reliability commensurate with the economics of production and efficiency of operation.

The importance of recognizing responsibilities to consumers was emphasized in a survey of top management by *Business Week* ("Corporate Clout," 1977). The survey found that executives by and large stress the value of recognizing the consumer as an integral part of product manufacturing and marketing decisions. In this way the organization gains a competitive edge by making a consumer orientation an integral part of the philosophy.

Figure 19.6
The Most Hazardous Products: The Top Twenty

The twenty goods that the Consumer Product Safety Commission rates most hazardous, based on frequency and severity of accidents involving them are:

1. Bicycles and equipment
2. Stairs, steps, ramps, landings
3. Football equipment, apparel
4. Baseball equipment, apparel
5. Swings, slides, seesaws, other playground equipment
6. Nonglass tables
7. Swimming pools, related equipment
8. Beds
9. Liquid fuels
10. Nails, carpet tacks, screws, thumbtacks
11. Basketball equipment, apparel
12. Chairs, sofas, sofa beds
13. Bleaches, dyes, cleaning agents, caustic compounds
14. Architectural glass, including glass doors
15. Floors and flooring materials
16. Cooking ranges, ovens, related equipment
17. Lawn mowers
18. Skates, skateboards, scooters
19. Furnaces
20. Bathtubs and nonglass shower enclosures

Source: Data from Consumer Product Safety Commission, 1977, as cited in Starling, 1984, p. 339.

Responsibilities to Investors

Corporations have both a legal and a moral responsibility to investors to describe adequately and truthfully the current financial status of the organization. This responsibility typically is fulfilled by circulating audited annual reports to shareholders. One of the primary purposes of the Securities and Exchange Commission is to ensure the publication and accuracy of such data. But beyond reporting current financial activities, corporate officers also have a responsibility to be good trustees of the corporation's resources. This means that future investments and expenditures must be prudent and sound and must reflect the interests of those who are supplying the money for such activities.

Responsibilities to Employees

Perhaps the most difficult area of social responsibility, in terms of the sheer number of problems involved, is an organization's responsibilities to its employees. The contemporary work environment is changing rapidly. The changes require considerable effort by managers seeking to provide the most rewarding and effective work environment. What sorts of changes are occurring? According to Starling (1980, pp. 473–474), at least nine major changes in the work situation can be detected. These are:

1. New technology (such as voice analyzers, computer data banks, and television surveillance) has infringed on employee privacy in some companies.

2. Post–World War II economic trends have drastically reduced the percentage of the work force that labor unions have traditionally looked to for membership.

3. New economic trends, by increasing the number of technical people in the work force, have necessitated certain changes in the leadership style of managers.

4. New values and attitudes (such as suspicion of authority and desire for rewarding work) have placed new pressures on managers in general and human resources directors in particular.

5. New laws (such as the Civil Rights Act of 1964 and the Occupational Safety and Health Act of 1970) have established new regulators to look over the manager's shoulder.

6. Stiffer competition from overseas has, in several industries, resulted in the formation of new management-labor alliances in the United States.

7. Demographic change and federal legislation have forced employers to reconsider retirement policies.

8. Because so many married women are now working, both they and their husbands often find themselves with more money and less time to spend it than

ever before. As a result, many two-income couples have begun to pressure employers for new benefits (such as more flexible working hours or less work time).

9. During the 1980s, with the ranks of new entrants into the labor market severely thinned by the passing of the "baby-boom" years, employers will have to adjust to a relative shortage of labor for the entry positions in business.

Managers need to respond in concrete and creative ways to these pressures. We shall consider four such areas of management concern: equal employment opportunity and affirmative action, occupational safety and health, employee privacy, and quality of working life. Taken together, these four areas represent a blueprint for managerial action aimed at providing a fair, safe, productive, and satisfying workplace.

Equal Employment Opportunity and Affirmative Action. Recent history has seen numerous lawsuits and countersuits claiming discrimination. Most prominent among those initiating the complaints have been minority employees, older workers, and women. The picture that develops is one that seems to be substantiated by the facts: many organizations have historically favored the young, the white, and the male in decisions involving hiring, promotion, and compensation.

To realize the magnitude of the problem and the economic costs to organizations, consider the 1973 settlement against American Telephone and Telegraph Company, in which the company agreed to give 26,000 of its female and minority employees immediate wage increases totalling $35 million in the first year alone, plus an additional $15 million for past discrimination. Other examples can be cited. The point is that job discrimination, besides being unfair, can be costly.

In an effort to remedy past problems, Congress passed a series of laws and presidents have issued executive orders aimed at equalizing employment opportunity and correcting past practices. Although a detailed examination of these laws is beyond the scope of our analysis, we can briefly summarize several of the more important laws and orders:

* *Civil Rights Act of 1964.* Commonly known as Title VII, this act forbids discrimination by employers of fifteen or more persons on the basis of race, color, religion, sex, or national origin. Under this act, employees who feel unfairly treated can file a charge with the Equal Employment Opportunity Commission. If found guilty by this agency, employers can be fined and instructed to change their personnel practices.
* *Equal Pay Act of 1963.* This act requires that women be paid the same wage as men for doing substantially the same work — that is, work requiring equal skill, equal effort, and equal responsibility.
* *Age Discrimination in Employment Act of 1967.* Under this act, age discrimination is outlawed in hiring and promotion decisions, and in any other aspect of work.

- *Federal Rehabilitation Act of 1973.* Disabled or handicapped workers are protected from discrimination under this act.
- *Executive Orders 11246 and 11375.* President Lyndon Johnson issued two executive orders that require all companies doing business with the federal government to initiate results-oriented affirmative action programs aimed at redressing past discriminatory practices in hiring, compensation, and promotion.

As a result of these various laws and orders, considerable progress has been recorded in reducing or eliminating job discrimination and attempting to build a new order based on equality and equal opportunity. If this progress is to con-

---

Feature 19.4
Suit May Change Salary System

For years now Allstate Insurance Co. has paid its new agents with a combination of commissions and a minimum salary guarantee, based in part on previous earnings. The object, presumably, was to give trainees an assurance that they wouldn't starve, while still keeping them hungry for their commissions.

Sound reasonable? Well, it didn't to Lola Kouba, 35, who took a job with Allstate about ten years ago. "Soon after she began working, it became clear to her that all the men had a higher minimum monthly guarantee than she did," says her lawyer, Judith Kurtz, a staff attorney with Equal Rights Advocates, Inc., a public interest law firm in San Francisco that deals exclusively with sex discrimination suits. "My client agitated and she was given a slightly higher minimum guarantee. But she still felt she was being treated unfairly, so she filed suit on behalf of all the other female sales agents and trainees at Allstate."

Kouba received a summary judgment in her favor. The judge concluded that since Allstate used prior earnings information to help set its minimum guarantee, the company should make sure previous employers weren't discriminating. Otherwise, Allstate's policies merely reinforced existing inequities.

That decision was overturned on ap-

peal, but the Kouba case isn't over. Lawyers for both sides think it may ultimately be resolved in the Supreme Court. In the meantime corporate lawyers are watching the proceedings carefully. If Kouba wins, not only will Allstate have to fork over millions of dollars to a sizable number of female sales personnel, but thousands of other firms soon may be in court facing similar complaints. . . .

Allstate and its lawyers . . . claim that Kurtz and her client totally misunderstand the purpose of the minimum guarantee. "It is not intended as pay," says Shayle Fox, a partner at the Chicago law firm of Fox & Groves. "After new employees are trained, in eight weeks or so, they should be earning in excess of their guarantees. That money is simply an estimate of what it would take for a person to survive during the period of time when he starts selling insurance. And a measure of survival is what someone was surviving on before he took the job."

So, Allstate's lawyers claim, the company was hardly discriminating. It was just trying to do business in the best way it knew how. . . .

Source: Forbes, September 26, 1983, "A Measure of Survival?" pp. 124–128. Reprinted by permission. © Forbes Inc., 1983.

tinue, however, it is important that corporations take the initiative and accept responsibility for continued improvement in the workplace.

Occupational Safety and Health. A second area receiving considerable attention in recent years is the corporate responsibility to provide a safer working environment. Although scientific investigations into worker safety and industrial accidents can be traced back to the fifteenth century, little serious effort was made to improve the safety of the workplace until the early 1900s. Before this time the employee suffered the cost of industrial accidents. Several attempts were made by various states, including Maryland in 1902, Montana in 1909, and New York in 1910, to introduce workmen's compensation laws, but these laws were overturned quickly by the state supreme courts. It was only after a March 1911 fire at the Triangle Shirtwaist Company factory in New York City that the situation began to change. In this fire 154 employees, mostly young women, died because the doors to the factory had been kept locked "to safeguard employers from the loss of goods by the departure of workers" (Schnapper, 1972, p. 358). As a result of this tragedy, workmen's compensation laws and factory safety inspection laws began to be enacted.

In 1970 an attempt was made by the United States Congress to provide a systematic legal framework for enforcing occupational safety. This *Occupational Safety and Health Act* aimed to ensure "so far as possible every working man and woman in this nation safe and beautiful working conditions." The Occupational Safety and Health Administration was established to enforce laws in this area. The extent of these regulations can be seen in Figure 19.7, which lists the top ten industrial safety violations as determined by the Occupational Safety and Health Administration.

Although this agency has been criticized for being overly zealous and heavy handed in its enforcement procedures, major changes in regulations and enforcement procedures were made in 1977. The responsibility still rests with management to take serious steps to ensure employee safety and health on the job, however. This responsibility can be demonstrated in serious efforts to eliminate hazardous working conditions, such as faulty or unsafe machines, cluttered workspaces, or improper work clothes, and in employee training programs that enable employees to contribute to the effort.

Employee Privacy. Although less legislation exists in this area, employers do have a responsibility to protect their employees from unwarranted invasions of their personal privacy. Invasion of privacy can happen in many ways: irrelevant questions may be asked during employment interviews, one-sided information or memos may be placed in an employee's personnel file, or confidential information from personnel files may be given to outsiders.

Often the issue is more perceived than actual. Although abuses by employers exist, a more common problem is the rumors and misconceptions that are created in employees' minds about possible management abuses. As Westin

Figure 19.7
The Top Ten Safety Violations

1. National electrical code requirements (from loose wires to underground equipment)

2. Safety of abrasive wheel machinery

3. Construction and placement of compressed gas containers

4. Marking of exits

5. Safety of pulleys in mechanical power-transmission gear

6. Maintaining portable fire extinguishers

7. Safety of drives in mechanical power-transmission gear

8. Guarding floor and wall openings, platforms, and runways

9. General housekeeping requirements (from unmopped puddles to flammable rubbish piles)

10. Effectiveness of machinery guards

Source: Occupational Safety and Health Administration, 1975, as cited in Starling, 1980, p. 503.

("Private Files," 1978) notes, "You have to worry about the fantasies of workers about what is in the record; employee access to records is the only way to hold down wild rumors and misconceptions." As a result, many corporations go to great length to provide employees with information about the contents of their personnel files. For example, International Business Machines Corporation tells employees precisely the purpose of their health questionnaire, and Cummins Engine Company tells employees all the possible uses of its employee-profile form within the corporation.

Managers have a dual responsibility. They must ensure that employee privacy on such matters as employment records is protected, and they must reassure the employees of this protection. In this way greater trust and confidence are established as employees come to feel that they are indeed being treated as responsible adults.

Quality of Working Life. In 1973 a landmark study of worker attitudes in the United States was published by the Department of Health, Education, and Welfare. The book, entitled *Work in America,* drew three conclusions concerning the problems of the American worker. First, it concluded that employees were becoming increasingly dissatisfied with their jobs and that this disaffection negatively influenced the economic and social strength of the country. Second, it concluded that various forms of dysfunctional social behavior relating to work were on the rise. These included absenteeism and turnover, boredom, alcoholism and drug abuse, family instability, and "unbalanced" political ideas. The study concluded that the two primary causes of these work-related problems were the diminishing opportunities for employees to be their own bosses and a continued belief by many managers in the outmoded ideas of scientific management.

These findings are not new. As early as 1835 Alexis de Tocqueville came to the same conclusion:

> When a workman is increasingly and exclusively engaged in the fabrication of one thing, he ultimately does his work with singular dexterity; but at the same time he loses the general faculty of applying his mind to the direction of the work. He every day becomes more adroit and less industrious; so that it may be said of him that in proportion as the workman improves, man is degraded. What can be expected of a man who has spent twenty years of his life making heads for pins? [1956, p. 217]

Recent times have witnessed significant efforts by organizations to improve the quality of working life and make better use of their human resources. These efforts are occurring on several fronts. For example, many companies are attempting to increase employee participation in decisions affecting their jobs. One lesson evident from the recent economic problems in the United States is that Japanese firms make far better use of their employees' skills and knowledge in the decision-making process. We sometimes assume that one needs a college diploma to be qualified to make a decision. Greater employee input into decision making, combined with greater autonomy and responsibility — often together called "job enrichment" — provides employees with a more challenging and rewarding work environment. From such efforts the organization derives the benefits of a more motivated, productive work force, and the employee sees increased meaning in the tasks performed.

Thus, an organization's responsibilities to its employees are widespread and costly in terms of both time and money. The decision for the organization is whether to attempt to "drag its feet" in many of these legally mandated areas or to take an active role in ensuring that its employees are fairly treated and are provided with opportunities for personal growth on the job. Legally, morally, and on the grounds of increased organizational effectiveness, evidence suggests the need to recognize employees as partners in the corporate enterprise. In this way greater human resources are available to contribute in meaningful ways to attaining organizational objectives.

Responsibilities to Society

The final area of corporate social responsibility focuses on an organization's debt to society. We have already discussed many such responsibilities, because employees, investors, and consumers are all part of society. There are at least two other areas of responsibility, however.

First, organizations — particularly manufacturing organizations — have a responsibility in the area of environmental pollution. Figure 19.8 shows how various business operations, such as production, processing, and use, can have detrimental effects on the environment. Various laws have been passed in the

Figure 19.8
The Environmental Effects of Resource Use in Business Operations

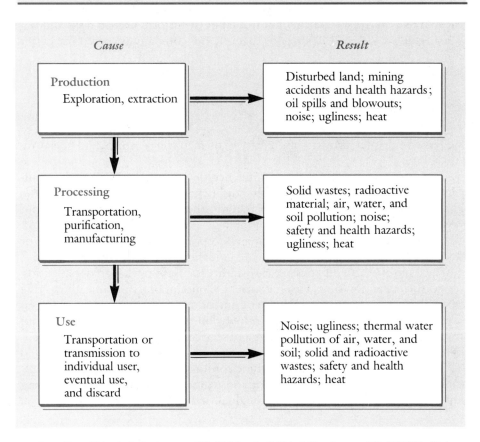

Cause	Result
Production Exploration, extraction	Disturbed land; mining accidents and health hazards; oil spills and blowouts; noise; ugliness; heat
Processing Transportation, purification, manufacturing	Solid wastes; radioactive material; air, water, and soil pollution; noise; safety and health hazards; ugliness; heat
Use Transportation or transmission to individual user, eventual use, and discard	Noise; ugliness; thermal water pollution of air, water, and soil; solid and radioactive wastes; safety and health hazards; heat

Source: From *Living in the Environment,* Third Edition, by G. Tyler Miller, Jr., page 242. © 1982 by Wadsworth, Inc. Reprinted by permission of Wadsworth Publishing Company, Belmont, California 94002.

last decade aimed at minimizing pollution, but the costs of the efforts required can be staggering. For example, the Interior Department's environmental impact study for the Alaska pipeline stood ten feet high and cost $9 million to compile. The $9 million did not include the costs of environmental protection itself. Even so, a balance must be achieved between the impact of manufacturing processes on the environment and economic reality.

Organizations also have responsibility in the area of unemployment. All organizations are adversely affected by rising unemployment rates; therefore, the attitude of "let someone else do it" fails to be persuasive. In some countries it is believed that the national government should be the employer of last resort and that employment must be paid for by taxes collected from corporations. A wiser strategy may be for organizations to take a proactive stance again and assume some share of the burden. A good example of such responsibility is the decision by Kawasaki to use its "excess" employees at its Lincoln, Nebraska, factory to do civic work in the town instead of laying them off in 1981. As a result the city of Lincoln received the social benefit of free labor to perform needed tasks and Kawasaki retained a skilled labor pool that left the company prepared for better economic times.

Summary

The present chapter provides an overview of managerial ethics and social responsibility.

There are two general areas of influence on the ethical behavior of managers: (1) the manager's internal values and (2) external influences such as the behavior of a supervisor or peers on the job, the work situation climate, and pressures for money and achievement.

To overcome ethical pressures, many corporations have written codes of ethics to constrain behavior and provide guidelines for acceptable practices.

The issue of corporate social responsibility focuses on what an organization does to society and what it does for society. Contemporary organizations have responsibilities to various stakeholders, including consumers, investors, employees, and society. They have the responsibility to use good judgment and honesty in claims about their products and services and to produce safe and reliable products.

Responsibilities to employees include conforming to various laws and regulations concerning equal employment and worker safety and health, ensuring employee privacy, and maintaining the quality of working life.

Questions for Discussion

1. What is meant by managerial ethics? Why are ethics in business important? Why are they necessary?
2. What factors influence the development of managerial ethics?
3. How effective do you believe corporate codes of ethics are? How could corporations make them more effective?
4. Define *stakeholder*. What are some of the more important stakeholders of a typical business organization?
5. Are stakeholders different for a small business and a major corporation?
6. Of the various laws passed to improve employee rights and protection, which one do you believe has been most significant? Why?
7. How can companies balance the need for employee privacy against the "need to know" about employees in the legitimate pursuit of organizational effectiveness?

8. What in your opinion is a large corporation's most important responsibility to society at large? Defend your answer.

9. How does an organization know when it is doing a "good job" in the area of corporate social responsibility?

10. Do we need more laws to protect employees, investors, and consumers from corporate behavior? Explain your answer, and use relevant examples.

Case Study
Beneficial Builders

Beneficial Builders is a major subdivision home builder in southern California. During the last fifteen years it has developed seven large subdivisions in the Los Angeles area. Its policy is to buy large tracts of land on the edges of suburbs and build good-quality, low-cost homes for working families. In order to keep costs low, Beneficial Builders uses only a few house plans in each subdivision, enabling it to precut lumber and subassemble walls, door frames, windows, cabinets, and other house parts in its shops. There are several variations of the front, or "elevation," of the houses, so that the houses are not identical in appearance.

A shopping center and 800 homes had been planned for the Hills East subdivision, located in high foothills 50 miles east of Los Angeles. Over 700 homes had been built and sold when heavy winter rains started. After the ground had been thoroughly soaked, an unprecedented 12-inch rainfall occurred on Monday night in the foothills just above the subdivision. A stream that drained these foothills ran through the center of Hills East. In planning this subdivision, Beneficial Builders recognized that heavy thunderstorms did occur in the area, so it widened and straightened the stream bed according to a plan approved by county engineers.

The rain sent torrents of water down the steep stream bed at an estimated 30 miles an hour. It appeared that the stream bed was adequate until the fast, high water uprooted a giant eucalyptus tree on the edge of the stream and carried it ⅓ mile to a highway bridge. The tree lodged against the bridge and held fast, soon collecting other debris until it blocked an estimated 60 percent of the streamflow. The lake created behind the bridge soon flooded a few homes, and even worse, it caused a major streamflow over a low spot in the highway 100 yards

from the bridge. This overflow could not return to the stream bed, so it continued down a street for several blocks, horizontal to the stream but one block away.

Soon there was a torrent of raging water 3 to 5 feet deep in this overflow route. Homeowners were awakened suddenly about 5:30 A.M. by the sound of water running through their houses and cars crashing against carports and house walls. Water rose above 3 feet in over twenty-five houses, and occupants had to flee to roofs or to a second story if they had one. Walls and doors were torn away, but no house was swept from its foundation. Two persons were swept away by the current and drowned.

In a few hours the flood subsided, leaving a jumble of automobiles, uprooted trees, furniture, and house parts. Forty houses and thirty-five automobiles had damage estimated at $300,000. National Guard, civil defense, armed services, and city police helped restore order and provided trucks to haul away debris. Light showers continued, but the stream was back in its bed, and no further flooding was predicted. All utilities including water were disrupted, and none of the damaged homes could be occupied.

Glen Abel, president of Beneficial Builders, heard of the flood early in the morning and drove directly to his subdivision. He talked with public officials on the scene and with dazed and shocked residents. Although some were understandably bitter, there was no evidence that they thought the flood had been caused by poor design of the subdivision. Their homes had received the same heavy rains that hit the foothills, so they knew the rainfall was torrential. A flood victim described his experience to Abel as follows: "When I woke up, the water was leaking through the walls at the joints. We all started picking things off the floor so they wouldn't get wet, and then there was a crash as the water broke a plate-glass window and an outside door.

"The furniture started to float on top of the water, and big pieces like our dresser fell over. I knew then that we had to get out, but I didn't know how or where to go.

"I started to the boys' room, but before I got there the bedroom wall gave way and they came floating right by me out into the yard, both in their beds. I started after them, sort of swimming. Finally I reached one of the boys, still on his bed, and I handed him up to my neighbor on the roof of his house. I just handed him up; the water was so high, I didn't stand on a ladder or anything. Somebody else reached my other boy and put him on a roof.

"My house is still standing and the roof is good, but most of the walls are gone. I really don't know how it all happened, because you couldn't see anything in the dark."

Abel checked with city street engineers at the bridge, and they reported that the stream bed had proved large enough to hold the flood and that there was no overflow except that caused by the blocked bridge. On the basis of these discussions and all other evidence he had, Abel concluded that the subdivision drainage design was sound and that his firm had no liability for the damages.*

Although no company liability was evident, Abel was nevertheless distressed by suffering caused by the flood. He felt sure that the homeowners had no insurance protection against floods; hence many home buyers faced the loss of all their savings or might be forced into personal bankruptcy. He knew that these wage-earning residents, most with young families, were not financially prepared to cope with losses this large.

From a business point of view, Abel recognized that even though the Hills East subdivision was nearly sold out, any remaining sales would be handicapped by publicity about the flood. He reasoned that many persons would not be able to repair their homes, which would leave eyesores of wrecked buildings until mortgage settlements were made. He expected that various types of lawsuits and legal

---

* Weeks later a special engineering report requested by the city council and made by city engineers concluded that the flood was an "act of God" and that no negligence was evident.

entanglements would develop among homeowners, automobile insurers, real estate mortgagors, chattel mortgagors (furniture and appliances), finance companies, and others.

While on the scene Abel checked with city engineers and determined that they would work with civil defense and National Guard truckers to clear all debris and return furniture to homes. The city would rebuild streets. Abel also worked with officers of the Hills East Community Improvement Association to arrange for flood victims to live temporarily with neighbors. The improvement association was a voluntary community group encouraged by Beneficial Builders when the first home buyers moved to Hills East.

Later that afternoon Abel returned to his downtown office several miles from Hills East in order to discuss with his associates what might be done for the flood victims. They considered asking the state governor for state flood aid, but delayed for two reasons. First, they felt that government aid should be requested only when all private and public self-help, such as the American Red Cross, was insufficient. Second, government aid would probably require much red tape and delay, and action was needed now.

They were discussing what direct action Beneficial Builders might take, when Arch Smith, the union business agent for Beneficial workers, arrived and asked whether the union might help. He said that he had talked informally with several union leaders and could guarantee 200 volunteer carpenters and other selected skilled workers all day Saturday and Sunday to repair all structural damage to houses, if someone would supply materials, equipment, and supervision.

After extended discussion, Beneficial executives and Smith decided they would take direct action to repair all flood damage with donated labor and materials, provided Apex Lumber Company would donate lumber and building materials. Apex was considered the key to this plan, for lumber was the main building material needed. If Apex agreed, Abel and Smith believed that all lesser services would "fall in line." Apex was one of the largest building suppliers in the West, and it had been the principal supplier of Beneficial Builders since Beneficial Builders was organized.

If Apex accepted, the following plan would be

used. All services would be donated. All homes would be restored to approximately their original condition, except for furniture and household supplies. A newspaper release would announce that the restoration was a joint effort of businesses, unions, and community agencies. Appeals for help would be made privately through existing groups; there would be no public appeal playing upon emotions and possibly leading to disorganized action. Unions would provide sufficient skilled labor (an estimated 200 workers) for ten hours daily on Saturday and Sunday and the following weekend if necessary. Beneficial Builders would provide supervision, shop services, and construction equipment (worth an estimated $20,000 wholesale). Apex would provide all building materials (worth an estimated $30,000 wholesale). Community agencies would be asked to supply unskilled labor (about 100 workers). Other groups employed by Beneficial Builders to construct its subdivisions would be asked to donate services, such as plumbing and electrical work, appliance repair, landscaping, and painting. All services except painting would be donated for the forthcoming weekend so that homes would be livable on Monday. Painting would be donated the following two weekends. The Red Cross or some other service agency would be asked to provide food and coffee for all volunteer labor.

Abel and Smith were convinced that 95 percent of the repairs could be made in one weekend because of the fortuitous circumstance that Beneficial's shops had completed cutting and assembling all components for the last fifty houses in the Hills East subdivision on the Friday before the flood. These components provided a ready-made inventory matching most of the houses destroyed. In the few instances where necessary items were not as-

sembled, Abel promised to work his shops overtime to assure that all needed precut materials and subassemblies would be delivered to the carport of each home by 6:00 P.M. Friday. This procedure probably would delay by ten days the completion of the remaining fifty houses because new lumber would have to be cut and assembled. Some persons who had bought one of these fifty houses might be inconvenienced or have added expenses if they had already promised to vacate their present residence and move to Hills East on a certain date, believing that their homes would be available at that time.

By the time Abel and Smith completed their plans, it was 7:30 P.M. They telephoned Abe Silver, southern California manager of Apex Lumber, at his home near Los Angeles. When he learned the purpose of their call, he agreed to an appointment in his home at 9:00 P.M. that evening.

At 9:03 P.M. Abel and Smith rang the doorbell of Silver's palatial home.

Case Questions

1. If you were Abel, what presentation would you make to Silver? If you were Smith, what would you do? Role play the 9:00 P.M. meeting of Abel, Smith, and Silver.

2. Who are the different claimants in this situation, and what are their benefit expectations?

3. What general policies should the cooperating businesses adopt for managing this emergency?

4. What are the possible risks and rewards of involvement by Apex Lumber in this situation?

Source: Reprinted by permission from *Business and Society,* Fourth Edition, by K. Davis, W. Frederick, and R. Blomstrom, pages 573–577. Copyright © 1980 by McGraw-Hill, Inc.

PART V

The Future of Management

There are signs that smokestack America is reversing its aging process.

"Remarkable things are going on in numerous plants throughout the country — at auto, industrial engine, agricultural machinery, and steel factories," said the late William Abernathy, a Harvard Business School professor and co-author of *Industrial Renaissance.*

Abernathy called what now is happening in the nation's mills and factories "dematurity." It is a process using automation and innovative management that is returning these industries to a zestier stage of development.

"High tech with a dirty face and greasy fingernails," is what James Baker, a senior vice-

president at General Electric Company, calls the pioneering use of robots, computers, and telecommunications on the plant floor. "The technology to make our industries world-competitive has been here for years," Baker said. "We invented most of it. All that's needed is the guts to try it."

One example of this renaissance is the shoe industry, which had been struggling for years. New Balance Athletic Shoe Inc. of Boston, Massachusetts, is one of the companies at the forefront of the revival. New Balance doubled its sales each of the past three years. It has had great success with its line of running shoes, which are designed by an orthopedic surgeon

CHAPTER 20

Managing Effective Organizations in the Future

and made of new, high-tech materials. Now the company is branching out into other specialized footwear using the same innovative production techniques and materials.

There are other transformations too. General Electric's locomotive plant in Erie, Pennsylvania, and the Nucor Corporation, a steel company based in Charlotte, North Carolina, are using high-tech hardware and their workers more efficiently. And there is new life in the small truck industry and in plants like the Goodyear Tire and Rubber Company's Topeka, Kansas, tire plant, among others.

Analysts believe the United States has all it needs for an industrial renaissance. It has a healthy capital market, an abundance of raw materials, and a big edge in microprocessors, communications, industrial robots, and other technologies that can open up a new "golden age" for manufacturing.

Source: Reprinted with the permission of *Dun's Business Month,* (formerly *Dun's Review*), July 1983, Copyright 1983, Dun & Bradstreet Publications Corporation.

Chapter Outline

- Trends That May Influence Organizations
- Challenges of Managing in the Future

Chapter Objectives

After studying Chapter 20 you should be able to

1. See why it is important for managers to anticipate events.
2. Understand the implications of the shift toward decentralization.
3. Describe how computer technology is changing the workplace.
4. Determine how the changing work force will affect organizations.
5. Understand why top-level managers must be increasingly sensitive to what is happening in the world around them.

Introduction

It is often said that we can predict the past with a great deal of precision and the future with relative impunity.

Historians interpret past events, and those who predict the future usually deal with events few, if any, of us will live to witness. The business manager, however, must operate in an ever-changing, complex, often turbulent world. He or she must make decisions based on imperfect information about the present with only educated guesses about how future events will affect those decisions.

Few managers could have predicted the 1973 Mideast oil embargo, which was to have a tremendous effect on many organizations. Partially because of the oil shortage, automobile executives began the costly and time-consuming process of switching production from large to small cars. Then, when overcapacity in the oil industry resulted in declining fuel prices in the early 1980s, the consumer's taste for larger cars returned. Automobile manufacturers found themselves in an uncomfortable position: The demand for larger cars could not be met with existing plants and equipment. Companies that only a few years earlier had been heroes for quickly increasing their capacity to produce compact and subcompact cars found themselves competing with the Japanese in a segment of the market that was becoming less popular with their customers.

RCA, often considered one of the best-managed firms in the United States, increased its capacity to produce video discs ahead of consumer demand. Normally this would have been a very effective strategy. But a severe, prolonged recession cut consumer demand for most durable goods, particularly those with a disadvantage in price compared with more established technologies — such as video cassette recorders. Had this strategy worked, the wisdom of high-level executives at RCA would have been unquestioned. Unforeseen events made the strategy ultimately unsuccessful, however, and these same managers drew criticism about their effectiveness. Moreover, RCA accumulated losses totaling $580 million on video discs ("RCA Quits Making," 1984).

It is impossible to predict the future with precision. And because the consequences of managerial decisions often become evident in a short time, predictions seldom can be made with impunity either. Even so, it is important for managers to look into the future and anticipate events that can have important implications for what the organization does today. As technologies become increasingly complex, the costs of building production capacity increase. The investment in time and money required to make basic changes in production capacity limits management's future flexibility. Courses of action may not be changed or reversed without great cost. Therefore, it is increasingly important for managers to anticipate changes, even at a time when uncertainty about the future seems to be increasing.

The purpose of this chapter is to speculate about what it will be like to manage organizations in the next ten to twenty years. The discussion will focus on several forecasts about how the organization's internal and external environment will change in the future. As Bennis (1966, p. 10) observed: "A forecast falls somewhere between a prediction and a prophecy. It lacks the divine guidance of the latter and the empirical foundation of the former." When Bennis made his comments nearly twenty years ago on the changing conditions that would confront organizations in the future, he believed he was on empirical thin ice. The situation has not improved much since then. Some of the trends he mentioned have begun to become evident, although not all of them to the degree or with the speed that he expected.

Our discussion will be organized around the three managerial competencies mentioned in Chapter 1. The environment in which organizations must operate in the future is likely to change, but the importance of these basic competencies is not. Changing events may cause specific skills within each of these areas to shift over time, but the fact remains that managers in the future, like those of today, will need basic competence in technical, behavioral, and strategic areas. These general competencies provide a convenient framework for discussing future trends that may have significance for managers.

Trends That May Influence Organizations

Forecasting what our society and world will be like in the future, although it is not an easy task, has caught the attention of many serious scholars. Some forecasts represent the individual efforts of visionary thinkers like Warren Bennis (1966). Others emerge from the efforts of groups of scholars brought together in research institutes, perhaps the most productive and famous of which is the Hudson Institute founded by the late Herman Kahn. The importance attached to the ability to forecast and prepare for the future more adequately is evident in the widespread popularity of books on this topic. Efforts such as John Naisbitt's *Megatrends* (1982) have been widely discussed and debated. The ten new directions Naisbitt (1982) identified as having the greatest potential for transforming our lives are presented in Figure 20.1. The trends he believed to have the greatest relevance for managers, as well as trends mentioned by a number of other authors, will be discussed next in terms of their implications for managerial competencies.

Before we describe these trends in detail, several points must be made to place the discussion in perspective. First, these are general trends in society and it is possible to identify specific exceptions to them. But the fact that exceptions exist does not necessarily preclude the existence of the trend in the direction suggested. Second, some of these trends may not beome evident on a widespread basis for a number of years, whereas others are evident today. Finally, unforeseen events may either inhibit or accelerate some of these trends. For example, wars, economic embargoes, or changes in political leadership often are difficult to predict yet have significant implications for future directions.

Implications for Technical Competencies

The technical competencies of management discussed in Chapter 1 included the basic management functions of planning, organizing, staffing, di-

Figure 20.1
John Naisbitt's Megatrends

PREDICTED TRENDS

From	To	BRIEF DESCRIPTION
Industrial society	Informational society	Economy based increasingly on production, interpretation, and dissemination of information rather than manufacture of goods
Forced technology	High tech/ high touch	For every major new technology introduced into society, there will increasingly be a counterbalancing human response
National economy	Global economy	Shift from self-sufficient national economy to being part of an interdependent global economy
Short term	Long term	Increasing emphasis placed on long-term planning and performance; reassessment of what business organizations are in
Centralization	Decentralization	Decreasing centralized power in government and organizations; increased bottom-up emphasis
Institutional help	Self-help	Decreasing reliance on government institutions and large organizations for securing basic needs; increasing self-reliance
Representational democracy	Participative democracy	Increased participation of citizens in basic decisions that influence their lives; increasing use of referenda and initiatives
Hierarchies	Networking	Decreasing faith in hierarchical organizations; emphasis on horizontal communication and sharing (ideas, information, resources)
North	South	Shift in population and economic activity from North and East to South and West
Either/or	Multiple options	Decreasing importance of traditional options and roles; increasing individualism and creation of niches.

Source: Naisbitt, 1982.

recting, controlling, and coordinating. In addition, technical competencies include the basic skills and abilities required to perform the tasks under the manager's direction. Several general trends appear to have important implications for these competencies.

Increasing Decentralization. Naisbitt (1982) suggested that movement from a high degree of centralization to greater decentralization is evident at many levels of our society. A shift in power away from the federal government to regional, state, and local government is evidence of this trend. The trend also is evident within organizations. Although the stereotypic model of the large organization is the pyramid in which authority rests at the top, a number of factors may push decision making increasingly downward. As the technologies employed by organizations grow more complex, there is a tendency to make decisions at the level at which the relevant expertise and knowledge exist. In addition, organizations facing increasing competitive pressures and unstable environments have found that they can respond better when decision making is decentralized among operating divisions and smaller units. In many large organizations corporate staffs are shrinking as divisions increasingly assume many of the responsibilities previously performed at headquarters (Peters and Waterman, 1982). This does not mean that higher-level executives will lose their control over the direction of the organization. Naisbitt (1982) argued that it is increasingly irrelevant who holds leadership positions, however — including the presidency of the United States.

Naisbitt (1982) also suggested that organizations increasingly will be structured from the bottom up rather than from the top down. He believes that increasing economic pressures and the changing values of employees will result in much greater attention being paid to the quality of working life. Many managers have been influenced by the success of Japanese management and consider greater employee involvement an economic necessity to slow the decline in productivity. The result will be that more than token attention will be paid to creating more satisfying and fulfilling work environments for *all* employees, not just key executives or the hard-to-replace technical staff. This trend already is evident in many of the largest corporations in the form of quality circles and autonomous work group approaches to job design.

Computerization of the Workplace. Personal computer technology has the potential to change fundamentally the ways in which organizations are structured and managers perform their jobs. Managers have access to increasingly sophisticated computers that can provide more information much more rapidly for decision making. In addition, computers can simulate options to determine their impact on different parts of the organization, and decisions can be communicated instantaneously throughout the organization. The vice-president for planning and business development at Pfizer Pharmaceuticals, for example, uses a microcomputer to simulate the impact of cutting promotion expenses for different products. Computers make this task much easier, as the Pfizer vice-president indicated: "If you had to look through market research books, it would take four weeks. Now you can do it right away. You ask more questions and get more analytic" ("A New Era for Management," 1983, p. 68).

A poll of middle managers conducted for *Business Week* found that 85 percent currently use computer-generated data in their jobs and 91 percent believed that more direct access to computers would increase their productivity ("A New Era for Management," 1983). Perhaps more important from an organizational standpoint, 41 percent believed that the increasing use of computers in managerial work would lead to further consolidation of departments and functions. In addition, more widespread use of computers may alter fundamental power relationships within organizations by increasing access to important information that in the past had been available to only a limited few. Ben W. Heineman, president of Northwest Industries, used to rely on his finance department for summary reports, for example, but now his computer provides direct access to the company's data base ("A New Era for Management," 1983). He can receive detailed information on the performance of Northwest subsidiaries and compare these data with the company's past performance and that of other firms in the industry.

The computerization of the office and workplace is well under way and likely to increase as equipment gets more sophisticated and less expensive. Managers may perform their tasks more often at work stations that link their desks directly with other work stations, company data bases, word processors, and laser printers. Nowhere is the office computer revolution more evident than in Japan. Although it may seem surprising because of Japan's technological sophistication in manufacturing, their business offices are described as archaic:

> In sharp contrast to its highly automated factories, the majority of Japanese offices are still out of the nineteenth century. Few office workers use telephones except to convey simple messages, and scores of desks are often crammed together in a single room. New employees learn from old ones and develop their own filing and accounting methods, a long-honored custom that has led to unindexed filing systems that make it impossible for anyone to find a document without the person who actually filed it ["Office Automation," 1983, p. 122].

For managers in the United States and Japan, more sophisticated use of computers may be a prerequisite for effective job performance. Computers also may dramatically increase the manager's ability to monitor and control the work of others, enabling him or her to take corrective action when problems are uncovered in a far more timely fashion than is currently possible.

Fewer Managers with Greater Responsibility. One result of increasing decentralization and the use of computers in organizations is that often fewer managers are needed. *Business Week* ("A New Era for Management," 1983) reported that many large corporations have eliminated middle-management positions, pushing responsibility downward in the organization and creating more direct communication between operational levels and top executives. The Container Group at Crown Zellerbach Corporation recently eliminated three levels of management, for instance. Division presidents at Brunswick Corporation report directly to the chief executive officer now that the positions of chief operating officer and group vice-presidents have been abolished. The result is that many organizations have fewer hierarchical levels

Feature 20.1
Computers: The New Generation

Even as we marvel at the speed and the usefulness of the computer in the business office, a revolutionary new generation of these wonders in being born.

This next generation reportedly will not be limited to processing instructions from users. It will have the capability that now distinguishes people from computers — creating knowledge from raw information. The new machines will be able to summarize, shape, interpret, and transform the information they contain.

Systems already under development are being designed to assist doctors in diagnosing complicated medical problems. The INTERNIST/CADUCEUS system covers more than 80 percent of all internal medicine with a knowledge base that includes 500 diseases and 3,500 symptoms. Doctors and physicians' assistants using the sytem will be able to put in a patient's symptoms and be given a diagnosis.

Similar systems may have widespread application in business. Several oil exploration firms have begun development of expert computer systems to analyze problems encountered on site in oil drilling. Hitachi reportedly is developing several systems that will help diagnose manufacturing problems in their plants.

Digital Equipment Corporation is using an expert computer system to help design computers to customer specifications. The Digital system is said to plan correctly 99 percent of the time, eliminating costly errors that previously had gone undetected until well along in the production process.

Another corporation is said to be talking about an expert system that would be able to capture the knowledge and expertise of higher-level managers expected to retire soon from the firm. Their information would be available to the younger managers who would replace them.

Computers also are being designed that eliminate the need for managers to know programming languages. Instead, communication with the computer will take place through everyday conversational language, or even through handwriting or pictures.

Managers need not even be very precise about the problems they are dealing with, because the computer will be able to reason things out for itself or ask a series of questions that will lead to the answer. The computer and manager working together will be able not only to solve problems, but to formulate them as well.

Technological innovations in communication and computers have already changed how managers work. In the future, these changes could be even more dramatic.

Source: The Fifth Generation by Edward A. Feigenbaum and Pamela McCorduck, Reading, MA: Addison-Wesley, 1983, pp. 63–75.

and more direct communication among managers. If this trend continues, organizations in the future may have fewer managers but those who remain will assume greater responsibility and have clearer lines of authority and more direct communication with others. The problem of coordinating activities within organizations should become easier as hierarchies are streamlined and direct communication is made simpler.

The general trends discussed in this section suggest that the technical competence of managers will become even more crucial to effective job performance in the future. Although computerization and its consequences may make planning, directing, controlling, and coordinating the efforts of others easier, managers will need to become more sophisticated to use these tools properly. It may no longer be possible for managers to have a passing familiarity with computers and rely on the staff to perform the more complex operations. Rather, managers will need to know how to use computers themselves and will require access to complicated analytical techniques if the information made available by the computer is to be utilized effectively. As the technological sophistication of organizations increases, so will the demands placed on the technical competence of managers.

Implications for Behavioral Competencies

The behavioral competencies important for management largely involve interpersonal processes, including the ability to communicate with others, resolve conflict, manage group processes, motivate employees, and effectively influence what goes on in the organization. Several general trends have implications for these competencies.

Changing Work Force Demographics. The nature and composition of the work force in the United States have undergone dramatic changes in the past decade, and additional changes can be expected. Freeman (1979) identified several trends that appear especially important. First, the proportion of people aged from sixteen to twenty-four years in the work force is expected to decline 6 percent from 1975 to 1990, whereas the proportion aged from twenty-five to forty-four will increase by 55 percent. Thus, on the average the work force is becoming older. Fewer young people will be available to enter organizations, and the high proportion of employees at mid-career suggests that, once hired, there may be few places for them to advance.

The ability to reward employees with promotion may therefore decline in the future. Byrne and Konrad (1983) have noted that many organizations that established a management "fast track" when business was expanding and managers were in short supply have begun to slow the promotion process. Instead, these organizations are emphasizing higher-quality management development in job assignments for young managers with potential rather than highly visible and rapid advancement up the hierarchy.

Second, the work force is increasingly better educated. The proportion of employees who have completed college is expected to increase, particularly among those twenty-five to forty-four years of age. With fewer young people entering the work force, however, the rate of increase in mean years of schooling and the proportion of the total work force with higher education will decline.

Third, the participation of women and minorities in the work force has been increasing and should continue to increase in coming years. Naisbitt (1982) indicates that 19 million new jobs were created in the United States during the 1970s, and Freeman (1979) estimates that the total civilian labor force over the age of sixteen will increase by 23.7 percent between 1975 and 1990. A large number of new employees have entered the work force in recent years, many of whom are women who in the past might have been solely home-makers. Moreover, affirmative action plans and equal employment opportunity legislation have opened the career options available to women and minority group members, thus increasing competition for what might be considered the most desirable jobs.

Changing Employee Values. In part because of the increasing educational level of employees, basic work values and attitudes have undergone major changes. Katzell (1979) cites a number of important trends in work attitudes that have implications for how we manage in organizations. First, he believes, employees are increasingly concerned with the long-range career implications of jobs rather than their more immediate payoffs. Second, employees are placing greater importance on the intrinsic features of jobs, such as autonomy and responsibility, and less on material considerations. Third, employees want and expect a greater voice in what transpires in the workplace. Fourth, employees are increasingly concerned about the quality of their working life, even if this quality must come at the expense of corporate profits or productivity. Finally, employees are less inclined to work hard out of habit or conscience. Rather, Katzell believes, employees increasingly expect to know why they are being asked to do things and to see a connection between what they do and the larger goals of the organization.

Changes in work force demographics and basic work values have important implications for management in organizations. Managers may be able to rely less on traditional extrinsic rewards to motivate employees, with greater attention having to be paid to intrinsic rewards and quality of work life. Although the work force generally is growing older and better educated, the increasing participation of women and minorities may result in a more heterogeneous mix of employees. Conflict may become more apparent and consensus more difficult to achieve among groups of employees who come from very different backgrounds and share different values. This trend will make effective communication even more important, although perhaps more difficult, than when management was dominated by white, Protestant men. The challenges facing management in the area of interpersonal relations within organizations therefore should increase, making behavioral competence even more crucial in the future.

Implications for Strategic Competencies

Decisions about overall strategic direction and the maintenance of relations between the organization and its external environment are the important strategic tasks facing management. Because changing societal and world trends have significant implications for the ways in which decisions are made about these tasks, top-level managers must be increasingly sensitive to what is happening in the world around them.

Feature 20.2
Analysts Look Ahead

. . . (W)hile American business (went) into 1984 in much better shape than it went into 1983, it by no means face(d) a trouble-free future. (Says) consultant Michael Kami, who worked as chief long-range planner in the 1950s and 1960s for IBM, and before that, Xerox: "The right decisions will have to be made faster than in the past. Conservative executives who can't make quick decisions, and won't move in tune with the times, may be the losers." The past couple of years have seen plenty of losers, as companies that once seemed impregnable in their markets — International Harvester, for example — have been sinking toward insolvency or acquisition, or just plain closing their doors.

(Says) TRW's Pat Choate, senior policy analyst: "It's going to be a quick, fast-paced world. And we'll have to think globally. I think we've learned that success in the world economy is not our God-given right. That it's because of the basics of pricing, quality, service and innovation, and that we're not the only people who can do those things. We have to concentrate on the basics." As the Japanese have long done.

MIT economist Charles Kindleberger sees the situation in macroeconomic terms. . . . Says he: "We're seeing the inevitable erosion of the U.S. economic position internationally." It bothers Kindleberger that a lot of Americans react to erosion by wanting to throw up protective walls — just as the French and Japanese have done. But as the world's leading economy, Kindleberger says, the U.S. "has to pay the price in responsibility." He warns against quick fixes: "What's happening now is that the international

monetary system is breaking down. We ought to spend more time coordinating monetary policies with the other industrialized nations. And this business of trying to settle the Third World debt crisis with another big Bretton Woods–type meeting is a bad idea. We're at the edge of the precipice now, and we'll have to inch our way slowly back.

"If we get together and talk about all the debt in the world, it will make everybody nervous, and the odds are the trouble will get worse."

. . . (Then there's the) view expressed by novelist James Michener, 77, who's been in Texas . . . working on another book. "I think the preempting of the American market by Japanese and European products that are better made has frightened much of the country. And the tremendous amount of wealth we pour into funding our past debt is staggering and inhibits our national life.

"But down here in Texas things are different. If there is a place that ought to be in a depressed mood, it's here. The peso, oil, the collapse of some of the electronics markets and the big bank failures — it's been hard hit. But no one is depressed down here. The mood is ebullient, hopeful. Those mistakes can be corrected. People feel the marketplace will take care of all the empty buildings. And I think they're right. I can see the perils ahead, but we're not a stupid people."

Source: Forbes, January 2, 1984, "Where Do We Go from Here?" by Geoffrey Smith and Jane Sasseen, pp. 36–37. Reprinted by permission. © Forbes Inc., 1984.

From an Industrial to an Informational Society. One of the more interesting observations made by Naisbitt (1982) is that our economy is moving away from one based on the production of goods to one based on the production of information. Daniel Bell's (1976) vision of the postindustrial economy was largely interpreted to mean that growth would take place in the service sector. Naisbitt (1982) points out that the overwhelming proportion of these jobs involves the creation, processing, or distribution of information. Discounting the information-related occupations, employment in the service sector has remained relatively stable during the past thirty years. In contrast, currently 60 percent of all jobs involve work in some way related to information, such as teaching, programming, accounting, law, and stock-brokerage work. The comparable percentage in 1950 was 17 percent.

Jobs in the future are more likely to be characterized by intellectual endeavors than by physical effort. The fact that traditional manufacturing industries in the United States are maturing, if not declining, while jobs are being created in high technology, is evidence of this point. Naisbitt (1982) points out that innovations in computers and communication technology, particularly communication satellites, have increased the speed with which information is available throughout the world. The technological advances in the United States today may very well be known in other countries tomorrow, undermining any competitive advantage in this area.

From a Domestic to a Global Economy. A primary advantage United States industry has had since the turn of the century has been a relatively affluent domestic market characterized by increasing consumer demand. Industries in other countries have found it difficult or impossible to produce goods of equal quality or sophistication. Thus, American firms have enjoyed a competitive advantage based on the domestic market they served. The fact that Japan has enjoyed recent success in traditional industries such as automobile manufacturing, however, is evidence that the situation has changed.

Many American firms have been active in international markets, but only recently have international considerations played a prominent role in strategic thinking. Now markets are being considered in global terms, as suggested by Ford's promotion of the Escort as the "world car." Engines for many Chrysler products now are made in Germany and Japan, and parts made in the United States often are assembled in Singapore and Taiwan. Naisbitt (1982) estimates that by the year 2000, Third World countries will manufacture 30 percent of the world's goods. The importance of national boundaries to economic production is declining, a fact that top-level executives can ignore only at their peril.

The Move South. In the United States a dramatic shift is underway from the North and East to the South and West. Population, wealth, and economic activity have all increased in the "sun belt" states, often at the expense of the industrial Northeast and Midwest. In terms of economic potential, Naisbitt (1982) identifies Florida, Texas, and California as the most important centers of business in the future.

Higher Expectations of Business Organizations. Katzell (1979) believes that society generally is expecting more from large business organizations. More and more it is believed that they have an obligation to contribute to the quality of life and to society, even at the expense of return on investment for their shareholders. Business is being held increasingly accountable for improving the quality of the environment, making safe products, providing a safe work environment, and serving the broader goals of society, such as equal opportunity and affirmative action. Many of these expectations have been formalized in federal legislation and regulations that govern business activity. Although some people consider the role of the federal government in regulating business less important today than it was twenty years ago, the social obligations of organizations are less likely to change. Recent court cases and proposed legislation in such areas as employee dismissal and plant closure — traditionally viewed as management prerogatives — are examples of the changing standards by which organizations will be judged. The public relations campaigns of many large corporations, demonstrating what a good job they are doing in protecting the environment, for example, may reinforce and increase these expectations.

During this time of increasing expectations about the role of organizations, Naisbitt (1982) believes, general confidence in large organizations is decreasing. For example, the ability of a highly centralized and powerful federal government to satisfy the basic needs of citizens and provide for their welfare seems to be declining. This may even be true of business, in which the trend toward large conglomerate organizations existing in the 1970s appears to be declining. It is unrealistic to expect that large organizations will disappear entirely. Many managers, however, have discovered that size and diversification present difficult management problems. For instance, the level of financial performance International Telephone and Telegraph Corporation achieved during its period of rapid acquisition and growth under Harold Geneen has proved difficult to match. Corporate acquisitions undoubtedly will continue, although the trend toward decentralization suggests that acquired firms may retain greater autonomy and independence within larger corporate structures.

The nature of business in the United States appears to be changing. Unlike business in the past, which was characterized by manufacturing oriented toward the domestic economy, business in the future will likely be information based, operating in a global economy. In addition, people may expect more from business in the future, both in the employment relationship and in the broader contributions of business to society. It is safe to say that managers in the future will operate in an environment different from the one that exists today. Managers who understand these changes and adapt their organizations to them are likely to be more effective than those who do not.

Challenges of Managing in the Future

The challenges associated with managing in the future always appear far more formidable than the tasks facing managers today or in the past. This is because there is tremendous uncertainty about future events and how they will affect our activities. We are familiar with the past and the present, but no one can forecast what will happen in the next ten to twenty years with a high degree of certainty.

We are not suggesting that the tasks managers faced in the past were easy or presented fewer challenges. Things certainly must not have seemed that way to Cornelius Vanderbilt in the 1860s as he attempted to acquire the Erie Railroad, for example. While Vanderbilt was buying all the Erie shares available on the market, the men in control of the railroad, Daniel Drew, Jay Gould, and James Fisk, were simply printing more as a result of secret and complicated bond-conversion transactions. Even after Vanderbilt had acquired more Erie Railroad shares than were known to exist, additional shares continued to appear on the market and Vanderbilt still was not in control. Vanderbilt could not buy stock as fast as the men at Erie could print it. As Fisk was reported to have said, "If this printing press don't break down, I'll be damned if I don't give the old hog all he wants of Erie" (Josephson, 1934, p. 127). Two years after Vanderbilt began his quest to acquire the Erie Railroad, he gave up in disgust, swearing never to have another thing to do with that particular railroad — and he never did. The environment Vanderbilt faced in the 1860s presented unique challenges, just as the environment of the 1980s was challenging to William Agee in his attempt to acquire Martin Marietta Corporation for Bendix Corporation.

It is difficult to say whether the environment facing managers will be any more or less challenging in the future. There is no doubt, however, that it will be *different*. If there is one thing managers can count on, it is that things will change. As a result, it will be extremely important for organizations to scan their environments carefully and make changes to adapt to new conditions. Business literature is filled with stories of companies that failed to adapt to a changing environment. There also are stories of firms that anticipated changes that did not materialize, often with equally disastrous results.

After deregulation of the airline industry, Braniff International Airlines quickly expanded its route system, fearing that there would be pressures to return to regulation. Such pressures never materialized but a recession did, leaving Braniff with overcapacity and a poorly planned route structure. After competitive pressures from other airlines, Braniff failed. Anticipating and adapting to changes in the environment may be important for organizations, although not as important as anticipating the *correct* change and adapting appropriately.

The changing nature of the environment facing business also has important implications for students preparing themselves for management careers. Business schools have suffered their share of blame for recent problems in the performance of companies. One cynic suggested that the secret to meeting the Japanese challenge would be to export our masters of business administration programs. Another equally cynical commentator suggested that we send Japan one lawyer for every one of their cars we import, although it is likely Japan would run out of cars long before we exhausted our supply of lawyers.

Business schools often have been criticized for preparing their students in an overly narrow fashion, sacrificing a broader understanding of society and the world for the ability to calculate discounted cash flows. Business education has come a long way from the historical situation described by Bennis (1966,

p. 182), in which it was viewed as "a haven for fools, adventurers, and anemic heirs of industrialists who needed a college degree on the minimum of brains and the maximum of tuition." Bennis suggested that business education in the past was "ranked in the academic hierarchy somewhere between football and a curiously indigenous American course known colloquially as 'home economics,' a curriculum cocktail of cooking, etiquette, and good housekeeping" (p. 166).

It is clear that business schools have achieved a high degree of stature in professional education on most campuses. Business schools can provide students with good training in the complex and sophisticated analytical tools that are needed to manage organizations effectively. There is little doubt that these analytical skills will become even more important as the environment facing managers becomes more complex and changes rapidly.

In addition to these tools, however, business students also require a broader knowledge, which can be acquired through study outside the business schools. Events in society and in the international environment will have increasingly important implications for managers and business organizations. It is important for future managers to be informed about and understand those events if, as seems likely, business increasingly operates on a global rather than a domestic scale and the expectations of society for business keep changing. The management skills discussed in this book provide a good foundation for a future career in organizations, but additional skills also will be required for success.

Summary

It is increasingly important for managers to look to the future and anticipate changes, even though uncertainty about the future is increasing. The business environment of the future is likely to be different, but the importance of basic competence in technical, behavioral, and strategic areas will remain.

In the technical area, there is a shift toward decentralization in organizations. Decisions are being made more often at the level at which the expertise and knowledge exist. Naisbitt suggests that future organizations will be increasingly structured from the bottom up rather than from the top down.

Computer technology is changing the way organizations are structured and managers do their jobs. For many managers, more sophisticated use of computers may be a prerequisite for effective job performance. Decentralization and the greater use of computers often has meant that fewer managers are needed.

Behavioral competencies also are important for managers. The work force is aging and better educated and has an increasingly higher proportion of women and minority group members. Basic work values and attitudes also are changing. Employees are more concerned with long-range career implications of jobs and consider the quality of their working life and such features as autonomy and responsibility important. Employees also are less inclined to work hard out of habit or conscience.

Decisions about the organization's strategic direction and its relations with its external environment are the important strategic tasks facing management. Our economy is moving from the production of goods to the processing of information. The importance of national boundaries to economic production is declining.

Within the United States, a dramatic shift in wealth, population, and economic activity is underway from the North and East to the West and South. Society expects more of business and believes business has an obligation to contribute to society, even at the expense of profits.

Challenges facing managers in the future appear more formidable than those facing managers today. In addition to the knowledge they gain in business schools, students require broader knowledge acquired through study elsewhere.

Questions for Discussion

1. Identify and discuss several examples in which companies either failed to anticipate changes in the environment or anticipated changes that subsequently did not take place. How might these problems have been avoided?
2. What skills will be required by managers to manage effectively in work environments characterized by increasing decentralization?
3. Describe the major impacts on managers and employees of increasing computerization in the work place.
4. What challenges will managers face as the work force ages and the proportion of the work force composed of women and minority group members increases?
5. Compare the changing work values of employees mentioned by Katzell with Naisbitt's views on increasing decentralization and bottom-up organization design. Are these general trends moving in the same or different directions?
6. How will the shift from a domestic to a global economy change the strategic focus of managers?
7. What are the implications faced by managers as a result of the increased societal expectations of the role played by business coexistent with decreasing confidence in large organizations?
8. Are the increasingly technical and analytical skills required to manage effectively in the future likely to be sufficient by themselves for success in a management career? Why or why not?

Exercise 20.1
1995: The Year in Review

Beyond the "here and now" aspects of management — supervising employees, scheduling production, dealing with customers — there remains a strong need for vision, creativity, and proaction concerning the future and the environment of business. As one moves up the organizational hierarchy, this time perspective shifts from tomorrow or next week to one, five, ten, or twenty years into the future. Given this perspective, consider the following assignment:

The year is 1995. You are the editor of the business section of an internationally recognized daily newspaper. At year's end, your job is to prepare a list of the five major stories in the business world for the preceding year. Write the headline and draft (or be prepared to elaborate) the first sentences of each of the five major business stories that you would expect for that year.

Questions

1. What are the implications for business of each of the stories you identified?

2. Research or speculate on predictions made in the *past* concerning how futurists predicted the way life would be *today*. Were the predictions fulfilled? What events were not anticipated?

Source: Reprinted with permission of Macmillan Publishing Co., from *Experiential Organizational Behavior* by Theodore T. Herbert and Peter Lorenzi. Copyright © 1981 by Macmillan Publishing Company.

Case Study
Capitalizing on Social Change

When it comes to predicting the future, most managers have long been preoccupied with financial plans and economic forecasts, nearly to the exclusion of any attempts to foresee many long-term social and political changes that can affect their operations dramatically. Yet many have found that such social short-sightedness — particularly in an age of consumer activism and societal protest — can be just as costly as laxity in tracking economic trends.

General Motors Corp. and other auto makers paid dearly for failing to recognize early enough that Ralph Nader's objection to the Corvair model was a forerunner of a broad-based consumer movement for safer products and tougher liability standards. Similarly, by ignoring early warnings from environmentalists, hundreds of manufacturers were forced to retrofit plants with pollution-control gear that could have been incorporated more cheaply in the original plant design. More recently, Nestlé Co. faced a worldwide boycott of its products after it seemingly ignored the public outcry against its marketing of infant formula in underdeveloped countries where it was a far too expensive substitute for mother's milk.

Such costly mistakes, however, may at last be driving home the importance of watching social trends, and recently a number of companies have begun expanding their forecasts well beyond the realm of economics. Some have set up internal departments to predict the future social and political environment in which they will operate, while others are relying on a growing number of consultants who specialize in such crystal-ball gazing. Social predictions even are trickling into strategic plans, and line managers increasingly are called to task for not following them as closely as technical or pricing trends. The ultimate goal is to prevent unexpected social changes from wreaking havoc with profitability. As Robert L. Thaler, a senior vice-president at Security Pacific National Bank, puts it: "If we don't manage social change, change will manage us."

Cooperative Effort

While this new interest in assessing the business impact of future social changes often goes no further than informal discussions among managers, some formal forecasting programs do exist, and occasionally, they even transcend traditional corporate rivalries. For example, executives from such companies as AT&T, IBM, and Sperry — all fierce competitors — are sharing their techniques under the auspices of the Diebold Corporate Issues Program (DCIP), sponsored by Diebold Group Inc.,

New York–based management consultants. For nearly three years, the 20-member corporate group has been meeting periodically to discuss such questions as whether communications breakthroughs will push more employees into working at home, or how companies should change their product development techniques to anticipate any future environmental or consumer concerns.

The executives also explore changing demographics and value systems and, most important, tell each other about structures — new research departments, shifting lines of authority, and the like — they have set up within their organizations to forecast and react to social change. The group's main concern, says Robert F. Kamm, DCIP's director, is that "more and more traditionally non-P&L items are affecting profit and loss."

Corporations within and outside the DCIP are experimenting on their own with ways to keep that effect positive by focusing more closely on social trends. One popular method is "environmental scanning," which involves extensive reading of publications to identify various social and political factors that will help shape the future business environment. For example, PPG Industries Inc. recently hired Cynthia S. Angrist, a Carnegie-Mellon University sociologist, to fill the newly created post of manager of public policy research. She scans the publications of government agencies, public interest groups, research institutes, and other periodicals. She pays particular attention to politically extreme publications or to futurist journals, such as *Alternative Future,* all of which usually run counter to the way corporate America thinks. At management's request, Angrist also researches specific issues, such as a proposed law or an apparent cultural trend, and prepares reports on the issue's long-term ramifications for the company. Although Angrist admits that PPG has not yet managed the formal integration of social, political, and economic trends into its strategic plans, she says her weekly briefings with the company's chairman are evidence that there is "interest at the highest level."

Scanners

Still other corporations are increasingly employing outside research services and consultants specializing in the kind of scanning work that Angrist does.

For example, IU International Corp. retains consultant Kurt Lewin, a New York–based economist and specialist on social and political developments abroad, and IU Vice-Chairman Robert F. Calman says Lewin has helped his company ascertain the "mood" of foreign countries. IU also uses Williams Inference Service, a private environmental scanning group, which monitors and analyzes 150 publications each week.

Calman believes that nearly every social trend that will affect business 20 years from now is being "previewed" today somewhere, and he says he employs scanners out of "fear of missing a big opportunity or stepping into a crack." Apparently, Calman's concerns are shared. Although Williams Inference has been around for 15 years, it shuffled along with about six clients for the first 11 years, then signed on nearly 60 more in the last four years alone.

Ironically, even founder James S. Williams admits that scanning reports are often read for entertainment. Nevertheless, some companies are now making organizational changes to make sure that these reports and other social indicators are heeded by managers.

A prime example is Mead Corp.'s Human & Environmental Protection Dept. In just six years, the group has evolved from a run-of-the-mill environmental watchdog staff, sequestered in the research department, to a major part of the company's planning function. Russell E. Kross, the department's director, says it now reviews each of Mead's one- and five-year plans to make sure that they meet regulatory requirements. But in Mead's site-selection process for new plants, the company goes beyond legal issues to include such things as community sentiment. "In the past, we would say 'We've got to build here,'" Kross recalls, noting that the decision to zero in on one site was often based solely on conventional economic factors. Now, he says, Mead routinely selects three or four potential sites for new plants and evaluates each one for impact on local schools, traffic patterns, and the like before committing itself to a single site.

Hiring Its Critics

A few corporations are even eliciting the help of their critics in identifying future trouble spots. Velsicol Chemical Corp., apparently tired of its costly fights with the Environmental Protection Agency and various environmentalists, recently hired two former EPA officials and gave one of them line responsibility — complete with a full budget — to make sure that Velsicol's plants and products meet current safety standards. But a major part of their job is preventing any future problems as well. For example, Velsicol recently trucked fresh water at a cost of $1,200 a week for five months to homes in Tennessee when a preliminary report showed a possible chance that the company's landfill could contaminate wells.

A handful of companies have become downright formal about factoring social and political concerns into strategic plans. Every Wednesday, for example, 13 top vice-presidents at Security Pacific National Bank check all plans against a rundown of relevant external factors provided regularly by the 16-person in-house staff that handles the company's environmental scanning. When that staff projected that 75% of married women will be working by 1990, the committee decided that the trend calls for more automatic teller machines, pay-by-phone setups, and automatic payroll deposits to speed up banking for busy women. Concurrently, it is looking carefully at its original plan to build more suburban branches.

All of these companies, however, still face a major hurdle in getting operating managers to think beyond the next quarter. "Managers with profit-and-loss responsibility only look at larger issues when they are dragged in kicking and screaming," admits Richard R. Mau, vice-president of corporate and government relations for Sperry Corp. Thus, Sperry, Allied Chemical Corp., and others are tinkering with traditional employee education, appraisal, and incentive plans to spur line managers to grapple with social developments.

Measuring Success

Allied has perhaps the most ambitious program. Since 1974 it has been sending high-level managers through three-day corporate ethics seminars, which deal with situations ranging from questionable gifts and payments to handling employees during a plant closing. Charles J. Bischoff, Allied's director of management resources, says the seminars will eventually include middle managers. Moreover, since 1976, Allied has included a manager's contribution to the community in evaluations for incentive bonuses. "We felt the pocketbook was a good place to attract people's attention," Bischoff says.

Measuring the results of a company's increased awareness to social trends is anything but an exact science. "We measure success by the lack of negative results," concedes DCIP's Kamm.

Still, DCIP members seem to feel they get their money's worth. J. Paul Lyet, Sperry chairman, claims that once a company indicates to its own employees that it is a positive force in the communities in which it operates, the bottom-line payout comes in lowered turnover and improved morale. But Lyet, too, stresses that concentrating on social and political factors is as important as preventive medicine. "It dawned on me," he says, "that it was external factors over which we have no control that influence the stock." As he sums it up, "I realized that many little seeds could flower into bushes of poison ivy."

Case Questions

1. List and discuss potential sources for information about the future. What sort of information would be useful to (a) a computer manufacturer, (b) an automobile manufacturer, (c) a national fast-food franchise corporation, or (d) a regional grocery chain?
2. What does "demographics" mean? How do changes in demographics affect business decisions concerning (a) marketing, (b) personnel selection and training, (c) job design, or (d) the traditional 40-hour work week?
3. What is meant by the statement: "If we don't manage social change, change will manage us"? Give examples.

Source: Reprinted from the October 29, 1979 issue of *Business Week* by special permission, © 1979 by McGraw-Hill, Inc.

Glossary

Absolute Advantage A country's edge in efficiency of producing goods and services as compared to other countries.

Acceptance A potential barrier to effective communication; a communication cannot be effective unless it is accepted by the receiver (e.g., source is viewed as credible).

Achievement Motivation A motive of an individual that focuses on performing up to high standards.

Achievement-Oriented Leadership Leadership that sets challenging goals, emphasizes improvement in performance, and establishes high expectations for subordinates; part of the path-goal theory of leadership.

Acognitive Models of Motivation Models of human motivation that emphasize the relationship between behavior and external stimuli in the environment.

Actual Efficiency The cost/benefit ratio an organization actually achieves.

Adaptive Cycle The decisions of management on what strategies to adopt, which technologies are appropriate, and what structures accommodate the given strategies.

Administrative Management Theory A theory developed by Henri Fayol and holding that good or enlightened management is able to motivate workers to perform according to management guidelines or expectations.

Anchoring A judgmental heuristic in which individuals make estimates by adopting initial values that are typically insufficient; bias occurs when different starting points yield different estimates that are biased toward the initial values.

Antidumping Duties Import duties imposed when imported goods have a price lower than they command in their country of origin; the low price exists because the foreign exporter (1) wants to profit from the economies of scale resulting from operating at full capacity or (2) wants to gain early monopolistic control of the export market and later profit by charging higher prices.

Aspiration Levels A psychological notion that describes the level of satisfactory performance of an individual; it is theorized that over time aspiration levels adjust to the level of performance.

Autarky National economic self-sufficiency.

Availability A judgmental heuristic in which individuals assess the frequency of a class or the probability of an event by the ease with which instances or occurrences can be remembered.

Avoidance Learning The process involved in behavior that is performed to avoid an unpleasant condition; an aspect of reinforcement theory.

Backward Integration A company's entrance into its supplier's business and direct competition with the supplier.

Balance Sheet A summary statement of what an organization owns and what it owes at any given time.

Balance Sheet Budgets Financial budgets that summarize and integrate all the operating and financial budgets and project the balance sheet at the end of the year; a final check on plans and objectives of an organization; also known as pro forma budgets.

Bargaining Power Actual and potential power exerted by buyers and suppliers on host organizations in an industry; in general, stronger bargaining power is associated with lower industry profitability.

Behavioral Competencies Skills in social and political relationships.

Behavioral Decision Making An area of research and study that attempts to specify, both prescriptively and descriptively, how decision makers' beliefs and values are incorporated into their decisions.

Behaviorally Anchored Rating Scale A performance evaluation system in which anchor points describe specific behavior.

Behavior Modification A technique that assumes that individuals are passive and reactive, and respond to stimuli rather than assuming responsibility for initiating behavior.

Bounded Rationality A condition in which an individual attempts to solve a problem as rationally as possible within the limits of incomplete and inadequate information.

Budget A statement of future expenditures and revenues that helps managers plan and control the use of financial and other resources.

Bureaucratic Organizational Theory A design theory that championed bureaucratic structures, particularly their precision, stability, and reliability; can be traced to the work of Max Weber.

Business/Divisional-Level Plans Plans that address how a particular business or division can best compete in a particular market.

Capital Money, equipment, machinery, buildings, and other physical assets necessary to produce a product or provide a service.

Capital Expenditure Budgets Financial budgets that focus on new buildings, property, equipment, or other physical assets.

Capital Requirements The amount of expenditures needed to effectively enter and compete in a given industry.

Carrying Costs The costs of keeping inventory, associated with obsolescence, depreciation, theft, the maintenance of storage facilities, breakage, and capital costs.

Cash Budgets Financial budgets that project revenues and expenses for the year or appropriate budget period, providing managers with data on how well cash is flowing through a particular unit.

Cash Cows Slow-growing products that have a large market share and usually yield substantial cash flows; they generate more cash than required for reinvestment.

Cash Flow Statement A financial statement indicating where funds come from and where they are spent.

Choices Activities jobholders can perform but do not necessarily have to perform.

Code of Ethics A set of beliefs concerning what constitutes acceptable behavior.

Cognitive Models of Motivation Models of human motivation that assume individuals make conscious decisions about their behavior based on internal processes.

Collaboration An approach to problem solving in which each party may obtain its desired goal and each is satisfied.

Comparable Worth A concept that holds that equal wages should be paid to men and women performing tasks of equal value.

Compensatory Processing An information processing strategy in which the individual is assumed to have assimilated cues, which are then weighted equally or differentially; the alternative with the highest overall utility measure is selected.

Competencies Abilities necessary for a manager's success; managers should have technical, behavioral, and strategic competencies.

Competitor Analysis A systematic way of appraising a firm's competitors; that is, the goals, assumptions, strategies, and capabilities of competitors in terms of their impact on the firm.

Compromise An approach to solving a problem in which one or both parties give up something to reach a solution.

Concentric Diversification Company expansion resulting from movement into related fields.

Conceptual Skills The manager's ability to organize information to understand or perform his or her job more effectively; skills necessary to coordinate departments or divisions.

Conflict A condition that results when the goal-directed activities of groups block or are thought to block the goal-directed activities of other groups.

Conglomerate Diversification Company expansion resulting from movement into areas unrelated to the company's present focus.

Conjunctive Processing An information processing system in which cutoff points are set up and alternatives falling below these points are rejected.

Consideration Those aspects of leader behavior that focus on looking after employee welfare.

Constraints Internal and external limitations on the jobholder, including resource and technical limitations, legal and trade union restraints, physical location, organizational policies and procedures, and attitudes.

Contigency Approach Organizational design theory that attempts to outline conditions or circumstances that favor either organizational perogatives or employee welfare, instead of defining one best way to organize.

Contingency Planning A proactive method of anticipating changes in planning assumptions through the use of simulations and alternative representations of future events (scenarios).

Contingency Theory (a) A perspective of organizational design that postulates that there is no one best way to organize, and that different ways of organizing are not all equaly effective. (b) A theory advanced by Fred Fiedler, in which leadership effectiveness is defined in terms of group performance, and leaders are viewed as either relationship oriented or task oriented.

Continuous Reinforcement Schedule A system that rewards desired behavior each time it occurs.

Contract Manufacturing Manufacture for sale of a company's product by a foreign producer in the foreign market.

Control A systematic effort to set performance standards with planning objectives, to design information feedback systems, to compare actual performance with predetermined standards, to determine whether there are any deviations and to measure their significance, and to take any action required to assure that all corporate resources are used as effectively and efficiently as possible in achieving corporate objectives.

Conversion Process See Transformation Process.

Corrective Duties Duties imposed on imported goods suspected of having been export subsidized by their country of origin; take the form of countervailing duties or antidumping duties.

Cosmopolite An individual who links the organization or group with its external environment.

Cost (Expense) Centers Operating budgets relating to the efficiency of operations that closely monitor and minimize costs associated with production or the provision of a service.

Cost Leadership Strategy Based on the concept of the experience curve, this strategy aims at placing a company in the low-cost position through efficient scale economies, cost minimization, and cost control.

Countervailing Duty A corrective import duty set at the amount of the suspected export subsidy.

Cross-Elasticity A general measure of the ways in which two products are related to, or substitute for, each other; the cross-elasticity of demand for products A and B, for example, can be defined as the affect on the quantity demanded for product A by a change in the price of product B.

Decisional Roles The decision-making responsibilities of management; managers serve an entrepreneurial role, acting as disturbance handlers, resource allocators, and negotiators.

Decision Making A process through which a decision or choice is made; specific and discrete actions taken to close the gap between what is desired and what is available.

Decision Support System (DSS) A computerized information system that provides managers with the data they need when they need them.

Decision Tree A graphic representation of the sequential decisions and events that constitute decision making.

Declining Industries Industries characterized by different rates and patterns of decline.

Demands What a manager has to do; include minimum criteria of performance and the performance of certain kinds of work.

Deregulation A substantive reform of government control over business or industry.

Destructive Competition A situation in which a dominant firm sets prices low enough to drive out its competitors and then raises prices before new firms can enter the market.

Dialectic Processes Methods of examining underlying assumptions in the planning process through the use of team interaction.

Differentiation Cognitive and emotional differences in formal structure, goal orientation, time orientation, and interpersonal orientation in the units of an organization.

Differentiation Strategy A strategy that involves offering unique and distinct products and services to broad markets with the aim of protecting or insulating certain market segments through customer loyalty.

Direct Foreign Investment Acquisitions by domestic firms of foreign-based operating facilities that give the investor effective managerial control over the assets of the acquired firm.

Directive Leadership Leadership that provides specific guidance, standards, schedules of work, rules, and regulations for subordinates; a part of the path-goal leadership theory.

Disjunctive Processing An information processing system in which cutoff points are set up and alternatives that surpass these points are selected for further consideration.

Distortion A barrier to effective communication; intentional or unintentional change in the meaning of a message or information.

Diversification A company's development of new and improved products in new markets with the goal of increasing sales.

Divisional Structure An organizational structure that groups a product line into divisions.

Dogs Products that are growing very slowly and have a small market share.

Downward Communication The transmittal of information downward in the organization, often about the goals of the organization or specific directions about tasks to be performed from management to employees.

Dynamic Equilibrium A balance that is maintained in the presence of change within the framework of an international system.

Economic Regulations Government regulations that relate to the control of prices and conditions for entry in certain industries.

Economies of Scale The decline in unit costs as the volume of a product produced per period increases.

Efficiency The cost/benefit ratio incurred in pursuing organizational effectiveness; the extent to which resources are utilized in the pursuit of organizational goals.

Emerging Introductory Industries Industries characterized by uncertainty, the absence of product differentiation, and the lack of technological know-how to arrive at good estimates of costs.

Environmental Scanning The monitoring of changes and developments in the environment that have potential impact on the organization; normally done by executive management.

Ethics An individual's personal code concerning acceptable behavior and beliefs about what is right and wrong.

Executive Management Senior administrators who set long-term objectives and general operating policies; a level of management including chief executive officer (CEO), president, and vice-president.

Expectancy A belief about the likelihood or probability that a particular behavioral act will lead to a particular outcome; two types are effort-performance expectancy ($E \rightarrow P$) and performance-outcome expectancy ($P \rightarrow O$).

Expectancy/Valence Theory A cognitive theory of motivation that answers questions about the bases of motivation and job performance.

Experience Curve The representative relationship between the unit cost of producing and distributing a product and the accumulated output over time.

Expert Power The power that derives from the possession of specialized skills or knowledge.

Exponential Smoothing A technique used to remove the influence of random fluctuations in demand that places more weight on certain data, such as recent sales.

External Audit An appraisal of a firm's financial statements by a qualified independent agent.

External Environment Those factors outside the organization that have the potential to influence organizational actions and success.

External Equity A state existing when compensation is comparable to what employees might earn in other organizations for performing the same work.

Externalities External costs that occur whenever the total cost of producing or consuming a product is not covered by either the producer or the consumer.

External Status Characteristics Individual importance or prestige within a group based on factors originating outside the group.

Extinction The notion that undesirable behavior that is ignored or not followed by positive reinforcement will decline in frequency over time; an aspect of reinforcement theory.

False Negative Error A selection error in which a person is predicted to fail but ultimately succeeds.

False Positive Error A selection error in which a person is predicted to succeed and he or she ultimately fails.

Feedback Controls Controls that are activated after a process is complete.

Feedback Loop Information from the receiver to the sender in the communications process; used to check the accuracy of the received message.

Feed-Forward Controls See Steering Controls.

Financial Budget Plans that detail how the organization will spend money for a particular period, as well as where the money will come from.

Financial Statements Statements that help determine the long- and short-term financial standing of the organization; they assist managers in analyzing how financial resources have been used, and help determine the organization's liquidity and profitability.

Financing Budgets Financial budgets developed to ensure that the organization has sufficient funds to meet both short- and long-term borrowing obligations.

First-Line Management Supervisors who are responsible for day-to-day activities within the various departments of an organization who ensure that short-term goals are met.

Fixed Interval Schedule A partial reinforcement schedule that rewards performance at prespecified times.

Fixed Ratio Schedule A partial reinforcement schedule that provides rewards when a certain number of responses have been completed.

Flat Structure An organizational structure in which a large number of subordinates report to a superior.

Focus Strategy Concentrating resources and attention on a particular market segment in order to earn above average return in the industry.

Forecasting Predicting future events through structured analysis.

Forward Integration A company's entrance into its retailer's business and direct competition with the retailer.

Franchising A form of licensing in which the supplier of a product or service grants a dealer the right to sell it in exchange for a fee.

Functional Structure An organizational structure that fosters specialization through functional groupings.

Gatekeeper A person who controls the flow of messages and information in the communications process.

Gatekeeper (Yes-No) Controls Primary checkpoints that must be passed before moving on to a new checkpoint in a production process.

General-Purpose Tool A tool that has more than one function.

Geographic Structure An organizational structure divided on the basis of physical location.

Global Enterprise A multinational corporation that sells a fairly uniform product in all its markets and coordinates all of its sections to work together.

Goal Displacement An unintentional shift in organizational goals by management.

Goal Optimization Recognizing and accounting for a series of constraints such that an organization sets realistic goals.

Goal Relevancy The importance of a particular organizational goal as compared to other goals faced by a particular organization or individual.

Goal Succession A conscious attempt by management to shift an organization's course.

Government Regulatory Agencies Agencies with statutory power to issue rules and standards.

Great Man Theory of Leadership The theory that great leaders are born rather than developed; popular throughout the nineteenth century.

Grid Organization Development An approach to organization development in which change agents analyze organizational processes by use of a specific grid technique that evaluates management styles in terms of the relative emphasis on people and production.

Group A collection of individuals who have relationships to one another that make them interdependent to some significant degree.

Group Norms Rules of conduct or behavior that regulate members of a group; unwritten rules that generally apply to overt behavior and not to private beliefs.

Groupthink The psychological drive for consensus at any cost that suppresses dissent and appraisal of alternatives in cohesive decision making.

Growth Industries Industries characterized by widespread demand for the product, a wider buyer group, and an influx of competition.

Halo Error Generalization by supervisors from one important performance dimension to all other performance dimensions.

Heuristics Exploratory problem-solving techniques to improve performance.

Horizontal Communication Communication among employees or work groups at the same level of the organization.

Human Relations Movement A school of thought in management theory, developed by Elton Mayo, that emphasized employee imperatives and social work groups.

Human Resource Management The personnel department, in many organizations.

Human Resource Planning The translating of organizational goals into specific human resource objectives.

Human Skills The ability to understand human motivation and group processes, and to work well with others; skills necessary for a manager to become involved with and lead work groups.

Hurwicz Strategy A decisional strategy that combines mini-max and maxi-max strategies; it employs a coefficient of optimism to balance pessimistic and optimistic preferences.

Income Statement A financial statement indicating how much money a company has made over a given time period.

Individual Change An approach to organization development that focuses on modifying attitudes and behaviors of individuals.

Industrial Policy As defined by Leone and Bradley, the sum of a nation's efforts to shape business activity and influence economic growth.

Industry Life Cycle The characterization of an industry into distinct phases; that is, emerging, growing, maturing, and declining phases.

Inertia Conditions within an organization that facilitate or limit the organization's responsiveness to change; the more inertia, the less responsiveness.

Informational roles Activities that help a manager gain valid information useful in identifying problems and opportunities.

Initiating Structure Those aspects of employee behavior that focus on insuring task performance.

In-Place Production A type of unit or small-batch production in which workers come to a fixed construction site.

Input-Throughput-Output A systems perspective of organizations that views organizations as acquiring inputs from their environment, transforming these inputs into products and services (outputs), and providing these outputs to relevant parties in their environment.

Inside Recruitment   Seeking job candidates from among those already within the organization.

Integration   The process of achieving unified effort among various organizational units.

Intendedly Rational   The approach of individuals seeking to be rational in the face of incomplete information and limited computational skills.

Internal Audit   An assessment of the accuracy and reliability of a firm's financial statement, carried out by staff personnel.

Internal Equity   A state existing when employees' salary levels are relatively comparable in an organization, taking into account the employees' skills, background, performance level, and importance to the firm.

Internal Representation   A decision maker's interpretation of problem components. The components include the initial situation as presented to the decision maker, the desired goal situation, various intermediate states, as well as any concepts used by the decision maker.

Internal Status Characteristics   Importance or prestige within a group based on individuals' position or contributions to the group.

International Business   A multifaceted system linking countries, governments, firms, and people that is less encumbered by national borders than by political processes; it involves all kinds of public and private business activities and transactions involving goods and services, skills and technology, raw materials, and information.

International Management   The process of accomplishing the international and global objectives of an organization.

Interpersonal Communication   Communication among employees that has a more direct and personal focus, ranging from praise from manager to employee for a job well done to inquiries about the health of an employee's family.

Interpersonal Roles   A manager's efforts to deal effectively with others on behalf of the organization.

Inventory   The amount of input or output kept on hand in an operations management system.

Iron Law of Oligarchy   The tendency for revolutionary leaders to become more conservative in their objectives once they gain power in order to protect and maintain their new positions.

Job Analysis   Analysis of the component tasks required in a job and the skills necessary for effective performance of each task.

Joint Venture   A cooperative enterprise with a foreign firm or government in a manufacturing facility abroad to meet local demand or to provide an export platform to boost that country's export sales.

Jurisdictional Ambiguities   Unclear responsibility among individuals or groups for the performance of a specific task.

***Kanban* System**   A Japanese control system pioneered by Toyota with the objective of producing goods in the necessary quantity at the required time.

Labor   An organization's human resources, employees, involved in either making a product or providing a service.

Laissez-faire   A doctrine stipulating that every individual, if led to pursue his or her own individual desires, will achieve the best results for all.

Leadership   The influential increment over and above mechanical compliance with routine directives of the organization.

Lead Time   The amount of time needed between placing an order and completing a job.

Least-Preferred Co-worker Scale (LPC)   A measure designed by Fred Fiedler to assess the extent to which a person is relationship-oriented or task-oriented.

Legitimate Power   Power sanctioned by the organization and derived from the official position of authority of an individual in the organization.

Lexicographic Processing   An information processing system in which the individual rank orders the judgmental dimensions in terms of their relative importance.

Liaison   A person who provides a communications linkage between or among two or more groups and facilitates the exchange of information.

Licensing   An agreement by an international company, the licensor, to provide access to its patents and trademarks to another company abroad, the licensee; a form of direct foreign investment.

Line Managers   Managers directly involved in the production of goods and services.

Management   The process of planning, organizing, directing, and controlling the activities of employees in combination with other organizational resources to accomplish stated organizational objectives.

Management Audit   An assessment of the general effectiveness of management in an organization; done every three to five years by outside professionals.

Management Information System (MIS)   Computerized information systems that provide management with regular reports.

Managerial Ethics   A manager's personal code concerning what constitutes acceptable managerial behavior.

Managerial Role Constellation   The set of roles managers must perform if they are to be successful in their jobs.

Manifest Needs Model   Henry Murray's model of employee motivation that classifies people according to the strengths of their needs.

Market Development   A company's introduction of its current products into new markets with the goal of increasing sales.

Market Penetration   A company's use of more aggressive advertising, product design, and sales campaigns with the goal of increasing sales of its current products.

Mass Production   The production of large volumes of identical or similar goods.

Material Requirements Planning   A computerized data information system that keeps track of scheduling and inventory functions for manufacturing.

Materials   Physical items directly used in producing a product or providing a service.

Matrix/Mixed Structure   An organizational structure that combines the elements of functional and product management structures in an ad hoc or temporary manner to remain flexible in the face of complex environmental conditions; popularly known as project management organization.

Mature Industries   Industries characterized by a slowing of industry growth, a strengthened hold on repeat buyers, an emphasis on cost and service, and a decrease in product and technological innovation.

Maxi-Max Strategy   A decision aid that assumes the best outcome; the opposite of the mini-max strategy.

Means-ends Inversion   The conversion of the means for attaining an organization's goals into goals themselves.

Mercantilism   An international trade philosophy prevalent in the seventeenth and eighteenth centuries that favored increased export of goods so the surplus could benefit the nation.

Middle Management   The level of management responsible for interpreting the general, long-range goals of executives and setting goals for divisions and departments.

Mini-Max Strategy   A decision aid that assumes the worst will happen and that losses should be minimized by selecting the alternative with the best of the worst possible outcomes.

Mission Statement   A general statement defining a company's business in long-range terms.

Modal Technology   The technology of the primary flow of products in a manufacturing unit; the three types are unit or small-batch, mass or large-batch, and process production.

Motivation   That which energized, directs, and sustains human behavior; a force that causes people to behave in certain ways and that is goal directed.

Moving Averages   A mathematical way of removing the influence of random fluctuations in demand by smoothing data.

Multinational Corporation   A company that views each of its businesses around the world as independent and that encompasses both domestic and overseas markets; it engages in a variety of business activities, including direct and indirect exporting, portfolio investment, and direct foreign investment through contract manufacturing, licensing, franchising, turnkey projects, joint ventures, and wholly owned subsidiaries.

Natural Monopolies Firms or entities that, by virtue of edict, government policy, or other reasons, represent the sole supplier of particular goods and services.

Need for Achievement Behavior directed toward competition with a standard of excellence.

Need for Affiliation Attraction to others based on a need for reassurance as to one's acceptability.

Need for Power A need to influence others and to control one's environment.

Need Hierarchy Model Abraham Maslow's model of human motivation; it assumes that people are primarily motivated by a desire to satisfy specific needs, which are arranged in a hierarchy.

Neocontingency Design Theory An organizational design theory emphasizing the strategic choices of management relating to structures and processes.

Noise Anything that can influence the reception of a message, ranging from actual noise to contextual factors.

Noncompensatory Processing An information processing strategy in which an individual uses selected information, depending on the manner in which the problem is structured and presented.

Nontariff Barrier A trade control device that may include surtaxes, government participation in trade, corrective duties, quantitative limitations or quotas, customs and entry regulations, government standards, monetary or exchange control and quotas, and import charges.

Nonverbal Communication Messages that can be inferred from the behavior or actions of others.

Non-Zero-Sum Game A situation in which someone's win does not necessarily mean someone else's loss.

Normative Decision Making An area of study concerned with prescribing courses of action suitable to particular decisions.

Normative Theory Victor Vroom and Phillip Yetton's leadership theory; it assumes that no single leader behavior is appropriate for all situations and that leaders develop a repertoire of behavioral responses ranging from autocratic to consultative.

Occupational Psychosis The development, among people in bureaucracies, of special preferences as a result of routine, daily activities — for example, the refusal by workers to perform a task outside their job description.

Official Goals Formal statements made by an executive about the nature of the organization's mission.

Omission A barrier to effective communication in which only part of a larger message is transmitted.

Operating Budget Plans for the use of raw materials, goods, and services for a specified period of time, usually incorporating physical quantities and cost figures.

Operational Goals Goals with clearly measurable assessment standards.

Operations Management The process of obtaining and utilizing resources to produce goods and services in ways that are consistent with the goals of the organization.

Operative Goals The real intentions of an organization.

Opinion Leader A person with a highly influential position in a group; often an informal role.

Order Costs The managerial and clerical costs of placing an order for more goods to be added to the inventory.

Organization A system of consciously coordinated activities of two or more persons, with stated purposes or goals, communication networks, and people willing to cooperate with one another on jobs necessary to meet organizational goals.

Organization Development A long-range effort to improve an organization's problem solving and renewal processes, particularly through a more effective and collaborative management of organizational culture — with special emphasis on the culture of formal work teams — with the assistance of a change agent, or catalyst, and the use of the theory and technology of applied behavioral science, including action research.

Organizational Effectiveness An organization's ability to acquire and efficiently use available resources to achieve its goals; the extent to which operative goals have been met.

Organizational Goal A desired state of affairs that indicates where an organization is going; a frame of reference for understanding and evaluating what an organization does.

Organizational Slack An organization's total resources in excess of the necessary side payments.

Outside Recruitment Seeking job candidates from among those individuals who are not already within the organization.

Overcapacity A situation in which supply exceeds demand, leading to pressure to reduce prices.

Overload A barrier to effective communication in which too much information is received.

Path-Goal Theory Robert House's theory of leadership; it states that leaders can improve subordinates' performance by showing them how performance results in desired rewards.

Partial Reinforcement Schedule A system that rewards desired behavior at specific intervals; types of partial reinforcement schedules are fixed ratio, fixed interval, variable interval, and variable ratio.

Participative Leadership Leadership that involves consultation with subordinates and elicitation of their suggestions and advice before job-related decisions are made; part of the path-goal theory of leadership.

Performance Gap A disparity between planned or intended and actual performance.

Perks Perquisites, special benefits that come with a job, such as a private, corner office or a company car.

Personnel Objectives Statements that provide direction for specific actions needed to manage human resources effectively, and standards for judging success in doing so.

Planning The process by which managers define goals and adopt necessary steps to ensure that those goals are achieved; an anticipatory or future-oriented process involving multiple parties, interdependent decisions, and actions that lead to future states that would otherwise not occur.

Planning-Programming-Budgeting System or **(PPBS)** An approach to developing budgets aimed at identifying and eliminating costly program duplications and providing a more efficient overall budget.

Political Activity The process through which power is exercised to gain compliance with desired actions.

Political Decision Making Decision making influenced by the politics underlying the situation.

Political Processes The processes through which power is exercised to gain desired outcomes.

Pooled Interdependence The result of individuals performing independent tasks the sum of which is necessary to create the group or unit's product.

Portfolio Investment A type of business activity involving the purchase of securities in the form of stocks, bonds, or commercial paper in order to obtain a return on that investment in the form of dividends, interest, or capital gains.

Positive Reinforcement The provision of a reward after a desired behavior has occurred.

Postaction Controls See Feedback Controls.

Potential Efficiency The top level of efficiency at which organizations theoretically can function, given their unique characteristics, processes, products, and goals.

Power Force that is sufficient to overcome others' resistance to compliance with requested actions.

PPBS See Planning-Programming-Budgeting System.

Problem Children Products that are growing fast yet have low margins because of low market share.

Process Consultation A method used in organization development in which an outside change agent is brought into the organization to make observations concerning the organization's processes.

Product Development A company's development of new and improved products for current markets with the goal of increasing sales.

Product Management Structure A business organized by product.

Product/Market Expansion Matrix A representation of management's choices of growth opportunities in its present and future products and markets.

Product Portfolio Strategy The strategy in which some products generate cash and others use cash, resulting in a balanced growth pattern and minimized risk.

Profit Centers Operating budgets that measure performance by comparing revenues with expenditures, assessing how well a unit has used what it has to maximize profits.

Programmability The relative ease with which transformational rules defining the solution to the problem can be specified.

Protectionism The political and economic measures taken by a government to safeguard domestic goods from the competition of less expensive imported goods.

Punishment The administration of unpleasant or adverse outcomes as a result of undesired behavior.

Punishment Power The use or threatened use of punishment associated with failure to comply with a specific request for action.

Quality Circles A group of employees that meets regularly to identify work problems and discuss their solutions with the aim of increasing the productivity and quality of the organization's management system.

Quality Control A quality process in which items are sampled and compared with standards.

Random Fluctuation Changes in demand that have no pattern and cannot be forecasted.

Rational Decision Maker An individual with complete knowledge of the relevant aspects of the environment, a well-organized and stable system of preferences, and almost infinite computational skills.

Recession A slowing down in the growth of the economy, often characterized by high unemployment.

Reciprocal Interdependence Task interdependence in which the performance of one task is dependent upon the completion of both preceding and subsequent tasks.

Recruiting The process of identifying and attracting candidates for positions in an organization.

Referent Power The ability to influence others because they identify with you or want to be like you.

Regression Analysis A sophisticated method of dealing with sales forecasting that uses knowledge of the relationship of one variable to another.

Regulations A government agency's written statements designed to interpret law, policy, and the intent of legislation that have the force of law within the authority given to the agency by the legislature.

Regulatory Budget A regulatory reform measure in which the state or federal government sets a budget figure for a regulatory agency, providing an incentive for the agency to adopt cost-effective regulations.

Regulatory Costs All costs attributable to regulations or resulting from adherence to regulations, including direct compliance costs, administrative costs, and mitigation and noncompliance costs.

Regulatory Inefficiencies Those regulatory costs that result from conflict or unnecessary duplication among regulatory requirements, or regulatory requirements that do not permit a firm to comply in the most efficient, least costly manner.

Regulatory Review Program A regulatory reform mechanism in which regulatory agencies are required to analyze the costs and benefits of particular regulatory programs and to examine the feasibility of alternate methods of achieving the objective.

Reinforcement Anything that causes certain behaviors to be repeated or inhibited.

Reinforcement Theory An acognitive theory of motivation that assumes behavior that leads to positive or pleasurable outcomes will tend to be repeated, and behavior that leads to negative behavior or punishment will tend to be avoided.

Representativeness A judgmental heuristic in which individuals assess the probability of an event by the degree to which it is representative of or similar to the stereotype.

Return Potential Model A model that can be used to portray group norms in terms of approval or disapproval associated with different levels of specific behavior.

Revenue Centers Operating budgets that measure outputs in monetary terms instead of by input costs, to maximize the revenues generated by the sales and distribution of the product or service.

Reward Power The use of rewards to gain compliance with a request for action.

Role An organized set of behaviors related to an identifiable office or position.

Satisfice To select the most acceptable solution.

Satisficing Decision Maker An individual who finds the most acceptable solutions by using heuristics and limited alternatives.

Scanlon Plan A bonus system that ties bonuses directly to specially designed organization-wide or plantwide performance standards.

Schedules of Reinforcement The patterns according to which reinforcement is administered; schedules can be continuous or partial.

Scheduling The process of establishing the specific time when a job or some task is to be accomplished.

Scientific Management Theory A theory developed by Frederick Taylor; it held that the key to reconciling differences between management and the individual was to design jobs using scientific methods.

Seasonal Variation A variation in demand caused by a fluctuation associated with the season of the year.

Self-contained Task A task in a system in which all the resources required for performance are placed in a single unit.

Sequential Interdependence Task interdependence in which the performance of one task is dependent upon the successful completion of preceding tasks.

Setup Costs Costs incurred in getting equipment ready and prepared for producing a product.

Shortage Costs Carrying costs associated with not selling an item; the difference between what is received and what might have been received if there had been an inventory to sell; also called opportunity costs.

Side Payments Incentives given to various members of an organization to secure their participation in achieving certain organizational goals.

Simulations The generation of sequences of events on a hypothetical basis, normally done with a computer.

Slack Resources Additional resources beyond those minimally required to perform a task efficiently; can be used to reduce the need to process information.

Social Loafing The tendency of individuals not to work quite as hard in a group as they would performing the same task alone.

Social Regulations Government regulations covering areas in which unregulated activity may pose significant threats to public health, safety, or the environment.

Span of Control The number of subordinates who directly report to a supervisor.

Staff Managers Managers who serve a supporting role in an organization and do not deal directly with production.

Stagflation Rising prices accompanied by stagnation and increasing unemployment.

Stakeholder An individual or group that has a distinct interest in the organization; for example, a labor union, stockholder, or employee.

Standard Operating Procedures (SOPs) Standardized responses to recurring problems.

Stars Market-leading, fast-growing products that need a great deal of cash to sustain or improve their growth rate.

Status Differentiation The varying importance or prestige of different individuals in a group.

Status Inconsistencies Differences in the importance or value of an individual that result from different dimensions being used for assessment.

Steering (Feed-Forward) Controls Controls in which results are predicted and corrective actions taken before the total operation is complete.

Stoplight Strategy General Electric's strategy that rates companies in terms of their competitive position and industry attractiveness using the concepts of red, yellow, and green lights.

Strategic Choice A recent school of thought in management theory that emphasizes the role of managerial discretion and choices in the development of organizational structures and processes.

Strategic Communication Communication involving the future direction and goals of the organization and information relating to the external environment.

Strategic Competencies The manager's skill in dealing with changes in the environment, competitors, international markets, and organizational change.

Strategic/Corporate-Level Plans Plans that are aligned with the development of the company's mission and that address questions such as: What is our business? Who is our customer? What products and markets should we be in?

Strategic Gap The difference between the current, existing state and a desired or alternate state.

Strategic Management A dynamic and adaptive management process; a systematic way of relating a company to its environment.

Strategies A pattern of decisions made by a firm to achieve its corporate mission and objectives.

Structural Change An approach to organization development that focuses on modifying organizational design.

Structural Characteristics The total pattern of differentiation and relationships that develop among parts of a group.

Structure A pattern of stable and relatively fixed relationships that exists among jobs in an organization; stable or enduring relationships reflecting task differentiation and coordination.

Suboptimization The intentional pursuit of objectives below those that are realistically feasible.

Substitute Product A product that is complementary to, or a substitute for, another product; for example, coffee and tea.

Sunset Laws Laws that require regular legislative review of the effectiveness of government agencies.

Supportive Leadership Leadership that shows concern for the status, well-being, and personal needs of subordinates; part of the path-goal theory of leadership.

Support Personnel Workers not directly involved in the production process but responsible for such duties as accounting, data processing, or maintenance.

Survey Feedback A method used in organization development in which employees are surveyed with a questionnaire or interview and the results are given back to them in an aggregate or summarized form.

Tall Structures Organizational structures in which fewer subordinates report to several superiors.

Tariff A trade control device including export, transit, and import tariffs.

Task Specialization The assignment of group members to perform specific and unique tasks.

Team Building An approach to organization development which attempts to analyze the effectiveness of a work group and help it discover how to work more effectively as an integrated and cohesive team.

Technical Communication Instructions, policies, and procedures related to the performance of jobs in an organization.

Technical Competencies A working knowledge of the requirements of management in a particular field, including planning, organizing, staffing, directing, controlling, and coordinating, as well as the basic skills and abilities needed to perform the tasks under the manager's direction.

Technical Skills Skills involving the tools, procedures, and techniques of their particular area that are required of successful managers.

Technological Change   An approach to organization development that focuses on changing the way work is actually performed.

Timeliness   The need to receive critical information in time to act on it.

Trained Incapacity   A potential problem for bureaucratic structures, in which actions successfully applied to a previous problem may result in incorrect responses when applied to new problems.

Transformational Rules   Programs or processes used in problem solving.

Transformation (Conversion) Process   The basis of operations management; how inputs are converted into desired goods or services.

Turnkey Project   A form of direct investment in which a firm sets up an operation abroad involving the design and construction of an entire project, then turns over the operation of the project to local personnel upon its completion.

Unfair Discrimination   Selection decisions that are based on criteria that are not job related; for example, age, sex, religion, or race.

Unit/Functional-Level Plans   Plans concerned with getting the best mix of strategic variables; e.g., price, promotions, advertising, distribution, product output, and personnel policies that are generally under the control of the functional manager.

Unit (Small-Batch) Production   The custom manufacture of small numbers or individual pieces; also called a job shop.

Universalistic Approach   Organizational design research that attempts to define the one best way to organize.

Upward Communication   Communication flowing upward in the organization; it often provides feedback to management on the performance of the company's operational parts.

Valence   The value an individual places on available outcomes or rewards.

Value Programming   The formation of personal values as the result of observing and imitating role models such as parents, friends, and national heroes, particularly during the period from ten to twenty years of age.

Variable Interval Schedule   A partial reinforcement schedule according to which rewards are administered at random times that cannot be predetermined or detected by the subject.

Variable Ratio Schedule   A partial reinforcement schedule in which rewards are administered in a certain overall ratio of performances to rewards, the number of responses to reward varying during the period of reinforcement.

Wholly Owned Subsidiary   A form of direct investment in which a company owns 100 percent of an affiliate.

Work Redesign   A concept that assumes workers want a larger voice in decisions concerning their workplace and are willing to increase their involvement and productivity when given a chance to participate.

Yes-No Controls   See Gatekeeper Controls.

Zero-Base Budgeting (ZBB)   An approach to developing budgets in which managers must justify each line item in a new budget from scratch.

References

AGUILAR, F.J. (1967). *Scanning the business environment*. New York: Macmillan.

THE AIRLINES' INVISIBLE WARLORDS. (1983, August). *Frequent Flyer,* pp. 36–39.

ALDERFER, C.P. (1977). Group and intergroup relations. In J.R. Hackman & J.L. Suttle (Eds.), *Improving life at work* (pp. 227–295). Santa Monica, CA: Goodyear.

ALLISON, G.T. (1971). *Essence of decision: Explaining the Cuban missile crisis*. Boston: Little, Brown.

AMERICA'S RESTRUCTURED ECONOMY. (1981, June 1). *Business Week* (Special Issue).

ANDERSON, H., Ma, C., Lampert, H., & Cane, B. (1983, May 30). The dynamite issue. *Newsweek,* pp. 34–36.

ANSOFF, I., Avner, J., Brandenberg, R., Portner, F., & Radosevich, R. (1970). Does planning pay? The effect of planning on success of acquisitions in American firms. *Long Range Planning, 3*(2), 2–7.

ANTHONY, R., & Dearden, J. (1980). *Management control systems* (4th ed.). Homewood, IL: Irwin.

ARGYRIS, C. (1962). *Interpersonal competence and organizational effectiveness*. Homewood, IL: Dorsey Press.

ARGYRIS, C. (1974). *The applicability of organizational sociology*. New York: Cambridge University Press.

ARVEY, R.D. (1979). *Fairness in selecting employees*. Reading, MA: Addison-Wesley.

BALES, R.F. (1950). *Interaction process analysis*. Reading, MA: Addison-Wesley.

BALES, R.F. (1953). The equilibrium problem in small groups. In T. Parsons, R.F. Bales, & E.A. Shils (Eds.), *Working papers in the theory of action* (pp. 111–161). New York: Free Press.

BALL, D.A., & McCulloch, W.H., Jr. (1982). *International business: Introduction and essentials*. Plano, TX: Business Publications.

BARNARD, C.I. (1938). *The functions of the executive*. Cambridge, MA: Harvard University Press.

BARTLETT, F.C. (1958). *Thinking*. New York: Basic Books.

BASIC ANALYSIS: PERSONAL COMPUTERS. (1981, October 28). New York: Paine, Webber, Mitchell, Hutchins, p. 10.

BASS, B., & Vaughn, J. (1966). *Training in industry: The management of learning*. Belmont, CA: Wadsworth.

BEALS, A.R., & Siegel, B.J. (1966). *Divisiveness and social conflict: An anthropological approach*. Stanford, CA: Stanford University Press.

BEAUVOIS, J.J. (1966). International intelligence for the international enterprise. In J.J. Coyle & E.J. Mock (Eds.), *Readings in international business*. Scranton, PA: International Textbook.

BEER, M. (1980). *Organizational change and development*. Santa Monica, CA: Goodyear.

BEHIND THE BLOODLETTING OVER TOYOTA'S SALES. (1981, June 1). *Business Week,* p. 44.

BELL, D. (1976). *Coming of a post-industrial society: A venture in social forecasting*. New York: Basic Books.

BENJAMIN, D. (1978). Is planned obsolescence a serious problem? In M.B. Johnson (Ed.), *The attack on corporate America* (pp. 233–235). New York: McGraw-Hill.

BENNIS, W.G. (1966). *Changing organizations.* New York: McGraw-Hill.

BERVIRT, J.L. (1978). The cost impact of federal government regulation on the Dow Chemical Company. *Proceedings of the American Statistical Association,* pp. 345–358.

BIRCH, D., & Veroff, J. (1966). *Motivation: A study of action.* Monterey, CA: Brooks/Cole.

BLAKE, R., & Mouton, J. (1969). *Building a dynamic organization through grid organization development.* Reading, MA: Addison-Wesley.

BLAKE, R., & Mouton, J. (1978). The new managerial grid. Houston, TX: Gulf.

BLAU, P. (1970). A formal theory of differentiation in organizations. *American Sociological Review,* 35(2), 201–218.

BLODGETT, T.B. (1968). Slowdown on business bluffing. *Harvard Business Review, 46,* 162–170.

BRANCH, M.C. (1975, April 28). Piercing future fog in the executive suite. *Business Week,* pp. 46–54.

BRENNER, S., & Molander, E. (1977). Is the ethics of business changing? *Harvard Business Review, 55,* 64–65.

BURNS, T., & Stalker, G.M. (1971). *The management of innovation.* London: Tavistock.

BUSINESS FAILURE RECORD, 1977. (1977). New York: Dun & Bradstreet.

BYRNE, J.A., & Konrad, W. (1983, July 18). The fast track slows down. *Forbes,* pp. 77–78.

CAMPBELL, J.P., & Dunnett, M.D. (1968). Effectiveness of T-group experiences in managerial training and development. *Psychological Bulletin,* 70(2), 73–104.

CAMERON, K., & Whetten, D. (1982). *Organizational effectiveness.* New York: Academic Press.

CANTO, V.A., & Laffer, A.B. (1982). The incidence of trade restriction. *Columbia Journal of World Business,* 19(3), 10.

CARR, A.Z. (1968). Is business bluffing ethical? *Harvard Business Review, 46,* 143–153.

CARTWRIGHT, D. (1968). The nature of group cohesiveness. In D. Cartwright & A. Zander (Eds.), *Group dynamics* (3rd ed., pp. 91–109). New York: Harper & Row.

CARTWRIGHT, D., & Zander, A. (1968). Groups and group membership. In D. Cartwright & A. Zander (Eds.), Group dynamics (3rd ed., pp. 45–62). New York: Harper & Row.

CHANDLER, A.D. (1969). *Strategy and structure.* Cambridge, MA: MIT Press.

CHARLESWATER ASSOCIATES, INC. (1975, September). The impact on small business concerns of government regulations that force technological change. Final report prepared for the U.S. Small Business Administration, Washington, DC.

CHILD, J. (1972). Organizational structures, environment, and performance: The role of strategic choice. *Sociology, 6,* 1–22.

CHILD, J. (1977). *Organization: A guide to problems and practice.* London: Harper & Row.

CHIP WARS: THE JAPANESE THREAT. (1983, May 23). *Business Week,* pp. 80–85, 87, 90.

COLE, R.J., & Tegeler, P.D. (1979, March). *The impacts of government requirements on small business in Washington state.* Seattle, WA: Battelle Human Affairs Research Center.

CONSUMER PRODUCTS SAFETY COMMISSION. (1977). Hazard index, FY 1977. Washington, DC: U.S. Government Printing Office.

COOK, D.T. (1983, June 9). U.S. recovery contributes to balloning trade deficit. *Christian Science Monitor,* p. 10.

COOMBS, C.H. (1964). *The theory of data.* New York: Wiley.

CORPORATE CLOUT FOR CONSUMERS. (1977, September 12). *Business Week,* pp. 144, 148.

COSER, L.A. (1956). *The functions of social conflict.* Glencoe, IL: Free Press.

COSTELLO, T., & Zalkind, S. (1963). *Psychology in administration.* Englewood Cliffs, NJ: Prentice-Hall.

COX, W.E., Jr. (1967). Product life cycles as marketing models. *Journal of Business, 40*(4), 375–384.

CRAY, E. (1980). *The chrome colossus: General Motors and its times.* New York: McGraw-Hill.

CYERT, R., & March, J.G. (1963). *A behavioral theory of the firm.* Englewood Cliffs, NJ: Prentice-Hall.

DALTON, D., & Cosier, R. (1982, May–June). The four faces of social responsibility. *Business Horizons,* pp. 19–27.

DANIEL, D.R. (1966). Reorganizing for results. *Harvard Business Review, 44,* 96–104.

DANIELS, J.D., Ogram, E.W., Jr. & Radebaugh, L.H. (1982). *International business: Environments and operations.* (3rd ed.). Reading, MA: Addison-Wesley.

DAVIS, S., & Lawrence, P.B. (1977). *Matrix.* Reading, MA: Addison-Wesley.

DAWES, R.M. (1964). Social selection based on multidimensional criteria. *Journal of Abnormal and Social Psychology, 68,* 104–109.

DEARBORN, D.C., & Simon, H.A. (1958). Selective perception: The identifications of executives. *Sociometry, 21,* 140–144.

DELBECQ, A.I., Van de Ven, A.H., & Gustafson, D.H. (1975). *Group techniques for program planning.* Glenview, IL: Scott, Foresman.

DIGAENTANI, J.L. (1982, March–April). The Sperry Corporation and listening: An interview. *Business Horizons, 25,* 34–39.

DOWNS, A. (1967). *Inside bureaucracy.* Boston: Little, Brown.

DRAKE, R.L., & Caudill, L.M. (1981, May–June). Management of the large multinational: Trends and future challenges. *Business Horizons,* pp. 83–87.

DRUCKER, P., (1980). *Managing turbulent times.* New York: Harper & Row.

DUERR, M.G., & Roach, J.M. (1973). *Organization and control of international operations.* New York: Conference Board.

ECONOMIC REPORT TO THE PRESIDENT. (1983, February). Washington, D.C.: Superintendent of Documents, U.S. Government Printing Office.

EINHORN, H.J. (1970). The use of nonlinear, noncompensatory models in decision making. *Psychological Bulletin, 73,* 221–230.

ENGLAND, G. W. (1967). Organizational goals and expected behavior of American managers. *Academy of Management Journal, 10,* 102–112.

ETZIONI, A. (1964). *Modern organizations.* Englewood Cliffs, NJ: Prentice-Hall.

EUGENE REGISTER GUARD. (1983, February 9). Eugene, OR.

EVANS, R., & Novak, R. (1966). *Lyndon B. Johnson: The exercise of power.* New York: Signet.

FAYERWEATHER, J. (1978). *International business strategy and administration.* Cambridge, MA: Ballinger.

FAYOL, H. (1949). *General and industrial management.* London: Pitman.

FIEDLER, F. (1967). *A theory of leadership effectiveness.* New York: McGraw-Hill.

FIEDLER, F. (1971). *Leadership.* Morristown, NJ: Silver Burdett Company.

FIERMAN, J. (1982, August 9). The 50 leading exporters. *Fortune,* p. 68.

FISCHHOFF, B., Slovic, P., & Lichtenstein, S. (1977). Knowing with certainty: The appropriateness of extreme confidence. *Journal of Experimental Psychology: Human Perception and Performance, 3,* 552–564.

FORD, J., & Slocum, J.W. (1977). Size, technology, environment and the structure of organizations. *Academy of Management Review, 2*(4), 561–575.

FREEMAN, R.B. (1979). The work force of the future: An overview. In C. Kerr & J. Rosow (Eds.), *Work in America: The decade ahead* (pp. 58–79). New York: Van Nostrand Reinhold.

FRENCH, E.G. (1958). The interaction of achievement motivation and ability in problem solving success. *Journal of Abnormal Social Psychology, 57,* 306–309.

FRENCH, J.R., & Raven, B. (1959). The bases of social power. In D. Cartwright (Ed.), *Studies in social power.* Ann Arbor: University of Michigan, Institute for Social Research.

FRENCH, W., & Bell, C. (1973). *Organization development.* Englewood Cliffs, NJ: Prentice-Hall.

FRITSCHLER, A.L., & Ross, B. (1980). *Business regulation and government decision making.* Cambridge, MA: Winthrop.

GALBRAITH, J.K. (1981). *A life in our times.* New York: Ballantine.

GALBRAITH, J.R. (1973). *Designing complex organizations.* Reading, MA: Addison-Wesley.

GARDNER, B. (1945). *Human relations in industry.* Chicago: Irwin.

GERSTNER, L.V., Jr. (1980). Can strategic planning pay off? In R.A. Kerin & R.A. Peterson (Eds.), *Perspectives on strategic marketing management* (pp. 52–65). Boston: Allyn & Bacon.

GHISELLI, E. (1966). *Explorations in managerial talent.* Pacific Palisades, CA: Goodyear.

GLUECK, W.F. (1980). *Management.* Hinsdale, IL: Dryden.

GLUECK, W.F. (1982). *Personnel: A diagnostic approach* (3rd ed.). Plano, TX: Business Publications.

GOLDSTEIN, I. (1975, 1980). *Training: Program development and evaluation.* Monterey, CA: Brooks/Cole.

GOODMAN, P., & Pennings, J. (1977). *New perspectives on organizational effectiveness.* San Francisco: Jossey-Bass.

GOTCHER, J.W. (1981). Strategic planning for multinationals: The views of government and scientists. *Long Range Planning, 23*(2), 13–25.

GUZZARDI, W., Jr. (1983, March 21). How to foil protectionism. *Fortune,* p. 86.

HACKMAN, J.R. (1976). Group influences on individuals in organizations. In M. Dunnette (Ed.), *Handbook of industrial and organizational psychology* (pp. 1455–1525). Chicago: Rand McNally.

HACKMAN, J.R. (1977). Work design. In J.R. Hackman & J.L. Suttle (Eds.), *Improving life at work* (pp. 96–162). Santa Monica, CA: Goodyear.

HACKMAN, J.R., & Morris, C.G. (1975). Group tasks, group interaction process, and group performance effectiveness: A review and proposed integration. In L. Berkowitz (Ed.), *Advances in experimental social psychology* (Vol. 8, pp. 45–99). New York: Academic Press.

HACKMAN, J.R., & Oldham, G. (1976). Motivation through the design of work. *Organizational Behavior and Human Performance, 16,* 250–279.

HAGEN, M.C. (1966). Employee relations and the free enterprise image. In J.J. Coyle & E.J. Mock (Eds.), *Readings in international business.* Scranton: PA: International Textbook.

HALL, R.H., & Tittle, C.R. (1966). Bureaucracy and its correlates. *American Journal of Sociology, 72,* 267–272.

HAMERMESH, R.G., & Silk, S.B. (1979). How to compete in stagnant industries. *Harvard Business Review, 57,* 161–168.

HAMNER, W. (1977). Reinforcement theory. In H. Tosi & W. Hamner (Eds.), *Organizational behavior and management* (pp. 93–111). Chicago: St. Clair.

HAMNER, W., & Hamner, E. (1976). Behavior modification on the bottom line. *Organizational Dynamics, 4*(4), 3–21.

HARRIGAN, K.R. (1980). *Strategies for declining industries.* Lexington, MA: D.C. Heath.

HARRIS, J.F., & Klepper, A. (1970). Corporate philanthropic public service activities. In *Research Papers,* Vol. 3, sponsored by the Commission on Private Philanthropy and Public Needs. Washington, DC: Department of the Treasury.

HATVANY, N., & Pucik, V. (1981). Japanese management practices and productivity. *Organizational Dynamics, 9*(4), 5–21.

HAYES, R.H. (1981). Why Japanese factories work. *Harvard Business Review, 59*(4), 56–66.

HEALY, R. (Ed.). (1979). *Federal regulatory directory, 1979–1980.* Washington, DC: Congressional Quarterly.

HEDBERG, B., Nystrom, P.C., & Starbuck, W.H. (1976). Camping on seesaws: Prescriptions for a self-designing organization. *Administrative Science Quarterly, 21,* 41–65.

HEENAN, D. (1983). *The Re-United States of America.* Reading, MA: Addison-Wesley.

HEILBRONER, R.L., & Thurow, L.C. (1981). *Five economic challenges.* Engelwood Cliffs, NJ: Prentice-Hall.

HELLRIEGEL, D., & Slocum, J. (1976). *Organizational behavior contingency views.* New York: West Publishing.

HENEMAN, H.G., Schwab, D.P. Fossum, J.A., & Dyer, L.D. (1980). *Personnel/human resources management.* Homewood, IL: Irwin.

HEROLD, D.M. (1979). The effectiveness of work groups. In S. Kerr (Ed.), *Organizational behavior* (pp. 95–118). Columbus, OH: Grid.

HEROLD, D. (1972). Long-range planning and organizational performance: A cross-valuation study. *Academy of Management Journal, 15*(1), 91–102.

HICKSON, D., Pugh, D.S., & Pheysey, D.C. (1969). Operations technology and organizational structure: A reappraisal. *Administrative Science Quarterly, 14,* 378–397.

HOFFMAN, L.R. (1965). Group problem solving. In L. Berkowitz (Ed.), *Advances in experimental social psychology* (Vol. 2, pp. 99–132). New York: Academic Press.

HOFFMAN, L.R. (1979). *The group problem solving process.* New York: Praeger.

HORNE, J., & Lupton, T. (1965). The work activities of middle managers: An exploratory study. *Journal of Management Studies, 2,* 14–33.

HOUSE, R. (1971). A path-goal theory of leader effectiveness. *Administrative Science Quarterly, 16,* 321–338.

HOUSE, R., & Baetz, M. (1979). Leadership: Some generalizations and new research directions. In B.M. Staw (Ed.), *Research in organizational behavior* (pp. 341–422). Greenwich, CT: JAI Press.

HOUSE, R.J., & Dessler, G. (1974). The path-goal theory of leadership: Some *post-hoc* and *a priori* tests. In J.F. Hurt & L.L. Larson (Eds.), *Contingency approaches to leadership.* Carbondale, IL: Southern Illinois University Press.

HOUSE, R.J., & Mitchell, T.R. (1974). Path-goal theory of leadership. *Journal of Contemporary Business, 5,* 81–94.

HUBER, G. (1980). *Managerial decision making.* Glenview, IL: Scott, Foresman.

HURWICZ, I. (1953). Whatever has happened to the theory of games? *American Economic Review Supplement, 43,* 398–405.

INDUSTRIAL POLICY — YES OR NO. (1983, July 4). *Business Week.*

IRVINE, V.B. (1970). Budgeting: Functional analysis and behavioral implications. *Cost and Management, 44*(2), 6–16.

JACKSON, J. (1965). Structural characteristics of groups. In I. Steiner & M. Fishbein (Eds.), *Current studies in social psychology* (pp. 301–309). New York: Holt, Rinehart & Winston.

JACOBY, J. (1975). Examining consumer information acquisition behavior via an emerging process methodology. Paper presented at Tillburg University, The Netherlands.

JAIN, S.C. (1981). *Marketing planning and strategy.* Cincinnati, OH: South-Western Publishing.

JANIS, I.L. (1972). *Victims of groupthink.* Boston: Houghton Mifflin.

JANSSEN, R.F. (1981, March 11). U.S. companies profit from investments they made years ago in plants overseas. *Wall Street Journal,* p. 48.

JEMISON, D.B. (1981). The importance of an integrative approach to strategic management research. *Academy of Management Review, 6,* 601–608.

JERSTAD, F.E. (1979). An administrator's manual of planning. In R.J. Alio & M.W. Pennington (Eds.), *Corporate planning: Techniques and applications* (pp. 251–259). New York: American Management Association.

JOSEPHSON, M. (1934). *The robber barons.* New York: Harcourt Brace Jovanovich.

KAHNEMAN, D., & Tversky, A. (1973). On the psychology of prediction. *Psychological Review, 80,* 237–251.

KAHNEMAN, D., & Tversky, A. (1979). Intuitive prediction: Biases and corrective procedures. *TIMS Studies in Management Science, 12,* 313–327.

KANE, J.S., & Lawler, E.E. (1979). Performance appraisal effectiveness: Its assessment and determinants, In B.M. Staw (Ed.), *Research in organizational behavior* (Vol. 1, pp. 425–478). Greenwich, CT: JAI Press.

KANTER, R.M. (1977). *Men and women of the corporation.* New York: Basic Books.

KAPOOR, A., & Boddewyn, J.J. (1973). *International business — government relations: U.S. corporate experience in Asia and Western Europe.* New York: AMACOM.

KAST, F., & Rosenzweig, J. (1974). *Organization and management.* New York: McGraw–Hill.

KATZ, D., & Kahn, R.L. (1978). *The social psychology of organizations* (2nd ed.). New York: Wiley.

KATZ, R. (1974). Skills of an effective administrator. *Harvard Business Review, 52,* 90–102.

KATZELL, R.A. (1979). Changing attitudes toward work. In C. Kerr, & J. Rosow (Eds.), *Work in America: The decade ahead* (pp. 35–57). New York: Van Nostrand Reinhold.

KERR, S. (1975). On the folly of rewarding *A,* while hoping for *B. Academy of Management Journal, 18,* 769–783.

KERR, S., & Jermier, J. (1978). Substitutes for leadership: Their meaning and measurement. *Organizational Behavior and Human Performance, 22*, 375–403.

KIECHEL, W., III. (1979, June 18). Harvard Business School restudies itself. *Fortune,* pp. 48–61.

KIECHEL, W., III. (1981, November 16). Playing the global game. *Fortune.* pp. 111–114.

KIMBERLY, J. (1976). Organizational size and the structuralist perspective: A review, critique, and proposal. *Administrative Science Quarterly, 21*, 571–597.

KIPNIS, D., Schmidt, S.M., & Wilkinson, I. (1980). Intraorganizational influence tactics: Explorations in getting one's way. *Journal of Applied Psychology, 65*, 440–452.

KOLDE, E.J. (1982). *Environment of international business.* Boston: Kent.

KOTLER, P. (1980). *Marketing management.* Engelwood Cliffs, NJ: Prentice-Hall.

KOTLER, P., & Fahey, L. (1982, Summer). The world's champion marketers: The Japanese. *Journal of Business Strategy, 3*(1), 3–13.

KRAAR, L. (1980, March 24). The multinationals get smarter about political risks. *Fortune,* pp. 86–92.

LASKY, V. (1981). *Never complain, never explain: The story of Henry Ford II.* New York: Richard Marek.

LATANÉ, B., Harkins, S., & Williams, K. (1979). Many hands make light the work: Causes and consequences of social loafing. *Journal of Personality and Social Psychology, 37*, 822–832.

LAWLER, E.E. (1981). *Pay and organization development.* Reading, MA: Addison-Wesley.

LAWLER, E.E., & Hackman, J.R. (1969). The impact of employee participation in the development of pay incentive plans: A field experiment. *Journal of Applied Psychology, 53*, 467–471.

LAWLER, E.E., & Rhode, J. (1976). *Information and control in organizations.* Santa Monica, CA: Goodyear.

LAWRENCE, P.R., & Lorsch, J.W. (1967). *Organization and environment: Managing differentiation and integration.* Boston: Harvard University, Division of Research, Graduate School of Business Administration.

LEAVITT, H.J. (1964). Applied organization change in industry: Structural, technical and human approaches. In W.W. Cooper, H.J. Leavitt, & M. W. Shelly (Eds.), *New perspectives in organization research* (pp. 50–66). New York: Wiley.

LEAVITT, H.J. (1975). Suppose we took groups seriously . . . In E. Cass & F. Zimmer (Eds.), *Man and work in society* (pp. 65–77). New York: Van Nostrand Reinhold.

LEONE, R., & Bradley, S. (1981, November–December). Toward an effective industrial policy. *Harvard Business Review, 59*(6), 91–97.

LEONTIEF, W. (1954, February). Domestic production in foreign trade: The American capital position re-examined. *Economia Internazionale.*

LEWIN, K. (1947). Frontiers in group dynamics: Concept, method, and reality in social science. *Human Relations, 1*, 5–41.

LICHTENSTEIN, S., Fischhoff, B., & Phillips, L.D. (1977). Calibration of probabilities: The state of the art. In J. Jungerman & G. deZeeuw (Eds.), *Proceedings of the Fifth Research Conference on Subjective Probability, Utility, and Decision Making* (pp. 58–67). Dordrecht, The Netherlands: D. Reidel.

LICHTENSTEIN, S., Slovic, P., Fischhoff, B., Layman, M., & Combs, B. (1978). Judged frequency of lethal events. *Journal of Experimental Psychology: Human Learning and Memory, 4*, 551–578.

LINCOLN, W.B. (1981). *The Romanovs.* New York: Dial Press.

LINDHOLM, R., Cole, C., Brown, W., James, C., Ramsing, K., Smith, R., Spicer, B., & Unsgon, G. (1981). *A study of state and local regulation of business in Oregon.* Eugene, OR: University of Oregon, Business Regulatory Study Center, College of Business Administration.

LINDSAY, W., & Rue, L. (1980). Impact of the organization environment on the long-range planning process: A contingency view. *Academy of Management Journal, 23*, 385–404.

LOCKE, E.A., Saari, L.M., Shaw, K.N., & Latham, G.P. (1981). Goal setting and task performance: 1969–1980. *Psychological Bulletin, 90*, 125–152.

LOOMIS, C.J. (1982, July 12). The madness of executive compensation. *Fortune,* pp. 42–52.

LUND, R. (1977, January). Making products live longer. *Technical Review, 15,* 49–55.

MAGAZINER, I.C., & Reich, R.B. (1983). *Minding America's business.* New York: Random House.

MAGEE, S.P. (1980). *International trade.* Reading, MA: Addison-Wesley.

MAIN, J. (1981, June 15). Westinghouse's cultural revolution. *Fortune,* pp. 74–93.

MAIN, J. (1982, May 3). The executive yearn to learn. *Fortune,* pp. 234–236, 240, 244, 248.

MALABRE, A.L., Jr. (1980, November 13). Trade is playing fast-growing role in economic picture of the U.S. *Wall Street Journal,* p. 48.

MALABRE, A.L., Jr. (1981, August 3). World trade suffers as economies slow. *Wall Street Journal,* p. 1.

MALABRE, A.L., Jr. (1982, February 10). Service transactions keep balance of trade in surplus despite the large deficit on goods. *Wall Street Journal,* p. 48.

MALABRE, A.L., Jr. (1983, August 9). As economy continues to revive from slump, country's balance of trade grows sicklier. *Wall Street Journal,* p. 60.

MARCH, J.G., & Olsen, J.P. (Eds.). (1976). *Ambiguity and choice in organizations.* Bergen, Norway: Universitetsforlaget.

MARCH, J., & Simon, H. (1958). *Organizations.* New York: Wiley.

MAREK, J. (1966). Conflict, a battle of strategies. In J. Lawrence (Ed.), *Organizational research and the social sciences.* London: Tavistock.

MASLOW, A. (1954). *Motivation and personality.* New York: Harper.

MASON, R.O., Mitroff, I.I., & Barabba, V.P. (1982). Creating the manager's plan book: A new route to effective planning. In A.J. Rowe, R.O. Mason, & K.E. Dickel (Eds.), *Strategic management and business policy: A methodological approach* (pp. 82–86). Menlo Park, CA: Addison-Wesley.

MAYO, E. (1971). Hawthorne and the Western Electric Company. In D.S. Pugh (Ed.), *Organization theory* (pp. 215–229). Middlesex, England: Penguin.

MCCLELLAND, D. (1971). *Assessing human motivation.* New York: General Learning Press.

MCCLELLAND, D. (1976). Power is the great motivator. *Harvard Business Review, 54,* 100–110.

MCCLELLAND, D.C., Arkinson, J.W., Clark, R.A., & Lowell, E.L. (1953). *The achievement motive.* New York: Appleton-Century-Crofts.

MCNICHOLS, T.J. (1983). *Policymaking and executive action.* (6th ed.). New York: McGraw-Hill.

MERTON, R. (1940). Bureaucratic structure and personality. *Social Forces, 18,* 560–568.

METZNER, H., Watt, J.L., & Glueck, W.F. (1975, August). Product life cycle and states of growth: An empirical analysis. *Proceedings: Academy of Management* (pp. 61–63). 35th Annual Meeting, New Orleans, LA.

MEYER, H.E. (1976, February). Personnel directors are the new corporate heroes. *Fortune,* pp. 84, 87–89.

MEYER, M. (1972). Size and the structure of organizations: A casual analysis. *American Sociological Review, 34,* 434–440.

MICHELS, R. (1949). *Political parties.* New York: Free Press.

MILES, R.E., Porter, L.W., & Craft, J.A. (1966). Leadership attitudes among public health officials. *American Journal of Public Health, 56,* 1990–2005.

MILES, R., & Snow, C.C. (1978). *Organizational strategy, structure, and process.* New York: McGraw-Hill.

MILES, R. (1965). Human relations or human resources? *Harvard Business Review, 43,* 148–163.

MILES, R.H. (1980). *Macro organizational behavior.* Santa Monica, CA: Goodyear.

MILLER, B.C. (1980). "Hire in haste, repent at leisure" — the team selection approach at Graphic Controls. *Organizational Dynamics, 8*(4), 3–26.

MILLER, G.T. (1975). *Living in the environment: Concepts, problems, and alternatives.* Belmont, CA: Wadsworth.

MINTZBERG, J. (1973). *The nature of managerial work.* New York: Harper & Row.

MIRVIS, P. (1980). Assessing physical evidence. In E. Lawler, D. Nadler, & C. Camman (Eds.), *Organizational assessment* (pp. 418–443). New York: Wiley-Interscience.

MIRVIS, P.H., & Lawler, E.E. (1977). Measuring

the financial impact of employee attitudes. *Journal of Applied Psychology, 62,* 1–8.

MOCKLER, R. (1972). *The management control process.* Englewood Cliffs, NJ: Prentice-Hall.

MONDEN, Y. (1981). What makes the Toyota production system really tick? *Industrial Engineering, 13*(1), 36–46.

MORRISON, A.M. (1981a, May 4). Renault takes its hit show on the road. *Fortune,* p. 284.

MORRISON, A.M. (1981b, November 2). Revlon's surprising new face. *Fortune.* pp. 72–80.

MOUZELIS, N. (1967). *Organization and bureaucracy: An analysis of modern theories.* Chicago: Aldine.

MOWDAY, R.T., Porter, L.W., & Steers, R.M. (1982). *Employee–organization linkages.* New York: Academic Press.

MURDICK, R.G., Eckhouse, R.H., Moor, C.R., & Zimmerer, T.W. (1980). *Business policy: A framework for analysis,* Columbus, OH: Grid.

NADLER, D.A., Hackman, J.R., & Lawler, E.E. (1979). *Managing organizational behavior.* Boston: Little, Brown.

NAISBITT, J. (1982). *Megatrends: Ten new directions transforming our lives.* New York: Warner Books.

A NEW ERA FOR MANAGEMENT. (1983, April 25). *Business Week,* pp. 50–86.

NEWELL, A., Shaw, J.C., & Simon, H.A. (1958). The elements of a theory of human problem solving. *Psychological Review, 65,* 151–166.

NEWELL, A., & Simon, H.A. (1972). *Human problem solving.* Englewood Cliffs, NJ: Prentice-Hall.

NEWMAN, W. (1975). *Constructive controls.* Englewood Cliffs, NJ: Prentice-Hall.

NISBETT, R., & Ross, L. (1980). *Human inference: Strategic and shortcomings of social judgement.* Englewood Cliffs, NJ: Prentice-Hall.

NORTHWEST'S BIAS SETBACK. (1982, December 13). *Business Week,* p. 36.

O'CONNOR, W.F. (1983, May). New globalism: A game every multinational will have to play. *Management Review, 72,* 29, 31.

OCCUPATIONAL SAFETY AND HEALTH ADMINISTRATION, Office of Data Systems. (1979). Violations and penalty data from SIC code, FY 1975. Washington, DC: U.S. Government Printing Office.

OFFICE AUTOMATION FEVER STRIKES JAPAN. (1983, January 17). *Business Week,* pp. 122–124.

O'REILLY, C.A. (1978). The intentional distortion of information in organizational communication: A laboratory and field approach. *Human Relations, 31,* 173–193.

O'REILLY, C.A., & Pondy, L.R. (1979). Organizational communication. In S. Kerr (Ed.), *Organizational behavior* (pp. 119–150). Columbus, OH: Grid.

OUCHI, W. (1981). *Theory Z: How Americans can meet the Japanese challenge.* Reading, MA: Addison-Wesley.

PACE OF OVERSEAS INVESTMENTS BY U.S. TRAILS GROWTH OF CAPITAL INFLOWS. (1982, September 13). *Peat Marwick Executive Newsletter,* pp. 5–6.

PEARCE, J.A., & Robinson, R.B. (1982). *Formulation and implementation of competitive strategy.* Homewood, IL: Irwin.

PENSION PLANS GET MORE FLEXIBLE. (1982, November 8). *Business Week,* p. 82.

PERROW, C. (1961). The analysis of goals in complex organizations. *American Sociological Review, 26,* 854–866.

PERROW, C. (1965). Hospitals: Technology, structure and goals. In J. March (Ed.), *The handbook of organizations* (pp. 910–971). Chicago: Rand McNally.

PERROW, C. (1970). *Organizational analysis: A sociological view.* Belmont, CA: Wadsworth.

PERROW, C. (1979). *Complex organizations: A critical essay.* Glenview, IL: Scott, Foresman.

PETERS, T.J., & Waterman, R.H. (1982). *In search of excellence.* New York: Harper & Row.

PFEFFER, J. (1981). *Power in organizations.* Marshfield, MA: Pitman.

PHATAK, A.V. (1983). *International dimensions of management.* Boston, MA: Kent.

PHYRR, P. (1970). Zero-based budgeting. *Harvard Business Review, 48,* 111–121.

PIERCING THE FUTURE FOG IN THE EXECUTIVE SUITE. (1975, April 28). *Business Week,* pp. 46–54.

PONDY, L.R. (1973). Budgeting and intergroup conflict in organizations. In H. Leavitt, & L. Pondy (Eds.), *Readings in managerial psychology* (2nd ed., pp. 595–600). Chicago: University of Chicago Press.

PORTER, L., & Lawler, E. (1968). *Managerial attitudes and behavior.* Homewood, IL: Irwin.

PORTER, L.W., Lawler, E.E., & Hackman, J.R. (1975). *Behavior in organizations.* New York: McGraw-Hill.

PORTER, M. (1980). *Competitive strategy.* New York: Free Press.

PRASAD, S.B. (1983). *Policy, strategy, and implementation.* New York: Random House.

PRIVATE FILES. (1978, April 24). [Manager's Journal]. *Wall Street Journal,* p. 18.

PUGH, D.S., Hickson, D.J., & Hinings, C.R. (1973). *Organizations.* Middlesex, England: Penguin Books Ltd.

PUGH, D.S., Hickson, D.J., Hinings, C.R., & Turner, C. (1969). The context of organizational structures. *Administrative Science Quarterly, 14,* 91–114.

RAIFFA, H. (1968). *Decision analysis: Introductory lectures on choices under uncertainty.* Reading, MA: Addison-Wesley.

RAISE YOUR FARES 20 PERCENT. (1983, March 7). *Business Week,* p. 38.

RCA QUITS MAKING VIDEODISC PLAYERS. (1984, April 16). *Business Week,* p. 60.

THE REINDUSTRIALIZATION OF AMERICA. (1980, June 30). *Business Week,* pp. 58–140.

REUSS, J. (1981). Can American industry be born again? In M. Wachter & W. Wachter (Eds.), *Toward a new U.S. industrial policy* (pp. 23–29). Philadelphia: University of Pennsylvania Press.

ROBERTS, K.J., O'Reilly, C.A. Bretton, G., & Porter, L.W. (1979). Organizational theory and organizational communication: A communication failure? *Human Relations, 27,* 501–524.

ROBERTSON, T.S., Ward, S., & Caldwell, W. (1982). Deregulation: Surviving the transition. *Harvard Business Review, 61,* 20–24.

ROBINSON, R.D. (1978). *International business management* (2nd ed.). Hinsdale, IL: Dryden.

ROBOCK, S.H., & Simmonds, K. (1983). *International business and multinational enterprises* (3rd ed.). Homewood, IL: Irwin.

ROETHLISBERGER, F.J., & Dickson, W.J. (1939). *Management and the worker.* New York: Wiley.

ROGERS, E.M., & Agarwala–Rogers, R. (1976). *Communication in organizations.* New York: Free Press.

RUMMELL, R.J., & Heenan, D.A. (1978). How multinationals analyze risk. *Harvard Business Review, 56,* pp. 67–71.

SARBIN, T. & Allen, V. (1968). Role theory. In G. Lindzey & E. Aronson (Eds.), *Handbook of Social Psychology* (Vol. I, pp. 488–567). Reading, MA: Addison–Wesley.

SAYLES, L. (1964). *Managerial behavior.* New York: McGraw-Hill.

SCHEIN, E. (1961). Management development as a process of influence. *Industrial Management Review, 2*(2), 62–63.

SCHENDEL, D.E., & Hofer, C.W. (1979). *Strategic management.* Boston: Little, Brown.

SCHMIDT, S.M., & Kochan, T.A. (1972). Conflict: Toward conceptual clarity. *Administrative Science Quarterly, 17,* 359–370.

SCHNAPPER, M. (1972). *American labor.* Washington: Public Affairs Press.

SCOTT, W., & Mitchell, T. (1976). *Organization theory: A structural and behavioral approach.* Homewood, IL: Irwin.

SELZNICK, P. (1949). *TVA and the grass roots.* Berkeley, CA: University of California Press.

SHAW, M. (1981). *Group dynamics* (3rd ed.). New York: McGraw-Hill.

SHILLINGLAW, G. (1982). *Managerial cost accounting* (5th ed.). Homewood, IL: Irwin.

SILLS, D. (1957). *The volunteers.* New York: Free Press.

SIMON, H.A. (1947). *Administrative behavior.* New York: Macmillan.

SIMON, H.A. (1965). *The shape of automation for men and management.* New York: Harper & Row.

SIMON, H.A. (1976). *Administrative behavior* (3rd ed.). New York: Free Press.

SKINNER, B. (1971). *Beyond freedom and dignity.* New York: Knopf.

SLOVIC, P. (1976). Toward understanding the improving decisions. In E.I. Salkovitz (Ed.), *Science technology and the modern navy: Thirtieth anniversary, 1946-1976* (pp. 113-119). Arlington, VA: Office of Naval Research.

STARLING, G. (1980). *The changing environment of business.* Boston: Kent.

STARLING, G. (1984). *The changing environment of business.* (2nd ed.). Boston: Kent.

STAW, B.M. (1981). The escalation of commitment to a course of action. *Academy of Management Review, 6,* 577-587.

STEERS, R.M. (1975). Problems in the measurement of organizational effectiveness. *Administrative Science Quarterly, 20,* 546-558.

STEERS, R.M. (1977). *Organizational effectiveness: A behavioral view.* Santa Monica: Goodyear.

STEERS, R.M. (1981). *Introduction to organizational behavior.* Santa Monica: Goodyear.

STEERS, R.M. (1984). *Introduction to organizational behavior* (2nd ed.). Glenview, IL: Scott, Foresman.

STEWART, R. (1982). *Choices for the manager.* Englewood Cliffs, NJ: Prentice-Hall.

STOGDILL, R. (1948). Personal factors associated with leadership: A survey of the literature. *Journal of Psychology, 25,* 35-71.

STONE, T.H. (1982). *Understanding personnel management.* Chicago: Dryden.

STONNER, J. (1978). *Management.* Englewood Cliffs, NJ: Prentice-Hall.

STRAUSS, G. (1976). Organization development. In R. Dubin (Ed.), *Handbook of work, organization and society* (pp. 617-685). Chicago: Rand McNally.

SZILAGYI, A. (1981). *Management and performance.* Glenview, IL: Scott, Foresman.

TAKAMIYA, S. (1981). The characteristics of Japanese management. *Management Japan, 14*(2), 6-9.

TAYLOR, F.W. (1911). *The principles of scientific management.* New York: Harper.

TEAMWORK PAYS OFF AT PENNEY'S. (1983, April 12). *Business Week,* pp. 107-108.

THIBAUT, J., & Kelley, H. (1959). *The social psychology of groups.* New York: Wiley.

THOMAS, K. (1976). Conflict and conflict management. In M. Dunnette (Ed.), *Handbook of industrial and organizational psychology* (pp. 889-935). Chicago: Rand McNally.

THOMPSON, A., Jr., & Strickland, A.J., III. (1981). *Strategy and policy: Concepts and cases.* Plano, TX: Business Publications.

THOMPSON, J.D. (1967). *Organizations in action.* New York: McGraw-Hill.

THOMPSON, J., & McEwen, W. (1958). Organizational goals and environment. *American Sociological Review, 23,* 23-30.

THORNDIKE, E. (1911). *Animal intelligence.* New York: Macmillan.

THUNE, S.S., & House, R. (1970). Where long-range planning pays off. *Business Horizons, 13*(4), 81-87.

THUROW, L.C. (1983, February 2). If the debtors default. *Newsweek,* p. 68.

TORRANCE, E.P. (1954). Some consequences of power differences on decision making in permanent and temporary three-man groups. *Research Studies* (Vol. 22, pp. 130-140). Pullman, WA: Washington State College.

TSURUMI, Y. (1983). *Multinational management: Business strategy and government policy.* Cambridge, MA: Ballinger.

TVERSKY, A. (1972). Elimination by aspects: A theory of choice. *Psychological Review, 79,* 281-299.

TVERSKY, A., & Kahneman, D. (1973). Availability: A heuristic for judging frequency and probability. *Cognitive Psychology, 5,* 207-232.

TVERSKY, A., & Kahneman, D. (1974). Judgment under uncertainty: Heuristics and biases. *Science, 185,* 1124-1131.

URWICK, D.F. (1947). *The elements of administration.* London: Pitman.

VERNON, R. (1966). International investment and international trade in the product cycle. *Quarterly Journal of Economics, 80,* 190-207.

VERNON, R.F. (1971). *Sovereignty at bay*. New York: Basic Books.

VERNON, R. (1972). *The economic and political consequences of multinational enterprise*. Boston: Harvard College.

VON NEUMANN, J., & Morgenstern, O. (1944). *Theory of games and economic behavior*. Princeton, NJ: Princeton University Press.

VROOM, V. (1964). *Work and motivation*. New York: Wiley.

VROOM, V.B., & Yetton, P.W. (1973). *Leadership and decision making*. Pittsburgh, PA: University of Pittsburgh Press.

WAVERMAN, L. (1975). Regulation of intercity telecommunications. In A. Phillips (Ed.), *Promoting competition in regulated markets* (pp. 270–278). Washington, DC: Brookings Institute.

WEBER, M. (1947). *The theory of social and economic organization*. New York: Free Press.

WEIDENBAUM, M.L. (1978). *The impacts of government regulation* (Working Paper #3). St. Louis, MO: Washington University, Center for the Study of American Business.

WEIDENBAUM, M. (1979). *The future of business regulation*. New York: American Management Association.

WEIDENBAUM, M. (1981). *Business, government and the public*. Englewood Cliffs, NJ: Prentice-Hall.

WELSCH, G. (1976). *Budgeting: Profit planning and control*. Englewood Cliffs, NJ: Prentice-Hall.

WEXLEY, K., & Yukl, G. (1977). *Organizational behavior and personnel psychology*. Homewood, IL: Irwin.

WHAT WE CAN LEARN FROM OUR RIVALS. (1980, June 30). *Business Week*, pp. 138–141.

WHO'S WHERE IN THE INDUSTRY GROUPS. (1983, January 3). *Forbes*, pp. 224–225.

WHY THE GENERALS CAN'T COMMAND. (1983, February 14). *Newsweek*, pp. 22–24.

WITCHER, S.K., & Rout, L. (1983, June 8). New crisis has begun in international debt, banking experts warn. *Wall Street Journal*, p. 1.

WOOD, D.R., & LaForge, R.L. (1979). The impact of comprehensive planning on financial performance. *Academy of Management Journal, 22*, 516–526.

WOODWARD, J. (1965). *Industrial organization: Theory and practice*. London: Oxford University Press.

WREN, D.C. (1979). *The evolution of management thought* (2nd ed.). New York: Wiley.

WRIGHT, J.P. (1979). *On a clear day you can see General Motors*. New York: Avon.

WRIGHT, P. (1975). Consumer choice strategies: Simplifying vs. optimizing. *Journal of Marketing Research, 12*, 60–69.

YOST, C. (1975, November 19). Living with interdependence. *Christian Science Monitor*, p. 39.

ZANDER, A. (1982). *Making groups effective*. San Francisco: Jossey-Bass.

Name Index

Subject Index